Rethinking careers education and guidance

Rethinking careers education and guidance

Theory, policy and practice

A. G. Watts, Bill Law, John Killeen,
Jennifer M. Kidd and Ruth Hawthorn

Routledge
Taylor & Francis Group

LONDON AND NEW YORK

First published 1996
by Routledge
2 Park Square, Milton Park, Abingdon, Oxon, OX14 4RN

Simultaneously published in the USA and Canada
by Routledge
270 Madison Ave, New York, NY 10016

Reprinted 1998, 1999, 2000, 2002 (twice), 2003 (twice), 2005

Routledge is an imprint of the Taylor & Francis Group

Typeset in Palatino by Florencetype Ltd, Stoodleigh, Devon
Printed and bound in Great Britain by
T.J. International Ltd, Padstow, Cornwall

British Library Cataloguing in Publication Data
A catalogue record for this book is available from the British Library

Library of Congress Cataloging in Publication Data
A catalog record for this book is available from the Library of
Congress

ISBN 0–415–13974–0 (hbk)
ISBN 0–415–13975–9 (pbk)

Contents

Figures

Tables

Preface

This is to our knowledge the first book published in the United Kingdom to cover theory, policy and practice in all sectors of careers education and guidance provision. Traditionally, such provision has been fragmented and sector-bound. The establishment of the National Advisory Council for Careers and Educational Guidance (NACCEG) and of the Advice, Guidance, Counselling and Psychotherapy Lead Body have however brought the sectors into closer contact with one another. The rapid changes that are taking place in the world of work are also producing increased recognition of the need for lifelong access to guidance in support of lifelong career development. This is encouraging practitioners in different sectors to pay more attention to the whole of which they are part.

At the same time, careers education and guidance is receiving greater public-policy attention in the UK than ever before. This offers new opportunities but also new threats. There is a danger that development will be narrowly policy-focused, and will lose touch with the field's theoretical roots. Theory, policy and practice are mutually dependent: each is impoverished without fertile links with the others.

The present book is designed to help practitioners to develop a broader and deeper intellectual base for their work. It is aimed particularly at students in initial training, those engaged in in-service and higher-degree work, and reflective practitioners.

We are immensely indebted to the Esmée Fairbairn Trust, for a grant which supported the writing of the book. It provided us with reflective space in which to bring together some of the main work we have carried out over the last two decades since the launch of the National Institute for Careers Education and Counselling (NICEC) in 1975, and to rethink and re-invigorate it. We have met regularly over the last two years to brainstorm chapters and to review drafts. Although we have different viewpoints and different styles, we hope that the text is reasonably coherent and cohesive, and displays the fruits of the conversations we have had with one another.

We have tried to harmonise our terminology where possible. In general, we adopt a broad definition of the term 'careers education and guidance', covering a range of processes designed to enable individuals to make informed choices and transitions related to their learning and to their work. Where appropriate, we distinguish between 'careers education' and 'careers guidance': Chapter 12 includes an extended discussion of the relationship between the two. Sometimes, however, we follow the common convention of using the term 'guidance' as a shorthand version of 'careers education and guidance'. In the light of the changes that are taking place in the structure of work and the concept of career, we contend that there is a growing case for adopting the singular usage 'career education and guidance', on the grounds that the individual has a single career, representing his or her development in learning and in work. We have, however, retained the more conventional plural usage for the purposes of this book.

We are grateful to many colleagues who have commented on drafts of particular chapters, including David Andrews, Diane Bailey, Malcolm Ballantine, Anthony Barnes, Val Butcher, Ruby Coldicott, David Guest, Peter Heaviside, Ed Herr, Peter Herriot, Phil Hodkinson, Jill Hoffbrand, Bernard Kingston, Frans Meijers, Mary Munro, Marcus Offer, Peter Plant, Richard Pethen, David Raffe, Gabrielle Rowe, Jim Sampson, Tom Snow, Andrea Spurling, Rob Stickland and Margaret Wallis. In addition, we are indebted to the Careers Research and Advisory Centre (CRAC) for its continuing support for NICEC, and to Daphne Ewen, Deborah Parr, Simone Shadrack and Suzanne Williams for their patience and skill in typing various drafts of the chapters. Responsibility for any deficiencies in the text is, of course, ours.

Tony Watts
Ruth Hawthorn
Jenny Kidd
John Killeen
Bill Law

Cambridge
January 1996

Part I

Theory and context

All careers education and guidance policy and practice is based on theory: on some model of the reality with which it is dealing. The task of formal theory is to offer policy-makers and practitioners a variety of such models, fleshed out and supported by evidence, against which their own model can be explicated and tested.

Chapter 1 examines the changing social context in which careers education and guidance has to operate. It pays particular attention to the ways in which the concept of 'career' is changing, including the increasing emphasis on functional flexibility and non-standard work patterns. Arguably, these changes greatly strengthen the case for lifelong access to careers education and guidance.

Chapter 2 reviews a wide range of career theories, disentangling some of the key elements that distinguish them. It pays particular attention to recent theoretical work, which has placed more emphasis than hitherto on economic factors. Indeed, as a crude generalisation, it could be argued that whereas in the 1940s and 1950s the careers field was dominated by psychology, in the 1960s and 1970s this dominance was challenged in the UK by sociology, and in the 1980s and 1990s by economics. Career theories need to be distinguished from guidance theories: career theories are concerned with describing, explaining and predicting what happens; guidance theories with providing a basis for action. Nonetheless, since effective interventions have to based on an understanding of the processes in which they are intervening, guidance theories are necessarily based on career theories.

Chapter 3 presents a new career theory, focusing on career learning. It contends that career development proceeds through four 'capacities': sensing, sifting, focusing and understanding. Each of these stages is divided into two sub-stages. It is suggested that such a framework may be particularly valuable in designing progressive careers education programmes.

Chapter 4 looks at the outcomes of guidance. It distinguishes learning and economic outcomes, and examines the existing evidence on the extent of such outcomes. It also explores the relationship between the two forms of outcome, arguing that if such a relationship could be definitively demonstrated, learning outcomes could be used as proxies for economic outcomes. This would have the additional merit that learning outcomes are considered by many practitioners to be the most *appropriate* outcome measure in terms of professional practice.

Chapter 1

The social context of guidance

John Killeen

1.1 INTRODUCTION

It is difficult to think of an element of the social context which does not have implications for, or is unconnected from, working life and careers. This context is a changing one, and the rapidity of change is becoming central to our thinking about the role of guidance. The writing about careers, and hence guidance, is increasingly dominated by images of disorder and unpredictability, as if the direction and speed of history have become overwhelming in their consequences for individuals and their families. We shall first consider some of the sources of change in the organisation of work and the character of labour markets. We shall then look at some of the main implications for organisations and careers, and conclude by examining their implications for guidance.

1.2 SOURCES OF CHANGE

Technological change

Technological change is deeply embedded in the restructuring of developed economies. The most recent wave of technological transformation is the micro-electronic and information technology revolution, which is powerfully shaping the world of work. Most obviously, it is making process technologies practicable in an ever-increasing range of industries. The general outlines of this particular application of information technology were the first to be recognised, leading some commentators to treat industries such as petro-chemicals as the model for the future. Machine-paced, de-skilled, minutely sub-divided assembly-line work would give way to process-control work, and the trend in worker alienation would be reversed (Blauner, 1964). More recently, attention has shifted to the new forms of capital-intensive 'flexible specialisation', or batch production, which rapidly re-programmable technologies permit (Piore and Sabel, 1984). A more general conception of 'post-Fordist' production has emerged which (prematurely) announces the death of repetitive assembly-line work.

But of course, information technology is deeply implicated in many other changes in the character of work organisation. For example, it is changing most forms of work which involve the manipulation of symbols and images. The most routine forms of manipulation, once performed by an army of clerks, are being reduced to data input. Change extends to expert intellectual and artistic work, creating a new stratum of expert system-users. It also challenges the spatial concentration of work organisations. At one pole, this is represented by 'home-working'; at the other, by the emergence of new forms of industrial organisation which depend upon real-time knowledge of internal operations, irrespective of geographical location.

Globalisation and regional free trade

Globalisation is the term used to describe the way in which national economies are increasingly becoming local ones, so that in order to understand what happens in them, we must attend to the whole of which they are parts. Most obviously, glob-alisation implies a reduction in national barriers to trade (for example, through the General Agreement on Tariffs and Trade), so that an increasing proportion of firms compete on world markets. But regional alliances such as the European Union have also arisen within which barriers to trade are even more sharply reduced (Robson, 1993). These developments can be viewed as *intensified competition*. Under very intensely competitive conditions, the way firms operate and the kinds of careers they can offer are constrained in ways we shall consider in detail later.

But globalisation means much more than the internationalisation of product markets. Capital markets, too, are increasingly international. Capital may move on open markets, and the ownership of firms may consequently become inter-nationalised. Capital also, however, flows across national boundaries within multinational companies: these acquire or create subsidiaries in each regional market, often dispersing both production and research-and-development activ-ities; in addition, they move production around the globe with increasing ease, pitting plants against one another in an internal product market. Parallel to this, alliances are forged between companies across regional markets in order to share research-and-development costs and marketing facilities. This can lead to merger and the creation of new multinationals (Adams, 1993).

Britain's ability to attract inward investment is sometimes considered in isola-tion from its ability to export capital. Historically, it has been a net exporter of capital; even in the 1980s, the influx of US, continental and far-eastern compa-nies into the UK, and the jobs they created, did not match the outflow of capital from UK firms (CBI, 1991). A study of 25 large UK companies in this period (Williams *et al.*, 1989) showed the rate of growth in the number of their foreign employees (28 per cent) to be almost exactly matched by the rate of reduction in their UK employees (29 per cent). Britain can with some justice claim to be one of the most globalised of developed economies: 80 per cent of its overseas trade in manufactured goods is conducted by multinationals, and 40 per cent of the employees of UK-based multinationals are overseas; in addition, an increasing proportion of UK jobs are in foreign-owned companies (United Nations, 1988).

An obvious possible consequence is the internationalisation of careers, both by conventional labour mobility and, for the upper echelons, by mobility inside international organisations. Thus the European dimension of guidance, in partic-ular, has become increasingly prominent (Watts *et al.*, 1994). But undoubtedly the most discussed potential consequence is the domestic impact of non-UK corporate cultures on working life.

Unfortunately, there is a wide measure of disagreement about what those cultures are and the degree to which they have permeated Britain. A general view which covers US companies such as IBM and Japanese ones such as Nissan includes high rates of pay and job security, the exclusion of trade unions or conclusion of single-union deals, highly evolved human-resource-development and training strategies, a superficial form of egalitarianism which is reflected in little movement between the main employment strata, close and individualised performance monitoring and appraisal, and, in the Japanese case, sweatshop work intensities, all resulting in high productivity. In order to compete, it is assumed that British firms must either emulate this strategy, or retreat into low-skill, low-wage sectors. Ashton *et al.* (1989) pointed to the absence of plans for training in up to 70 per cent of UK firms as evidence of the latter, but most firms are small-to-medium enterprises, not involved in direct competition with either foreign or British-owned multinationals.

Turning to 'Japanisation', this is often taken also to include 'Toyotaism' ('lean' and 'just-in-time' production), which involves the minimisation of buffer stocks and the elimination of all obstacles to the continuity of production (Womack *et al.*, 1990). This, in turn, is associated with features such as team-based, shop-floor problem-solving of production-engineering problems, and the embedding of responsibility for quality in all production tasks and teams. A second feature commonly noted is the creation of intimate, long-lasting relationships with suppliers, based upon the assumption that they will continually strive to surpass contractual obligations (for a review, see Wood, 1991). The implications for careers within the hierarchy of corporations and favoured suppliers is one of organisational employment stability, in return for extremes of commitment, effort, obedience and flexibility. But Japanese 'transplants' have gone to exceptional lengths to select young, fit, and psychologically-adapted workforces (Berggren, 1993). It remains to be seen if, like football players, their playing days are numbered.

Industrial restructuring and the rise of the service sector

Viewed in terms of employment share, and even in terms of the absolute numbers of people employed, primary industries, such as agriculture, mining, energy and water supply, have been in long decline. But until recently, falling employment in failing manufacturing sectors, or sectors shedding labour due to productivity gains, was more than offset by new employment in emergent ones. The 1960s were the high-water mark of manufacturing employment, and since then there has been an absolute decline. In 1971, 6.8 million people were employed in (non-primary) manufacture, comprising approximately 30 per cent of the labour-force. By 1986, these figures had declined to 4.5 million and 21 per cent respectively (CSO, 1990), prompting fears that Britain was de-industrialising. Since that time, decline has been much slower, but is projected to continue.

On definitions which focus upon financial services and the knowledge professions, the trend towards service employment has been observable since the mid-nineteenth century, in the sense that its growth rates exceeded those of other sectors (Bell, 1974). On the broadest conventional definitions, the sector is very heterogeneous, including activities as diverse as tourism, the arts (the economic importance of which is consistently underestimated in the popular imagination), transportation, catering, repair, banking and medicine. But even taking the broadest definition, the service sector is dramatically expanding. It accounted for half of all jobs in 1971, but two-thirds by the early 1990s (*Employment Gazette*, various issues). All developed countries are treading a similar path and, as part of this process, all are losing manufacturing jobs to developing ones, such as those of the Pacific Rim. Unlike countries such as Germany, however, Britain is particularly dependent on the export of 'invisibles' (services) to replace the manufacturing capacity it has lost. The optimistic view of industrial transformation is sometimes expressed in the proposition that Britain is becoming a 'post-industrial society', characterised for 1970s commentators by the dominance of knowledge-based professions (Bell, 1974), or in its more up-to-date formulation by the dominance of information and knowledge-based private-sector industries dependent upon advanced information technologies, coupled with a large arts, leisure and tourism sector.

Unemployment

The price of technological change, globalisation and restructuring has been unemployment. During the post-war boom years, unemployment was mainly 'frictional' – a short-term consequence of movement between jobs, rather than a long-term consequence of the inability to find work. It was assumed that frictional unemployment of about 0.5 million people was consistent with 'full employment'. But in the later 1970s there were more than a million unemployed, rising to more than 3 million in 1982. Fast growth in the late 1980s reduced this figure by about a half, but by 1993 the figure of 3 million was again exceeded, declining slowly thereafter (*Employment Gazette*, various issues). Unemployment is notoriously difficult to measure. The 'claimant count' upon which the foregoing figures are based is a by-product of a changing benefits system and therefore lacks a stable definition. The tendency of changing definitions is to minimise the number of unemployed. The Labour Force Survey estimate does not take benefit entitlement into account, treating someone who is not working but is actively seeking work as unemployed. Used in conjunction, the methods can be used to produce a higher estimate than either one taken alone, as the people they count as unemployed do not fully coincide. But whatever the true rate, mass unemployment, on a scale similar to the period 1921–39, has become a normal condition.

The paradox of modern unemployment, however, is that it accompanies labour-force growth. Despite a decline in full-time employment, the number of people in work of some kind (part-time or full-time, employed or self-employed) in 1990 was 25.8 million, which was 1.4 million more than in 1979. Since then, the number of people in work has fluctuated, but not below the 1979 figure. So if the same number, or even more people, are in work, why are so many unemployed? The short answer to this question is that the labour-force has grown faster than the number of jobs. Although immigration briefly fuelled labour-force growth during the post-war boom, today the books are approximately in balance; and as we shall see, population growth is not the reason. Moreover, there has been a long-term trend to increase the age at which people become economically active; and men, at least, are tending to be economically active for a shorter part of the life-span. When the post-war economic boom came to an end, this tendency was accelerated, in the sense that unemployment was concentrated among the young and the old, and subsequently converted into 'non-employment' or economic inactivity.

The unemployment of older people has been partially converted into non-employment, in the form of early retirement, as reflected in the apparent fall in the unemployment rates of those over 55 years of age between 1983 and 1992 (see Figure 1.1). A similar effect has been achieved amongst the young, in two stages. In the first, youth unemployment was treated as a temporary phenomenon, to be met by temporary measures. In part, young people were absorbed into conventional post-16 education, so that, for example, staying-on rates were higher in unemployed Liverpool than in prosperous St Albans (Roberts *et al.*, 1986). This was the era of the O-level / GCSE resit, and of pre-vocational courses, often at the equivalent of National Vocational Qualification level 1. But it was also the era of Manpower Services Commission 'special programmes', which offered the opportunity of work experience and/or training, often in charitably-based community schemes. It was possible to justify these measures as 'warehousing', maintaining – rather than significantly raising – the employability of those exposed to them. But in the sharp recession of 1981/82, the scale of the problem increased, and there occurred what came to be known as the 'death of apprenticeship': large numbers of employers ceased to recruit young trainees. Subsequently, in the second stage, there has been a government policy to increase the proportion of the 16–19 age-group undergoing systematic education and training, without raising the age of compulsory education (Ashton *et al.*, 1989). Policy has also favoured dramatic expansion of higher education, thus accommodating an increased proportion of the 19–22 age-group (see 'Increasing and restructured education', below).

Successive policies have therefore abolished much unemployment by fiat, and training schemes for adults unemployed longer than six months have had the incidental effect of reducing the apparent volume of long-term unemployment: when people return to unemployment upon the completion of such schemes, they begin a new spell. Without these measures, the picture would look very grim. But if people are being removed from unemployment

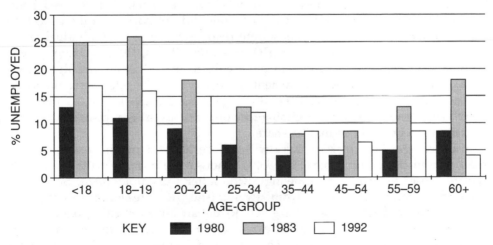

Figure 1.1 Registered unemployment rate by age, 1980—92

Source: Employment Gazette, various issues

Note: The 1992 <18 figure (17 per cent) is taken from the Labour Force Survey for 1993 (*LFS Rapid Release*, October 1994), as the nearest available comparator. (Changes in benefit regulations have led to the exclusion of this age-group from the statistical series on which the rest of the chart is based.)

into non-employment, the population is barely growing, the migration books balance, and we are working for fewer years, why is the workforce growing? The answer is, of course, increased rates of participation by women.

Gender composition of the labour-force

In the mid-nineteenth century, more than 40 per cent of adult women were in the labour-force. The depression of the 1870s cut this figure back very quickly: by the turn of the century, women made up about one-third of the labour-force, only 30 per cent of girls and women over the age of 10 were 'occupied', and 53 per cent of all girls and women in employment were aged less than 20 (Hakim, 1993). Although both World Wars brought women into employment in exceptional numbers, the underlying pattern for the first half of the twentieth century remained that of the final decades of the nineteenth. National policy gave priority to the sharing of employment opportunities between families and the payment of a 'family wage' to men. Although there were centres of demand for female labour (e.g. Nottingham), the general pattern was for women to be paid at lower rates than men. Married women were excluded from some forms of employment, for example in the Civil Service. It took the exceptional circumstances of the post-war boom to return the proportion of adult women in the peace-time labour-force to that of the 1860s. Indeed, one commentator has gone so far as to claim that, until quite recently, rising female employment was a myth (Hakim, 1993).

Despite legislative changes, it was the slump of the early 1980s which finally dispelled the notion that women were a 'dispensable' labour-force group. Hitherto (Barron and Norris, 1976), their relative absence from managerial and professional work, and from the full-time, skilled and unionised forms of work which seemed to enjoy employment protection, had led commentators to think that in times of economic recession they would be expelled from the labour market in favour of men. But in the 1980s this did not happen at the collective level, not least because employers sought dispensability at the individual level. Contrary to the indications of earlier research (Hunt, 1975), women were employed in female occupations in preference to men (Killeen and Robertson, 1988). Their conditions of employment (hours, wage rates, etc.) were unattractive to men, who still sought a 'family wage', and the kinds of work they did were less concentrated in declining sectors. So, as a group, women have continued to gain labour-market share.

It is projected that in 2001 there will still be about 3 million fewer women than men in the labour force (ED, 1992), although the number actually in work will be closer to that of men, owing to the latter's unemployment. But as the pool of economically inactive women diminishes, it is reasonable to suppose that increasing attention will be given to enhancing women's preference to supply labour, notably through an extension of child-care arrangements, such as crèche and nursery education. The impact of increasing female labour-force participation upon the family has two facets: the 'dual career family', and the increased possibility of family dissolution permitted by the dwindling economic dependence of women on men. Both of these depend not upon women acting as part-time 'supplementary wage earners', but upon sexual equality in the labour market.

Men and women continue to work in different sorts of jobs, in different places and in different industries. For most of this century, occupational desegregation has been glacially slow (Hakim, 1979; 1981), and on some definitions undetectable in the periods investigated (Blackburn *et al.*, 1993). Women's employment level relative to men is a complex matter because they have lost share in some sectors, such as professional and skilled manual work, and gained share in others, such as clerical, sales, and unskilled manual work. On conventional definitions, there was no overall reduction in 'vertical segregation' in the period up to 1971 (Hakim, 1979). In more recent times, the pay gap between men and women has been closing only very slowly. For full-timers, this reflects both differences in hourly rates, and premium payments for overtime and shift working which go more often to men. In the period 1988–93, the gross weekly earnings of women rose from 67 per cent to 72 per cent of those of men. But proportionately more women are in non-manual work, and here the gap is more exaggerated than in manual jobs (ED, 1993). Figure 1.2 shows why this is so. The growth areas for non-manual male employment are professional and managerial work. This growth is taking place for women, too, but from a lower base, and female 'intermediate' work is both a much higher proportion and still growing, whereas such work is static for men. Moreover, the decline in manual work, where men predominate in skilled trades, has included a small increase in unskilled female work.

An ageing labour force

Changing demography is one of the key factors influencing careers today. In the late nineteenth century, the UK population contained more than four times as many people aged 15–19 than were aged 55–59; in the early 1990s, their numbers were nearly equal. A century ago, more than a third of the labour force was under 20 years of age; this figure is now around 7 per cent and falling (see Figure 1.3). An ageing population brings both an ageing workforce and, with increasing longevity, a larger retired population. While the total GB population grew by about 1.8 million from 1971 to 1991, those of working age increased by little more than half a million, and this was more than offset by a reduction of the number of young people waiting to enter the labour-force. Fluctuations in birth rates of the sort which produced the latter decline send ripples through the age structure of the labour-force. But overall, the combination of demography and increasing educational participation (see below) mean that we have moved decisively from the era of youth labour into that of middle-aged labour.

The workforce is not merely getting older, it is also being compressed into a somewhat narrower age-band and, within that band, is displaying a somewhat flatter age-profile. This poses a long-term challenge to the maintenance of a pyramidal, seniority-based system of work organisation. It may also be a stimulus to mid-career change, since structural change increasingly means redeploying established workers. This, in turn, implies a diminution of certainty, in the sense that – irrespective of career progression – transition through an age threshold to security and career stability is less easy to assume. Similarly, it implies retraining, and hence a new general conception of education and training as being 'lifelong'.

Men
%

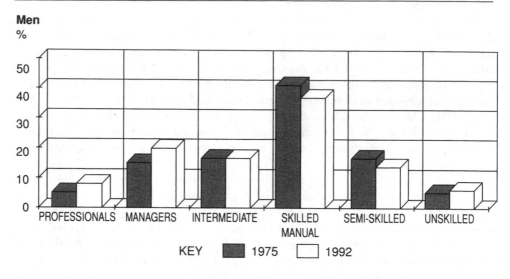

KEY   ■ 1975   □ 1992

Women
%

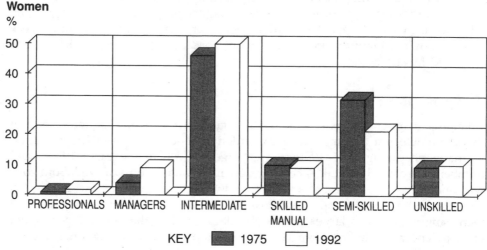

KEY   ■ 1975   □ 1992

Figure 1.2   Occupational class of men and women (GB), 1975–92
Source: OCPS (1992, p. 108)

Increasing and restructured education

There has been a long-term trend towards increasing educational participation, but the rate of participation particularly exercises us today for a variety of reasons. Concern with the UK 'skills gap', which has been voiced since the 1840s, is currently very marked. For example, in Germany and the Netherlands almost three-quarters of the workforce holds qualifications at (approximately) NVQ level 2 and above. A series of influential studies have indicated that this allows similar plant to be operated more productively with less 'down time', and new plant and working methods to be introduced more easily (Prais, 1995). Moreover, it is routinely asserted that economic expansion is inhibited by skill shortages and that inward investment is attracted by education and training provision. The argument that 'credential inflation' wastes resources by over-educating people

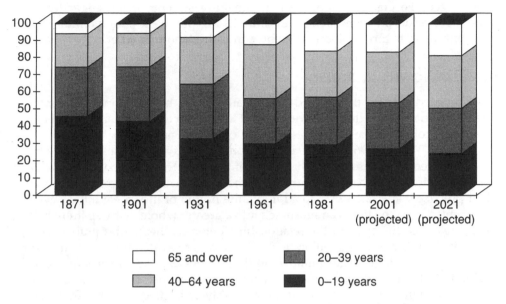

Figure 1.3 Age structure of the population, 1871–2021

Source: Mitchell (1992, pp. 41–42); CSO (1993).

whose occupations cannot make use of high educational attainment is now routinely ignored or dismissed (e.g. Halsey *et al.*, 1980). Employment chances and rewards are related to educational level, and the ability of the economy to absorb unskilled labour is projected to decline (Wilson *et al.*, 1990).

High levels of youth unemployment have created the conditions for a sharp upward step in post-compulsory participation, and the rapidity of this rise is itself a matter for comment. In 1976, 27 per cent of 16–18-year-olds were in full-time education, and the rest were in the labour-force, either employed (65 per cent) or unemployed (8 per cent). By 1990, 36 per cent were in full-time education, 15 per cent were in youth training schemes, and less than half (49 per cent) were in the labour-force. Educational participation reduces with age, even inside this group. For 16-year-olds, participation of some kind was at 76 per cent in 1992 and projected to rise to 84 per cent in 1997 (DfE, 1994). By early 1993, conventional working by those who had reached the minimum school-leaving age was a minority activity: only about 8 per cent of 16-year-olds and one-third of 17-year-olds were in full-time employment (*Employment Gazette*, 101(8), LFS3). Higher education participation rates rose from 13 per cent in 1981 to just over 30 per cent in 1994, and the 'push' from increasing rates of GCSE success had not yet abated by that year (DTI, 1995). Thus it is quite possible that over one-third of all young people will be entering higher education by the end of the century.

Another aspect of increasing participation is allied to structural change. The 'front-loaded' or 'end-on' model of education and training is being replaced by a 'continuing' or 'lifelong' one (e.g. Killeen and Bird, 1981) in which the periodic retraining and updating of people in employment, personal strategies for maintaining employability through education and training, and the recycling of unemployed adults into employment through training, are all recognised and encouraged. Formal education and training investments increasingly tend to taper over adult life, consistent with diminishing pay-back periods, rather than stopping dead before or soon after entry into the labour market.

1.3 CHANGING CAREERS

It is repeatedly asked if the word 'career' any longer has meaning. Attempts to rescue the integrity of careers have plunged into subjectivity, hoping to find there the form, continuity and progression the objective career now seems to lack (Collin and Watts, 1996). This is as a personal narrative: a sense-making which lends coherence because it is in the nature of the narrative to do so. Careers guidance practitioners are being encouraged to incorporate narrative construction into their practice (Savickas, 1993). In addition, the notion of life-career allows even a fragmented working life to be subsumed into a greater whole, with a pattern being found over the life-span in the relationships between these roles (Super, 1994). There is a danger of exaggeration here. All seems predicated on a particular sort of career, available to larger numbers in the recent past: the career which could be made in large companies or in the employment of the state during the postwar era of high employment. But it can plausibly be argued that at both the subjective and objective levels, a reorientation is occurring, and that there is a range of career possibilities to which guidance should attend.

Much of what has been written about careers has been focused upon what dual-labour-market theorists (e.g. Doeringer and Piore, 1971; Gordon *et al.*, 1982) call the 'primary labour market', and especially upon those who make their careers within one of the 'internal labour markets' of the great corporations and the state. In the recent past, it was often realistically assumed that these large, multi-layered employing organisations would provide employment security and respect the principles of equity and due process in the treatment of their employees. Many private employers occupying dominant positions in stable or growing product markets were prepared to enunciate non-contractual 'no redundancy' employment policies. Employment contracts were usually full-time and permanent. Both the state and firms defending their share in mature product markets resembled what Sonnenfeld (1989) calls 'clubs': organisations whose employment conditions permitted deep socialisation into and understanding of internal processes, products or tasks, and their markets. The concept of 'career' which applied to the managerial and administrative superstructures of these internal labour markets was one of progress up clearly-defined career ladders determined, at least in part, by seniority or order of entry. It was these organisations which seemed to offer the natural home for what Kanter (1989) has called the 'bureaucratic career'.

More generally, this sort of internal labour market is recognised in the British literature as its traditional form, offering a career in which seniority and experience are the conventional basis for progression (Lovering, 1990). A career of this kind was available to employees other than bureaucrats. In order to permit this, the organisation had to be made up of a hierarchy of hierarchies. The hierarchy in which a career took place generally depended upon the 'port of entry' into the organisation: movement *between* hierarchies was much less common than movement *within* them. This pattern was applied to professional, scientific and technical workers in two ways: by grading structures which reflected experience and might be related to the difficulty or responsibility of the tasks undertaken within their field of competence; and by the hierarchical supervision of all functional areas. Worried by labour turnover, dominant employers competed with one another to provide such careers, even for production workers: careers of minutely graduated steps, which were often allied to demarcations established by collective bargaining and the grading of pay by work study. Such careers could scarcely be called bureaucratic and did not necessarily correspond to increasing authority. To the undiscerning eye, they might appear to be made up of merely lateral moves, but to those involved they constituted progress.

These forms of career are defined by security, stability, continuity, and progression. They are emblematic of their age, and thus easily overgeneralised, so that they become the fictional common origin from which all change is charted. But they are emblematic precisely because the sense of security most people felt in the post-war boom years was far greater than it is today, irrespective of their place of work. Stability seemed achievable when labour was in short supply. So strong was this impression that young people who took the opportunity the age afforded to change jobs as often as they wished, and older people who failed to 'stabilise', were easily thought to be 'immature' and to be doing themselves unnecessary harm. Much attention was given by researchers to this imaginary problem (for a review, see Clarke, 1980).

The sorts of career we have just considered were always, however, only part of the picture. Internal labour markets differed from one another in ways which shaped career patterns; the state and large 'club-like' firms made up only part of the structure of opportunities; and the underlying assumption of a static organisational structure is almost wilfully perverse. Moreover, if people had been less prone to change employers, it would not have been so necessary to structure organisations in ways which might persuade them to stay. And, of course, many workers were, when considered in terms of the dominant imagery, 'careerless'.

In addition to *clubs*, Sonnenfeld (1989) sketches three further types of firm and career system. *Fortresses* are out-competed firms, or firms which must react to unpredicted change or volatility in their markets. Recruitment is confined to that of 'turn-around talent', careers are by seniority and sponsorship, but labour shedding means that remaining employees feel at risk. *Academies* occupy dominant positions in evolving product markets and must maintain an ability to introduce new products and production processes. These recruit at the outset of a person's career, offering employment security in exchange for a high degree of internal lateral mobility, allied to training which extends and updates skills and knowledge. *Teams* grow through product innovation and opening-up of new markets. They tend therefore to be newer and smaller than the 'academies' into which they may evolve, and to recruit both young trainees and older persons of reputation from the external labour market. Those no longer able to contribute are shed. It is tempting to characterise the recent evolution of larger employing organisations as moving away from 'clubs' to 'fortresses' and, for those that succeed, towards the 'academy' (see Herriot and Pemberton, 1995). More simply, we might speak of a transition from traditional to modern, often by wholesale closure and subsequent replacement by inward investment, as has happened in Wales. Lovering (1990) describes a modern form, somewhat akin to the 'academy', in which hierarchies are flat, and rewards and career progression are dependent upon a highly individualised form of performance appraisal.

But what of those beyond the charmed circle? Let us first consider the 'career-less'. The existence, in large numbers, of people who failed to stabilise was acknowledged, somewhat grudgingly, by the developmental theorists of careers (e.g. Super, 1957) in terms which did the theorists little credit. Such people were viewed as being engaged in 'multiple trial': they were 'vocationally immature'. They were also concentrated in the semi- and unskilled stratum. And then there were women, most of whom would leave the labour market for an extended period and only a modest proportion of whom would return, often to part-time work and to jobs of inferior status to those they had left when forming families (Martin and Roberts, 1984). Contrary to the views of the developmental psychologists, women, immigrants, youths who might later stabilise, and a much smaller proportion of indigenous adult men, were often thought unwillingly to populate the 'secondary labour market' (Barron and Norris, 1976). The conditions of working life in the secondary labour market correspond much more closely to the classical economic notion of a labour market. Employers tend to be small, to operate in intensely competitive, low-tech, and labour-intensive sectors, and are 'price-takers'. Trade-union or professional organisation is weak. Wage rates are low, employment insecure and, perhaps, casual, and careers no more than a succession of jobs.

In addition, we must consider those who can construct careers, but are not tied to internal labour markets. Kanter (1989) has distinguished 'professional' and 'entrepreneurial' careers, attempting in each case to preserve the idea of progression. 'Professional careers' are characterised by the possession of a skill or craft in short supply, and by the pursuit of 'reputation' and, hence, of increasing responsibility and rewards within a specific field of expertise. They are not confined to internal labour markets, and when employment occurs in them, the probability of movement between employers is greater than for the 'bureaucrat'. By 'entrepreneurial career', Kanter means the career not merely of one who 'grows' a business but also that of anyone whose career consists of expanding the territory, volume of business, or returns from what is within his or her existing scope, and who shares in the rewards that accrue.

Many of these ideas have been brought together in a model which purports to describe the way in which internal labour markets react to intensified price competition, and competition to introduce new technologies and new products (Atkinson, 1984; Atkinson and Meager, 1986). The firm responds to increased competition, market instabilities, and the continual need to introduce new products, by becoming flexible. The core workforce shrinks, and is made functionally flexible. This means organisational flattening (or delayering), and multi-skilling. It also means that promotion prospects are reduced, whilst the likelihood of redeployment or lateral mobility is increased. But as we have seen, additional forces are at work, which cannot simply be reduced to intensified competitive pressures and market volatility. These include the rise of process technologies, which not only displace labour, but imply a different kind of production work for those who remain. In part, it is because production processes can be rapidly reprogrammed and adapted, that 'flexible specialisation' can be practised; this preserves the cost advantages of capital intensity, but exploits 'niche markets' and consumer demand for variety and change in products.

In addition, inward investment has brought with it foreign, notably Japanese, approaches to production, with – as noted in Section 1.2 – emphasis upon team-working, production staff responsibility for quality assurance, and resistance to trade unions, together with strong preference for 'green' labour which lacks a collective memory of past labour-relations practices. Irrespective of the spur of competition, many indigenous employers have long sought to achieve this sort of reorganisation of production, maintenance, quality assurance and other shop-floor functions, resentful of demarcations and minute sub-divisions which come to appear particularly irrational when capital-intensive process technology is introduced. Thus part of flattening and multi-skilling is the creation of new kinds of jobs which combine process-control, quality-assurance and maintenance functions; while another part is the creation of rapidly redeployable labour, capable of a range of semi-skilled tasks. More recently, however, downsizing, either from loss of markets or technical innovation, devolution of control to point of production or point of sale, and the advent of computerised management information systems which allow this to happen, have led to delayering of the managerial superstructures of companies, with similar effects upon the careers of managers as upon those of the managed.

In Atkinson's model, the core workforce is surrounded by a periphery, through which numerical flexibility is achieved. Non-standard employment relations such as short-term contracts, use of 'agency' and self-employed sub-contractors, and use of part-timers (whose employment rights have been more limited), mean that the labour-force can be varied according to fluctuating demand. This creates an 'internal secondary labour market' differentiated from those with a more permanent relationship to the employer. Increased sub-contracting achieves a similar effect, passing on the consequences of market volatility to suppliers. The model, therefore, assumes a 'market' relationship, rather than an intimate and pervasive Japanese-style relationship, between corporation and supplier. The net effect of an expanded periphery is an expanded secondary labour market which stretches across the boundary of the organisation, out into sub-contracting, increased 'casualisation', and insecurity.

This model has been controversial. Many regard it as a useful idealisation, rather than an empirical generalisation, and only a small minority of firms claim it as conscious policy (Hakim, 1990), although in a CBI membership survey many said that they were practising some forms of 'flexibility' (CBI, 1994). Moreover, much of the evidence for increasing flexibility at the aggregate national level arises from privatisation and other changes in the state sector, rather than changes in the private sector to which the concept was originally directed (Pollert, 1988). Many of the practices identified are not new, and it is difficult to isolate, from the perspective of employment practices and labour processes, those changes which go on in firms as they grow, achieve dominance, and decline; changes which respond to general and persistent increases in competitive pressures; changes which are necessary responses to new technology; and changes which reflect the altered bargaining positions of employers and workers in an era of high unemployment and weakened trade unions.

But even if the model is no more than an idealisation, it does collect together a large number of recent preoccupations. The new career realities which such tendencies imply are uncertainty, unpredictability, insecurity, reduced likelihood of promotion, increased likelihood of mobility out of one's initial occupational field, non-standard employment contracts, and other non-standard working (part-time work and self-employment). However, the notion is preserved that employment insecurity is not equally distributed. Firms are still social organisations, not top-hatted entrepreneurs who hire a new labour-force every day, and, of course, employers remain as dependent as they ever were upon the maintenance of the human fabric of their companies.

As Figure 1.4 shows, non-standard working is on the increase among both men and women. Between 1978 and 1991, the number of men in full-time employment fell from 12.4 to 10.3 million. The number and proportion of male part-timers increased, but the number who took this kind of work because they could not get full-time jobs varied considerably from year to year, being as high as 28 per cent in 1987, but declining to 14 per cent in 1990. Far fewer women part-timers (only 5 per cent in 1990) were in this position (Meulders *et al.*, 1994). These percentage figures must, however, be set against the more naively benign interpretations of the inexorable rise in the number of part-timers.

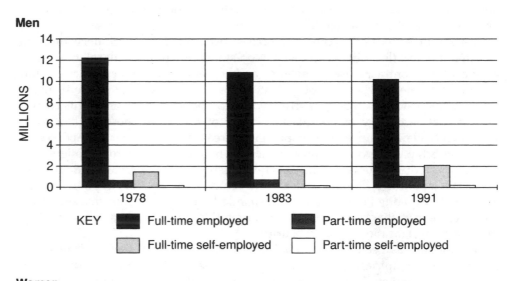

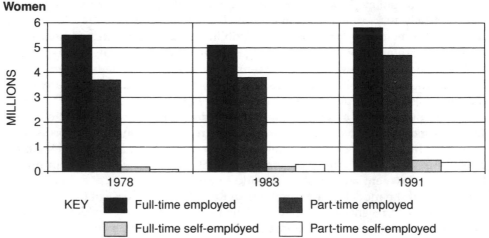

Figure 1.4 Numbers of men and women in standard and non-standard work (agriculture excluded), 1978–91

Source: Blanchflower and Freeman (1994, p.73)

For men, the rise in self-employment during the same period is better characterised as an increase in 'disguised unemployment' than as the burgeoning of enterprise. The increase was due to transitions from non- and unemployment, not from employment, and there was also an increase in the rate of transition back into non- and unemployment (Blanchflower and Freeman, 1994). Temporary working, however, stayed at a fairly constant 3 per cent (*ibid.*; Meulders *et al.* [1994] give a higher and more fluctuating figure) for men and 7 per cent for women, throughout the 1980s. But about 15 per cent of part-timers were in temporary jobs, and a fifth of recently unemployed people found themselves in temporary jobs, as did a similar proportion entering work from non-employment (Payne and Payne, 1993). A high but fluctuating proportion of those in temporary work were doing it because they could not find permanent jobs. This proportion reached 53 per cent for men in 1987, but by 1990 had fallen back to 29 per cent of male and 20 per cent of female part-timers (Meulders *et al.*, 1994). It would be wrong to suggest that non-standard work is inevitably second-best. Many people want part-time or temporary work, or to be self-employed. But equally, these sorts of work may be all that is available for those who want full-time and permanent employment.

We can characterise much non-standard working as insecure underemployment. It is connected to relatively high probabilities of unemployment: an expansion of secondary conditions of employment. To this we should now add a number of other considerations. Trade-union membership has declined. Unemployment and underemployment occur in local concentrations which greatly exceed the national rate. In 1993, ethnic minorities made up 5.8 per cent of the working population, but 9.4 per cent of the under-16s waiting to enter the world of work, and their elders already had to accept a disproportionate share of unemployment (*Equal Opportunities Review*, 56, 1994, 25–26). From about 1977, the post-war trend towards household income equalisation was reversed, returning by the end of the 1980s to the degree of inequality obtaining in the later 1940s. An analysis by Stark (1989) indicates that the main cause was changing employment income. Full-time earnings were influenced by changes in industrial and occupational composition and by a 'market' or flexibility effect. Guidance must, therefore, confront an increasingly polarised society.

1.4 IMPLICATIONS FOR GUIDANCE

The non-contractual 'no redundancy' promises of corporations such as IBM proved impossible to keep. Small but growing companies may provide continuity of employment contingent upon their success, but of course this cannot be anticipated before the event. So despite the fact that, for those in employment, job-tenure durations have not declined (Income Data Services, 1995), in each case the *expectations* which constitute psychological security are lacking. In addition, too many people who could make a contribution are denied the opportunity to do so. These include those officially unemployed, those hidden in education and training which fails adequately to raise their competence, 'non-employed' women who under happier circumstances would seek work, and those eased into premature retirement by a raid upon the pension funds. It is against this unpleasant backdrop that guidance must make its contribution.

But even if the conditions under which people offer their labour improve, the economy will continue to require 'flexibility'. The flow of people between employers is greater in times of full employment than in those of unemployment, and this is not a result of aimless experimentation. The role of guidance in initial education and training is becoming increasingly important, not merely because more decisions must be made, over an increasing period of time, without direct experience of the work to which one is being oriented, but also because a complex and increasingly modularised system of education and training cannot really work without it. The extension of education and training in the 16–22 age-group is, however, only part of the story. An ageing labour force is one in which human resource development becomes increasingly imperative, not merely for the favoured few as an accompaniment to promoted responsibility, but for a very high proportion of workers.

Lifelong flexibility and lifelong education and training are creating the conditions for lifelong guidance. We shall therefore conclude by briefly considering the role of guidance in the labour market. This may be classified according to the nature of the *employment contract* and the degree of labour-force *attachment* of the client group. It is simplistic to assume that individuals *either* have protected careers inside internal labour markets, *or* have professional or entrepreneurial careers, *or* have 'careers' on secondary-labour-market terms; it is also simplistic to assume that people are *either* strongly attached *or* weakly attached to the labour market. People can flow between employment conditions, and their attachment to the labour-force may alter over the course of their working lives. However, simplification is necessary to clear exposition. We shall consider the role of guidance in relation to three groups: those with (modifying Herriot and Pemberton, 1995; 1996) *conditional relational* psychological contracts, those with *transactional* psychological contracts who are *closely attached* to the labour market, and those who are *weakly attached* to the labour market.

Conditional relational psychological contracts

Many people continue to strike a more or less explicit bargain with their employers, entailing a set of mutual expectations of security and reciprocal loyalty (see Chapter 2). As Herriot and Pemberton (1995; 1996) have observed, with the waning of the traditional internal labour market, security is now offered in exchange for functional flexibility, in the manner described by Atkinson and Meager (1986): it is the form of career possible at the 'core' of the labour-force. Careers consist of a series of renegotiations of organisational roles and their associated training requirements. It is advisable to qualify the term 'relational contract', since any such set of mutual expectations is conditional upon the state of competition and other factors, such as technical change: security is only relative. This sort of career is not confined to managers, professionals or other highly-skilled workers. It also applies to protected sectors of the production workforce, which may include workers trained in an increasing range of semi-skilled tasks. Guidance provided by the employer focuses upon the need to recruit from within, both for lateral mobility and for up-skilling, and may lie on a continuum of activities which include performance appraisal and other coercive measures. However, employers are often persuaded of the need to preserve a distinction between the more coercive aspects of their labour-management regime and guidance provided on a voluntary basis.

There are, however, two other functions for guidance provided by employers to this category of worker, each of which hinges on the 'conditional' nature of their relationship. The first is to encourage self-development and the maintenance of employability through education and training, not merely because any increase in these things adds to the auditable stock of competence within the firm (which conventionally trains in a firm-specific manner), but also in recognition of the inability of the employer to offer absolute guarantees of security. In this respect, guidance is part of the contingency planning for redundancy and premature retirement. It is often argued that employers' expressions of interest in guidance for such a reason are rhetorical, but there are examples of practice, such as the Employee Development and Assistance Programme (EDAP) at the Ford Motor Company.

The second function is to facilitate outplacement. This is designed not only to help those leaving the organisation, but also to maintain morale among those who remain. The hope is that it will shore up commitment and maintain the 'relational' contract, under circumstances which might otherwise lead those who remain to become demoralised, perform less effectively, seek alternative employment, unionise, or adopt a narrow view of their obligations to their employer. Of course, once shed, the guidance needs of workers who have previously enjoyed a sense of some security must be met externally, like those of people with transactional psychological contracts.

Transactional psychological contracts

Herriot and Pemberton (1995; 1996) describe transactional contracts as explicit, purely economic, and tending to be short-term. They therefore correspond to the conditions of employment on the secondary labour market, and to life at the periphery of internal labour markets, such as 'agency' workers (often self-employed) and other non-standard workers whose relationship with companies is recognised not to involve expectations of security. They also, however, characterise the relationships of the most mobile professional and other skilled groups to their employers, described in Kanter's (1989) 'professional' career. The essential point, from the perspective of guidance, is that whereas mobility tends to be high, attachment to the labour-force is also high. The guidance needs of this group must be met externally, since there is neither the incentive nor, because of the group's concentration in the small-to-medium enterprise sector, the capacity for employers to provide guidance internally. A similar point may be made of formal training, which employers have no incentive, and often no capacity, to provide (although the once-despised 'Nellie', who has now been accorded the dignity and title of 'mentor', no doubt still does as well or ill as ever). Guidance provided externally may be from professional and trade associations, from private-sector guidance agencies or from the state. The range of people involved is very wide, and includes those with a preference for this sort of career, and those forced to adopt it. Many may be hoping to enter or return to a relational form of psychological contract. It is difficult to think of a form of guidance which is not potentially required, since job search, entry into self-employment, and the use of education and training to increase or extend employability, may all figure. The development of a comprehensive range of guidance services for adults may play a role in reducing the duration of unemployment spells, increasing access to training, and allowing novices, such as those displaced from employment for the first time, to manage the remainder of their careers for themselves.

Weak attachment

Unemployment is, as we have seen, locally and racially concentrated. Employment opportunities are related to educational attainment and, often, geographical mobility. This has led to the belief that an increasingly middle-class society will be attended by an 'under class'. This under-class may more and more become spatially concentrated, owing to the outward flow of those able to obtain work. Its educational attainments will be few. It will suffer much of the burden of long-term unemployment. Its jobs, as opposed to participation in government programmes, will be ill-paid – close to the threshold dictated by benefit payments – and infrequent, insecure, temporary, or casual; it will often be part of the black economy. Its female members will retreat into parenthood, rather than elect for it from a position of strength. Its men will be unable to support families. Its attachment to the labour market will be weak, and this will become an accepted way of life.

This is really no more than a dramatisation of the existing position. Increasingly coercive and punitive methods may be adopted to re-establish labour-force attachment, including workfare-like methods, perhaps on the Swedish education and training model which, since they make benefit conditional on attendance, have the theoretical effect of reducing the (reservation) wage at which people are prepared to accept open employment. This represents perhaps the most challenging environment in which guidance, wedded to voluntaristic and client-centred principles, must work. It is perhaps one in which guidance practitioners will continue to argue, as through their professional bodies they have often argued, that one of the tasks of guidance is to draw forcibly to our attention the plight of its most disadvantaged clients.

REFERENCES

Adams, N. A. (1993) *The North South Divide and the International System*, London: Zed Books.
Ashton, D., Green, F. and Hoskins, M. (1989) 'The Training System of British Capitalism: Changes and Prospects', in Green, F. (ed.) *Restructuring of the UK Economy*, Hemel Hempstead: Harvester Wheatsheaf.
Atkinson, J. (1984) 'Manpower Strategies for Flexible Organisations', *Personnel Management* 16(8): 28–31.
Atkinson, J. and Meager, N. (1986) *Changing Working Patterns: How Companies Achieve Flexibility to Meet New Needs*, London: National Economic Development Office.
Barron, R. D. and Norris, G. M. (1976) 'Sexual Division and the Dual Labour Market', in Barker, D. L. and Allen, S. (eds) *Dependence and Exploitation in Work and Marriage*, London: Longman.
Bell, D. (1974) *The Coming of Post-Industrial Society*, London: Heinemann.
Berggren, C. (1993) 'Lean Production: the End of History?' *Work, Employment and Society* 7(2): 163–88.
Blackburn, R. M., Jarman, J. and Siltanen, J. (1993) 'The Analysis of Occupational Gender Segregation over Time and Place: Consideration of Measurement and Some New Evidence', *Work, Employment and Society* 7(3): 335–62.

Blanchflower, D. O. and Freeman, R. B. (1994) 'Did the Thatcher Reforms Change British Labour Market Performance?', in Bassell, R. (ed.) *The UK Labour Market: Comparative Aspects and Institutional Developments*, Cambridge: Cambridge University Press.

Blauner, R. (1964) *Alienation and Freedom: the Factory Worker and his History*, Chicago: Chicago University Press.

Central Statistical Office (1990) *Social Trends*, London: HMSO.

Central Statistical Office (1993) *Annual Abstract of Statistics 1993*, London: HMSO.

Clarke, L. (1980) *The Transition from School to Work: a Critical Review of Research in the United Kingdom*, London: HMSO.

Collin, A. and Watts, A. G. (1996) 'The Death and Transfiguration of Career – and of Career Guidance?', *British Journal of Guidance and Counselling* 24(3): 385–98.

Confederation of British Industry (1991) *Competing with the World's Best: Report of the CBI Manufacturing Advisory Group*, London: CBI.

Confederation of British Industry (1994) *Flexible Labour Markets: Who Pays for Training?*, London: CBI.

Department for Education (1994) 'Education Statistics for the United Kingdom', *Statistical Bulletin* 1/94, London: DfE.

Department of Trade and Industry (1995) *Competitiveness: Forging Ahead*, London: HMSO.

Doeringer, P. B. and Piore, M. J. (1971) *Internal Labor Markets and Manpower Analysis*, Lexington, MA: Heath.

Employment Department (1992) 'The Labour Force to 2001', *Labour Market Quarterly Review*, May, 9.

Employment Department (1993) *New Earnings Survey 1993, Part A*, London: HMSO.

Gordon, D. M., Edwards, R. and Reich, M. (1982) *Segmented Work, Divided Workers: the Historical Transformation of Labor in the United States*, Cambridge: Cambridge University Press.

Hakim, C. (1979) *Occupational Segregation: a Comparative Study of the Degree and Pattern of the Differentiation between Men's and Women's Work in Britain, the United States and Other Countries*, Research Paper No. 9, London: Department of Employment.

Hakim, C. (1981) 'Job Segregation: Trends in the 1970s', *Employment Gazette* 89(12): 521–29.

Hakim, C. (1990) 'Core and Periphery in Employers' Workforce Strategies: Evidence from the 1987 ELUS Survey', *Work, Employment and Society* 4: 157–58.

Hakim, C. (1993) 'The Myth of Rising Female Employment', *Work, Employment and Society* 7(1): 97–120.

Halsey, A. H., Heath, A. F. and Ridge, J. M. (1980) *Origins and Destinations*, Oxford: Clarendon Press.

Herriot, P. and Pemberton, C. (1995) *New Deals*, Chichester: Wiley.

Herriot, P. and Pemberton, C. (1996) 'Contracting Careers', *Human Relations* 49(6): 757–90.

Hunt, A. (1975) *Survey of Management Attitudes and Practices towards Women at Work*, London: HMSO.

Income Data Services (1995) *The Jobs Mythology*, IDS Focus 74, London: IDS.

Kanter, R. M. (1989) 'Careers and the Wealth of Nations: a Macro-Perspective on the Structure and Implications of Career Forms', in Arthur, M. B., Hall, D. T. and Lawrence, B. S. (eds) *Handbook of Career Theory*, Cambridge: Cambridge University Press.

Killeen, J. and Bird, M. (1981) *Education and Work*, Leicester: National Institute for Adult Education.

Killeen, J. and Robertson, E. (1988) *Technological Change and the Work of Women in Industry*, Cambridge: National Institute for Careers Education and Counselling.

Lovering, J. (1990) 'A Perfunctory Sort of Post-Fordism: Economic Restructuring and Labour Market Segmentation in Britain in the 1980s', *Work, Employment and Society*, Special Issue, 9–28.

Martin, J. and Roberts, C. (1984) *Women and Employment Survey: a Lifetime Perspective*, London: HMSO.

Meulders, D., Plasman, O. and Plasman, R. (1994) *Atypical Employment in the EC*, Aldershot: Dartmouth.

Mitchell, B. R. (1992) *International Historical Statistics: Europe 1750–1988*, Basingstoke: Macmillan.

Office of Population Censuses and Surveys (1992) *General Household Survey*, London: HMSO.

Payne, J. and Payne, C. (1993) 'Unemployment and Peripheral Work', *Work, Employment and Society* 7(4): 513–34.

Piore, M. and Sabel, C. (1984) *The Second Industrial Divide: Possibilities for Prosperity*, New York: Basic Books.

Pollert, A. (1988) 'The "Flexible Firm": Fixation or Fact?', *Work, Employment and Society* 2: 281–316.

Prais, S. J. (1995) *Productivity, Education and Training: an International Perspective*, Cambridge: Cambridge University Press.

Roberts, K., Dench, S. and Richardson, D. (1986) *The Changing Structure of Youth Labour Markets*, Research Paper No. 59, London: Department of Employment.

Robson, P. (1993) *The Economics of International Integration* (3rd edn), London: Routledge.

Savickas, M. L. (1993) 'Career Counseling in the Postmodern Era', *Journal of Cognitive Psychotherapy* 7(3): 205–15.

Sonnenfeld, J. A. (1989) 'Career System Profiles and Strategic Staffing', in Arthur, M. B., Hall, D. T. and Lawrence, B. S. (eds) *Handbook of Career Theory*, Cambridge: Cambridge University Press.

Stark, T. (1989) 'The Changing Distribution of Income under Mrs Thatcher', in Green, F. (ed.) *Restructuring of the UK Economy*, Hemel Hempstead: Harvester Wheatsheaf.

Super, D. E. (1957) *The Psychology of Careers*, New York: Harper & Row.

Super, D. E. (1994) 'A Life Span, Life Space Perspective on Convergence', in Savickas, M. L. and Lent, R. W. (eds) *Convergence in Career Development Theories: Implications for Science and Practice*, Palo Alto, CA: Consulting Psychologists Press.

United Nations (1988) *Transnational Corporations in World Development*, New York: UN Centre for Transnational Corporations.

Watts, A. G., Guichard, J., Plant, P. and Rodriguez, M. L. (1994) *Educational and Vocational Guidance in the European Community*, Luxembourg: Office for Official Publications of the European Communities.

Williams, K., Williams, J. and Haslam, C. (1989) 'Why Take the Stocks Out?: Britain vs Japan', *International Journal of Operations and Production Management* 9(8): 91–105.

Wilson, R. A., Bosworth, D. L. and Taylor, P. C. (1990) *Projecting the Labour Market for the Highly Qualified*, Coventry: Institute for Employment Research, University of Warwick.

Womack, J., Jones, D. and Roos, D. (1990) *The Machine that Changed the World*, New York: Rawson Associates.

Wood, S. L. (1991) 'Japanisation and/or Toyotaism', *Work, Employment and Society* 5(4): 567–600.

Chapter 2

Career theory

John Killeen

2.1 INTRODUCTION

Career theory is a source of guidance strategies and techniques, and can offer a rationale for guidance to those who control its destiny. More fundamentally, it is a powerful formative influence on what we think careers are.

There are many theories of or about careers, any one of which would, if allowed to do so, occupy all of the pages which follow. So it is important to acknowledge at the outset that summary presentations of theory are simply no substitute for the real thing, and that anyone who determines to become theoretically aware faces a demanding, but ultimately very rewarding, journey.

Here, we shall consider some of the basic building-blocks of career theory, go on to review some recent theoretical developments, and conclude by considering the uses of theory. Detailed exposition will be avoided, but part of the work of particular theorists will be summarised, albeit sometimes in dismembered form, in answer to three simple questions. First, who is the 'agent' – that is, the person who has a career? Second, what are the 'environments' in which careers are made? Third, what is the nature of career 'action'? These are the *who*, the *where* and the *what* of career theory. As we shall see, there are many possible answers to each of these questions.

The *agent*, or person who has a career, may be seen as someone who does, or does not, have sufficient power to make effective decisions and thus to be in control of his or her career. He or she may be thought essentially the same as other people in the main respects which determine how happily any particular occupation will be performed, or as fundamentally different from most other people in these respects. In the latter case, the 'fit' between the person and the working environment really matters. If we decide to view people as different from one another, then the ways in which they differ must be identified, and how they become different can come to be considered an important aspect of career development. Finally, assuming that people have at least some power to exercise volition over their careers, the question arises as to what sort of decision-maker we envisage. Is the agent to be conceived as a rational actor, or in a more complex psychological light?

Turning to the *environments* in which careers are made, these are most commonly thought of as labour markets, or as occupational structures, or as social structures more broadly conceived. Alternatively, like biologists, psychologists may simply speak in terms of a general 'environment', echoing the tendency of earlier generations of psychologists sometimes to regard their object of study as the behaviour of the 'organism' in its environment.

Finally, concerning *action* – what happens in careers – we can reasonably say that, until recently, the focus has most often been upon how some sort of harmony or equilibrium – usually thought of as 'correspondence' or 'congruence' between people and their work – is achieved, and upon the nature of that state. The three simple underlying ideas have been: first, that people move towards 'suitable' occupations and environments; second, that people are moulded to fit their careers; and third, that people act upon and change their environments and roles in ways which reflect what they can do and what they find satisfaction in.

This brief sketch should be sufficient to indicate that even from a set of simple ingredients, a great many theoretical recipes can be created. Broadly, theorists can be divided into two stylistic camps. Those who attempt, in the manner of decision science and much of economics, to argue out the logical consequences of a restricted set of initial assumptions, aim at the precision of mathematical expression. Others, to be found amongst the developmentalists and sociologists who have contributed to career theory, adopt a more inclusive, discursive and descriptive approach. There are virtues in each, and our understanding is enriched if we are prepared to engage with both styles of theorisation.

At the substantive level, theorists may not merely make choices, but actively *reject* what they take to be opposing ideas about the agent, environment, and action in careers. Theories may become polarised and antagonistic to one another. Alternatively – and this is common – theorists may ingest elements of the work of their predecessors, so that their theories may be thought of as cross-breeds. This makes much of career theory very difficult to classify. Perhaps the clearest example is developmental theory, which cheerfully incorporates virtually every other approach.

So two further trends in the development of career theory must be noted. The first is the tendency to examine polarised positions and to seek to decide between them by means of research. This may lead to new 'compounds' when it comes to be thought that neither of the original, polarised positions is sufficient, but that each has some virtue. Later in this chapter we shall give an example of this process, considering what happens when structural and rational decision theories are allowed to coalesce. The second is the renewed tendency, previously evident in early forms of developmentalism, to expand theories or develop new ones which are ever more inclusive, attending now not only to the classical problems of choice and equilibrium, but also to new preoccupations. One of these is the increasing prevalence of disrupted and fragmented adult careers, prompted by the changing context of careers outlined in Chapter 1.

2.2 THE ELEMENTS OF CAREER THEORY

The agent in career theory

The first component of career theory is the agent: the person who 'acts' – that is who has intentions which are in some way reflected in what he or she does. Career theories differ, in the main, in their approach to the motives which underlie such intentions and to the behavioural processes through which the intentions are pursued. In some sociological theories, 'agency' hides in the shadows, not because it is denied, but because the *power* of each individual is regarded as

slight. Even when they appear to themselves to be following their own preferences, people tend to be treated as acting-out the consequences of their
socialisation, so far as it has formed their identities as men or women, as members
of this or that social class, and so on, thus fulfilling a social destiny to which
they have been assigned (Roberts, 1968; 1981).

Many theorists assume *universal* needs and preferences. Job satisfaction varies
by occupational class (Quinn *et al.*, 1974), and a multi-disciplinary literature on
worker alienation (e.g. Argyris, 1964) has generally assumed that there is a lack
of correspondence between the demands of routinised, machine-paced, repetitive work and the needs of any normally-developed adult. Goldthorpe and Hope
(1974) take a more extensive view, basing their scale of occupations on a criterion of 'general desirability'. The critical perspective represented by Roberts
demands, despite its views about the socialisation of preferences, a superordinate, generally recognised view that there are 'good' and 'bad' jobs. Simple
economic theories treat jobs as better or worse according to wage rates, although
an ancient debate concerned the extent to which high wages *compensated* for the
demands of work (the view of Adam Smith) or were *associated* with the quality
of work measured in other ways (the view of J. S. Mill). Universalism directs
us away from over-optimistic assumptions about the scope for 'free choice'. If
a hierarchy of opportunities is universally recognised (cf. Goldthorpe and Hope,
1974) so that, in effect, 'everyone wants the same', this focuses attention on the
competition between individuals, families, or wider groupings.

Other theories focus upon the way in which people are *different* from one
another as to their needs and interests, and also their capacities. This allows
person–environment fit to occur, in principle, without a need for further changes
in individuals. If people differ in their wants and capacities, then merely by
movement into suitable kinds of work, they will achieve higher levels of reward
for themselves without necessarily diminishing the rewards available to others.

Within this person–environment fit tradition, *psychodynamic theory* is concerned
with what moves people to act (motives), as applied to careers. Theories about
the role of personality in careers can include attention to psychodynamics because
personality types may be thought to embody, or represent, needs. Similarly, theories of career development often include attention to psychodynamics because
the expression of personality in career may be explained developmentally, as rest-
ing upon early experiences in the family (e.g. Roe, 1956; Bordin *et al.*, 1963; Bordin,
1990). Indeed, there is a tendency for psychoanalytic theorists to see the family as
the source of career behaviour: 'the enlarged perspective offered by the family system can encompass all theories' (Bordin, 1994, p. 61).

Bordin distinguishes six intrinsic motives:

1 *Precision* – the satisfaction of 'neat, clear, error-free thought and action'.
2 *Nurturance* – the desire to care for and foster living things.
3 *Curiosity* – the wish to know and understand, which may take an object- or
   people-centred form.
4 *Power* – which may take a physical/mechanically-augmented form, or one in
   which others are dominated by skill, knowledge, personal charisma, etc.
5 *Aesthetic expression* – sensory and rhythmic satisfactions.
6 *Ethics* – concern with right and wrong, which is a concern for defining and
   enforcing rules, rather than for doing good.

Conceptions like this can, in principle, contribute to the analysis of 'work values', or of the rewards people seek from work; they can thus become the 'content' of decision models. They may also be treated as sources of personality types, and of distinctions such as 'orientation to people or things', and hence of preferences for occupational types.

Trait-and-factor theory also considers the stable psychological characteristics of individuals which distinguish them from other people, and thus make them better adapted to and more likely to prefer some kinds of work than others. Perhaps the trait-and-factor theory best known in the world of career theory is Holland's (1985) theory of occupational personalities. These are preferences for and skills appropriate to six environments and activities: *realistic* (concrete, physical activities); *investigative* (intellectual, problem-solving activities); *artistic* (self-expressive performance as a means of relating to others); *social* (close human contact and supportive or succourant activities, allied to the development of interpersonal skills); *enterprising* (manipulation and domination of others; preference for power and status); and *conventional* (closely-regulated, structured, rule-bound environments with clear hierarchies; respect for authority; self-control and subordination of personal needs). Holland showed that these types or dimensions form a hexagon (in the sequence RIASEC, so that C (conventional) becomes adjacent to R (realistic)). The scores individuals obtain in any one dimension tend to be most strongly correlated with adjacent dimensions and most weakly correlated with the opposite dimensions. Thus, for example, 'artistic' is strongly correlated with 'investigative' and 'social', and weakly correlated with 'conventional'.

Thereafter, concepts of the agent differ somewhat, on disciplinary lines. The agent may be seen as a maker of self-interested rational decisions, an important instance of which is the economic actor – that is, someone who attempts to maximise utility. We need give no further attention to this view here. However, the agent may also be seen, from the viewpoint of either social or cognitive psychology, as someone with a self-concept which he or she is driven to 'implement' in work. Self-concepts or their analogues can be: 'identity'; self-evaluations; self-esteem; ideas we have of how others see us; ideas of ourselves as we are, would like to be, or could be; ideas of how others would see us if we were like who we would like to be, or could be; ideas of ourselves as or as like a role model or person with whom we identify (significant other); and so on. The place of the self-concept in personality, and hence its role in promoting or shaping actions, varies accordingly.

In the psychology of careers, the best-known exponent of *self-concept theory* is Super (1953; 1957) who made a variety of statements ranging from the assertion that self-concepts are based on self-observation and comparison to others, to a more social–psychological formulation in which identification with significant others becomes central. Holland (1985) asserts that preferences for occupations are based upon stereotypes of the people who perform them, and that people use the same stereotypes to organise their perceptions of themselves: their self-concepts are essentially occupational. More recently, *social learning theory* has reinforced the tendency to treat self-concepts as self-observation generalisations (Krumboltz, 1994). However, some sort of 'self idea' seems necessary to any theory of careers which assumes *conscious* attempts to identify occupations that will be within one's capacities, and more, rather than less, rewarding.

The environment in career theory

The second main component of career theory is its conception of the *environment* in which careers are made. In economic theories, the environment is a market: the labour market. Neo-classical theory deals with perfectly informed competitive labour markets in which job search and mobility are cost-free. Wage offers signal the productivity with which employers can make use of labour, and determine the flow of labour into and out of jobs. Contemporary theories of job search recognise the artificiality of these assumptions and consider 'imperfect' markets in which information, mobility, etc. all have costs. Theories of organisational careers focus upon the internal labour market afforded by larger organisations (see Chapter 1), and students of segmented labour markets (see below) consider the effects of barriers in the market-place. Theories of markets assume rational decision-makers, but in some rational decision theories, market concepts may not be explicit, and the environment may simply be viewed as an option set.

Many theoretical traditions work with a two-dimensional option set. The vertical dimension is thought to correspond to the socio-economic status of occupations, and to be subject to competitive or other pressures; whereas the horizontal dimension is thought to correspond to occupational activity types among which mutually-compensating preferences reduce competitive pressure. It is upon this latter dimension that theorists concerned with interests and choice concentrate their attention (e.g. Holland, 1985). Sociologists are more concerned with the vertical dimension (e.g. Roberts, 1981), and often view it as a set of social classes rather than as a continuum. This is part of a general tendency to view the environment as a structure, or as an organised social formation. Indeed, structural theory may go so far as to abolish the distinction between person and environment characteristic of psychology, so that individuals become the medium through which social structures exist and social processes occur. We will, however, consider such theory in its more familiar garb.

Structural theory, as already indicated, tends to explain careers in terms which refer almost exclusively to the systematically differentiated social environments of individuals, such as coercively-maintained gender-related social institutions which determine occupational type, or in terms of the collectivities to which individuals belong. The latter include families that bequeath social position, in the form of actual and cultural capital (e.g. Bowles and Gintis, 1976; Bourdieu and Passeron, 1977), and that in turn belong to more or less 'closed' social classes within which information and friendship networks are confined, marriages contracted, political groupings formed, etc. In other words, social classification determines the type of career an individual is likely to have. This brief portrayal strips the approach of its historical dimension: for example, gender-related social institutions are evidently changing in ways related to careers (see Chapter 1). It also omits the consideration given to competitive systems of role allocation, regarded as social institutions. But structural theory is, nonetheless, the site of opposition to the tendency of some (but not all) career psychologists, when regarding status attainment, to assume – as if it were a natural condition – that a 'meritocratic' competition takes place between individuals, whose success is determined by their general intelligence and effort, perhaps mediated by aspects of their self-concepts such as self-esteem and self-efficacy (i.e. their belief that tasks can be mastered) – or, in Holland's (1985) formulation, their 'perceived intelligence'.

In British guidance circles, the best-known structural theory is Roberts's 'opportunity structure' thesis. This is probably because it was formulated in explicit opposition to the psychology of careers and what Roberts took to be its excessive interest in choices, decisions and self-realisation in work. In its earliest formulation, which was made in the days of tripartite education (Roberts, 1968), it simply stated that opportunities were (class) structured by access to different types of schooling and their relationship to selection criteria, and by the position of the home in networks of information and influence. These were held to determine or delimit the real option-set from which a young person is able to choose, to the point of indifference with respect to rewards that really matter. It will be noted that the thesis is equally at variance with the idea of 'fair competition'. Ancillary elements of the theory proposed, first, that a 'free-choice ideology' existed which had the purpose of hoodwinking people into believing that they exercised much greater choice than was in fact the case; second, that young men [sic] could gain self-esteem merely by taking on the role of adult worker, irrespective of the occupations they entered; and third, that early (or 'anticipatory') socialisation aligned expectations to realities. In each respect, individuals became reconciled to and accepting of an unjust system of allocation and distribution of rewards. Roberts also went on to deny that people's preferences played any part (as a supply-side pressure) in determining changes in the shape of the occupational structure and, reflecting changes in the school system, to re-emphasise that the real holders of power are educational and occupational gatekeepers (Roberts, 1975; 1977; 1981). Attacks on the 'myth of free choice' rumble on (e.g. Sawdon et al., 1977–81; Cockburn, 1987) despite the fact that neither psychologists (e.g. Roe, 1956) nor even proletarian 'lads' (Willis, 1977) subscribe to the myth.

In recent years the segregation of the labour market by sex has been considered in a similar way to its division on class lines, and there has been a coalescence of opinion between many sociologists (e.g. Ashton et al., 1982) and some economists around the concept of 'segmented labour markets'. The occupational structure is viewed as a set of market segments, surrounded by barriers within which careers are made and in terms of which traditional concerns about the nature and injustice of social allocation may be expressed.

Finally, we may note the tendency of psychologists to continue to use the classical distinction between the individual (or organism) and its environment. This produces conceptions of the environment which are both generous and weak. In recent years an attempt has been made to impose order by using ecological notions of a hierarchy of 'systems' to organise thinking about the environment, in a manner reminiscent of a past generation of sociological thought. *Career ecology theory* (e.g. Young, 1983) has used the more general 'ecological' ideas about human development proposed by Bronfenbrenner (1977; 1979) to describe the habitat in which adolescent career development occurs. This is taken to be made up of *microsystems* (face-to-face contact groups such as school, home, peer-group and workplace, which figure so large, for example, in Law's [1981] community-interaction theory, and in social–psychological approaches generally); *mesosystems* (the inter-relationships of microsystems – for example, school and workplace may be inter-connected); the *exosystem* (specific social structures, such as the parents' social network or school-district policies: the developing person does not participate in the exosystem but is connected to it, so that it 'impinges' upon or 'encompasses' that person's 'immediate settings'); and the *macrosystem* (the pervasive system of beliefs, values and institutions – such as gender, or 'the role of work in life' – which impresses itself upon every subordinate system level). To date, these ideas have been used heuristically rather than theoretically: in other words, ecological notions have been used to organise what we know, rather than to generate new kinds of knowledge about careers which would be unavailable without them.

Action in career theory

The third component of career theory is some conception of what the agent *does*. As should be evident, some theorists assume that choice-making is a minor and unproblematic aspect of careers, barely worth consideration. But a great deal of career theory concerns decision-making, regarding this as the key behaviour. In economic terms, the important decision may be to supply or not to supply labour, or to invest or not invest in education and training, or to accept or not accept a job offer; but elsewhere the object of decision is more often an educational option or an occupation (this often implies that the individual must decide how much to compete with others). However, decision-making is seldom thought to be an instantaneous event. Thus theories of decision-making may be embedded in theories of search or of decision 'process': a 'known' option set may not be assumed, and the individual may be considered as accumulating information over time which permits a decision, or a series of tentative decisions, to be made.

General rational decision theory includes economic theories of the sort we shall consider below and is in its simplest form concerned with perfectly informed decisions (for an introduction, see Hargreaves Heap *et al.*, 1992). At the core of such theory is the assumption that options can be ranked according to the total bundle of utility or rewards they offer. But its most familiar form in career theory is as 'expectancy value' theory (Vroom, 1964; Fishbein and Ajzen, 1975; 1977). This assumes that decision-makers are uncertain whether, or to what degree, any job or career yields any given reward, but that they subjectively perceive the *probabilities* of rewards; it can be extended to assume that decision-makers rate each available reward according to their own subjective preferences. Within this view, the most preferred option is that which can be calculated (from the information just described) to have the highest 'expectancy-value' score. Even 'dependence' can be introduced into rational decision models. The easiest way to do this is to define a decision-making unit (e.g. the family, or the individual and his or her advisers) which goes wider than the individual (e.g. Halsey *et al.*, 1980). Psychologists do not like to do this, so they have to introduce motivation to comply with the views of others as a modification of the basic, individualistic theory of rational choice (Herriot and Ecob, 1979).

Rational theories do not consider, but are compatible with, theories of decisional conflict and stress and its consequences (Janis and Mann, 1977) and cognitive dissonance resolution (Festinger, 1957). The strongest challenge they face comes from theories which assume individuals to be driven by forces of which they are unconscious and which treat rationalisation as a shadow-play without genuine effect. Theories which deny that people have the power to implement their preferences may simply set the issue aside, but may, in a manner similar to theories of unconscious motivation, treat people as prompted to think they have chosen to do what they cannot easily escape (Roberts, 1968).

Economic job-search theory (e.g. Narendranathan and Nickell, 1989) applies best to labour market entrants, the unemployed, etc. It assumes that individuals have 'reservation wage levels' (the minimum net wage levels they will currently accept). Job search is prompted when the reservation wage exceeds current net income/current offers, and occurs under uncertainty about the length of time (and cost) which will elapse before the reservation wage is met by an offer, although the probability of success is known or discovered. This probability determines the decision to supply labour (begin search), and the accepted cost of search. Search yields information, which may lead to either revision of the probability estimates, or revision of the reservation wage. As the reservation wage converges with current net income/offers, job search ceases in a decision either to accept the current offer or not to supply labour. Modifications to job-search theory propose (Granovetter, 1973; 1974) that social networks are information channels which reduce information costs. Therefore job search may be considered as a networking activity and as determined by access to networks (see 'Structural theory', above).

Human capital theory (Becker, 1964) complicates the economic analysis by treating wages as, in part, a form of investment income. The complications of this theory need not detain us, save to say that the decision to invest (even in the form of missed earning opportunities) in education and training is treated like any other investment, as subject to rational calculation of the probable rate of return.

Search or decision stage theories tend, unlike economic theories of job search, to assume that an occupational option will be entered, and consider, at a high level of generality, the way decision tasks are approached. Perhaps the most well-known model is that of Tiedeman (1961) and Tiedeman and O'Hara (1963), who distinguished two stages, each comprising sub-stages:

1 *Anticipation*, involving exploration (awareness raising/information gathering), crystallisation (of alternatives), choice, and clarification of the manner of implementing choice.
2 *Implementation and adjustment*, involving induction (to the option and exposure to the consequences of entry into it), reformation (reaction to these consequences), and maintenance (balance of efforts upon and demands of the environment).

This is a model not merely of decision-making, but of work adjustment (see below). Other models, such as Krumboltz *et al.*'s (1986) DECIDES model, are similar but prescriptive, reflecting counsellors' concern with the 'quality' of decision processes by enjoining actions and the acquisition of skills which seem to make normative rational decision-making possible.

Following on from the work of Tiedeman and O'Hara, Harren (1979) outlined a sequential model of awareness, planning, commitment and implementation, and considered factors which might influence the process. This led to a *decision styles theory* and an instrument to assess such styles (Buck and Daniels, 1985). Three styles are identified which have subsequently been shown (Phillips *et al.*, 1983) to yield four empirical 'types' owing to their patterns of inter-correlation. These are: *rational* (personal sense of responsibility for decision, deliberation, planful strategies, future-directedness); *intuitive* (personal sense of responsibility, reliance on feelings, fantasy, inner experience, impulsiveness); *dependent* (denial of personal responsibility, and compliance with, deference to, or projection of responsibility upon, others, such as family, friends, and authority figures); and *intuitive–dependent*.

Developmentalism extends this process over so long a period that the notion of a static decision-maker and a single decision task breaks down. A developing, learning self forges and revises ideas about self relevant to careers, accumulates a body of knowledge about the world of work from diverse sources, comes to think about careers in new ways, finds itself trapped by childish decisions, and acts tentatively, so that even entry into a job may be part of the search process, providing experiential knowledge. Such theories are sometimes focused on maturation; sometimes on the whole life-span. Although there is at least one early British example (Hill, 1969) (see also Chapter 3), American theorists have been more influential. Ginzberg *et al.*'s (1951) developmental theory (many of the implications of which were subsequently repudiated by Ginzberg [1972] himself) described, in Freudian terms, a shift from the (infantile) pleasure principle to the reality principle, allied to increasing instrumentalism and deferral of gratification, increased compromise, and extending time horizons. This was characterised as movement through a 'fantasy' stage (to 11/12 years), in which 'pleasure' dominates childish occupational wishes; a 'tentative' stage (aged 11/12 to 17/18), in which occupational preferences become influenced in sequence by interests, capacities and values; and a 'realistic' stage (aged 18+), in which 'exploration' is followed by 'crystallisation' (or a more fixed orientation to a particular part of the occupational structure, e.g. through educational specialisation), and finally by 'specification' or final commitment to a career.

But perhaps the best-known developmental theory is that of Super (1957). Super's ingestion of new ideas continued over his entire career, but in his early theory, occupational choice was viewed as the attempt to implement a self-concept in an occupation, by matching one's self-image to images of people already in occupations in which one has an interest (this idea was later used by Holland, 1966). The natural history of the occupational self-concept was superimposed on Buehler's (1933) characterisation of the life-cycle as comprising five stages: growth, exploration, establishment, maintenance, and decline. Although Super considered the whole life-span, most attention was given to the exploration and establishment stages, when the occupational self-concept is formed, tentatively implemented, revised, and finally implemented. Ginzberg *et al.*'s 'fantasy', 'tentative' and 'realistic' stages were incorporated, as was the idea that the occupational self-concept progressively includes interests, capacities and values. Buehler's stages were superimposed, in turn, on Miller and Form's (1951) characterisation of careers as comprising five stages: preparatory (childhood socialisation relevant to work); initial work period (work-related experience prior to full entry to the labour market); trial work period (first full-time job, and possibly others, prior to commitment); stable work period (characterised by occupational immobility and long job tenures); and retirement. This made it appear that occupational stability and long job tenures were a result of maturation. In its classic formulation, therefore, developmentalism saw the developing individual as eventually coming to *the* decision: the choice of a stable career, for which everything else has been a preparation. Thereafter, the task changes. The agent now does different things.

The second major group of activities considered by career theory are summarised in the terms 'adjustment', 'movement', and 'environmental modification and role innovation'. Many theories embody what might be called 'pre-adjustment'. This may be in the form of socialisation and other pressures during development which lead to differences in occupational personalities, capacities, etc. When structural theorists speak of anticipatory socialisation, they draw attention to regularities in what other theorists tend to treat as idiosyncratic. We shall consider pre-adjustment no further here. Originally, theories of work adjustment focused, as their name implies, upon changes which take place in people that lead to greater correspondence between them and their roles: on the more or less automatic forms of learning and extinction or suppression of needs, and on the 'occupational socialisation' through which capacities, preoccupations, beliefs, habits of action, etc. are modified. But, somewhat confusingly, modern theories also attend to the *alternatives* to personal adjustment. These ideas are all assimilated in outline to Super's developmentalism. They are also assimilated to Holland's theory in the proposition that people seek out work environments of people like themselves, viewed through occupational stereotypes, and that congruence between self and environment leads to reinforcement and satisfaction; whereas lack of congruence leads to changes in people, adapting them to their environments, or to a propensity to change environments, or make changes in the environment.

But the best-known *work adjustment theory* takes a 'trait-and-factor' approach to the process of adjustment itself. Work adjustment is theorised (Dawis and Lofquist, 1984) on the assumption that for the individual the goal is correspondence between needs and rewards (or reinforcers), whereas for the employer (or, in Dawis and Lofquist's terminology, the 'environment') the goal is congruence between abilities and the demands of work. Thus equilibrium is reached when job satisfaction and satisfactoriness are achieved, and the spur to action is dissatisfaction. There are four possible targets of adjustment: work demands, work capacities, work rewards, and individual needs. What *kind* of action is undertaken by the individual as a result of dissatisfaction is governed by four 'personality style variables'. These are *celerity* (or the speed with which interaction is typically initiated with the environment), *pace* (the typical intensity of this interaction), *rhythm* (of interaction as sustained, cyclical, or erratic), and *endurance* (or persistence of interaction). A parallel line of reasoning is used to suggest that the 'styles' of 'environments' also differ. Four additional *adjustment style* variables were ultimately identified which are an attempt to explain how adjustment behaviour is triggered. The more *flexible* people are, the greater their initial tolerance for dissatisfaction. The more *persevering* they are, the longer they will tolerate dissatisfaction. They may be *active*, seeking to change the environment, or *reactive*, changing as a result of impetuses originating in the environment.

Much of the terminology in which this theory is expressed has been translated in this short exposition and many of its complications set aside. In fact, the theory is developed symmetrically from the perspective both of the individual and of the employing organisation. In the United Kingdom, Nicholson (1984; Nicholson and West, 1989) has taken a somewhat similar and equally complicated approach to the study of work role transitions, distinguishing personal development from role development, and replication (when a change brings few new demands) from absorption (when personal adaptation or development is paramount), determination (when there is latitude for role creation and exploration), and exploration (when people with special expertise negotiate their roles). The style of adaptation is thought to be determined by role novelty and discretion, and by earlier work experiences, induction and socialisation procedures, the availability of role models, etc. (Schein, 1971; Van Maanen and Schein, 1979). But, as in the theory of Dawis and Lofquist, personality and allied differences (rendered as four 'motivational types' based on desire for feedback and control) also influence the outcome.

Like decision theory, work adjustment theory can also be concerned with the steps or sequence of activities or events through which adjustment occurs. Here we shall briefly allude only to the later analysis of the whole transition cycle made by Nicholson (1987) and Nicholson and West (1989), who propose: *preparation*, in which there is some prior anticipation or rehearsal of the perceived, impending change; *encounter*, or the affective and 'sense-making' response to the first experiences of the new or changed role (see, in this connection, studies of 'surprise', e.g. Arnold, 1985); *adjustment*, as already considered; and *stabilisation*, or the state of 'settled connection' to the role.

A general view of career theory

So far we have implicitly put the 'agent' and his or her 'action' centre-stage. As should by now be plain, this does not sit equally happily with every approach. But there is another tension which we should acknowledge. Theorists may be more or less 'universalistic' in their thinking. Arguing from fundamentals is characteristic of rational decision theory, but also of much of the psychology of careers where starting-points are found, for example, in 'social learning' and other universal human processes. But we must also acknowledge that careers are part of biography, and take place in, not outside, history. So career theory has to attempt to bridge the gap between the two – between universality and history.

At the end of the day, therefore, we may define careers as work histories, and go on to say that any theory of work histories – that is, any theory which is intended to help us understand the time dimension and dynamics of, and succession or change in, the working lives of individuals – may be regarded as a theory *of* or *about* careers. A career theory may include:

1 A set of dimensions and/or possible states which are used to describe work history or career, or some part of it.
2 Propositions about the trajectories, steps and events which occur in careers.
3 Propositions linking changes across dimensions.
4 Explanations of these various propositions.

As we have seen, a career theorist may consciously attend to the whole time-span, or to many dimensions and possible states, or may be concerned only with some small part of these matters.

The limits of explanation

We should be modest about what theory can do. One aspect of common-sense is the belief of some people in the rule of chance over their careers. This has been characterised as a 'folk-theory' deriving from the impact of unanticipated events on careers, and their unanticipated consequences (see Crites, 1969). If we reflect that careers are first of all an aspect of biography, which occur in history, then this belief may be regarded as partially true. Even systematic changes in the environment, which have effects on careers that future generations of theorists will be able to take into account, are now only a matter for speculation (see Chapter 1). Recently, Vondracek and his collaborators (Vondracek *et al.*, 1983; 1986; Vondracek, 1990) have gone so far as to attempt to recognise the role of 'chance' in theory, by treating development, and hence career development, as 'probabilistic'. As development occurs in interaction with the environment, and as the environment changes (or varies between individuals) unpredictably, individual development – and hence career development – can be predicted only 'probabilistically'.

2.3 PUTTING THE ELEMENTS TOGETHER

From what has already been said, it should be clear that to call what follows 'putting the elements together' is a little disingenuous. Career theorists have a magpie-like tendency to borrow ideas. But it is possible to identify a number of bodies of theory and research which express or recombine the elements of career theory in new and interesting ways. We shall confine ourselves, here, to attempts to develop theories which resolve the problem of agency and constraint. In the first group, this is done by making career-related aspects of development essentially conservative in their implications. Krumboltz's social learning theory (Krumboltz, 1979; 1981; 1994; Krumboltz *et al.*, 1976), which amplifies some of the possibilities of the theory of self-concept development, has been combined with Gottfredson's (1981) reworking of developmentalism, which answers a perceived need to bring the constraints on choice typically associated with structural theory *into* the decision process itself, by making them the most fundamental components of the self-concept. Second, we shall examine the attempt to combine structural and rational decision-making theories: a trend observable in the sociology of educational decision-making (e.g. Gambetta, 1987; Halsey *et al.*, 1980) and in the psychology of occupational choice (e.g. Herriot and Ecob, 1979).

Social learning and circumscription

Every career theory acknowledges or assumes 'learning', and the purpose of Krumboltz and his associates (Krumboltz, 1979; 1981; 1994; Krumboltz *et al.*, 1976) is to show how one such theory (Bandura, 1969) can be used to explain career decisions. Activity preferences are 'learned'. Two sorts of learning are distinguished: instrumental and associative learning. *Instrumental* learning is based upon rewards for successful performance and the negative reinforcement of unsuccessful ones. Preference and performance become bound together. *Associative* learning occurs vicariously, when significant others (who act as role models) are seen to be rewarded and punished. In the most recent statement of this position, a more general interpretation is emphasised: the general milieu, including the mass media, loads activities and especially occupations with positive and negative associations, which may be conflicting (Krumboltz, 1994).

According to this view, people construct schemata, or beliefs about themselves and the world, which organise their learning, and which subsequently guide their selection of goals and the choices they make. *Self-observation generalisations*, as their name implies, are beliefs about self, but they may be false beliefs. Another key concept within this theory, *task-approach skills*, is more difficult to grasp. On one level, they are the feelings people have about each type of task and the habitual ways in which tasks are approached, including 'work habits, mental sets, perceptual and thought processes, performance standards and values, problem orientations and emotional responses' (Krumboltz, 1994, p. 18). But in Krumboltz's hands, they are, equally, the means by which people make inferences from self-observation generalisations and their knowledge of the outside world (for an extension of these ideas, and also those discussed later in this chapter as 'Interpretivism', see Chapter 3).

Gottfredson (1981) offers a theory which focuses on the ways in which occupational decisions are delimited or circumscribed, so that people do not actively consider most of the occupations or jobs which make up the full structure of opportunities. The two key circumscribing criteria are sex-type and class (or prestige level). These are produced according to the stages of cognitive development identified by Van den Daele (1968). First, the association of roles with 'concrete' categories (e.g. male/female) is perceived and identification with own-sex roles occurs. At age 9–13, abstract general categories and dimensions are perceived, and class consciousness and occupational-prestige-level perception become sophisticated. Class of origin and of peers constitute a reference group fixing the 'floor' below which options are excluded. However, the 'ceiling' above which options are excluded is determined, in conventional psychological fashion, by perceived general ability and tolerance of 'effort'. At age 14 and above, orientation to 'internal unique self' occurs, leading to initially unstable orientations to occupations which are compatible with the sort of personality a young person would like to develop, or be seen to have. This period corresponds to that of formulating an occupational self-concept, in the work of Super and others. Nonetheless, 'unique self' provides the final circumscription. Thereafter, subject to numerous constraints external to the theory (e.g. those of geography), circumscribed search occurs.

In the context of rational search, 'compromise' can be thought of as the relaxation of a stipulation about the tolerable range of one or more option attributes (interests, work values, abilities) when an 'ideal' option is not located (e.g. Gati *et al.*, 1993). Gottfredson rephrases this idea to contend that when search fails, circumscription barriers are moved out, increasing the zone of search. In particular, she advances a specific hypothesis, arising from her characterisation of circumscription: that people 'will tend to sacrifice interest in field of work to maintain sex-type and prestige, and to some extent will sacrifice prestige level for sex-type, if this is also necessary' (Gottfredson, 1981, p. 572). Thereafter, adjustment to compromise occurs.

Perhaps the most obvious potential criticism comes from the structural determinist position. From this point of view, Gottfredson's description of development would be regarded as an unduly 'naturalised' account of anticipatory socialisation. But Pryor (1987) has pointed out that even if the order of emergence of circumscriptions is as Gottfredson describes, this order does not in itself explain their relative importance. He tries to fill this gap by introducing ideas from Krumboltz's social learning theory. Pryor argues that if gender conceptions are the first 'self-observation generalisations', they determine the later experiences upon which less fundamental 'self-observation generalisations' and 'task-approach skills' are based. Moreover, sex-stereotyped self-observation generalisations may be the most resilient because they do not have to be altered and adapted to fit existing symbolisation in memory.

Unfortunately, however, there is a current lack of empirical support for the basic premise of this exercise. Studies conducted under a variety of artificial conditions have been at best only partially supportive (Pryor and Taylor, 1986; Leung and Plake, 1990; Davidson, 1986; Hesketh *et al.*, 1989). Indeed, Elmslie (1988) has proposed a revised version of the theory to the effect that the most recently emergent elements of self-concepts (such as interests), which incorporate earlier ones (such as gender and class), are more important and less likely to be compromised during search.

Structure, social causation and rational choice theories

Halsey *et al.* (1980) and Gambetta (1987) are important examples of researchers who attempt to decide the relative merits of structure, social causation and rational choice theories, on the assumption that these may all be more or less applicable. In consequence, they elaborate complex theories which combine elements from these different theoretical positions.

In each case, the object of research is educational participation decisions. The key questions are fourfold. First, are such decisions 'rational', in the sense that they are predictable from the rewards expected from education and the perceived probability of success in it? Second, do family 'material circumstances' determine the degree of risk aversion, so that as they decline, the perceived probability of success must be greater, in order to lead to participation? Third, does the culture or 'climate' of the family (e.g. as measured by parental education) independently influence this calculation? Fourth, and related to this, are preferences and 'life plans' systematically related to social class (and gender, etc.) so that educational participation is more imperative to the realisation of highly valued rewards for the children of some classes than of others? If in each case the answer is 'yes', then structural accounts of life chances, socialisation accounts of preferences and intentions, and 'agentic' accounts of rational decision-making, begin to cohere.

Halsey *et al.* (1980) presented evidence for each of the first three propositions. Gambetta's (1987) results were complex, but suggested the following resolution of the issues. First, there is rational calculation which takes in constraints, notably the cost (including income forgone) of education and ability (past performance) and expected benefits in the labour market. But, second, this occurs on the basis of 'personal life-plans' and preferences which are in part class-socialisation effects and in part idiosyncratic or 'personal'. It is to these class-biased life-plans and preferences that rational procedures of decision-making are applied. The more strongly life-plans or preferences (e.g. for an interesting career) imply education, the greater the level of cost accepted and the higher the probability of participation, irrespective of other factors such as ability or perceived probability of success. Even so, working-class children remain more sensitive to signals of ability such as bad school reports, and to economic constraints (family income), and their participation is more elastic relative to expected income; they are therefore less likely to stay on than are 'middle-class' children of similar ability and family income, both in the school system and at the point of entry to university. Finally, within each economic class, family 'climate' (indicated by parental education) shifts life-plans and preferences in favour of education.

When considering *intentions*, from the psychological expectancy-value perspective, Herriot and Ecob (1979) reasoned, in a fashion parallel to that of the sociologists we have just considered, that the perceived probability of access to options becomes relevant. They used a sample of engineering students to test these and other ideas, including the possibility, noted earlier, that beliefs about the way in which significant others rate options, and strength of motivation to comply with those beliefs ('subjective norms'), may also be influential. Each contributed to expressed intentions.

This is a complex picture, but more realistic than simple notions about class determining everything on the one hand, or free choice on the other. We are no longer forced to choose between seemingly antagonistic theories; however, the price of integration is complexity.

2.4 MODERN TIMES

Each of the developments so far considered can be thought to have taken place on the terrain of 'post-war' career theory. But, as already noted, in the last two decades forces have been at work which make career theorists want to think about different things. One factor has been declining faith in the 'predictability' of careers and in the 'stability' or orderliness of adult working life. Associated with uncertainty is the 'problematisation' of adult careers. Career theory has been refocusing itself on the whole span of career: adults – including adult women, and hence 'dual career families' – and the continuing relationship between working and non-working life have been rediscovered. At least three general consequences are evident. The first is the increasing propensity of work-adjustment theory to consider movement into new, ill-defined and malleable positions. The second has been an urge towards ever more comprehensive theorisation, both in terms of the object of study (the 'life career') and in terms of the range of explanatory factors to be considered. The third has been an 'interpretivist' resurgence in the study of careers.

Beyond work adjustment?

As we have already seen, work adjustment theory does not any longer imply a once-for-all adjustment to a particular role. Recently, the perception that organisations and the people in them necessarily change has stimulated the view that careers can be seen, when in organisations, as repeated 'renegotiation' between the organisation and the individual. Psychologists have extended a number of ideas to be found in the economic literature on employment relations, characterising contracts as 'psychological' – as sets of expectations between employers and employees – in addition to their more formal legal component (Argyris, 1960; Rousseau, 1989; Herriot and Pemberton, 1996) (see also Chapter 1).

According to this view, organisational careers consist of psychological contracts in which the 'match' (or congruence) between the wants and offers of employees and organisations is central. 'Negotiation' is not merely formal, but also implicit in much of the behaviour of organisations towards their employees, and vice versa. Each is seen to attempt to optimise the cost-benefit to him or herself, and the capacity of each to do so is dependent on his or her relative power. Harmony is achieved when the individual and the employing organisation (or rather, those who represent it to the individual) perceive the existing contract to be equitable and honoured. Contracts may be more or less 'transactional': in other words, they may be more or less a matter for a fixed, limited, explicit set of agreements. 'Relational' contracts, characteristic of managers and professional workers, are more a matter for mutual trust, loyalty and commitment. This means that when they are perceived to be inequitable or dishonoured, reactions become correspondingly more emotional, involving anger, grief and mistrust.

Negotiation involves an initial stage in which each party assesses the match of wants and offers. Thus when this match is destabilised, and inequity or dishonoured agreements come to be perceived on either side, negotiation is triggered. The second stage is one in which a deal, or new deal, is struck. However, as the respective power of each party changes, so do initial bargaining positions. This means that as people or organisations develop or change, there are stimuli to renegotiation, irrespective of the original 'deal'. This process model, which is of much greater complexity than can be summarised here, clearly shifts attention away from the idea of careers as being determined at the outset, to one of careers as dynamic phenomena.

Adult development and life-span, life-space theories

In relation to adult development theory, the ideas of Jung (1933) and of Erikson (1963) have been influential, as has Vaillant's (1977) thirty-year longitudinal study of 268 Harvard graduates. However, at least as great an influence has been exercised by Levinson et al.'s (1978) four-year study of forty men aged 35–45.

During the middle years of life, Vaillant (1977) identifies an early phase, in which mentors are left behind and consolidation occurs, and a later one of 'generativity'. Over-arching these phases are processes of instinctual reawakening and 'self-reappraisal'. Levinson et al. (1978) identify 'settling down' and 'becoming one's own man' in the thirties, which gives way to 'mid-life transition'. Other students of the middle years often use similar terms, such as 'deadline decade' and 'switch forties' (Sheehy, 1976). As people become aware of limited time (and, perhaps, failing powers) they reorient themselves to their careers. The consequences of this reorientation may vary (a 'big push', instability, resignation, etc.), but underlying all of these accounts is the idea that some sort of re-orientation occurs. This occurs regardless of any external impositions upon careers leading to involuntary job moves, organisational de-layering and constriction of career pathways. So we can think of these theories as describing what might happen in a stable occupational environment.

Sonnenfeld and Kotter (1982) take up this point in their criticism of earlier traditions in career theory for paying insufficient attention to the way in which jobs and their relative status positions change, to changes in individuals during adult life, to the interaction between work and non-work roles, and to 'biography'. Sonnenfeld and Kotter's purpose is to characterise career theory as increasingly 'dynamic', 'adding more variables and complexity' along two dimensions – time and life-space. However, their resultant model, like many such models formulated in the past (e.g. Blau et al., 1956), is not an explanation of anything in particular: it merely attempts to show how interconnected the world is.

Super responded to the changing *Zeitgeist* by extending his developmental theory to become a 'life-span, life-space' theory intended to cover shifting saliences between types of role, and their associated decision points. As ever, he made hypothetical generalisations about what is typical at each developmental stage, calling the resultant diagram a 'career rainbow' (e.g. Super, 1981). Super distinguished two groups of determinants, the situational and the personal, eventually representing them in a symmetrical diagram or 'career arch', intended to show how remote or proximate are various groups of determinants, such as 'historical change' or 'the family' (e.g. Super, 1994). Super's essential message is similar to that of Sonnenfeld and Kotter. He identifies four principal 'theatres' in which nine major 'roles' are played. The 'theatres' are the home, the community, the school (education generally) and the workplace. Roles tend to be played more in one theatre than in others, but the compartments are not watertight. The nine principal 'roles' are child, student, 'leisurite', citizen, worker, spouse, homemaker, parent and pensioner. Over the course of the life-cycle, role expectations change. Current roles and role performance can have implications or consequences for other current roles, and for other roles in the future. These can include inter-role conflict, and the possible personal benefits of role 'balance' and of role 'extension' (i.e. playing a greater or lesser number of roles at any one time). The time given to each theatre and to each role varies during the life-cycle. 'Life-style' at any point in time can be described as the set of roles played (number, types), their 'width' and their 'depth'. Decision points occur when roles are taken up, cease, or change significantly. With this, Super broke decisively with the earlier spirit of developmentalism, which pivoted upon *the* career decision, taken in late adolescence or early adulthood, and focused thereafter on a 'stable' career.

Interpretivism

Generally speaking, one may say that the current of career psychology, like that of general psychology, has been flowing for many years in a 'cognitive' direction. For example, 'self-efficacy' (belief in one's eventual ability to perform given actions) and 'outcome expectations' have been introduced into the career development literature as cognitive phenomena (e.g. Hackett and Betz, 1981; Betz and Hackett, 1986; Lent and Hackett, 1987). Similarly, one might say that, owing to the strength of the phenomenological and self-concept tradition, there has been no prohibition on studies of the 'subjective career' (e.g. Collin, 1990).

However, a more fundamental 'interpretivist' reawakening has occurred. A relatively early UK attempt to reorient theorisation around the issue 'How do people construct meaningful careers?' is to be found in the work of R. J. Roberts (1980). It was influenced by the Chicago school of sociology, which for decades treated social space as if static and organised. As 'status passages', transitions were between sets of role expectations, and identities and careers were seen as double-sided: as 'objective' expressions of social organisation, and as the 'subjective' set of meanings people constructed, or their 'sense-making' of their own lives. This construction was seen to change. Part of this change might result from the acquisition of new vocabularies of motive. Barley's (1989) sociological agenda for the study of careers focuses upon the relationship between subjective and objective career, and the role of career 'scripts' or rationalisation, not merely in allowing people to 'make sense' of their lives, but also as constituents, supports and possible sources of change in the organisational structures in which careers occur.

As organisations have come to be seen as less and less able to provide orderly, progressive careers, the study of subjective careers has become more and more attractive, as if in response to perceived social dislocation and disorder (see Chapter 1), rather than in the terms originally envisaged for it. Recently, the adoption of a *narrative* approach has been advocated. This is in effect a call to find a 'pattern' or 'narrative', by the retrospective study of careers in the form of a dialogue between the subject of study and the investigator (e.g. Polkinghorne, 1990; Cochran, 1990). It is almost as if the job of guidance were increasingly to become one of helping people to find something that has been taken away from them: a career.

2.5 WHAT USE IS THEORY?

Theories often have technical implications. Examples are the prescriptive (or 'normative') models of decision science which can be the basis of 'paper-and-pencil' decision-making exercises or built into computer-assisted guidance; the psychometric aptitude- and personality-matching techniques of trait-and-factor theory; or the diagnostic questionnaires which are used to investigate decision style. Thus Krumboltz's main recent practical application has been a questionnaire, the Career Beliefs Inventory (Krumboltz, 1991), intended to assess 'dysfunctional' career beliefs with a view to intervention. But outside their incorporation to computer-assisted guidance, are such technical applications put to widespread use in the United Kingdom?

It is often not entirely clear what the technical implications of theory are. It is, therefore, necessary to resist the view that theories without immediate technical implications are useless. We can scarcely avoid having ideas about careers, and the ideas we subscribe to are likely to determine, for example, whether we think guidance is worthwhile and what we think guidance *is*. The most obvious examples are the economic theories considered earlier. They represent policy rationales for guidance (see Chapters 4 and 21). They also suggest forms of practice, emphasising information and prescriptive or normative strategies for taking specific forms of rational decisions. Similarly, Super's earlier and later developmental statements may each be said to carry a strong message about what guidance can be, and the things to which it should attend: the early statement directs guidance to supporting the maturation and exploratory behaviour of the decision-maker; the later statement draws attention to the developmental tasks involved in balancing roles across the whole life-cycle. The work on psychological contracts, too, directs attention away from initial career choices to the tasks of career management. Structural theories, on the other hand, can be used to underwrite guidance as a counsel of despair (or facilitating no more than realistic accommodation to one's social destiny), as a radical or critical form of practice, and as an equal-opportunities activity, dependent upon the small print of the form of structural theory to which one subscribes.

Given the current lack of support, one would be unwise to derive too many implications from the details of Gottfredson's (1981) theory for practice. Practitioners are already aware of 'self-stereotyping' in the occupational choice process, and the young ages at which this is evident, from quite different sources, and they do or do not attempt to counter it according to their degree of commitment to equal opportunities, or simply to the avoidance of premature foreclosure. Gottfredson's message is probably a conservative one: gender and social-class identity are real and shape preferences. When people are forced to compromise them in their job search, they forgo things they want. Thus exclusion of the gender composition of occupations, and of some means of identifying the social-class ranges which they occupy from the computerised matching systems and other devices used to facilitate search, may make them unrealistic.

It is possible to argue that the approach taken by Krumboltz (1994) suggests forms of guidance practice which are directed to structuring the conditions under which learning occurs, with the aim of broadening aspirations. This would be, for example, by giving opportunities for positive reinforcement in hitherto negatively reinforced domains, exposure to role models, and encouraging the expression of positive valuations of a wider range of options by 'significant others'.

Like Vondracek et al. (1986), who also use Bronfenbrenner's (1977) systems approach to describe 'context' in their 'developmental–contextual' approach to careers, Young (1983) argues that there has been a neglect of the reciprocal (or interactive) relationship between individuals and their environment, particularly at the microsystem and mesosystem levels, where the possibility is strongest that individuals will be able to influence the conditions of their own development. Young considers that guidance should assume a wider role, taking in interaction at these levels. This tends to underwrite such practice as the involvement of parents, or the use of school–industry links, in careers education. It parallels part of Super's (1994) final statement about adults.

Each form of theory, and each particular theory, has implications of these kinds (see also Watts et al., 1981). The tortured attempts to 'find applications' in the concluding passages of the journal articles in which they are outlined often result from a failure to recognise that what is really being addressed is, as noted at the beginning of this chapter, the fundamental understanding of careers by the guidance profession. Theories are useful if they help us to interpret careers, seeing them in ways which, without the theory, would remain invisible to us. This may influence the way practitioners approach the task of careers guidance, without directly providing a technology for doing it. The price we pay for this is, of course, that theories may blind us to what lies beyond their scope. This is why it is so important for guidance practitioners to be aware of *theory*, not merely of *a* theory – enabling them to test against alternatives the implicit theory they bring with them to the profession.

REFERENCES

Argyris, C. (1960) *Understanding Organizational Behavior*, Homewood, IL: Dorsey.
Argyris, C. (1964) *Integrating the Individual and the Organization*, New York: Wiley.
Arnold, J. (1985) 'Tales of the Unexpected: Surprises Experienced by Graduates in the Early Months of Employment', *British Journal of Guidance and Counselling* 13(3): 308–19.
Ashton, D. N., Maguire, M. A. and Garland, V. (1982) *Youth in the Labour Market*, London: Department of Employment.
Bandura, A. (1977) *Principles of Behavior Modification*, New York: Holt, Rinehart & Winston.

Barley, S. R. (1989) 'Careers, Identities and Institutions: the Legacy of the Chicago School of Sociology', in Arthur, M. B., Hall, D. T. and Lawrence, B. S. (eds) *Handbook of Career Theory*, Cambridge: Cambridge University Press.

Becker, G. S. (1964) *Human Capital*, New York: National Bureau of Economic Research.

Betz, N. E. and Hackett, G. (1986) 'Applications of Self Efficacy Theory to Understanding Career Choice Behaviour', *Journal of Social and Clinical Psychology* 4: 279–89.

Blau, P. M., Gustad, J. W., Jessor, R., Parnes, H. S. and Wilcock, R. C. (1956) 'Occupational Choice: a Conceptual Framework', *Industrial and Labor Relations Review* 9(4): 531–43.

Bordin, E. (1990) 'A Psychodynamic Model of Career Choice and Satisfaction', in Brown, D. and Brooks, L. (eds) *Career Choice and Development* (2nd edn), San Francisco, CA: Jossey-Bass.

Bordin, E. (1994) 'Intrinsic Motivation and the Active Self', in Savickas, M. L. and Lent, R. W. (eds) *Convergence in Career Development Theories: Implications for Science and Practice*, Palo Alto, CA: Consulting Psychologists Press.

Bordin, E., Nachmann, B. and Segal, S. (1963) 'An Articulated Framework for Vocational Development', *Journal of Counseling Psychology* 10: 107–16.

Bourdieu, P. and Passeron, J. C. (1977) *Reproduction in Education, Society and Culture*, London: Sage.

Bowles, S. and Gintis, H. (1976) *Schooling in Capitalist America*, London: Routledge & Kegan Paul.

Bronfenbrenner, U. (1977) 'Towards an Experimental Ecology of Human Development', *American Psychologist* 32: 513–31.

Bronfenbrenner, U. (1979) *The Ecology of Human Development: Experiments by Nature and Design*, Cambridge, MA: Harvard University Press.

Buck, J. N. and Daniels, M. H. (1985) *Assessment of Career Decision-Making (ACDM) Manual*, Los Angeles, CA: Western Psychological Services.

Buehler, C. (1933) *Der Menschliche Lebenslauf als Psychologisches Problem*, Leipzig: Hirzel.

Cochran, L. R. (1990) 'Narrative as a Paradigm for Career Research', in Young, R. A. and Borgen, W. A. (eds) *Methodological Approaches to the Study of Career*, New York: Praeger.

Cockburn, C. (1987) *Two-Track Training*, Basingstoke: Macmillan.

Collin, A. (1990) 'Mid-Life Career Change Research', in Young, R. A. and Borgen, W. A. (eds) *Methodological Approaches to the Study of Career*, New York: Praeger.

Crites, J.O. (1969) *Vocational Psychology: the Study of Vocational Behavior and Development*, New York: McGraw-Hill.

Davidson, A. (1986) 'The Relative Importance of Prestige and Sex-Type in Career Compromise', unpublished thesis, University of New South Wales, Sydney (cited in Hesketh *et al.*, 1989).

Dawis, R. V. and Lofquist, L. H. (1984) *A Psychological Theory of Work Adjustment*, Minneapolis: University of Minnesota Press.

Elmslie, S. (1988) 'A Test of Gottfredson's (1981) Compromise Theory Controlling for Gender and Social Class', unpublished thesis, University of New South Wales, Sydney (cited in Hesketh *et al.*, 1989).

Erikson, E. H. (1963) *Childhood and Society* (2nd edn), New York: Norton.

Festinger, L. (1957) *A Theory of Cognitive Dissonance*, London: Tavistock.

Fishbein, M. and Ajzen, I. (1975) *Belief, Attitude, Intention and Behaviour*, London: Addison-Wesley.

Fishbein, M. and Ajzen, I. (1977) Attitude–Behavior Relations *Psychological Bulletin* 84: 888–918.

Gambetta, D. (1987) *Were They Pushed or Did They Jump?*, Cambridge: Cambridge University Press.

Gati, I., Shenhav, M. and Givon, M. (1993) 'Processes Involved in Career Preferences and Compromises', *Journal of Counseling Pyschology* 40(1): 53–64.

Ginzberg E. (1972) 'Toward a Theory of Occupational Choice: a Restatement', *Vocational Guidance Quarterly* 20(3): 169–76.

Ginzberg, E., Ginsburg, S. W., Axelrad, S. and Herma, J. L. (1951) *Occupational Choice: an Approach to a General Theory*, New York: Columbia University Press.

Goldthorpe, J. M. and Hope, K. (1974) *The Social Grading of Occupations*, London: Oxford University Press.

Gottfredson, L.S. (1981) 'Circumscription and Compromise: a Developmental Theory of Occupational Aspirations', *Journal of Counseling Psychology* 28(6): 545–79.

Granovetter, M. (1973) 'The Strength of Weak Ties', *American Journal of Sociology* 78: 1360–80.

Granovetter, M. (1974) *Getting a Job: a Study of Contacts and Careers*, Cambridge, MA: Harvard University Press.

Hackett, G. and Betz, N. E. (1981) 'A Self-Efficacy Approach to the Career Development of Women', *Journal of Vocational Behavior* 18: 326–36.

Halsey, A. H., Heath, A. F. and Ridge, J. M. (1980) *Origins and Destinations*, Oxford: Clarendon Press.

Hargreaves Heap, S., Hollis, M., Lyons, B., Sugden, R. and Weale, A. (1992) *The Theory of Choice: a Critical Guide*, Oxford: Blackwell.

Harren, V. A. (1979) 'A Model of Career Decision Making for College Students', *Journal of Vocational Behavior* 14: 119–33.

Herriot, P. and Ecob, R. (1979) 'Occupational Choice and Expectancy-Value Theory: Testing Some Modifications', *Journal of Occupational Psychology* 52(4): 311–24.

Herriot, P. and Pemberton, C. (1996) 'Contracting Careers', *Human Relations* (in press).

Hesketh, B., Elmslie, S. and Kaldor, W. (1989) 'Career Compromise: an Alternative Account to Gottfredson's Theory', *Journal of Counseling Psychology* 37: 49–56.

Hill, J. M. M. (1969) *The Transition from School to Work*, London: Tavistock Institute of Human Relations.

Holland, J. (1966) *The Psychology of Vocational Choice*, Waltham, MA: Blaisdell.

Holland, J. (1985) *Making Vocational Choices: a Theory of Vocational Personalities and Work Environments* (2nd edn), Englewood Cliffs, NJ: Prentice-Hall.

Janis, I. L. and Mann, L. (1977) *Decision-Making: a Psychological Analysis of Conflict, Choice, and Commitment*, New York: Free Press.

Jung, C. G. (1933) *Modern Man in Search of a Soul*, New York: Harcourt, Brace & World.

Krumboltz, J. (1979) 'A Social Learning Theory of Career Decision Making', in Mitchell, A., Jones, G. and Krumboltz, J. (eds) *Social Learning and Career Decision Making*, Cranston, RI: Carroll Press.

Krumboltz, J. (1981) 'A Social Learning Theory of Career Decision Making (Revised)', in Mitchell, A., Jones, G. and Krumboltz, J. (eds) *Career Development in the 1980s: Theory and Practice*, Springfield, IL: Thomas.

Krumboltz, J. (1991) *Career Beliefs Inventory*, Palo Alto, CA: Consulting Psychologists Press.

Krumboltz, J. (1994) 'Improving Career Development Theory from a Social Learning Perspective', in Savickas, M. L. and Lent, R. W. (eds) *Convergence in Career Development Theories: Implications for Science and Practice*, Palo Alto, CA: Consulting Psychologists Press.

Krumboltz, J., Kinnier, R. T., Rude, S. S., Scherba, D. S. and Hummel, D. A. (1986) 'Teaching a Rational Approach to Career Decision-Making: Who Benefits Most?', *Journal of Vocational Behavior* 29: 1–6.

Krumboltz, J., Mitchell, A. and Jones, G. (1976) 'A Social Learning Theory of Career Selection', *The Counseling Psychologist* 6: 71–81.

Law, B. (1981) 'Community Interaction: a "Mid-Range" Focus for Theories of Career Development in Young Adults', *British Journal of Guidance and Counselling* 9(2): 142–58.

Lent, R. W. and Hackett, G. (1987) 'Career Self-Efficacy: Empirical Status and Future Directions', *Journal of Vocational Behavior* 30: 347–82.

Leung, S. A. and Plake, B. S. (1990) 'A Choice Dilemma Approach for Examining the Relative Importance of Sex Type and Prestige Preferences in the Process of Career Choice Compromise', *Journal of Counseling Psychology* 37(4): 399–406.

Levinson, D. J., Darrow, C. N., Klein, E. G., Levinson, M. H. and McKee, B. (1978) *The Seasons of a Man's Life*, New York: Knopf.

Miller, D. C. and Form, W. H. (1951) *Industrial Sociology*, New York: Harper.

Narendranathan, W. and Nickell, S. (1989) 'Modelling the Process of Job Search', in Nickell, S., Narendranathan, W., Stern, J. and Garcia, J., *The Nature of Unemployment in Britain*, Oxford: Oxford University Press.

Nicholson, N. (1984) 'A Theory of Work Role Transitions', *Administrative Service Quarterly* 29: 172–91.

Nicholson, N. (1987) 'The Transition Cycle: a Conceptual Framework for the Analysis of Change and Human Resources Management', in Rowland, K. M. and Ferris, G. R. (eds) *Research in Personnel and Human Resources Management*, Greenwich, CT: JAI Press.

Nicholson, N. and West, M. (1989) 'Transitions, Work Histories and Careers', in Arthur, M. B., Hall, D. T. and Lawrence, B. S. (eds) *Handbook of Career Theory*, Cambridge: Cambridge University Press.

Phillips, S. O., Strohmer, D. C., Berthaume, B. L. J. and O'Leary, J. C. (1983) 'Career Development of Special Populations: a Framework for Research', *Journal of Vocational Behavior* 22: 12–29.

Polkinghorne, D. E. (1990) 'Action Theory Approaches to Career Research', in Young, R. A. and Borgen, W. A. (eds) *Methodological Approaches to the Study of Career*, New York: Praeger.

Pryor, R. G. L. (1987) 'Compromise: the Forgotten Dimension of Career Decision-Making', *British Journal of Guidance and Counselling* 15(2): 158–68.

Pryor, R. G. L. and Taylor, N. B. (1986) 'What Would I Do If I Couldn't Do What I Wanted To Do?: Investigating Career Compromise Strategies', *Australian Psychologist* 21: 363–76.

Quinn, R. P., Staines, G. L. and McCullough, M. R. (1974) *Job Satisfaction: Is There a Trend?*, Manpower Research Monograph 30, Washington, DC: Manpower Administration, US Department of Labor.

Roberts, K. (1968) 'The Entry into Employment: an Approach Towards a General Theory', *Sociological Review* 16: 165–84.

Roberts, K. (1975) 'The Development Theory of Occupational Choice: a Critique and an Alternative', in Esland, G., Saloman, G. and Speakman, M. (eds) *People and Work*, Milton Keynes: Open University Press.

Roberts, K. (1977) 'The Social Conditions, Consequences and Limitations of Careers Guidance', *British Journal of Guidance and Counselling* 5(1): 1–9.

Roberts, K. (1981) 'The Sociology of Work Entry and Occupational Choice', in Watts, A. G., Super, D. E. and Kidd, J. M. (eds) *Career Development in Britain*, Cambridge: Careers Research and Advisory Centre/Hobsons.

Roberts, R. J. (1980) 'An Alternative Justification for Careers Education: a Radical Response to Roberts and Daws', *British Journal of Guidance and Counselling* 8(2): 158–74.

Roe, A. (1956) *Psychology of Occupations*, New York: Wiley.

Rousseau, D. M. (1989) 'Psychological and Implied Contracts in Organizations', *Employee Responsibilities and Rights Journal* 2: 121–39.

Sawdon, A., Pelican, J. and Tucker, S. (1977–81) *Study of the Transition from School to Working Life* (3 vols), London: Youthaid.

Schein, E. H. (1971) 'The Individual, the Organization, and the Career: a Conceptual Scheme', *Journal of Applied Behavioral Science* 7: 401–26.

Sheehy, G. (1976) *Passages: Predictable Crises in Adult Life*, New York: Dutton.

Sonnenfeld, J. and Kotter, J. P. (1982) 'The Maturation of Career Theory', *Human Relations* 35: 19–46.

Super, D. E. (1953) 'A Theory of Vocational Development', *American Psychologist* 8: 185–90.

Super, D. E. (1957) *The Psychology of Careers*, New York: Harper & Row.

Super, D. E. (1981) 'Approaches to Occupational Choice and Career Development', in Watts, A. G., Super, D. E. and Kidd, J. M. (eds) *Career Development in Britain*, Cambridge: Careers Research and Advisory Centre/Hobsons.

Super, D. E. (1994) 'A Life Span, Life Space Perspective on Convergence', in Savickas, M. L. and Lent, R. W. (eds) *Convergence in Career Development Theories: Implications for Science and Practice*, Palo Alto, CA: Consulting Psychologists Press.

Tiedeman, D. V. (1961) 'Decision and Vocational Development: a Paradigm and its Implications', *Personnel and Guidance Journal* 40: 15–20.

Tiedeman, D. V. and O'Hara, R. P. (1963) *Career Development: Choice and Adjustment*, New York: College Entrance Examination Board.

Vaillant, G. E. (1977) *Adaptation to Life*, Boston: Little, Brown.

Van den Daele, L. (1968) 'A Developmental Study of the Ego-Ideal', *Genetic Psychology Monographs* 78: 191–256.

Van Maanen, J. and Schein, E. H. (1979) 'Towards a Theory of Organizational Socialization' in Shaw, B. M. (ed.) *Research in Organizational Behavior*, vol. 1, Greenwich, CT: JAI Press.

Vondracek, F. W. (1990) 'A Developmental–Contextual Approach to Career Development Research', in Young, R. A. and Borgen, W. A. (eds) *Methodological Approaches to the Study of Career*, New York: Praeger.

Vondracek, F., Lerner, R. and Schulenberg, J. (1983) 'Career Development: a Life-Span Developmental Approach: the Concept of Development in Vocational Theory and Intervention', *Journal of Vocational Behavior* 23: 179–202.

Vondracek, F., Lerner, R. and Schulenberg, J. (1986) *Career Development: a Life-Span Developmental Approach*, Hillsdale, NJ: Erlbaum.

Vroom, V. H. (1964) *Work and Motivation*, New York: Wiley.

Watts, A. G., Law, B. and Fawcett, B. (1981) 'Some Implications for Guidance Practice', in Watts, A. G., Super, D. E. and Kidd, J. M. (eds) *Career Development in Britain*, Cambridge: Careers Research and Advisory Centre/Hobsons.

Willis, P. (1977) *Learning to Labour: How Working Class Kids Get Working Class Jobs*, Farnborough: Saxon House.

Young, R.A. (1983) 'Career Development of Adolescents: an Ecological Perspective', *Journal of Youth and Adolescence* 12(5): 401–17.

Chapter 3

A career-learning theory

Bill Law

3.1 INTRODUCTION

As Chapter 2 has indicated, there is no shortage of ideas about influences on career. Some are supported by research; many have been incorporated into formal theory. This chapter takes another look at these ideas, and reconfigures them. The configuration is as a progressively learned sequence of career-development capacities and behaviours. Progression is important for two related reasons: first, it identifies what is 'basic' and what is 'developed' in people's career experience; second, it indicates how the more basic experiences prepare the ground (or fail to prepare the ground) for later development.

This is a matter of some practical importance. Career development is increasingly problematic. Anticipating the consequences of one's own actions is ever more troublesome; plans laid today commonly require adjustment – and, possibly, abandonment – later. Notions of career planning based on a once-and-for-all (or even once-in-a-while) review of the options and priorities are weak because both the options and the priorities will change. The requirement is that people need repeatedly to review career choices and transitions, with thought and care. All of this argues for supporting people through a lifelong process of career-related thinking and rethinking, action and new action.

The progression developed in this chapter therefore refers to how people learn to manage their careers. Like all theories, it offers *descriptions* of what happens; *explanations*, suggesting why they happen in the way they do; and *predictions*, anticipating what can happen in what conditions. A strong justification for any career-development theory is its ability, through prediction, to suggest useful models for careers education and guidance.

The chapter will first examine similarities and differences between existing career-development theories. It will next present a new career-learning theory, first as a set of ten propositions, and then as a series of four stages and eight sub-stages. Finally, it will locate this theory in relation to existing theories, and explore implications for practice.

3.2 KEY COMPONENTS IN CAREER-DEVELOPMENT THEORIES

Career-development theory is not unitary. It comprises a range of theories, offering a variety of configurations, each offering foreground significance to different aspects of work, role and self. The similarities and differences between theories are dealt with in more detail in Chapter 2. For our present purposes, it is useful to identify four broadly distinguishable clusters: trait-and-factor theories; self-concept theories; opportunity-structure theories; and community-interaction theories.

Trait-and-factor theories

Trait-and-factor theories offer foreground significance to specifically identified features of the self, such as abilities or personal orientations. They suggest matching models for careers education and guidance, assuming the usefulness of making a link between particular people and suitable work, for example through structured interviewing and computer-assisted guidance. Much of Rodger's (1952) 'seven-point plan' – with its use of such descriptors as 'aptitude' and 'personality' – relied upon such thinking. Psychometric testing is also based on such assumptions (Kline, 1975), as were some early attempts at profiling (see Chapter 14).

At its simplest this is 'pegs-and-holes' thinking, but it is capable of more sophistication. For example, Dawis (1994) explains satisfactory career development in terms of a person–fit match, taking account of four sets of individual differences: (1) ability; (2) reinforcement values – that is, personal needs, settling over time into stable values; (3) satisfaction by the employee; and (4) person–environment fit – that is, 'harmony with the environment'. Match and mismatch between person and position may, therefore, be dynamic and interactive.

Self-concept theories

The 'self-concept' connotes a more interactive self, developing through life stages, and – in so doing – experiencing changing motivations and other feelings about work (Super, 1957). Such theories yield more subtle descriptions of an individual, difficult to fit to the ready-made categories of trait-and-factor thinking (Roe, 1951). They emphasise the importance for careers education and guidance of the expression and use of the affective, changing, multi-layered and unique experience of each person (Daws, 1968).

A well-defined use of such highly individualised ideas appears in the application to careers education and guidance of personal-construct theory (Edmonds, 1979; Offer, 1995). It suggests counselling models in guidance, and experiential learning in careers education. Some aspects of recording achievement and individual action planning also call upon self-concept theory (Watts, 1991), as do some aspects of computer-assisted guidance (Law, 1994). All invite helpers to work sensitively, in the learner's own terms, seeking bases for the learner's choices and actions.

Accommodation of interaction between person and position is found in Gottfredson's (1981) work. She argues that children orientate by stages to: (1) size and social power – noticing the differences between *child* and *adult*; (2) sex roles – noticing the differences between *masculine* and *feminine*; (3) social valuation – using more abstract concepts to discriminate levels of *status* and *prestige*; and (4) internal unique valuation – noticing the differences between *me* and *others* in term of interests, abilities and values. These 'selves' are not conceived as growing in a social vacuum.

Opportunity-structure theories

That social position is an important determinant of career-related life chances is a central feature of opportunity-structure theories. These offer foreground significance to the labour economy and its supporting education-and-training and social structures. People are thought of not so much as choosing work as being chosen for it. They do not need to agonise about what they want because, it is argued, they take what is available to them. If they like their work, this is because they have learned to like what they can secure – through 'anticipatory socialisation' (Roberts, 1977). This explains, for example, the willingness with which the sons of working-class families assume – and even celebrate – menial work (Willis, 1977). Willis is, however, more interested than Roberts in the interactive processes through which family, peer and neighbourhood attachments mediate social-class influence. His ethnography identifies significant variations in *individual* responses to social experience.

A more recent ethnography comes from Banks *et al.* (1992), who maintain that social class has a variety of entwined effects on career: educational attainment, participation in post-compulsory education and subsequent labour-market position are the interwoven 'manifestations of inequality'. The conclusion is pessimistic: 'many young people are allowed, if not actively encouraged, to set themselves adrift in the labour market without adequate preparation' (p. 188). No model for practice is developed.

Models for gradualist careers education and guidance interventions are not much elaborated by these theories. However, the theories can suggest the value of career-development coaching, which helps learners to identify, practise and refine the competencies needed to secure the opportunities open to them, and to cope and (where possible) thrive in a demanding and competitive working environment.

Community-interaction theories

Community-interaction theories offer foreground significance to direct-and-personal encounters between individuals and their community. People act, it is argued, for and in response to other people; encounters with and attachment to individuals and groups are both the cause and the effect of career development. Social exchanges such as interpersonal feedback, modelling and expectation are important in this process (Law, 1981b). Such thinking sets career development in its more immediate community context: emphasising, for example, the importance of both the entrapping and the liberating effects of learners' roles in their own neighbourhoods.

Although presented as a 'social *learning* theory', Krumboltz's (1994) theory is concerned with community interaction. He explains career development in terms of person–environment interactions, distinguishing between *instrumental* interactions where preferences favour activities in which people succeed, and *associative* interactions where preferences favour activities valued in the culture. In both cases, individual *schemata* (beliefs about self and the world) are assembled and modified to take account of the learning from these interactions. Krumboltz specifies feedback, modelling and influence as features of this process.

Such theories suggest that the wider the range of these contacts, the broader the framework for choice a person can construct. They therefore direct attention to the uses of work experience and other strategies which introduce people to a range of perspectives on career (Law, 1981b). The model encourages developing a human-resource network and helping people to make constructive use of it.

A theoretical synopsis

The relationships between these theories is less tidy than analyses and diagrams can adequately portray. There are important within-cluster differences, and some theories permeate the boundaries (Dawis, Gottfredson and Willis being identified above as examples, but there are many others – see Chapter 1). Nonetheless, Figure 3.1 suggests how each type of theory tends to identify different foreground phenomena, offer different explanations, and imply different models.

There are further significant differences between the four broad types of theory (Table 3.1). Both trait-and-factor and self-concept theories substantially understand career in *psychological* terms; whereas opportunity-structure and

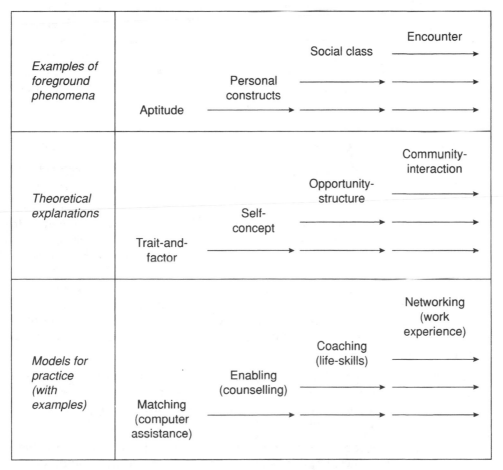

Figure 3.1   Focuses of different career-development theories

Table 3.1 Distinctions between different career-development theories

	Psychological	*Sociological*
Structured	Trait-and-factor theories	Opportunity-structure theories
Interactive	Self-concept theories	Community-interaction theories

community-interaction theories are more strongly expressed in *sociological* terms. Attention has thus been expanded from what is 'in here' – the person and the self – to include more attention to what is 'out there' – the working world and its positions. Furthermore, trait-and-factor theories and opportunity-structure theories focus on more or less firmly *structured* categories of self (suggesting the possibility of relatively stable relationships between self and work) and of socio-economic phenomena (producing generation-on-generation effects) respectively; whereas self-concept theories and community-interaction theories focus on relatively *interactive* concepts, suggesting that links change within self, and between self and community, and that this may provoke intra- or inter-personal conflict and thus catalyse changes-of-mind.

Figure 3.1 is based on the historical sequence in which these four sets of ideas have emerged in Britain over nearly half a century. Each has responded to social concerns prevalent at the time of its first coinage (Law, 1981a). But each has also proved persistent: none has been discarded; all have provided the basis of a sustained addition to the repertoire of careers thinking (and practice). There may be no central congruence to be found here (cf. Savickas and Lent, 1994). But theory reflects the field's conversation with itself, developing new questions which previous contributors have left unanswered.

3.3 A CAREER-LEARNING THEORY

The question in this chapter is, then, 'what new questions might a career-learning theory seek to answer?' There are three in particular, ranging from the specific to the general:

1   When a person's attention shifts from one of these multifarious influences to another, or when a person decides for the first time to start paying conscious attention to *something* in her or his experience, why does that change come about?
2   How is it that different people attend to different influences: some to some parts of the structures and interactions outlined above, some to others?
3   How do people embark upon the discovery of and response to these influences, how is that voyage developed and extended into adulthood, and what enables and hinders it?

The concept of progression addresses all three questions. As we shall see, it can accommodate extant theoretical material. But it does so in a different foreground-and-background configuration, and with different implications for practice. The theory is set out as ten propositions:

1   Some career-development activities depend upon relatively 'basic' capacities, in the sense that these capacities are innate, or are easier to acquire, or can be acquired without the benefit of much prior learning.

2 Other activities depend on more 'developed' capacities, in the sense that they are needed to deal with more complex, dynamic, abstract or emotionally laden experiences.

3 Whether basic or developed, these capacities include both intellectual and behavioural elements, but they also include capacities to acknowledge and manage one's own and others' feelings.

4 The more basic activities require that a person is able to *sense* career-related information and impressions, and to *sift* that material into recognisable patterns that can become the basis for action.

5 The more developed activities require a person to *focus* the material more tightly (for example, by differentiating elements in terms of point of view or ascribed value) and to *understand* it (for example, by being able to identify causes and probable effects in specific scenarios).

6 Some career-development activities require no more than the basic capacities: such activities can be characterised as a 'sense, sift and act' type, used by everyone in more or less routine situations.

7 But everyone will, from time to time, need to engage more developed capacities, where the action is critical or its ramifications are extensive. Here sensing and sifting need to be extended into a 'focus, understand and act' type.

8 The more developed capacities cannot be engaged unless some basic capacities have been successfully developed to support them. In simple terms, a person cannot concentrate upon and properly grasp information she or he has not first sensed and sifted. In more complex terms, the capacity to focus and understand requires a foundation of prior learning.

9 Where prior learning has not been accomplished, or has been accomplished in a form which distorts rather than represents the information, further development may be hindered. Put specifically: a person is likely to misunderstand on the basis of flimsy or misperceived evidence. Put generally: the sifting of knowledge into stereotyped, or other habitually biased frames, will distort further development.

10 Like other learning, career development can be educated. A programme which builds a cycle or cycles of learning, developing from sensing through sifting and focusing to understanding, will equip a person with an educated repertoire of capacities to support career-development actions.

The product of progression is thus conceived as a repertoire. A repertoire is a progressively acquired range of material – some basic, some developed – any part of which can be called into play as it proves appropriate. The notion is not foreign to learning theory (Meadows, 1993). The extent of the repertoire is important: career development requires deep background knowledge of changing causes and effects, speed and accuracy in gathering and organising specific information, flexibility and resilience in negotiating contracts, and a capacity to manage the resulting complexity, ambiguity and probable conflicts.

The key elements in the repertoire are set out in Figure 3.2, using the four levels indicated in propositions 4 and 5, in ascending order. The assumption is that most people have the potential to develop such a repertoire, but that they may need help to do so – for use and re-use in lifelong career development.

The four sections that follow assemble ideas and evidence into a case for career-learning theory. They draw upon much extant career-development

Understanding	8 Anticipating consequencies 7 Developing explainations	⟶ ⟶
Focusing	6 Taking one's own view 5 Dealing with points of view	⟶ ⟶
Sifting	4 Using concepts 3 Making comparisons	⟶ ⟶
Sensing	2 Assembling sequences 1 Gathering information	⟶ ⟶

Figure 3.2 The developing repertoire of career-development capacities

thinking. But they also look for useful suggestions concerning how people learn in more general terms. Like other theories, career-learning theory relies on the probability that the way in which people 'do' their career is much like the way they 'do' everything else. The argument is therefore infused with elements from developmental psychology, social-learning theory and other bodies of thought.

3.4 SENSING

The assumption is that people work from information about work, role and self. The acquisition of that information is here called sensing. It is argued to entail *gathering information*, and *assembling sequences*.

Gathering information

Opportunity-structure theory points to the basic importance of gathering information. Its sole explicit practical concomitant is that people need accurate information to identify opportunities 'actually open to them', and 'where they can be found' (Roberts, 1977). A less rigidly structured conception of information is found in community-interaction theory, which characterises information as impression, feedback and modelling (Law, 1981b). All are a matter of report or encounter, requiring direct and personal contact. They are argued to be an important means through which young people build a picture of how – in career terms – things are.

Assembling such material begins early. From before they go to school, children assemble impressions of work in the family, neighbourhood and community. They learn something of the work of the adults in their home, through sight and sound, and even touch, smell and taste. Biographies are full of such encounters, assembling them into what opportunity structure terms 'anticipatory socialisation'. An example is the recollection of an adult philosopher remembering his childhood in the family library: 'with a creak like a shoe . . . pale, dank, slightly blistered pages, covered with small black veins, which drank ink and smelt of mildew . . . holy objects!' (Sartre, 1964, p. 28). Of course, what is thought 'holy' among the *fin de siècle* bourgeoisie may or may not be much revered in turn-of-the-century Basildon. Elsewhere, other encounters, articulated perhaps in the images of television and tabloids, offer different – and perhaps more attenuated – impressions of work.

It may seem fanciful to call such impressionistic material 'careers information'. But early frames-of-mind, into which fragments of child learning are assembled, shape the accommodation for more formal and more urgent learning later in life. A variety of frames-of-mind are used to accommodate and give order to career learning. A natural frame appears to be a map, connoting opportunity-structure concepts of 'where-it-can-be-found'. Maps locate starting-points and directions, as well as barriers and destinations. Terms and phrases such as 'route' ('career' is cognate with 'carriage'), 'cross-roads', 'prospects' and 'coming a long way' occur repeatedly in ordinary conversations about career. This process of map-making is sustained into adulthood. Gowler and Legge (1989) refer to what they call 'patterns of symbolic construction', representing work as 'a race to be won', 'a mountain to be climbed', 'a maze to be run': all locations for the accommodation of aspects of the working world.

Maps can be both topographical and metaphorical. Expanding the boundaries of the map might mean that the child locates work roles undertaken (topographically) *in other places*, but also (metaphorically) *in other ways*. In both cases, proximity and distance are connoted. Proximity is about how different examples of work are close to each other, but also how they are close to me. It therefore locates self on the map. I can visualise myself as at a starting-point, on a journey, negotiating a barrier or arriving at a destination. In Gowler and Legge's uses of the metaphor, the person sees her or his self as a kind of competitor, mountaineer or maze runner. But long before such fraught images are conjured, a child experiences self as 'customer' and 'helper', as well as in roles with close metaphorical ties to work – 'friend', 'team-member', 'brother' or 'sister'. Again, such early learning frames later thinking – not only concerning work, but also concerning role and self (see Chapter 12).

Whether as a map, or – as we shall see – in other ways, fragments can be assembled into forms which will preserve and organise them for future use. Otherwise they remain a confusing muddle of unusable impressions. The cogency of gestalt psychology is that finding order gives pleasure (Storr, 1992).

Assembling sequences

But work is not just located in (topographical or metaphorical) space: it is located in time. Some remembered moments survive, unattached except perhaps to some palpable location (such as a grandfather's library). We all carry such minikins: scenes and voices, often aromas, difficult – now – to date or sequence. But where such fragments are located in a narrative – with a beginning, a middle and an end – the impression is put into a more durable form. Hence the importance to progression of assembling sequences.

Narrative is, like a map, a natural accommodation for information about work, role and self. Much career talk is embedded in the 'tales we tell', which narrate 'episodes' calling for new adjustments (Nicholson and West, 1989). Much of what people say about work they say through narrative. Hill (1969) reports 7–9-year-olds speaking of work in what he calls 'story-book' form, developing narratives to say what they know of their parents' work. Narrative contains information, preserves it, and makes it more readily transmittable.

There are, of course, always gaps in any story – posing questions ('what did she do then?', 'why did he do that?'). The value of narrative to childhood thinking is argued to be precisely this: that it conveys 'the given' and – through questioning – suggests 'the new' (Feldman, 1987). Hill notes that younger children will sometimes bridge the gaps in their knowledge by simply inventing new narratives. The capacity of frames-of-thought to assimilate the material they receive is, as we shall see, an important feature of career-learning theory. Questioning the gaps is a good thing; but one must not infer from this that any answer to the question is, *ergo*, also a good thing. We shall return to this issue.

Support for the importance to adults of narrative, in thinking about social situations, comes from Fiske (1993). The best 'story', she concludes, is the one that covers most of the evidence, and is coherent (consistent, plausible and complete). Such stories, she says, help people to make decisions – a claim we shall also examine in more detail later in this chapter. Career is, then, a narratable story, moving across a mappable terrain, from episode to episode, each with its own decisions and transitions. The usefulness of narrative to career learning is worth analysing. Like maps, narrative both puts impressions into durable form and poses questions which suggest the possibility of new learning. But narrative extends the accommodation offered by maps by (1) portraying roles in reciprocating relationships – mother with daughter, player with player, shopkeeper with customer, employer with employee – linking what one person does in her role to what another does in his; (2) moving from episode to episode, each with its own decision or transition; and (3) presenting sequences, inviting the investigation of causes and effects.

Story-telling is, of course, the prototypical teaching-and-learning method. As we shall see, both mapping and narrative form a foundation for what will become more developed career-development capacities. As Howard (1987, pp. 30ff.) characterises it, such schemas ('scenes, events, actions, persons, and stories') prepare for the formation of concepts ('mental representations of a category which allows a person to sort stimulus into instances and non-instances').

The central narrative is, of course, autobiography – a term not far distant in meaning from the term 'career' itself – accommodating the ever more episodic experience of my work, my roles and my self. If we still have careers, it may now be in the sense that we each try to make of that story.

3.5 SIFTING

Mapping and story-telling assemble sensory information into frames which locate here-and-there, proximate-and-distant, earlier-and-later, then-and-now. Such maps and stories may be limited or extensive, general or detailed, and more or less complete.

There is more to be done. Career-learning theory suggests that making sense of learning entails a process of sifting: of *making comparisons*, and of *using concepts*.

Making comparisons

Useful maps and stories portray different places, different people, different acts. Such variety invites comparisons.

Children learn to make such comparisons: the postman's job is like the crossing attendant's and not like the shopkeeper's, because . . . The comparisons establish role classifications: '. . . you wear a uniform', or '. . . it is done outdoors', or '. . . it doesn't involve maths'. 'Postman' and 'crossing attendant' can appear alike in all these respects; while 'shopkeeper' may be filed elsewhere. As other cases are encountered, they are appropriately located. The resulting system can be extended to accommodate new cases.

This process is construct-formation. Without such a mental system, the clamour of experience would prove overwhelming and, therefore, unusable (Kelly, 1955). Constructs constitute a multi-dimensional framework for locating information, like-with-like. Their most important feature is that they are internally generated: each person construes her or his experience idiosyncratically. Personal constructs form the basis for much of what is meant by the term 'point of view' (Bannister and Fransella, 1986). Personal construct formation is thus argued to be an important potential contributor to our understanding of how careers develop (Edmonds, 1979).

We forget much of what we learn. Maps, stories and, now, constructs frame the material into more durable form. Indeed, a construct such as 'women's work' can survive the recollection of whatever it was that first suggested it. Constructs can be formed on the basis of very few cases. Stereotyping is the pre-emptive construing of life-roles; and stereotypes, though ill-founded, often prove durable.

The affirmation 'I don't want to do that because it doesn't involve maths' employs a construct as an explanation. While maps locate career in *space*, and stories locate it in *time*, constructs move career thinking towards the issue of *causality*. Maps and narratives may raise questions about what is known and not known; constructs – for good or ill – can suggest answers. Career-learning theory therefore sets construct formation in a progressive sequence, drawing upon awareness, assembling information, leading towards understanding.

Using concepts

Some personally developed constructs are similar to shared concepts (Meadows, 1993). The relationship between construct and concept is subtle: at times, the two terms appear interchangeable (Bannister and Fransella, 1986). But while constructs are internally generated from direct experience, concepts can be learned from others – 'ready-made'. The capacity to learn concepts is as important to career learning as the capacity to develop constructs.

In child-development theory, Piaget (Piaget and Inhelder, 1969) explicitly traces this emerging use – internally organising the material of experience into concepts – to the mature capacity of the young woman or man to think about a career. Hill (1969) finds children engaged in such tasks at 9 years of age, earlier than Piaget would have predicted.

Some such shared classification of data is necessary if communication is to be at all possible. Suppose, as a redundant teacher, that I construe 'teacher', 'comedian' and 'barrister' as involving a standing-up-and-talking person engaging the attention of a sitting-down-and-listening audience. There is no ready-made career concept corresponding to this construct. To engage in public communication, I may need to use other, learned concepts, such as education and training, arts and entertainment, and the law. The fact that I do not associate teaching with training, that I do not think the most important thing about humour is entertainment, and that serving the law is not something that has ever occurred to me, means that my linking of the three roles may be missed by the rigid and impatient. Yet it would be unreasonable of me to expect a guidance service to re-organise its library to file all of my three instances in one place. To get any further, we must link my personal construct to the library's public concepts. Communication requires such transpositions – if not on your part, on mine.

Yet in a fast-changing economy it may be of considerable importance that shared concepts are not allowed to crystallise information into unadaptable frames-of-thought. Idiosyncratic constructs may be liberating, in an otherwise constricting experience. Such lateral thinking may be highly functional in a society constantly needing to redraw its career paths. What counts as 'teaching', 'arts and entertainment', 'sunrise industries', 'in the public sector' and 'women's work' have all changed; and will change again.

The interchange between (shared) concept and (personal) construct is, therefore, critical, connecting the personal-and-individual with the social-and-economic. Such thinking will transform matching processes in careers education and guidance. For example, computer-assisted guidance has not yet solved the problem of linking the user's 'subjective' frame to the 'objective' frames required to access a database. But it will (Law, 1994).

Personal constructs and public concepts represent one analysis of how classifications are developed. There are many others. This chapter develops a macro-analysis of descriptive (sensing), organising (sorting), prioritising (focusing) and explanatory-and-anticipatory (understanding) concepts. A complete career-learning theory would be able to identify more. Such classifications will outline what we need to recognise and communicate about work, role and self. Indeed, the very terms 'work', 'role' and 'self' are themselves generic concepts within each of which are layered ever more detailed ways of describing and locating career-related learning.

An examination of cognitive structure in adult vocational development (Neimeyer et al., 1985) suggests that this degree of detailed differentiation, together with its integration, may be – in varying respects – significant to career choice. While differentiation makes finer discriminations between micro-constructs, integration perceives the linkages between them. These notions are also considered later in this chapter: in Section 3.6, as 'wide-angle' and 'close-up' focusing of information; in Section 3.7, in the building of cause-and-effect links between impressions.

Meanwhile, Howard (1987), more immediately to our present purpose, suggests that concepts may be analysed in the same terms as the eight parts-of-speech: nominal concepts of things, verbal concepts of action, and so on. This is attractive, because it suggests a basic relationship between the way we talk and the way we think. In the same spirit, the categorisation of concepts in Table 3.2 presents the six core forms of question as a basis for identifying career-related concepts.

Table 3.2 Identifying career-related concepts

Category	Question	Classifications
Location	'Where?'	'At home', 'In the street', 'In a shop', 'Far away', 'In a laboratory', 'In the public sector', 'In employment'
Activity	'What?'	'Talking', 'Using tools', 'Writing with pens and papers', 'Travelling', 'Thinking', 'Helping people'
Condition	'How?'	'Wearing a uniform', 'Noisy', 'Clean', 'Busy', 'Being popular', 'Stressful', 'Unhealthy', 'Away from home'
Time	'When?'	'9 to 5', 'In shifts', 'At leisure', 'In spare time', 'Not any more', 'In the present', 'In the future'
People	'Who?'	'Physically strong', 'My family', 'Other people', 'The brainy', 'The enterprising', 'Black people'
Cause	'Why?'	'Runs in my family', 'Well-paid', 'Safe', 'Interesting', 'Important', 'Modern', 'Wealth-creating', 'Voluntary'

But even here, there are cross-analyses: some classifications are relatively concrete, others more abstract. Work that 'runs in my family' is a matter of veri-fiable observation. But 'safe' is more abstract (in part, because it integrates a variety of more concrete 'safeties'). According to Piaget (1932), we can expect younger children to classify social and moral experience in more specific, oper-ational and concrete terms. Abstract concepts for assigning significance to experience emerge later, he argues. Applied to education, a consequence of such thinking is that teachers might prematurely introduce children to concepts they cannot yet use (cf. Goldman, 1964).

Beginning too early might be a danger; but so is beginning too late. The work of Feuerstein (1977), developed from Piagetian theory, shows how children's and adolescents' general ability to learn is damaged by concepts ill-formed in earlier life. Our consideration of the function of narrative in framing career informa-tion warned us of this possibility. Classification errors damage development. Classification can be improved, according to Feuerstein, by targeting remedial help on the way in which people conceptualise their experience.

But as Feuerstein suggests, this cannot be done on the instant. It requires that people are helped to sense and sift a range of material concerning work, role and self; to receive feedback on how they do that; to identify where the matches and mismatches between personal and shared classifications occur; and to see how to bring about a 'useful conversation' between them.

3.6 FOCUSING

Such a programme might be undertaken in 'wide-angle' terms – articulated, for example, to general ideas about 'women's work'. But it might also require a 'close-up' focus. That would mean attending to personally pressing instances of what is perceived to be women's work, and identifying how it is that I – and others – see these instances that way. In order to do that, a person would need to build from sensing and sifting, into knowing that point of view is a possibility, and that it alters how the information is perceived. Career-learning theory therefore argues that focusing will entail *dealing with points of view*, and *taking one's own view*.

Dealing with points of view

All of this means that career learning cannot occur in a social vacuum. It is a bridge connecting what a person receives from the culture to what he or she is going to do about it. It is signposted both by the social-and-verifiable and by the individual-and-subjective. It therefore entails understanding both what a person can and cannot agree with others. All of this means dealing with points of view.

In child-development theory, Meadows (1993) cites a research-based model for the development of variously conceived senses of self. The model offers parallels to the account given above: (1) *categorical* identification refers to some actual or assumed fact; (2) *comparative* assessment takes account of another person or of self in other circumstances; and (3) *interpersonal* implications of self are often drawn from communication with others – so that the self is set in a social context. As we shall see, there is more than this; but we must first examine what the third of these levels means to career learning in more general terms.

The earliest settings for the process of agreement and disagreement about career are in homes, and – soon after – among friendship groups. Growing up both extends and adds to these encounters. In adulthood, the different point of view of an employer becomes important.

Bruner and Haste (1987) summarise findings from more recent work on child development, pointing to the importance to learning of community relationships and wider sociological influences. Within this body of thought, developmental psychology characterises the sense of self in early childhood as stemming from an acknowledgement of the existence of others (Donaldson, 1978). Early social behaviour is said to interpret the influence of others as though it is rule-bound – 'out there', ready-made, the-same-for-everybody and unchangeable. But children do not forever accept the imposition of rules. Subsequent appreciation of the variability of points of view is seen as an important milestone in that learning. Seeing the other person as an individual, together with the development of formal and conceptualised thought, allows other people's purposes to be appreciated and their 'rules' to be questioned. 'The consciousness of autonomy dispels the myth of revelation!' (Piaget, 1932).

Of course, there are some career 'rules': these include entry requirements, more or less objective facts about the current labour economy, and reasonably verifiable probabilities concerning health risks in certain roles. But there are no rules about what constitutes 'women's work', the necessity of following 'family traditions', or the 'right to paid employment'. Propositions on such matters derive from points of view. There is, therefore, disagreement.

Nonetheless, the childlike persist in the search for certainties, to script what they, and others, do. Arendt (1978) dramatically recognises the child-mind in an adult worker. Reporting the functioning of a senior official, she identifies the way in which, when confronted with situations for which routine procedures did not exist, he was said to be 'helpless', dealing in 'clichés, stock phrases, adherence to convention, standardised codes of expression and conduct' (p. 4). The official was Adolf Eichmann.

This counter-positioning of unproblematic rules-and-right-answers with problematic points of view has two important consequences. One of these has to do with changes-of-mind. Changes-of-mind in biography not uncommonly ensue from encounters with others. One example of community-interaction theory

(Law, 1981b) suggests that people are helped by encounters with new points of view on work, role and self. The theory identifies the dynamics of feedback, modelling and expectation as influential in this process. In childhood, such influences are from parent to child; in adolescence, from peer to peer; in later life, the influence might as likely be from child to parent. In all cases, the converse hypothesis is also made: that structural influences, of (say) social class or media images, will be stronger where they are re-transmitted, unchallenged, in a dominant culture (cf. Willis, 1977). Community interaction can therefore confirm the status quo or catalyse a change-of-mind. It has important potential concerning the education of ethnic, gender and social-class stereotypes.

A further consequence follows from this. If career development were signposted wholly by 'facts' and 'rules' which everybody agreed, then we could more readily agree about who should do what in the working world. Outgrowing the acceptance of such certainty brings doubt and conflict. Their occurrence and resolution evoke, in turn, fear and hope, hostility and alliance, apathy and motivation. Career development is always emotionally charged, sometimes painfully so. Withdrawal, into a 'safe' group or away from all groups, might anaesthetise the pain, but it does not help the learning. Failure to move into and through the pain renders me a passive recipient of other people's points of view, or an un-self-critical celebrant of my own. Dealing with other people's points of view, though at times tiresome, is a necessary precursor to taking one's own view, not least because it demonstrates that that point of view is a possibility.

Taking one's own view

Having a point of view means that what I learn is more than a compliant reaction to the last thing that happened to me. In the simplest of all learning theories, stimulus evinces an intended response. But children do not appear to see it that way! This chapter has traced the complications for learning of work, role and self. It shows how I may have once known: but I have 'forgotten' it because it has not been incorporated into a *schema*; or I have dropped it when I realised how different it was from what I had always assumed; or I ignore it because it is derided by significant others. Any 'stimulus' must compete for *my* particular attention, if it is to shape any sustained 'response'.

On the other hand, if new learning can be fitted to what I already know (or think I know), I may use it, shaping and re-configuring it to a form that I can reconcile with prior learning. Early learning will have established the frames for that: mapping identifies what I see as proximate and distant; narrative identifies what I see as significant characters and episodes; and classifications identify what is more or less important. These are all foreground-and-background configurations. They show that I stand 'here' rather than 'there' in relation to what I know, so that what I learn is different for me than for other people.

Child-development theory emphasises the importance to understanding of new configurations brought about by changed points of view (Bruner and Haste, 1987). In careers guidance, the client-centred concept of 'empathy' expresses an appreciation of that personal and unique configuration of experience (Natale, 1972).

There are, however, problems in developing a distinctive point of view. Willis's (1977) work with the wayward but tribal 'lads' is valuable for its documentation of the difficulty experienced by some (those with 'ear-'ole' tendencies) in maintaining a minority point of view in a proximate and valued ('laddish') culture. A telling problem for careers education and guidance concerns how to help people to develop and sustain for themselves a distinctive point of view in the face of peer, family and other community pressures.

How do we know that a point of view is developing? The model of developing self-awareness cited by Meadows, outlined earlier, in fact comprises not three but four stages, the fourth being that self can be thought of as a set of systematic beliefs and principles, involving evaluation of past actions and purposes for new actions. It is in this sense that point of view begins to become recognisable, and to take on some of the characteristics of what might be called an 'inner life'.

Community-interaction theory suggests that developing a point of view is not an introspective event but a series of selective responses to other people's points of view. Autonomy, then, is not freedom from influence: it is deciding to whom one is going to pay attention (Law, 1981a; 1992). An inner life unfurnished with what other people offer would be a poor one.

Attraction and repulsion concerning other points of view evoke considerations of motivation, concerned with what a person likes, finds interesting, needs or values. This is another respect in which career development evokes feelings, here voiced as valence – seeking 'this' rather than 'that'. That career development is motivated appears to be beyond doubt (Law and Ward, 1981). Roe (1951) imported motivational ideas to career-development theory, linked to Maslow's (1954) theory of *organismic* needs. But motivations also express *cultural* expectations – the values to be found in 'music *we* play', 'stories *we* tell', 'people *we* admire', 'work *we* think important'. Much of what we value, we *learn* to value from family, neighbourhood, religion or ethnic group. The process becomes more than anticipatory socialisation when I begin to consider 'their' as well as 'our' values.

We are speaking here of a *learning* individual who knows why he or she is doing this rather than that. Expanded cultural attachments do not inevitably lead to choice. If all that happens is the usurping of earlier by later cultural influences, then we are speaking not of choice but of the substitution of an earlier compliance by a later one. This is not flexibility but malleability. Choice means being able to say 'I know why I no longer want to do that, and why I now want to do this!' Learning must be subjected to test, whereby *some*, but not just *any*, points of view are accepted.

A condition for learning is, therefore, that two or more points of view are concurrently held in place, while they are examined. Personal-construct thinking offers the metaphor of 'the community of self' (Mair, 1977), developing the meaning of the conversational phrase 'being in two minds', and betokening a readiness to 'open out'. A person voluntarily enters and leaves different points of view by assigning to each other the roles of 'self' and 'other', as bases for construct-building comparisons. Point of view is then, at least for some of the time, not a fixed but a changing perspective. A person may change her or his response to a single repeated stimulus. More than that, a person may perpetuate one of the new responses in a new sense of sustained self. This would be a move from 'in-two-minds' to 'change-of-mind'. The process is described in some detail for adult career development, where it is characterised as 'perspective transformation' (Mezirow, 1977).

The mental processing entailed here is characterised in child-development theory (Piaget and Inhelder, 1969) as twofold: accommodation and assimilation.

Accommodation alters current mental organisation to take account of new experience; *assimilation* filters and modifies new experience so that it fits existing mental organisation. Piaget and Inhelder characterise the change as a process of forming new concepts from the observation of new cases: as 'the spontaneous development of an *experimental* spirit' (p. 145; my italics). The mind is not simply a stimulus–response processor, but is in a creative relationship with its experience – sometimes using experience to support a current point of view, sometimes changing its configuration.

Adult career-development theory appeals at this point (Arnold, 1994) to 'post-formal' thinking, implying a movement beyond Piaget's ascription to adolescents of conceptualised thought. Arnold cites (without approval) a number of models for that continuing career-development processing, each more or less characterising the following beliefs as bases for action: (1) that truth is absolute, known to everyone; (2) that truth exists, but might remain uncertain and unknown; (3) that reality is subjective, any being as good as any other; (4) that truth is subjective, so that action upon it must be founded in values; and (5) that both reality and the means of ascertaining it are uncertain. One can only hope that these are not the only choices we have. The statement 'housework is women's work' may not qualify as an 'absolute truth, known to everyone', but it is certainly not a view 'as good as any other'. Must credibility rest upon either the rule-bound 'fundamentalism' of the earlier levels or the 'post-modern' capitulation of the later ones? Piaget's experimenting adolescents seem to be more mature than either!

What, then, is a mature test here? Career-learning theory proposes that the process is, as Piaget and Inhelder suggest, experimental – inductive rather than deductive. For example, on the issue 'housework is women's work', I could ask myself, 'have I enough to go on?' (on the experimental analogy of sampling); and I could also ask, 'would somebody with a different point of view agree?' (on the experimental analogy of replication). Such credibility testing occurs: one of the 'lads' in the study by Willis (1977) is clearly documented as having checked out his own point of view (concerning the futility of success at school) to the extent where he could see it from the point of view of the 'ear-'oles'.

The transitional state is, however, confusion. Piaget calls this 'disequilibrium' – a condition in which I may find myself thinking 'that is not what I have always believed' or 'that doesn't make any sense' or 'I just can't get this straight in my head'. We are talking here, not of a lack of intellectual power, but of a willingness to find room for new ideas – perhaps by changing existing ideas. Learning here is not so much about being bright enough; it is more about being open enough. Disequilibrium is discomfort. It may, therefore, be more comfortable not to think.

In her account of Eichmann's career, Arendt (1978) spectacularly documents the lack of inner life in an unthinking man. She speaks of the 'manifest shallowness' of his functioning, rendering it impossible to trace behaviour to any deeper level of roots or motives, and offering no sign of firm ideological convictions. His actions were, she says, the products 'not of stupidity but *thoughtlessness!*' (p. 4).

A bi-polar analysis of relative 'depth' in child learning (Meadows, 1993) similarly treats thoughtfulness as being different from intelligence, and more to do with being prepared to be troubled. She characterises the poles as: (1) surface learning, instrumentally concerned with getting results for minimal effort, focusing only on the essentials; and (2) deep learning, with an intrinsic interest in the material, developing and using a personal understanding of it, and more likely to relate facts to one another, with amendment and with reference to underlying principles.

Parallel support for the importance to learning of focused 'thoughtful-ness' comes from social learning theory. Fiske (1993) cites a four-level analysis (given here with my added characterisations of level). *Pre-conscious auto-maticity* is unaware of both the occasion and the response. This might be called the 'knee-jerk' level. *Post-conscious automaticity* is aware of the occasion, but not its effects on judgement or actions. It can be strong where the information is ambiguous and difficult to clearly sort, and is used to explain some stereotyping behaviour. This might be called the 'suggestible' level. *Goal-dependent automaticity* is where the response to the occasion might be unaware and unintended, and therefore spontaneous; but where there is sufficient aware-ness that it might be shaped by one's own purposes. A person may interrupt his or her automatic response to the occasion by suppressing the old thought with new – occurring sometimes in the form of 'rumination', which is argued to be capable of changing behaviour. This might be called the 'awakening' level. Finally, *full intentionality and control* is where attention to the occasion elicits what is required for response. The direction of attention is central to this process, constituting much of what is meant by an act of 'will', a particular feature of which is to attend to the unexpected or unwanted information in the situation. People here are seeking diagnostic rather than confirmatory informa-tion, with the intention of shaping their own behaviour. This might be called the 'wide-awake' level. It closely parallels earlier characterisations of point of view as inner life.

Let us return, then, to the question: why is that a person will attend to some influences in developing a point of view, but not others? A summary of this sec-tion suggests that focus might be achieved by what is salient, valued or credible:

1 It is *salient* if it belongs centrally to my map, narrative or conceptual struc-ture. I will then perceive it as 'recognisable', 'in-tune', 'relevant' or 'of concern to me'.

2 It is *valued* if it offers a positive valence – attracting rather than repelling. That may be because it entails action which is in some way 'like us' or 'like me', or something 'I like' or 'we like', or in these and other senses 'inter-esting', 'welcome', 'comfortable' or 'right'. These descriptors can also include variations on 'like those-that-I-like' and 'like those-who-like-me'.

3 It is *credible* if it makes sense and can, therefore, be believed. It might be said to be 'sensible', 'thought-through', leading to 'a wise decision' or – better still – 'a decision made wisely'. Elements in the process of achieving credibility for a point of view are inductive – involving sampling ('I've enough to go on now') and replication ('a sane onlooker would confirm it').

The feeling and thinking elements in this layered processing may be in contention with each other. Yet, if we are to speak of '*a point of view*', thoughts and feelings must cohabit. The parallel case is made in rational-emotive coun-selling theory (Ellis, 1973), which argues that thoughts and feelings are the same thing differently expressed. Career-learning theory has identified three respects in which thought and feeling are integral:

1 My career idea is linked to, or separated from, some organismic need or cultural value of importance to me.
2 My career idea is applauded or rejected by significant others.
3 Focusing itself confirms or challenges prior learning – taking me into or out of a 'comfort zone'.

Like Ellis, career-learning theory assigns arbitrating (yet not exclusive) force to credibility: 'your feelings are important, and nobody is saying that you should not attend to them; but *think* about them too!' This approach does not exclude the acknowledgement that the links between feeling and career occur subliminally (Hood, 1995).

If there is any validity in this analysis, people – in working through their career plans – will experience confusion, discomfort, unfocused unease and (on occasions) anguish. There are important implications. Among them is the consequence that careers guidance cannot offer instant gratification for 'customers' who – in a market-place – might prefer to patronise 'feel-good' vendors. Neither can careers education invariably be quick-and-easy: it is as demanding as any other 'subject' – and more demanding than many (see Chapter 12).

Career-learning theory must assume that people are able to cross the difficulty thresholds and are willing to confront the discomfort zones! Indeed, in this and other ways to be examined below, career-learning theory implies that avoidance of difficulty and discomfort is, itself, living dangerously.

3.7 UNDERSTANDING

Moving directly from information to action would not be planning: it would be impulse. Career-learning theory argues that, for at least some of the time, we must all do some serious reflecting: locating, comparing and conceptualising the information; invoking – from others and within ourselves – alternative points of view; so that we can establish for ourselves what is salient, valuable and credible. All of this prepares for understanding. Understanding, it is further argued, then entails *developing explanations* and *anticipating consequences*.

Developing explanations

Information, and the points of view which configure it, suggest *action*: 'having formed that impression, she decided . . .', 'her sense of responsibility was such that she . . .', 'once he realised that, he was bound to . . .'. The sequence in such narratives invites a linking of causes to their effects. Howard (1987) argues that it is the function of such *schemas* to provide for such inferences. He offers 'enrolment–study–examination–graduation' as an example.

The interaction of narrative and understanding is not accidental. The themes of behavioural science and literature overlap. It is the open question which offers the greater insight: as Meadows (1993) herself observes, 'I remember seeing a performance of an early play by Chekhov in which he seemed to anticipate twentieth-century psychology with extraordinary specificity, forty or fifty years before these ideas occurred to psychologists' (p. 236). Indeed, literature – from classical myth to television soap-opera – offers other people's stories as a clue to our own. We may, then, find telling traces of explanation-for-career in

Table 3.3 Literary examples of career-development explanations

Explanation	Literary figure	Parallel theory
A specific characteristic	Achilles	Trait-and-factor
Person as 'self'	Don Quixote	Self-concept
Dealing with obstacles	Odysseus	Opportunity-structure
Social attachment	Romeo	Community-interaction
Point of view	Shylock	Career-learning

literature (Table 3.3). Of course, any story has plot and sub-plot; most touch more than one row in the chart. That is the point of this chapter.

All narrative, then, provokes the question 'why?': 'why couldn't she . . .?', 'why do they . . .?', 'why did I . . .?' The answers to such questions are explanatory hypotheses, suggesting 'this came about because . . .'.

Forming explanatory hypotheses might suggest an unusual and élite form of thought, but it is commonplace – what we all do when we seek to 'figure it out'. Seeking explanations for specific phenomena is often deductive, reciprocating the earlier inductive classifying process by making cases contingent upon concepts: 'she couldn't have done that, because . . . she is a *woman*!'; 'it is not *well enough paid*'; 'her sense of her own *importance* wouldn't let her!'

Deductive credibility depends upon what Piaget (1932) calls 'experimental' thinking. The scientific parallels are not too far-fetched: 'theory building' ('so that's what makes the difference'); 'hypothesis building' ('how can we check that out?'); and 'control groups' ('do *other* people like her do that?').

This is 'conversational science': street use of refined theory. Concepts are characterised in social learning theory (Fiske, 1993) as tools to locate explanations, which are accepted if they work 'well enough' for most people most of the time – in particular, if they permit people to predict the future from the past. We all do 'science' for some of the time; and, as a breed, we do it comparatively well. We are a theory-building species: it is part of our finger-hold on survival.

The faster the rate of change, the more critical the requirement for such thought. So argues Sparkes (1994), who complains about a contemporary over-reliance on mere competence as a measure of performance in vocational behaviour. He argues for the acknowledgement of understanding, which he defines as 'the capacity to use explanatory concepts'. Furthermore, he argues that understanding is critical for the solution of new problems. The recycling of predefined skills developed from familiar problems cannot deal with a changing world. Learning theory concurs: the essential importance of formal thought (what experimenting adolescents can do) is that it is no longer bounded by what is perceived, but instead 'grasps possible transformation, and assimilates reality in terms of imagined or deduced events' so that the world is 'not bound by the concrete and perceptible, but encompasses many interpersonal and social possibilities' (Piaget and Inhelder, 1969, p. 149).

We have spoken so far in terms of a *personal* narrative – with a 'close-up' focus on particular people confronting particular episodes in their stories. But there are also broader – 'wide-angle' – focuses. They would incorporate such statements as: 'people *like that* generally prefer this, because . . .', 'the effects of *technological change* have been . . .', 'changes in the qualification *system* have led to . . .', and '*work is offered* on short-term contracts, because . . .'. Such statements are explanatory, but at a different level of analysis. They draw as much upon a scientific as upon a literary paradigm. Yet they form a backdrop to any personal narrative, offering a parallel series of generalities, some of which will sometimes touch the particulars of experience. They are a *meta*-narrative.

The relative usefulness of *personal* narrative and *meta*-narrative is an issue in career-development theory. Roberts's (1977) case is that career development is best explained in terms of meta-narrative. Willis's (1977) ethnography recounts personal narrative, but the Marxist analysis he imposes upon it is wholly meta-narrative. On the other hand, community-interaction theory (although itself a meta-narrative) argues that career development is best understood as personal narrative – as biography. It contends that where the culture does not re-transmit a meta-narrative into personal narratives, it will be less attended to, and less influential. Conversely, where it is re-transmitted, it will shape behaviour. People do have some idea of what is going on in larger (sociological, psychological, or economic) terms. But generally, those terms are absorbed into biography through a proximate culture.

At a time of large-scale change in society and economy, the practical implications for helping people to understand and explain 'the meta', so that they can act upon it, would be extensive. There is a possible implication here that people should be helped, through reflection upon their own and other people's career biographies, to become their own career-development theoreticians (cf. Munro and Law, 1994) as a basis for their own action.

Anticipating consequences

Acting on understanding is where we are headed. Without understanding of how things came to be the way they are, we are at a disadvantage in knowing what to do about them. Career learning accordingly hypothesises a progression from attempting explanation of the past to anticipating future consequences.

Cogent explanation suggests the possibility of action: 'so, if it's this that makes the difference, why don't I ...?' The process includes the possibility of further experimentation: 'how can I try it out first?' And further inference: 'if it works like that for her, maybe I can risk ...'. Autonomous action must involve some such visualisation (whether rational or not) of 'this is what will probably happen if I do this ...'. It requires the imagination of possible selves in possible futures.

There are, of course, few sure-fire predictions. Action always entails risk. But risks can be assessed so that probabilities are cogently estimated (Sutherland, 1992). Indeed, not to be able to assess risk is to live in insouciant peril.

An empirical enquiry by Arroba (1977), directly addressing decision-making, reported decisions being made in six distinguishable styles: (1) a *logical* decision, 'coldly and objectively appraised'; (2) a *no-thought decision*, concerning 'a routine matter, frequently encountered'; (3) a *hesitant* decision, characterised by an 'inability to make the decision', which was therefore postponed; (4) an *emotional* decision, based on 'subjective preferences or feeling ... what a person likes or wants'; (5) a *compliant* decision, made in accordance with 'perceived expectations' of others; and (6) an *intuitive* decision, which is 'inner-oriented ... a sense or rightness or inevitability'. Most people are said to use different styles in different situations.

Table 3.4 Relationship between career-learning theory and decision-making styles

Career-learning theory	Salience – having immediacy and recognisability	Value – being culturally or personally attractive	Credibility – appearing cogent in induction and deduction
Decision-making styles (Arroba)	Compliant (?) No-thought	Emotional Intuitive (?)	Logical Hesitant (?)

Table 3.4 suggests that Arroba's findings are by no means inconsistent with career-learning theory's analysis of point of view into considerations of salience, value and credibility (the correspondence is not exact, and queries appear in the table where the parallel is not manifest). Career-learning theory assigns arbitrating but not exclusive significance to credibility in effective career decision-making. The majority of Arroba's sample appear to agree, in so far that they see career as among the 'most important' decisions, which – most report – require a logical style.

A practical implication would be that, if I wanted to defend my untenable position with the assertion 'I am entitled to my opinion', a teacher or counsellor would know that I need help. But it is the *kind* of help that theory most valuably identifies: do I have enough information? . . . well-enough remembered? . . . reliably-enough classified? . . . understood to be influenced by others? . . . seen from alternative points of view? . . . tested by cogent thought? A person does not have to be a genius in order to benefit from such help. Indeed, the importance of such reflection to people with learning difficulties is advocated, because it: (1) helps the learner to think about possible demands; (2) provides an opportunity for ongoing reflection; and (3) enables remembered impressions to be organised into emerging theories (Powell and Makin, 1994).

Reflection takes many forms. There is no single route to cogent rationality. It is to be found through language, through mathematics, in spatial terms, and in kinaesthetic terms (Gardner, 1983; cf., for a more comprehensive account, Vernon, 1961). Most people – if they are open enough to do it – are capable enough to cross the difficulty thresholds, if not by one intellectual route, then by another.

Career-learning theory therefore suggests careers education and guidance models which will take people to a point where they can recognise the difference between evidence and rhetoric, fact and opinion, argument and leverage. Not much is to be gained from actions conceived in loosely-screwed heads.

3.8 IMPLICATIONS

It was argued at the beginning of this chapter that career-development theories respond to a receptive cultural ambience. This chapter's propositions are of particular contemporary pertinence. An increasingly problematic career structure demands a more incisively heuristic response – the harder it gets, the more we should think about it.

Career-learning theory is re-connected in this section to its provenance in career-development thought. Later in this section, it is also connected to areas in which its models for practice can be developed.

Theory and meta-theory

The chapter opened with an analysis of types of theory in terms of their historical and conceptual relationships. As Figure 3.3 suggests, career-learning theory's fit to the conceptual model now requires a third dimension. The diagram is adapted from an earlier three-dimensional analysis (Law, 1981a).

The third dimension discriminates between *differentialist* theories which assume that the important differences are between people, and *progressive* theories which assume that the important differences are between different stages of learning progression. At one extreme, I may be best understood in terms of being better-than-average with my hands. At the other, I may be best understood in terms of not yet having assembled this information into any understanding of the work roles it opens for me. This opposition is not adequately covered by the two-dimensional model used at the beginning of the chapter.

All of the theories cited at the beginning of this chapter can, then, be sorted on this new dimension – between the front and back of Figure 3.3. Career-learning theory appears at the back: perhaps further back than Roberts's version of opportunity-structure theory (with its slightly-developed use of anticipatory socialisation as a 'learning' process); and perhaps rather lower than Rodger's (1952) seven-point version of trait-and-factor theory (with its self-contained assumptions about the structure of abilities). But most theories fit *along* the dimensions, rather than at particular *points* on them.

For example, Super's (1957) version of self-concept theory has elements of both differential *and* progressive thinking within it. The idea of a self-concept is plainly differential in its effect; its development, on the other hand, is described in progressive terms. But the progressive element is less developed than for career-

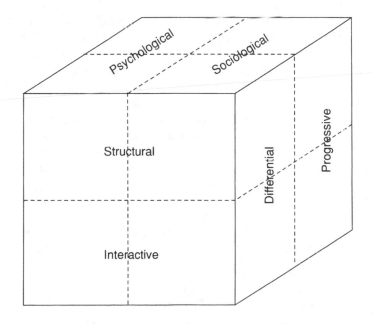

Figure 3.3 A three-dimensional representation of career-development theories

learning theory as outlined in this chapter. Super's main developmental stages are not learning-stages, but life-stages. They are defined in terms of the kinds of roles that a person is likely to occupy at different stages in a life-span. Each stage no doubt affords learning opportunities; but each is primarily articulated to requirements-for-help at a particular stage of social positioning (see especially Super, 1981).

The contribution to meta theory of career-learning theory is, then, to add to the terms in which thinking may be framed. At this stage, however, it is no more than a series of unconfirmed propositions. Confirmation may be a matter for research; but experience with models of careers education and guidance can also validate theory.

Practical implications

The chief justification for a theory is its capacity to suggest predictive hypotheses which can be formulated into models for effective action. In this respect, career-learning theory's elaboration of the third dimension in Figure 3.3 is important.

Wholly differentialist theories offer strong support to models where the task is to identify key features in a person's presentation of self, and what she or he wants – here and now – to do about it. Differentialism therefore identifies the client's personal *agenda* as the occasion for help. Guidance interviews (see Chapter 11) and small-group work lend themselves well to that formulation; as do some uses of psychometrics and computer-assisted guidance (see Chapter 15). Indeed, a pure and highly structured version of differentialism would be an assumption that the innate and unchanging tendencies of the individual are the most powerful determinants of career behaviour, and that the best way to help would be (psychometrically) to determine these tendencies and build career planning upon them.

The implications of progressive formulations are different. They assume that career behaviour is learned and, therefore, can be educated. They identify a *scheme-of-work* as the occasion for help. Careers education, together with open-learning and distance-learning programmes, lend themselves to that formulation (see Chapter 12); as do the formative use of psychometrics, of computer-assisted guidance and of recording-and-planning techniques (see Chapter 14).

The two sets of activities – curriculum and guidance – are, of course mutually dependent (see Chapter 12). A use of career-learning theory in guidance would, then, be diagnostic. Guidance providers would be able to assess where the strengths and weaknesses are in what people are able to learn of a career. This could be provided as 'feedback': indicating where – among sensing, sifting, focusing and understanding activities – a group needs more curriculum-based help.

More detailed implications of career-learning theory in curriculum terms can be identified within four professional frames (for the detailed content of such programmes, see Chapter 12):

1 *Foundation learning* is comprehensive in the sense that it is for everybody and covers all the stages of learning progression, bringing people into command of the full repertoire of capacities. The implications of the theory are that this should begin (in some form) in primary school, and be aimed at the progressive enrichment, diversification and verification of bases for action. The expectation would be that earlier stages would require higher concen-

trations of sensing and sifting activity (engaging children in finding out about work, role and self, and in sifting and sorting what they find into useful orders). This would lay an informed and explored basis for later expansion, and more demanding reflection, at later stages in the foundation programme. It might usefully link exploration of specifically 'career' roles to other life-roles; in schools, it might be undertaken in personal and social education programmes. In adulthood, open-learning and IT-based schemes of careers education offer promising prospects for such help.

2 *Connecting learning* ensures that career applications of learning are, from time to time, re-examined in specific contexts. Such work in school could be under-taken on a 'long-block' integrated basis (see Chapter 5). This provides for the re-focusing of career learning, enabling connections between foundation learning and specific learning projects. Programmes would move, with vari-ations, in 'mini-progressions', touching upon sensing, sifting, focusing, understanding and action. The 'whole-curriculum' opportunities are exten-sive: career-learning theory suggests links to the full range of investigating, mapping, narrative, classifying, experimenting and practising activities within the curriculum.

3 *Pivotal learning* is concerned with the depth as well as the extent of career learn-ing. It provides necessary learning at crucial stages. It *systematically* revisits all levels of sensing, sifting, focusing and understanding, in increasing detail and depth. In sensing, for example, people need to learn how to access official sources of information; but probably not *until* they are 13 or 14 years old, and best *after* they have had an opportunity to set 'public' information into a personal and interpersonal context. Such work requires trained helpers, calling upon understanding and skill that only experts can provide. In particular, it must be able to deal with the affect-laden responses that are embedded in career development.

4 *Recovery learning* is a special form of pivotal learning for people needing to recover lost learning opportunities and to undertake 're-building' work. It will probably be concerned – as much as with anything – with re-examining and re-shaping damaging constructs.

Work, role and self cannot be learned in short order. If we do not help people with their career learning earlier, we should not be surprised if, later, help needs more time than we can readily find.

REFERENCES

Arendt, H. (1978). *The Life of the Mind*, vol. 1, New York: Harcourt Brace Jovanovich.

Arnold, J. (1994) 'The Applications of Theory and Research in Adult Cognitive Development to Career Management', Paper presented to the 23rd International Congress of Applied Psychology, Madrid.

Arroba, T. (1977) 'Styles of Decision Making and their Use: an Empirical Study', *British Journal of Guidance and Counselling* 5(2): 149–58.

Banks, M., Bates, I., Breakwell, G., Bynner, J., Emler, N., Jamieson, L. and Roberts, K. (1992) *Careers and Identities*, London: Open University Press.

Bannister, D. and Fransella, F. (1986) *Inquiring Man: the Psychology of Personal Constructs* (3rd edn), Beckenham: Croom Helm.

Bruner, J. and Haste, H. (1987) *Making Sense: the Child's Construction of the World*, London: Routledge.

Dawis, R. V. (1994) 'The Theory of Work Adjustment as Convergent Theory', in Savickas, M. L. and Lent, R. (eds) *Convergence in Career Development Theories*, Palo Alto, CA: Consulting Psychologists Press.

Daws, P. P. (1968) *A Good Start in Life*, Cambridge: Careers Research and Advisory Centre.

Donaldson, M. (1978) *Children's Minds*, Glasgow: Fontana.

Edmonds, T. (1979) 'Applying Personal Construct Theory in Occupational Guidance', *British Journal of Guidance and Counselling* 7(2): 225–33.

Ellis, A. (1973) *Humanistic Psychotherapy: the Rational-Emotive Approach*, New York: Julian Press.

Feldman, C. F. (1987) 'Thought for Language: the Linguistic Construction of Cognitive Representations', in Bruner, J. and Haste, H. (eds) *Making Sense: the Child's Construction of the World*, London: Routledge.

Feuerstein, R. (1977) 'Mediated Learning Experience: a Theoretical Basis for Cognitive Modifiability during Adolescence', in Mittler, P. (ed.) *Research Practice in Mental Retardation*, vol. 2, Baltimore, MD: University Park Press.

Fiske, S. T. (1993) 'Social Cognition and Social Perception', *Annual Review of Psychology* 44: 155–94.

Gardner, H. (1983) *Frames of Mind*, Glasgow: Fontana.

Goldman, R. (1964) *Religious Thinking in Childhood and Adolescence*, London: Routledge & Kegan Paul.

Gottfredson, L. S. (1981) 'Circumscription and Compromise: a Developmental Theory of Occupational Aspirations', *Journal of Counseling Psychology* 28(6): 545–79.

Gowler, D. and Legge, K. (1989) 'Rhetoric in Bureaucratic Careers: Managing the Meaning of Management Success', in Arthur, M. B., Hall, D. T. and Lawrence, B. S. (eds) *Handbook of Career Theory*, Cambridge: Cambridge University Press.

Hill, J. M. M. (1969) *The Transition from School to Work*, London: Tavistock Institute of Human Relations.

Hood, V. (1995) 'Work-Related Counselling: a Psychodynamic Approach', *Psychodynamic Counselling* 1(2): 239–52.

Howard, W. R. (1987) *Concepts and Schemata*, London: Cassell.

Kelly, G. A. (1955) *The Psychology of Personal Constructs*, New York: Norton.

Kline, P. (1975) *The Psychology of Vocational Guidance*, London: Batsford.

Krumboltz, J. D. (1994) 'Improving Career Development from a Social Learning Perspective', in Savickas, M. L. and Lent, R. W. (eds) *Convergence in Career Development Theories: Implications for Science and Practice*, Palo Alto, CA: Consulting Psychologists Press.

Law, B. (1981a) 'Careers Theory: a Third Dimension?', in Watts, A. G., Super, D. E. and Kidd, J. M. (eds) *Career Development in Britain*, Cambridge: Careers Research and Advisory Centre/Hobsons.

Law, B. (1981b) 'Community Interaction: a "Mid-Range" Focus for Theories of Career Development in Young Adults', *British Journal of Guidance and Counselling* 9(2): 142–58.

Law, B. (1992) 'Autonomy and Learning About Work', in Young, R. A. and Collin, A. (eds) *Interpreting Careers: Hermeneutical Studies of Lives in Context*, New York: Praeger.

Law, B. (1994) 'On the Importance of Interwagulation!', in *The Future Use of Information Technology in Guidance*, Coventry: National Council for Educational Technology.

Law, B. and Ward, R. (1981) 'Is Career Development Motivated?', in Watts, A. G., Super, D. E. and Kidd, J. M. (eds) *Career Development in Britain*, Cambridge: Careers Research and Advisory Centre/Hobsons.

Mair, J. M. M. (1977) 'The Community of Self', in Bannister, D. (ed.) *New Perspectives in Personal Construct Theory*, London: Academic Press.

Maslow, A. (1954) *Motivation and Personality*, New York: Harper & Row.

Meadows, S. (1993) *The Child as Thinker*, London: Routledge.

Mezirow, J. (1977) 'Perspective Transformation', *Studies in Adult Education* 9(2): 153–64.

Munro, M. and Law, B. (1994) *The Morrisby Careers Education Programme*, Hemel Hempstead: Morrisby Organisation.

Natale, S. (1972) *An Experiment in Empathy*, Slough: National Foundation for Educational Research.

Neimeyer, G., Nevill, D. D., Probert, B. and Fukuyama, M. (1985) 'Cognitive Structures in Vocational Development', *Journal of Vocational Behaviour* 27: 191–201.

Nicholson, N. and West, M. (1989) 'Transitions, Work Histories and Careers', in Arthur, M. B., Hall, D. T. and Lawrence, B. S. (eds) *Handbook of Career Theory*, Cambridge: Cambridge University Press.

Offer, M. (1995) 'Personal Construct Theory: a Complete Programme for Careers Education and Guidance?', *Careers Education and Guidance*, October, 21–24.

Piaget, J. (1932) *The Moral Judgement of the Child*, London: Routledge & Kegan Paul.

Piaget, J. and Inhelder, B. (1969) *The Psychology of the Child*, London: Routledge & Kegan Paul.

Powell, S. D. and Makin, M. (1994) 'Enabling Pupils with Learning Difficulties on their Own Thinking', *British Educational Research Journal* 20(5): 579–93.

Roberts, K. (1977) 'The Social Conditions, Consequences and Limitations of Careers Guidance', *British Journal of Guidance and Counselling* 5(1): 1–9.

Rodger, A. (1952) *The Seven Point Plan*, London: National Institute of Industrial Psychology.

Roe, A. (1951) *Psychology of Occupations*, New York: Wiley.

Sartre, P. (1964) *Words*, Harmondsworth: Penguin.

Savickas, M. L. and Lent, R. (eds.) (1994) *Convergence in Career Development Theories*, Palo Alto, CA: Consulting Psychologists Press.

Sparkes, J. (1994) *The Education of Young People Aged 14–18 Years*, London: Royal Academy of Engineering.

Storr, A. (1992) *Music and the Mind*, London: HarperCollins.

Super, D. E. (1957) *The Psychology of Careers*, New York: Harper & Row.

Super, D. E. (1981) 'Approaches to Occupational Choice and Career Development', in Watts, A. G., Super, D. E. and Kidd, J. M. (eds) *Career Development in Britain*. Cambridge: Careers Research and Advisory Centre/Hobsons.

Sutherland, S. (1992) *Irrationality: the Enemy Within*, London: Constable.

Vernon, P. B. (1961) *The Structure of Human Abilities*, London: Methuen.

Watts, A. G. (1991) 'Individual Action Planning: Issues and Strategies', *British Journal of Education and Work* 5(1): 47–63.

Willis, P. (1977) *Learning to Labour: How Working-Class Kids Get Working-Class Jobs*, Farnborough: Saxon House.

Chapter 4

The learning and economic outcomes of guidance

John Killeen

4.1 INTRODUCTION

Does careers education and guidance work? In order to answer this question, we need to know what guidance (as we shall henceforth refer to it in this chapter) is supposed to do. From a policy perspective (cf. Chapter 21), the main objectives of guidance can, rather loosely, be called 'economic'; we accordingly use the term *economic outcomes* to describe them. From the viewpoint of the guidance practitioner, the main objectives are changes in people exposed to guidance, many of which (but not all) can be called *learning outcomes*. In this chapter we shall be concerned with both economic and learning outcomes, but we shall not exclude other outcomes just because they are not commonly encompassed within these terms.

Table 4.1 presents a model which summarises the relationships we need to take into account when we examine the learning and economic effects of guidance. The value of such a model is as a summary statement of logically and perhaps (although the term seems a little grandiose) theoretically plausible connections, and as a tool of analysis which can be used to generate the more localised 'predictive' models which we might actually seek to test. The model follows a time-line, but it is *analytical*, not *descriptive*. Feedback loops have been avoided (for example, as a result of guidance, individuals may alter their personal situation; as a result of learning and search, individuals may return to guidance). Furthermore, no attempt has been made to link the model to the life-span, as this would either greatly complicate the analysis, or introduce a set of descriptive generalisations. Of course, people and their situations change: they may return to guidance at various points in their lives. But in reality, when we try to assess the outcomes of guidance, we either study the impact of a particular intervention, or of a recent accumulation of guidance, over a limited period of time. In these circumstances, Table 4.1 describes what we can, and sometimes must, consider.

The remainder of the chapter examines the existing evidence in relation to this model. It looks first at some of the methodological problems in measuring and demonstrating outcomes. It then examines the evidence on learning and other immediate outcomes, their conceptual relationship to economic outcomes, and the evidence on intermediate and ultimate economic outcomes. Finally, it outlines some unfinished business in relation to research in this area.

4.2 MEASURING AND DEMONSTRATING OUTCOMES

Most of the methodologically adequate studies of the outcomes of guidance have been conducted in educational settings by American counselling psychologists. For practical reasons, and by virtue of their main interests, these investigators have usually considered only the most immediate effects of guidance. This means that a considerable body of evidence has been accumulated about short-run changes in individuals, rather than about the economic consequences to which these changes are thought to give rise. Many of the short-run changes considered in the research literature are learning outcomes. We shall now look at the practical reasons why so much of the evidence available to us concerns learning, and associated short-run effects in individuals.

Some guidance outcomes are hard to measure but easy to demonstrate, whereas others are easy to measure but very difficult to demonstrate. This seems like a highly contradictory statement, but what it really means is this. Some of the outcome criteria of guidance, such as wage rates or employment status, are in principle very easy to observe or record. They pose very few measurement problems. For the most part we can use administrative records, or can ask people straightforward questions. Providing that we take some fairly simple steps to ensure the validity of our information, the job is done. One of the strengths of this sort of information is that the outcome criterion and the measured variable are so close to one another that we would be hard pressed to distinguish them. We feel that we are standing on firm ground. But what if the criterion is something like 'productivity'? Economic theory tells us that there should be a close relationship between an individual's productivity and his or her wage rate. However, the world (and economists) tell us that this relationship is not clear-cut. This means that when we measure 'productivity', wage rate is just one possible indicator of the criterion we have in mind. There is always a danger that such indicators are partial, contradictory, biased, or just plain wrong.

Matters become even worse when we consider learning outcomes. It is important to remember that classifications such as 'self-awareness' are precisely that: classifications. It is quite another matter to show that there is something called 'self-awareness' which increases or decreases in a consistent way, so that we can represent it in a single score. It is likely that there are many ideas and possible objects of measurement jostling beneath such classification schemes. Thus the problem we have just considered returns with a vengeance. *Self-awareness* is particularly difficult to measure (one expedient is to measure the degree of correspondence between people's self-ratings, and their scores on tests of aptitudes or other personal characteristics). *Opportunity awareness* has never been measured generically, but there are a number of American tests of occupational knowledge. In order to satisfy the usual requirements that these tests be reliable and valid, they are necessarily long and of restricted application; they are also difficult and time-consuming to construct, and date rapidly. Again, skill-testing for vocational *decision-making* and for *transition* are ill-developed.

Not unnaturally, therefore, evaluators have tried to devise easier ways of showing that individual change results from guidance. This has led them towards the use of attitude measures, such as Crites's (1978) Career Maturity Inventory Attitude Scale (CMI-AS), and, more recently, towards the use of subjective

Table 4.1 A simplified model for the analysis of guidance outcomes

---

CONTROL FACTORS AND DETERMINANTS OF GUIDANCE

Individual	Gender, age, educational attainment, employment status; current decision state, information needs, anxiety, conflict, etc.
Personal situation	Local labour market conditions, access to information sources, domestic situation, etc.
Institutional	Employer requirements, conditions for receipt of welfare benefits, school and college policies, etc.

↓

GUIDANCE

Advice, information, counselling, instruction, etc.	Exposure to objectives, intensity/duration, types, techniques, etc.
Ancillary outputs	Placement, advocacy, feedback, etc.

↓

IMMEDIATE OUTCOMES

Knowledge and skills	Decision skills, opportunity awareness, transition skills, career management skills, etc.
Attitudinal/affective	Optimism, sense of personal control, anxiety reduction, etc.
Decision state	Decidedness, etc.

↓

INTERMEDIATE OUTCOMES

Motivational commitment	Motivation to work, motivation to train, etc.
Search	Search strategy, intensity, channels, duration
Decision-making	Decision behaviour, decision outcomes

↓

ULTIMATE OUTCOMES AT THE INDIVIDUAL LEVEL

Training and education effects	Take-up, attainment level, match to skills, relevance to employment, drop-out rates, etc.
Labour supply effects	Reservation wage, entry into labour market, withdrawal from labour market, etc.
Job effects	Job entry, job quality, functional flexibility/job change, performance, productivity, adaptation to role, role innovation, etc.

↓

ULTIMATE OUTCOMES AT THE SYSTEM LEVEL

Employing organisations	Increased labour productivity, reduced recruitment and turnover costs, increased numerical flexibility, other organisational flexibility, rate of introduction of new processes, etc.
Education and training providers	Student recruitment and retention, adaptation of schemes, management costs for complex schemes, attainment levels, income, etc.
National	GDP growth rate, rate of structural economic change, reduced skill shortages, lowered unemployment and exchequer savings, etc.

self-report scales, often called measures of 'career indecision' (e.g. Osipow, 1987). These do not 'test', but simply allow people to report upon, things such as their clarity of self-perception, possession of information, and so on (for a review, see Killeen *et al.*, 1994). We do not currently know whether such subjective measures are acceptable substitutes for objective tests, in two crucial respects. First, there are some worrying indications that self-reports do not agree with corresponding objective tests, and are thus measuring something rather different (Lowman and Williams, 1987; Westbrook *et al.*, 1987). Second, with a few exceptions (e.g. Holland *et al.*, 1980), there has been as little interest in assessing the predictive validity of self-report scales against later economic outcomes, as there has in assessing their criterion validity against objective tests.

Broadly, we can say that the 'economic' outcomes we have in mind at the individual level, such as employment, entry into training, qualifications obtained, wage rates, and so on, tend to be fairly easy to measure, whereas more confusion and difficulty surrounds the measurement of learning outcomes. But when we turn to demonstration, the reverse applies. Learning outcomes emerge immediately or soon after guidance, whereas economic ones emerge over longer periods of time. This means that studies of economic outcomes are inevitably more protracted: taken to the extreme, they would cover the whole working life of individuals after guidance, so as to demonstrate that 'lifetime income' or 'lifetime unemployment' are affected by it. But it also means that experimental control cannot be exerted – it simply breaks down over time – so that controlled experiments are less feasible.

A second problem concerns the scale of anticipated effects. Guidance is a small investment when set against, for example, the total investment made in the compulsory education of each child, and many guidance investments are really very small indeed, when considered at the individual level. But from the economic point of view, what matters is the rate of return to this small investment, not the absolute size of subsequent benefits.

How does this translate into the terminology of research into guidance effectiveness? First, we would expect the subsequent income distributions of those exposed and not exposed to guidance (in a controlled trial) to overlap to a very considerable degree, and the mean salaries (or lifetime incomes) of the two groups to lie fairly close together. This means that the 'effect size' of guidance would be small, and that in consequence we would require large samples in order to be confident, in the statistical sense, that the observed effect was real. If we consider the difficulties of mounting this experiment, the further practical problems of demonstration should be apparent. Thus a quite high rate of return, sufficient – were it known – to justify investment in guidance, may be compatible with a small 'effect', which is difficult to detect with confidence. It is

---

Notes to Table 4.1:

1   Groups of factors within each category can interact, and factors can exert direct influences on categories of factors additional to those shown immediately below them. But causal pathways have been selectively shown only to indicate the chief considerations when assessing the contribution of guidance to outcomes.

2   The outcomes shown here are confined to those which most commonly figure in analyses of the learning and economic objectives and outcomes of careers guidance. Possible effects upon the family (e.g. guidance for dual-career couples), upon social cohesion (e.g. disruption of ethnic barriers to recruitment) etc. can all, in principle, find a place in such a model.

reasonable to assume that *economic* outcomes will be modest, whereas a similar restraint does not necessarily apply to *learning* outcomes.

For all of these reasons, it is much easier to make a convincing demonstration of learning outcomes than it is to make a convincing demonstration of economic gains, *providing* that we are in possession of convincing measures of the former. This means that in our discussion of the evidence we will have quite a lot to say about some kinds of learning outcomes, relatively little to say about economic outcomes, and even less to say about their connection.

4.3 LEARNING AND OTHER IMMEDIATE OUTCOMES

Table 4.1 employs a conventional set of distinctions between immediate, intermediate and 'ultimate' outcomes (Thorndike, 1949). Immediate outcomes include, in particular, learning outcomes. The intended learning outcomes of guidance have been defined (Killeen and Kidd, 1991) as the skills, knowledge and attitudes which facilitate informed and rational occupational and educational decision-making and the implementation of occupational and educational decisions. This definition should be read as encompassing training decisions. It should also be read as covering decisions between participation in education or training on the one hand and immediately productive work on the other; and decisions about whether or not, or to what extent, to participate in the labour market.

But what are these skills, knowledge and attitudes? The fairly obvious central idea is that individuals should possess self-knowledge, occupational knowledge, and the skill of 'correct reasoning' of relationships between these matters (Parsons, 1909) – or, as we would now say, 'decision-making skills'. This central idea has been elaborated in numerous ways. In Britain, the most widely-known listing (DOTS) adds a fourth category of skills, those of 'transition' or 'transition learning', and broadens occupational knowledge into 'opportunity awareness' – for it is not merely occupational decisions which guidance assists (Law and Watts, 1977; see Chapter 12). The skills of transition have been defined broadly as those needed 'to cope with the consequences of particular decisions' (Watts and Kidd, 1978), pointing to the possibility that guidance, or some parts of it, should be concerned both with transition into jobs and education, and with successful adjustment.

In the United States, students of career development defined and measured career maturity in ways which echoed Parsons's early prescription, considering knowledge of occupations and of the 'world of work', self-appraisal skills and decision-making skills. However, they extended the central idea in a different way, by considering, also, planfulness, involvement, and independence of decision-making, regarding them as 'attitudinal' (as distinct from 'cognitive') components of career maturity (Crites, 1978; Super and Thompson, 1979). Crites's Career Maturity Inventory Attitude Scale (CMI-AS) has probably been more frequently used as an outcome measure in subsequent American studies of guidance effectiveness, than any other learning-outcome measure.

More recently (Killeen and Kidd, 1991), these traditions have been brought together, and a further category of 'career management skills' added (Kidd and Killeen, 1992). This recognises that, under changed economic circumstances, individuals less commonly stabilise and are often in a more or less permanent state of adjustment. In their earlier publication, Killeen and Kidd did not confine their consideration to learning outcomes, properly so-called, and were content to include factors such as decision anxiety, together with attitudes, as subjective factors which might be beneficially influenced by guidance. A further subjective change – 'decidedness' – has frequently figured in outcome research and is included in Table 4.1.

All of the categories of outcome so far considered appear in the careers education curriculum (see Chapter 12), which now contains strong messages about the need for continuing education, flexibility, adaptability and other characteristics implied by economic change and career uncertainty (e.g. DES, 1988). Employers' statements also embody the assumption that guidance achieves its objectives through its impact on these sorts of knowledge, skills and attitudes (CBI, 1993).

Why should this be so? Some decision-makers are 'dependent' (Harren, 1979), but it has long been known that even young school-leavers do not, for the most part, do as they are told by guidance practitioners. It was the developmental movement of the 1950s and 1960s (Super, 1953; 1957; Ginzberg et al., 1951; Hill, 1969) – responsible, incidentally, for the career maturity measures discussed earlier – which captured with least ambiguity the resultant view that if guidance was to be effective with the generality of people, it must, rather than issue recommendations, exert an influence upon their own knowledge, thinking, skills and attitudes, and hence upon their own search behaviour and decision-making.

But of course, much guidance is of very short duration, and increasingly given to adults, for whom it is often unreasonable to expect large learning gains. The needs being served may range from that for a very simple and straightforward piece of information, to the opportunity less to learn than to think matters through. So even the educative model underlying terms such as 'learning outcomes' has its limits: limits which we shall not rigidly impose here.

Does guidance actually lead to learning gains and allied subjective changes? The short answer to this question is (if one is prepared to accept that the American evidence derived mainly from studies of young people applies here): 'Yes, it does!' Successive reviewers have searched the literature, selecting only properly-conducted trials, or uncontrolled 'before and after' studies in which measurement occurs soon before, and soon after, guidance. Repeatedly they conclude that positive findings far outweigh null results. Negative findings – that guidance does the reverse of what is intended – are virtually unknown (Baker and Popwicz, 1983; Clarke, 1981; Fretz, 1981; Holland et al., 1981; Killeen and Kidd, 1991; Krumboltz et al., 1979; Myers, 1971; Oliver and Spokane, 1988; Pickering and Vacc, 1984; Spokane and Oliver, 1983; Watts and Kidd, 1978). Killeen and Kidd's (1991) review of the more recent evidence classified outcomes as 'precursors and correlates' (i.e. attitudes and allied measures), decision-making skills, self-awareness, opportunity awareness, certainty of preference, and transition skills. Forty studies reported outcomes in these categories, only four reported no gains, thirty reported wholly positive results, and gains were reported in each outcome category more often than null results. Moreover, positive results were reported for each main type of guidance intervention (classes and courses, workshops and groups, individual guidance, test interpretation and feedback, experience-based interventions, and multi-method interventions).

American reviewers have often grouped together many of the outcomes we have so far distinguished. Myers (1971) considers most of them under the generic heading 'readiness for decision-making', concluding that the run of evidence strongly favours the proposition that guidance has a beneficial effect. A meta-analysis combining the results of fifty-eight good-quality US controlled trials (Spokane and Oliver, 1983; Oliver and Spokane, 1988) produced a similar conclusion in a more precise form. Studies which specifically focused upon self-knowledge, self-concept changes, career-related knowledge, decision skills, transition-related skills and other relevant variables (from locus of control to career decidedness) were relatively few in number, but in each category the aggregate result was a gain by those exposed to guidance. In comparison, many studies looked at information-seeking behaviour, number of options considered/time given to consideration, and career maturity (or its components). Gains were reported in each case, although not of similar magnitudes. Career maturity gains, measured as 'effect size' (or standardised mean score gains), were highest, on average.

We will not dwell too much on differential gains here, because reasonable expectation differs between types of outcome (some are more easily shifted than others), and because the kinds and intensities of intervention varied, so that like was not necessarily compared with like. Spokane and Oliver tentatively concluded that individual guidance has the biggest impact per hour; that classroom (or careers education) interventions, sometimes conferring grade-points in US college courses, had the biggest overall effects, owing to their intensity or duration; but that 'workshop' (group guidance) interventions were the most 'cost-effective', in part at least because they involved the highest client-to-counsellor ratios. Spokane and Oliver used counsellor hours as the basis for their input calculation, and thus counsellor-free methods were excluded. As the use of computers grows, this will be less and less tenable as a way of forming cost-effectiveness estimates.

But of course, cost-effectiveness, as considered by Spokane and Oliver, is very different from cost-benefit. In cost-benefit analysis, we need to assign a monetary value to the effects of guidance, discounting them to adjust for the length of time they may take to be realised, and then compare this to the *total* cost of guidance 'production'. Only by assuming that learning outcomes lead to economic ones can we translate this sort of 'cost-effectiveness' analysis into an indicator of 'cost-benefit'.

Nonetheless, the general case for learning outcomes is made. Guidance can and does lead to learning outcomes and associated changes in individuals. This means that we should now be focusing upon more precise questions. Which sorts of guidance produce each sort of outcome best? Which sorts of guidance work best with which sorts of client? What is the relative importance of each sort of learning outcome (or to what extent must a variety of learning outcomes be achieved in order for learning to be translated into changed vocational behaviour)? Our ability to answer each of these questions is very limited. The outcomes, client groups, and guidance interventions considered from study to study vary so wildly that it is difficult to draw clear conclusions. At present, we may *tentatively* assert that people of low ability are less able to benefit from 'counsellor-free' intervention (Melhus *et al.*, 1973; Roselle and Hummel, 1988); that personality and interests (for example, 'people-centredness'), and even current level of decidedness, may determine whether group or individualised methods are more effective (e.g. Kivlighan *et al.*, 1981; Kivlighan and Shapiro, 1987); that decision styles (dependent, intuitive, rational) call for congruent forms of intervention

(Rubinton, 1980); and that closely similar interventions are interchangeable, but without additive effect (Slaney, 1983; Slaney and Dickson, 1985; Slaney and Lewis, 1986).

When general treatment methods are compared, it is generally found that, if deliberately constructed as realistic alternatives, computerised methods seem to be as effective as face-to-face ones (e.g. Johnson, 1985; Wiggins, 1987), and group methods as effective as individual ones (e.g. Cooper, 1986; Kivlighan *et al.*, 1981; see also the review by Fretz, 1981). This does not mean that one method is always as good as another, as we have already seen. It does mean that one general method is not inevitably superior to another.

But perhaps one of the most important questions to be asked is: do learning outcomes lead to economic benefits? We are currently unable to answer this question – but an answer must soon be attempted. If it becomes possible to assume that they do, learning outcomes will, in future, legitimately come to play the role which evaluators have, de facto, attributed to them: they will act as proxies, or substitutes, for economic assessment, in routine, low-cost, well-controlled experimental studies of the effectiveness of guidance.

4.4 THE CONCEPTUAL RELATIONSHIP BETWEEN ECONOMIC AND LEARNING OUTCOMES

In the period of full employment following the Second World War, there was enormous interest in job satisfaction and its causes. Academic studies of this subject conducted at that time are numbered in their thousands (see e.g. Locke, 1976). Employers believed that labour productivity might be higher if workers were more satisfied, and that labour turnover might be reduced. Some used job enrichment in an attempt to achieve these ends. In other words, the non-wage 'rewards' of work were seriously regarded as part of the total bundle of 'utilities' available from work. It was therefore possible to treat job satisfaction as a guidance objective, and to assert, without blushing, that this was an 'economic' outcome, both directly and for its possible consequences on productivity and turnover. But over the last two decades priorities have changed, so that it is necessary to consider a more complete statement of the economic rationale.

For the economist, the starting-point is the market and, in particular, the 'perfect' market, in which resources, including people, are put to their most productive use (see Chapter 2). This is because of the operation of the price mechanism. If a firm can make more productive use of labour than its competitors, then that firm can offer a higher price for labour, and labour therefore flows towards it until a new equilibrium is reached. Similarly, if labour is homogeneous and all units of labour are equally productive, there is no basis for persistent wage inequalities. But if productivity can be raised by education and training (and experience), then differences in productivity determine differences in wage levels.

The world is, of course, much more complicated than this, and one of the main complications discussed by economists is *market imperfection*. Labour markets are imperfectly 'informed', and information has a cost. Individuals do not, therefore, seek information in a vacuum. The decision to seek information, and the intensity with which this is done, implies cost, even though this cost may be made up largely of what is forgone in order to permit search. That is, to the economist the decision to do one thing is always, simultaneously, a decision *not* to do the *other* things which might otherwise have been done. The value of these other things is called 'opportunity cost'.

The economic conception of 'information' is more generous than that conventionally found in the world of guidance. It does not just mean opportunity awareness. It means any information relevant to search and decision-making, including self-awareness. It further means organising and processing information, which also has a cost. So guidance activities which sort, select, package and otherwise process information, and at least some aspects of decision learning, might be included. If we consider transition skills, then at least part of these relate to *transmitting*, rather than *receiving*, information. So quite a lot of what is done in the world of guidance from the perspective of the educationalist or vocational psychologist fits the economist's conception of what guidance is about. Either directly, or indirectly (through learning), guidance may make search and decision-making more efficient. The market becomes more informed, and less imperfect.

When should guidance lead to economic benefits? We can consider this at the *individual*, *corporate* and *national* levels. It is important to consider each of these levels because, despite guidance practitioners' focus upon the individual, the future of guidance will depend to a substantial degree on the advantages it offers to institutions and its 'public' or 'social' returns.

The individual

There are three kinds of decisions which are likely to be improved by guidance (White, 1992). The first are *labour-supply* decisions: that is, decisions to participate, or to participate more, or less (e.g. full- or part-time), in the labour market. The second are *human-capital* decisions, or decisions about the amount and kinds of competence (education, training, competence-raising experience) to acquire. The third are *job-search* decisions, or decisions about the kinds of jobs and wage levels to aim at, how long to search before changing one's goals, and so forth.

The analysis by White (1992) suggests that for individuals a number of benefits may follow (although in recessionary times it is particularly necessary to stress that benefits are relative to their times). First, more people will supply labour and do so to the degree (e.g. full-time/part-time) that they prefer. Women returners are a case in point. Second, more people will be able to perceive the longer-run risks of and returns to education and training of different kinds, and be prepared to accept the costs (such as income forgone) of investment in it, so that more people will enter education and training, succeed in it, and reap the eventual benefits. These benefits can be summarised as the discounted rate of return to this investment through increased 'lifetime income' (in everyday terms, this means higher wages and less unemployment sufficient to justify the investment in training). This applies with special force and poignancy to minimally-qualified minimum-age school-leavers, who under-invest, and for whom the world offers fewer and fewer possibilities. But it increasingly applies to *all* people, at *all* stages of their careers. It also applies to the smaller but real risk of *over*-investment. Third, if search costs are reduced and the amount of information processed in any given period of time is increased, people will tend to 'match' themselves quicker and better in two ways: by adjusting their 'reservation wage' in a more realistic manner, not necessarily downwards, and by being less inclined to accept jobs below their skills and abilities. This will lead to more rapid re-employment and/or wage benefits. They will also (and this is linked to wage rates) be less likely to enter 'over-supplied' or contracting industries and occupations, thus reducing their chances of unemployment in the longer term.

The organisation

Two kinds of organisation must be considered – employing organisations and education and training organisations – and two sorts of benefit, which we may call 'external labour market' and 'internal labour market' benefits.

External-market benefits to employers are those that affect the volume and nature of their labour supply, and relate in the main to guidance provided externally, for example by the Careers Service. They follow quite directly from what has already been said about the individual, and have long been incorporated into the rationale for guidance. If, on balance, the supply of labour is increased by guidance, this increases the probability that employers will be able to recruit, and damps-down upward pressure on wage rates. If, on balance, guidance encourages individuals to invest in 'human capital', this may make individuals more trainable, and reduce the employers' share of training costs (an assumption of human capital theory is that the objective of such investments is to raise productive potential). Finally, if job-search decisions are enhanced, employers will benefit from the increased 'suitability' of applicants, and from reduced recruitment costs, wastage of training and labour turnover costs (e.g. CBI, 1993). It is, however, far from clear that all employers benefit equally. In particular, employers in unskilled and contracting sectors should, in principle, do less well than others.

Internal-market benefits are those which enhance employers' ability to achieve their objectives amongst their existing labour forces, and relate to the guidance provided *by* employers to their own staff (see Chapter 8). These include raising the levels of training and skill of existing employees, and thus reducing reliance on the external labour market for recruits to skilled positions; and promoting functional flexibility, by increasing both the range of skills at employees' disposal and their preparedness to work 'flexibly' across job boundaries. Allied to these, guidance is intended to promote both vertical and horizontal mobility. A further group of objectives concerns what is now delicately called 'downsizing'. Guidance may be used to facilitate this, and to raise or at least maintain employee commitment to the company amongst those whom it retains, by demonstrating that it has acted humanely to those being shed. This means, in turn, that employers want guidance to work (raise employment chances) for those leaving the company. Companies also see guidance as a more general means of raising commitment, and reducing absenteeism, indiscipline, and avoidable turnover. In a nutshell, employers see guidance as a means of reducing costs and increasing their productivity and prospects of survival or growth.

Turning to education and training institutions, much of the analysis above continues to apply: increased recruitment, more suitable initial student choices, and hence, reduced drop-out and failure rates and increased student performance. Even the successes of its own 'outplacement' services (such as graduate careers advisory services) may contribute to the long-term reputation of an institution, and hence to the number and quality of its recruits. But educational systems are becoming more complex, so that 'internal' guidance is perceived to contribute to the aims of student retention and success by providing the means for students to understand and navigate the modular and credit-accumulation pathways available to them, and to use 'assessment of prior learning'. Whether or not these sorts of objectives are economic ones when viewed exclusively from the perspective of the education or training institution is a moot point. But when viewed from the perspective of human capital theory, or from that of the efficiency of investment in education, plainly they become so.

The nation

Government policy statements and documentation associated with guidance tend to endorse what has been said so far about economic benefits, associating it in a general way with national economic performance (e.g. Bruce and Evans, 1990; Employment Department, 1992; Coopers & Lybrand, 1994). If guidance benefits us all, rather than just those who are exposed to it, we say that it confers a *social* benefit. This social benefit is a major consideration in the economic analysis. There are two chief arguments: first, that relating to the direct costs of unemployment; and second, that relating to gross domestic product (GDP). Each follows from what has already been said about the economic benefits to individuals.

Unemployment might be reduced in three main ways. The first is by increasing the efficiency of search, so that unemployment durations are reduced and vacancies filled more quickly. Second, guidance may re-stimulate some 'discouraged workers'. These are people who have ceased to search for opportunities, because their past experience of search has led them to believe that they will not find employment. Awareness of high local unemployment rates, and membership of groups (e.g. older workers, persons without skills) known to have lower-than-average re-employment prospects, may reinforce this belief, and pessimism may be realistic. Moreover, fatalistic acceptance of unemployment (Jahoda *et al.*, 1933/1972) can have a positive side, allowing individuals and families to make some sort of new life (Bakke, 1940). But few of us accept that it is just, or socially desirable, to encourage the emergence of a permanently unemployed underclass. The unemployed were estimated in the early 1990s (White, 1992) to include 200,000 to 400,000 'discouraged workers', some of whom guidance might help to become active in the labour market, perhaps by exposing them for the first time to the possibility of training. The third possibility concerns 'mismatch'. Up to a third of all unemployment has been attributed to mismatch: misalignment between the industries and occupations people enter, and actual patterns of demand for labour (White, 1992). In rapidly changing economies, mismatch is endemic, but nonetheless improved decision-making may help to reduce it. The essential point is that quite *small* reductions in the rate of unemployment can lead to quite *large* exchequer savings. So by working at the margin, guidance may lead to social benefits far outweighing its cost.

If unemployment is reduced, and those actually in employment increase in number, not only are exchequer savings significant, but also the consequent increase in gross domestic product (GDP). The potential impact of guidance upon GDP arises in so far as it encourages absolute labour-force growth – for example, by easing the entry of women returners into the labour market (increasing labour supply) – well-focused human capital investment, and labour market matching, so as to allow output growth, productivity growth and the growth of new industries, respectively. Per capita GDP and its growth rate reflect, and are determined by, these things. Once again, even a marginal impact upon GDP would be sufficient to justify the modest level of public investment in guidance.

4.5 INTERMEDIATE OUTCOMES

It is extremely difficult to make more than a heuristic distinction between imme-diate (often learning) outcomes and intermediate ones. At the conceptual level, the intention is plain enough: to distinguish the learning and other changes in people which happen directly as a result of guidance from consequent changes in their behaviour when they engage in option search. A temporal sequence is involved, together with an assumption that, for example, just because people learn decision-making skills or job-search skills, it does not necessarily follow that their actual decision-making and job search will be changed when they come to do these things. Roughly speaking, there is a distinction to be made between what people get from guidance and what they do with it later on. The underlying model is an educative one, but also one which makes simplifying assumptions about time. From the standpoint of a conventional economic analysis, 'intermediate effects' include at least three types of effect noted in Section 4.4: effects upon the intention to *supply labour*, upon the intention to *acquire human capital*, and upon *job search*.

It is easy to point to deficiencies and complications. Some guidance inter-ventions (and careers education) are protracted, so that only by the closest monitoring would it be possible to distinguish 'intermediate' effects which might occur *after* rather than *during* the complete intervention; moreover, these 'intermediate' effects might influence the direction of guidance, further compli-cating matters. At the other extreme, people may take real decisions, or formulate intentions, during quite short interventions, so that it would be necessary to monitor what happened in guidance in order to disentangle the temporal sequence. Furthermore, if learning outcomes now legitimately include 'career management skills', then one cannot really confine intermediate outcomes to a discrete period of search *prior* to entry into an option: 'career management' does not stop at this point. Also, we can often characterise guidance as something individuals use *in* and *as part of* search: perhaps as a way of accessing and processing information on options. This slices the conceptual cake, and treats time in a very different way to that implied in Table 4.1. Alternatively, we must not assume that guidance practitioners and careers educators never attempt to exert influence *directly* upon things such as intention to train or search behav-iour. This might be thought bad practice, but we must consider practice as it is rather than as it should be.

But for the present purpose, we will assume that it is at least reasonable to ask if there is evidence of consequential changes in intention and search behav-iour arising from guidance. Most of the evidence available to us relates to *search intensity* and *search channels*. Myers's (1971) review of the American evidence concluded that information-seeking behaviour is increased by exposure to guid-ance. Studies (mostly American) which have shown an effect upon the amount of exploration or search activity of young people, or upon the range (channels) of search, include those by Kivlighan *et al.* (1981), Chamberlain (1982), Cooper (1986), Remer *et al.* (1984), Lent *et al.* (1986), Robbins and Tucker (1986) and Mostsch (1980). Fairbairns and Coolbear (1982) in the UK, and Azrin *et al.* (1975) in the USA, showed rates of job application by unemployed adults to be increased, but in each case the intervention under evaluation, which included guidance, also provided facilities and direct encouragement for job search.

Other 'intermediate' outcomes pose more problems. Decision-making is a case in point. Some guidance interventions are deliberately constructed to help people to take a decision (form an intention), or become 'more decided' (more committed to an intention). The 'decidedness', and sometimes the suitability or appropriateness of decisions, have been used as criteria of evaluation. Provisionally, we may think of these as immediate outcomes, but it should be clear that 'decidedness' or for that matter 'suitability' may emerge much later, as a result of search patterns influenced by guidance. A similar point may be made about influences upon motivation, and especially motivation to supply labour (or to work) and motivation to train (see below), which contribute to decisions and intentions. What does seem clear, however, is that during search following guidance, we might expect the way in which decisions are made, the way in which options are evaluated, their motivational value, and hence the kinds of decisions taken *during search* (intentions formed and pursued), to be influenced, in turn, by the earlier effects of guidance.

The evidence available to us in these respects is very limited. Researchers have usually been content to quantify the amount and range of search, and have paid little attention to the other effects guidance may have upon it. Myers (1971) was content that the appropriateness or realism of vocational preferences was increased by guidance, and studies published after Fretz's (1981) review (e.g. Fretz and Leong, 1982; Krumboltz *et al.*, 1982) tend to support the view that guidance increases 'decidedness'. But as we have seen, dependent upon circumstances these may be classified as 'immediate' outcomes. Moreover, follow-up periods tend to be short. A study by Slaney and Dickson (1985) failed to show an effect after one year, but the interventions under investigation were very modest and the (student) sample may not have been engaged in search over this period. We also have to be careful when we assess American studies, as the measures of career indecision they employ often turn out, upon inspection, to be self-report scales relating to the possession of information and so on, rather than measures of intentions.

In short, we know far too little about the intermediate effects of guidance and, for this reason, we do not know directly if guidance induces individuals to behave in ways which the economic analysis suggests they may. We can only *infer* that this *may* be so, from studies of 'ultimate effects'.

4.6 ULTIMATE ECONOMIC OUTCOMES

Attempts to assess the economic outcomes of guidance are far fewer in number than those concerning learning outcomes. Methodological deficiencies are common, so that only a small proportion of studies are worth consideration. We do not know if employers' aspirations for the guidance they provide to their own employees are met, because published studies (mostly American) are descriptive, or fail to substantiate their conclusions, or confine themselves to reporting opinion data (for reviews, see Cairo, 1983; Russell, 1991). The best of these (Schlossberg and Leibowitz, 1980) merely reports the success outcomes for all those participating in a 'job separation' programme, leaving us without any point of comparison. Again, well-conducted studies of the effects of guidance upon educational participation and attainment – once more mostly American – are 'confounded'. Guidance is part, but only part, of each intervention, and its effects cannot be disentangled from those of other components (for a review of early studies, see Campbell, 1965). This is unfortunately true, also, of many studies of the effects of guidance on job search and unemployment durations: guidance, narrowly defined, is mixed together with other forms of help, such as social support and practical facilities for making job applications.

This means that we are excessively reliant on a handful of studies, some of them very old, which concern benefits to individuals, and benefits to employers only as *recruiters* of labour. Two main lines of approach have been taken. The first is studies which assume that guidance of the young should lead to better 'matching' in the person–environment fit rather than the economic sense, and hence reduced turnover, enhanced job quality, greater satisfaction, employer approval of recruits and, perhaps, improved long-term career prospects. The second is studies of interventions for the unemployed, which have been primarily concerned with speed of re-employment, coupled with job quality.

'Matching'

By 'matching', psychologists mean person–environment fit and, hence, adjustment. This differs greatly from the economic conceptions of labour-market 'matching' (see Section 4.4). There is however a relationship between the two, in that both would lead one to expect lower rates of labour turnover, together with the avoidance of productivity losses assumed to arise from the appointment of unsuitable recruits.

We can distinguish two linked issues. First, does guidance lead to retention of the first job entered after it? Second, does guidance reduce the 'rapid job changing', associated with notions of labour-market 'floundering'? These issues have most commonly been considered in relation to compliance or 'congruence' with guidance recommendations. However, if people are little influenced by the recommendations made to them, the evidence concerning 'congruence' with, or entry into work thought congruent with, allows us to argue a net gain to those exposed to guidance, or to one sort of guidance as opposed to another. The issue is not: 'Do people who *seem* to do as they are told, benefit?' We want to know if guidance improves the outcomes for those exposed to it.

Older studies of young people permitting this calculation (Earle, 1931; Allen and Smith, 1932; Hunt and Smith, 1944) indicate a somewhat lower turnover rate amongst those who were 'scientifically advised' (using a 'talent-matching' approach – see Chapter 11). But the margin was greatest in the study (Hunt and Smith, 1944) which suffered the greatest sample attrition (loss of contact with sample members), and was statistically non-significant in its precursor (Allen and Smith, 1932). It is the consistency of the finding across studies, coupled with the fact that controls were given the usual forms of guidance available to young people, which is persuasive, rather than the results of any one study taken in isolation. Weaker, survey evidence is consistent with the view that exposure to guidance has a small effect on early job retention (Ives, 1985). A study by Hopson (1970), which adopted a quasi-experimental form, failed to demonstrate that retention of first job was influenced by the introduction of careers education into a school, but did show a reduction of rapid job changing.

But even if we accept that the run of evidence suggests that guidance reduces job changing by new entrants into the labour market, is this necessarily indicative of economic benefit? Not all turnover is dysfunctional to individuals, to employing organisations, or nationally. When regarded in a positive light, it is called 'flexibility', and of course may involve career progression. So some evaluators have tried to separate good or progressive movements from bad or floundering change, by going beyond simple counts of 'rapid job changers' to look at *kinds* of change. Hopson (1970) defined 'floundering' change as movement between, rather than within, occupational areas: it was less common in the cohort which had experienced careers education. Lancashire (1971; Lancashire and Cohen, 1971) found over an extended period that those following occupations congruent with guidance recommendations had a higher ratio of 'upward' to 'sideways' moves, but this does not tell us about the net impact of guidance. The results of the pre-war experimental studies differed here. Defining functional movement as measurement *towards* congruence with recommendations, Hunt and Smith (1944) found the incidence of 'good' movement to be associated with exposure to 'scientific guidance', whereas Earle (1931) did not. On balance, therefore, the available data suggest that exposure to guidance may have a small positive effect on job retention, but the evidence for a positive impact on the *quality* of job movement is too limited even for a preliminary conclusion to be drawn. And of course, the ways in which 'good' and 'bad' forms of movement have been assessed are crude and inconsistent.

'Congruence' has also been found to be associated with job satisfaction in the earlier years of employment, and in one study (Burt *et al.*, 1926) with wage level, albeit this result was not reported in a way which allows us to determine its statistical significance. Earle (1931) and Hunt and Smith (1944) produced conflicting results in relation to job satisfaction. Only in the latter study, after four years, and in a sample subject to much attrition, were 'scientifically advised' young people markedly more inclined to say that their jobs were 'suitable'. In Hopson's (1970) study, young people exposed to careers education were not more satisfied than others. Indeed, only one group of studies, of US Job Clubs, has provided convincing evidence of enhanced job quality, reporting both higher socio-economic status and wage rates (see below).

The British evidence of effects on human capital investment and success rates (e.g. Nelson-Jones and Toner, 1978; Wankowski, 1979; NFER, 1987; Closs *et al.*, 1985) is uncompelling, because adequate comparisons are not made. American evidence is quite old, and concerns interventions wider than guidance, but arises from more satisfactory studies. At present all we may say is that guidance *may*, for example, have contributed to the 25 per cent higher graduation rate reported for counselled students in a well-matched non-random trial (Campbell, 1965), and to similar gains in other studies (e.g. Brown, 1965).

Efficiency of job-search and unemployment duration

If guidance improves the efficiency of job search, then it should be capable of reducing job-search and unemployment durations. Aspirations or reservation wages may sometimes be lowered following guidance, but this should be as a result of 'search' rather than of their artificial deflation. Thus when we examine the impact of guidance on unemployment duration, we should also pay attention to job quality.

Remarkably few methodologically adequate studies of these important effects have considered them together, and indeed, job-search duration (or unemployment duration) has itself seldom been examined except in a somewhat confused way. Interventions for the adult unemployed have generally included guidance alongside other forms of support in the preparation of CVs, facilities for search, etc. (e.g. Fairbairns and Coolbear, 1982; Davison, cited in Carroll, 1987), or have been very wide-ranging, so that guidance is only a modest part of the whole (e.g. Pearson, 1988). The largest body of evidence concerns North American group activities which depend heavily upon instruction and social support (for a review, see Amundson and Borgen, 1988), and the best-conducted studies of all are of the Job Club, as originally designed (e.g. Azrin *et al.*, 1975; 1980; 1981).

None of the British evidence derives from random assignment trials. Fairbairns and Coolbear (1982) matched their 'control' sample on a *post hoc* basis to unemployed volunteers. They found that the intervention reduced unemployment durations somewhat (a median reduction of two weeks). Others (Davison, cited in Carroll, 1987; Pearson, 1988) have compared re-employment rates and unemployment durations to those of the general populations, or of the target-group from which subjects have been drawn. In each case, guidance, together with other activities, was associated with enhanced employment chances. Goldman (1976) conducted a quasi-experiment similar in general approach to Hopson's (1970) study cited above, in which career-undecided students about to graduate achieved shorter job-search durations, when targeted for further guidance. The US studies of the Job Club show much larger reductions in job-search periods (e.g. median search period reduced to 14 days compared to 53 days for controls [Azrin *et al.*, 1975]), but as already noted, this is a much wider intervention than conventional guidance.

Turning to job quality, Fairbairns and Coolbear (1982) and Pearson (1988) made 'old-job/new-job' satisfaction and salary comparisons, finding no evidence of 'trading down'. Azrin *et al.* (1975) made a more convincing comparison between Job Club and control samples, showing that Job Club participants attained significantly higher salaries and socio-economic status, despite shorter search. So the British evidence is encouraging, but uncompelling for methodological reasons. The best US evidence is of high quality, and suggests substantial gains – but awaits replication and, in any event, concerns an intervention focused much more on supported search than on guidance narrowly defined.

Beyond the evidence reported here, there are fragmentary indications of possible effects upon job performance and other criteria. These are reviewed more fully in Killeen *et al.* (1992). However, little point would be served in this short chapter by listing yet more studies, only to complain how equivocal or tangential their results are, or how confused, or how they fail in design and execution, as they all too commonly do, to measure up to the difficulties of the task they essay. It is really very striking how little we know of economic effects, especially in the modern British, as distinct from the pre-war or American, contexts.

4.7 UNFINISHED BUSINESS

There is plentiful evidence for the learning outcomes of guidance, although a high proportion of this evidence is either attitudinal, or based upon measures *other than* objective tests either of skills or of knowledge. Over-reliance on US evidence relating to young people aside, one of the chief limitations of guidance effectiveness research is, however, that it is usually short-term and thus overly focused upon immediate effects, among which learning outcomes are prominent. Confidence in this sort of demonstration will be raised if intermediate effects and ultimate effects, especially the economic ones which weigh so heavily with the sponsors of guidance, are subjected to greater scrutiny, and if it is shown that immediate effects are predictive of these later ones. We therefore need a new generation of studies which measure each type of effect, and are sufficiently longitudinal to encompass at least entry into and adjustment to (or success in) the options for which guidance has been preparatory. One or two big studies are not enough. We need to assess the impact (and cost-benefit) of differing types and intensities of guidance over a wide range of client groups, and we need enough studies to be able to form judgements about the generalisability of results, not least between investigations (the methodological problems of guidance evaluation are considered more fully in Chapter 18).

But we can go further. It is increasingly the case that guidance is integral to a wider initiative – often to an educational innovation or training initiative. In the United Kingdom, credit accumulation and transfer in higher education, Youth/Training Credits, and Training for Work (training for unemployed adults) are three recent examples of innovations in which, from the outset, it has been assumed that effective functioning would depend upon guidance, or upon enhanced guidance. This takes us from the traditional economic preoccupation (making markets work) to an organisational one (making systems work). There is, to date, no experimental or quasi-experimental evidence of the value of guidance *in* systems, or of the relative effectiveness of different types of guidance, or means of delivering guidance, *in* systems. But closed environments, be they firms or educational institutions, offer suitable locations in which to obtain evidence of these kinds. So it may be the case that evidence from systems will, in future, be used to illuminate the functioning of guidance in the place that it is commonly designed, at least in policy terms (see Chapter 21), to serve – the market.

REFERENCES

Allen, E. P. and Smith, P. (1932) *The Value of Vocational Tests as Aids to Choice of Employment: Report of Research*, Birmingham: City of Birmingham Education Committee.
Amundson, N. E. and Borgen, W. A. (1988) 'Factors that Help and Hinder in Group Employment Counseling', *Journal of Employment Counseling* 25(3): 104–14.
Azrin, N. H., Flores, T. and Kaplan, S. J. (1975) 'Job-Finding Club: a Group Assisted Program for Obtaining Employment', *Behavior Research and Therapy* 13: 17–27.

Azrin, N. H., Philip, R. A., Thienes-Hontos, P. and Besalel, V. A. (1980) 'Comparative Evaluation of the Job Club Program with Welfare Recipients', *Journal of Vocational Behavior* 16: 133–45.

Azrin, N. H., Philip, R. A., Thienes-Hontos, P. and Besalel, V. A. (1981) 'Follow-Up on Welfare Benefits Received by Job Club Clients', *Journal of Vocational Behavior* 18: 253–54.

Baker, S. B. and Popwicz, C. C. (1983) 'Meta-Analysis as a Strategy for Evaluating Effects of Career Education Interventions', *Vocational Guidance Quarterly* 31: 178–86.

Bakke, E. W. (1940) *Citizens Without Work*, New Haven, CT: Institute of Human Relations, Yale University.

Brown, W. F. (1965) 'Student-to-Student Counseling for Academic Adjustment', *Personnel and Guidance Journal* 53: 811–17.

Bruce, D. and Evans, B. (1990) *Review of Careers Guidance*, London: Employment Department (mimeo).

Burt, C., Gaw, F., Ramsey, L., Smith, M. and Spielman, W. (1926) *A Study in Vocational Guidance*, MRC Industrial Fatigue Research Board Report No. 33, London: HMSO.

Cairo, P. C. (1983) 'Counseling in Industry: a Selected Review of the Literature', *Personnel Psychology* 36: 1–18.

Campbell, D. P. (1965) *The Results of Counseling: Twenty-Five Years Later*, Philadelphia: Saunders.

Carroll, P. (1987) *The Potential of Guidance for Making Job Search More Effective*, ES Research and Evaluation Branch Report No. 27, London: Manpower Services Commission (mimeo).

Chamberlain, P. J. (1982) 'Careers Lessons and Career Awareness of Fifth-Form Students', *British Journal of Guidance and Counselling* 10(1): 74–82.

Clarke, L. (1981) *The Practice of Vocational Guidance: a Critical Review of Research in the United Kingdom*, London: HMSO.

Closs, S. J., Maclean, P. R. and Walker, M. V. (1985) *An Evaluation of the JIIG-CAL System*, Sevenoaks: Hodder & Stoughton (mimeo).

Confederation of British Industry (1993) *A Credit to Your Career*, London: CBI.

Cooper, S. E. (1986) 'The Effects of Group and Individual Vocational Counseling on Career Indecision and Personal Indecisiveness', *Journal of College Student Personnel* 27: 39–42.

Coopers & Lybrand (1994) *Gateways to Learning: Summary of Findings from First Round Pilots*, London: Coopers & Lybrand.

Crites, J. O. (1978) *Career Maturity Inventory: Theory and Research Handbook* (2nd edn), Monterey, CA: California Test Bureau/McGraw-Hill.

Department of Education and Science (1988) *Careers Education and Guidance from 5 to 16*, HMI Curriculum Matters 10, London: HMSO.

Earle, F. M. (1931) *Methods of Choosing a Career*, London: Harrap.

Employment Department (1992) *Assessment and Guidance Credits Initiative: Consultative Document*, London: ED.

Fairbairns, J. and Coolbear, J. (1982) *Career Development Counselling: an Experiment*, Sheffield: Manpower Services Commission.

Fretz, B. R. (1981) 'Evaluating the Effectiveness of Career Interventions', *Journal of Counseling Psychology* 28: 77–90.

Fretz, B. R. and Leong, F. T. L. (1982) 'Career Development Status as a Predictor of Career Intervention Outcomes', *Journal of Counseling Psychology* 29(4): 388–93.

Ginzberg, E., Ginsburg, S. W., Axelrad, S. and Herma, J. L. (1951) *Occupational Choice: an Approach to a General Theory*, New York: Columbia University Press.

Goldman, G. (1976) 'Career Decision-Making and Interview Frequency', *British Journal of Guidance and Counselling* 4(2): 195–201.

Harren, V. A. (1979) 'A Model of Career Decision Making for College Students', *Journal of Vocational Behavior* 14: 119–33.

Hill. J. M. M. (1969) *The Transition from School to Work*, London: Tavistock Institute of Human Relations.

Holland, J. L., Daiger, D. C. and Power, P. G. (1980) *My Vocational Situation*, Palo Alto, CA: Consulting Psychologists Press.

Holland, J. L., Magoon, T. M. and Spokane, A. R. (1981) 'Counseling Psychology: Career Interventions, Research and Theory', *Annual Review of Psychology* 32: 279–305.

Hopson, B. (1970) *The Effectiveness of a Careers Course in a Secondary School*, London: Vocational Guidance Research Unit, University of Leeds (mimeo).

Hunt, E. P. and Smith, P. (1944) *Scientific Vocational Guidance and its Value to the Choice of Employment Work of a Local Education Authority*, Birmingham: City of Birmingham Education Committee.

Ives, R. (1985) 'Careers Advice and Obtaining a Job', *Careers Journal* 5(3): 33–36.

Jahoda, M., Lazersfeld, P. F. and Zeisel, H. (1972; first pub. 1933) *Marienthal: the Sociography of an Unemployed Community*, London: Tavistock.

Johnson, R. G. (1985) 'Microcomputer-Assisted Career Exploration', *Vocational Guidance Quarterly* 33: 296–304.

Kidd, J. M. and Killeen, J. (1992) 'Are the Effects of Careers Guidance Worth Having?: Changes in Practice and Outcomes', *Journal of Occupational and Organizational Psychology* 65: 219–34.

Killeen, J. and Kidd, J. M. (1991) *Learning Outcomes of Guidance: a Review of Research*, Research Paper No. 85, Sheffield: Employment Department.

Killeen, J., White, M. and Watts, A. G. (1992) *The Economic Value of Careers Guidance*, London: Policy Studies Institute.

Killeen, J., Kidd, J. M., Hawthorn, R., Sampson, J. and White, M. (1994) *A Review of Measures of the Learning Outcomes of Guidance*, Cambridge: National Institute for Careers Education and Counselling (mimeo).

Kivlighan, D. M. and Shapiro, R. M. (1987) 'Holland Type as a Predictor of Benefit from Self-Help Career Counseling', *Journal of Counseling Psychology* 34: 326–29.

Kivlighan, D. M., Hageseth, J. A., Tipton, R. M. and McGovern, T. V. (1981) 'Effects of Matching Treatment Approaches and Personality Types in Group Vocational Counseling', *Journal of Counseling Psychology* 28: 315–20.

Krumboltz, J. D., Becker-Haven, J. F. and Burnett, K. (1979) 'Counseling Psychology', *Annual Review of Psychology* 30: 555–60.

Krumboltz, J. D., Scherba, D. S., Hamel, D. A. and Mitchell, L. K. (1982) 'Effect of Training in Rational Decision-Making on the Quality of Simulated Career Decisions', *Journal of Counseling Psychology* 29(6): 618–25.

Lancashire, R. D. (1971) 'Changing Needs in Vocational Guidance Follow-Up', paper presented to Annual Conference of the British Psychological Society (mimeo).

Lancashire, R. D. and Cohen, B. J. (1971) *Validation of Vocational Guidance: a Follow-Up of Selected Groups*, London: National Institute of Industrial Psychology (mimeo).

Law, B. and Watts, A. G. (1977) *Schools, Careers and Community*, London: Church Information Office.

Lent, R. W., Larkin, K. C. and Hasegawa, C. S. (1986) 'Effects of a "Focused Interest" Career Course Approach for College Students', *Vocational Guidance Quarterly* 34: 151–59.

Locke, E.A. (1976) 'The Nature and Causes of Job Satisfaction', in Dunnett, M. D. (ed.) *Handbook of Industrial and Organizational Psychology*, Chicago: Rand McNally.

Lowman, R. L. and Williams, R. E. (1987) 'Validity of Self-Ratings of Abilities and Competencies', *Journal of Vocational Behavior* 31: 1–13.

Melhus, G. E., Hershenson, D. B. and Vermillion, M. E. (1973) 'Computer Assisted versus Traditional Counseling with High and Low Readiness Clients', *Journal of Vocational Behavior* 3, 137–44.

Mostsch, P. (1980) 'Peer Social Modeling: a Tool for Assisting Girls with Career Exploration', *Vocational Guidance Quarterly* 28: 231–40.

Myers, R.A. (1971) 'Research on Educational and Vocational Counseling', in Bergin, A. E. and Garfield, S. L. (eds) *Handbook of Psychotherapy and Behavior Change: an Empirical Analysis*, New York: Wiley.

National Foundation for Educational Research (1987) *Job Ideas and Information Generator: Computer Assisted Learning (JIIG-CAL): Evaluation Report*, Slough: NFER (mimeo).

Nelson-Jones, R. and Toner, H. L. (1978) 'Assistance with Learning Competence and Decision-Making in Schools and Further Education', *British Journal of Guidance and Counselling* 6(2): 183–90.

Oliver, L. W. and Spokane, A. R. (1988) 'Career Intervention Outcome: What Contributes to Client Gain?' *Journal of Counseling Psychology* 35: 447–62.

Osipow, S. H. (1987) *Career Decision Scale Manual*, Odessa, FL: Psychological Assessment Resources.

Parsons, F. (1909) *Choosing a Vocation*, Boston: Houghton Mifflin.

Pearson, R. W. (1988) 'Creating Flexible Careers: Some Observations on a "Bridge" Programme for Unemployed Professionals', *British Journal of Guidance and Counselling* 16(3): 250–67.

Pickering, J. W. and Vacc, N. A. (1984) 'Effectiveness of Career Development Interventions for College Students: a Review of Published Research', *Vocational Guidance Quarterly* 32: 149–59.

Remer, P., O'Neill, C. D. and Gohs, D. E. (1984) 'Multiple-Outcome Evaluation of a Life-Career Development Course', *Journal of Counseling Psychology* 31: 532–40.

Robbins, S. B. and Tucker, K. R. (1986) 'Relations of Goal Instability to Self-Directed and Interactional Career Counseling Workshops', *Journal of Counseling Psychology* 33(4): 418–24.

Roselle, B. E. and Hummel, T. J. (1988) 'Intellectual Development and Interaction Effectiveness with DISCOVER', *Career Development Quarterly* 36(3): 241–50.

Rubinton, N. (1980) 'Instruction in Career Decision-Making and Decision-Making Styles', *Journal of Counseling Psychology* 27: 581–88.

Russell, J. E. A. (1991) 'Career Development Interventions in Organizations', *Journal of Vocational Behavior* 38(3): 237–87.

Schlossberg, N. K. and Leibowitz, Z. (1980) 'Organizational Support Systems as Buffers to Job Loss', *Journal of Vocational Behavior* 17, 204–17.

Slaney, R. B. (1983) 'Influence of Career Indecision on Treatments Exploring the Vocational Interests of College Women', *Journal of Counseling Psychology* 30(1): 55–63.

Slaney, R. B. and Dickson, R. D. (1985) 'Relation of Career Indecision to Career Exploration with Reentry Women: a Treatment and Follow-Up Study', *Journal of Counseling Psychology* 32(3): 355–62.

Slaney, R. B. and Lewis, E. T. (1986) 'Effects of Career Exploration on Career-Undecided Reentry Women: an Intervention and Follow-Up', *Journal of Vocational Behavior* 28: 97–109.

Spokane, A. R. and Oliver, L. W. (1983) 'The Outcomes of Vocational Intervention', in Walsh, W. B. and Osipow, S. H. (eds) *Handbook of Vocational Psychology*, vol. 2: 99–136, Hillsdale, NJ: Erlbaum.

Super, D. E. (1953) 'A Theory of Vocational Development', *American Psychologist* 8: 185–90.

Super, D. E. (1957) *The Psychology of Careers*, New York: Harper & Row.

Super, D. E. and Thompson, A. S. (1979) 'A Six-Scale, Two-Factor Test of Vocational Maturity', *Vocational Guidance Quarterly* 27: 6–15.

Thorndike, R. L. (1949) *Personnel Selection: Test and Measurement Techniques*, New York: Wiley.

Wankowski, J. (1979) 'Statistics and Economics of Educational Counselling in One University', *British Journal of Guidance and Counselling* 7(1): 31–41.

Watts, A. G. and Kidd, J. M. (1978) 'Evaluating the Effectiveness of Careers Guidance: a Review of the British Research', *Journal of Occupational Psychology* 51: 235–48.

Westbrook, B. W., Sanford, E. R., Mervin, G. A., Fleenor, J. and Renzi, D. A. (1987) 'Reliability and Construct Validity of New Measures of Career Maturity for 11th Grade Students', *Measurement and Evaluation in Counseling and Development* 20(1): 18–26.

White, M. (1992) 'The Potential of Guidance: Ideas from Economics', in Killeen, J., White, M. and Watts, A. G.: *The Economic Value of Careers Guidance*, London: Policy Studies Institute.

Wiggins, J. D. (1987) 'Effective Career Exploration Programs Revisited', *Vocational Guidance Quarterly* 35(4): 297–303.

Part II

Provision

This part of the book examines in turn the development and current state of the six main sectors of careers education and guidance provision in the UK. These can be divided into three clusters.

Chapters 5–7 deal with provision within the education system: Chapter 5 with schools, Chapter 6 with further and adult education, and Chapter 7 with higher education. In all three cases, there is a clear move from relatively marginalised provision to much closer integration into the mainstream educational process within the institutions in question. This move has been particularly marked in further education, where guidance was traditionally less well-developed but has now become more strongly institutionalised than elsewhere. In higher education, more attention is focused on specialist services within institutions (unlike schools and further education colleges, higher education institutions do not have access to the statutory Careers Service).

Chapter 8 focuses on a relatively new area of provision: career planning within work organisations. Such provision bears some similarities to provision within educational institutions. There tend, however, to be stronger tensions between individual interests and organisational needs. Nonetheless, this is a growing and potentially important area of guidance provision.

Chapters 9 and 10 address guidance provided from an 'external' or 'free-standing' base, in the sense that clients commonly go *to* the agency in question, rather than being provided with guidance in institutions in which they are already located. Chapter 9 examines the Careers Service, while Chapter 10 looks at other sources of guidance on learning and work. The Careers Service is a key provider, not least because of its statutory nature. The agencies examined in Chapter 10 are very diverse. An important issue for the future is whether they can be brought together within a more systematic framework to attend to the needs of individuals who fall outside the Careers Service's statutory client-group and are unable to find the help they need within education or work organisations.

While most of this part of the book relates to the United Kingdom as a whole, some relates more specifically to England and Wales. There are important differences between the various parts of the United Kingdom, which are not covered here: for example, the structure of 'promoted posts' in guidance within Scottish schools; and the fact that the Careers Service in Northern Ireland has long been part of the employment services, currently run by the Training and Employment Agency.

Chapter 5

Careers work in schools

Bill Law

5.1 INTRODUCTION

Careers education and guidance at school poses the question 'What do you want to do when you leave here?' The answer can be specific ('to train as a teacher!') or more encompassing ('to find something with meaning and purpose!'). But we can no longer assume that the specific answers will serve for a working life: both the possibilities and the priorities may change. A career is becoming episodes, linked by transitions, stretching into an unforeseeable future. The question, therefore, is protean, manifesting itself differently to each rising generation. It might now engage students at school in:

1 Understanding how working opportunities came to be the way they are now and how they continue to change.
2 Being able to see themselves in relation to those opportunities – a better fit for some than others.
3 Knowing what they want to change in their sense of their possibilities in the working world.
4 Equipping themselves to making those changes.
5 Knowing what they will do at the coming career transition, and why.
6 Appreciating what other things they might have done.
7 Appreciating the reactions of other people to their action.
8 Anticipating the possible consequences of that action for themselves and their life-style.
9 Being able to deal with frustration, disappointment and rejection.
10 Recognising how what they learn at school can help them with all of this.
11 Being committed to continuing to learn for new choices and transitions throughout life.

This chapter examines actions in schools to develop and pursue such aims. First, a historical section identifies trends in, and influences on, careers work. It shows how a range of learning settings for careers work has evolved in schools, and how a variety of educational, economic and social factors have influenced these developments. Second, an analysis of these learning settings provides a framework for identifying options for further development. This indicates how the settings complement each other and how they can be co-ordinated into a coherent whole within a particular school. Finally, a review of the current situation identifies priorities for new action in the future. (Training of teachers involved in careers work will be covered in a broader discussion of staff development in Chapter 16).

5.2 HISTORY

Three main periods can be identified in the development of careers work in schools. It can be seen at different periods to have been: (1) a *supplementary* service; (2) an optional part of the *curriculum*; and (3) an emergent *requirement*. The boundaries between these 'periods' are artificial, each stage moving through overlapping sub-stages into its successor. More is happening at each stage than any three headings can adequately label: there are developments towards more formal structures; towards a more educational conception; towards more integrated curriculum provision; and towards a concern for all students at all stages of their education. There are also cross-flows: consequences are sometimes unintended and unanticipated; schools are sometimes the originators, sometimes the recipients, of change. History is tidier than reality.

A supplementary service

The protean question was asked by kindly aunts long before teachers took an interest. Answers may well have been predictable on the basis of what was known of a person's social class, sex, neighbourhood and family. Most people could get most of the information and help they needed about their life chances from family and neighbourhood contacts. Careers education and guidance services emerged where such markers and resources were no longer sufficient to predict, and enable, the individual's plan.

The Juvenile Employment Bureaux (forerunners of the Careers Service) were first established around 1910 (see Chapter 9). Within schools, the earliest 'careers teachers' were headteachers offering help where it was needed. Designated school staff for careers in schools are mentioned from the late 1920s (Daws, 1972). But their role was separated from the curriculum. Careers work was not thought of as (like English) part of the curriculum, as (like the library) a resource for the curriculum, or as (like a 'house' system) a reinforcement of the curriculum. Where it was provided, it was (like a lost property office) offered independently of the curriculum – for those who needed it.

By the 1960s, 'careers teachers' were being widely appointed: the National Association of Careers (later 'and Guidance') Teachers was set up in 1966. Their tasks included managing incoming information (from the Central Youth Employment Executive and commercial publishers, and recruitment literature from employers and professional associations) and co-ordinating the work in the school of the youth employment officer (later called the careers officer) (for a detailed account of the important and changing relationship between the Careers Service and schools, see Chapter 9).

The first disturbances to this pattern came from an American tradition of humanistic psychology, celebrating autonomous individual development in careers (Super, 1957). The emerging rationales were developed with British resonance, in particular by Daws (1968) who articulated the new thinking as an attack on mere 'talent-matching'. Daws urged an alternative 'comprehensive-matching' model, which could accommodate motivations and feelings as well as abilities and aptitudes, but would require more sustained and more skilful help to be offered to students. Daws conceived of this help primarily in terms of an individual service offered not now through traditional interviewing, but through the more sustained and layered contacts implied by the term 'counselling'; he also, however, anticipated a classroom course that might be arranged by a counsellor to promote the general development of pupils.

An optional part of the curriculum

The idea of careers *education* was not mooted until the late 1960s and early 1970s. Prior to this there had been talks by 'visiting speakers' (often scheduled at the lunch break), plus early forms of work-experience programmes (see Jamieson and Miller, 1991). But a rationale was evolving, concerned to avoid the inefficient use of individual guidance to cover the same basic information: help could be 'more economically and, probably, more effectively' provided in the classroom (Watts, 1973).

By the early 1970s, government publications (e.g. DES, 1973) were beginning to specify coverage for careers education and guidance: careers education was to be addressed to 'an understanding of self', 'thinking about opportunities' and making 'considered choices'. This was subsequently elaborated into the DOTS model (Law and Watts, 1977):

1 Self awareness – 'who am I?'
2 Opportunity awareness – 'where am I?'
3 Decision learning – 'what will I do?'
4 Transition learning – 'how will I cope?'

The model was developed as an analytical tool for both careers education and guidance (see Chapter 12). It deepened and extended beyond matching, with consequences for a curriculum seeking to involve active students in participative learning experiences.

At the end of the 1960s, half of schools reported that 'careers' figured as a subject on the timetable for final-year leavers (Rodknight, 1969). Subsequent surveys indicated further advances over the next few years. Thus DES (1973) found that two-thirds of schools offered careers education. It also however discovered that careers education was less likely to be provided in grammar than in secondary modern and comprehensive schools, and that many schools still offered such courses for leavers only: 'the concept of careers education as a continuous process for all from the age of 13 onwards is in no sense realised' (p. 7).

Some ideas for careers education continued to be based on American rationales. Particularly influential was Samler's (1961) argument that career development is too narrowly conceived if it excludes the 'life-style' concomitants of choice (cf. Hopson and Hough, 1973). During the late 1970s the Schools Council Careers Education and Guidance Project developed a range of curriculum materials explicitly addressing many of these 'life-style' concomitants of work (see Bates, 1990). These materials also raised questions about the way 'careers' happen in our society, examining respects in which this might be unfair or need to be changed. Such work extends the protean question into 'How did things get to be this way?', 'Are we sure we should just be accepting this?' and 'What can we do about it?' They are asked by students thinking of themselves as citizens as well as workers, transposing careers work into a more social, more comprehending and more moral domain – part of the radical–liberal tradition in the British curriculum (Bates, 1989; Wirth, 1991; see also Chapters 12 and 19).

Such a conception of education fitted well with the egalitarian spirit of the times. But 'the times they were a-changing' – more than we knew. From the mid-1970s, education was required to take account of the rising levels of school-leaver unemployment. A government response was the Youth Opportunities Programme (YOP), a forerunner of Youth Training. Curriculum development for YOP drew upon ideas being assembled into the concept of pre-vocational education, an early attempt to bridge the 'academic–vocational divide' (FEU, 1979). The concept is broader than careers education, concerned not only with planning and decision-making, but also with enabling students to learn *how to do* things in the working world (Pring, 1987). It is, moreover, as much driven by concerns for economic performance as for personal development or for the fabric of a liberal democracy. Through a post-secondary programme, it soon exerted its influence on schools too, particularly in the form of life-skills programmes (Hopson and Scally, 1980) addressed to coping and thriving in a demanding and competitive labour economy and society. In schools such programmes were as likely to appear in personal and social education (PSE) as in careers education.

In addition to separate careers education provision or provision within PSE, there was also encouragement during this period for the idea of cross-curricular careers work: inviting English, geography and other 'non-specialists' to recognise and develop the help they offer students in dealing with some aspect or other of the protean question. Law and Watts (1977) used the term 'integrated careers work', the intersections linking the DOTS aims to the material of the school's overall programme – including its academic curriculum (see Chapter 12). The term for the teacher in charge of this process of integration was the 'careers co-ordinator' (see Law *et al.*, 1991). But a project set up specifically to encourage such approaches, the Careers Guidance Integration Project, found resistance in schools. It concluded that integrated development must be based upon finding common ground between teachers' subject concerns and what careers co-ordinators wanted them to do (Evans and Law, 1984; see also Chapter 17); there were, therefore, limits to what could be integrated. This has important implications for the pursuit of careers education as a requirement.

An emergent requirement

In 1976 Prime Minister James Callaghan launched a 'great debate' about changing not just the structure but the content of education. Careers education was not exempt: indeed, in the initial government discussion paper for the subsequent debate, it was named as one of five 'fixed points in the curriculum' in, particularly, the fourth and fifth years of secondary school (DES, 1977). This notion was subsequently dropped. But the idea that schools should be *required* to provide careers education and guidance has been a recurrent theme through the 1980s and early 1990s. This section identifies three more or less sequential attempts to move in the direction of mandatory provision: *targeted funding* (largely for pre-vocational work in schools); *policy imperatives* (from business, other interests, and government); and *quality standards* (kite-marking schools that measure up to requirements).

Targeted funding

The Technical and Vocational Education Initiative (TVEI), launched in 1983, provided 'labelled money' for approved programmes in the 14–18 curriculum. From the government's perspective, it represented an attempt to strengthen vocational education within secondary education. But labelled money requires negotiation, which in turn requires compromise on both sides. In the event, most of what TVEI achieved had as much to do with a broadly liberal as with a narrowly vocational education. The concern of TVEI that secondary education should be made relevant to the future working lives of students, placed in a broader context, provided a hospitable environment for careers education and guidance (Jones, 1989). Among its particular achievements was a significant strengthening in schools of work experience (see Chapter 13) and of recording achievement and action planning (see Chapter 14).

Policy imperatives

The 'great debate' led in due course to the Education Reform Act of 1983, which established a National Curriculum as a statutory requirement. It specified that the curriculum should, among other things, prepare students for the 'opportunities, responsibilities and experience of adult life'.

The intention of TVEI was very different from that of the National Curriculum (Table 5.1). The former developed a culture of relevance; the latter a culture of standards. There is no necessary tension between relevance and standards: a good education needs both. The tension lies in the priorities. This tension was anticipated by Bernstein (1971; 1973) who characterised the curriculum as being variably classified and framed – 'closed' programmes protecting purity, 'open' programmes permitting connections. A culture of relevance requires new connections for learning (for a more detailed discussion, see Chapter 12).

To be fair, some interest in such connections was expressed in the cross-curricular 'themes', 'skills' and 'dimensions' of the National Curriculum (NCC, 1990a). Careers education and guidance was identified as one of five life-relevant 'themes', from age 5 to age 16 (NCC, 1990b). But the themes were neither mandated by statute nor supported by funding. Indeed, they were announced after the main structure of the National Curriculum had been set in place, and appeared to respond, as much as anything, to five clusters of constituencies concerned that their interests were being neglected. The skills and dimensions fell out of favour before the themes. Moreover, little thought was given to how the intersections between ten subjects and five themes could be managed. Whitty *et al.* (1994a) examine this problem in detail, concluding – in line with Bernstein's predictions – that the 'closed' nature of the National Curriculum made it difficult for most teachers to establish such links between subject discourses and everyday life. Cleaton (1993) estimated that only one-sixth of schools were attempting any cross-curricular careers education, and concluded that 'careers education is being squeezed out of the curriculum by

Table 5.1   Contrasting cultures of TVEI and the National Curriculum

	The TVEI culture	The National Curriculum culture
Government sponsorship	Employment Department	Department for Education
Objectives	Defined by applicability to working life	Defined by content of 10 school subjects
Coverage	Negotiated and developed at departmental, school, consortium and LEA levels	Defined as an entitlement for all students
Logistics	Assumed internal co-operation in schools, active learning methods – including links with community – and modified ('long-block') timetabling	No particular logistics assumed
Sanctions	Labelled money for programme development, delivery, training and formative evaluation	Statutory
Assessment and evaluation	Assessment through recording methods – for summative and formative purposes; separate evaluation and accountability procedures	Through 'standard assessment tasks' – for both school evaluation and student diagnosis

the core and foundation subjects'. In the architecture of the National Curriculum, careers work became an outhouse.

In more general terms, Cleaton's study found some evidence that the position of careers work was strengthening: 74 per cent of schools had a written policy for careers education; and 97 per cent had a designated careers co-ordinator, 79 per cent of senior careers teachers having head of department status. But in practical terms the news was less good: 57 per cent of these heads of department had 3 hours or less timetable remission for their careers work; about the same number had no more than 5 hours of secretarial support. Although more than 80 per cent of schools allocated some of years 9, 10, 11 and 12 timetable time to careers education, in year 11 (for example) only 14 per cent of schools allocated the equivalent of a period a week. The study showed that only one-fifth of secondary schools provided separately timetabled specialist careers education in the last two years of compulsory education. The most common form of provision was as part of personal and social education (PSE) (42 per cent of schools in year 11).

PSE has many more things to do than careers education. But it is in a position to draw upon a broad liberal-education tradition. In particular, PSE is well placed to help students examine and relate the life-style implications of their actions, seeing how work choices have causes and consequences for consumer, citizen, family and other roles and one's health in them. PSE has a broader canopy than careers education and is nourished by deeper roots. However, PSE is itself marginal to the National Curriculum. Indeed, Whitty *et al.* (1994a) found that PSE in schools is not usually related to other subjects in any structured way, a common rationale being to teach what would not be covered elsewhere. PSE is under-resourced. It is too frail a vessel to carry all the freight required for contemporary concerns with career development.

Policy pressure for the provision of careers work persists. Dearing (1993), in examining the scope for releasing timetabling to teacher discretion, mentioned careers education and guidance as important for supporting students in choosing between new academic and vocational options. The National Commission on Education (1994), noting the erosive effects of National Curriculum overload and the tendency to underfund careers work, specifically supported an entitlement to 'guidance' in schools. The Confederation of British Industry proposed a broader entitlement including careers education, as well as pressing for stronger links with the business world (CBI, 1988; 1989; 1993).

The CBI (1988) case for improved links between school and industry influenced the establishment of government support for education–business partnerships (ED, 1990) – useful structures for supporting much of the life-relevant use of the curriculum, including careers work. Some of the problems of managing such schemes had been set out earlier (Law, 1986), acknowledging the work of the School Curriculum Industry Project (SCIP) and school-based initiatives over more than a decade. There are more interests in life-relevant education than business interests. It is not surprising to find, therefore, that educators want to negotiate for a social as well as economic value to be gained from such links; or, indeed, to find that business people are often open to such negotiation (Law, 1991).

Nonetheless, CBI arguments stemmed from the assertion that 'individuals are the key to the UK's competitiveness'. Government concurred. Its Competitiveness White Paper (DTI, 1994) examined education in general, and careers work in particular, in the context of a general review of British competitiveness. The document set out, for the first time, an 'entitlement to careers education and guidance' from 11 to 16. The statement was voiced as a directive, specifying what 'schools will provide'.

Other statements by government departments and agencies closer to schools have, however, been more cautious. A joint publication of the Employment Department and Department for Education (1994) satisfied itself with a characterisation of an 'effective' careers-work programme, reiterating *inter alia* the expectation (first set out in DES/ED/WO, 1987) that schools should produce a policy statement on careers work. The School Curriculum and Assessment Authority (1995) used the slightly stronger formula an 'essential part of the curriculum', without adopting the language of requirements and directives. The SCAA document asserted that careers work should feature in primary as well as secondary schools, involving roles for both senior and middle management. It focused substantially on the curriculum, outlining elements for schemes of work and specifying the need for auditing, planning, implementation and evaluation. It urged the use of both 'continuing' (progressive) and 'blocked' (critical-phase) units of work.

In 1995, the government canvassed proposals for, among other things, a statutorily required careers education programme in secondary schools (ED/DfE, 1995). This begged three important questions: (1) what would count as a careers education programme; (2) could a statutory requirement be adequately resourced; and (3) could it be adequately policed?

Quality standards

OFSTED inspections are means for maintaining quality standards in schools. There has however been dissatisfaction concerning the attention paid to careers work within the OFSTED framework (Westergaard and Barnes, 1994). A case for more stringent quality standards for careers work in schools and elsewhere was part of Ball's (1993) argument for the National Advisory Council for Careers and Educational Guidance. The council should have, among other things, an advisory role in defining standards and monitoring quality. A feasibility study (Hawthorn, 1995) suggested that this might be delivered through a system of 'kite-marking' run by an independent body, much like the 'Investors in People' system. Various providers of such kite-marks have emerged (Law, 1995).

While not strictly providing a 'quality standard', the London Enterprise Agency (1995) set out a verifiable set of descriptors for an adequate programme in this field. It was framed as a unified approach to what had previously been known as the cross-curricular themes. The scheme concentrated on the curriculum, and set out objectives for primary and secondary education. The objectives were framed much like the attainment targets of the National Curriculum, and – like them – were designed to be used to provide assessment for students and evaluation for schools.

Establishing criteria for the identification of value raises serious problems for the reliability and validity of the evidence upon which awards are based, as the experience with both OFSTED inspections and with standard assessment tasks for monitoring performance in the National Curriculum attest. There are, furthermore, problems for the use of a single system for assessing the quality of provision (input) and activity (process) and their impact (outcome). There are also problems in deriving central standards for local provision: organisational priorities, local traditions, the community and the state of its labour economy must all moderate the assessment of input, process and outcome. Much depends upon the skill and insight with which the perpetrators of 'kite-marks' manage these tasks. At the time of writing, it is too early to assess their impact on the quality of careers work.

'Loose ends'

Despite rumours to the contrary, history is not over yet. There are many loose ends. There has been no sustained attempt to support what primary-school teachers do to help their children lay good foundations for their career development; nor a national initiative to bring better career help to young people with special educational needs. But, perhaps most seriously of all, there has been little attention to what careers educators can do to help those many young men and women who, every calculation estimates, are not likely to secure worthwhile jobs in any readily foreseeable future. The issues have been addressed and some school-based efforts have been documented (Watts, 1983). Curriculum material has been developed (Law and Storey, 1987). But few policy statements say much about this. The issue extends the protean question – 'Suppose I can't get a job?'

5.3 LEARNING SETTINGS

It may seem curious to some that careers work, first undertaken on the basis of a few rather straightforward assumptions about what is required, should have become so complicated. If you are not confused, you are simply not paying attention! This section re-examines the story in two ways: by disentangling the *elements* of change, and by probing the *dynamics* of change.

The elements of change

The argument here is that careers work is more complicated because it has to be. The rationale, the experience of students, changes in society: all require more than a few rules of thumb in support of a supplementary service.

In the first place, there are various reasons for doing the work:

1 The *humanistic* rationale argues that careers work is an investment for personal choice: a means by which we motivate our young men and women for their lifelong learning and work, and help them to develop and implement a sense of personal purpose in and for that life.
2 The broader *liberal education* rationale argues that careers work is an investment in the social fabric: a means by which we attach our young men and women to their working and learning communities, help them to arrive at a questioning understanding of that attachment, and thereby offer them a sustainable stake in their own and their society's future.
3 The *vocational education* rationale argues that careers work is an economic investment in the preparedness for working life of our young men and women, so that they can acquire the knowledge, skills and attitudes, and make the decisions, that an effective economy requires.

These rationales do not exclude each other; but they are different (for a more sustained account, see Chapter 12). What we do about the 'loose ends' of our history will be changed by how we balance these rationales.

In the second place, a young person's approach to career planning is more deeply layered than simple solutions can deal with. Career learning is interwoven with all learning – with perception, understanding, feeling and attachment. Young people need information, but they also need skills, concepts, and explanations and anticipations. They need this at progressively more demanding levels of complexity and depth. They need to be able to identify the feelings of self and others in times of disappointment and elation. And they need all of this for continuing use. Begun in early childhood, and perpetually unfolding, influential impressions and thinking are in place long before school-leaving hoves into view. And what happens earlier can both help and hinder what children may do later (see Chapter 3).

In the third place, in our society – continuously adjusting its social and economic structures – career planning is harder than ever to focus. The concern must be broader than for employability: young women and men need to understand and be ready for a working life in all its changing manifestations.

Understanding careers can be thought of, then, as being as demanding as anything else that children learn at school. Such learning cannot be gained from a combination of occasional individual guidance and marginal careers education. Schools have accordingly sought to develop a range of learning strategies. Over time, each of the following has become established:

1 *Careers resource centres* – providing visitors with up-to-date, accessible and multi-media information on work and opportunity.
2 *Face-to-face help* – offering individuals or small groups help on their own decisions and transitions, staffed by careers-service staff along with their pastoral-care and careers teacher partners.
3 *Recording, action planning and 'portfolio' work* – helping students to identify, record and review key information on their experiences, abilities, potential and intentions concerning work-life.
4 *Personal and social education* – offering a planned series of learning experiences setting work-life concerns in a more general personal, social and moral context, staffed by designated teachers.
5 *Specialist careers education classroom work* – offering a planned series of schemes-of-work examining key aspects of work-life, staffed by expert teachers.
6 *Integrated work* – where the career relevance of a subject is specifically developed, as it commonly can be in English, geography, technology and science; a useful but necessarily piecemeal strategy which can develop into a wider programme linking subject learning to work-life situations; most effectively organised as 'long-block' events, and – in developed forms – staffed from across the timetable.
7 *Community-linked work* – linking careers work to its clients, resources and partners in the community; in particular, offering students an expanding range of useful human and physical learning resources – such as are found in work experience.

Some parts of this range appear in one school, some in another; few schools do them all, some do very few. But the potential directions for development are now much richer than they were.

The dynamics of change

Careers work, then, is a range of learning settings, capable of responding to a range of needs, offering differentiated knowledge, at different stages of learning, responding to different learning styles, at various levels of feeling and complexity.

Table 5.2 organises the elements in relation to two explanatory dimensions. Growth in this framework can be characterised both as expansion and as development. *Expansion* means that more settings are used (upward movement in the table); where more people are involved, more agreement is needed and the work becomes more publicly visible and more political. *Development* means that more time, skill and other resources are invested (rightward movement in the table).

As we have seen, growth is driven both by rationale and by perceptions of need. The table offers a narrative which suggests how that might be so. Having picked up and read a leaflet (setting 1), a student might ask to talk to a teacher or careers adviser (setting 2). Either might suggest that the student should write out a possible plan of action (setting 3) to inform the process. To do so, the

Table 5.2 Progressive levels of development within seven learning settings in schools

Learning setting	Levels of development		
	A	B	C
7 *Community-linked work*	Communicating with parents, employers, and other clients about what the school does and how students are doing in careers	Engaging work experience, community projects and other community bases which students can use as learning resources	Working with business and other community partners in development work so that they contribute to influencing the development of careers work in the school
6 *Integrated work*	Relatively informal linking with individual partners, acknowledging careers work done by others	Developing more sustained partnership between careers work and at least one other subject	Negotiating formal agreements to co-operate on specific programmes at inter-departmental level
5 *Specialist careers education classroom work*	Designing and running planned careers education classes	Bringing in the use of active learning-by-doing: with enquiries, projects and decision-making and problem-solving simulations	Bringing methods which disclose and share whole-person thoughts and feelings about careers: in role-plays and actual decision-making and problem-solving activities
4 *Personal and social education*	Incorporating careers as a formal part of a carousel or other scheme of work	Running active tutorials incorporating careers work	Establishing a comprehensive and coherent PSE programme, engaging work roles in the context of other adult roles
3 *Recording, action planning and 'portfolio' work*	Using information about each student's progress and qualities: in reports, assessment schedules or scientific tests and questionnaires	Recording achievement: helping students to develop their own accounts of what they are gaining from school and other experiences	Individual action planning: where the individual student's progress is talked through and made the basis for future action
2 *Face-to-face work*	Interviewing students: taking them through a schedule concerning their preferences and intentions	Counselling students: offering time, space, atmosphere and skills, so that students can disclose	Negotiating with students: offering them opportunities to influence what the school offers, in exchange for their commitments
1 *Resource-centre work*	Displaying and lending leaflets, books and other material to students, colleagues, parents and others	Cataloguing and labelling the centre to make it and its information accessible and easy-to-find, e.g. using an index system and other aids to access and search	Using graphic, computer and other media, e.g. software, videos, posters

student needs to link career plans to other hopes – as consumer, citizen, house-holder, whole person: PSE (setting 4) can help students to make, understand and use those links. In any event, detailed and expert help is required, and 'interviews' inefficiently cover the ground, so some specialist 'classroom' space (setting 5) is needed to get this basic learning in place. A student's plans might stem from something that another teacher said, linking interest in work-life to the school subject: such links by colleagues can be built (setting 6) into more opportunities for students to recognise the relevance to their lives of all that they learn at school. Such work will certainly need the co-operation of parents and others in the community (setting 7).

The learning settings may be thought of, as we have seen they sometimes are, as a series of fragmentary and free-standing (even, perhaps, independently funded) programmes. But they are better thought of as elements in an overall, interdependent and coherent programme. The content of such a programme cannot be adequately specified from outside the school. The distinctive philos-ophy of the school, its social setting, and the experience and readiness of its people, will all make a difference to what can and should be done.

However generated, no movement occurs unhampered. As *expansion* occurs, more people need to be involved. It may be possible to provide a walk-in resource centre without bothering, or being bothered by, too many other people. But inte-grating a work-experience programme into the school's programme is a more public undertaking, needing more negotiation, more co-operation and more agreement with more people. This means more possibilities for conflicting inter-ests and priorities – the 'hassle' factor. Similarly, *development* in any of the settings involves more time, or more equipment, or more material, or more training and support – in a word, more money. While the pressure from hassle is downward on the table, the pressure from expense is leftward.

The model has planning value. The table can be used to analyse what is currently being provided, what is being provided but needs further develop-ment, what could soon be embarked upon and what would at best have to be a long-term aim. The concept of 'the best next thing to do' (Law et al., 1995) rests upon such an analysis of potentiality for growth. Each school will yield its own plan, nominating its own priorities. The task is to identify upon what well-established bases new expansions and developments can be built.

5.4 PRIORITIES FOR NEW ACTION

The model outlined above provides a basis for establishing priorities for new action, in two respects: for linking careers work more closely to the mainstream curriculum; and for strengthening local as well as national bases for developing careers work.

Careers work and the mainstream curriculum

Careers work is perceived as marginal when its links to the curriculum are weak. Where new activities are introduced – interest inventories, work experi-ence, recording experience, computer-assisted guidance – they share that marginality until they achieve such integration. Yet few have argued that careers education should gain mainstream status as a subject in the National Curriculum.

That is not argued here, but neither is leaving careers education on the margins of the timetable.

Subject-by-subject infusion into separate subjects is unsustainable (Whitty *et al.*, 1994a). Main-subject concerns override and obscure other concerns, both for teachers and for their students. Whitty *et al.* conclude that specialist careers education may be of more value than cross-curricular work.

But any obituary for integrated work may be premature. As Whitty *et al.* indicate, a minority of skilful teachers *can* manage the 'background and foreground' configuration of main-subject content and its connections in the lives of students. During the early days of the National Curriculum, in which their study was conducted, it was not surprising that for most teachers their highest priorities were focused narrowly on subject content. Furthermore, standard lesson-length timetable slots set severe limits to the way in which students can make the connections that integration requires. But there are other ways of organising the timetable. Again, cross-curricular work is presented as though it must be undertaken more or less independently of support from learning in other settings, such as formative recording and reviewing (see Chapter 14), the use of resource centres and community links; but this is not the case. No conclusions can yet be drawn concerning the viability of the whole range of integrated possibilities.

To indicate the other possibilities, Table 5.2 suggests (left-to-right in setting 6) three levels of integrated development:

Level-A *links* require an alert and open careers teacher, ready to acknowledge the careers value of subject teachers' work, finding colleagues ready to develop these links, and accepting that not all colleagues will be. Such work must be free of heavy accountability or control procedures – from either senior or departmental management.

Level-B *partnerships* develop from level-A links, where a colleague is sustaining action to a point that others are interested and the work can become embedded. Such movement requires that the school accepts inter-departmental initiatives instigated at 'classroom' level, subject only to reports to management, and not insisting that everything conforms to existing expectations.

Level-C *co-ordination*, the necessary basis for a long-block project, requires head-of-department involvement in a shared – though still contained – scheme of work. Such a movement requires an organisation where inter-departmental agreements can be made on resources and evaluation, where there is a co-ordinator to manage the shared action, and where senior management will support the action with a mandate and resources.

The assumption that the initial link will lead to school-wide subject-by-subject *infusion* is avoided here. If this were to occur, it would be difficult to monitor, and (on the evidence of the Whitty *et al.* [1994a] study) would be likely to be extremely variable in its effects. The preferred strategy is to follow the available energy, drawing upon the skills and motivations of colleagues who want to be involved, and not dragging the unready into unwilling and uncomprehending compliance. The strategy particularly favours short-run schemes of work, in long-block timetabling, achieving palpable impact in a short time. Work experience, mini-enterprise and other community-linked task projects all rely upon such a strategy.

Cross-curricular links to life relevance are sometimes characterised (e.g. Whitty *et al.*, 1994b) as a way of dealing with curriculum overload – added value, on the cheap. The arguments in this chapter are different: that students need to recognise the intrinsic relevance to their lives of their education, and that career development cannot thrive in a culture where that relevance is never manifested in mainstream activity. These arguments lead to reassertions of the life-role-relevant purposes of education. They require the local, gradual but ultimately radical re-structuring of a curriculum currently too completely defined by *subject-by-subject* concerns. School improvement requires a culture of relevance as well as one of standards.

Partnerships for progress

Of course the state has an interest in education. In careers work, schools are expected to produce a policy statement on careers education and guidance, to enter into a service-level agreement with the Careers Service, and – in general terms – to use discretionary time released by the contracted National Curriculum to improve careers-work provision. Leaving aside the problematic question of whether targeted but temporary funding can achieve any sustained impact, these are the effects of more than a decade of policy interest.

A feature of targeted funding and policy imperatives has been their central generation – they come from government and its quangos. But there are other legitimate interests in education (cf. Law *et al.*, 1995), at three levels at least:

1 In *school* – at departmental, organisation-wide and school-network levels. Each has voices for priorities, policies and culture, for what is distinctive and valuable about the school's work, and for the ability and willingness of its staff to undertake particular new commitments, based on an understanding of the needs of its specific students.
2 In *community* – at neighbourhood, area and regional levels. In recent history, the main forums have been the TVEI consortium, the Local Education Authority, the Careers Service and the Training and Enterprise Council – all now in radical transition. But, with or without such help, new action can take account of what is distinctive about a community's labour economy, its social fabric, its work traditions, the hopes and expectations of its people, and their special needs in relation to the way in which work in that area is changing.
3 In *society* – at trans-national, national, and 'big-constituency' (e.g. CBI and TUC) levels. These express concerns for the macro-economy, but also – we may hope – for the social fabric, and for the maintenance of a liberal democracy in which rising generations can find and value a legitimate stake in their society.

As we have seen, careers work can be viewed as being capable of helping with all these matters.

To illustrate this, a selection of priorities for the future development of careers work, drawn from the discussion in this chapter, is set out in Table 5.3. Suggestions are made concerning where actions on each might usefully be undertaken. The three columns on the right correspond to the three constituency areas and their agencies outlined above. Typically one finds a school management in the first column, a local education authority in the second, and national govern-

Table 5.3 Possible priorities for development

Priorities	School	Community	Society
Developing a culture of relevance in education	✓	✓	✓
Defining learning outcomes at key transition points			✓
Identifying requirements for minimum levels of acceptable provision		✓	✓
Defining what each learning setting can achieve	✓	✓	
Understanding how a coherent programme can be co-ordinated, appropriate to a particular school	✓	✓	
Relating that programme to the local social fabric and to its social and economic conditions and concerns	✓	✓	
Establishing specific partnerships between school, the Careers Service and other local providers of formal and informal career-development help	✓	✓	
Appointing a curriculum co-ordinator with authority and time for careers work	✓		
Training OFSTED inspectors in what constitutes effective careers work			✓
Targeting government resources for careers work		✓	✓
Developing education and training for careers co-ordinators	✓	✓	✓
Implementing staff development for 'other subject' and PSE staff, specialist careers teachers and school management	✓	✓	✓
Developing initial teacher training that links careers work to the delivery of 'main' subjects and PSE	✓	✓	✓
Developing curriculum material and methods progressing students from basic to developed careers learning		✓	✓
Developing curriculum material for students with special educational needs		✓	✓
Attending in primary schools to the helping and hindering effects on careers of early learning	✓	✓	✓

ment in the third. But, as we have seen, there are other possibilities for all three sets of interest.

Central government cannot think of everything that needs to be done, and should not try. People sequestered in schools cannot think of everything either; though the immediate responsibility for action is theirs. Vague pleas for improvements in resources, status and policy attention will no longer do. Fifty-plus years of progress have at least shown us more precise compass bearings for future journeying: pointing (in terms outlined above) to work on curriculum, in neighbourhoods and for resources.

1 *On curriculum*: careers work requires a curriculum frame which can accommodate both the need for improved standards and the need for an education which is *relevant* and useful to people's present and anticipated lives, and how they plan their lives.
2 *In neighbourhoods*: careers work, though nationally supported and monitored, needs to be based on informed *local* action responding to the needs of people – in their communities, with their identities, and in their social and economic conditions.
3 *For resources*: careers work requires materials, research-and-development and training at a level and with a rigour *commensurate* with the enormity and complexity of its task.

None of this requires new legislation, nor further centrally-directed initiatives. It does, however, depend upon a willingness continually to rethink the education of our young men and women. And it requires that attention in all parts of our society.

REFERENCES

Ball, C. (ed.) (1993) *Guidance Matters: Developing a National Strategy for Guidance in Learning and Work*, London: Royal Society of Arts.
Bates, I. (1989) 'Versions of Vocationalism: an Analysis of Some Social and Political Influences on Curriculum Policy and Practice', *British Journal of Sociology of Education* 10(2): 215–31.
Bates, I. (1990) 'The Politics of Careers Education and Guidance: a Case for Scrutiny', *British Journal of Guidance and Counselling* 18(1): 66–83.
Bernstein, B. B. (1971) 'Open Schools, Open Society', in Cosin, B. R., Dale, I. R., Esland, G. M. and Swift, D. F. (eds) *School and Society*, London: Open University/Routledge & Kegan Paul.
Bernstein, B. B. (1973) 'On the Classification and Framing of Educational Knowledge', in Brown, K. (ed.) *Knowledge, Education and Cultural Change*, London: Tavistock.
Cleaton, D. (1993) *Careers Education and Guidance in British Schools*, Stourbridge: National Association of Careers and Guidance Teachers/Institute of Careers Guidance.
Confederation of British Industry (1988) *Building a Stronger Partnership*, London: CBI.
Confederation of British Industry (1989) *Towards a Skills Revolution*, London: CBI.
Confederation of British Industry (1993) *A Credit to Your Career*, London: CBI.
Daws, P. P. (1968) *A Good Start in Life*, Cambridge: Careers Research and Advisory Centre.
Daws, P. P. (1972) 'The Role of the Careers Teacher', in Hayes, J. and Hopson, B. (eds) *Careers Guidance: the Role of the School in Vocational Development*, London: Heinemann.
Dearing, R. (1993) *The National Curriculum and its Assessment: Final Report*, London: School Curriculum and Assessment Authority.
Department of Education and Science (1973) *Careers Education in Secondary Schools*, Education Survey 18, London: HMSO.
Department of Education and Science (1977) *Educating Our Children*, London: HMSO.
Department of Education and Science/Employment Department/Welsh Office (1987) *Working Together for a Better Future*, London: DES/ED/WO.
Department of Trade and Industry (1994) *Competitiveness – Helping Business to Win*, London: HMSO.
Employment Department (1990) *The Partnership Handbook*, London: HMSO.
Employment Department/Department for Education (1994) *Better Choices*, London: ED/DfE.
Employment Department/Department for Education (1995) *Careers Education and Guidance Proposed Legislation: a Consultation Paper*, London: ED/DfE (mimeo).
Evans, K. and Law, B. (1984) *Careers Guidance Integration Project: Final Report*, Hertford: National Institute for Careers Education and Counselling (mimeo).

Further Education Unit (1979) *A Basis for Choice*, London: FEU.

Hawthorn, R. (1995) *First Steps: Quality Standards for Guidance Across Sectors*, London: Royal Society of Arts/National Council for Careers and Educational Guidance.

Hopson, B. and Hough, P. (1973) *Exercises in Personal and Career Development*, Cambridge: Careers Research and Advisory Centre.

Hopson, B. and Scally, M. (1980) *Life Skills Teaching*, Maidenhead: McGraw-Hill.

Jamieson, I. and Miller, A. (1991) 'History and Policy Context', in Miller, A., Watts, A. G. and Jamieson, I.: *Rethinking Work Experience*, London: Falmer.

Jones, A. (1989) 'The Real Aims of TVEI', *Education*, 14 April, 351–52.

Law, B. (1986) *The Pre-Vocational Franchise*, London: Paul Chapman.

Law, B. (1991) *Side by Side*, Cambridge: National Institute for Careers Education and Counselling (mimeo).

Law, B. (1995) *Key Concepts for Careers Work*, Manchester: Open College.

Law, B. and Storey, J. (1987) *Is It Working?*, Cambridge: National Institute for Careers Education and Counselling.

Law, B. and Watts, A. G. (1977) *Schools, Careers and Community*, London: Church Information Office.

Law, B. et al. (1991) *Co-ordinating Careers Work*, Sheffield: Careers and Occupational Information Centre.

Law, B. et al. (1995) *Careers Work* (revised edn), Manchester: Open College.

London Enterprise Agency (1995) *Pathways Towards Working Life*, London: LEntA.

National Commission on Education (1994) *Learning to Succeed*, London: Heinemann.

National Curriculum Council (1990a) *The Whole Curriculum*, Curriculum Guidance 3, York: NCC.

National Curriculum Council (1990b) *Careers Education and Guidance*, Curriculum Guidance 6, York: NCC.

Pring, R. (1987) 'The Curriculum and the New Vocationalism', *British Journal of Education and Work* 1(3): 133–48.

Rodknight, E. (1969) 'A Survey of Careers Work in Schools', *Journal of the Careers Research and Advisory Centre* 4(2): 3–10.

Samler, J. (1961) 'Psycho-Social Aspects of Work: a Critique of Occupational Information', *Personnel and Guidance Journal* 39: 458–65.

School Curriculum and Assessment Authority (1995) *Looking Forward: Careers Education and Guidance in the Curriculum*, London: SCAA.

Super, D. E. (1957) *The Psychology of Careers*, New York: Harper & Row.

Watts, A. G. (1973) 'A Structure for Careers Education', in Jackson, R. (ed.) *Careers Guidance: Practice and Problems*, London: Arnold.

Watts, A. G. (1983) *Education, Unemployment and the Future of Work*, Milton Keynes: Open University Press.

Westergaard, J. and Barnes, A. (1995) *Inspecting Careers Work*, Chelmsford: Essex TVEI.

Whitty, G., Rowe, G. and Aggleton, P. (1994a) 'Subjects and Themes in the Secondary-School Curriculum', *Research Papers in Education* 9(2): 159–81.

Whitty, G., Rowe, G. and Aggleton, P. (1994b) 'Discourse in Cross-Curricular Contexts: Limits to Empowerment', *International Studies in Sociology of Education* 4(1): 25–41.

Wirth, A. G. (1991) 'Issues in the Vocational–Liberal Studies Controversy (1900–1917): John Dewey v. the Social Efficiency Philosophers', in Corson, D. (ed.) *Education for Work*, Clevedon, Avon: Multilingual Matters.

Chapter 6

Careers work in further and adult education

Ruth Hawthorn

6.1 INTRODUCTION

The post-compulsory, non-advanced further education sector in Britain is easier to define than to describe. Compared with secondary and higher education, its evolution has been relatively recent and rapid; to make matters more complicated, it varies greatly at local level. The careers education and guidance needs of its students are equally complex.

The sector consists mainly of colleges providing education and training for two groups: young people who have left school, but are still entitled to state-funded initial education (that is, aged between 16 and 19); and people over that age who are commonly returning to education or training. Most colleges offer both vocational and academic courses across a broad range of subjects, but the sector also includes specialist institutions devoted to, say, agriculture or fine art. It further includes separate sixth-form colleges, as well as tertiary colleges (where sixth form and further education colleges have been combined into single comprehensive institutions).

Many accounts of careers work refer to 'schools and colleges' as if the provision is closely similar. Certainly there are some similarities, particularly between post-16 work in schools and what is offered in sixth-form colleges, and in more academic courses in further education and tertiary colleges. In other respects, however, further education is a unique sector, shaped by different funding arrangements, and by the complex nature of further education colleges themselves, as well as by the greater variety of students. As in all post-compulsory education, the decision to be there is an explicit career step in itself. But in further education, the spectrum ranges more broadly, from those disadvantaged educationally or socially, for whom enrolment may have been experienced as an absence of employment choices, to those already well-established in their careers, undergoing specialist training to take them further.

Older people who are returning to education or training in Britain now constitute a majority of the students in the further education sector as formally defined, and one area of debate (as in higher education) is the extent to which they have the same careers education and guidance needs as young people (FEU, 1993a). But adult education also forms a distinct sector of its own. It has traditionally been understood as consisting of those vocational and non-vocational courses that are provided by local authorities (through their adult or community education services) and voluntary organisations. These are mostly part-time, but the sector also includes some residential colleges which offer full-time courses, often as alternative entry routes to higher education. Open, distance and independent learning have all extended the nature of adult education, and the guidance necessary to it.

In this chapter we will first examine the evolution of the structure of further and adult education in more detail. We will then, against this background, explore the paths of development for careers education and guidance provision within these sectors. Next, we will look at current provision within a framework adapted from that now used for funding and inspection purposes in further education: pre-entry and entry guidance; and on-course and exit guidance. Finally, we will discuss a number of issues related to the development of guidance provision: management and organisation, quality assurance, the role of the Careers Service, and training and staff development.

6.2 STRUCTURAL BACKGROUND

The two main functions of further education have been to provide training in technical and vocational skills, and an alternative or second-chance route to academic study. These have developed from distinct traditions in education and training in Britain, and neither has come about as a result of central or coherent planning.

The college's vocational role continues that initiated in the second half of the nineteenth century by the mechanics' institutes and continued during the first half of the twentieth century by technical colleges, partly in response to a demand from individuals and partly also to meet the training needs of local employers (Hall, 1990). It was not until the 1944 Education Act that the colleges became the responsibility of local authorities, and the term 'further education' was linked to this area of vocational education and training. The creation of industrial training boards in the 1960s strengthened the role of colleges in the training of apprentices, on a block- or day-release basis (Cantor and Roberts, 1986). With the rise in youth unemployment in the 1970s and 1980s, new kinds of 'pre-vocational' courses were developed which frequently included aspects of careers education and guidance within their curriculum.

The provision of academic courses in colleges for young people, and of educational classes for adults, has a different origin. During the nineteenth century and the first half of the twentieth, the demand for academic courses from adults who had not had the chance of secondary education was met by a range of voluntary organisations. Again, it was the 1944 Act which gave the responsibility to local authorities to ensure adequate provision for adults (Legge, 1982), either by supporting the voluntary sector or by providing it directly themselves. This gave rise to different arrangements in almost every local authority area. In some, adult education was incorporated wholesale into colleges. In others, colleges shared provision with local authority adult (and later community) education services, frequently in competition for resources and students.

The 1944 Act also required local authorities to make broad educational provision for young people who wanted to continue their education after the statutory school-leaving age (then 15) but did not want, or were not able, to continue at their secondary school. One consequence of the Act, and the responsibility it gave to local authorities to assume management quickly of such a broad range of small, formerly independent providers, is the number of large colleges and adult education centres which are now run on multiple sites. To complicate the picture further, many colleges and adult education centres also offer courses away from their own premises, for example in local schools or community centres.

The system of further and adult education that had developed by the late 1980s was thus broadly recognisable in each local authority area, but had local differences on almost every count. Colleges varied considerably in size, and in the range of what they offered. Subject departments within the colleges, particularly those responsible for vocational subjects that were supported by strong industrial boards such as construction and engineering, had great autonomy. There was no guarantee that all colleges would include the same range of courses.

The 1988 Education Reform Act resulted in some rationalisation of advanced and non-advanced further education, and the 1992 Further and Higher Education Act then gave colleges independence from local authorities. The incorporation of colleges after the 1992 Act was part of a much broader range of measures designed to introduce market principles into education and training. This had particularly significant consequences for further education. Schools too now had financial autonomy, and the possibility of opting out of local authority control. There had always been an element of rivalry between colleges in the same local authority area, between them and schools, and, where they existed independently, between further education and local authority adult education services; now, funding, and therefore growth and survival, became more closely linked to student numbers. The local authority was no longer in a position to plan provision, or adjudicate between institutions, or arrange collaborative activities – including impartial guidance.

A further development which has affected the context of guidance in the further education sector has been the introduction of the new system of unit-based National Vocational Qualifications, with its emphasis on work-based assessment. This has been linked to increasing moves to modularise the curriculum, which have increased the number of choices and transition points students are asked to face.

There can therefore be no single response to careers work in this sector. The students on each type of course have different kinds of need, and are building on very different previous careers learning. Some attend the college full-time; some may only attend for two hours each week; some may never set foot in the college at all: any of these may attend over a period of a year or more, or may spend no more than a single day at the college. Few colleges have the same mixture of these different groups, or the same balance of needs between them. Their lecturers have very different backgrounds, and vary in the extent to which their subjects keep them in contact with careers issues or with the job market for their students (FEFC/OFSTED, 1994). For some courses, funding or validation depends on the inclusion of a careers element, but this is not the case for all.

There are also sub-groups with distinctive guidance needs. An area of adult education where careers education and guidance is particularly important is basic skills: students acquiring or improving on basic numeracy and literacy are often involved in career transitions, as are people enrolled on English for speakers of other languages (ESOL) courses. Careers education and guidance has a similar significance for people on educational programmes in prison. It also presents a particularly important challenge in programmes for adults with

learning difficulties, often run through social services departments, or in rehab-
ilitation programmes for people who have suffered from mental illness (offered
by health authorities and voluntary organisations).

The boundaries between further and adult education have been altered by the
incorporation into the further education sector, under the 1992 Further and
Higher Education Act, of the vocational courses for adults offered by adult or
community education services. This sharpens a distinction between vocational
and educational courses that is particularly problematic in relation to adults,
whose leisure activities often develop into 'second careers'.

Adult education so-defined is only one of many places where adults seek or
receive education; or rather, the sector overlaps with others. Besides constituting
a majority of students in further and higher education, there are higher education
institutions expressly for adults (for example, Birkbeck College in the University
of London), and an increasing number of courses in other institutions specifically recruiting adults. The Open University was founded in 1964 to provide
second-chance higher education, and open learning more generally developed
during the subsequent decades with the Open Tech and later the Open College.
There are many training organisations which provide training for or within
companies. There is also a more informal area where learning is an integral part
of leisure, or health, or community development activities, involving other public
services such as district councils or health authorities. An increasing number of
adults study as independent learners, sometimes using open-learning materials,
but also simply by buying or borrowing books, and many public library services
take an active interest in developing this side of their work. This broader area
overlaps into the work discussed in more detail in Chapter 10.

The need for impartial educational guidance for students on all of these pathways is now more widely acknowledged, but not so readily available. As all
careers become less predictable, the question is also emerging of how to provide
all adults with some of the rudimentary skills of career planning: this will involve
devising imaginative approaches to careers education in the adult sector, possibly
within, but more likely alongside, existing classes and learning materials (see
Chapter 12).

6.3 PATHS OF GUIDANCE DEVELOPMENT

Historically, careers education and guidance was less well developed in further
education than in other sectors of education. This was due in large measure to the
strength of the vocational tradition within the colleges. It was assumed that
students on vocational courses had already made a vocational commitment, and
therefore had no further need of guidance. Moreover, since many students were
sponsored by employers, senior management were 'often wary of undermining
relationships with employers by overtly providing careers guidance within their
colleges' (Stoney and Scott, 1984, p. 8). Thus a report in the mid-1970s noted that
college careers work was located almost exclusively in departments, and that in
this respect colleges were ten to fifteen years behind schools (Marks, 1975).

In the late 1970s and early 1980s, interest in careers education and guidance
within further education began to grow, partly because of the increasing number
of students on non-vocational courses, and partly because of the development
of the new forms of 'pre-vocational' provision which were vocationally oriented

but not vocationally specific. The latter courses brought into colleges a large number of low-achieving students with particularly acute guidance needs (Miller *et al.*, 1983).

Stoney and Scott (1984) identified two different growth patterns for guidance provision. The first resulted formally from decisions taken by college senior management, and commonly involved the appointment of a member of staff to a cross-college guidance role and/or asking the (then) local education authority Careers Service to provide personnel; either way, it gave rise to the appointment of staff with specialist guidance and counselling qualifications. The second resulted more informally from the enthusiasm and 'solitary efforts of an interested staff member (frequently from a general or academic studies department)' (p. 33). This person was gradually given more responsibility for careers co-ordination across the college, but often with insufficient time and recognition to carry out the work. As the service grew, it tended to be staffed on a part-time basis by enthusiastic but untrained college staff.

By the time of Stoney and Scott's study, colleges with a head of student services were still in a minority, though a quarter did have either someone with that title, or a careers co-ordinator; heads of department and vice-principals were also involved in a co-ordinating capacity; and guidance work was carried out by different combinations of college-appointed careers specialists, careers officers from the Careers Service, and departmental careers tutors or other academic staff. Stoney and Scott reported that only 17 per cent had appropriate accommodation including interviewing rooms, a reception/browsing area, and open storage for careers literature and display boards. At the other end of the scale, 7 per cent managed with only some careers literature stored in the college library, and display boards around the college.

This model of provision focused mainly on the careers education and guidance needs of 16–19-year-olds, and was broadly similar to that for secondary education. Alongside it, however, there emerged a rather different model, focused around the educational guidance needs of adults. Advice on educational opportunities for adults had been the responsibility of the adult education centre or provider concerned. The need for more specialist and impartial guidance was highlighted by a report from the Advisory Council for Adult and Continuing Education (1979), promoting the growth of educational guidance services for adults (see Chapter 10). This tradition emphasised the provision of guidance that is independent of educational provision: impartiality, and links with wider guidance networks, were both of prime importance. Careers education is not easily included in this perspective, but the activities of guidance on which this approach is based (the seven activities identified by UDACE [1986], discussed further in Chapter 10, were informing, advising, counselling, assessing, enabling, advocating and feeding back) imply participation by departmental tutors as well as staff attached to guidance or student services departments. The definition was later expanded (SCAGES, 1992) to include teaching, managing, networking and systems change, in order to create a better fit with careers work in schools and colleges, but the resulting list is an uncomfortable blend of two perspectives and has not had the impact of the original.

Although the recommendations from ACACE (1979) and UDACE (1986) stressed the links between educational and vocational guidance, some in the field saw it as important to separate decisions, and therefore guidance, about education from those to do with work (Edwards, 1989). This was partly to resist the 'vocational imperative' – the trend, strengthening through the political climate of this period, for learning to be justified only in terms of its employment applicability, thus challenging the liberal adult education tradition. It was also partly because many adult clients who sought or needed help did not regard themselves as being in the labour market, and partly too in order to establish a professional right to offer such help in the face of Careers Service claims to exclusive expertise.

During this period more attention was paid to access, progression and credit-accumulation issues for 'non-traditional' students. Access courses were developed to offer alternative routes for adults without A-levels to enter higher education; they also offered encouragement to students to review existing skills and broaden their interests. Credit Accumulation and Transfer Schemes made higher education more accessible to adult students who might face interruptions to their courses, and the Open College Networks extended the concept of credit accumulation to include non-vocational adult education. All these developments helped to highlight the guidance needs of adult students, and indeed the inspection framework proposed by the Office for Standards in Education for adult education following the 1992 Act included information and guidance (FEU, 1994a). Guidance was also recognised as important by some open-learning organisations: student counselling was integrated into the structure of the Open University from the outset; the Open Tech developed guidance strategies (Bailey, 1987); and the Open College developed training for staff in open-learning centres.

Although adult education has not traditionally used the term 'careers education', during the 1980s there was a proliferation of courses which were specifically aimed at helping adults to plan and develop their career. They were given impetus from European and other funding for courses to help women into the labour market (such as New Opportunities for Women programmes: e.g. Aird, 1980), and later from the Employment Department with short 2–5 day programmes to help unemployed adults with career planning and job-search skills (e.g. Weatherley, 1982; also Watts and Knasel, 1985). But 'return to work (or study)' courses and events, with a strong guidance component to help these and other groups of disadvantaged adults, had existed before that and continued to develop alongside the government-subsidised ones.

Training and guidance entitlements for adults who had been unemployed for more than six months were introduced through the 1980s. Employment Training, and later Training for Work programmes, incorporated a guidance element. Provision for the unemployed included colleges, but also adult education centres and others (Watts and Knasel, 1985). In some areas the guidance was provided by specialist guidance services, and in others by the trainers themselves.

This is a particularly difficult area of careers work. Young people and adults on government training schemes are under pressure to find any work, or to choose between an often limited range of available opportunities, and they are not usually in a position to reflect for long on which would suit them best. Funding for training and guidance is frequently linked directly or indirectly to 'positive outcomes' – the subsequent employment of clients or trainees (which neither can guarantee) – and this does not favour impartiality on the part of the staff.

Two government-funded schemes specifically for adult guidance were based on the credit or voucher model (Gateways to Learning and Skill Choice) and in both cases colleges were among the many agencies authorised to redeem vouchers. This is discussed in more detail in Chapter 10, but what is relevant here is the impact they had on guidance provision in the further education colleges involved. Some colleges developed guidance centres through funding under these voucher schemes; others incorporated the funding into their arrangements for helping people enquiring about 'mainstream' opportunities at the college, at the 'pre-entry' stage (see below). These arrangements were often as transient as the funding programmes on which they were based, but in some cases they led colleges to explore ways of charging 'clients', or prospective students, for guidance of that kind.

At the time of the transition to corporate status, and the introduction of new funding arrangements through the Further Education Funding Council (FEFC) in England, the Audit Commission gave guidance in further education a new prominence with the publication of a report which showed the high cost of people not completing courses (OFSTED/Audit Commission, 1993), and recommended that more attention be paid to the choice of course on entry to colleges. The FEFC in England introduced arrangements to link funding to the provision of assessment and guidance on entry to the course, during the course itself, and on exit (FEFC, 1993b). This in effect brought together elements of the educational guidance tradition derived from the adult guidance perspective with the careers education and guidance tradition derived from the 16–19-year-old perspective. We will now examine the FEFC arrangements against the range of current provision, looking first at pre-entry and entry guidance, and then at on-course and exit guidance.

6.4 CURRENT PROVISION

Entry and pre-entry guidance

The FEFC arrangements attached particular importance to guidance on entry to learning programmes. They also included audit procedures to ensure that colleges could demonstrate that students were satisfied with the entry guidance they had received (FEFC, 1994a; 1994b). Full individual guidance with all students on entry is however enormously time-consuming, and is disproportionately expensive in relation to the income that is attracted by part-time students in particular. Colleges have argued that full guidance may not be needed by many people registering for part-time or short courses. Accordingly, some colleges have developed active screening procedures, which check that potential students realise the implications of their choice.

The FEFC regards pre-entry guidance as the guidance needed before making a decision about which institution to apply to. Pre-entry guidance for young people coming straight from school is provided in part through the careers advice they receive there from teachers and careers officers, but college staff are also involved through their liaison work with schools. Colleges frequently see potential students in the spring before they want to enter the college, and then see them again for entry guidance at the beginning of the new academic year. For adults, pre-entry guidance could be provided by other agencies in the adult guidance network (see Chapter 10), or by a guidance unit in the college itself.

In practice, a large number of students probably arrive at the entry stage without any independent advice, so it is important that the entry stage be monitored carefully for impartiality. Training credit schemes give this added importance: young people may be sent by their employers for training which is not the most relevant for them, and they will not have another chance to spend their credit (Martin, 1993). The FEFC lays down clear guidelines on the kinds of activities to be covered at entry, including impartiality (FEFC, 1994a). But it will only authorise funding if this work leads to an enrolment, and this potentially undermines the impartiality of the guidance offered at this stage. It need not do so, however. In principle, only truly impartial guidance could prevent inappropriate enrolments and subsequent drop-out: a non-enrolment at the start could be seen as a financial advantage if it saved a subsequent drop-out. A more limited definition of impartiality in terms of even-handedness between courses within the same institution (Watts, 1994) is likely to be less effective in improving retention.

The distinctions between entry and on-course guidance are not sharply defined. Induction could reasonably be provided at entry, but in reality often takes place as part of the chosen course, and the Further Education Unit (FEU) put it at the next stage, in its 'on-programme' category, suggesting that responsibility for it lies with teaching staff (FEU, 1994b). Entry guidance in adult education centres may be offered by course tutors on enrolment evenings, or by the adult education centre head or assistant, either then or at some other time. Centre heads and assistants are increasingly seeking basic training in adult guidance. Where the course attracts FEFC funding, the students must sign learning agreements and a declaration that they have received guidance, but in this sector too it is possible to meet this requirement after a very cursory conversation with unqualified staff. Adult education centres are likely to run a mixture of courses which are funded with help from FEFC and courses which are not, and it is not necessarily apparent to the student which are which (fee levels will be set to reflect other factors besides the actual cost of the course). It is therefore possible that requirements for vocational (FEFC-funded) courses could raise expectations and procedures for all adult education courses, but this is unlikely to happen unless adult (and further) education staff are able to take these guidance requirements seriously.

On-course and exit guidance

On-course and exit guidance can include individual guidance interviews with Careers Service advisers or careers specialists in the college, the support of a tutor, work on records of achievement, and work experience, as well as a careers education curriculum. The boundaries with exit guidance are unclear: few courses in further education last more than two years, and help with career choices on exit should properly have started at the pre-entry stage, particularly where students are considering courses leading to specific vocational skills.

On-course guidance is an area where the differences between individual courses are the most significant, and where generalisations are of limited use. For example, work experience is a compulsory element of some vocational courses, but is less likely to form part of the programme for post-16-year-old students on academic courses than it is for comparable students who stay on at secondary schools (FEFC/OFSTED, 1994), partly because they spend less time in the institution outside the classes associated with their specific subjects. 'Pre-vocational' courses such as those leading to General National Vocational Qualifications provide a particularly hospitable environment for careers education, often including blocks of work experience and strong links with employers.

Some colleges, and some individual departments, run careers education modules alongside certain courses, and arrange programmes of speakers on different occupational areas, with work-shadowing opportunities and supported by open-learning careers education materials (FEDA, 1995a). Service-level agreements with the Careers Service can include support in the development of careers education programmes. There are interesting examples of colleges where individual careers advisers work with nominated departmental careers co-ordinators to plan careers education, but this is not universal, and other institutions report difficulties in making the most of this potential resource. This may be caused partly by the structural complexity of colleges, and difficulties of communication between departments, the cross-college careers co-ordinator, and senior management; or sometimes by sheer pressure of work on people who are not necessarily specialists (ibid).

The connection between careers guidance, counselling and the role of the tutor has been a key issue in shaping on-course guidance in colleges. Professional guidelines for guidance work in colleges have stressed the need for skilled one-to-one counselling (e.g. Hamblin, 1983). Influential reports from the FEU in the early 1980s emphasised the role of the tutor (Miller, 1982) in relation to the needs of students on pre-vocational courses in particular; they also advocated the concept of a 'personal guidance base' (Miller et al., 1983), attending to personal, educational and vocational decisions in an integrated way, with support from a team of qualified counsellors, youth workers, social workers and careers specialists.

The Further Education Development Agency identified three functions of tutoring in college: academic, personal, and acting as a link to specialist support (e.g. careers guidance, counselling or financial advice) (FEDA, 1995b). Its study found that while there was enthusiasm for the benefits of a well-organised and supported tutorial system, time constraints and work overload, as well as inconsistency of staff attitudes and performance, combined to make this difficult to deliver. Respondents also reported difficulties stemming from the needs of different student groups, including part-time students and some 'reluctant' students, and from lack of college support in the form of clear policy guidelines, as well as from more practical considerations such as inadequate accommodation. However, the need for tutorial support is growing as colleges become larger, and students follow increasingly individualised programmes of learning and assessment.

The continuity with records of achievement and action plans developed in schools is patchy, partly because of the disappointingly low numbers of students who take their record of achievement from school to college even for admission purposes (ED, 1994; FEFC/OFSTED, 1994). Colleges have introduced their own systems, partly prompted by the increased administrative complexity introduced by modularisation of courses (FEU, 1993b). However, the study by FEDA (1995b) showed that while a third of their sample undertook recording of achievement for students once in further education, this was seen by college tutors as ranking only fourth in importance, behind subject-related action planning, general feedback on progress, and monitoring attendance. Action planning is a more pressing concern: colleges must draw up 'learning agreements' for all students at the entry stage, and these can develop into individual action plans which can be maintained with the help of the tutor (FEU, 1994b) and provide a basis for ongoing exit guidance. This is more feasible on some kinds of course than others, though the Association of College Principals is committed to developing this area of work across the curriculum (ACP/ICG, 1994).

Records of achievement are potentially as useful for older students as for the 16–19 age-group, and they could form the basis for a career planning/careers education strategy for adult students in all sectors. FEDA (1995b) found that one further education college was accrediting personal and social education programmes through its local Open College Network. Colleges are putting 'tracking' arrangements in place to monitor student progression through further education, and these could be used to record the extent to which students make use of these various services.

The Careers Service tends to have a particularly important role in relation to exit guidance. We will examine this in detail as one of the issues to be covered in the next section.

6.5 ISSUES

Management and organisation

The report by FEFC/OFSTED (1994) on careers education and guidance for 16–19-year-olds found that colleges were much more likely than schools to have documented procedures on guidance, but commented that few schools or colleges had policy documents which set out clearly their underlying philosophy, objectives, or procedures for evaluation. Earlier, Stoney and Scott (1984) had found fewer policy statements in further education than in the (then) public-sector higher education institutions. A survey conducted by the Further Education Unit (1994b) commented on the relatively *high* proportion of colleges with written policies on guidance entitlement for full-time students: this possibly reflects a rapid response to the FEFC funding arrangements introduced that year. Colleges were much less likely to have policies covering guidance for part-time students; though even here, the figure was over 40 per cent of those surveyed.

The FEFC/OFSTED report commented that in larger tertiary and general further education colleges, the most effective practice occurred where there was a central services unit, often known as 'student services', which co-ordinated and managed the whole process from admissions through to students leaving the college. Student services can cover a wide range of activities. One survey by FEU (1993b) found that colleges included at least fifteen activities within student services management: action planning, admissions arrangements, accreditation of prior learning, core skills, educational and vocational guidance, examination entries, exit and progression arrangements, health education, induction programmes, initial advice and assessment, libraries and study centres, records of achievement, recreational and cultural activities, tutorial arrangements, and work-experience placements.

Even in colleges where the amalgamation of these different functions into a central service has gone furthest, this still involves collaboration with subject departments, and in some cases with individual departmental staff who take on a specialist or liaison role in relation to one or more of the functions. The rationalisation of all of the functions within a single management area has clear advantages, but may also make it difficult to give due attention to each. Student service managers who lack professional experience in one or more areas may not have enough staff to whom responsibility for these areas can be delegated.

The FEU (1994b) distinguished four different models for defining the balance between central and devolved student support:

1 *The integrated model*. This comprises a central admissions and guidance unit (CAGU) 'where specialist guidance is delivered through an admissions, guidance and information team providing an impartial, centralised service'. While this is an effective way of addressing pre-entry and entry guidance, it leaves responsibility for on-course and exit guidance unclear.
2 *Dispersed functions*. Here individual services exist for careers, counselling, information, or records of achievement; they may be responsible to the same line manager (perhaps through student services), but they operate independently. Responsibility for each of the four stages can be given to separate services, but co-ordination can be difficult.
3 *The informal approach*. This is more common in small colleges, and is based on personal contacts, with all staff, including senior management, playing a role. Restricted division of labour has the benefit of supporting a greater understanding of the interconnection between guidance, careers education and the curriculum, but lack of specialist expertise affects the quality of the work and can result in reduced impartiality.
4 *Tutor-led*. This is focused on the tutorial programme at the on-course stage, delivered through the completion of records of achievement. This gives a strong on-course emphasis, though the recording-of-achievement process is likely only to be available to full-time students. Otherwise the advantages and disadvantages are similar to the 'informal approach' system.

Quality assurance

Careers education and guidance in colleges in England is inspected by the FEFC, against guidelines which include reference to 'recruitment, guidance and support' (FEFC, 1993a). In spite of this, there is still variation in the nature and quality of provision which is acceptable to the FEFC. Early inspection reports of individual colleges described and graded activities very differently, partly as a result of the difficulties in prescribing precise standards for such a broad range of types of institution. Colleges are required to develop their own charters based on the national Charter for Further Education (DfE, 1993) and this includes an entitlement to guidance and support. It is unclear, however, whether the charter has raised expectations about careers education and guidance, or has contributed to their being met.

The report by FEFC/OFSTED (1994) noted that students were more aware of their responsibilities than their rights. Neither FEFC guidelines nor the charter contains any detail on this area of work. The Further Education Unit published numerous documents on ways of developing and enhancing all aspects of careers education and guidance in further education, and more specific reports on monitoring and developing quality overall (FEU, 1994b), but these were not linked to funding requirements in the way that FEFC requirements are, and could not be enforced. The FEFC/OFSTED report commented that relatively few colleges formally monitored the non-completion and failure rates of their students, although they were beginning to do this in response to the fact that funding arrangements are linked to completion rates; also, although colleges collected information about student destinations, they rarely analysed them in order to reflect on the effectiveness of their guidance.

The Careers Service

The 1973 Employment and Training Act gave the Careers Service (see Chapter 9) a responsibility to offer the same service to full-time students in further education as it offered to young people in schools, as well as to some part-time students – the latter group was clarified following the 1993 Trade Union Reform and Employment Rights Act as referring to part-time students involved in education 'commonly undergone by the persons in order to fit them for employment'. The actual provision is negotiated locally by the local careers service with each college, and can include (adapted from ED, 1993):

1   Ensuring that the curriculum is informed by an understanding of the world of work.
2   Developing and implementing careers education and guidance policies.
3   Developing and maintaining careers information resources.
4   Ensuring that institution-based staff are aware of the requirements of various education, training and employment routes.
5   Promoting education–business partnerships and similar initiatives.
6   Collecting, disseminating and analysing destinations data for future planning.

This work was spelled out in the 1993 Act and in the *Advice and Guidance to Providers* (ED, 1993), and monitored through the Careers Service inspection arrangements (with periodic reports such as ED, 1994). Some of the careers services inherited arrangements where staff had been seconded to work in colleges; some had set up separate careers offices on college premises; and some had distributed responsibility for further education institutions between careers officers in each area (in some cases, careers officers had mixed workloads of one college and several schools). The 1993 Act required that these arrangements should be negotiated and agreed within service-level agreements.

Careers services' links with colleges have never been so strong as those with schools. A survey of Careers Service work in schools and colleges carried out in 1993 showed that colleges were less likely than schools to have a written policy on careers education and guidance, and that careers services were less likely to have a written statement on their arrangements with colleges. Careers services in their work with colleges were also less likely than in schools to offer help with first-destination information, to involve parents, to arrange work experience, to be involved in education–business partnerships, and to help with careers conventions (ED, 1994).

Nonetheless, the proposals published in *Working Together for a Better Future* (DES/ED/WO, 1987), and updated in *Better Choices* (ED/DfE, 1994), underlined the importance of close links between the careers services and colleges as well as schools. Government White Papers published in 1994 and 1995 sought to strengthen such links (DTI, 1994; 1995).

The Careers Service has not had any statutory links with adult education, although some careers services have offered outreach support to courses helping adults to return to education or work.

Training and staff development

The staff development implications of each of the aspects of careers work discussed in this chapter are considerable, and FEFC/OFSTED (1994) called for a continuing programme of in-service training. Some colleges have used guidance training and accreditation designed for guidance work with adults (Hawthorn and Wood, 1988); some college staff have qualifications designed for careers education and guidance work in schools; some staff working as careers specialists have previously worked as careers officers and hold a Diploma in Careers Guidance. The FEDA study on tutoring found that only a small proportion of the colleges was providing accreditation for tutors, through a range of further education tutor qualifications, National Vocational Qualifications for training, and a specialist qualification for work in adult basic education (FEDA, 1995b). Some colleges provide open-learning materials in tutoring skills in the form of tutorial handbooks for staff. Although qualifications have been uncertain in the past, a system of National Vocational Qualifications for advice, guidance, counselling and psychotherapy, covering the full range of specialist activities within the student services spectrum, is being put in place at the time of writing which is likely to transform the accreditation and training of guidance staff in colleges. Government funding programmes to support in-service training links between college staff and their careers services, introduced in 1995, is likely to accelerate this development. *Better Choices* (ED/DfE, 1994) advocated that management training for college principals should include careers education and guidance. Staff development in general is discussed in more detail in Chapter 16.

6.6 CONCLUSION

Many of the questions surrounding careers work in further and adult education have parallels both in school-based provision and in higher education: how to ensure that the students understand the career implications of their educational choices; how to provide a personal service to individuals at a time of increases in student numbers and staff workloads; and how to determine the optimum division of labour, and collaboration, between guidance specialists, tutors and academic staff. Successive legislation and policy directives have highlighted the needs of students in both sectors, and more resources are now available for guidance provision. But the rapidity of growth and change, particularly in further education, has made it difficult for guidance providers to keep pace; at the same time, students, for a variety of reasons, are not making the fullest use of what is available. Within education it is possibly the area of careers work in greatest flux, closest both to changes in the labour market, and to government strategies to develop this market. These uncertainties are likely to continue to affect both the nature and the content of the work itself.

REFERENCES

Advisory Council for Adult and Continuing Education (1979) *Links to Learning*, Leicester: ACACE.

Aird, E. (1980) 'The Place of Counselling in "New Opportunities for Women" Courses', *British Journal of Guidance and Counselling* 8(1): 92–98.

Association of College Principals/Institute of Careers Guidance (1994) *Working Together in the New Era*, Stockport: ACP/ICG.

Bailey, D. (1987) 'Open Learning and Guidance', *British Journal of Guidance and Counselling* 15(3): 237–56.

Cantor, L. M. and Roberts, I. F. (1986) *Further Education Today: a Critical Review*, London: Routledge & Kegan Paul.

Department for Education (1993) *Further Choice and Quality: the Charter for Further Education*, London: DfE.

Department of Education and Science/Employment Department/Welsh Office (1987) *Working Together for a Better Future*, London: DES/ED/WO.

Department of Trade and Industry (1994) *Helping Business to Win*, London: HMSO.

Department of Trade and Industry (1995) *Forging Ahead*, London: HMSO.

Edwards, R. (1989) *Separating Educational and Vocational Guidance*, Occasional Publication No. 13, Canterbury: National Association for Educational Guidance for Adults.

Employment Department (1993) *Requirements and Guidance for Providers*, Sheffield: ED.

Employment Department (1994) *The Work of the Careers Service in Schools and Colleges*, Sheffield: ED.

Employment Department/Department for Education (1994) *Better Choices*, London: ED/DfE.

Further Education Development Agency (1995a) *College Careers Education and Guidance: Developing a Service*, London: FEDA (mimeo).

Further Education Development Agency (1995b) *Developing Effective Tutoring Systems*, London: FEDA (mimeo).

Further Education Funding Council (1993a) *Assessing Achievement*, Circular 93/28, Coventry: FEFC.

Further Education Funding Council (1993b) *Recurrent Funding for 1994–95: Guidance to Institutions*, Circular 93/39, Coventry: FEFC.

Further Education Funding Council (1994a) *Recurrent Funding Methodology: Audit Evidence for Entry Units*, Circular 94/16, Coventry: FEFC.

Further Education Funding Council (1994b) *Modified Audit Evidence for Entry Units for 1994–95*, Circular 94/23, Coventry: FEFC.

Further Education Funding Council/Office for Standards in Education (1994) *16 to 19 Guidance*, Coventry: FEFC.

Further Education Unit (1993a) *Paying their Way: the Experiences of Adult Learners in Vocational Education and Training in FE Colleges*, London: FEU.

Further Education Unit (1993b) *Learning Support Services in Further Education*, London: FEU.

Further Education Unit (1994a) *Adequate Provision for Adult Learners – a Framework*, London: FEU.

Further Education Unit (1994b) *Managing the Delivery of Guidance in Colleges*, London: FEU.

Hall, V. (1990) *Maintained Further Education in the United Kingdom*, Bristol: Further Education Staff College.

Hamblin, D. (1983) *Guidance 16–19*, Oxford: Blackwell.

Hawthorn, R. and Wood, R. (1988) *Training Issues in Educational Guidance for Adults*, Leicester: Unit for the Development of Adult Continuing Education.

Legge, D. (1982) *The Education of Adults in Britain*, Milton Keynes: Open University Press.

Marks, H. (1975) 'Careers Guidance in Further Education', *Careers Bulletin*, Spring, 36–40.

Martin, L. (1993) 'Training Credits', in Tomlinson, H. (ed.) *Education and Training 14–19*, Harlow: Longman.

Miller, J. (1982) *Tutoring*, London: Further Education Unit.

Miller, J., Taylor, B. and Watts, A. G. (1983) *Towards a Personal Guidance Base*, London: Further Education Unit.

Office for Standards in Education/Audit Commission (1993) *Unfinished Business*, London: OFSTED/Audit Commission.

Standing Conference of Associations for Guidance in Educational Settings (1992) 'Statement of Principles and Definitions', in Ball, C. (ed.) *Guidance Matters*, London: Royal Society of Arts.

Stoney, S. M. and Scott, V. M. (1984) *Careers Guidance in Colleges and Polytechnics*, Windsor: NFER–Nelson.

Unit for the Development of Adult Continuing Education (1986) *The Challenge of Change*, Leicester: National Institute of Adult Continuing Education.

Watts, A. G. (1994) *Guidance in Further Education*, CRAC/NICEC Conference Briefing, Cambridge: Careers Research and Advisory Centre.

Watts, A. G. and Knasel, E. G. (1985) *Adult Unemployment and the Curriculum*, London: Further Education Unit.

Weatherley, M. J. (1982) 'Counselling in Career Self-Management Courses for the Mature Executive', *British Journal of Guidance and Counselling* 10(1): 88–96.

Chapter 7

Careers work in higher education

A. G. Watts

7.1 INTRODUCTION

In Britain, careers services within higher education are the strongest example of specialist careers guidance services within educational institutions. In schools, and in further and adult education, careers education and guidance tends to be more closely linked to teaching roles: any specialist services are accordingly likely to be less strongly 'bounded'. In higher education, on the other hand, careers guidance has tended to be separated more markedly from the teaching process.

This is linked to the relative size of higher education institutions, which provides sufficient critical mass to justify their own specialist services (accordingly – unlike most students in the other sectors – higher education students are explicitly excluded from the statutory Careers Service examined in Chapter 9). It is also linked to the non-vocational tradition within British higher education. There is, for example, much more occupational flexibility on graduation than elsewhere in Europe. Around half of graduate 'current vacancies' are for students from any discipline, and this proportion rose during the 1980s (Bee and Dolton, 1990). There is much less rigid 'tracking' than in other European countries, where there tends to be a more widespread assumption that university students have already committed themselves to certain occupational areas by the nature of the courses they have chosen. The need for separate help outside course structures is accordingly more acute.

At the same time, higher education institutions in Britain have tended to assume stronger *in loco parentis* responsibilities than in other European countries. This has been linked to their residential tradition, supported by a grants structure which has permitted students readily to go to institutions away from their homes. Support structures to help students with their vocational as well as their personal and educational problems have grown naturally out of this tradition.

7.2 ORIGINS

The most important and authoritative report on the role of careers services in higher education was the Heyworth Report produced under the auspices of the University Grants Committee (1964). Published shortly after the influential report of the Robbins Committee (1963) on higher education, it was supported by extensive surveys of students, employers and universities. It provides a valuable account of the origins of the services, as well as a well-researched snapshot of their nature and operations in the early 1960s, against which our discussion of their subsequent development can be set.

The Heyworth Report noted that up to the end of the nineteenth century, most university graduates – which at that time meant almost exclusively men from Oxford and Cambridge – became parsons, schoolmasters or civil servants. A few went into politics or law or medicine. In general, it was considered eccentric and ungentlemanly for a university man to go into business. There was no need for careers services, because the older universities were part of a social pattern in which dons, undergraduates and parents all knew what careers were approachable from the university and how to get into them.

The origins of university appointments boards – as they were still called in the mid-1960s – were traced by the Heyworth Report to the foundation in Oxford around 1892 of an intercollegiate committee set up to pool dons' patronage in the public and grammar schools. It gradually extended its activities to the civil service and, around 1904, to industry. By 1914 appointments services had been set up at Cambridge and five other universities; a further nine followed between the two World Wars; and by the mid-1950s all universities had such a service.

The activities of university appointments boards as defined by the Heyworth Report were threefold: advisory *interviews*; the provision of *information* about careers, employers and jobs; and *placement* activities, including notifying vacancies to students, and arranging selection interviews between students and employers. Most of the professional staff had been 'in business, in teaching, or in some other activity closely related to that on which they were liable to be asked to give advice' (ibid., p. 10). The 'cornerstone' of the service was the interview: pressures of numbers at particular times of the year meant that there were often long waiting lists for such interviews. While the professional staff tended to stress the advisory side of their role, few had any training for it. For many students, job-finding was the service's only function of any consequence: 'the service exists, so far as many students can see, solely to tell them what vacancies there are and how to get in touch with those who offer them' (ibid., p. 44). Of particular interest in this respect were the 'circuses' of selection interviews arranged with employers on the university campus, normally in the spring term: what subsequently became familiarly known as the 'milk round'.

The Heyworth Report recommended that the advisory side of the services needed strengthening, through increased staffing. It also recommended that there should be 'more space, since much of the work is of a confidential and private nature and therefore requires a fairly large number of separate rooms, so that conversations can be carried on without any likelihood of being overheard' (ibid., p. 76). Among its other proposals was setting up a central services unit for the universities as a whole to carry out functions (for example, providing a register of employers) which involved individual services in unnecessary duplication of effort. In short, the report was concerned with reinforcing the existing model of university appointments boards rather than moving towards any new model.

7.3 FROM APPOINTMENTS BOARDS TO CAREERS SERVICES

Since 1964, the number of universities has expanded considerably, with the foundation of the new universities in the 1960s and the elevation to university status of the colleges of advanced technology in 1965 and of the polytechnics in 1992. In 1960/61 there were 23 universities and around 92,000 full-time first-degree students in the UK (UGC, 1967); by 1994/95 these figures had risen to 86 and around 829,700 respectively (as well as 162,700 part-time students) (HESA, 1995). This expansion has meant that students have entered higher education from more varied social backgrounds; it has also meant that graduates have moved into much wider areas of the labour market than before. Both of these factors placed severe strains on the 'appointments' model. Moreover, many of the newly elevated universities and colleges had very different cultures from the traditional universities. In particular, many had strong vocational traditions, with guidance being regarded either as unnecessary or as part of teaching responsibilities. Their careers services tended to be of more recent origin, and less well resourced (Kirkland and Jepson, 1983; Kirkland, 1988).

Partly as a result of the interaction of these traditions and cultures, considerable changes have taken place since the Heyworth Report. The old appointments boards have been transformed, both in function and in title, into careers services. This transformation has involved changes in their relationships with teaching departments, and in their institutional role. It has also involved changes in their training and professional structures. These matters will be considered later in this chapter. First, though, we will examine the three sequential changes in their core guidance activities which characterised the transformation: the impact of *counselling*, the growth of *careers education*, and the move towards an *open-access* style of delivery.

The impact of counselling

The rise of the counselling movement in Britain in the 1960s – strongly influenced, particularly in its early stages, by the USA – had a major impact on education in general, including higher education (Daws, 1976). The first counselling service to be established in a British university was set up as an 'appointments and counselling service' at Keele in 1963. While most of the university counselling services established subsequently were structured separately from careers services (see Mackintosh, 1974; Breakwell, 1987), the Keele service celebrated the relationship between its two functions. The 'appointments' work provided a respectable cover to any students who felt that going to 'counselling' implied some personal stigma. At the same time, the 'counselling' work meant that vocational decision-making came to be viewed not as a separate entity but as a vital strand in the student's overall personal development. Moreover, the counselling skills of the staff – based significantly but not exclusively on Rogerian principles (see Chapter 11) – meant that they had more skilled help to offer to students who were confused and uncertain about their futures. The often-heard criticism in other universities that appointments services provided effective assistance to those who had already decided what they wanted to do, but little to those who had not, ceased to be valid (Newsome *et al.*, 1973).

The Keele model was emulated organisationally only by a few polytechnics. It had, however, a considerable influence on the philosophy of careers services. Some staff in other institutions began to adopt similar approaches. In the mid-1970s the Keele team began to run counselling courses for groups of careers staff in other institutions, which changed the style in which their interviews were conducted. These courses also led to the establishment of more professional training structures (Thorne, 1985) (see Section 7.6 below). While careers staff continued to conduct careers interviews in very different ways, and most remained reluctant to become too involved in counselling related to students' deeper personal issues, many began to make more use of counselling techniques in their work. There also emerged a widespread recognition that offering information and advice to the decided was not enough: that guidance was an equally and perhaps more important aspect of the service than placement (Kirkland, 1988).

The growth of careers education

Following hard on the heels of the counselling movement was the emergence in higher education of the concept of careers education (Watts, 1977). The juxtaposition of the two was not accidental. Counselling was concerned with facilitating the process of decision-making, and helping students to take responsibility for the decisions that emerged, rather than being passively dependent on the advice of experts. Counselling on its own could however be a very lengthy and hence expensive way of achieving this goal. For students to make decisions wisely, they needed a conceptual vocabulary, a range of experiences, and a set of decision-making skills, to draw upon. Developmental theories of careers (see Chapter 2) suggested that such concepts, experiences and skills developed to some extent in the normal process of social maturation. Careers education was based on the premise that such development could be facilitated and, perhaps, accelerated by programmes of deliberate intervention, designed on a group basis (see Chapter 12).

The growth of careers education was thus in part theory-driven, and in part resource-driven. It offered a way of working which was closely attuned to the emerging redefinition of the role of careers services, influenced by the counselling movement. It also offered a strategy which recognised the limitations of the services' resources and sought to use these resources to optimum effect. Working more with groups rather than with individuals offered possibilities for more student time 'on task' for each unit of careers adviser time. There were also potential benefits to be harnessed from the interaction between the students themselves.

The nature of the services developed varied considerably. At the most cynical level, 'careers education' could be used as a new label for the careers talks which had been a long-standing element of most careers programmes (they were mentioned by the Heyworth Report, which disparagingly commented that they were 'not very highly regarded' [UGC, 1964, p. 44]). Such talks might cover particular occupations or more general themes such as self-presentation. But they were one-off informational events, with no developmental intent.

An analysis of more elaborate careers education programmes in higher education, drawing on American as well as British examples, distinguished three main forms: courses leading to credit; courses not leading to credit; and intensive experiences (Watts, 1977). At the time, a few examples of courses leading to credit were reported, mainly in the (then) polytechnics, as well as more widespread examples of intensive experiences, ranging from short life-planning workshops to five-day courses making heavy use of simulations and business games. No courses leading to credit were recorded, but Ross (1988) later reported the development of such a course within a modular degree scheme, and further examples have since been developed, including the Open University's influential module on Personal and Career Development.

Careers education programmes within higher education continued to grow into the 1980s. Kirkland and Jepson (1983) asked heads of careers services whether they knew of any cases in which courses in their institution included some element of specific careers education: 44 per cent of universities, 75 per cent of polytechnics, and 66 per cent of colleges replied 'yes'. When asked whether in their view the degree courses at their institution should include more careers education, around three-quarters in each sector were in favour. It should be noted that these questions were not confined to courses in which the careers service was actively involved (see Section 7.4 below). When individual advisers were asked what proportion of their own time was spent lecturing on careers, only 22 per cent (8 per cent in universities, 39 per cent in polytechnics, and 44 per cent in colleges) gave figures of over 5 per cent.

While careers education programmes *per se* thus remained a relatively limited feature of careers services, they started to wean the services from the heavy focus on formal individual interviewing which had hitherto characterised their work. They thus helped to pave the way for the third aspect of the transition from the old appointments board model: the move to an open-access approach.

Towards an open-access approach

In the 1980s many careers services reviewed their work patterns. They recognised that the traditional hour-long interview was highly labour-intensive, and not always the most effective way of using their professional resources. They realised in particular that many students' information needs might be met more effectively by upgrading the services' information resources and making use of computer technology.

The result was, in some services, a radical redesign both of work patterns and of work spaces. Instead of the one-to-one interview being seen as the core activity, with a careers library available as a supportive resource, an open-access information room was now viewed as the heart of the service. Students were able to come in when they wished, to browse through a wide range of information files, videos and other materials, and to have access to personal help not only from upgraded information staff but also from careers advisers who were available on a rota 'surgery' basis for brief informal interviews. These were designed partly to respond to 'quick queries', and partly to diagnose students' guidance needs and signpost them to other services where these needs might be met. Such services might include not only the resources in the information room but also group sessions, work-experience opportunities, and the like. The traditional hour-long interview was then available for those students who needed intensive personal help.

This shift of focus was greatly strengthened by the growing use of computer-aided guidance systems (see Chapter 15). A number of limited systems had been introduced in higher education from the 1970s. The most notable of these was GRADSCOPE, a matching system available first on a batch-processing and subsequently on an interactive basis (Wilson, 1980; Hesketh *et al.*, 1987). Then in the 1980s, following a feasibility study by Pierce-Price (1982), a major learning system was developed: PROSPECT (HE). It was designed to be *comprehensive*, including as many as possible of the main components of the careers guidance process; it was also to be capable of use on a *stand-alone* basis, without any need for support, though it was expected to be more effective when fully integrated with the other facilities offered by careers services (Watts *et al.*, 1991). The active involvement of careers services in its development significantly facilitated the move towards a more open-access approach (Sampson and Watts, 1992). Despite many political obstacles, PROSPECT (HE) was by 1992 being used extensively in most higher education institutions (Watts, 1993).

The organisational changes in careers services were often reflected in physical changes. Traditionally, many services had comprised a small reception area leading to a number of separate rooms occupied by individual careers advisers, with a further room for the careers library. Now, large open spaces were created, in which a wide range of resources could be attractively presented and workspaces for individual students provided. There were still rooms for individual one-to-one interviews, but these were less prominent.

The extent of the move towards an open-access approach has varied considerably. In some institutions, progress has been limited by constraints on physical changes. In some cases, the one-to-one interview has remained a strong feature of the service; in others, it is now barely advertised, and offered only in exceptional circumstances (see e.g. Watts *et al.*, 1989). In general, though, most services have been touched by the change to some extent. It is part of a wider European trend in which the concept of an expert guidance specialist working with individual clients in a contextual vacuum is replaced, or at least supplemented, by a more diffuse approach in which a more varied range of interventions is used, with a greater emphasis on the individual as an active agent rather than a passive recipient within the guidance process (Watts *et al.*, 1988; see Chapter 20).

Through these changes, the level of student contact with the work of careers services has been maintained and even increased despite the massive growth of student numbers. Under the old appointments board model, students using the services were required to 'register'. The Heyworth Report found that the number of students doing so varied considerably from university to university, but that the national proportion of registrants was 66 per cent (UGC, 1964). Kirkland's (1988) survey of nine institutions found that 84 per cent of respondents had had some contact with the service at their institution; 77 per cent acknowledged, either strongly or with reservations, that they were satisfied with the work of advisers; and only 29 per cent found it difficult to get enough individual attention. Whether the latter figure can be kept as low despite the growing pressures on resources is an issue that needs to be monitored on a regular basis.

7.4 RELATIONSHIPS WITH TEACHING DEPARTMENTS

Alongside the work of careers services, teaching departments have always considered themselves as having some responsibilities in relation to their students' career planning. In part, this is linked to the *in loco parentis* tradition noted in Section 7.1. Most institutions have tutorial systems, and these are often based in teaching departments. In a large survey of university teachers, Williams *et al.* (1974, p. 490) found that 84 per cent thought it part of their job to give guidance on career choice (this probably says more about what they saw as being possible expectations of their role than about delivery intentions). Moreover, departments running vocational courses have tended to provide information on related job opportunities and to put students in touch with employers with whom they have ongoing links.

In both of these respects – guidance and placement – there has therefore been some overlapping of roles between careers services and teaching departments. The emergence of careers education noted in Section 7.3 has provided a third area of overlap where the boundaries are even less clear. Although, as we have seen, many careers services have now set up careers education programmes, they have not been resourced to provide such programmes on any significant scale: many students have been untouched by them, and few students have had access to more than two or three short sessions. Moreover, the delivery of the mainstream curriculum is the core responsibility of teaching departments. Although the notion of careers education may be less familiar to such departments, their claims on it, and the scale of their potential contribution to it, are in principle much greater (Watts and Hawthorn, 1992).

In practice, the extent of role overlap has tended to vary between different types of course (ibid.):

1 In *vocational* courses such as medicine and architecture – which are linked to a specific occupational role, are regarded as essential to that role, and are viewed as completing occupational training for the role – the department tends to regard careers education and individual guidance as being irrelevant, but job placement and more specific professional guidance as being its own responsibility; only students who decide to change vocational direction – usually regarded by the department as 'deviants' or 'drop-outs' – are referred to the careers service.

2 In *semi-vocational* courses such as chemistry and psychology – where the course leads to a wide range of occupational fields, but with the expectation that it will be regarded as essential or desirable for entry to those fields, and as providing at least a relevant base for occupational training – the department is more likely to regard careers education, individual guidance and job placement as being a *shared* responsibility with the careers service.

3 In *non-vocational* courses such as English and history – where it is common for students to enter a wide range of occupational fields, to which the content of their courses is irrelevant – the department tends to view careers education, individual guidance and job placement as being the *sole* responsibility of the careers service.

In the late 1980s, however, a number of development programmes were set up which had the effect of encouraging some non-vocational courses to view themselves as 'semi-vocational' in terms of skills, if not of knowledge. The Pegasus programme (e.g. Findlay *et al.*, 1987), the Education for Capability programme (Stephenson and Weil, 1992) and the much larger Enterprise in Higher Education (EHE) programme (Macnair, 1990; Watts and Hawthorn, 1992) were all concerned with advancing, under different titles, the concept of 'personal transferable skills': the notion that, alongside their knowledge components, higher education courses can develop generic intellectual, problem-solving, communication, teamwork, inter-personal and other skills, and that it is from the transferability of such skills that the general employment value of degrees largely stems.

Careers services, it should be noted, played an important role in the development of the concept of 'personal transferable skills'. In particular, they were important *message-bearers* about the importance which employers attached to such skills. They also increasingly incorporated into their guidance programmes elements designed to help students to *identify* their skills and the forms of employment to which they were transferable. A few services also developed programmes designed to *develop* particular skills. But they were not equipped to do this latter except on a limited residual basis. The EHE and other programmes in effect allocated this task primarily to teaching departments.

The concepts of personal transferable skills and of careers education are by no means coterminous, but they overlap considerably: the decision-making and transition skills which careers education is concerned with developing are themselves personal transferable skills; self-awareness and opportunity awareness can help students to identify respectively their skills and the arenas to which they are transferable. The concept of personal transferable skills has accordingly been a powerful vehicle for developing careers education – in practice if not always in name – in teaching departments within higher education. Relevant initiatives have included profiling systems, support for work-experience programmes as vocational exploration, lectures or workshops on particular aspects of careers education, and even – in a few cases – more comprehensive careers education courses (Watts and Hawthorn, 1992; see also Ball and Butcher, 1993).

These initiatives have posed new challenges to careers services in developing closer relationships with teaching departments. Traditionally, such links have tended to be limited. Some services have set up liaison networks with particular individuals in various departments, but these have often been restricted to narrow informational tasks. Where, however, teaching departments have developed a significant role in the delivery of careers education, new possibilities for partnership have emerged. Possible roles for the careers service have included those of *contributor*, responding to departmental requests for particular contributions; of *consultant*, assisting the department in planning the activities; and/or of *partner*, organising jointly planned events, possibly including co-tutoring. Such forms of partnership have been facilitated by the Higher Education Funding Council's teaching quality assessments, which have raised awareness of the interrelationship of teaching, the development of personal transferable skills, and the role of careers services; and by the Higher Education Quality Council's quality-assurance framework for guidance and learner support in higher education, which included attention to career planning as part of the on-programme phase (HEQC, 1995).

7.5 THE INSTITUTIONAL ROLE OF CAREERS SERVICES

The diversity of roles played by careers services raises questions about where they should be located organisationally within higher education institutions. Traditionally, they tended to be separated from mainstream organisational structures, particularly within institutions with mainly non-vocational (or semi-vocational) courses. Their organisational separation enabled them to respond to the career-development needs of individual students without challenging the non-vocational (sometimes, indeed, anti-vocational) culture of the institutions themselves. The curriculum-development programmes based around the concept of personal transferable skills (see Section 7.4 above), however, have made their own challenge to this culture, and have raised new questions about the careers service's role. At the same time, the funding pressures on higher education institutions have meant that the institutional value of all their activities have begun to be scrutinised more closely.

As a result of these and other factors, steps have in some cases been taken to align careers services with other activities within particular institutions. At least three forms of such alignment can be distinguished.

The first is to align the careers service to other *student* services. In some cases this has involved integration, to some extent on the Keele model (see Section 7.3) but also including welfare services, accommodation services, and the like: this model has been followed in a number of former polytechnics (Kirkland, 1988). It tends to identify the careers service as essentially a service to individual students, outside the academic process.

A second option is to align the careers service to other *academic* services, and to view an important part of its role as being to support the work of teaching departments. This may include partnerships in the delivery of careers education, as outlined in Section 7.4. It may also mean involvement in course planning, on the basis of feeding back data on the first destination of students, and students' and employers' perceptions of the employment value of the course provision. This option has tended to be less well-developed than the others, though it has begun to attract growing interest (Watts and Hawthorn, 1992). Moves have been made in a number of institutions to establish closer links between careers services and other services concerned with educational guidance and learner support, including access and credit accumulation/transfer (Herrington and Rivis, 1994).

The third option is to align the careers service to other *marketing* services within the institution. The then director of the Cambridge University Careers Service, Kirkman (1982), suggested that the service should be viewed by institutions as their 'marketing department': 'careers advisers need to keep themselves fully informed about what the market requires, to ensure the information is fed back to their institutions, and to encourage the students and graduates with whom they are dealing to appreciate these requirements and to fit themselves to fulfil them'. In at least one university, the careers service was made part of the University Relations Service, a unit concerned with the university's external relations (Watts *et al.*, 1989). The notion of taking fuller institutional advantage of the careers service's employer links has been explored elsewhere as well. In some cases, too, the notion of marketing has been extended to align careers services to marketing the institutions to potential students – including schools liaison work, access initiatives for non-traditional students, and overseas recruitment operations – and to maintaining links with alumni.

These three options are not mutually exclusive, but they emphasise different aspects of the careers service's role. They also pose different problems in terms of reconciling the careers service's institutional role with its guidance role. The marketing option, in particular, can pose difficulties in this respect. In relation to access activities, for example, Wallis (1990) has pointed out that 'our professional objectivity and impartiality can be compromised if our institutions insist ... that intending students are actually encouraged to register for our own courses rather than more suitable ones elsewhere'. Marketing roles in relation to employers, too, can raise questions about who is the primary client: the student, the institution, or the employer.

In practice, most careers services view the students as their primary client. This is partly because they recognise that unless they provide an effective service to students – which in turn requires them to command students' trust and confidence – they are unlikely to be able to serve the interests of their other potential clients. At the same time, in order to serve the interests of students, they need to command the support and involvement of employers. To do this, they need to regard employers as clients too, and to provide them with an effective service. To a significant extent, the interests of students and employers are sufficiently congruent for this to pose no problems. At times, however, tensions may emerge: for example, employers are interested in selecting the 'best' students, whereas student interests require services to be concerned with the needs of *all* their students. At these tension points, services usually affirm that the interests of employers are secondary (Watts and Sampson, 1989).

The argument becomes more complex if the issue of direct charging is introduced. For example, the restrictions on higher education resources in the 1980s and early 1990s led to increasing pressure to exert charges for services to employers (e.g. Steptoe, 1990). This gave rise to concerns that if extended significantly, employers might no longer be content to accept the position of secondary clients: they would expect full value for their money. This might pose much greater difficulties to services in reconciling the interests of students and employers, especially if the employer charges were used to reduce the core funding provided by the institution. Some institutions, for example, rejected fee-charging altogether on the grounds that it might discourage employers from visiting their institution, to the disadvantage of their students (HMI, 1990) (there was indeed evidence that it had this effect in at least one institution [Harris, 1992]). It is worth noting that the stance of the Heyworth Report on this issue had been unequivocal: 'we think that the Board's primary responsibility is to the students and that, therefore, it is undesirable that Boards should be in any way financially dependent on employers' (UGC, 1964, p. 8). In the straitened financial climate of the 1980s and early 1990s, however, many institutions felt that they could not afford to take such a clearly principled position. Indeed, some university administrators went so far as to discuss the possibility of making careers services completely independent of public funding, instead being financed by charging employers for the graduates they recruited (*Financial Times*, 8 July 1989). This was fiercely resisted by services and employers alike on the grounds that it would mean careers services becoming no more than employment agencies.

If, however, institutions were to continue to fund careers services, there was increasing pressure for the benefits of such services to be argued in terms not only of private benefits to individual students but also of organisational benefits to the institutions themselves. Where the goals of the institution gave priority to serving the interests of students, including their career interests, no conflict of interest with a student-centred orientation need arise. Indeed, the careers service could be viewed as a crucial support to the institution as a whole in achieving its goals. Some services accordingly sought to become closely involved in strategic planning within their institutions, to ensure that there was as much congruence as possible between institutional goals and the service's goals (Watts and Sampson, 1989); a few successfully built strong roles within their institutions' policy structures. The use by the Government of first-employment destinations as a 'performance indicator' for higher education institutions (see Cave *et al.*, 1988), though open to question in terms of its validity and appropriateness, helped to focus institutions' attention on employability as a goal.

Interviews with policy-makers in institutions of higher education in the early 1990s indicated two different views of the institution's responsibility for helping students with their career decisions and transitions. One was that such help was an integral part of the *core offer* made to students: it helped to sustain a virtuous circle in which the student experience was enhanced by addressing the vocational aspirations which drove or underpinned most students' motivations for entering higher education, thereby increasing the chances that these aspirations would be met, which in turn provided evidence of enhanced employability that helped with the recruitment of new students. The other was that such help was an *additional service* which was open to review in terms of its own specific costs and benefits. Where this help was regarded as being solely a careers service responsibility, it was more likely to be seen in the latter terms. Where, however, it was also regarded as being partly the role of teaching departments, with the careers service available as a support and specialist resource to such departments, it was more likely to be viewed as part of the core offer (Watts and Hawthorn, 1992).

The balance of allegiances which a careers service has to maintain is delicate and intricate. Their source of 'power' within their institution (Pfeffer, 1981) is based largely on their responsiveness to students' demands and their links with employers. In institutions which wish to restrict the links between these perspectives and the teaching process, the careers service can be a means of containing their influence: in such cases it will tend to be marginal organisationally and more open to questioning as an additional service. On the other hand, in institutions which are concerned to develop strong interaction between the content of courses, the personal development of students, and their future careers, the careers service is likely to be more central organisationally, with more scope for influence – but also more open to questioning on the grounds that its functions need to be integrated into the institution as a whole.

7.6 TRAINING AND PROFESSIONAL DEVELOPMENT

As a counter-balance to the institutional pressures on careers services, there has also been a significant strengthening of the professional identity of careers advisers. Gouldner (1957/58) distinguished between 'locals' who are primarily concerned with institutional loyalties, and 'cosmopolitans' whose primary reference group is their professional colleagues in different organisations. Since the Heyworth Report, there has been a significant growth of 'cosmopolitan' orientations within careers services in higher education.

The first significant steps to establish operational links between university appointments boards was the establishment of a Statistics Committee in 1955 to pool information on first destinations of graduates and to make them available nationally. This provided a base for the services not only to collaborate but also to achieve media prominence and policy influence. In 1967 the Standing Conference of University Appointments Services (SCUAS) was created, which made it possible for the services to look at their work as a whole on a national basis. A decade later, in 1977, SCUAS transmuted itself into the Association of Graduate Careers Advisory Services (AGCAS), with four primary objectives: to encourage and facilitate the exchange of views and information; to foster and co-ordinate investigations and promote improvements in services; to encourage training in the skills and techniques appropriate to the work of its members; and to express a collaborative viewpoint. Meanwhile, in 1972 the Committee of Vice-Chancellors and Principals belatedly acted upon the recommendation of the Heyworth Report to set up a Central Services Unit to provide a specialist resource for common tasks such as the collection of vacancy and statistical information (Scott, 1993; Thorne, 1985).

The patterns of recruitment of careers advisers have changed considerably over this period, merging two very different traditions. The pattern of the old university appointments boards was, as we have seen, to recruit people with experience in the fields of work on which they were advising. This tradition has continued to some extent: Kirkland and Jepson (1983) found that 69 per cent of advisers had previously worked in the private sector (presumably in industry or commerce). Careers staff in the former polytechnics, on the other hand, had often been trained as Local Education Authority careers officers (the polytechnics were under the control of LEAs, and many of them had originally been serviced by the LEA Careers Service). This background has become increasingly common among higher education careers advisers. Kidd *et al.* (1993) found that 51 per cent of such advisers had previously worked as an LEA careers officer.

These backgrounds are not mutually exclusive, of course. Nonetheless, there have been some tensions between careers advisers whose professional authority stemmed from their own career experience, and those (often younger) advisers whose authority stemmed from their specialist guidance training. The former can be criticised stereotypically for their lack of formal training in guidance theory and skills; the latter for their lack of first-hand knowledge of the 'real world'.

In practice, AGCAS has sought to bring together the strengths of the two traditions through a variety of training and development activities. Its working parties on a wide variety of different topics have in effect provided opportunities for professional development through sharing of skills in relation to particular tasks. This and its other activities – including its links with CSU – have enabled it to act as a rich network for professional growth.

An AGCAS activity of particular importance has been its programme of short training courses to provide remedial or updated training in particular skills. This has provided the basis for further professional evolution. In 1992, a Certificate and Diploma in Careers Guidance in Higher Education were launched by the University of Reading in association with (and on the initiative of) AGCAS to provide a more formal training and accreditation structure. Designed on an open-learning basis, they included validation of the AGCAS short courses, accreditation of prior learning, and also new opportunities for distance learning (Ford and Graham, 1994). An important principle was that careers advisers should be able to work towards these qualifications while remaining in post. To support the work-based learning, a mentoring scheme was developed under which trainees were supported by experienced practitioners (Graham, 1994).

The development of a qualification specifically for careers advisers in higher education reflected the professional maturation of careers guidance in higher education. Its flexibility enabled it to encompass some of the strengths of the tradition of the old appointments boards, but finally to bury its amateurism. It thus gave careers services in higher education a greater chance of surviving the market pressures to which they were increasingly being subjected.

7.7 CONCLUSION

The place and roles of careers services in higher education are likely to remain matters of dispute. This is partly because of their merging of guidance and placement roles. The interaction between the two is perceived by many to be one of the strengths of the services: Kirkland (1988) quoted one adviser as arguing that 'placement without counselling was irresponsible, but counselling without placement was sterile'. But placement is a highly marketable activity, and the careers service's hold on it is likely to remain contested. In effect, careers services regulate the placement operation, in a way that so far has been perceived to be in the interests of institutions, employers and students alike. Periodically, however, private-sector organisations challenge the careers service's dominant role in this respect. This seems likely to continue.

A further issue for continuing debate is likely to be the extent to which careers services should provide not only for their own current students but also for students from other institutions and for past students. AGCAS has for some time organised a 'mutual aid' scheme to enable students during vacations and on graduation to use services near their home. This has become linked with the assumption of some 'after-care' responsibility, particularly for students who experience difficulties in finding employment on graduation: indeed, Brennan and McGeevor (1988) suggested that a national policy on graduate education and training might usefully involve a reappraisal and extension of the role of careers services to enable them to provide information and counselling for at least the first two years after graduation. At the same time, many institutions are now concerned to build their links with alumni, who represent potential sources of financial support. It is also argued that maintaining such links provides a network of contacts for current students, and valuable feedback on career patterns. All these arguments have, however, to be reconciled with funding pressures on institutions. And their relationship with other structures of guidance for adults needs to be clarified.

As noted at the beginning of this chapter, higher education is the only sector of education excluded from the remit of the guidance structures set up under the Trade Union Reform and Employment Rights Act 1993. All other full-time students – whether in schools, further education or adult education – may have access to guidance services within their institutions but are also part of the statutory remit of the Careers Service answerable to the Secretary of State for Employment. In a sense, therefore, higher education represents a lacuna within current statutory guidance structures. If careers services within higher education are to maintain their current position, their strategic links with these structures are likely to be of growing importance.

REFERENCES

Ball, B. and Butcher, V. (1993) *Developing Students' Career Planning Skills*, Sheffield: Employment Department.

Bee, M. and Dolton, P. (1990) 'Patterns of Change in UK Graduate Employment, 1962–87', *Higher Education* 20(1): 25–45.

Breakwell, G. (1987) 'A Survey of Student Counselling in Higher and Further Education in the United Kingdom', *British Journal of Guidance and Counselling* 15(3): 285–96.

Brennan, J. and McGeevor, P. (1988) *Graduates at Work*, London: Jessica Kingsley.

Cave, M., Hanney, S., Kogan, M. and Trevett, G. (1988) *The Use of Performance Indicators in Higher Education: a Critical Analysis of Developing Practice*, London: Jessica Kingsley.

Daws, P. P. (1976) *Early Days: a Personal View of the Beginnings of Counselling in English Education during the Decade 1964–74*, Cambridge: Careers Research and Advisory Centre/Hobsons.

Findlay, P., Martin, C. and Smith, S. (1987) 'The Pegasus Programme at Portsmouth Polytechnic', *Industry and Higher Education* 1(1): 67–69.

Ford, C. and Graham, B. (1994) 'The New Qualification on Careers Guidance in Higher Education: a Collaborative Partnership', *British Journal of Guidance and Counselling* 22(1): 127–41.

Gouldner, A. W. (1957/58) 'Cosmopolitans and Locals: Towards an Analysis of Latent Social Roles', *Administrative Science Quarterly* 2(3): 281–306; 2(4): 444–80.

Graham, B. (1994) 'Mentoring and Professional Development in Careers Services in Higher Education', *British Journal of Guidance and Counselling* 22(3): 261–71.

Harris, N. (1992) 'The Talent Scouts are Coming', *New Scientist*, 4 January, 46.

Her Majesty's Inspectorate (1990) *A Survey of Measures of Performance and Reporting Procedures in Polytechnic Careers Services*, London: Department of Education and Science.

Herrington, M. and Rivis, V. (1994) *Guidance and Counselling in Higher Education*, London: Higher Education Quality Council.

Hesketh, B., Wilson, L., Faulkner, A. and Jackson, C. (1987) 'GRADSCOPE: an Analysis of the Item Structure and a Survey of Usage', *British Journal of Guidance and Counselling* 15(2): 197–213.

Higher Education Quality Council (1995) *A Quality Assurance Framework for Guidance and Learner Support in Higher Education: the Guidelines*, London: HEQC.

Higher Education Statistics Agency (1995) *Data Report, July 1995*, Cheltenham: HESA.

Kidd, J. M., Killeen, J., Jarvis, J. and Offer, M. (1993) *Working Models of Careers Guidance: the Interview*, London: Department of Occupational Psychology, Birkbeck College, University of London (mimeo).

Kirkland, J. (1988) 'Careers Advisory Service', in Boys, C. J., Brennan, J., Henkel, M., Kirkland, J., Kogan, M. and Youll, P., *Higher Education and the Preparation for Work*, London: Jessica Kingsley.

Kirkland, J. and Jepson, M. (1983) *Expectations of Higher Education: the Role of the Careers Adviser*, Expectations of Higher Education Project, Paper No. 8, Uxbridge: Department of Government, Brunel University (mimeo).

Kirkman, B. (1982) 'A Good Career with Prospects?', *Times Higher Education Supplement*, 21 May.

Mackintosh, J. (1974) 'Counselling in Higher Education: Some Basic Issues', *British Journal of Guidance and Counselling* 2(1): 55–63.

Macnair, G. (1990) 'The British Enterprise in Higher Education Initiative', *Higher Education Management* 2(1): 60–71.

Newsome, A., Thorne, B. J. and Wyld, K. L. (1973) *Student Counselling in Practice*, London: University of London Press.

Pfeffer, J. (1981) *Power in Organizations*, Marshfield, Mass.: Pitman.

Pierce-Price, R. P. (1982) *Report on the Feasibility of Developing a Computer-Aided Careers Guidance System for Use in Higher Education, Including a Proposed Specification for the System*, London: City University (mimeo).

Robbins Committee (1963) *Higher Education*, London: HMSO.

Ross, R. P. (1988) 'Establishing Careers Education within a Modular Degree System', *British Journal of Guidance and Counselling* 16(2): 203–9.

Sampson, J. P. and Watts, A. G. (1992) 'Computer-Assisted Careers Guidance Systems and Organisational Change', *British Journal of Guidance and Counselling* 20(3): 328–43.

Scott, N. (1993) 'The Birth of SCUAS/AGCAS', in Dunsmore, R. (ed.) *Graduate Recruitment: a 25-Year Retrospective*, Cambridge: Careers Research and Advisory Centre/Hobsons.

Stephenson, J. and Weil, S. (eds.) (1992) *Quality in Learning: a Capability Approach in Higher Education*, London: Kogan Page.

Steptoe, B. (1990) 'Fortune Favours the Solvent!', *Phoenix* 51: 2–5.

Thorne, B. (1985) 'Guidance and Counselling in Further and Higher Education', *British Journal of Guidance and Counselling* 13(1): 22–34.

University Grants Committee (1964) *University Appointments Boards* (Heyworth Report), London: HMSO.

University Grants Committee (1967) *Statistics of Education 1967, Volume 6: Universities*, London: HMSO.

Wallis, M. (1990) 'Access: Morality and Professionalism', *Phoenix*, 55, 13–14.

Watts, A. G. (1977) 'Careers Education in Higher Education: Principles and Practice', *British Journal of Guidance and Counselling* 5(2): 167–84.

Watts, A. G. (1993) 'The Politics and Economics of Computer-Aided Careers Guidance Systems', *British Journal of Guidance and Counselling* 21(2): 175–88.

Watts, A. G. and Hawthorn, R. (1992) *Careers Education and the Curriculum in Higher Education*, NICEC Project Report, Cambridge: Careers Research and Advisory Centre/Hobsons.

Watts, A. G. and Sampson, J. P. (1989) 'Strategic Planning and Performance Measurement: Implications for Careers Services in Higher Education', *British Journal of Guidance and Counselling* 17(1): 34–48.

Watts, A. G., Dartois, C. and Plant, P. (1988) *Educational and Vocational Guidance Services for the 14–25 Age-Group in the European Community*, Maastricht: Presses Inter-universitaires Européennes.

Watts, A. G., Kidd, J. M. and Knasel, E. (1989) *PROSPECT (HE) Pilot Evaluation: First Report*, Cambridge: National Institute for Careers Education and Counselling (mimeo).

Watts, A. G., Kidd, J. M. and Knasel, E. (1991) 'PROSPECT (HE): an Evaluation of User Responses', *British Journal of Guidance and Counselling* 19(1): 66–80.

Williams, G., Blackstone, T. and Metcalf, D. (1974) *The Academic Labour Market: Economic and Social Aspects of a Profession*, Amsterdam: Elsevier.

Wilson, L. M. (1980) *A Machine-Aided System for Exploration of Occupations by Undergraduates*, PhD thesis, University of Aston in Birmingham.

Chapter 8

Career planning within work organisations

Jennifer M. Kidd

8.1 INTRODUCTION

As noted in Chapter 1, profound changes are taking place in the structure of career opportunities within work organisations. Pressures to adapt to more competitive and changing environments are leading to 'downsizing', internal restructuring, 'delayering' and rapid changes in skill requirements. The new 'career realities' which have resulted include uncertainty, insecurity, increased mobility between occupations, non-standard employment contracts, and increased part-time working. Significantly, many employees are being told that their organisations can no longer take responsibility for their long-term careers. Career management is coming to be seen as the individual's own responsibility; 'objective' career paths are being replaced by 'subjective' careers which emphasise self-direction and personal autonomy.

The term 'boundaryless careers' (Arthur, 1994) goes some way to capture the essence of these changes. It encompasses notions of careers that involve frequent changes of employer, the 'non-organisational' careers of many professions and the self-employed, and careers within organisations which progress relatively independently of well-trodden career paths. It also has the additional benefit of allowing a broader, less organisationally-centred approach to career theory. For the last twenty years or so, writers on adult career development have been predominantly concerned with the careers of managers within organisations with internal labour markets; the careers of other workers and those working outside large organisations have been largely ignored.

A number of organisations have responded to the challenge of managing changed expectations and encouraging employees to assume more control of their career development by expanding and elaborating their career management activities, and, in some cases, introducing new initiatives. These developments have been facilitated in Britain by a range of policy initiatives from private- and public-sector organisations alike to promote self-development, both generally and with regard to career planning. The Investors in People initiative and the emerging National Vocational Qualifications system, for example, both emphasise the importance of employees taking responsibility for their own development. Furthermore, there is policy interest in developing 'individual learning account' schemes, whereby employers and employees jointly contribute funds to finance the employee's training (Commission on Social Justice, 1994; Commission on Wealth Creation and Social Cohesion, 1995).

This chapter provides an overview of the various types of career interventions offered by organisations. It also discusses some of the potential benefits of these activities to individuals and employers, and highlights some of the issues that need to be resolved in the further development of guidance provision in this area.

8.2 TYPES OF CAREER INTERVENTIONS

Career development within organisations was traditionally seen as synonymous with succession planning, where employees' careers (usually those of senior managers) are designed and corporately managed to meet future business needs. The emphasis tended to be upon activities designed to meet the career management needs of the organisation, rather than those of employees. The main focus of organisational career interventions, then, was to design, implement and monitor employees' careers.

During the 1970s, however, isolated initiatives began to emerge which acknowledged, and in some cases emphasised, the importance of individual career planning. Employee-centred or individual career interventions began to be offered by a few large organisations. The central thrust of these activities was helping individuals to manage their own careers by identifying career and life goals and implementing their plans for achieving these goals. Hopson (1973), for example, described the introduction of a programme in one organisation which involved career planning workshops, access to an external counsellor, and the development of a pool of internal counsellors. Other writers raised issues concerning the introduction of career interventions which, as we shall see, still resonate today. Williams (1979), for instance, identified a number of core requirements for 'participative' career development programmes. These included training employees in self-managed approaches to career development and the sharing of career-relevant information with them. Another researcher writing at the same time urged organisations to consider whether they were willing to introduce activities which might lead some employees to leave, and argued the case for integrating individual career interventions within existing related activities such as performance appraisal and human resource planning to ensure congruence between individual and organisational goals (Ritchie, 1979).

Organisations in the 1990s are increasingly offering a range of career interventions which address both their own and their employees' concerns. Moreover, interventions that were previously focused on organisational concerns are now beginning to incorporate self-development features. Some companies, for example, are offering 'third-generation' development centres which aim to involve participants in identifying their development needs and producing development plans, rather than simply to assess competencies or identify potential (Griffiths and Goodge, 1994).

Employee-focused activities frequently involve self-assessments of interests, values and skills, information about career opportunities both inside and outside the organisation, and the development of action plans. The term 'personal development planning' is often used to describe these activities (Seabright, 1993). These may run alongside interventions which attend primarily to the organisation's needs for effective decision-making about individual employees, such as

Table 8.1　Types of employee-focused career interventions within organisations

Interventions	Examples of provision
Career planning work-shops Individuals engage in self-assessment exercises and receive feedback from others in the workshop to check the realism of their plans and to decide on strategies for implementation.	The Wellcome Foundation (Jackson and Barltrop, 1994) offered employees career and personal development workshops consisting of a mix of sessions involving individual and small-group exercises. Workshops had three stages: exploring self-concepts, skills, values and interests; understanding future needs; and action planning. They were staffed by a mixture of internal and external tutors, including personnel and training staff. Participants were volunteers, typically young scientists, who might be at a 'first career crisis stage'.
Individual career counselling Individuals are helped to examine their goals in one-to-one counselling sessions, sometimes over a period of time. Self-assessment exercises may be used, and educational and occupational information provided.	In 1992, as part of the Department of Employment's 'Gateways to Learning' initiative, Sainsbury's began a pilot scheme using guidance vouchers, entitled 'Choices' (Deaves, 1994). The programme offered a 45-minute guidance interview to weekly-paid staff in 37 stores, who were not in full-time education. The interviews were conducted by branch personnel managers, who had been given some training in guidance; participants had opportunities to identify skills and development needs, and to draw up action plans. As a result of the scheme, some staff took up educational sponsorship, others embarked on in-store training (including management training), and some made plans to achieve personal goals.
Self-assessment materials Workbooks, videos or computer-aided guidance systems are provided on a stand-alone basis. These resources may be tailored to specific career opportunities within the organisation.	Staff working for the BBC had the opportunity to use 'Career Point' (CBI, 1993), a resource centre with a library of information about BBC jobs, career workbooks, and 'Career Builder' (an interactive computer program). Career Builder was customised for the BBC: it helped staff to identify skills, interests and work values and related them to around 2,000 internal jobs. Career planning workshops and individual career counselling were also available.
Development centres Individuals participate in group exercises, often based on simulations of work tasks, and are given feedback on their strengths and development needs.	W. H. Smith redesigned its development centre to make it more compatible with the management style it wanted to promote (Griffiths and Goodge, 1994). A new set of competencies was developed, emphasising teamworking, innovation and flexibility, and new company-specific work-simulation exercises were designed. Line managers were given more help in their role of supporting subordinates' development, and a post-centre follow-up process was implemented, with clear steps for the participant and the line manager.
Mentoring programmes Superiors or peers are assigned to individuals to provide sponsorship, coaching, counselling or general support with career development. Alternatively, individuals are encouraged to find their own mentors.	In 1992, Lewisham Council in London launched its 'Sponsor Scheme' (Lewisham Personnel, n.d.) which involved a white manager sponsoring a more junior black manager. Each sponsor helped the sponsee with his/her development by one-to-one coaching, job shadowing, providing information about the organisation and its culture, personal and career counselling, and providing introductions to people. There were benefits for the sponsors too: involving white managers, many of them senior, in an initiative for black staff helped them to learn to manage diversity.

performance appraisals, assessments of potential and new job assignments. The main types of employee-focused interventions, with examples of provision, are outlined in Table 8.1.

These interventions vary in their availability to different categories of employees. Most will only be on offer to employees in large organisations. Many will only be available to white-collar and managerial staff (exceptions include government-funded programmes such as those at Sainsbury's, where all employees are offered individual counselling to identify their training and development needs [West, 1994], and guidance within employer-based but government-sponsored youth training schemes [Knasel et al., 1982]).

Relatively little is known more generally about the extent of usage of these kinds of interventions in Britain. To date, the most comprehensive survey of provision involved 582 organisations of varied sizes, across all industrial sectors (Metcalf et al., 1994). Eighty-two per cent of these employers provided careers guidance to at least some of their employees. The larger the organisation, the more likely they were to offer guidance: 92 per cent of the largest organisations did so, compared with 34 per cent of the smallest. Only 22 per cent, however, offered guidance on careers outside the organisation: they were reluctant to provide such guidance because they felt it would encourage employees to leave, and so reduce their return on investment in training. Some were also concerned that advice on external careers would be construed by employees as dismissal. When asked whether they saw it as their responsibility to provide guidance, 90 per cent agreed that they should offer advice on careers inside the organisation, but only 40 per cent felt it was their responsibility to provide guidance on external careers.

Other surveys have used severely restricted samples. Iles and Mabey (1993), for example, surveyed 120 managers undertaking an MBA programme. The findings showed that the most frequently used techniques were career reviews with superiors (77 per cent reported these being used in their organisations), followed by informal (self-selected) mentoring (reported by 43 per cent). Only 19 per cent of the sample said that their organisations used self-assessment materials, 18 per cent development centres and 14 per cent career planning workshops. In a survey of a sample of 12 per cent of its members in 1992, the Industrial Society (cited in Iles and Mabey, 1993) showed an increase in the proportion of the Society's member companies which were using mentoring (41 per cent as compared to 3 per cent in 1989).

The examples in Table 8.1 describe programmes where the aim is usually to manage and develop employees' careers in the context of the opportunities provided by the organisation, or occasionally to give participants the option of planning a voluntary career move out of it. Other programmes manage the exit from organisations. Outplacement is one element here; another is the resettlement services offered by 'short-career' organisations, such as the armed services. Pre-retirement schemes could fall into this category too, though these tend to emphasise the practical problems of coping with retirement, such as health, finance and housing (see Coleman, 1983).

Outplacement programmes

In recent years, even companies which previously espoused a 'no redundancy' policy, such as Marks & Spencer and IBM, have had to make reductions in their labour force. Outplacement services have become an important feature of managing redundancies for staff at all levels. There are, as noted in Chapters 1 and 4, good business reasons for this – organisations wish to be seen as supportive and caring so that they can better retain the commitment of the survivors of a redundancy programme. Research does indeed suggest that decreased motivation is somewhat alleviated when survivors perceive the situation to be handled fairly (Brockner *et al.*, 1987). But it seems that few organisations pay enough attention to the needs of survivors themselves for information and support (Doherty and Horsted, 1995; Herriot and Pemberton, 1995).

A comprehensive outplacement service will involve personal and career counselling, possibly with group work, training in presentation and interview skills, career information resources, and the use of office facilities for preparing curricula vitae and job applications. In a survey of 614 organisations ranging in size from 200 to 50,000 employees, 88 per cent had recently been involved in enforced redundancies, and 56 per cent had used voluntary redundancy to reduce the labour force (Doherty and Tyson, 1993). Around 75 per cent offered an outplacement service: 36 per cent of these used only external services, while 25 per cent used a combination of in-house and external provision; this suggests that the majority (39 per cent) used only internal services. Larger organisations were more likely to use external services. The most common reasons given for this related to the quality of the services provided – expertise and professionalism were often cited. Some also felt that external agencies were better able to assist with the general practicalities of job loss, and more able to provide specific help with job contacts and skilled counselling. However, their services were often only seen as appropriate for those at senior levels. The most common reason for not using external services was cost, and those preferring in-house provision usually felt they had sufficient resources internally. Some organisations were offering distinct 'products' to different levels of staff. Not surprisingly, managers were more likely to be offered services than other staff; senior managers were most commonly offered one-to-one 'executive programmes', while those at lower levels were more likely to be offered group-based programmes or 'job-shop' services.

Instances of large-scale individual career counselling programmes for employees at lower levels do exist, however. In the 1970s, for example, the British Steel Corporation initiated a redundancy counselling scheme to cope with the reduction of jobs by 80,000 over 15 years. This involved trained peer counsellors conducting one or more individual interviews with those to be made redundant (Hopson, 1977).

Resettlement in the armed services

Retention and resettlement have become increasingly important issues in the armed services. Concerns about large numbers leaving after less than five years' service, together with extra redundancies created by restructuring, have led to substantial reorganisation of resettlement provision. Resettlement is now viewed as a 'whole career activity' – indirect assistance is given from the time an individual joins the services, and efforts are made to make the transferability of skills to civilian employment more explicit.

Those who have completed a term of five years or more, as well as those being made redundant, are eligible for the full range of resettlement services. This includes up to four weeks' pre-release training and briefings; by 1999 this is to be extended according to the number of years served, up to seven weeks for those serving more than 16 years. Initial advice is provided at unit level, but the collective aspects of provision are provided by the Tri-Services Resettlement Organisation. From two years to discharge point (2.5 years in the Royal Navy), there is a formal process of interviews, involving action planning, and of briefings, covering job-search skills, occupational information, and advice on finance and housing. A computerised job-search and job-matching service is also provided (Tri-Services Resettlement Organisation, 1994).

8.3 BALANCING INDIVIDUAL AND ORGANISATIONAL NEEDS

It may be the case that particular processes and interventions succeed to some extent in meeting the concerns of both the individual and the organisation. However, inherent within many, if not most, are tensions concerning the balance

Table 8.2 Possible tensions between individual and organisational interests in the provision of career interventions

Career interventions	Possible tensions between interests
Assessment of potential and development needs	Difficulty of offering individuals a supportive environment within which to explore strengths, whilst meeting the organisation's requirement for rigorous assessment. Individuals may be required to engage simultaneously in impression management and self-disclosure.
Assessment of interests and values	Enhanced self-awareness in these areas may lead employees to reject opportunities within the organisation.
Provision of information on opportunities within the organisation	Employees need realistic information; if there are few opportunities for advancement, organisational commitment may be difficult to sustain.
Provision of information on opportunities outside the organisation	May encourage employees to leave.
Preparation of action and development plans	Potential difficulty of producing realistic action plans where the organisation's own plans for the future are uncertain or unknown. Yet if individuals fail to plan, they may not be ready to respond to opportunities when these arise.
Provision of information	Individuals may want information on training and educational opportunities unrelated to work; organisations may want them to take up work-related training.
Assuring confidentiality	May lead to problems with implementing action plans, owing to failure to tap into human resource systems.
Involving line manager	May be overburdened, may lack the skills or power to help individual to develop or implement plans, or may feel threatened by the development of the subordinate.

that can be struck between the two sets of interests. One fairly obvious dilemma from the organisation's point of view is whether providing opportunities for career planning is likely to raise expectations about development within the organisation which cannot be met. Other potential difficulties are summarised in Table 8.2.

Some of these conflicts may, however, be more apparent than real. Confidentiality may not be a serious issue in some contexts, since many career interventions take place some distance from central personnel systems. Furthermore, offering information on non-job-related educational opportunities might encourage employees to be more open to change generally, to the benefit of the organisation. This was indeed one rationale for the introduction of the Employee Development and Assistance Programme (EDAP) at Ford, which offers all employees sponsorship for educational courses unrelated to the employee's current job. Moreover, encouraging employees to reflect on their interests and needs and regularly to monitor the direction of their careers is in line with current notions of the 'learning organisation' which 'facilitates the learning of all its members and continuously transforms itself' (Pedler *et al.*, 1991).

On the other hand, some of the tensions may originate from a much more deep-rooted scepticism regarding the value of investing resources in career interventions. When there is a plentiful supply of labour, why should employers be concerned with encouraging staff – who, after all, are their key economic assets – to take time out of their day-to-day responsibilities to plan more conducive life-styles? How is this going to help the company maintain its economic competitiveness? Some organisations have developed positive answers to these questions; others, however, are likely to be more negative.

8.4 BENEFITS TO INDIVIDUALS AND ORGANISATIONS

Although there is a fair amount of descriptive and anecdotal detail about the provision of different types of career interventions and the techniques used, we know very little about their impact. It is therefore difficult to develop compelling arguments to persuade organisations that the interventions will have an effect on 'bottom-line' productivity outcomes. Some empirical data on outcomes exist, but the benefits are far from well-established. Most of the research is American, and few studies have employed rigorous methodologies, with pre-post designs, control groups and follow-up of respondents.

Chapter 4 sets out four possible categories of guidance outcomes. At the individual level, we can distinguish between immediate, intermediate and ultimate outcomes. Immediate outcomes include knowledge of self and situation, and career-relevant attitudes and skills; the intermediate category covers motivational outcomes, including job satisfaction and organisational and career commitment; and ultimate outcomes at the individual level include behavioural effects, such as performance and employee productivity. The fourth category covers ultimate outcomes at the system level, which, from the organisation's point of view, include overall productivity plus recruitment and turnover costs.

Some evidence relating to individual outcomes is available from the United States. Kingdon and Bimline (1987), for example, evaluating a career development programme including self-development and job training for women, found outcomes that included increases in self-esteem, growth motivation, decision-making skills, and work commitment. Minor (1986), in an evaluation of an intervention using a computer-aided guidance system, produced evidence for increased organisational commitment. A study by Granrose and Portwood (1987) failed to show any effect of participating in a career management programme on job satisfaction (it is not clear what activities were offered), but it did demonstrate a relationship between matching of individual and organisational career plans and satisfaction. A little evidence for performance outcomes is also available. In a study of the effectiveness of workbooks, workshops and counselling, supervisor ratings six months later showed that participants had improved their morale and the quality and quantity of their work. Furthermore, many had undertaken self-development programmes, and felt that they were more in control of their careers (Hanson, 1982). One indication of possible organisational effects is evident in the findings of a British study evaluating development centres (Iles *et al.*, 1989), but the evidence presented is simply participants' ratings of increased organisational effectiveness – no objective indicators were used.

The key question for employers will be the extent to which any individual outcomes actually make a difference to productivity. In the absence of firm evidence of organisational benefits, and bearing in mind the limited evidence on individual performance, one way to answer this is to examine the literature on linkages between employee attitudes and performance. Unfortunately, the only clear benefit of high organisational commitment is a lower level of turnover (Guest, 1992). Common sense might suggest that if participating in career interventions increases job satisfaction, this too would impact on performance. But the relationship between performance and job satisfaction is extremely modest: meta-analyses produce correlations of around 0.15 (see, for example, Iaffaldano and Muchinsky, 1985).

So the case has to be developed along different lines. One line of thought could be to view career interventions as manifestations of a psychological contract which is predominantly relational rather than transactional (Rousseau and Parks, 1993) – that is, where the expectations of both the employee and the organisation are more concerned with mutual commitment than with instrumental exchange (of, say, pay for performance). Herriot and Pemberton (1996) argue that the honouring of relational contracts leads to perceptions of 'procedural equity' where both parties pay more attention to the fairness of the career-management process than to its outcomes. Support for career development and clearly defined opportunities for progression, for example, are seen as more important outcomes of relational contracts than are pay and job satisfaction.

Taking this perspective leads to a search for evidence on the impact of perceptions of procedural equity and support on ultimate outcomes. Some data are available. Eisenberger *et al.* (1990) showed that perceptions of being valued and cared about by the organisation related to attendance, job performance (assessed mainly by supervisors' ratings), and innovation. One explanation for the increased performance was that social exchange processes played an important role. Perceived support led the employee to have confidence that the organisation would fulfil its reciprocal obligations of taking notice of and rewarding efforts made on behalf of the organisation. Another study also produced evidence for innovation as an outcome. Noe *et al.* (1990) found that perceived support, in the form of performance feedback and encouragement to set career goals, resulted in more behaviours designed to develop innovations on the job, as well as to obtain increased visibility and more performance feedback.

The psychological contracting model, then, with its emphasis on reciprocal expectations and obligations, seems to have potential in interpreting the indirect evidence on the likely benefits of career interventions. Rather than attempting to accrue data directly relating outcomes at the various levels of analysis (for example, asking whether setting development plans affects organisational commitment, and whether commitment, in turn, leads to increased performance), this model draws attention to employees' perceptions of provision, and the implications of these for performance outcomes. Taken to the extreme, one hypothesis under this model would be that even those employees who had not participated in career interventions offered by their employer would show enhanced performance, as long as they were informed about the kinds of support available! Indeed, as we saw earlier, there is some evidence that offering outplacement services to redundant employees affects the commitment of those who remain.

Returning to the potential effects of individual career 'learning' on organisations, a number of arguments regarding organisations' need for functional and numerical flexibility are possible. First, in an era of rapid organisational change, organisations will increasingly need up-to-date information on employees' skills in order to facilitate succession planning and reduce reliance on the external labour market for recruitment. If it could be shown that those participating in career interventions become more clear about their skills and more articulate in describing their goals and development needs to management, this would be of benefit to organisations. One study (albeit small-scale and exploratory) suggests that this may indeed be an outcome of such interventions (Moses and Saltrese, 1989).

Second, providing opportunities for career planning within the context of wider dissemination of information about opportunities within the organisation is likely to lead employees to recognise the value of lateral and functional moves where vertical mobility is less likely. This can make it easier to encourage more flexible transfers within the organisation.

Third, offering opportunities for employees to assess long-term career aims and preferred balances between work and other life-roles could lead to changes in perceptions of work centrality. Initiatives such as job sharing and periods of parental leave might then seem more desirable, and this could facilitate the introduction of more flexible working arrangements. As far as the author is aware, these relationships have not yet been supported empirically, but they suggest areas where organisational benefits distinct from performance and productivity indices might be demonstrated.

In essence, then, one important rationale for the introduction of career interventions which is likely to have credence with employers is that they increase employees' openness to change or their 'career adaptability'. The latter term is not new. Super and Knasel (1981) originally proposed its use as a substitute for 'vocational maturity', which was seen to be inappropriate in describing career development in adulthood. If promoting career adaptability is the aim, then interventions need to be designed with this in mind, and studies of effectiveness need to attend to outcomes in these terms. However, we lack an adequate model which addresses the skills, attributes and knowledge needed in dealing with the tasks of individual career management within organisations.

8.5 A MODEL OF INDIVIDUAL CAREER MANAGEMENT

Kidd and Killeen (1992) have argued for a new model of individual career management that incorporates dynamic interactionist perspectives on career development (e.g. Vondracek *et al.*, 1986) and focuses on the skills necessary for coping with and adjusting to change as well as decision-making. These skills include exploring resources (including networking), planning, monitoring and negotiating career systems, and understanding labour markets. The model also needs to take account of learning derived from previous work experience, to be set within the context of both the employing organisation and the individual's other life-roles (Ballantine, 1993), and to incorporate affective characteristics. Building on Herriot and Pemberton's (1996) work, a satisfactory model of individual career management must therefore:

1 Include notions of the individual's career *purpose* or direction. Understanding aspirations within a framework of values, life-style and life-roles is the starting-point for further exploration.
2 Focus on *skills* for lifelong planning and negotiation and *attitudes* towards change, as well as *knowledge* and *understanding* of self and situation.
3 Be *contextualised*, reflecting knowledge of the organisational career context as well as other potential contexts. Knowledge and monitoring of human resource systems and features of the wider labour market are key features of career planning.
4 Be *interactive*, taking account of the relationship between the individual and the organisation and their conflicting interests. Individuals need to develop an understanding of power relationships within organisations, and the skills to negotiate career development.
5 Have a *temporal* perspective, encompassing constructions of the past and ideas about future possibilities. The skills of systematic reflection on experience and action planning are fundamental in the face of changing labour markets.
6 Incorporate notions of career *resilience*, the capacity to cope with uncertainty and insecurity, and the confidence to challenge exploitative practices in the workplace.

So how far do the types of career interventions described in Table 8.1 match up to these requirements? Career planning workshops, individual career counselling and self-assessment materials are potentially capable of meeting most of them, though they may not be sufficiently interactive or linked into formal human resource systems and processes (Iles and Mabey, 1993). Simply providing self-assessment materials on their own, however, is unlikely to facilitate the development of career planning skills. Development centres are interventions which are firmly couched within the organisational context, and are also likely to meet the need for a temporal perspective on career development. But they may be weak on helping individuals to take a long-term view of development which encompasses personal as well as career concerns, and on developing their career planning skills. The intervention which arguably is most likely to help individuals to attend to relationships with their organisation and to areas where interests may conflict is mentoring. Consequently, mentoring is also likely to meet the requirement of contextualisation and encouraging career resilience. It is unlikely, though, to involve structured self-assessment activities.

One is left with the suspicion, then, that employee-centred interventions may be relatively ineffectual in promoting development within the organisation because of their marginal relationship to human resource systems and processes. Many of these types of interventions do seem to give less attention to helping individuals to implement decisions than to the decision-making process itself. On the other hand, those which are more firmly anchored into these systems may give individuals insufficient opportunities to explore values, interests and long-term goals.

This issue of integration with organisational systems is discussed in more detail in Chapter 17. It raises important questions about the way career interventions are introduced and managed. Hirsh *et al.* (1995) argue that the way in which initiatives are implemented is crucial, and that any strategy for career management needs to be tailored to the needs of the organisation and its employees. As they suggest, effective implementation needs the support of top management, a willingness to wait for medium- to long-term payoffs, and, as far as possible, the use of common frameworks for different activities so that the outputs from one can be used as inputs to others.

In Section 8.1, attention was drawn to the need for employees to take charge of their own careers within changing and potentially more flexible career paths and systems. Furthermore, a self-development approach has been espoused recurrently as the way forward in organisational career management (see e.g. Jackson, 1990). A truly employee-centred system would place the individual's needs and desires centre stage. Within many companies, however, the current climate is hardly conducive to individual development. From the employee's point of view, disclosing career aims and negotiating career opportunities requires a degree of risk-taking in a climate of trust and support. Yet many find that job insecurity is greater than ever before and that feelings of powerlessness are overwhelming (Herriot and Pemberton, 1995). And from the perspective of the organisation, it could be argued that companies cannot be trusted to generate and facilitate career management skills in their employees, since they know they are unlikely to recoup their investment (there is indeed some evidence for this from the research of Metcalf *et al.* [1994] cited earlier). As Streeck (1989) has argued in relation to vocational training, institutions may be required that 'constrain the rational self-seeking behaviour of firms and make the enterprise do its duty as a cultural institution'. This may mean more regulation, and a greater role for the state in encouraging firms to engage in development activities, perhaps by setting up co-operative ventures.

What may be underestimated, then, is the extent of cultural change and attendant shifts in power relationships that career planning initiatives require within organisations. This is perhaps particularly so in those with 'unitary' characteristics, where employees and management are assumed to co-operate harmoniously in the achievement of common goals. Unitary features are commonly found in organisations that have developed 'strong', cohesive cultures based on respect for managers' right to manage, especially those who have had a long history of a paternalistic approach (Morgan, 1986). Their managers tend to view conflict as a source of trouble, and attempts are made to eliminate or suppress it. If self-directed career planning initiatives were able to attain a more central position within human resource management, this would require a much more 'pluralist' perspective, where it is accepted that individuals' values and goals may not coincide with the collective purposes of the organisation.

Nevertheless, as we have seen, some large organisations are introducing career interventions successfully. Although there is considerable diversity in content, scope and implementation strategy, closer monitoring and evaluation of these initiatives should enable others to learn more about the basic prerequisites necessary to provide effective career planning opportunities for employees at all levels within work organisations.

REFERENCES

Arthur, M. B. (1994) 'The Boundaryless Career: a New Perspective for Organizational Inquiry', *Journal of Organizational Behavior* 15: 295–306.

Ballantine, M. (1993) 'A New Framework for the Design of Career Interventions in Organisations', *British Journal of Guidance and Counselling* 21(3): 233–45.

Brockner, J., Grover, S., Reed, T., DeWitt, R. and O'Malley, M. (1987) 'Survivors' Reactions to Lay-offs: We Get By With a Little Help from Our Friends', *Administrative Science Quarterly* 32: 526–41.

Coleman, A. (1983) *Preparation for Retirement in England and Wales*, Leicester: National Institute for Adult Continuing Education.

Commission on Social Justice (1994) *Social Justice: Strategies for National Renewal*, London: Vintage.

Commission on Wealth Creation and Social Cohesion (1995) *Wealth Creation and Social Cohesion in a Free Society*, London: CWCSC.

Confederation of British Industry (1993) *A Credit to Your Career*, London: CBI.

Deaves, J. (1994) 'Choices: Personal Development at Sainsbury's', *Adult Learning* 5(9): 223–24.

Doherty, N. and Horsted, J. (1995) 'Helping Survivors to Stay on Board', *People Management*, January, 26–31.

Doherty, N. and Tyson, S. (1993) *Executive Redundancy and Outplacement*, London: Kogan Page.

Eisenberger, R., Fasolo, P. and Davis-La Mastro, V. (1990) 'Perceived Organizational Support and Employee Diligence, Commitment and Innovation', *Journal of Applied Psychology* 75: 51–59.

Granrose, C. S. and Portwood, J. D. (1987) 'Matching Individual Career Plans and Organizational Career Management', *Academy of Management Journal* 30(4): 699–720.

Griffiths, P. and Goodge, P. (1994) 'Development Centres: the Third Generation', *Personnel Management*, June, 40–43.

Guest, D. E. (1992) *The Continuing Search for the Happy Productive Worker*, Inaugural lecture, Birkbeck College, University of London (mimeo).

Hanson, M. E. (1982) 'Career Development: Maximising Options', *Personnel Administrator* 23: 58–61.

Herriot, P. and Pemberton, C. (1995) *New Deals: the Revolution in Managerial Careers*, London: Wiley.

Herriot, P. and Pemberton, C. (1996) 'Contracting Careers', *Human Relations* 49(6): 757–90.

Hirsh, W., Jackson, C. and Jackson, C. (1995) *Careers in Organisations: Issues for the Future*, IES Report No. 287, Brighton: Institute for Employment Studies.

Hopson, B. (1973) 'Career Development in Industry: the Diary of an Experiment', *British Journal of Guidance and Counselling* 1(1): 51–61.

Hopson, B. (1977) 'Setting up a Counselling Network', in Watts, A. G. (ed.) *Counselling at Work*, London: Bedford Square Press.

Iaffaldano, M. and Muchinsky, P. (1985) 'Job Satisfaction and Job Performance: a Meta-Analysis', *Psychological Bulletin* 97: 251–73.

Iles, P. and Mabey, C. (1993) 'Managerial Career Development Programmes: Effectiveness, Availability and Acceptability', *British Journal of Management* 4: 103–18.

Iles, P., Robertson, I. and Rout, U. (1989) 'Assessment-Based Development Centres', *Journal of Managerial Psychology* 4(3): 11–17.

Jackson, C. (1990) *Careers Counselling in Organisations: the Way Forward*, IMS Report No. 198, Brighton: Institute of Manpower Studies.

Jackson, C. and Barltrop, J. (1994) 'Career Workshops', Paper presented at Careers Research and Advisory Centre conference, *Improving Career Development in Organisations*, February.

Kidd, J. M. and Killeen, J. (1992) 'Are the Effects of Careers Guidance Worth Having?: Changes in Practice and Outcomes', *Journal of Occupational and Organizational Psychology* 65: 219–34.

Kingdon, M. A. and Bimline, C. A. (1987) 'Evaluating the Effectiveness of Career Development Training for Women', *Career Development Quarterly* 35: 220–27.

Knasel, E. G., Watts, A. G. and Kidd, J. M. (1982) *The Benefit of Experience*, Special Programmes Research and Development Series No. 5, London: Manpower Services Commission.

Lewisham Personnel (n.d.) *Sponsor Scheme Information Pack*, London: Lewisham Personnel.

Metcalf, H., Walling, A. and Fogarty, M. (1994) *Individual Commitment to Learning: Employers' Attitudes*, Research Series No. 40, Sheffield: Employment Department.

Minor, F. J. (1986) 'Computer Applications in Career Development Planning', in Hall, D. T. (ed.) *Career Development in Organizations*, San Francisco: Jossey-Bass.

Morgan, G. (1986) *Images of Organization*, London: Sage.

Moses, B. and Saltrese, K. (1989) 'Implementing a Career Planning Program', *International Journal of Career Management* 1: 19–24.

Noe, R. A., Noe, A. W. and Bachhuber, J. A. (1990) 'Correlates of Career Motivation', *Journal of Vocational Behavior* 37: 340–56.

Pedler, M., Burgoyne, J. and Boydell, T. (1991) *The Learning Company*, New York: McGraw-Hill.

Ritchie, J. (1979) 'Fair and Effective Career Development in the Air Transport and Travel Industry', *Training Research Bulletin* 8(1): 15–20.

Rousseau, D. M. and Parks, J. M. (1993) 'The Contracts of Individuals and Organisations', in Cummings, L. L. and Staw, B. M. (eds) *Research in Organizational Behavior*, vol. 15, Greenwich, CT: JAI Press.

Seabright, V. (ed.) (1993) *Building a Learning Culture: Personal and Career Development Plans in Higher Education and Employment*, Cambridge: Careers Research and Advisory Centre.

Streeck, W. (1989) 'Skills and the Limits of Neo-Liberalism: the Enterprise of the Future as a Place of Learning', *Work, Employment and Society* 3(1): 89–104.

Super, D. E. and Knasel, E. (1981) 'Career Development in Adulthood: Some Theoretical Problems and a Possible Solution', *British Journal of Guidance and Counselling* 9(2): 194–201.

Tri-Services Resettlement Organisation (1994) *Outline of Resettlement Provision*, London: Tri-Services Resettlement Organisation (mimeo).

Vondracek, F. W., Lerner. R. M. and Schulenberg, J. E. (1986) *Career Development: a Life-Span Development Approach*, Hillsdale, NJ: Erlbaum.

West, M. (1994) 'Gateways with Sainsbury's and Vauxhall', *Guidance Update* 9: 1.

Williams, A. P. O. (1979) 'Career Development and Employee Participation: Current Trends and their Implications', *Personnel Review* 8(4): 15–21.

Chapter 9

The Careers Service

John Killeen and Jennifer M. Kidd

9.1 INTRODUCTION

The Careers Service, which is funded by the Department for Education and Employment (DfEE), is required by legislation to secure the provision of a careers guidance and placement service to certain groups of individuals, mainly young people and those in further education. An increasing number of careers services, however, also offer guidance to adults not falling into these categories. Clients' needs are met by two types of staff – careers advisers and employment officers. In general, careers advisers are responsible for guidance, and employment officers for placement, although the division of responsibilities varies somewhat from service to service. The professional qualification for careers advisers is the Diploma in Careers Guidance, though some services recognise other guidance and counselling qualifications.

Despite the considerable changes which have taken place within the Careers Service over the last few years, many of the questions which are asked today about its role are persistent ones, and some of them emerged at the birth of its earliest precursors. One of the aims of this chapter is to identify some of these questions, and to discuss their relevance in the current context. The chapter is organised in two main parts. In the first, we outline the history of the development of the service, setting out some of the enduring dilemmas which have arisen as it has attempted to respond to the demands of successive governments, the changing requirements of the economy, and the needs of individual clients. This is followed by a deeper discussion of some of these issues, drawing on recent research into the service's work with schools, opportunity providers and individuals.

We begin, then, with an overview of the development of the service. This covers four broad phases. First, we outline its origins. Then we describe the emergence of dual provision, where the Local Education Authority (LEA) controlled the service in some areas, while in others control was exercised by central government. The third phase covers the period from the mid-1970s, when all services came under LEA control, to the early 1990s. Finally, the structure of competitive tendering introduced following the 1993 Trade Union Reform and Employment Rights Act is discussed.

9.2 EARLY YEARS

The early precursors of the Careers Service emerged at the beginning of the century, when the school-leaving age was 13 in some places but 14 in others, and when partial exemption from school attendance was permitted from the age of 11 or 12 if the child was in part-time employment (Heginbotham, 1951). At that time it was believed, as it has been ever since, that too many working-class children were taking inappropriate decisions about working life. This view represented two closely connected anxieties which already had a long history: first, that the British labour force was inadequately educated and trained, in comparison with those of its trading rivals; and second, that unskilled workers suffered more than others during times of high unemployment. It was also recognised that a youth labour market existed: that there were forms of unskilled work in which young people were preferentially employed, but which offered scant prospect of continued employment in adult life. Since at that time adult women often withdrew permanently from the labour force, concern was sometimes confined to the decisions made by boys, or by parents on their behalf. But irrespective of scope, the problem remained the same: that too many children drifted into unskilled work which offered poor long-term prospects. Moreover, so little was education valued by them or their parents that some young people might leave school at the earliest opportunity in the hope of finding work, even if there was no realistic prospect of employment.

The purpose of the earliest bureaux set up to advise young people and their parents was to convince them that they should take a much longer-term view, and especially to convince the more able to enter skilled forms of employment, to obtain training and to take advantage of educational opportunities available in the 'night schools' from which our system of further education has evolved (see Chapter 6). Such was the purpose, for example, of the Local Labour Bureau set up in Finchley in 1907 (Heginbotham, 1951). It is difficult to escape the conclusion that, viewed in sectoral terms, these bureaux were to act as recruiting sergeants, providing education with what it always needs: students.

But of course, this analysis has to be fitted into a broader conception of their role. The originators of the Finchley Local Labour Bureau were also concerned that children should enter 'suitable' employment. If guidance helps young people to find employment which matches their abilities and interests, they will be inclined to stay in it, and because they are productive, employers will want to retain them. In principle, then, everyone benefits. Young people avoid unemployment, enter suitable jobs in which they want to remain, and if their aspirations are below their capacities, are nudged towards a brighter future involving education, training, skilled work and better long-term economic prospects. Employers get more suitable recruits and minimise their turnover costs. Some employers, recruiting into skilled work, get a better supply of labour (whereas employers unable to offer 'suitable' employment should, in consequence, find life more difficult). And we all benefit from lower unemployment costs and more rapid economic progress (see Chapter 4).

But if the analysis is not shared by its clients, is the aim of the service guidance or persuasion? Certainly when Carter (1966) conducted his research half a century after the opening of the first bureaux, many children and their parents perceived it to offer attempted persuasion, and were accordingly indifferent to or irritated by the advice given to them. As we shall see, this issue has periodically resurfaced, and communication of the aims of the service continues to be problematic.

9.3 THE EMERGENCE OF TWO TRADITIONS

The Scottish Education Act (1908) and the Education (Choice of Employment) Act (1910) permitted but did not oblige local authorities to institute services that would help young people to make the transition to work. The Juvenile Employment Bureaux set up under this legislation were soon to become the Juvenile Employment Service. These were, in organisational terms, part of local educational provision, and were in later years, like other peripheral 'educational' agencies such as the Youth Service, often to view themselves as 'Cinderella services'. But in 1909, when Labour Exchanges were created on a national basis, distinct Juvenile Employment Offices were established. By 1919, only 28 per cent of local authorities provided a bureau (Bradley, 1990), and in the majority of places, where local authorities did nothing, Juvenile Employment Offices filled the gap. So two traditions emerged: a Local Authority tradition, closely if sometimes impotently connected to education; and a Board of Trade (later Ministry of Labour) tradition, primarily offering a labour exchange service (or 'placement') to young people. An attenuated form of this distinction was still observable many years after the creation of the modern Careers Service, associated with the question: just how 'educational' is the mission of the service, and how intimate should its working relationship be with schools and colleges? Many subsidiary questions follow. To what degree should careers advisers participate in careers education? Should the service take a lead in its development? Should the Careers Service, like the Youth Service, do 'outreach' work?

Conflict between the two kinds of service provided to young people in those areas where both co-existed led to the setting up of the Chelmsford Committee. In 1923, following the report of this committee, LEAs were permitted to assume responsibility for both elements of provision, and within a year approximately one-third had done so (Heginbotham, 1951; Roberts, 1971). The 'two traditions' were now entrenched on geographical lines.

Multiple roles

The Careers Service has long had duties which require it to exercise 'oversight': to know and record what is happening to young people, whether or not it offers guidance to them. This has been because the service has had administrative responsibilities regarding young workers for ensuring that the laws relating to their employment are observed, and for compiling statistics (although there has been no legislation which the service has been directly responsible for policing). More recently, the service has provided information on the likely volume of demand for training alternatives to youth unemployment. But oversight can also reflect a model of intervention in which the service assures itself that guidance is or is not needed, rather than one in which the onus is placed upon young people or their parents to use guidance as they think fit. As late as the mid-1980s, Killeen and Van Dyke (1991) found that oversight was one of the motives underlying the 'blanket interviewing' policy which continued to be adopted by many services.

But after young people leave education, the service has always had difficulty in exercising oversight. In the 1920s, a major problem facing the service was its lack of contact with 14–16-year-olds, since only at 16 did they have to register for unemployment insurance. This was overcome in two ways. First, a scheme of 'working certificates' was introduced, which employers had a statutory obligation to require young recruits to produce. Second, with reduction of the minimum age of unemployment insurance to 14, administrative contact was ensured.

This highlights two dilemmas which were to haunt the service over the years. Both concern tensions inherent in the administrative aspects of its role, performed to meet the requirements of government policy. Does the role of oversight and administration create a relationship with young people which conflicts with that of providing guidance? In its absence, will the service fail to reach young people who have left education? And what is the relationship with employers: is it to provide them with a service, or to ensure that they obey the law concerning the employment of young people? In the 1920s, the latter referred most obviously to under-age workers, prohibited occupations, and hours and conditions of work. In the 1980s and 1990s, the most obvious example has been breaches of the law concerning racial and sexual discrimination.

During the 1920s and 1930s, youth unemployment increased to such an extent that the main concern of the service was to find work for school-leavers, so that much of its attention was focused upon those who might, or did, have difficulty in finding work. This focus on placement, coupled with administrative duties, was perhaps one of the chief reasons why guidance remained ill-developed, and why a well-trained guidance profession was not created in the inter-war years.

The Youth Employment Service

The Employment and Training Act of 1948 inched the service further towards uniformity. This act required all schools to register their pupils with the service before they left. It assembled what it termed the 'Youth Employment Service' from existing provisions, by enabling LEAs which did not currently provide a service to set one up, taking over this responsibility from the local offices of the Ministry of Labour. The central government grant, channelled through the Ministry of Labour, was raised from 50 per cent to 75 per cent. However, the Ministry continued to exercise its responsibilities, including that of inspection, through the Central Youth Employment Executive, which was staffed by civil servants drawn from the Ministry of Labour, the Ministry of Education and the Scottish Education Department. The anomaly of an LEA service funded and inspected by an employment ministry continued to affront notions of organisational tidiness into the 1990s. And in practice, much of the pre-war pattern remained.

The number of LEA services more than doubled to 129 in England, Scotland and Wales within three years of the legislation; but over a decade later a third of local authorities continued to have direct provision by the Department of Employment. The functions of the Youth Employment Service remained as before, but the age-range of clients was extended: it was to now to provide information, vocational guidance and placement to school-leavers and up to the age of 18. The service continued to exercise oversight, or 'keep in touch', with young people to that age, and was responsible for the administration of their National Insurance and Assistance (unemployment benefit). In other words, it had responsibilities towards them similar to those which the Labour Exchanges of the day had to adults, but it combined these with a stronger emphasis on guidance. Carter (1966), however, was still able to speak of two traditions and two sorts of staff, divided on the question: is it primarily an educational or an industrial matter? That is, is its main purpose to help young people make sensible choices, or to help employers find young workers?

The creation of the Youth Employment Service was quickly followed by the post-war 'boom' and by rising demand for youth labour. Those who measured the utility of the service exclusively by the proportion of school-leavers it placed were made a little nervous by the ease with which other channels were used. By the 1960s, only one-quarter to one-third of school-leavers were 'placed' by the service. For others, the *quality* of young people's decisions again became paramount. The assumed adverse consequences of youthful 'job-hopping' came to play a key role in the rationale for a strengthened guidance role (Clarke, 1980). By the 1970s, placement was generally regarded as of lower priority than guidance and familiarisation/liaison visits to employers.

There has always been a tension in the service between, on the one hand, the identification of its role with specific 'problem groups' – such as able working-class children who fail to continue in education and training, or those at risk of unemployment (e.g. ex-offenders, and those with special needs) – and, on the other hand, the idea that guidance may be a universally beneficial resource for wise decision-making and job search. In practice, and with limited resources, some sort of targeting has generally been evident. The Youth Employment Service, which was universally available to young people up to the age of 18, actually worked, in the main, with working-class minimum-age leavers in secondary modern schools, rather than with other young people who were not perceived as being 'part of the problem'.

9.4 AN LEA-BASED SERVICE

The new Careers Service created by the 1973 Employment and Training Act finally ended the pattern of dual provision that had characterised the preceding half-century. For the first time, it became a statutory duty of all LEAs, funded through the Rate Support Grant, though ministerial responsibility, including that for inspection, remained with the Department of Employment (later, government was to use discretionary funding mechanisms, such as the direct funding of unemployment specialist careers officers, to exert further control). The legislation drew in part on the proposals of the Albermarle Committee (NYEC, 1965; 1968). As well as recommending an end to the dual system of provision, this committee proposed that the upper age-limit of the statutory client group be increased, that more attention be given to older leavers, and that new youth employment officers – soon re-labelled 'careers officers' – should be required to complete an approved full-time training course. It also emphasised the importance of co-operation between careers teachers and careers officers, and recommended an increase in staffing. A minority recommendation advocated a new all-age service which would incorporate the guidance and placement service of the Careers Service with the adult employment services. These proposals were unpopular with the Careers Service, however, and were not implemented.

The Employment and Training Act still assumed that the core task of the service was to assist the transition from education to work, and that it should be universally available to young people at this transition point. The age limit for mandatory provision was raised to 18 or one year after the cessation of full-time education, whichever was the later. The service was permitted, but not obliged or centrally funded, to offer guidance to adults. Responsibility for the administration of unemployment benefit was removed. The first Memorandum of Guidance, issued after some delay in 1980, listed the aim of the service as 'satisfactory transition'; among its objectives was the provision of vocational guidance 'at appropriate stages during . . . educational life'. Plainly, therefore, the focus on transition was not seen to imply merely a 'point of transition' service. In 1988, a revised memorandum replaced the statement concerning vocational guidance with a more general one about helping 'young people to reach informed, realistic decisions', and added, as a specific objective, the promotion of equal opportunities.

Although it was not fully recognised at the time, the creation of the Careers Service coincided with a decisive change in employment conditions. The youth unemployment rate rose dramatically in the 1970s, but it was hoped that this was to be a temporary phenomenon. The provisions made for the young unemployed had a makeshift air, captured in the designation 'special programmes'. Only in the following decades did it come to be accepted that a more permanent institutional arrangement was required. It was inevitable that the new Careers Service would become a rather different service from its immediate predecessor, and that it would have to cope with youth unemployment, be a channel to 'special programmes', and later, adjust to much higher staying-on rates in education, delayed entry to work, and increasingly complicated (or 'unstable') career trajectories (Banks et al., 1992).

Placing young people in government schemes was a major feature of many careers officers' work at this time: Watts (1986) cites Department of Employment figures showing that the service recruited around 85–90 per cent of entrants to the Youth Opportunities Programme in the early 1980s, and 80 per cent of entrants to the Youth Training Scheme in the middle of the decade. Monitoring the progress of young people through the schemes was also part of the role of the service – this was particularly important near the end of a young person's time on a scheme, since most subsequently had to find work elsewhere. This continuing involvement with young people also enabled careers officers to give feedback to training providers on the schemes themselves, and they often became involved in scheme design. Arguably, this close involvement with government programmes allowed the service to continue without any radical reappraisal of its role, which could have been substantially threatened by large-scale youth unemployment. It was still possible, for example, to give guidance precedence over placement, since Youth Training placements were considered the functional equivalent of jobs (Killeen and Van Dyke, 1991; Lawrence, 1994). A further role, less welcomed by careers officers, involved the recruitment of young people on to these schemes. Many services experienced pressure from government to act as recruiting agencies for the programmes, and to report those who turned down placements so that benefits might be adjusted or withheld (Watts, 1986; Ranson and Ribbins, 1988).

Several important educational initiatives were also introduced at this time, many of which linked with the 'new vocationalism' movement in education, and required substantial careers education and guidance inputs. In schools, careers education became an integral part of the Certificate of Pre-Vocational Education (CPVE) and the Technical and Vocational Education Initiative (TVEI) (see Chapter 5). The latter initiative in particular sometimes led to the creation of specialist careers officer posts, and offered officers opportunities to increase their involvement in curriculum development. The service also became more involved in education–business partnerships and in facilitating links between educational institutions and employers generally.

During this time, it began to be difficult to generalise about the role and functions of the Careers Service nationwide. Responding to their views of local needs, services increasingly varied in their priorities concerning tasks and in their judgements about the best ways of organising themselves. In one authority, Coventry, officers were based entirely in schools, giving them more opportunities to influence the curriculum and more contact with school pupils from an early age. In East Sussex, too, many careers officers were placed in schools and colleges. These were radical developments, which raised a number of questions. Were the activities of careers officers and teachers, especially careers teachers, to coalesce? Could the school, acting as a community school, become a 'pastoral base' for its local community? Within the Careers Service, should work with employers and placement be split off, as a set of central functions, from the guidance activities taking place in schools (Ranson and Ribbins, 1988)? In addition, fears about the 'impartiality' or 'honest broker' role of the service as between schools and other post-16 opportunity providers could easily surface.

9.5 COMPETITIVE TENDERING

Some twenty years of LEA control (with occasional Department of Employment funding for specialist work) ceased in the 1990s, following the 1993 Trade Union Reform and Employment Rights Act. A White Paper on education and training (DoE, 1991) had made clear the government's aims of reducing the influence of LEAs on services and increasing the influence of local employers. The Act permitted organisations other than LEAs to run careers services: bids were invited from all kinds of private- and public-sector organisations, whether separately or as partnerships or consortia. Following the initial, phased tendering process, most services administered under the 'new arrangements' were run by various forms of partnerships between LEAs and Training and Enterprise Councils (TECs). A minority were run by private- or voluntary-sector agencies, or by services from other areas. The statutory client group comprised: those in full-time education at any institution outside the higher education sector; part-time students in work-related further education; and young people under 21 who had left education up to two years previously. Work with other adults was still encouraged, and if they wished, services were allowed to charge clients outside the statutory group.

These changes reflected several aspects of the Conservative government's ideology and policies: for example, marketisation of the public sector (see Chapter 21);

increasing the influence of central government over local government (in particular, the progressive removal of powers and functions from LEAs); and the creation of mechanisms which allowed greater influence of employers over education and training provision. The new emphases on contracts and account-ability were bound to have a profound impact on the culture, policies and working practices of individual services, and seemed likely to create tensions that would be difficult to resolve. For example, the relationship with govern-ment was dominated by the constraints of a contractual relationship, but the new 'market' in guidance services demanded innovation and flexibility. And output-related funding (15 per cent of funds was based on completed action plans) brought with it the danger of an emphasis on meeting targets rather than on the underlying quality of service to individuals.

An early evaluation of the first, 'pathfinder' services (Watson et al., 1995) described many of the predictable consequences of 'privatisation'. Most obvi-ously, each service had become a business organisation, with 'crisper' decision-making by a board with real power, with a more independent and longer-term approach to strategic planning in its own interest, and in possession of its own management (or financial) information system attended by a new kind of business-function appointee. Management and service-delivery personnel had become more sharply distinguished, and middle-management delayering had occurred. Staff performance targets and monitoring had been sharpened, and non-standard employment contracts introduced. Stress had increased and morale had declined. Performance-related pay was on the horizon. However, it was expected that, with staff turnover and adjustment, morale would return. Quality assurance was given a high priority, but it was acknowledged that this was a focus of concern before the new arrangements. It was said that these services were becoming more responsive to their customers, and expanding into non-core activities, such as redundancy counselling or the co-ordination of work experience, but the examples given were of activities which at least some services had carried out in the past.

As we have seen, several themes and dilemmas concerning the role and func-tions of the Careers Service have persisted over the years. Some of these raise fundamental questions about its aims and purpose, while others involve debates about the best tactics for achieving them. In the following sections, we discuss how some of these issues have been debated recently, and identify some of the key challenges facing the reorganised services of the late 1990s. We will deal in turn with the three main areas of the work of the Careers Service: relationships with schools; relationships with employment and training providers; and work with individual clients.

9.6 RELATIONSHIPS WITH SCHOOLS

A recurring issue has to do with the educational aims of the Careers Service, and the nature of its work with schools. Many senior figures in the service have long been persuaded that the effectiveness of guidance by careers advisers (as careers officers are now called) is enhanced when it follows careers education in schools (Bedford, 1982). They have complained, correctly or incorrectly, that in its absence, vocational guidance interviews are often used, inappropriately, to deliver careers education rather than guidance. They have also taken the view

that if the aim of the service is to perform its own work *in* schools efficiently –
for example, by using group methods – more extensive co-operation *with* schools
is necessary. But until 1995, the Careers Service was the responsibility of the
Department of Employment, not of the Department for Education; in consequence, national policy for the work of the service in schools had not, save at
a very minimal level, been binding upon schools. On the other hand, careers
services and schools were linked at the level of the LEA. We now have a
situation in which a common ministry (the Department for Education and
Employment) is presiding over a system in which more independent careers
services enter into 'service-level agreements' in the schools. There is a widely-
perceived danger that the net effect of the new arrangements will be to reinforce
a *contractor–supplier* relationship, rather than a *collaborative* one, between the
service and schools.

As we have seen, there have always been considerable local variations in the
kinds of relationships that educational institutions and careers services have
forged with one another. Moreover, individual careers advisers have viewed
their roles in planning and delivering careers education and guidance differently: some favouring a predominantly consultative role; others preferring to
spend more of their time in delivering guidance to individuals. How the line
is to be drawn between the respective roles of careers teachers and careers
advisers has been a matter for discussion for decades. Watts (1986) identified
several different models which have been used to differentiate the roles of
careers teachers and careers advisers. One points to 'complementary expertise':
for example, careers teachers being responsible for curricular work, and careers
advisers for individual work (e.g. Avent, 1974). Another relates to 'level of
involvement', using the medical analogy of the careers adviser as consultant
and the careers teacher as general practitioner (Gray, 1973). A third refers to
stages of the guidance process: Peck (1975) suggested, for instance, that careers
teachers should be responsible for the early stages of orientation, information
and assessment, and careers advisers for guidance, placing, adjustment and
readjustment.

Some careers advisers, too, have always been more successful than others
in their influence on guidance practice in schools generally. In Merseyside in
the late 1960s, for example, only 26 per cent of a sample of 50 youth employment officers (as they were then called) reported that they had been able
to persuade more than half of the schools for which they were responsible to
institute careers education; 71 per cent said schools obstructed their attempts
to develop guidance, refusing to allow them more than a single talk and interview. They complained that they were seen as 'poor relations' or 'intruders'
(Roberts, 1971).

The term 'partnership' is commonly used to describe the relationship between
careers services and schools. As studies carried out over the last decade have
shown, this term conceals a diversity of ways in which services and individual
staff conceive, and are enabled by schools to enact, their roles. Killeen and Van
Dyke (1991), for example, in a study involving case-studies of eight services and
eight schools plus a survey of principal careers officers, identified three 'ideal
types' of careers-service strategies in their school-based work. The first was *isolation*, where a standard service was provided to schools by a careers service
operating as a 'disinterested outsider', with few attempts actively to develop

careers education programmes. The second was *local integration*, where careers officers were encouraged, as a matter of policy, to engage in joint planning with schools and to make local innovations. This tended to create integrated careers programmes and to erode traditional boundaries between their responsibilities and those of teachers. Two services based careers officers permanently in schools, giving continuity of service to ex-pupils, one as part of an (abortive) LEA policy for the creation of community schools which would act as pastoral bases for their localities. The third strategy, *central integration*, was to offer specialised central services to schools, intended to develop and support their own careers education and guidance activities, so that careers officers could concentrate on 'deeper' forms of guidance with a minority of pupils.

Under each of the two forms of integration, there was a willingness to abandon traditional boundaries between what teachers and careers officers do, on the assumption that guidance is 'part of' education; whereas a key feature of the 'isolated' strategy was their preservation, articulated in a rigid distinction between careers education, which was seen to be the task of the school, and careers guidance, which was viewed as the main role of the careers service. This latter strategy usually meant that careers officers spent most of their time in schools carrying out individual guidance interviews, and that little time remained for more developmental or consultancy roles.

A more recent survey (Morris *et al.*, 1995) suggests that this model still prevails in some schools in the 1990s. It also demonstrates that there is still considerable variation between schools regarding the extent of integration of the activities of careers advisers and teachers. The study involved eleven careers services in England and Wales and 66 schools. Three broad models of practice were identified. In a minority of schools, the model was characterised as *parallel provision*: interaction and information flow between the school and the service were minimal, and careers education was viewed as the responsibility of careers teachers, while guidance, in the form of interviews, was the province of careers advisers. Within most of the schools in the sample, however, provision seemed to be somewhat more integrated, in a model of practice described as *pyramidal provision*. Here, there was a greater exchange of information, and the interview was seen as the culmination of the guidance process; however, although young people were better prepared for the interview than in the parallel provision model, there was little feedback from the interview process to inform the development of the curriculum. In the third, *guidance community* model, careers advisers were more actively involved in planning the curriculum and they were also provided with more detailed information about the interests and abilities of young people attending interviews. Furthermore, general information from interviews was fed back into the curriculum planning process. There was also some evidence from this study that, in schools with a high degree of involvement with careers advisers, pupils had developed greater opportunity awareness, decision-making skills and transition skills. These schools were those where careers advisers were more involved in curriculum planning, review and development; where clear systems for information flow and feedback had been developed; where the respective skills of teachers and careers advisers were identified and used appropriately; and where the guidance interview was viewed as just one element of an ongoing strategy for careers education and guidance.

Killeen and Van Dyke (1991) found that the autonomy of schools was a limiting factor on integrationist strategies. The discretion of head teachers was wide, co-operation might have adverse resource implications for schools (or at least, result in the transfer of resources to careers work from competing areas), and much depended upon the priorities of careers co-ordinators or teachers. Morris *et al.* (1995) showed that, significantly, in most cases the degree of interaction between schools and careers services was determined by the school rather than the service. It seems that, therefore, as Roberts found some twenty-five years earlier, many careers advisers still lack the power and status to make an impact on guidance strategies in schools. Morris *et al.* suggest a number of areas which, if attended to, could make it easier for careers service staff to work with increased confidence in schools and to develop relationships of greater mutual trust and esteem with school staff. These include continuity of staffing in careers advisers' attachments to schools, joint training exercises, and more co-operation between senior managers in each organisation.

School/careers-service partnerships of the future would seem to demand a more proactive stance on the part of the careers service. This role is increasingly apparent in government documents and guidelines, which encourage services to find ways of helping individuals apply their learning progressively to their thinking and planning, and to become active members of guidance communities (ED, 1993; Careers Service Quality Assurance and Development Unit, 1995). The latter document explicitly contrasts this approach with the practice of offering a discrete guidance intervention towards the end of a guidance programme. The introduction of service-level agreements is likely to be an important initiative in this respect, since they encourage greater interaction between school and careers service staff, clear frameworks for working together, and closer monitoring of progress.

One source of leverage careers advisers may have over schools is their position in relation to the boundary of the institution. Although the organisational base of most careers advisers is clearly outside the school, those advisers who achieve strong partnerships with schools begin to move towards internal roles, as members of a guidance team. This places careers advisers in a potentially more powerful position, since they can draw simultaneously on the roles of 'outsider' and 'insider' in initiating change. As outsiders, they can draw on the strengths of being external change agents, with access to experience of policy and practice in other schools, and with a more objective view; but as insiders, they are also able to appreciate the broad context of provision and the political realities of the institution.

9.7 RELATIONSHIPS WITH EMPLOYMENT AND TRAINING PROVIDERS

A second set of issues arises from a consideration of the service's links with the world of employment. Recruitment and placement have always been seen by some members of the Careers Service as conflicting with guidance, and decisions have to be made within individual services regarding the relative emphasis given to employer liaison on the one hand and to work with educational institutions and individual clients on the other. In addition, the service still has responsibilities to ensure that employers are obeying the law in their employment practices – for example, in relation to health and safety and equal-opportunities legislation. Employers, on the other hand, see the Careers Service as a recruitment channel, and it is natural that they should try to export the costs of recruitment to it, as if it were acting as an (unpaid) recruitment agency on their behalf. Thus, for example, in areas of high unemployment, employers complain that it does not act as a sufficiently discriminating filter, leaving them to deal with too many applicants; whereas in buoyant local economies, they make the opposite complaint – that the service does not advertise their vacancies widely enough, or attract sufficient applicants (Maguire and Ashton, 1983).

As we have seen, a persistent theme over the years has been the question of who are the primary clients of the Careers Service – young people or employers. When control of the service was in the hands of LEAs, responsibilities towards young people seemed to predominate, but criticisms of bias in favour of their needs periodically resurfaced in the late 1970s and the 1980s. So long as careers advisers provide a recruitment service to employers, potential bias towards one party or the other will continue to be an issue, and the possibility of its aims being seen as persuasion rather than guidance will persist. When the new contractual arrangements have been in place long enough to take effect, it seems likely that the lessons learnt from different kinds of partnerships and modes of operation will sharpen this debate.

In general, there seem to be two bodies of opinion on the balance of responsibilities. On the one hand, it seems fairly clear that most careers advisers take the view that their main allegiance is to the individual (Roberts, 1971; Lawrence, 1994). On the other hand, however, government officials, as well as some employers, commonly see the main aim of the service as meeting the needs of the economy, and they have periodically expressed concern about its undue emphasis on the needs of young people. But even accepting the view that young people's needs should predominate far from negates the importance of attending to employers' requirements. Good relationships with employers are necessary for informed guidance to individuals, and are also essential for influencing local opportunity structures in the interests of the client group as a whole. Furthermore, employers will only continue to notify the service of vacancies if they are confident that it can submit suitable candidates, and effective follow-up of young people in training schemes and in employment also requires the trust of employers.

Nevertheless, there is still the potential for some conflict within the aims of the service in relation to placement activities, particularly with respect to the decisions that careers advisers have to make concerning which young people to recommend to employers for interview. Bradley (1992) has set out the options analytically in terms of how far careers advisers might take an interventionist approach to the demands of either party. Allowing unrealistic employer and client requirements (in terms of wages, for example) to remain unchallenged merely reinforces the status quo, and in times of low demand for youth labour will reinforce the employer's labour market power. Clients, in turn, will spend longer searching for work. If both parties are challenged as to the realism of their requirements, greater congruence between supply and demand can be achieved. Stronger effort needs to be made to inform employers of the type of youth labour available, and more information on job availability and job content

needs to be disseminated to young people. This may not meet employers' immediate needs to fill certain vacancies, but this analysis suggests that the needs of
young people might be met more effectively by giving *more* attention to work
with employers and providers of training opportunities.

More specifically, effectiveness is likely to depend on how successful the
service is in its information-gathering activities, and the extent to which it is
able to influence clients and employers. At the very least, the Careers
Service/TEC partnerships established in the 1990s may help to bring more coherence to the analysis of supply and demand within local labour markets. However,
in the views of some careers advisers, there may still be conflicts with the client-
centred ethos of the service, and it is possible that some staff may be resistant
to the cultural changes that may be necessary.

Organisational theory suggests that problems almost inevitably arise when an
organisation is required to deal with different sectors in its external environment whose demands are volatile and uncertain. Its further argument –
supported by the work of, among others, Lawrence and Lorsch (1967) – is that
the organisations which deal most successfully with these kinds of turbulent
environments are those that pay attention to 'differentiation' of structure and
management style, coupled with sophisticated mechanisms for collaboration and
'integration'. Ideally, organisations need to set up specialised units to deal with
different sectors of the environment, staffed by managers with differing orientations to the work, and at the same time develop appropriate strategies for
linking and co-ordinating these units.

The implication of this analysis for the Careers Service is that one way of
coping with the conflicts inherent in its dual responsibility to the worlds
of education and employment is to consider instituting specialised functions
to work with each sector, as Ranson and Ribbins (1988) have suggested, staffed
by individuals with preferences for the different roles and with different
working styles. Some services have moved towards this approach by having
employment officers deal with placement, leaving careers advisers freer to fulfil
their guidance functions. This strategy is unlikely to succeed, however, without
amalgamation of smaller services and without paying attention to co-ordination,
which may require an additional layer of management.

9.8 WORK WITH INDIVIDUALS

Lastly, we can identify a series of issues concerning the service's client group
and how it relates to this group. More specifically, should its primary client
group be extended? Should clients in special need of guidance be targeted in
some way? And how can the service ensure that its aims are understood by
potential clients? Although the post-1973 legislation has permitted services to
offer guidance to adults, and has included the provision of a service to adults
in further education, the emphasis is still on young people. Most non-statutory
adult work (see Chapter 10) has to be paid for from LEA funds, from TECs or
from other sources such as the European Social Fund, and in some areas fees
are charged to adult clients. Initiatives such as Gateways to Learning and Skill
Choice have increased guidance provision for adults in recent years, and some
careers services have been involved in these schemes. Funding, however, has
been short-term, and channelled through TECs.

There is little doubt that a coherent national strategy for adult guidance is needed (see Chapters 10 and 21), and the emphasis on guidance at the point of initial entry into work can be, and has been, questioned. Roberts (1971), for example, pointed out that much of the work of the service has been rooted in assumptions concerning the problematic nature of the transition from school to work, yet research suggests that, at least when the youth labour market has been buoyant, most young people experience few problems in moving into employment. Clarke (1980) was unable to show that 'job-hopping' harmed the young people involved. Moreover, it has repeatedly been shown that more young people want to enter skilled work than can actually do so (e.g. Dex, 1982). The situation may be different in times of high unemployment and when initial choices concern entry into Youth Training and other government special programmes. And just because young people want 'good jobs', this does not mean that they understand the way in which the occupational structure is changing or how best to position themselves for good new employment possibilities. But the general claim that people are in particular need of guidance at this stage in their lives needs questioning. In a similar vein, Ballantine (1993) has argued that greater job mobility of adult workers within and between employers, and more uncertainty generally over the course of their working lives, lead to the conclusion that mid-career planning and decision-making should be seen as fundamental, and initial entry seen as the 'special case'.

But to what extent are careers advisers equipped to deal with adults? Despite the increasing diversity of their client group, training has traditionally focused on work with school-leavers. With experience, many careers advisers become skilled in developing the flexibility to adapt to a range of client needs, although recent research has suggested that few appear to be able to make the fundamental changes in approach which they feel are demanded by adult clients (Kidd et al., 1993; 1997). This study also suggested that careers advisers see adults as generally requiring more personal counselling than young people, partly because the issues they present are often intertwined with other aspects of their lives. They further tend to be more assertive about what they want from guidance, and when these demands are unrealistic, the careers adviser in turn may need to be more assertive and challenging. Many adults also need in-depth assessment of skills, interests and personality. Psychometric assessment may be valuable in this respect, and although many careers advisers are trained in the use of interest measures, few services use aptitude or ability tests (National Test Users Group, 1994).

Careers advisers have long been dissatisfied with the amount of guidance they are able to give to individuals within the statutory client group: a significant number conduct 600 or more interviews each year, in addition to their other duties. One response has been to try to distinguish those individuals who are 'at risk', and thus in need of more extensive guidance, from those who are not. The problem here is that if blanket interviewing were used for this diagnostic purpose, most of the resources necessary for more extensive guidance would be consumed. Experiments have, therefore, repeatedly been conducted in an attempt to find a method of screening young people, providing 'routine' forms of guidance – such as information giving – in a more cost-effective way, and thus freeing advisers to give more time to those in real need. An example is the use of computer-aided guidance systems for this purpose.

Most services have moved to a more selective approach to interviewing, using a variety of methods to prioritise clients, including self-referral, referral by careers teachers or tutors, and referral by interest questionnaires (Le Gro and Cavadino, 1991); at the same time, however, there is an increasing emphasis on the statutory client group's entitlement to a wider guidance process which includes careers education, other group work, and occupational and educational information. The majority of services now have certain criteria they use to select clients for interview, the most important of which are: those leaving education for jobs or courses that require early application; those whose aspirations do not match their academic achievements; those with no job ideas; and special-needs pupils. The success of any selective system of interviewing will depend on relationships with individual schools and their staff, and the careers advisers' access to documentation from schools. It will also be influenced by the adequacy of the school's careers education programme, since pupils are unlikely to be able to make an informed decision about whether they need an interview unless they have some awareness of their guidance needs and what guidance can offer them. At the time of writing, there is some concern that developments such as action planning and youth credits will require a return to blanket interviewing.

Careers services have also had to grapple persistently with the issue of how to promote themselves to their primary clients. Services have been encouraged to give more emphasis to marketing and communications in recent years, and bids for the provision of services in the mid-1990s were required to include 'clear proposals for achieving and maintaining the confidence, trust and support of . . . clients, other customers and the wider community interests' (ED, 1993). Guidance, however, is a complex and multi-faceted process, and communicating what it entails is far from straightforward. The image of careers advisers operating in a talent-matching mode has been hard to shake off, and this still leaves the service open to allegations of persuasion and lack of client-centredness.

There is evidence to suggest that careers adviser involvement in careers education activities in the school affects the progress that young people make during careers interviews (Bedford, 1982; Cherry and Gear, 1987b). But for many, their first contact with a careers adviser is in the individual guidance interview. Knowledge of the guidance process is therefore likely to be sketchy, and expectations misconceived (Bates, 1990; Cherry and Gear, 1987a). Spending some time at the beginning of the interview discussing the nature of guidance and agreeing objectives for the interview has come to be regarded as a necessary part of good practice, even for clients with some experience of guidance (Kidd *et al.*, 1997). But this in itself is unlikely to overcome long-established misconceptions, especially where a pupil's experiences of one-to-one discussions are limited to those where a teacher's authority is in no doubt.

Communicating the aims of guidance to potential clients outside the education system is even more problematic. Recognising this, some services have initiated 'outreach' activities, making contact with young people in youth clubs and other centres, and 'open-door' sessions in schools and colleges in lunch hours. Ranson and Ribbins (1988) describe an outreach project in the North-East of England where a team of careers advisers and youth workers held a series of group discussions on local employment opportunities, and helped young people to produce curricula vitae which stressed positive personal achievements. According to the careers advisers working on the project, one of the reasons for the project's success was that alienating aspects of the bureaucracy involved in running the service were distanced, allowing good relations to develop. Furthermore, meeting young people on their own territory shifted the balance of power towards more adult–adult relationships.

The potential value of outreach activities was also noted in a study of the use of the Careers Service in Lambeth (Rolfe, 1994). Representatives of local organisations with an interest in young people suggested that outreach work might help the service to overcome some of the barriers to its use – for example, too close an association with school and mistrust of its work. Outreach work was also suggested as a way to obtain feedback about the service from other organisations working with young people.

9.9 CONCLUSION

Throughout this chapter we have alluded to various dilemmas and tensions arising from the need for the Careers Service to act within certain constraints in its attempts to implement government policy. To a greater or lesser extent, guidance principles and guidance practice have always been at odds, for various reasons. Some of these concern actual or potential role conflicts; some are to do with time constraints and role overload; others relate to careers advisers' professional autonomy.

As we have seen, conflicts of allegiance and loyalty have persisted throughout the history of the service, and these are inherent even in the so-called 'honest broker' role. How far does being an honest broker require the service to stand aloof from schools and colleges, for example? And does being an honest broker also imply impartiality between the supply side and the demand side of the youth labour market, providing an even-handed service to young people who want jobs and employers who want to recruit labour, and thus, at the end of the day, not being the agent of the ostensible client, the young person? With the growing involvement of TECs and commercial organisations in the management of services, impartiality will continue to be a contentious issue.

Time constraints have always affected the balance of activities between work with individual clients, work in educational institutions, and liaison with employers. They have always been particularly severe in guidance interviewing, especially in schools. The problem of how to give effective guidance in one session, sometimes of less than one hour's duration, has exercised the service since its inception. Many of the approaches now covered in initial training have been imported from the field of personal counselling, and assume that the helping process will extend over several sessions. New models of interviewing are needed which are geared to the needs of careers advisers working with clients on predominantly vocational issues over a short period of time.

The professional status of careers advisers has never been entirely secure, though movements towards greater professionalisation have been given an impetus by the gradual development of a professional literature on guidance and by the formation of the Advice, Guidance, Counselling and Psychotherapy Lead Body to oversee training and qualifications in guidance and related fields (see Chapter 10). Recent developments which reduce careers advisers' discretion in their work – for example, the imposition of new systems of accountability and tighter performance measurement in the form of action plans – may threaten this position by 'proletarianising' their profession (Oppenheimer, 1973). As a consequence, services may find that staff turnover, which has always been high, will remain a problem.

These are just some of the issues that careers services will have to try to resolve in the next few years. The service probably faces a future with as many, if not more, uncertainties than at any other time since its establishment. What does seem clear, though, is that a stronger business ethic will prevail, and that cost-effectiveness will become increasingly important. More worryingly, the new competitive culture seems likely to have the effect of making services wary of sharing ideas about new management arrangements and models of practice, fearing that this could strengthen competitors' bids and so lead to the loss of their next contract. On a more positive note, the greater importance given to careers education and guidance by policy-makers seems likely to result in more resources for the service, and increased provision to a wider range of clients.

REFERENCES

Avent, C. (1974) *Practical Approaches to Careers Education*, Cambridge: Careers Research and Advisory Centre/Hobsons.

Ballantine, M. (1993) 'A New Framework for the Design of Career Interventions in Organisations', *British Journal of Guidance and Counselling* 21(3): 233–45.

Banks, M., Bates, I., Breakwell, G., Bynner, J., Emler, N., Jamieson, L. and Roberts, K. (1992) *Careers and Identities*, Buckingham: Open University Press.

Bates, I. (1990) 'The Politics of Careers Education and Guidance: a Case for Scrutiny', *British Journal of Guidance and Counselling* 18(1): 66–83.

Bedford, T. (1982) *Vocational Guidance Interviews: a Survey by the Careers Service Inspectorate*, London: Careers Service Branch, Department of Employment.

Bradley, S. (1990) 'The Careers Service: Past, Present and Future', *British Journal of Guidance and Counselling* 18(2): 137–55.

Bradley, S. (1992) 'A Case Study of the Careers Service Placement Function', *British Journal of Guidance and Counselling* 20(1): 90–107.

Careers Service Quality Assurance and Development Unit (1995) *Careers Education and Guidance: an Evaluative Framework*, Sheffield: Employment Department.

Carter, M. (1966) *Into Work*, Harmondsworth: Penguin.

Cherry, N. and Gear, R. (1987a) 'Young People's Perceptions of their Vocational Guidance Needs: I. Priorities and Pre-Occupations', *British Journal of Guidance and Counselling* 15(1): 59–71.

Cherry, N. and Gear, R. (1987b) 'Young People's Perceptions of their Vocational Guidance Needs: II. Influences and Interventions', *British Journal of Guidance and Counselling* 15(2): 169–81.

Clarke, L. (1980) *The Transition from School to Work: a Critical Review of Research in the United Kingdom*, London: HMSO.

Department of Employment (1991) *Education and Training in the Twentieth Century*, London: HMSO.

Dex, S. (1982) *Black and White School Leavers: the First Five Years of Work*, Research Paper 33, London: Department of Employment.

Employment Department (1993) *Careers Service Requirements and Guidance for Providers*, Sheffield: Employment Department.

Gray, L.T. (1973) 'If I Were You . . .', *Education and Training* 15(1).

Heginbotham, H. (1951) *The Youth Employment Service*, London: Methuen.

Kidd, J. M., Killeen, J., Jarvis, J. and Offer, M. (1993) *Working Models of Careers Guidance: the Interview*, London: Birkbeck College, University of London (mimeo).

Kidd, J. M., Killeen, J., Jarvis, J. and Offer, M. (1997) 'Competing Schools or Stylistic Variation in Careers Guidance Interviewing', *British Journal of Guidance and Counselling* (in press).

Killeen, J. and Van Dyke, R. (1991) *States of the Union*, Cambridge: National Institute for Careers Education and Counselling (mimeo).

Lawrence, D. (1994) 'The Careers Service: Threatened by Youth Unemployment – Saved by Youth Training', *British Journal of Education and Work* 7(2): 63–76.

Lawrence, P. R. and Lorsch, J. W. (1967) *Organization and Environment*, Boston: Graduate School of Business Administration, Harvard University.

Le Gro, N. and Cavadino, C. (1991) *Careers Service Interviews: Policy and Practice*, Sheffield: Careers Service Branch, Department of Employment.

Maguire, M. and Ashton, D. N. (1983) 'Changing Face of the Careers Service', *Employment Gazette* 91(3): 87–90.

Morris, M., Simkin, C. and Stoney, S. (1995) *The Role of the Careers Service in Careers Education and Guidance in Schools*, Sheffield: Careers Service Branch Quality Assurance and Development Unit, Employment Department.

National Test Users Group (1994) *Use of Psychometric Tests on the Diploma in Careers Guidance Courses* (mimeo).

National Youth Employment Council (1965) *The Future Development of the Youth Employment Service*, London: HMSO.

National Youth Employment Council (1968) *The Work of the Youth Employment Service 1965–1968*, London: HMSO.

Oppenheimer, M. (1973) 'The Proletarianisation of the Professional', *Sociological Review Monograph* 20: 213–27.

Peck, D. (1975) 'The Careers Officer and the Careers Teacher', *Careers Quarterly* 26(4): 9–11.

Ranson, S. and Ribbins, P. (1988) *Servicing Careers in the Post-Employment Society*, London: Falmer.

Roberts, K. (1971) *From School to Work: a Study of the Youth Employment Service*, Newton Abbot: David & Charles.

Rolfe, H. (1994) 'Careers Guidance and the Needs of Young Unemployed People', *Skills Focus* 4: 1–3.

Watson, A., Stuart, N. and Lucas, D. (1995) *Impact of New Management Arrangements in Pathfinder Careers Services*, Sheffield: Careers Service Branch Quality Assurance and Development Unit, Employment Department.

Watts, A. G. (1986) 'The Careers Service and Schools: a Changing Relationship', *British Journal of Guidance and Counselling* 14(2): 168–86.

Chapter 10

Other sources of guidance on learning and work

Ruth Hawthorn

10.1 INTRODUCTION

Although people generally only seek guidance at times of transition, it is now more widely acknowledged that they continue to face such transition points after they have left full-time education, and that their need for help with decisions about learning and work does not diminish. The need can be triggered for internal and personal reasons: we grow and change as individuals, and we need new skills as we face or seek out new roles, whether or not that is in paid work. It can also be triggered by domestic responsibilities: many women, and some men, will take time out of work for family reasons and may want to use that time to reconsider their options before they return. It is further triggered by changes in employment status such as unemployment or retirement. So even individuals who are able to make the most effective use of guidance at school, college or university, and then of the help offered by employers, still may experience periods in their lives when they need to make career-related decisions, but that help is not available. Also, people who are entitled to help from educational institution or employer may still want to get an independent opinion on their best options.

This area of provision, the 'third pillar' of guidance (Watts, 1993), is made up of a multitude of helping agencies. Some are specialist, publicly-funded services; some offer an equally specialist service funded through other means (including direct fees to the guidance client); some may offer guidance on learning or work as part of some wider support role to particular client groups. A number of these providers are statutory public services; some are in the private sector; many, however, are in the voluntary sector, operating on a not-for-profit basis.

This chapter will look briefly at the background and purposes of some of these providers of guidance that are independent of education or employment. The main groups of providers covered are shown in Table 10.1. The chapter will consider the extent to which they face similar issues in relation to their guidance work, and in particular the ways in which they have been able to work together. It will also discuss the possibilities for some kind of overall co-ordination strategy for this kind of guidance provision.

Table 10.1 Guidance providers which are independent of education or training institutions or employers

Guidance provider	Main provision	Funded by
Careers Service	Careers guidance for statutory groups outside formal education (for Careers Service provision for students in schools and further education, see Chapters 5–6 and 9)	Department for Education and Employment (DfEE) or relevant department of Welsh and Scottish Office; in Northern Ireland, Training and Employment Agency
	Guidance for non-statutory clients	Various sources, singly or combined, including Local Authority, European Social Fund, DfEE via TECs/LECs, direct charging to clients
Adult guidance provided by TECs or LECs	Generally TECs or LECs have been purchasers of guidance on behalf of clients, but some also make direct provision, for example through guidance 'shops'	DfEE (or Welsh or Scottish Office), through temporary funding programmes, or European Social Fund, or TEC/LEC itself though income generated locally
Guidance offered by the Employment Service	Job search and guidance programmes for registered unemployed: Jobclubs, Job Review Workshops, Restart courses, etc.	DfEE
Educational guidance services for adults	Educational guidance for people over 19 in various locations: free-standing, as well as the 'pre-entry' guidance offered by colleges or adult education provision	Various, including one, and often several, of the following: Local Education Authorities, District Councils, colleges, universities, European Social Fund, and DfEE via TECs/LECs
Private (fee-charging guidance services)	Educational or careers guidance for young people and adults	Client fees, sometimes subsidised through DfEE via TEC/LEC programmes
Guidance provided as part of broader support for specific client groups	Examples include the Prison or Probation Service, women's centres, centres for unemployed people, youth centres, projects working with socially excluded groups, community centres for ethnic-minority groups	According to provision: includes local government (either directly or through grants to voluntary organisations), Home Office, charitable trusts
Other agencies which offer learning- or work-related advice	Examples include public libraries, Citizens' Advice Bureaux	According to the agency concerned

10.2 PROVIDERS

Careers Service

The work of the Careers Service with its statutory target-groups is described in Chapters 5–6 and 9. There are two areas of its work which fall particularly within the remit of this chapter. As well as serving students in school and college, the Careers Service has also had a responsibility to offer a guidance and placement service to people under the age of 19 who have left education or training. This has included people who go into jobs and then want, or have, to change, but also young people who for various reasons drop out of school and the labour market. A proportion of these may also have problems to do with their families, with physical or mental health, or with housing; although this is equally true of some Careers Service clients who stay on in education or training, all these difficulties are compounded by unemployment and the fact that they may lose touch with the agencies that could help.

The second relevant area of Careers Service work has been the non-statutory work that it has been able to do with adults who are not in work-related education. This has varied from area to area throughout Britain, and over time: whether or not to provide such a service, and if so how much, was a matter for decision at Local Authority level, and depended on the resources and energies of individual services (see Chapter 9). Since 1993, it has been a matter for each careers service. In some areas, adults have been able to make appointments for full interviews with careers advisers, and to make use of specialist services such as psychometric testing; in others, adults have been able to make use of a more informal, drop-in information and advice service. In areas where the Careers Service has not offered full interviews to non-statutory adult clients, it has sometimes been able to offer the use of its careers library. More recently, encouraged by the emergence of the market model for adult guidance (see Chapter 21), an increasing number of services have been developing a policy of charging fees for specified services, often on a 'contribution' basis but sometimes moving towards a full-cost basis. This may result in some expansion of adult services, but to a limited clientele that are able and prepared to pay.

Training and Enterprise Councils/Local Enterprise Companies

Training and Enterprise Councils (TECs, in England and Wales) and Local Enterprise Companies (LECs, in Scotland) were set up in 1990, with responsibility – among other things – for training for unemployed adults, and the development of a training culture in companies. At first, TECs were able to bid for additional funds to introduce or develop guidance to support this work through annually agreed development funds. Later, in order to encourage TECs to explore ways of offering guidance for specific target groups, the Employment Department as it then was introduced a series of one- or two-year funding programmes specifically based on a 'voucher' system of funding (Gateways to Learning, aimed primarily at unemployed adults, from 1992 until 1996; and Skill Choice, primarily for employed adults, from 1993 to 1995). Typically, targeted individuals were issued with vouchers which they could redeem at one of a number of quality-assured guidance services in the TEC area. In many cases,

TECs enlisted and quality-assured existing guidance providers; in other cases, they set up their own guidance services. Where the latter happened, the services were sometimes located in centres which also offered information about other TEC programmes, and were known as guidance 'shops'. Not all of these funding programmes were available in Scotland, but some LECs were also involved with the development of local guidance provision during the same period.

Although guidance was not specifically mentioned in the National Training and Education Targets, agreed for the adult population as well as school-leavers by the National Advisory Council for Education and Training Targets (1993; 1995), TEC support for guidance was strengthened by their responsibility for the achievement of those targets. Government support for TEC provision of guidance after the end of the specific funding programmes was subsumed into a broader interest in the development of lifelong learning linked to the targets, and into ways of encouraging individuals to take responsibility for their own training; guidance was seen as a valid component of this, but was no longer shaped by any central strategy. One consequence of this was that, in the absence of a more strategic initiative (cf. Sections 10.3 and 10.4 below), an already very varied pattern of provision at local level seemed likely to continue to diversify.

Employment Service

The functions of the Employment Service have included help in placement for adults, and the administration of benefits associated with unemployment. These functions have been carried out in the same and separate premises at different periods, and the guidance component has also fluctuated. Occupational Guidance Units, available in some Jobcentres, for a time provided a free careers guidance service to adults, but this service was dismantled in 1981. A number of guidance-related schemes to help long-term unemployed adults back into the labour market were subsequently introduced during the recession of the 1980s. Jobclubs, Restart courses (one, and later two, weeks in duration), and two-day Job Review or Jobplan workshops, are examples.

Entry to such schemes has been negotiated at interviews associated with benefit entitlement. Individuals have had initial interviews with claimant advisers, and then again after 3 or 6 months if still unemployed, and there has been the potential for some element of guidance at these interviews. But claimant advisers have been seriously restricted in the time available for individual clients, and often have been able to do no more than refer people to other guidance providers (in many TEC guidance schemes, applications for vouchers were issued through claimant advisers). Their potential to develop as providers of client-centred guidance has been limited by their responsibility to report benefit fraud, and by the consequent perception held of them by some clients; it has also been limited by the requirement on them to meet employment or special-programme enrolment targets wherever possible. However, this has not affected all their work, and they do see and help individuals who would be unlikely to seek out other guidance providers.

The Jobclubs and short courses have offered greater scope for guidance, as well as careers education, which is more closely comparable with that offered by other specialist services. As with TEC provision, these are generally contracted out to careers services, to colleges of further education, and to other organisations. There has been a considerable variety in the organisations which provide these courses, and in the extent to which they draw in specialist help from guidance professionals.

Educational guidance services for adults

As discussed in Chapter 6, the movement to provide educational guidance for adults was not argued in terms of the labour market; instead, based on a report from the Advisory Council for Adult and Continuing Education (1979), it stemmed from the belief that individuals benefit personally from learning, and should have more equal access to it. What might appear to be non-vocational courses could lead on to vocational ones, but if not, they are still of value to the learner, and to society. The first educational guidance service for adults (EGSA) in the United Kingdom started in Belfast in 1967, and such services steadily grew in number on the mainland; in 1980 a professional association, the National Association of Educational Guidance Services (NAEGS, later NAEGA), was formed to bring together people working in them.

Some central and local government funding for these services was made available throughout the 1980s, prompted partly by government concern with the high unemployment in the first half of that decade, partly by growing pressures to redress inequalities experienced by women and ethnic-minority groups, and partly, towards the end of the decade, by anxiety about skill shortages (UDACE, 1990). In 1988 the Department of Education and Science introduced a category of Educational Support Grant provision to set up educational guidance provision for adults. Jointly the DES and the Employment Department funded first the Unit for the Development for Adult Continuing Education (UDACE), which commissioned a series of what became seminal reports for adult guidance, and later the National Educational Guidance Initiative.

Partly because of their origins in adult education, and partly because of the focused development work of UDACE and NAEGA during the second half of the 1980s, EGSAs have generally been referred to as a distinct sector of provision. However, the concept of the EGSA was bound up in that of a network of agencies which contributed one or more of seven activities seen as central to educational guidance (informing, advising, counselling, assessing, enabling and advocating on behalf of clients, and feeding back to providers of education information about their unmet needs) (UDACE, 1986). In some cases the EGSA itself was not an independent agency resourced directly by the Local Education Authority, but the agency within the network which undertook the co-ordinating role. The change in the role and resources of the LEAs has reduced the number of LEA-funded, network-co-ordinating EGSAs; in some cases these have given way to TEC-led local structures, more closely linked to employment targets (see Section 10.3 below).

Consequently it may now be less sensible to see EGSAs as a sector than as a way of working. Their distinctive focus is on educational rather than employment choices, and on redressing inequality of opportunity not for the sake of improving the pool of labour, but for the benefit of the individual. There are guidance agencies and individual guidance workers, in almost all of the sectors which work with adults, that subscribe to the model and underlying principles of the UDACE reports (see, in particular, UDACE, 1986). This is reflected in the broad membership of NAEGA.

Private (fee-charging) guidance services

The extent and growth of private, fee-charging guidance provision is hard to assess, particularly as a number of organisations which offer outplacement packages to companies (see Chapter 8) also offer services to individuals independently of an employer. Fees and services – and, probably, quality – vary considerably, but many are staffed by occupational psychologists, trained personal counsellors, or former staff from the Careers Service. The demand for such help, and probably the supply, increased during the periods of high unemployment in the 1980s, but contacts with other providers of 'neutral' guidance were limited until the early 1990s when some private providers took part in TEC voucher schemes.

Guidance provided as part of broader support for specific client groups

In addition to these sources of specialist advice, many adults and young people receive educational or vocational advice from organisations or centres where they go for help with some broader problem. Examples include community centres for ethnic minorities, a wide range of organisations specifically for women (from professional support networks, through mothers' groups run by Social Services, to the Women's Institute), centres for the unemployed run by City or District Councils, organisations to help physically or mentally handicapped people or people recovering from mental illness run by Health or Social Services or voluntary organisations, organisations to support retired or elderly people, and organisations for the resettlement of offenders. Services for young people include the Probation Service, and agencies which work with young people at risk of social exclusion. Some Youth Services have set up information or counselling centres for young people, which can involve an element of educational or work-related advice.

The main function of these organisations might be to provide training for their target group, or to provide advice on welfare support, or to provide a social centre; their guidance function might be to refer individuals to specialist guidance sources or to invite in specialist guidance professionals, but it might involve the use of one or more members of staff with specialist guidance training and is likely also to include some direct informal guidance delivered by generalist staff. Links with the local careers service, TEC, LEC or EGSA have varied considerably, but in some areas statutory or voluntary organisations of these kinds have been actively involved in adult guidance networks.

Other agencies which offer learning- or work-related advice

Other kinds of agencies have participated in guidance work at local or national level. Some offer advice relating to learning and work within a broader spectrum of help, such as Citizens' Advice Bureaux and public libraries. Again, generally there has been no overall pattern. In some Local Authority areas, for example, public libraries can do little more than provide appropriate reference books; others have actively supported local guidance networks and have even housed EGSAs; and yet others have entered into more formal arrangements through TECs to contribute to information collection and dissemination systems (UDACE, 1991). Some have set up centres for open learning, with staff who offer advice about appropriate courses (Allred, 1995).

Other organisations have provided specialist information on specific aspects of entry to learning or work. These have included, at a local level, Local Education Authority staff responsible for educational grants, and at a national level, the Educational Counselling and Credit Transfer Information Service (ECCTIS).

10.3 ISSUES

Collaborative networks

The idea of providing a full guidance service through the collaboration of a number of individual specialist services was central to the concept of the 'personal guidance base' (Miller *et al.*, 1981) (see Chapter 6), and was also adopted by NAEGS (Butler, 1984). It was developed and elaborated by UDACE (1986) at the beginning of its development programme for educational guidance for adults. This fuller model suggested a central co-ordinating organisation, and a collaborative network of a potentially large number of other agencies which offered one or more of the seven activities of guidance identified by UDACE (see Section 10.2 above). The argument for this approach was made in terms of the pooling of expertise and resources. A refinement of the model suggested an inner partnership of organisations or institutions which offered all seven guidance activities, a middle ring of more specialist agencies which offered some only, and a much larger outer ring of organisations which needed to know about the work of the guidance providers in order to be able to refer clients to them, or to which guidance agencies might want to refer clients with needs not directly to do with education or training (Alloway and Opie, 1987). The UDACE handbook for the development of guidance networks suggested that they could share staff development and professional support, the collection and dissemination of information on learning opportunities, and publicity for the work of its members; could develop referral procedures; and could set up arrangements to collect information about unmet needs and to feed it back to colleges and training organisations. Although some form of central co-ordination was necessary to arrange meetings, there were disadvantages in being 'too reliant on any one individual or agency' (Sadler, 1989).

The use of this model for collaboration was a condition of DES funding for adult guidance through subsequent rounds of Educational Support Grant and REPLAN funding (see Chapter 6) between 1986 and 1991, but was interpreted in very different ways at a local level, in keeping with the variety of different patterns of existing provision for the various constituent members of the networks. In some cases, an LEA-funded EGSA co-ordinated the network; in some, this was done by an adult unit within the Careers Service; and in some, networks grew up with no one agency in overall control (UDACE, 1990). In looking at links between guidance providers in Europe as a whole, Watts *et al.* (1988) identified five different forms: *communication* (explaining services to each other in order to, for example, improve referral), *co-operation* (on some joint task), *co-ordination* (where services alter their working patterns to bring them more in line with each other, but remain within existing professional boundaries), *cross-fertilisation* (sharing and exchanging skills with the possibility of redrawing such boundaries), and *integration* (where the boundaries disappear altogether). The adult guidance networks which developed by the end of the period of DES funding were engaged in most of these in relation to their different tasks: referral systems required regular and systematic communication; collaboration over information, marketing and feedback led to co-operation and co-ordination; and joint training in particular gave rise to cross-fertilisation.

The Employment Department was a joint sponsor of UDACE, and when TECs and LECs took a more active part in the development and funding of adult guidance from 1992, some of the ideas and terminology from EGSAs and the DES programmes reappeared in the conditions for ED funding to TECs. In particular, the idea of a quasi-market in guidance (see Chapter 21) – involving a choice of providers where individuals could 'spend' their voucher, and perhaps later, if they were in employment, pay for themselves – required there to be a number of different organisations which could offer a recognisably similar service. TECs were encouraged to map existing provision of the seven activities, and then set up 'guidance networks'. In some cases this task was carried out in areas which had set up networks on the UDACE model, and some TECs were able to build on this earlier work.

However, even where this happened, the TEC 'networks' which resulted differed from the earlier UDACE ones in important respects (and in some cases co-existed alongside them at least for a time). For the voucher system to work, TECs needed to quality-assure guidance providers, which meant that network members tended to be characterised by the similarity rather than the diversity of their services. Organisations took part in TEC networks for the income which they received from the vouchers, and for the other material advantages – in some cases, TECs would fund training for their staff, and the purchase of computer equipment for databases and computer-aided guidance (Marion Smith Associates, 1995). Most significantly, the notion of a market required the agencies to compete with one another to provide a good but economical service, and to that extent sharing of expertise and resources was replaced by competition (Coopers & Lybrand, 1994). By the nature of the association, the TEC was the dominant partner in networks of this kind and controlled the use of its funds (say, for professional development). A disadvantage of a network which is motivated by funding from one agency, and where collaboration is cultivated in a spirit of competition, is that if such funding diminishes beyond a certain point – as is possible with TEC resources for guidance – all collaboration can be endangered, and it may not be easy to revive the former more equal partnership of peers. In areas where funding was not made available for guidance voucher schemes, as in much of Scotland, co-ordination, co-operation and cross-fertilisation may have been more robust.

The transfer of interest in TECs and LECs to lifelong learning drew attention to the need for collaboration of a different kind: between providers of guidance for people at different stages of their lives. This focuses on links between the providers of guidance discussed in this chapter, and those who provide it in schools, colleges and universities, as well as in employing organisations. It could take the form of establishing some record of guidance (similar to, and perhaps contained within, a Record of Achievement) which could be kept by an individual; or it could take the form of stronger links – of communication, co-operation, co-ordination and cross-fertilisation – between the agencies, so that at the very least individuals could recognise that the help they received at school, college, Jobcentre, work, community centre and careers centre contained common features. Collaboration along this somewhat different dimension of 'all-age guidance' could build on the local adult guidance networks initiated by UDACE and the DES, and continued by TECs and the ED.

Funding

UDACE (1986) argued that the responsibility for provision of educational guidance for adults rested with the LEA. The principle behind the funding for adult guidance through the Educational Support Grant was that of 'pump-priming', so that by the end of the funding period the LEA in question would make resources available to continue the work at the same level. In fact, LEA budgets for adult education were badly affected by subsequent educational funding decisions, and by the end of the 1980s, only a limited number of EGSAs were fully funded by LEAs; in other cases, the Educational Support Grant had gone to careers services to make provision for adults. Not all EGSAs were dependent on LEA funds: a number were based in further education colleges, and some were supported by City or District Councils. But those that were wholly funded by LEAs, and those that were established as voluntary organisations and drew on funding directly or indirectly from LEAs, were insecure (UDACE, 1990). ED funding programmes through TECs were also seen as pump-priming exercises, with the intention that when they were over, guidance would be financed either by clients who could pay or, in the case of those who could not, by the TEC itself through forms of cross-subsidy. At the time of writing it is not clear whether this will be possible, but the evidence is that some TECs at least are using new short-term grants to pick up work initiated by earlier programmes. Both LEAs and TECs have also been able to bid annually for European Social Fund moneys to finance adult guidance work, and these have been enhanced by a number of forms of equally temporary funds available from the European Commission to redeploy staff in declining industries (defence and coal-mining, for example).

The unpredictability of these forms of funding has always been a serious problem for adult guidance. It has made it difficult to plan for periods of longer than one year, with consequent effects on staffing, on staff development, and on investment in equipment and premises. It has also made all provision susceptible to fundamental shifts in response to quite small additional and temporary sources of money, as the experiment in vouchers demonstrated. It raises a particular problem in relation to marketing: guidance providers are reluctant to give much publicity to a service which may not exist in a few months' time, but then are often only able to mount a case for funding on the basis of demonstrable demand (Coopers & Lybrand, 1994).

The voucher experiment had another significant influence on provision. DES funding, on the basis of the UDACE model, encouraged a mixture of provision including not only individual interviews, but also a drop-in service (staffed by experienced guidance workers and not just by receptionists), group work and outreach work. Vouchers, however, could only be redeemed against a fixed amount (often one or two hours) of individual guidance, and this removed the flexibility –

strongly valued by some services – to offer different kinds of activity according to the user's need. The voucher was based on a unit cost for standard interviews that often included staff time and accommodation, but not the more complex costs of developing and maintaining information bases, or of staff development (Wright, 1993). Although guidance providers were often invited to confirm whether the rate was set correctly, they were not always aware of the long-term consequences of unit costing on the basis of what were largely marginal costs. Few vouchers were increased in value in line with inflation in the second and subsequent years, and in some cases TECs reduced their value; the result was an even greater pressure to restrict any work other than one-to-one interviews. Although some TECs later abandoned vouchers as a way of promoting guidance, the principle of unit costing against interviews was still widely used.

Training

Before 1995, each type of guidance provider described in this chapter had different kinds of initial and in-service training (Hawthorn and Butcher, 1992). Advisers with the Careers Service were required to have a Diploma in Careers Guidance (see Chapter 9), and the Employment Service provided its own training for claimant advisers. But although a range of diplomas and certificates evolved to meet the needs of staff in educational guidance services for adults and in some other agencies within the guidance network (Hawthorn, 1995a), there was no overall pattern of requirements for these agencies.

In 1995, the Advice, Guidance, Counselling and Psychotherapy Lead Body completed its work to develop standards for staff in these fields, and a system of National Vocational Qualifications at levels 2, 3 and 4 was put in place. The aim is gradually to replace existing qualifications, and introduce accreditation in agencies where there was none before. In principle, staff in different but related agencies, such as benefit advice and careers guidance services, will be able to seek accreditation for the same units of competence against evidence related to their own fields. But it is also intended that this system of accreditation will make it possible for staff to move more freely than before between different types of guidance and advice-giving. These new qualifications are a system of accreditation: they do not necessarily involve training, as candidates can seek accreditation of prior learning. To some extent, NVQs influence the way in which staff will be trained, with their emphasis on theory only as manifested in professional competence, but this does not necessarily preclude the models of joint training that have been particularly associated with guidance networks of both the UDACE (Hawthorn and Wood, 1988) and TEC kinds.

Quality

Careers Service work has been subject to inspection by the Employment Department's Careers Service Branch (see Chapter 9). TECs and LECs have been required to submit all organisations that provide services to them to a quality-assurance procedure, including guidance. In the absence of any clear central direction, they have approached this in a variety of ways and against a number of different kinds of organisational standards. Some EGSAs were inspected by

Her Majesty's Inspectorate as part of adult education provision. In 1994, as its first major initiative, the National Advisory Council for Careers and Educational Guidance (the Guidance Council) undertook to embark on a programme to devise standards for each sector of guidance, within a a common framework (Hawthorn, 1995b). The success of this enterprise will depend on the extent to which these standards are consistent with, or can be incorporated into, other quality standards used by the many different organisations involved in guidance described in this and the other chapters in this part of the book. The obstacles in the case of the Careers Service, where standards are already embedded into the inspection system, will, for example, be different from those in guidance work in voluntary organisations with other remits: some of the latter may not have not embarked on quality-assurance procedures at all, or may be accountable to a number of different funding bodies.

Apart from formal standards, a number of independent providers of guidance for adults have drawn up policy statements, or statements of professional principles. EGSAs worked to one list of these (UDACE, 1986) and the Institute of Careers Guidance has drawn up its own in collaboration with NAEGA for careers and educational guidance work with adults (ICG/NAEGA, 1992).

Gaps in provision

The picture of multiplicity and variety may obscure the fact that some geographical areas have little provision, and that in other areas some potential users of guidance are not accommodated. People in rural areas (REPLAN, 1989), and well-qualified individuals at more advanced stages of their careers, are examples of groups who have particular difficulties not only in finding appropriate training, but in securing appropriate guidance.

10.4 CONCLUSION

Given the great variety of existing provision at a local level, but also its temporary nature and sometimes incomplete coverage, it is not easy to suggest a simplifying overall model to meet the needs of all individuals. The cost of extending the Careers Service's work with young people to everyone over 19 is agreed to be prohibitive, and the TEC National Council looked at alternatives from the many experiments carried out by TECs within the Gateways to Learning and Skill Choice programmes (TEC National Council, 1994). Many TECs have set up tiered provision, offering general guidance interviews as a first tier, and specialist activities such as psychometric testing, or advice on accreditation of prior learning, or help with constructing a CV, as a second tier. The TEC National Council gave its support to a proposal that a more limited 'foundation' level – comprising information and a signposting interview – should be provided free of charge to all adults, and that where the further services were recommended or sought, they should be paid for where possible by the individual, by his or her employer, or by a combination of the two; only in the case of the unemployed, the unwaged and possibly the low-waged would they be paid by the state, probably through the TEC or LEC (Watts, 1994; see Chapter 21). Questions remain about which agency or agencies should provide the foundation stage; who would be responsible to ensure that there was adequate provision for all client groups wherever they lived; and how the quality of the 'customised' level could be regulated.

The attention paid to the need by adults for guidance throughout their lives increased markedly in the 1980s and 1990s. The response has, however, been constrained by public-expenditure restrictions, and by the debate about how far it is desirable and/or feasible to develop a real 'market in guidance', in which the user will pay (see Chapter 21). In the meantime, funding for work with adults remains insecure and patchy, and no one agency at national or local level has yet definitively emerged to take responsibility for its coherent development.

REFERENCES

Advisory Council for Adult and Continuing Education (1979) *Links to Learning*, Leicester: ACACE.

Alloway, J. and Opie, L. (1987) *Setting Up Educational Guidance: Some Ideas*, Leicester: Unit for the Development of Adult Continuing Education.

Allred, J. (1995) *Open Distance Learning in Public Libraries*, Report for the Commission of the European Communities, Preston: Centre for Research in Library and Information Management, University of Central Lancashire (mimeo).

Butler, L. (ed.) (1984) *Educational Guidance: a New Service for Adult Learners* (2nd edn), Milton Keynes: Open University.

Coopers & Lybrand (1994) *Gateways to Learning: Summary of Findings from First Round Pilots*, London: Coopers & Lybrand.

Hawthorn, R. (1995a) 'Courses on Careers Education and Guidance', *NICEC Careers Education and Guidance Bulletin* 44, Spring.

Hawthorn, R. (1995b) *First Steps: a Quality Standards Framework for Guidance Across All Sectors*, London: Royal Society of Arts/National Advisory Council for Careers and Educational Guidance.

Hawthorn, R. and Butcher, V. (1992) *Guidance Workers in the UK: their Work and Training*, NICEC Project Report, Cambridge: Careers Research and Advisory Centre/Hobsons.

Hawthorn, R. and Wood, R. (1988) *Training Issues in Educational Guidance for Adults*, Leicester: Unit for the Development of Adult Continuing Education.

Institute of Careers Guidance/National Association for Educational Guidance for Adults (1992) *A Guidance Entitlement for Adults*, Stourbridge: ICG.

Marion Smith Associates (1995) *Lessons Learnt from Skill Choice*, Report for the Department for Education and Employment (mimeo).

Miller, J., Taylor, B. and Watts, A. G. (1981) *Towards a Personal Guidance Base*, London: Further Education Unit.

National Advisory Council for Education and Training Targets (1993) *First Annual Report on National Education and Training Targets*, London: NACETT.

National Advisory Council for Education and Training Targets (1995) *Report on Progress Towards the National Targets*, London: NACETT.

REPLAN (1989) *Country Learning: a Development Worker's Guide to Supporting Unwaged Rural Learners*, Leicester: National Institute of Adult Continuing Education.

Sadler, J. (1989) 'Developing Networks', in Rivis, V. (ed.) *Delivering Educational Guidance for Adults*, Leicester: Unit for the Development of Adult Continuing Education.

TEC National Council (1994) *Individual Commitment to Lifetime Learning*, London: TEC National Council.

Unit for the Development of Adult Continuing Education (1986) *The Challenge of Change*, Leicester: UDACE.

Unit for the Development of Adult Continuing Education (1990) *Educational Guidance for Adults in 1988–89*, Leicester: UDACE.

Unit for the Development of Adult Continuing Education (1991) *Educational Guidance for Adults and Public Libraries*, Leicester: UDACE.

Watts, A. G. (1993) 'How Are the Needs to be Met?', in Ball, C. (ed.) *Guidance Matters: Developing a National Strategy for Guidance in Learning and Work*, London: Royal Society of Arts.

Watts, A. G. (1994) *A Strategy for Developing Careers Guidance Services for Adults*, CRAC Occasional Paper, Cambridge: Careers Research and Advisory Centre/Hobsons.

Watts, A. G., Dartois, C. and Plant, P. (1988) *Educational and Vocational Guidance Services for the 14–25 Age Group in the European Community*, Maastricht: Presses Inter-universitaires Européennes.

Wright, E. (1993) *Calculating the Real Cost of Guidance*, paper prepared for a national conference as part of the Employment Department's Guidance and Assessment Development Programme, Stoke-on-Trent, November (mimeo).

Part III

Practice

This part of the book covers five areas of careers education and guidance practice.

Chapter 11 examines the career counselling interview, which has traditionally been considered to lie at the heart of the guidance process. It looks at ten main approaches to such interviews, clustered into four orientations. It also discusses some of the issues that guidance workers need to consider in applying these various approaches to their work.

Chapter 12 looks at careers education. It explores the relationship of careers education to careers guidance, and to the wider curriculum. It examines the components of careers education, including a review of the DOTS model, a proposal for a role-related curriculum, and a discussion of the need to attend to progression in careers education programmes. It investigates where such programmes might be found, and what forms they might take.

Chapter 13 reviews experience-based learning about work. It looks in particular at ways of using experience in the workplace – including work experience, work visits and work shadowing – for careers education purposes. It also looks at the use of work simulations. It discusses how to integrate such experience into learning.

Chapter 14 examines recording achievement and action planning. It clusters such methods into four groups: 'scientific', expanded, structured, and 'official'. It then looks at a number of issues relating to the use of these methods, including their purposes, their effects, their settings, their coverage, their sources, their trustworthiness, their control, and their acceptability.

Chapter 15 explores the use of computers in guidance. It maps existing 'mini' systems into eight categories, and also examines the advantages and disadvantages of 'maxi' systems which cover most of these categories in an integrated way. It discusses the possible roles of the computer – as a tool, an alternative, or an agent of change – and its general strengths and limits. It also explores how computer systems can be integrated into guidance programmes, and implications for the role of the counsellor.

The structure of this part of the book means that some topics do not receive separate attention. Psychometric tests are discussed to some extent in Chapters 11, 14 and 15. Using information on learning and work opportunities receives some attention in Chapter 15 in particular. Small-group work is mentioned briefly in Chapter 12; some of the approaches in Chapter 11 can also be related to such work.

Chapter 11

The career counselling interview

Jennifer M. Kidd

11.1 INTRODUCTION

The interview is probably the event that most lay people associate most directly with careers guidance. Many would be surprised, however, to learn of the variety of 'models' of interviewing that guidance practitioners may employ. Ten or fifteen years ago, the main differences in approach could be characterised quite simply: the choice was between a counselling-type interview using Rogerian relationship skills, and a content-oriented model where the aim was to obtain certain categories of information from the client and make recommendations as to the action he or she should take. Rodger's Seven-Point Plan (Rodger, 1952) was often used as a framework for this latter approach.

In recent years, though, there has been an increase in the range of approaches on offer to the guidance practitioner. To some extent this has been due to the pro-liferation of American writing on contemporary theoretical perspectives on career counselling, but the influence of British (more practice-oriented) work is also apparent. Crites's (1981) and Walsh and Osipow's (1990) volumes are good exam-ples of the contemporary American literature in this area: both contain compre-hensive reviews of a range of models, and attempt to describe and differentiate them along a range of dimensions. These are discussed later in more detail. There appear to be no British reviews of career counselling theories specifically, though Millar *et al.* (1992) deal thoroughly with the theoretical background to interview-ing practice in general, across a range of settings. Ball's (1984) and Nathan and Hill's (1992) discussions of practice have also made useful contributions.

The provision of interviews within the total guidance process varies some-what between professional groups. In higher education careers services, for example, there has been a move away from individual hour-long interviews, and in some cases more emphasis is now placed on access to information and group work (see Chapter 6). In other contexts, however, the interview is still seen as a central core of provision: for example, adults receiving guidance through Training and Enterprise Councils are sometimes given a voucher to 'pay' for an intensive interview as part of the service provided (see Chapter 10).

Whatever model for one-to-one career counselling is adopted, the interview should be seen as only one possible guidance activity among many. It might also be argued that where it is offered, the interview should come later rather than earlier in a sequence of activities, since research suggests that clients who have participated in careers education programmes before the interview gain more from the interview itself (Bedford, 1982a). It may further be noted that although individual guidance seems to be more effective, in terms of a range of learning outcomes, than other types of interventions, it is much more costly (Oliver and Spokane, 1988). Practitioners need to consider carefully, therefore, how far the one-to-one interview is the most appropriate intervention for a particular client or group of clients.

Guidance interviewing practice also varies between professional groups. It is dangerous to generalise, but practitioners working in independent career counselling and outplacement agencies are more likely than other guidance workers to offer clients a battery of tests (which may include interest and personality inventories and aptitude tests) and to make recommendations based on interpretations of their results. Outplacement counsellors are likely to focus on coaching and support in job hunting and also may be more prepared to devote more time to providing emotional support to clients who are recovering from the trauma of redundancy. In the face of limited information about their clients' interests and abilities, educational guidance workers may have to give a fair amount of attention to assessment too, though they are unlikely to be trained in the use of psychological tests and their assessment techniques may be more wide-ranging (Kidd, 1988). Recent research suggests that careers officers, higher education careers advisers and educational guidance workers vary considerably in their familiarity with different models of guidance interviewing (Kidd *et al.,* 1993) and for careers officers at least this seems to affect the way they describe their interviewing practice (Kidd *et al.*, 1994).

Space precludes a full discussion of the range of models of interviewing promulgated in the literature: the reader is referred to the reviews cited above for a detailed discussion of the orientations summarised here. What is attempted in this chapter is a fairly comprehensive (though, of necessity, broad-brush) overview of the main approaches to interviewing which appear to be applied in Britain. These are discussed within four general 'orientations': person–environment fit; developmental; person-centred; and goal-directed. Throughout, the techniques and methods derived from British theory and research are given more prominence than the American models, since reviews of the latter are more readily available. What some may consider as an important orientation, the psychodynamic, is not covered, because such approaches rarely inform practice in Britain. Even in the United States, where more use is made of them, the underlying psychodynamic theories have not been well applied, beyond the use of certain techniques such as card sorts and projective techniques, which are often used within other career counselling orientations.

The overall aim is to go some way towards reducing the gap between theory and practice by outlining some of the ways in which it is possible to learn from theory and by highlighting the main implications of the various orientations for career counselling methods and techniques. The orientations and approaches covered are set out in Table 11.1. To some extent this taxonomy describes ideal types, and categorising models in this way over-emphasises differences at the expense of similarities. Furthermore, the scheme may be too blunt, since it conceals some important distinctions between approaches within the same general orientation. Placing Egan and Krumboltz in the same category, for example, fails to draw attention to the fact that Egan's model is a framework for helping generally, whereas Krumboltz's model derives

Table 11.1 Major orientations and approaches to interviewing

Orientations	Approaches
Person–environment fit	Seven-point plan (Rodger) Congruence models (e.g. Holland) Information-processing principles
Developmental	Developmental careers counselling (Super) FIRST (Bedford)

Person-centred	Client-centred counselling
	  (Rogers)
	Personal construct theory
	  techniques

Goal-directed	Social learning model (Krumboltz) Skilled helper (Egan) Interpersonal interaction models

directly from his social learning theory of career decision-making (see Chapter 2). The scheme also fails to acknowledge differences in the degree of centrality of the interview itself within the various approaches. Within person–environment fit orientations, for instance, the interview is at the heart of the guidance intervention, but in Super's developmental approach it is only one component of the guidance process. Notwithstanding these caveats, a more elaborate classification of models is likely to be over-cumbersome for present purposes.

Following this overview of orientations and approaches, the final three sections of the chapter discuss some of the issues that guidance workers may need to consider in applying the various approaches in their work. Some general matters on the relationship between theory and practice are dealt with, and a classification scheme is presented which suggests how far each orientation and approach offers specific guidelines to the practitioner with respect to a number of criteria.

11.2 PERSON–ENVIRONMENT FIT ORIENTATIONS

Often called talent-matching or congruence theories, these models derive from trait-and-factor theories of occupational choice and guidance. They emphasise diagnosis and assessment, and the expected outcome is a recommendation to the client on an appropriate course of action. The practitioner is likely to use forms and questionnaires completed before the interview as aids to assessment. Sometimes the results of psychometric tests are used as well.

Perhaps the most well-known person–environment fit model in Britain is Rodger's seven-point plan (Rodger, 1952). This is simply a list of questions organised under seven headings. Rodger suggested that these should be regarded as a short list of items that need to be considered in guidance. The seven headings and their associated questions are shown in Table 11.2. For many years, this was the main model of interviewing used by careers officers. It has fallen out of favour in recent years, however, largely because of its diagnostic and directive

Table 11.2 Rodger's seven-point plan

Heading	Questions
1 Physical make-up	Has he [*sic*] any defects of health or physique that may be of occupational importance? How agreeable are his appearance, his bearing and his speech?
2 Attainments	What type of education has he had? How well has he done educationally? What occupational training and experience has he had already? How well has he done occupationally?
3 General intelligence	How much general intelligence can he display? How much general intelligence does he ordinarily display?
4 Special aptitudes	Has he any marked mechanical aptitude, manual dexterity, facility in the use of figures, talent for drawing or music?
5 Interests	To what extent are his interests intellectual? practical– practical–constructional? physically active? social? artistic?
6 Disposition	How acceptable does he make himself to other people? Does he influence others? Is he steady and dependable? Is he self-reliant?
7 Circumstances	What are his domestic circumstances? What do the other members of the family do for a living? Are there any special openings available for him?

Source: Rodger (1952)

nature, its perceived rigidity, and its focus on the content of the interview rather than process issues. Nevertheless, many guidance practitioners still appreciate the *aide mémoire* provided by the seven headings.

One of the most influential and widely researched person–environment fit models in the United States is that of Holland (1973), who proposed that people seek occupational environments that are congruent with their personalities. Holland's theory of occupational choice states that:

1 People fall into six personality or interests types (Realistic, Investigative, Artistic, Social, Enterprising, and Conventional).
2 Occupational environments can be classified in the same terms.
3 Individuals seek to achieve congruence between personality and environment.
4 Where congruence is achieved, optimum satisfaction and performance will result.

According to this model, one of the main activities of the career counsellor is to assess individuals along the six dimensions of occupational interests and to recommend occupations which match the individual's profile. A number of instruments have been developed to assess Holland's interest types. These include the Vocational Preference Inventory (Holland, 1985b), the Self-Directed Search (Holland, 1985a) and the Strong–Campbell Interest Inventory (Hansen and Campbell, 1985).

Holland's work has been criticised for its static view of individuals and occupations. Furthermore, as noted above, and as Rounds and Tracey (1990) have pointed out in their review of person–environment fit approaches, the historically pragmatic focus of these approaches fails to consider the counselling process in any detail. Until now, their emphasis has largely been upon the reliability, validity and type of information gathered about occupations and individuals; little attention has been given to how that information is processed. Rounds and Tracey argue that problem-solving and information-processing are inherent in the person–environment fit models. Theories of problem-solving can be applied to understand better how clients make decisions, how counsellors go about diagnosis, and how they might make decisions about the type of intervention most suited to a particular client. Anderson's (1985) Adaptive Control of Thought theory is used to discuss how information is processed. Vocational interventions need to facilitate the translation of declarative knowledge (facts) into procedural knowledge (ways of acting). This translation is a four-stage process of: (1) encoding (perception of information and appreciation of meaning); (2) goal setting; (3) development of plans and pattern matching; and (4) action.

Person–environment fit approaches have had a bad press in recent years, largely because of the move towards what have been perceived to be less-directive approaches where the guidance worker acts as 'facilitator' rather than 'expert'. It is undoubtedly the case, however, that guidance workers do make judgements and diagnoses in the course of interviews. It has been argued that we need to accept that this is so and to look more closely at these processes. Clarke (1994), for example, has drawn on the literature on medical diagnosis to put forward some hypotheses about the way in which careers officers use information cues to make judgements about clients in interviews. She suggests that an underlying feature of many interviews is a matching process using heuristics and cognitive maps of opportunities. Through this process, careers officers arrive at judgements about their clients, although they may not recognise that this is happening. She goes on to argue that this is an essential procedure within an effective mass careers guidance service, since it enables large numbers of clients to be interviewed in a limited amount of time.

11.3 DEVELOPMENTAL ORIENTATIONS

Although the term 'developmental' covers a range of models, these approaches have two basic features in common. First, all assert that choosing an occupation and adjusting to the world of work is a continuous process which carries on through life. Second, the language of developmental psychology is used to describe and explain the process of career development. Key variables in the various models are the notions of developmental stages, developmental tasks, and career maturity.

The process of career counselling can be broadly described as attempting to form an accurate and comprehensive picture of the client's career development, and encouraging the client to 'move on' in his or her development towards greater awareness of self and situation and competence in decision-making. It has been suggested (e.g. Healey, 1982) that all career counselling interventions need to be related to the client's developmental stage. For example, during the exploratory stage of career development (around ages 15–24) the focus of the interview will be on educational and occupational decision-making and placement, while in the establishment stage (ages 25–44) the emphasis will be broader, taking account of other life-roles in the client's career planning.

The writer most clearly associated with the developmental approach is Super (1957), though other writers have also used developmental theories to elaborate the process of career counselling (see e.g. Blocher and Seigal, 1981; Schlossberg, 1984). Perhaps in response to criticisms of the implicit values within the notion of career maturity, Super (1983) has suggested that developmental career counselling needs to attend to the relative importance of work to the individual (work *salience*) and the satisfactions sought from work (work *values*) as well as the client's career maturity.

Jepsen (1990) describes two general principles which are illustrative of developmental approaches: that 'descriptions and interpretations of a client's career help them construct fresh meanings and prepare to take action'; and that 'counseling techniques and methods are more effective when adapted to the client level of development' (p. 136). One tool which might be used in implementing the former principle is Super's (1980) life-career rainbow. The bands in the rainbow represent the different roles a person assumes during the course of a lifetime. This gives a graphic portrayal of the number and nature of roles that adults are likely to have to assume at any one time and the impact of internal and external forces on these roles.

The second principle finds expression in Bedford's (1982a) framework for describing and evaluating careers officers' interviews. This will be described in some detail, as those who have encountered it vouch frequently for its usefulness. Central to this framework is an initial diagnosis of the stage reached by the client at the start of the interview. This is assessed along five dimensions, using the mnemonic FIRST (Table 11.3). Progress made during the interview is assessed along the same dimensions, and each dimension is viewed as contributing cumulatively towards the goal of 'vocational awareness', which in the case of school-leavers is defined as being fully prepared for the transition from school to work. This suggests that Bedford's framework provides more than just an evaluative framework for the external observer. Rather, it can be seen as a fairly sophisticated framework for the assessment of career development.

The fundamental interviewer skills and techniques, which Bedford refers to as the 'process' aspect of the model, are seen as comprising seven distinct though related qualities (Bedford, 1982b):

1 Establishing the broad purpose of the interview.
2 Creating a friendly, encouraging atmosphere.
3 Gathering information.
4 Identifying the young person's needs.
5 Giving information.
6 Summarising progress made during the interview.
7 Clarifying the next steps to be taken.

Although Bedford does not describe these as stages, a temporal sequence is implied.

One strength of the FIRST framework is its simplicity and its potential for use in training situations. Behaviourally anchored rating scales derived from the framework can be applied in the evaluation of guidance interventions, although this requires observers to rate interviews individually and the reliability of the assessments depends on their skill in using the scales.

Table 11.3 The FIRST framework

Dimension	Question
Focus	How far has the young person narrowed down options?
Information	How well-informed is the young person about the career options s/he has in mind?
Realism	How realistic is the young person (both in relation to own abilities and the constraints of the market)?
Scope	How aware is the young person of the range of options available?
Tactics	To what extent has the young person worked out the practical steps necessary to achieve his/her career objective?

Source: Bedford (1982a)

11.4   PERSON-CENTRED ORIENTATIONS

Although the client-centred approach in personal counselling was first introduced by Rogers (1942), he himself had little interest in applying his approach to career counselling. Patterson (1964) was one of the first writers to elaborate how client-centred principles could be applied in careers guidance. The essence of the client-centred approach is that the most important influence on the progress made in the interview is the relationship between the interviewer and the client. Interview techniques are played down; the attitudes of the practitioner are the main focus. These are normally described as:

1 *Genuineness* – being integrated and real within the relationship.
2 *Unconditional positive regard* – respecting the client in a non-judgemental way.
3 *Empathic understanding* – understanding the client from his or her own internal frame of reference, and endeavouring to communicate this to the client.

The phrase 'person-centred counselling' appears to be the preferred term nowadays. Bozarth and Fisher (1990) suggest two reasons why this is a more appropriate term to describe how this approach informs the careers guidance interview. First, the term emphasises more clearly the importance of the interactive and egalitarian relationship between the practitioner and the client. Second, it highlights the importance of what they call the 'person to person' encounter of the two parties.

Bozarth and Fisher go on to describe four 'axioms' of person-centred career counselling (some of these are derived from Patterson's writings):

1 'The person-centered career counselor has attitudes and behaviors that focus on promoting the inherent process of client self-actualization.'
2 'There is an initial emphasis on a certain area of client concern, that of work.'
3 'There are opportunities for the client to test his or her emerging concept of personal identity and vocational choice with real or simulated work activities.'
4 'The person-centered career counselor has certain information and skills available to the client through which a career goal can be implemented.'

(Bozarth and Fisher, 1990, p. 53)

Axiom 1 suggests that the locus of control within the interview is with the client. In discussing Axiom 2, Bozarth and Fisher make the point that the choice of emphasis is made by the client and that the focus will normally be on occupational issues, although various other areas may be explored later. Axiom 3 points to the need to consider the interview within the broader framework of careers education and guidance; few other models acknowledge this need explicitly. In Axiom 4, we see a recognition of the importance of considering how information about opportunities should be made available. Information should only be introduced when there is a recognised need for it by the client; it should be introduced in a way that maximises client responsibility; and clients should be allowed to express their attitudes and feelings about the information.

In summary, then, the person-centred approach emphasises attitudes and beliefs rather than techniques and goals. It can be characterised as a phenomenological approach which implies a key role for the self-concept: indeed, Super's (1963) propositions concerning the role of self-concepts in career development are frequently referred to.

It is curious that so few links have been made between the person-centred approach and personal construct psychology (PCP) (Kelly, 1955). PCP is fundamentally a theory of personality which stresses the unique ways in which people make sense of the world. The lack of attention generally to the implications of PCP for careers guidance is surprising because it is essentially concerned with individual choice and change. The central building block of the theory is the *construct*, which is a bipolar discrimination made between objects of the individual's experience, and thus has choice built into it. Individuals are viewed as constantly testing out and elaborating their systems of constructs.

In Britain, following early work by Edmonds (1979), the person who has probably done most to elucidate how PCP might be applied to careers guidance is Offer (1989; 1990). A number of careers officers have become familiar with the guidance applications of PCP, largely through Offer's distance-learning materials and training courses.

At the heart of the PCP approach to guidance is the assumption that the effective guidance practitioner 'construes the construction processes of another' (Kelly, 1955, p. 104). Offer (1993) argues that the theory can encompass all of the four DOTS learning outcomes of guidance (see Chapters 4 and 12). Self awareness involves becoming aware of one's constructs; opportunity awareness is concerned with developing viable constructs about the world of work; decision learning involves framing a decision within the relevant constructs and preventing these becoming a 'cage'; and one of the tasks of transition learning is 'spreading one's dependencies', or gaining feedback from a wide range of other people.

In more theoretical terms, the guidance process is conceived as identifying the client's position in the 'experience cycle' and the 'CPC' (circumspection, preemption and control) cycle, and using certain techniques to help the client to move to the next stage in these cycles. The experience cycle starts with anticipation (a state of preparedness), followed by commitment (willingness to get involved with an issue or event), encounter (construing an issue or event), confirmation or disconfirmation (making sense of an event), and constructive revision (facing the implications of what has occurred). Overlapping with the experience cycle, the CPC cycle describes the process of decision-making. In the first phase, *circumspection*, constructs are floated which may be relevant to decisions. This equates to developing self awareness and opportunity awareness in careers guidance: the aim is to ensure that all the pieces of information that may affect the decision are available. In the next phase, *pre-emption*, one or more key issues concerning the decision are identified. The choice has not yet been made, but it becomes clear what the choice is to be between. The third phase, *control*, describes the actual choice (the term 'control' is preferred to 'choice' because the individual refers back to the 'control centre' of the construct system to assess the implications of a particular choice).

Techniques that the interviewer might use to enable the client to progress through these cycles include:

1 Eliciting constructs by asking the client to describe ways in which certain 'elements' (which might be jobs) are similar or different.
2 'Laddering' up the hierarchy of constructs from concrete subordinate constructs to superordinate constructs which have a wider application (one way of doing this is to probe *why* certain things are important to the individual).
3 'Pyramiding' down the hierarchy of constructs from superordinate constructs to subordinate ones (perhaps by asking *how* things differ).
4 Asking the client to complete a 'grid' using certain constructs on a small range of elements (possibly jobs).
5 Employing self-characterisation: for example, asking clients to describe how they see themselves in a year's time, or in a particular position at work.
6 Encouraging the client to develop action plans by moving towards tighter constructs.

Perhaps the main criticism that might be made of PCP as applied to guidance is its lack of attention to objective reality – specifically, hard data about the world of work. It is not clear, for example, how occupational information is to be incorporated into the interview.

11.5 GOAL-DIRECTED ORIENTATIONS

Contained under the heading of goal-directed orientations is a somewhat diverse range of models. Egan's (1990) prescriptive model of helping is placed alongside the descriptive framework offered by Millar *et al.* (1992), and these generic approaches to interviewing are linked with Krumboltz's exposition of the principles of learning that govern decision-making about careers specifically. What these approaches have in common is a recognition that career counselling is about, among other things, goal-setting and action planning. It is for this reason that they are considered together here.

We shall begin with Krumboltz's (1983) social learning approach. As noted in Chapter 2, Krumboltz argues that individuals acquire beliefs about themselves and about the world of work through two kinds of learning experiences: instrumental and associative. The term *instrumental learning experiences* refers to the way individuals develop preferences through participating in a range of activities, and the development of preferences for those in which they succeed or are rewarded. *Associative learning experiences* refer to the exposure of individuals to the ways in which occupations are associated with complex combinations of values. Two consequences of these learning experiences are *self-observation generalisations* (beliefs about one's own abilities, interests, values, etc.) and *task-approach skills* (relationships between self-observation generalisations and the external environment – for example, decision-making orientations, work habits, and emotional responses). Over a period of time, sequences of experiences enable individuals to generate self-observation generalisations and task-approach skills that form the basis for career development. These beliefs and skills are constantly changing as each new experience builds on previous ones.

One task of the career counsellor is to assess the 'accuracy, completeness and coherence' of clients' beliefs about themselves and about the outside world (Krumboltz, 1983). The problems that inaccurate beliefs can produce include:

1 Making inaccurate generalisations about the world of work from a single experience.
2 Making social comparisons with an idealised role model.
3 Over-reacting emotionally to negative events.
4 Making erroneous attributions of the causes of particular career outcomes.
5 Self-deception.

These types of inaccurate beliefs need to be countered and challenged by the career counsellor, using such strategies as: examining assumptions underlying expressed beliefs; looking for inconsistencies between words and behaviour; and confronting illogical frameworks of beliefs (Mitchell and Krumboltz, 1990). Also, more rational behaviour needs to be reinforced by expressions of approval and appreciation. The goal of more accurate self and occupational knowledge is also likely to be pursued by encouraging the client to learn by experience in the real world – for example, by participating in work-simulation and work-experience schemes (see Chapter 13).

The Career Beliefs Inventory (Krumboltz, 1988) may be used as a tool to identify attitudes that interfere with the client's ability to achieve his or her goals. Setting goals for career counselling is central. According to Krumboltz (1966), these should satisfy three criteria: They should (1) be capable of being set differentially for each client; (2) be compatible with the counsellor's values; and (3) be observable. The literature on rational–emotive therapy (RET) also suggests useful methods and techniques for challenging clients' irrational thinking (see, for example, Dryden, 1990). In an earlier article discussing some of the applications of RET to career counselling, Dryden (1979) argues that RET may be appropriate 'when the client is experiencing anxiety, depression, anger, guilt or boredom related to indecisiveness' (p. 185). In line with Krumboltz's views, the goal of counselling will then be to identify irrational and self-defeating assumptions, to challenge these, and to help the client work to change them.

As we have seen, then, central features of the social learning approach are cognitive restructuring and teaching decision-making skills. The three-stage model of helping set out by Egan (1990) has similarities with this approach since, like Krumboltz, Egan emphasises the importance of helping clients to identify their goals and make progress towards achieving them. A summary of Egan's model is provided in Table 11.4. Different communication skills are given emphasis at each stage. For example, within Step 1a, attending, listening, empathy and probing are most relevant, while in Step 1b, challenging is likely to predominate. Egan also emphasises the importance of the 'client–helper contract', which enables both parties to understand what their responsibilities are and helps them to develop realistic mutual expectations. The contract might include:

Table 11.4 Egan's model of helping

Stage	Steps
1 Identifying and clarifying problem situations and unused opportunities	1a Help clients to tell their stories. 1b Help clients to become aware of and overcome their blind spots and develop new perspectives on themselves and their problem situations. 1c Help clients to identify and work on problems, issues, concerns or opportunities that will make a difference.
2 Developing a preferred scenario	2a Help clients to develop a range of possibilities for a better future. 2b Help clients to translate preferred-scenario possibilities into viable agendas. 2c Help clients to identify the kinds of incentives that will enable them to commit themselves to the agendas they fashion.
3 Formulating strategies and plans	3a Help clients to brainstorm a range of strategies for implementing their plans. 3b Help clients to choose a set of strategies that best fit their environment. 3c Help clients to formulate a plan: that is, a step-by-step procedure for accomplishing each goal of the preferred scenario.
All stages	Help clients to act on what they learn throughout the helping process.

Source: Egan (1990).

1 An explanation of the helping process.
2 The nature of the client–helper relationship.
3 The helper's responsibilities.
4 The client's responsibilities.
5 The limits of the relationship (for example, whether the client can contact the helper between sessions).
6 The kind of influence exerted by the helper.
7 An explanation of the flexibility of the process.

An important additional feature of the contract may be an explanation to the client about the model of helping: various materials such as pamphlets and videotapes may be used to give clients a flavour of the process. Nathan and Hill (1992) call this 'screening' and point out that it usually occurs before the counsellor and client contract to meet. Screening may be in writing, by telephone or in person (though the Institute of Personnel Management [1991] recommended that counsellors in such settings should not accept clients without having a preliminary meeting with them to discuss their needs).

Many practitioners see Egan's clear definition of the stages of the helping process as an invaluable aid to strategy. It is covered on many of the initial training courses for careers officers, and a recent survey (Kidd *et al.*, 1994) showed that it is rated highly on practical relevance. This study also suggested, however, that Egan's work is not as well-known to practising guidance workers as are Rogers's client-centred approach or Rodger's seven-point plan. Given its perceived usefulness, more needs to be done to expose guidance workers to this model, particularly those who trained some time ago.

Our final model within the goal-directed category is the framework of interpersonal interaction described by Millar *et al.* (1992). They argue that this model is appropriate for the analysis of any type of interview, across a number of situations – for example, medical, research, selection, appraisal, counselling and careers guidance. Originally developed by Hargie and Marshall (1986), the model incorporates five processes concerning the behaviour of both the interviewer and the client: goal/motivation; mediating factors; responses; feedback; and perception. The model is outlined in Figure 11.1.

Space precludes a detailed account of the processes, so we shall focus primarily on two aspects of the model which, arguably, differentiate it most clearly from our other orientations. These are the attention paid to goals and goal-setting, and the use of social psychology (specifically attribution theory and social influence theory) to achieve a greater understanding of interviewing.

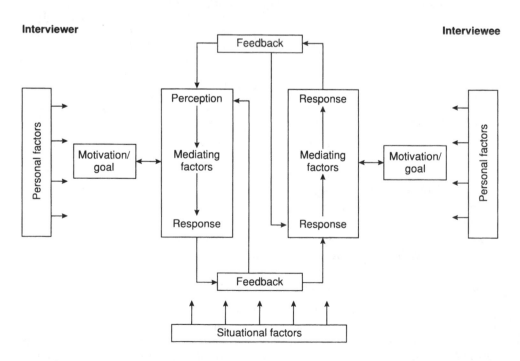

Figure 11.1 Model of interpersonal interaction
Source: Millar *et al.* (1992)

Table 11.5 The range of possible goals and sub-goals for vocational guidance interviews

Goals	Sub-goals
Enable the client to make realistic self-assessments	Develop self-awareness Develop informed self-discovery Encourage an exploration of aims, goals, attitudes and values Provide accurate and current information relating to the client's individualism (e.g. testing)
Enable the client to make realistic occupational/further education/higher education/training assessments	Provide relevant information Encourage critical evaluation of all available information Increase the client's awareness of all potential opportunities Promote a thorough exploration of opportunities Organise any activities deemed of assistance to the client (e.g. work visits, work experience)
Assist the client to make realistic decisions	Develop an awareness of the decision-making process including goal-setting Enable the client to explore the costs and benefits of all possible options (i.e. the implications) Facilitate reality testing of any tentative decisions made Note any interim or final decisions made by the client and act as agreed
Stimulate the client to act upon decisions reached	Provide necessary information (e.g. addresses, names, telephone numbers) Set goals for completion of sub-goals Help to increase the likelihood of action being taken by strengthening the facilitators and reducing the inhibitors Undertake any action promised as part of the agreement

Source: Millar et al. (1992)

Drawing on the goal-setting literature, Millar et al. (1992) argue that effective goals need to be:

1 Clear, specific, and stated in behavioural units.
2 Measurable or verifiable.
3 Realistic or achievable.
4 Internal rather than external.
5 In keeping with the client's values.
6 Appropriately time-scaled.

From these criteria, one can derive certain lessons for career counselling. These might include: the desirability of taking time to share and clarify expectations about the interview and its purposes; the need to monitor client progress and set goals for the interview which are in the control of the two parties; the need to ensure the client's commitment to the guidance process and avoid imposing one's own values on the client; and endeavouring to make the most effective use of the interview time. Some of these are issues which are frequently aired by guidance workers, and practice in various contexts has evolved to incorporate these features: for example, introducing 'contracting' and action planning, and discontinuing blanket interviewing within the Careers Service. What is instructive here is the exposition of how these practices are supported by well-established psychological theory.

Millar *et al.* identify two possible goals for careers guidance interviews: ultimate (e.g. helping the client make realistic decisions) and mediational (e.g. helping the client become aware of the decision-making process). A range of possible goals, based on an amalgam of previous work, is set out in Table 11.5. A number of 'mediating factors' (internal states or processes within the individual which mediate between goals, feedback and action) are incorporated into the model, including cognitions, emotions, beliefs, values and attitudes. Aspects of attribution theory are drawn on to explain these processes and to draw attention to various errors which may occur in the interview.

Perhaps the most important bias in the way we infer the causes of behaviour is the tendency to attribute the cause of our own action to the demands of the situation and the cause of others' behaviour to stable personal characteristics. This is the 'fundamental attributional error' (Ross, 1977). A careers officer, for example, may be too ready to explain the unco-operative behaviour of a client as a reflection of his or her disposition, rather than to what might be an unfamiliar or stressful interview situation.

The literature on counselling as a social influence process (e.g. Strong, 1968; Cormier and Cormier, 1985) is reviewed by Millar *et al.* to examine possible power bases within the interviewer's role. The potential for client change appears to be greatly increased when the client perceives the interviewer as expert, attractive interpersonally, and trustworthy.

The contribution of social influence theory to career counselling has been taken further by Dorn (1990), who identifies five social power bases: expert; referent; legitimate; informational; and ecological. *Expert* power is established as a result of the perceived expertness of the career counsellor. A *referent* power base results from the perception of the interviewer as socially attractive (defined as compatability with the client and having a positive regard for him or her). A *legitimate* power base emerges from the interviewer's standing in the community as a helper. An *ecological* power base results from the counsellor's suggestions about how the client can control his or her environment. Lastly, the *informational* power base develops as a result of the interviewer's awareness of information resources.

Although providing a useful language to describe the potential for social influence within the interview, these reviews pay little attention to how career counsellors might *recognise* and *realise* their power bases. As Bacharach and Lawler (1980) have pointed out, power is not an attribute, but a property of a relationship, and we have to take account of the characteristics of the party over whom the power is being exerted. Furthermore, power can only be exerted effectively when a degree of dependency exists, where one party is reliant on the other for an outcome. Dependency rests on the value of the outcome which is at stake, and the exertion of power is more likely to be effective when the outcome is highly desired than when the value attached to it is low.

One might deduce from this that in order to mobilise their power, career counsellors need first to be aware that certain power bases are possible, and second, to be able to identify the 'sources of dependency' within the client. Many clients see careers guidance as primarily an information-giving service (Cherry and Gear, 1984), and attempting to establish a relationship where clients can gain insight into their interests and abilities (that is, using a referent power base rather than an expert one) could explain why some clients who might benefit from further help fail to return for a second interview. This incongruence between the counsellor's influence attempts and the client's expectations is likely to be minimised by the 'screening' process discussed earlier.

A further practical feature of this framework lies in its implications for analysing the counselling process over a number of sessions. It is possible, for example, that legitimate power will be more important in first meetings, that expert and referent power will be important throughout the process, and that ecological power will play a key role in later stages.

11.6 WAYS TO LEARN FROM THEORY

As we have seen, the approaches described differ in a number of ways. But what difference does it make in practice which model is used? And how might practitioners begin to choose one or the other? These questions imply that career counsellors have some freedom to select a preferred approach, perhaps on the basis of how far a theory is in line with their own views about human nature, how far it seems to meet their clients' needs or the practical constraints of the context in which they interview, or the extent to which it meets various criteria of academic integrity. Yet for most practitioners, there is very little freedom of choice in relation to any of these criteria. How far particular theories are translated into practice depends not only on the nature of the theory itself, but also, and perhaps more significantly, on the 'gateways' through which they must pass in order to reach the practitioner (Tizard, 1990). Training courses are the most obvious of these gateways, and research suggests, in the case of careers officers at least, that students in their initial training are introduced to a narrow range of theories (Kidd et al., 1994). There are of course good reasons for this. Many careers officer trainers would take the view, for instance, that teaching any one approach requires an in-depth programme integrating theory and practical skills development, and it would be impossible to do justice to more than one or two models in a one-year college-based training course which has to cover all aspects of a careers officer's work.

But to what extent do the models have different and unique implications for practice? Some have argued (e.g. Krumboltz and Nichols, 1990) that the major theories are not in fundamental disagreement, and that their main differences are in emphasis and vocabulary. For example, Krumboltz's distinction between self-observation generalisations and task approach skills has a parallel in the 'psychtalk' and 'occtalk' described by Starishevsky and Matlin (1963) in their operationalisation of Super's theory.

A similar argument has been proposed with regard to theories of psychotherapy. Strupp (1973), for instance, takes the view that the commonalities in different forms of therapy are far greater than their differences. One way of identifying what the common therapeutic principles are, as Norcross and Grencavage (1989) observe, is to focus on an intermediate level of abstraction, lying between theory and techniques. They call this 'clinical strategy'.

Other attempts to integrate psychotherapy theories have been described as 'technical eclecticism' and 'theoretical integration' (Norcross and Grencavage, 1989). Put simply, advocates of technical eclecticism use methods and techniques drawn from different sources without necessarily subscribing to their parent theories, while theoretical integrationists attempt to synthesise conceptually diverse theoretical frameworks.

It may be that practitioners will want to develop their approach beyond the one or two models they may have become familiar with in their initial training. Furthermore, those in a training role may want to encourage trainees to use theory more consciously in their work. Given the plethora of models, how might they proceed? There is a range of options:

1 Stay with one or two models (if so, which and why?).
2 Identify the common features from various models that seem to produce client gains – the common factors approach.
3 Tease out the specific methods and techniques from the various models that produce client gains – technical eclecticism.
4 Try to come up with their own, unique, integrative model – theoretical integration.

It may be less important which option is chosen than that guidance workers appreciate that it is possible to learn from the models that exist in a number of different ways, so that tacit relationships between theories and interview styles become more explicit. An examination of the last two options – technical eclecticism and theoretical integration – illustrates some of these.

11.7 TECHNICAL ECLECTICISM

As was noted earlier, a number of schemata have been used to compare and contrast the main features of the various orientations. Walsh and Osipow (1990), for example, have used a framework originally developed by Crites (1981). This uses two main categories: model and methods. The 'model' category defines the theoretical framework of each approach, and this encompasses three chronological stages of the counselling process: diagnosis, process, and outcomes. The 'methods' category is more pragmatic, including interview techniques, test-interpretation procedures, and the use of occupational information.

It would be a relatively straightforward task to follow Walsh and Osipow's framework to classify the orientations described here, perhaps emphasising how the British methods and techniques flesh out their summaries of the techniques implied by each approach. But, consistent with the aim expressed at the outset of this chapter – to attempt to reconcile theory and practice – a schema is proposed which relates the methods and techniques suggested by the various approaches to specific and concrete criteria of effective interviewing. It is hoped that this will be more in tune with the needs of practitioners for guidelines on interviewing.

The rationale behind technical eclecticism is that it is not necessary to synthesise divergent models in order to use the various techniques they suggest.

As was shown earlier, the different approaches emphasise a range of different activities and techniques, and each of these is seen to contribute in some way to effective career counselling. Choosing appropriate techniques is difficult, however, without reference to any specific criteria of effective interviewing. An attempt is made here, therefore, to identify some of these criteria.

The criteria have been gleaned from a number of sources. Exploratory research into careers officers' perceptions of effective interviewing (Kidd *et al.*, 1993) suggests that interviews are seen to be most effective when the careers officer is able to *clarify clients' expectations* at the start of the interview (this may include drawing up a 'contract'), *establish rapport* with the client, effectively *challenge* clients to test their ideas against reality, and *structure* the interview clearly. Added to this list are two criteria derived from the key issues identified by Taylor (1985) and by Nathan and Hill (1992): namely, the most appropriate *provision of information about opportunities*, and the recognition of the *interdependence of personal and occupational concerns*. The final criterion is suggested by Holland *et al.*'s (1981) recognition that one of the main purposes of guidance is to *provide cognitive structures* for clients to help them to organise their thinking about self and situation.

Some of the activities suggested by each of these criteria are as follows.

1 *Clarifying expectations (or negotiating a 'contract')* – agreeing the objectives for the interview and the nature of the guidance process. The latter includes making explicit the responsibilities of the guidance worker and the client.
2 *Developing rapport* – using generic relationship skills, together with more specific skills such as listening and reflecting.
3 *Effective challenging* – helping clients to 'reality-test' their ideas about themselves and opportunities. This may include challenging uninformed ideas or plans, inconsistent beliefs, gender stereotyping, mismatches of job ideas with local opportunities or abilities, and strategically unsound plans.
4 *Structuring the interview* – having a clear sense of structure and being prepared to progress back and forth through interview stages in an iterative manner. This includes setting aside time at the end for action planning.
5 *Providing information appropriately* – helping clients to relate information to their self-assessments, express their feelings about information, and evaluate the information. This includes encouraging clients to research sources of information for themselves.
6 *Recognising the interdependence of personal and occupational concerns* – accepting that discussing career issues may involve sensitive personal issues, and helping clients to deal with these where appropriate. This includes recognising the boundaries between career counselling and personal counselling, and clarifying these for clients.
7 *Providing cognitive structures* – helping clients to develop a framework within which to organise their ideas, so as to increase the scope of their thinking about self and situation. This may be achieved through the use of self-report instruments, such as checklists or standardised psychometric tools, or through job classification schemes.

Table 11.6 indicates how far each orientation and approach identified in this chapter offers the clearest guidelines to the practitioner with respect to each of the criteria. It shows that it is unlikely that any one approach, in itself, will

Table 11.6 A classification scheme to inform practice

CRITERIA	ORIENTATIONS			
	Person–environment fit	Developmental	Person-centred	Goal-directed
Clarifying expectations				Egan Millar *et al.*
Developing rapport			Rogers	
Effective challenging			Kelly	Krumboltz Egan Dryden
Structuring the interview	Rodger	Bedford		Egan Millar *et al.*
Providing information appropriately	Holland		Bozarth and Fisher	
Recognising the inter-dependence of personal and occupational concerns		Super	Bozarth and Fisher	
Providing cognitive structures	Holland	Super	Kelly	

provide sufficient guidelines for effective career counselling. Offering training in just one approach, therefore, is likely to be inadequate. It can also be seen from the table that the more recent models of interviewing emphasise the role of the career counsellor as an active communicator and organiser of interview strategy. A core activity is managing the interview process, through contracting, structuring and challenging. This is in contrast with earlier models which, respectively, emphasised *content* (information-gathering and information-giving), and then non-interventionist interviewer *attitudes* (for example, facilitating the client–counsellor relationship).

Although technical eclecticism is helpful, then, in suggesting a range of practical methods, a word of caution is necessary. There may be a danger that career counselling comes to be seen solely as a pragmatic activity, and that practitioners lose sight of its overall purpose, or long-term direction. This may be a pitfall also in the emerging competence-based approach to skills development, since this seems likely to have the effect of encouraging practitioners to see interviewing simply as a cluster of techniques.

11.8 THEORETICAL INTEGRATION

Historically, guidance has proceeded through a series of stages which reflect different views of careers (Watts and Kidd, 1978; Kidd and Killeen, 1992). In the first stage, guidance was seen as making recommendations about initial job choices; in the second, it was viewed as a facilitative activity, promoting learning about self and situation; and most recently, it has become more concerned with helping individuals to develop the 'executive' skills for lifelong career management, so that they are able to shape their own careers within a changing labour market.

Different approaches to the interview reflect these various purposes for guidance. Holland's model, for example, focuses on occupational choice, while person-centred approaches see the interview as more facilitative of lifelong career development. Super's later writing is more in line with the career management view of guidance.

Practitioners should be aware of these differences in ideologies, so that they can judge how far each approach suits their own purposes in offering guidance to meet the needs of different clients in various contexts. They need to be helped to develop their own style, over and above a technical blend of methods, through the process of theoretical integration. This argues for an in-depth coverage of a range of theoretical models in training, helping trainees to develop the intellectual skills of critical analysis and evaluation, and offering them opportunities to reflect on their own values and goals. There is already some evidence that familiarity with a range of guidance and counselling theories leads practitioners to think strategically about aims and purposes in their interviewing (Kidd et al., 1994).

As is the case with psychotherapy, a single-school approach to career counselling is becoming less common, and is likely to be undesirable. Making more explicit the various ways in which it is possible to learn from career counselling models should lead to a greater recognition of the value of theory in the delivery of guidance and to a more productive dialogue between theory and practice. Two ways in which models can be linked to methods have been suggested – technical eclecticism and theoretical integration. In some respects these are complementary. If career counsellors are to become both effective practitioners and reflective professionals, using theory to identify particular techniques and synthesising theory to develop a personal counselling style are of equal importance.

REFERENCES

Anderson, J. R. (1985) *Cognitive Psychology and its Implications* (2nd edn), San Francisco, CA: Freeman.
Bacharach, S. B. and Lawler, E. J. (1980) *Power and Politics in Organizations*, San Francisco, CA: Jossey-Bass.
Ball, B. (1984) *Careers Counselling in Practice*, Lewes: Falmer.
Bedford, T. (1982a) *Vocational Guidance Interviews: a Survey by the Careers Service Inspectorate*, London: Careers Service Branch, Department of Employment.
Bedford, T. (1982b) *Vocational Guidance Interviews Explored*, London: Careers Service Branch, Department of Employment.
Blocher, D. H. and Seigal, R. (1981) 'Toward a Cognitive Developmental Theory of Leisure and Work', *Counseling Psychologist* 9: 33–44.
Bozarth, J. D. and Fisher, R. (1990) 'Person-Centered Career Counseling', in Walsh, B. and Osipow, S. H. (eds) *Career Counseling: Contemporary Topics in Vocational Psychology*, Hillsdale, NJ: Erlbaum.
Cherry, N. and Gear, R. (1984) *Young People's Perceptions of their Vocational Guidance Needs*, London: Careers Service Branch, Department of Employment.
Clarke, H. (1994) 'What Are Careers Officers Thinking Of?: How Information Cues are Selected and Used in Careers Interviews', *British Journal of Guidance and Counselling* 22(2): 247–59.

Cormier, W. H. and Cormier, L. S. (1985) *Interviewing Strategies for Helpers*, Monterey, CA: Brooks/Cole.

Crites, J.O. (1981) *Career Counseling: Models, Methods and Materials*, New York: McGraw-Hill.

Dorn, F.J. (1990) 'Career Counseling: a Social Psychological Perspective', in Walsh, W. B. and Osipow, S. H. (eds) *Career Counseling: Contemporary Topics in Vocational Psychology*, Hillsdale, NJ: Erlbaum.

Dryden, W. (1979) 'Rational–Emotive Therapy and its Contribution to Careers Counselling', *British Journal of Guidance and Counselling* 7(2): 181–87.

Dryden, W. (1990) *Rational–Emotive Counselling in Action*, London: Sage.

Edmonds, T. (1979) 'Applying Personal Construct Theory in Occupational Guidance', *British Journal of Guidance and Counselling* 7(2): 225–30.

Egan, G. (1990) *The Skilled Helper* (4th edn), Pacific Grove, CA: Brooks/Cole.

Hansen, J. C. and Campbell, D. P. (1985) *Manual for the SVIB SCII* (4th edn), Palo Alto, CA: Consulting Psychologists Press.

Hargie, O. and Marshall, P. (1986) 'Interpersonal Communication: a Theoretical Framework', in Hargie, O. (ed.) *A Handbook of Communication Skills*, London: Routledge.

Healey, C. (1982) *Career Development*, Boston, MA: Allyn & Bacon.

Holland, J. L. (1973) *Making Vocational Choices: a Theory of Careers*, Englewood Cliffs, NJ: Prentice-Hall.

Holland, J. L. (1985a) *The Self-Directed Search: Professional Manual*, Odessa, FL: Psychological Assessment Resources.

Holland, J. L. (1985b) *Manual for the VPI*, Odessa, FL: Psychological Assessment Resources.

Holland, J. L., Magoon, T. M. and Spokane, A. R. (1981) 'Counseling Psychology: Career Interventions, Research, and Theory', *Annual Review in Psychology* 32: 279–305.

Institute of Personnel Management (1991) *The IPM Code of Conduct for Career and Outplacement Consultants*, London: IPM.

Jepsen, D. A. (1990) 'Developmental Career Counseling', in Walsh, W. B. and Osipow, S. H. (eds) *Career Counseling: Contemporary Topics in Vocational Psychology*, Hillsdale, NJ: Erlbaum.

Kelly, G. A. (1955) *The Psychology of Personal Constructs*, New York: Norton.

Kidd, J. M. (1988) *Assessment in Action: a Manual for those Involved in the Educational Guidance of Adults*, Leicester: National Institute of Adult Continuing Education.

Kidd, J. M. and Killeen, J. (1992) 'Are the Effects of Careers Guidance Worth Having?: Changes in Practice and Outcomes', *Journal of Occupational and Organizational Psychology* 65(3): 219–34.

Kidd, J. M., Killeen, J., Jarvis, J. and Offer, M. (1993) *Working Models of Careers Guidance: the Interview*, London: Birkbeck College, University of London (mimeo).

Kidd, J. M., Killeen, J., Jarvis, J. and Offer, M. (1994) 'Is Guidance an Applied Science?: the Role of Theory in the Careers Guidance Interview', *British Journal of Guidance and Counselling* 22(3): 385–403.

Krumboltz, J. D. (1966) 'Behavioral Goals for Counseling', *Journal of Counseling Psychology* 13: 153–59.

Krumboltz, J. D. (1983) *Private Rules in Career Decision Making*, Columbus, OH: National Center for Research in Vocational Education, Ohio State University.

Krumboltz, J. D. (1988) *Career Beliefs Inventory*, Palo Alto, CA: Consulting Psychologists Press.

Krumboltz, J. D. and Nichols, C. W. (1990) 'Integrating the Social Learning Theory of Career Decision Making', in Walsh, W. B. and Osipow, S. H. (eds) *Career Counseling: Contemporary Topics in Vocational Psychology*, Hillsdale, NJ: Erlbaum.

Millar, R., Crute, V. and Hargie, O. (1992) *Professional Interviewing*, London: Routledge.

Mitchell, L. K. and Krumboltz, J. D. (1990) 'Social Learning Approach to Career Decision Making: Krumboltz's Theory', in Brown, D. and Brooks, L. (eds) *Career Choice and Development: Applying Contemporary Theories to Practice*, San Francisco, CA: Jossey-Bass.

Nathan, R. and Hill, L. (1992) *Career Counselling*, London: Sage.

Norcross, J. C. and Grencavage, L. M. (1989) 'Eclecticism and Integration in Counselling and Psychotherapy: Major Themes and Obstacles', *British Journal of Guidance and Counselling* 17(3): 227–47.

Offer, M. S. (1989) *Exploring the Construct System: 'Laddering'* (mimeo).

Offer, M. S. (1990) *Life Cycles* (mimeo).

Offer, M. S. (1993) *The Usefulness of the Psychology of Personal Constructs to Occupational Choice Theory and the Theory of Vocational Guidance*, paper presented at NICEC Seminar (mimeo).

Oliver, L. and Spokane, A. R. (1988) 'Career Counseling Outcome: What Contributes to Client Gain?', *Journal of Counseling Psychology* 35: 447–62.

Patterson, C. H. (1964) 'Counseling: Self Clarification and the Helping Relationship', in Borow, H. (ed.) *Man in a World at Work*, Boston, MA: Houghton Mifflin.

Rodger, A. (1952) *The Seven-Point Plan*, London: National Institute of Industrial Psychology.

Rogers, C. (1942) *Counseling and Psychotherapy*, Boston, MA: Houghton Mifflin.

Ross, L. (1977) 'The Intuitive Psychologist and his Shortcomings: Distortions in the Attribution Process', in Berkowitz, L. (ed.) *Advances in Experimental Social Psychology*, vol. 10, New York: Academic Press.

Rounds, J. B. and Tracey, T. (1990) 'From Trait-and-Factor to Person–Environment Fit Counseling: Theory and Process', in Walsh, W. B. and Osipow, S. H. (eds) *Career Counseling: Contemporary Topics in Vocational Psychology*, Hillsdale, NJ: Erlbaum.

Schlossberg, N. K. (1984) *Counseling Adults in Transition: Linking Practice with Theory*, New York: Springer.

Starishevsky, R. and Matlin, N. (1963) 'A Model for the Translation of Self-Concept into Vocational Terms', in Super, D. E., Starishevsky, R., Matlin, N. and Jordaan, J. P. (eds) *Career Development: Self-Concept Theory*, New York: College Entrance Examination Board.

Strong, S. R. (1968) 'Counseling: an Interpersonal Influence Process', *Journal of Counseling Psychology* 15: 215–24.

Strupp, H. H. (1973) 'On the Basic Ingredients of Psychotherapy', *Journal of Clinical and Consulting Psychology* 41: 1–8.

Super, D. E. (1957) *The Psychology of Careers*, New York: Harper & Row.

Super, D. E. (1963) 'Toward Making Self-Concept Theory Operational', in Super, D. E., Starishevsky, R., Matlin, N. and Jordaan, J. P. (eds) *Career Development: Self-Concept Theory*, New York: College Entrance Examination Board.

Super, D. E. (1980) 'A Life-Span, Life-Space Approach to Career Development', *Journal of Vocational Behavior* 16: 282–98.

Super, D. E. (1983) 'Assessment in Career Guidance: Toward Truly Developmental Counseling', *Journal of Counseling and Development* 63: 555–62.

Taylor, N. B. (1985) 'How Do Career Counsellors Counsel?', *British Journal of Guidance and Counselling* 13(2): 166–77.

Tizard, B. (1990) 'Research and Policy: Is There a Link?', *The Psychologist* 3: 435–40.

Walsh, W. B. and Osipow, S. H. (eds) (1990) *Career Counseling: Contemporary Topics in Vocational Psychology*, Hillsdale, NJ: Erlbaum.

Watts, A. G. and Kidd, J. M. (1978) 'Evaluating the Effectiveness of Careers Guidance: a Review of the British Research', *Journal of Occupational Psychology* 51: 235–48.

Chapter 12

Careers education in a curriculum

Bill Law

12.1 INTRODUCTION

Careers guidance evokes an image of an 'adviser' working on a 'plan' with a 'client' in an 'interview'; while careers education evokes a 'teacher' teaching a 'lesson' with 'pupils' in a 'classroom'. But it would be a mistake to leave it at that. The teacher might be offering guidance in the classroom; the adviser could be teaching. Moreover, other scenarios can be assembled. Either of the helpers might be a 'counsellor', 'mentor', 'tutor' or 'facilitator'. The help might be characterised as a 'chat', an 'agenda', a 'scheme-of-work', or a 'programme'. The person they are helping can be a 'client' or 'pupil' but can also be a 'student' or 'customer'.

Furthermore, the location need not be in a careers service, or in a school or college; it might be in a place of employment, or at home. Any of these encounters will involve both talking-and-listening and observation, and might easily involve role-play, simulation or keyboarding. All are linked to other sources of learning: careers resources centres and libraries, psychometric tests or interest inventories, recording achievement, planning action, other aspects of curriculum, life experience, other helpers. So:

1 The terms 'careers education' and 'careers guidance' together characterise a range of activities.
2 The boundaries between them, though important, are not always clear.
3 The similarities between them are as salient as the differences, so that skill and understanding in the one can often be used in the other.
4 A single programme of work can integrate them into a whole, each supplying mutually supporting contributions.

There is, therefore, no wholly stable relationship between careers education and careers guidance: the relationship is dynamic, in constant re-negotiation within a larger nexus. This chapter will examine these relationships and trace present and possible future developments for careers education in relation to careers guidance. It will first seek to identify their distinctive contributions; then to explore the relationship of careers education to the wider educational curriculum; next to describe what careers education comprises and where it might be found; and finally to outline implications for its methods and manifestations.

12.2 CAREERS EDUCATION AND CAREERS GUIDANCE

Careers education and careers guidance are both similar and different. Part of the difference is that careers education is usually undertaken in groups, and guidance with individuals. Other differences are more significant. Whether we call it a 'curriculum' or not, we are *educating* when we try to help people to question, explore and understand what is happening. In a curriculum, this process is designed as a 'scheme of work'. Learners work through the scheme stage-by-stage, until they can go on to use its learning independently. A scheme of work for careers education might involve learners in systematically gathering and organising information, recognising and adapting useful frames-of-thought, trying out strategies and skills in a simulation or trial, taking a sustained look at a wide range of points of view, working out where the main issues and problems are, and grasping what kinds of causes are likely to lead to what kinds of effects.

Table 12.1 suggests where the main focuses lie in careers education and careers guidance respectively. Neither, of course, is this tidy. Some activities straddle the boundary: for example, small-group work can be articulated from both the left and the right of the table. It can offer a developing sequence, covering material known to be useful to the group. But it can also identify the preoccupations of participants, developing personal agendas from their concerns. Indeed, this capacity concurrently to draw upon *group* processes, but to focus on *personal* experience, appears to be a key feature of successful group work.

There are other activities which do not exactly fit the model in Table 12.1. Some of these activities are assembled in Figure 12.1 into a more subtle two-dimensional analysis. It indicates that there may be some instructional elements in careers education, as there are counselling elements in careers guidance. But many aspects of careers work occupy a more centre-ground position, with some areas of overlap between careers education and careers guidance at the centre of the diagram. This is where a scheme-of-work and personal agendas overlay each other.

Table 12.1 Distinctions between careers education and careers guidance

	Careers education	Careers guidance
Contact	Often in a *group*, using group processes	Requires *individual or small-group* work, using inter-personal processes
Relevance	Emphasises learning *generally* relevant to the group	Emphasises learning *differentially* relevant to the individual
Basis	*Ready-made programme*, articulated to what is known in advance to be useful	*Negotiable*, not necessarily known in advance
Development	Movement *through the material*, from 'basic' to 'advanced'	Movement *through experience*, towards what the client needs to do now
Outcome	Acquisition of a *general* framework of learning (though capable of incorporating and supporting individual responses)	Readiness to deal with a *specific* problem or decision faced by one person now

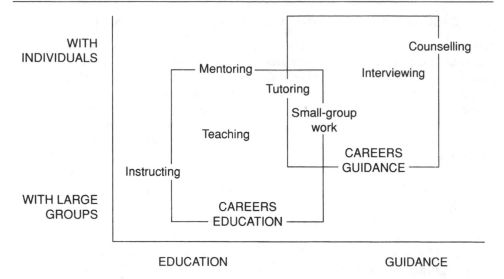

Figure 12.1   A two-dimensional analysis of careers education and careers guidance

12.3 CAREERS EDUCATION AND THE WIDER CURRICULUM

Much of what educational institutions have to offer is transmitted through their curriculum: in such organisations, the importance of careers work is measured by its relation to the wider curriculum. A lot depends upon the balance and relationship between two cohabiting cultures: of *standards*, and of *relevance*.

A culture of standards

A great deal of school or college transmission is characterised, often in contrast with careers education, as 'academic'. The term is much abused. Yet the academic intention – to identify, expand and communicate a culture's narratives, beliefs, dispositions, technologies and values – must count as a 'good idea'. A society which makes no effort to develop a shared culture is likely to fragment.

Academics may not be interested in such concomitants of their work. They are often at their best when insisting on rigour in the processes of acquisition and transmission. The knowledge they pursue should be, therefore, better than opinion: a challenge to superstition, politically unrectified and impervious to fashion. To the extent that this is so, we all need it. This culture of standards requires: (1) that the knowledge, concepts and methods are reliable and valid; (2) that learners rise as closely as they can to command of that material; and (3) that – as Goodson (1994) argues – the object of enquiry is thought worthy of such rigorous attention. These are legitimate interests, to which careers education must pay attention if it is to be taken seriously where the curriculum is taken seriously.

Academic knowledge is not set in stone. Bernstein (1973) characterises the possibility of change in terms of how educational knowledge is classified and framed. Re-classification changes internal boundaries, between elements in learning such as subjects. Re-framing changes an external boundary – identifying what counts as legitimate knowledge. Bernstein conceives of these processes in terms of degrees of control. Knowledge may be 'collected' behind tightened boundaries, or 'integrated' across loosened boundaries. In the latter case, integration permits re-classifying extant knowledge and re-framing new knowledge. This chapter contains examples of how careers educators do both things. The concept of boundary control usefully clarifies both the extent and the direction of such changes. Careers educators cannot usefully disregard an academic 'culture of standards'; but, as we shall see, they can also look elsewhere for directions for desirable change.

New knowledge creates 'curriculum squeeze': with finite resources, curriculum is a zero-sum game. Whether careers education can maintain a more formidable case than (say) Latin, or a less precarious fingerhold on the curriculum than (say) geography, will depend upon how effectively it can make its case for re-classifying and re-framing knowledge. Careers education, as a contender for anything better than highly marginal curriculum status, will not develop without having to confront formidable and legitimate opposition.

A culture of relevance

At its worst, the academic curriculum can be arcane, arbitrary, and usable only for passing examinations. Learning should be for something more than that – whether in society or in the learners' lives. Passing examinations is too narrow and sterile a reason for learning; and is surely not what the most rigorous and stimulating contributors to our culture had in mind for the use of their material. The culture of standards needs a cohabiting 'culture of relevance'. No teacher and no learner ever meet without some notion that what is being transmitted is, so to speak, '*for* something' – whether for pleasure, for interest or for application. Without standards, such anticipations are misdirected; without anticipation, such standards are futile.

In Bernstein's terms, changed classification and framing may be ascribed not only to the legitimation of new knowledge but also to the acceptance that learning can be applied to further uses. Both cultures change the curriculum: as changes occur in the idea of what knowledge is for, so what is taught is changed. An example of such re-classification in schools is how the subject 'technology' has unified and redirected previously fragmented material. As we shall see, careers education may be characterised in such terms (though, as Goodson [1994] warns, the classification 'applied' subject does not achieve equal status with 'academic' subjects).

Arguments for cultures of relevance are not necessarily as narrowly utilitarian as the epithet 'for something' implies. Hamlet's dilemma may be reduced to the elements of functional insight into decision-making; but to read it so would be to abuse the text, diminish the mind, sour the pleasure, and – as a matter of fact – trivialise decision-making.

Careers education has more options. At least three can be identified. None of them quarrels with what is best in the academic tradition; each argues for more. The three are:

1 A *guidance* culture. This derives from careers guidance and transposes its purposes into the schemes of work required for a curriculum, where the learner is thought of as a person with well-defined career-related decisions to make and transitions to accomplish.

2 A *liberal-education* culture. This derives from a long-standing educational tradition addressed to the human uses of learning. It has recently been represented in some aspects of what is called personal and social education, where the learner is thought of in terms of her or his relationships with others.

3 A *vocational-education* culture. This is ultimately derived from the liberal tradition, but is more sharply focused on functional roles in a productive economy, tending therefore to point education towards specific skills and competencies which the learner is seen as requiring in order to cope and thrive in that economically significant setting.

These cultures are not exclusive of each other. The guidance culture has already absorbed much of the other two. An important question, however, is whether such cross-fertilisation is yet in appropriate balance. We are dealing with a highly variegated spectrum of educational purposes capable of kaleidoscopic combinations and recombinations. But the centres of each segment are distinguishable and – for the purposes of understanding careers education – worth highlighting. How any careers education programmes can draw upon more than one culture is illustrated for three specimen programmes in Table 12.2.

A *guidance culture* transposes the aims of guidance into the aims of a curriculum. The most common framework is the DOTS analysis (Law and Watts, 1977), which argues that careers work should be pursuing four broad aims: (1) *opportunity awareness*, where the learner discovers what is available in the working world; (2) *self awareness*, where the learner explores her or his own abilities, motivations and potentialities; (3) *decision learning*, where the learner addresses what is entailed in making career decisions; and (4) *transition learning*, where the learner anticipates how to implement such decisions and deal with their consequences.

First developed for schools (see Chapter 5), this frame of thinking is substantially the product of humanistic ideology, which is optimistic about both the capacity of and opportunity for people to act on the basis of raised awareness. Much of the criticism of it therefore has to do with what would be a proper balancing of attention between the 'inner life' and the 'real world'. Some critics point out that career is best understood as a sociological, not a psychological,

Table 12.2 Examples of elements drawing on different cultures for careers education programmes in different settings

Culture	Personal and social education in a school	A university enterprise skills programme	A pre-retirement programme in a commercial company
Guidance	Knowing what you want from your work	Taking responsibility for yourself	Budgeting on a lower income
Liberal-education	Understanding the impact of work on the environment	Developing wider concepts of work	Making a difference through senior citizenship
Vocational-education	Developing job-seeking skills	Making a good curriculum vitae	Developing self-employment enterprise skills

event: that most people are not free to make choices in the way DOTS implies (Roberts, 1977). Some are critical of the failure of guidance to make the substance of working life visible and useful to learners (Taylor, 1991); some also argue that most learners need to know only about what is available to them (Jarvis, 1994; Steedman, 1994).

By contrast, others argue that the aims of careers education should be concerned not so much with learning how things *are* but with learning how they might be *changed* (Roberts, 1980), in some cases implying a radical route to change (Willis, 1977) (see also Chapter 19). Yet others are troubled by the ideological conflict between on the one hand a curriculum which celebrates personal autonomy, and on the other the dominant facts of organisational life, which often deny it (Hargreaves, 1972; Musgrove and Taylor, 1969; Lee, 1980; Watts and Herr, 1976). Others still have argued that early humanistic ideals have on occasions been abandoned, characterising one programme struggling with the issues as a 'politically malleable ideological resource' (Bates, 1989)!

The DOTS analysis has proven resilient in the face of such criticisms. There is, however, a further problem: one which is specific to the idea of curriculum. The DOTS analysis does not address progression: it offers no indication of what is basic and what is advanced, what must be learned early and what can be learned later, and what less-demanding activities lay the foundations for what more-demanding activities. Such considerations are central to the development of any curriculum. A later section of this chapter will re-examine these objections to DOTS and suggest how new accommodations can now be made by drawing more fully upon what is most promising in the liberal-education and vocational-education cultures.

A *liberal-education culture* has deep roots in Anglo-Saxon education (Wirth, 1991). Lee (1980) identifies a key characteristic in acknowledging the need to take account of learners' attachments to society as well as their individual and personal development. Both assent and dissent are forms of attachment to society, and Dewey (1915) argued for an education which develops the qualities of mind required to reform society. The liberal rationale, accordingly, supports an education not only 'for matters of importance and relevance to young men and women' but also for 'matters of widespread and enduring significance' (Stradling, 1984). In schools, personal and social education (PSE) is argued to be, among other things, concerned with reforming the institutions of society, a process which entails the search for a shared moral basis for action (Hargreaves *et al.*, 1988).

The liberal tradition has been characterised (Coffey, 1992) as an application of learning for life. The person doing the applying may at first have been thought of as 'a gentleman', and the life as one of 'leisure'. But such narrow connotations are not necessary to the concept. It has, more recently, acquired elements of political education, industrial awareness, multi-cultural education, moral education, environmental education, health education and community service (Lee, 1980). Accelerating change, in both personal lives and social experience, has increased the pressure on education to deliver also on sex education, substance abuse, AIDS – and careers education.

The liberal rationale is as likely to commend itself to adults as to children. It can relate personal career development in the context of a person's other roles and responsibilities in family, community and society. Most significantly, it is prepared to confront issues in moral terms, including where they relate to social conflict. It entertains 'impertinent questions' and 'dissent', as well as 'skills' and 'co-operation', as bases for achieving both personal and social change.

It would be a mistake to ascribe support for such thinking to education but not to industry and commerce. Informed business people understand that they cannot trade except in a consenting society, where people can weigh their influence on how things get done, whether in the organisation or in its impact on its social and physical environment. The trade union movement is a long-established contributor to both the understanding and use of such influence.

Liberal education has its problems. As a rationale for careers work, it has not recently attracted much political clout or economic leverage. In schools, PSE has a heroic record of maintaining a liberal curriculum through a period of accelerating change. But PSE is itself a marginal form of curriculum provision in schools (see Chapter 5).

Daws (1968) was among the first in Britain to seek a liberal commitment from careers education, urging its pursuit of 'moral awareness' and 'social criticism'. There is in all of this an underlying concern for social fabric as well as personal choice; more specifically, there is a concern for the maintenance of an open society in which sceptical and moral – as well as humanistic – *choice* is a real and not merely a rhetorical construct.

A *vocational-education culture* offers an economic justification for the curriculum: arguing that people must learn in order usefully to occupy positions in the working world. It stems from the need to remove the insulation which protects the academic curriculum from social change, and to enlist the curriculum in a strategy to rescue a 'nation at risk' (Goodson, 1994). It is capable of specific application to careers education, which – if it is effective – influences who-does-what in the nation's economy. The mechanisms by which careers education may improve macro-economic performance are set out by Killeen *et al.* (1992) (see Chapter 4).

Vocational education in schools is subject to detailed liberal criticism (Holt, 1987; Cohen, 1984). There is doubt about its underpinning concept of personal transferable skills. There is suspicion about the extent to which skills (rather than say motivation) are good predictors of vocational performance. There are also questions about whether a supply-side solution can deal with a demand-side problem: helping people to be more employable will not necessarily deal with underlying structural problems in the economy.

It may, however, put individuals in a *personally* more competitive position, so that the pecking order for available work is changed. The idea that a vocationally driven careers education programme can improve life chances has an appeal to both children and adults, despite the fact that its concerns for social fabric may not be as well developed.

There is no necessary contradiction between the liberal and vocational traditions. It is when 'vocation' is narrowly interpreted that problems extrude: compressing education into too narrow a frame, excluding social, moral or questioning processes, and assuming only economic motivation for learning. A worst case would be where careers education became a means of limiting options, restricting vision and sidelining scepticism, all in the interests of a hoped-for macro-economic gain.

To summarise: careers education is part of a larger system in continuous process of re-classifying and re-framing knowledge. That process responds to cultures both of standards and of relevance. Some of the relation-ships are suggested in Figure 12.2. A basic and legitimate concern is for (1) academic standards, most proximately expressed in (2) a transmitted curricu-lum, organised as disciplines or 'subjects'. Guidance, and liberal and vocational education, are parts of a further process focused on (3) anticipation as well as transmission. However, an anticipatory curriculum depends upon acad-emic subjects, for no plan can be made and no problem solved without the use of well-founded knowledge, concepts and methods. The process of re-classification and re-framing will have outcomes both for academic subjects and for the anticipatory curriculum. Each can be influenced from both direc-tions – with new considerations of what is reliable and rigorous, and what is useful and relevant.

Curriculum relevance is not an alternative to academic standards: it *depends* upon such standards. Indeed, it *is* such material, put to further uses. The case is for *one* curriculum with both 'retrospective' (academic) and 'prospec-tive' (relevant) faces (Law, 1981). The analysis applies more generally to the 'academic–vocational divide', which may better be understood as a single system with complementary elements (Spours and Young, 1990). A culture of standards and a culture of relevance are mutually dependent.

Careers education is engaged in two sets of negotiation – with its roots in the academic curriculum, and with its manifestations in guidance, vocational-education and liberal-education cultures of relevance. The argument here is

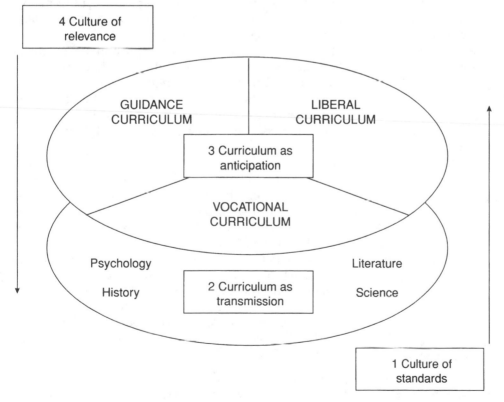

Figure 12.2   The curriculum as a system

that careers education must re-negotiate the guidance curriculum in some combination of vocational and liberal terms. The following section elaborates elements for consideration in that process. It indicates that, in its present form, the guidance curriculum is too ambiguous, too narrow and too static.

12.4 SUBSTANCE

We have, by implication, raised questions concerning the 'body of knowledge, concepts and methods' that represents careers education. What do they comprise? How are they constructed? What sorts of gains can be expected from them? This section examines possible answers to these questions, in three phases: (1) by relating DOTS to the transmitted curriculum; (2) by proposing a role-related curriculum – adding ideas from liberal and vocational education; and (3) by attending to the need for progression.

The DOTS analysis and the transmitted curriculum

DOTS (Law and Watts, 1977) offers four broad clusters of aims:

1 *Opportunity awareness*. This involves helping learners to know and understand what work is available, including both employment and other forms of work, showing routes into them: to know what work there is and what is available to whom; to know what work offers – in terms of interest and satisfaction as well as rewards and incentives; to know what work demands – in terms of commitment and motivation as well as skills and qualifications; and to understand how and why work is changing in all these respects.
2 *Self awareness*. This involves helping learners to know and understand their 'self' in career-relevant terms: to be able to communicate what they have done and can do; to know how others see that information-about-self, and identify what is important from different points of view; to know what they can offer to work – in terms of performance; to know what they can seek from work – in terms of motivation; and to understand how and why, in all these ways, a self can change.
3 *Decision learning*. This involves helping learners to be ready to make decisions for which they accept responsibility: to know what they are going to do, that they could have done something else, why they are going to do this thing, and what the likely consequences of that decision will be; to be practised in the skills and styles of decision-making; and to be able appropriately to apply these skills and styles to real decisions.
4 *Transition learning*. This involves helping learners to be ready constructively to solve the problems that attach to decisions: to be able to anticipate what needs to be done to implement a decision, and to deal with the consequences of other people's decisions; to be practised in transition skills – such as those for enquiry, self-presentation, communication, self-management, assertiveness and conflict resolution; and to be able appropriately to apply these skills to real transitions.

The DOTS analysis has proven adaptable. Indeed, it *needs* to be reshaped for use in different sectors. It can also be shaped to reflect the interests of different stakeholders in careers education.

Table 12.3 Examples of links between academic disciplines and the DOTS analysis

	Economics	Psychology	Sociology	Literature
Opportunity awareness	'Sunrise' and 'sunset' industries		Organisation of work	
Self awareness		Concepts for 'self' and 'behaviour'		Autobiography as insight
Decision learning	Estimating 'utility' and 'disutility'			Narrative as resolution
Transition learning		Stress management	Social pressure	

All of the elements of DOTS are rooted in academic knowledge. Table 12.3 suggests how that is so for four illustrative disciplines, showing how knowledge, concepts and methods embedded in these disciplines can be imported into the analysis. The table is merely suggestive. Other entries could be made for these disciplines, and other disciplines could be included (cf. NCC, 1990; Barnes and Andrews, 1995; Law *et al.*, 1995). The framework in the table can be adapted to review any current curriculum in any organisation, identifying how academic material and careers education purposes might be better integrated. Indeed, this is the purpose for which DOTS was originally designed.

A role-related curriculum

Like DOTS, liberal and vocational education are not a rejection of the academic curriculum, but represent the academic curriculum used for further 'prospective' purposes. One of the problems for the prospective face of the curriculum is the multiplicity of its constituency interests. Industry, government, community, family and education-based groups, as well as helpers and their students and clients, seek a say in what education is for. The concept of role-relatedness is a way of unifying these constituencies (Law, 1995). The concept is much less vulnerable than 'liberal', 'vocational' and 'careers' to being hijacked by ill-judged sectional constituency interests. Yet, like these other terms, it acknowledges the needs of learners to relate what they acquire to what they do, both as individuals and in their attachments to society. Its merits can be listed in the following terms:

1 Role unifies concepts of 'self' and 'opportunity'. All role terms ('mother', 'friend', 'worker') speak in one breath of a self in a position, thus using a single vocabulary for *'person-engaged-in-task'*. The term avoids the abstract and context-free use of 'self' in the DOTS analysis. Role insists that self is conceived in a position, on a task, with other people.
2 Role is a social term, identifying interdependencies and attachments. Role terms are commonly reciprocal relationships ('parent-and-child', 'producer-and-consumer', 'man-and-woman'). Such usage evokes both a psychological and a social self: much of who we are, what we feel, and what we do, lie in

Table 12.4   Relationship of different roles to the DOTS analysis

	Opportunity awareness	Self awareness	Decision learning	Transition learning
Citizen	Analysing land-use for new factories			Using the media
Consumer		Prioritising 'needs' and 'wants'	Reading between the lines of advertising copy	
Worker	Mapping the opportunity structure	Communicating self to others	Recognising work-related dilemmas	Assessing probabilities of employment
Parent		Understanding the influence of one's parents on one's parenting		Helping child grow into adult
Householder	Maximising options for occupancy		Calculating costs and benefits of accommodation options	

Table 12.5   A model for progression within the DOTS analysis

	Opportunity awareness	Self awareness	Decision learning	Transition learning
Sense	Mapping work distributions	Identifying models	Surveying approaches	Gathering feedback
Sift	Classifying examples of work	Comparing self 'here' and 'there'	Examining different reactions	Locating alternative strategies
Focus	Identifying occupational stereotypes	Articulating values	Empathising with points of view	Identifying preferred styles
Understand	Explaining and anticipating social and economic change	Anticipating future experience	Assessing risk and commitment	Explaining failed strategies and anticipating successful ones

such attachments. To be without a role is to be in a precarious and powerless position – indeed, in a sense, to be in no position at all.

3 Role extends the basis for understanding attachment to work, by suggesting alternatives to the concept of 'employee'. Other possible selves in other possible work futures include 'entrepreneur', 'volunteer' and 'parent'.

4 Role acknowledges how a person's various roles influence each other. An 'employee' is also a 'citizen', a 'partner', a 'consumer', and perhaps a 'debtor', and these roles are intimately entwined: decisions and transitions negotiated in one role will have causes and consequences elsewhere.

The concept of role is highly congruent with DOTS, offering it breadth, depth and resonance. Table 12.4 suggests how. DOTS can indeed be applied to all aspects of a role-related curriculum. Learning in any role will inform and influence learning in other roles. Academic knowledge, DOTS and role-relatedness combine here into a development model for programmes drawing on liberal-education and vocational-education cultures. People already holding down adult roles should readily be able to see their value. They restore work roles to their context in a whole life.

Making DOTS progressive

The concept of a curriculum requires that we know where to start and how to develop a programme of learning. It means understanding the difference between, on the one hand, what is 'basic', 'simple' and 'easy', and on the other, what is 'advanced', 'complex' and 'troublesome'. Then we can know what people will be ready for at different stages in the programme. We can also know what has to be learned before anything else *can* be learned. Progression shows how prior learning leads to subsequent learning.

Career-learning theory has been developed to address this task (see Chapter 3). It suggests that career learning moves from gathering information to taking action in a more or less progressive sequence:

1 'Sensing' – gathering and framing impressions.
2 'Sifting' – making comparisons and using concepts.
3 'Focusing' – appreciating alternative points of view and developing one's own.
4 'Understanding' – explaining past effects and anticipating future consequences.

These activities accumulate into a repertoire of career-development ability; and they can be taught.

The analysis provides DOTS with progression, illustrated in Table 12.5. The practical use of the model is in the design of learning sequences. 'Sensing' and 'sifting' identify what people need to do if useful 'focusing' and 'understanding' are to develop. This model, like the other planning devices set out in this section, could be used in different settings. In schools, it could help to avoid applying to 13- or 14-year-olds material developed for school-leavers. In adult work, it could provide a basis for establishing prior learning, and building upon it.

12.5 SETTINGS

This section examines the relationship between careers education and its organisational settings. It raises questions concerning where it *is* done, and where it *might* be done. The development of a careers-education programme requires:

1 Curriculum developers who can understand what is needed, how curriculum works, and how these ideas can be translated into effective learning sequences and processes.
2 Teachers, lecturers, mentors or tutors who recognise the programme ideas as relevant and useful and can manage the 'teaching' processes they require.
3 Physical resources – appropriate space and equipment to support these processes, whether in a 'classroom' or in other ways.
4 A mandate from the organisation to put these ideas into operation.

These conditions are found in educational organisations; although, even with these advantages, the position of careers education in such organisations is often marginal and precarious (see Chapters 5–7). Larger business organisations have much of the personnel and hardware, and can buy any additional help required; if they regard themselves as a 'learning organisation' (Senge, 1990), this will develop the mandate. It is with adult learners who are neither in a college nor a member of a 'learning organisation' that the needs may be greatest but the capacity to meet them weakest. This is the 'Catch-22' of contemporary careers education and the biggest challenge for its future.

Careers education in educational organisations

An organisation's mandate supports action as worthwhile, worthy of acknowledgement and resources. Such mandates spring from organisational cultures (see Chapter 17). We will examine two such cultures in particular: schools and higher education.

The difficulty which *schools* have in maintaining an appropriate culture can be examined by an extension of Bernstein's (1971) analysis. He characterised schools as 'closed' or 'open'. A relatively 'closed' school maintains tight boundaries around ready-made categories for its roles as well as its curriculum. This 'frames' what happens inside the school, isolating it from what happens outside. Such a school also maintains clear lines of separation within itself, maintaining 'classifications' which separate different curriculum courses along with their teachers and students. Such relatively closed schools restrict differentiation. The ability to achieve re-classified and re-framed differentiation is necessary to any useful response to external change.

More open organisations are less concerned with such ritual and purity. They are prepared to dismantle, extend and reassemble aspects of both framing and classification, in a manner which favours the achievement of new roles, re-mixes the curriculum and instils it with values from outside. Such organisations, Bernstein implies, can deal both with the changing demands of academic standards and with the changing life-role relevance of what they teach.

Bernstein's description of open schools, with both inter-departmental and community-linked co-operation, anticipated the organisation of the Technical and Vocational Education Initiative (TVEI) in schools by more than a decade. TVEI re-classified and re-framed the curriculum and its institutional support.

This was done ostensibly in response to vocational imperatives; although the local implementation of TVEI also resonated with liberal as well as vocational concepts. The subject-based National Curriculum serves priorities concerning academic standards rather than relevance, and is closer to what Bernstein characterises as a tightly classified and framed curriculum. The National Curriculum has crystallised the classification and framing of the curriculum, as a comparison of the 1904 and 1983 regulations and statutes demonstrates (Goodson, 1994). The dilemmas posed by Bernstein are therefore perennial, both in the pre-TVEI curriculum (King, 1976) and in the relationship between TVEI and the National Curriculum (Merson, 1992) (see Chapter 5).

Like schools, *higher education* (HE) developed careers education from careers guidance (see Chapter 6). Unlike schools, the earliest programmes were designed and staffed by university, polytechnic and college guidance services, rather than by teachers or lecturers. Curricular provision includes group work; one-off lectures, workshops and other events; short programmes, including work experience; and guided self-study or open-learning material (e.g. Hopson and Scally, 1984, first developed for the Open University). All such programmes may be analysed in terms of DOTS (Watts, 1977).

The Enterprise in Higher Education (EHE) programme was a vocational-education influence with many of the characteristics of TVEI. EHE proved hospitable to careers education in its use of personal transferable skills (Watts and Hawthorn, 1992) and its emphasis upon career planning (Ball and Butcher, 1993). Both can be argued to be closely identified with the aims of careers education, but both also resonate in varying degrees with vocational and liberal cultures. However, as in schools, the pervasive tension is with academic concerns (Watts, 1977).

Further examination suggests continuing diversification. Bray (1995) and McChesney (1995) identified different forms of careers education in higher education. McChesney's analysis of 'accountability' and 'developmental' models is articulated to attachment to the host organisation: the former seeks stronger attachments than the latter. Thus the accountability model acknowledges the importance of institutional and structural relationships; while the developmental model pursues objectives to do with learner well-being and professional integrity.

Bray's analysis further elaborates McChesney's model. His 'economic-and-vocational' form of careers education pursues 'functional' job-seeking-and-securing behaviour; it does so through help with application forms and curricula vitae, decision-making exercises and occupational information. His 'developmental' form of provision, by contrast, pursues more 'humanistic' outcomes, through the exploratory use of self-assessment exercises and work-experience placements.

There is some, but not yet complete, correspondence between McChesney's analysis and that of Bray and the analysis of vocational-education and liberal-education cultures. McChesney counterpoises organisationally utilitarian and professional service ideologies; Bray discriminates economically and personally significant outcomes.

However, higher education already accommodates vocational and liberal, as well as academic, cultures. Engineering and medicine on the one hand, and history and literature on the other, draw differentially upon these cultures. In Bernstein's terms, the integration of careers education into each will, accordingly, be different (see Watts and Hawthorn, 1992). The possibility for further integration in higher education will depend in some measure not only on how well-founded academically the guidance culture is thought to be, but also on whether its attachments to the vocational and liberal cultures are appropriately balanced.

For Bernstein, the problem for the curriculum is not only – and perhaps not mainly – one for academic standards, but for deciding how we connect and separate the elements of knowledge within and between disciplines. Applied to careers education, this is a problem for how we demonstrate the relevance of the knowledge to the lives of students, the interests of society, and the openness of the organisation. Whatever resolution careers education can make with its academic roots, its place in the curriculum will substantially be mandated on the strength of the rationale it uses for establishing these links. It is argued here that DOTS is too ambiguous, too narrow and too static a concept to be sufficient for use in a curriculum debate. Ultimately careers education must find a viable resolution between DOTS and some combination of the academic, vocational and liberal traditions. In order to transact that business, as Bernstein usefully demonstrates, careers education requires an open culture. A closed culture – with fixed subject content, analysed on a subject-by-subject basis, offering little room for the negotiation of new connections and new roles – is inhospitable to all future options for careers education (see Section 12.6 below).

These dilemmas have not been resolved in any education sector. While unresolved, they leave careers education vulnerable to continuing curriculum squeeze, to a persistent but narrowly focused academic drive for standards, and – perhaps most of all – to the imperatives of organisational survival.

Widening the constituency

Other organisations offer careers education. Business organisations do not employ high ratios of curriculum development and teaching staff; nonetheless, world-wide labour-economy changes are causing some employing organisations to consider themselves 'learning organisations'. This is frequently seen to imply the need for guidance at work (Savickas, 1994; see also Chapter 8) as part of 'lifelong career development' (Watts, 1994).

Additional careers education and guidance providers include further and adult education providers (see Chapter 6). They also include careers services, private (fee-charging) agencies, and guidance programmes attached to self-help, voluntary and community-based projects (see Chapters 9–10).

There are practical possibilities here. Careers education need not now depend upon the locations and apparatus of conventional 'classrooms'. Developments in information technology (Hunt, 1994; Law, 1994), in open learning (Paine, 1988), in supported self-study (Waterhouse, 1988), and in support for reflection upon experience-based learning (Boud et al., 1985), suggest new routes for needy learners. However, the 'we-must-do-it' argument is more compelling than 'we-can-do-it'. For it is the agencies outside the education–training–employment chain which are more likely to be in touch with the people in most pressing need of new learning for lifelong career development – many of whom are detached from ongoing institutional or social support.

The idea that careers education is mainly a provision of formal educational institutions, for young people, is clearly due for rethinking. The biggest constituencies for careers education have not yet been reached.

Table 12.6 Examples of learning activities within the DOTS analysis

	Opportunity awareness	Self awareness	Decision learning	Transition learning
Sense	Enquiring into work and available roles	Introspecting and receiving feedback from others	Examining biographical accounts of decision-making	Observing and reporting problem-solving
Sift	Mapping or classifying work and roles	Comparing points of view on self	Examining decision-making styles	Comparing transition strategies
Focus	Sceptical questioning on work on roles	Disclosing a point of view on self	Prioritising bases for action	Identifying immediate problems
Understand	Explaining and anticipating changes in work and roles	Explaining and anticipating changes in self	Identifying risks and probabilities, and ways to optimise them	Devising, practising, evaluating and negotiating strategies

12.6   METHODS AND MANIFESTATIONS

This section suggests the terms in which careers education can be developed for delivery. It identifies two practical concerns:

1 *Methods* – using what learning processes?
2 *Manifestations* – how is careers education best classified and framed?

Good practice means knowing how to manage learning settings so that learners can translate resources into gains. Examples of learning activities are set out (as a progression articulated to the DOTS analysis) in Table 12.6. The range of activities can be analysed into four broad types of method, each with a distinctive contribution to make to careers education: didactic, participative, experiential, and experience-based.

Didactic methods present knowledge in the form of words, graphics and models, so that learners are shown or told something. Tight control is maintained, whether by a teacher or by the structure of the learning programme. This may be necessary where time is short, where exactness, clarity and structure are important, or where there is unmanageable risk or difficulty in using other methods. Learners are required to attend to a presentation. There is however more than one way of managing such presentations. In Socratic management, the teacher or programme dialectically develops learning by open questioning. In group situations, whether in class or on the Internet, such interactions tend to be radial, arbitrated by a central authority.

Participative methods support learning-by-doing. Learners actively pursue, examine and practise knowledge – to carry out and reflect upon active experience. They may conduct an enquiry or carry out an experiment. The objective may be discovery, understanding or learning how to do things. By such methods, people may identify and sharpen skills, and learn to reapply them to new settings and applications – being responsible for themselves. In participative methods, a modified Socratic chairing supports orbital communication where participants help each other, although not losing touch with the 'expert'.

Experiential methods support learning by acknowledging and processing learners' personal and value-laden experience. This is where individual guidance, group work and classroom method most extensively share methodological common ground. Experiential work is value-laden: there is no known-in-advance 'right answer' to any issue; everything is a point of view. Experiential methods are essential where each learner needs to take a view of the material and relate it to her or his feelings, beliefs and attachments. The skills of neutral management, used in experiential learning, are similar to guidance skills. Neutral management invites learners to consider for themselves the validity of a decision or solution. It supports the interaction between learners without intruding expert or moralistic points of view. Conversations tend to become predominantly orbital – bypassing the 'chair'. The method supports, clarifies, restates, summarises and reflects the authority in the learners. A good neutral chairperson is an accurate and attentive listener – like a guidance worker.

Experience-based methods (see Chapter 13) support learning by establishing direct and personal contact with their objects. Learners engage in work, contact people and take roles. Other methods symbolise the material to be learned, with words, graphics, simulations and other representations. Experience-based learning engages actual (not postulated) people, places and tasks, in real (not pretend) processes and time. Work experience is an example of an experience base; as are teachers', learners' and community contacts' authentic experience, brought into the learning process. Adult–adult management is appropriate to experience-based methods, bringing the 'teacher' into the group as a member-with-other-members. The teacher might act as a consultant, manage resources on the learners' behalf, or respond to their cues. The method can become experiential, to the point where the teacher discloses irritation and confusion alongside the learners. In such a role, the teacher's statements have no more authority than anyone else's. Indeed, the teacher will acknowledge that the learners often have more authentic and relevant experience. A good adult–adult learning manager needs to be sure of her or his ability to sustain a relationship in which no appeal can be made to status or position.

The issue is not 'should we use traditional or progressive methods?' but rather 'what methods should we use for what purposes?' This more complicated question demands a more thoughtful answer. There are three sets of considerations:

1 *People learn in different ways.* Some people learn best from concrete specifics; others need a conceptual scan. Some cannot get on without actively engaging with the material; others need time to respond reflectively to it. Most people need to do all of this – but in their own sequence.

2 *Variety is interesting.* Everybody needs some change in method: 'lectures are boring' is a cliché, but other Johnny-one-note methods can also elicit the 'oh-no!-not-another-project' response from students.

3 *Depth, breadth and progression require varied methods.* Learning calls upon every part of our being, so careers education must engage thoughts, feelings, behaviours and attachments. Each is learned in different ways: some cannot be learned except with a clear head; for others, intellectualisation gets in the way.

Much remains to be to be done to harness new *communication* technologies to these *learning* requirements.

Manifestations

Much of the argument for a variety of methods *within* careers education can also be used to support a variety of manifestations *between* different forms of careers education. Developing a careers education curriculum may involve developing one or other of three different kinds of programme, each of which distinctively frames and classifies the material examined in this chapter:

1 *Pivotal* programmes, providing necessary career learning at particular stages.
2 *Foundation* programmes, supporting that learning with depth, breadth and progression.
3 *Connecting* programmes, identifying career learning in knowledge acquired for more general purposes.

The case for *pivotal* programmes hinges on the need for a clear and achievable focus on irreducible learning that everybody needs. Such programmes can usefully occur in cycles, beginning in secondary schools and extending into all subsequent settings for lifelong learning. At early stages in the cycle, they are basic; at all stages, they are necessary.

Such programmes are specialist and intensive. They require specifically trained 'teachers', able to deal with the expert knowledge and with the personal and affect-laden responses embedded in career development (see Chapter 3). Such people are either providers of guidance, or work closely with these providers. For these reasons, the most probable framework for identifying the aims and content of such programmes is DOTS; and, as we have seen, so it has proven.

There are problems for the cyclical use of such clearly focused material: repetition and lack of genuine progression result where providers at different stages are acting more or less independently of each other. But in principle, such programmes could be designed to set out and progressively revisit the essential learning required to support career development at each stage; and to explore and penetrate knowledge to greater breadth and depth as learners' experience and the demands of decision-making become more intricate and layered.

A special case of such a focused programme would be what might be called 'recovery' career learning, for people needing to make up for lost learning opportunities and to undertake 're-building' work. This would probably be concerned with re-examining and re-shaping damaged and damaging career-related constructs, such as work- or self-stereotypes (see Chapter 3).

Such pivotal schemes will enhance any organisation's overall programme, but they will occupy a limited position in order to do so. It is this 'marginal' position that careers education tends to hold in educational settings. This may be explained in terms of the re-framing strategy that such work requires. For it requires 'new' knowledge, not needed for the organisation's other purposes, and therefore more difficult to legitimate (where curriculum is being developed from scratch – as it often is in various 'adult' sectors – we must speak of 'new-framing' rather than 're-framing' the material). A pivotal careers education curriculum shows close parallels with what Watts (1990) characterises as a 'boundary' model for careers education (the apparent contradiction between Watts's use of 'boundary' and this use of 'pivotal' is less confusing when point of view is taken into account).

The case for establishing a *foundation* for career learning more fully acknowledges the depth, breadth and progression required for career-related learning. Career action in the contemporary world requires learning that is more dynamic and complex than can be accommodated by a series of marginal and short-run cyclical programmes. Changes in the working world require underpinning and flexible concepts for all aspects of work, role and self; and these concepts need to be capable of application, adaptation and re-application in changing circumstances and conditions. Moreover, such changes also require that connections are made between decision-making in one role and in other roles; the role of worker is intimately linked to causes and effects in all other life roles. In secondary schools, such connections are most readily made in personal and social education. The strategy has some parallels with what Watts (1990) calls an 'enclosed' model for careers education, set up as a separate subject.

An implication of the argument for progression is that such work should be begun in primary school, aimed at the progressive enrichment, diversification and verification of bases for present and future action. An expectation (see Chapter 3) would be that earlier stages would require higher concentrations of activity, engaging children in finding out about work, role and self, and in sifting and sorting what they find into useful order. This would lay an informed and explored foundation, for expansion to an understanding of specific bases for action in secondary education and beyond.

The culture would most appropriately be liberal – conveying a sense of how an educated person can deal with life's decisions and problems in all of her or his roles. In primary and secondary education, such a strategy would require both some curricular re-framing (introducing new elements of, for example, psychology and sociology) and re-classification (by linking elements, for example, literature, geography and history). Primary educators are, as Bernstein (1971) specifically points out, adept in re-framing and re-classifying curriculum into interesting, useful and workable packages. Pressure for a subject- and standards-based 'academic' curriculum will only hinder the development of a culture of relevance if it is exclusively and obsessively pursued.

The case for *connecting* programmes argues that learning in any part of any curriculum can have intrinsic value for career development. Geography portrays opportunity, literature explores self, mathematics assesses probability, science suggests causality; all other subjects inform career development in such ways. The connecting-programme strategy makes these links explicit.

The strategy is substantially concerned with re-classifying rather than re-framing the curriculum: making new connections between elements in the existing curriculum. Watts (1990) calls this a 'systemic' model, leading – in principle – to the possibility that all of the curriculum can be infused with links to careers education. This possibility has been examined by Whitty *et al.* (1994), who pessimistically conclude that the teacher's need to control the dominant 'academic' boundary generally overrides such considerations (see Chapter 5).

There are other possibilities for connecting programmes. The career applications of learning may be, from time to time, re-examined in limited and specific schemes of work. For example, careers, geography, literature and mathematics teachers might co-operate in taking learners into an enquiry into the biographical experience, work patterns and employment probabilities in a particular area of work. Such schemes need shared learning time and space. In schools, this is often undertaken on a 'federal' basis in set-aside long-block time. Work experience provides such opportunities, but there are others.

Connecting schemes share both academic and role-related objectives in a single co-operative learning programme. Such work improves the achievement of academic objectives by providing broader contexts for learning through association. Linking learning to a variety of settings is a necessary means for ensuring transferability (Meadows, 1993). Such schemes also improve role-related learning by drawing upon the 'academic' cultural capital which ultimately must inform all educated decision-making and problem-solving. In these ways, such schemes of work serve both the culture of standards and the culture of relevance: this is a reason for colleagues to get involved in this work for their own purposes, finding what Goodson (1994) calls 'the middle ground' for curriculum design.

Such programmes are unlikely to have the progression of either foundation or even pivotal schemes of work. But in longer 'long-block' slots (such as week-long projects), 'mini-progressions' can be established, integrating into a single progressive sequence investigating, mapping, narrative, classifying, experimenting and practising methods.

These types of programmes do not compete with each other. Career development needs the focus of the first, the progressiveness of the second, and the pervasiveness of the third. Table 12.7 suggests how different combinations might be appropriate for different stages in lifelong learning (the analysis includes people who, for some of their careers, will be out of paid employment, and therefore separated from the institutional and social support which employment affords). None of these types of programme can do everything that careers education in a curriculum might usefully do; each requires the others.

12.7 CONCLUSION

Careers education is a necessary part of careers work. It draws, as much as any other part of the curriculum, on academic knowledge, concepts and skills. Framing careers education as an academic subject is not a useful option; there are however many others, differentially applicable to all stages of lifelong learning. In educational institutions, the establishment of a climate of relevance – alongside the pursuit of standards – is a major priority for stimulating hospitality to the future development of careers education.

Some of the greatest opportunities may lie in other 'non-education' sectors, particularly those which can be brought close to the needs of people marginalised by contemporary careers education provision. These opportunities may best be approached through new and emergent learning technologies.

This chapter deliberately rejects notions of careers education as 'quick-and-easy' activities, free of challenge and rigour. Such activities discredit careers education's claim on the curriculum. They patronise learners with low expectations and refuse to engage the best of what people can bring to their lives. They assume that what people need to learn in order to manage their careers

Table 12.7 Possible manifestations of careers education at different life stages

	Pivotal	Foundation	Connecting
Primary education		Project work (liberal culture): re-framing and re-classifying	
Secondary, further and higher education	Careers education (guidance culture): re-framing	Personal and social education (liberal culture): re-framing and re-classifying	Long-block programme (liberal and vocational culture) (incorporating lifeskills/personal transferable skills): re-classifying
In employment	Career-development workshops (guidance culture): new-framing		
Out of employment	Career-development workshops (guidance culture): new-framing	Education-for-life programmes (liberal and vocational cultures): new-framing	
In the 'third age'	Personal-planning workshops (guidance culture): new-framing	Education-for-life programmes (liberal culture): new-framing	

can be achieved without much thought, or even much sustained attention. Contemporary and foreseeable worlds will not be kind to people socialised into such assumptions.

On the contrary, careers education is essential to any commitment to lifelong learning, if it is to be offered to autonomous citizens, perceived as members of an intelligent species, whose claim on survival is the use of their wits, and who therefore need to find rational bases for managing their experience. For any such commitment, the fullest use of the apparatus of curriculum development in careers education is a major priority.

REFERENCES

Ball, B. and Butcher, V. (1993) *Developing Students' Career Planning Skills*, Sheffield: Employment Department.

Barnes, A. and Andrews, D. (eds) (1995) *Developing Careers Education and Guidance in the Curriculum*, London: Fulton.

Bates, I. (1989) 'Versions of Vocationalism: an Analysis of Some Social and Political Influences on Curriculum Policy and Practice', *British Journal of Sociology of Education* 10(2): 215–31.

Bernstein, B. B. (1971) 'Open Schools, Open Society', in Cosin, B. R., Dale, I. R., Esland, G. M. and Swift, D. F. (eds) *School and Society*, London: Open University/Routledge & Kegan Paul.

Bernstein, B. B. (1973) 'On the Classification and Framing of Educational Knowledge', in Brown, K. (ed.) *Knowledge, Education and Cultural Change*, London: Tavistock.

Boud, D., Keogh, R. and Walker, D. (eds.) (1985) *Reflection: Turning Experience into Learning*, London: Kogan Page.

Bray, R. (1995) 'Careers Education in Higher Education: a Survey of Providers and a Case Study', MPhil thesis, University of Lancaster.

Coffey, D. (1992) *Schools and Work*, London: Cassell.

Cohen, P. (1984) 'Against the New Vocationalism', in Bates, I., Clarke, J., Cohen, P., Finn, D., Moore, R. and Willis, P.: *Schooling and the Dole?: the New Vocationalism*, London: Macmillan.

Daws, P. P. (1968) *A Good Start in Life*, Cambridge: Careers Research and Advisory Centre.

Dewey, J. (1915) *The School and Society*, Chicago: University of Chicago Press.

Goodson, I. F. (1994) *Studying Curriculum*, Buckingham: Open University Press.

Hargreaves, A., Baglin, E., Henderson, P., Leeson, P. and Tossell, T. (1988) *Personal and Social Education*, London: Blackwell.

Hargreaves, D. (1972) *Interpersonal Relations and Education*, London: Routledge & Kegan Paul.

Holt, M. (1987) 'Beyond the New Vocationalism', in Holt, M. (ed.) *Skills and Vocationalism: the Easy Answer*, Milton Keynes: Open University Press.

Hopson, B. and Scally, M. (1984) *Build Your Own Rainbow*, Leeds: Lifeskills Associates.

Hunt, M. (1994) 'On the Present and Future Use of IT to Support Guidance', in *The Future Use of Information Technology in Guidance*, Coventry: National Council for Educational Technology.

Jarvis, V. (1994) *Smoothing the Transition to Skilled Employment: How Can School-Based Vocational Guidance Be Improved?*, Discussion Paper No. 53, London: National Institute of Economic and Social Research.

Killeen, J., White, M. and Watts, A. G. (1992) *The Economic Value of Careers Guidance*, London: Policy Studies Institute.

King, R. (1976) 'Bernstein's Sociology of the School: Some Propositions Tested', *British Journal of Sociology* 27(4): 430–43.

Law, B. (1981) 'Careers Education and Curriculum Priorities in Secondary Schools', *Educational Analysis* 3(2): 53–64.

Law, B. (1994) 'On the Importance of Interwagulation!', in *The Future Use of Information Technology in Guidance*, Coventry: National Council for Educational Technology.

Law, B. (1995) *Key Concepts for Careers Work*, Manchester: Open College.

Law, B. and Watts, A. G. (1977) *Schools, Careers and Community*, London: Church Information Office.

Law, B., *et al.* (1995) *Careers Work* (revised edn), Manchester: Open College.

Lee, R. (1980) *Beyond Coping*, London: Further Education Unit.

McChesney, P. (1995) 'Yes, But How? Development and Evaluation of Careers Education in Higher Education by Careers Advisers', *British Journal of Guidance and Counselling* 23(3): 327–45.

Meadows, S. (1993) *The Child as Thinker*, London: Routledge.

Merson, M. (1992) 'The Four Ages of TVEI: a Review of Policy', *British Journal of Education and Work* 5(2): 5–18.

Musgrove, F. and Taylor, P. H. (1969) *Society and the Teacher's Role*, London: Routledge & Kegan Paul.

National Curriculum Council (1990) *Careers Education and Guidance*, Curriculum Guidance 6, York: NCC.

Paine, N. (ed.) (1988) *Open Learning in Transition: an Agenda for Action*, Cambridge: National Extension College.

Roberts, K. (1977) 'The Social Conditions, Consequences and Limitations of Careers Guidance', *British Journal of Guidance and Counselling* 5(1): 1–9.

Roberts, R. J. (1980) 'An Alternative Justification for Careers Education: a Radical Response to Roberts and Daws', *British Journal of Guidance and Counselling* 8(2): 158–74.

Savickas, M. L. (1994) 'Fracture Lines in Careers Counselling', *NICEC Careers Education and Guidance Bulletin* 42: 18–21.

Senge, P. M. (1990) *The Fifth Discipline: the Art and Practice of the Learning Organization*, New York: Doubleday.

Spours, K. and Young, M. (1990) 'Beyond Vocationalism: a New Perspective on the

Relationship Between Work and Education', in Moon, B. (ed.) *New Curriculum – National Curriculum*, London: Hodder & Stoughton.

Steedman, H. (1994) *Making Decisions about Education and Training: a Note on Practice and Procedures in Careers Guidance in France and Germany*, Discussion Paper No. 55, London: National Institute of Economic and Social Research.

Stradling, R. (1984) 'Teaching for Unemployment', in Stradling, R., Noctor, M. and Baines, B. (eds) *Teaching Controversial Issues*, London: Arnold.

Taylor, W. (1991) 'School to Work', in Corson, D. (ed.) *Education for Work*, Clevedon, Avon: Multilingual Matters.

Waterhouse, P. (1988) *Supported Self-Study*, Coventry: National Council for Educational Technology.

Watts, A. G. (1977) 'Careers Education in Higher Education: Principles and Practice', *British Journal of Guidance and Counselling* 5(2): 167–84.

Watts, A. G. (1990) 'The Role of Guidance in Educational Change', in Watts, A. G. (ed.) *Guidance and Educational Change*, Cambridge: Careers Research and Advisory Centre/Hobsons.

Watts, A. G. (1994) *Lifelong Career Development*, CRAC Occasional Paper, Cambridge: Careers Research and Advisory Centre/Hobsons.

Watts, A. G. and Hawthorn, R. (1992) *Careers Education and the Curriculum in Higher Education*, NICEC Project Report, Cambridge: Careers Research and Advisory Centre/Hobsons.

Watts, A. G. and Herr, E. L. (1976) 'Career(s) Education in Britain and the USA: Contrasts and Common Problems', *British Journal of Guidance and Counselling* 4(2): 129–42.

Whitty, G., Rowe, G. and Aggleton, P. (1994) 'Subjects and Themes in the Secondary School Curriculum', *Research Papers in Education* 9(2): 159–81.

Willis, P. (1977) *Learning to Labour: How Working-Class Kids Get Working-Class Jobs*, Farnborough: Saxon House.

Wirth, A. G. (1991) 'Issues in the Vocational–Liberal Studies Controversy (1900–1917): John Dewey v. the Social Efficiency Philosophers'; in Corson, D. (ed.) *Education for Work*, Clevedon, Avon: Multilingual Matters.

Chapter 13

Experience-based learning about work

A. G. Watts

13.1 INTRODUCTION

Origins

Guidance programmes in Britain and elsewhere have increasingly included, or taken advantage of, experience-based learning about work. Forms of such learning conventionally include work experience, work visits, work shadowing, and work simulation. All involve direct and personal contact with some mix of work roles, work tasks, work processes, and work environments.

The development of such provision within educational programmes is by no means solely guidance-related. In broad terms, it can be seen as a response to two factors (Watts, 1983). The first is the way in which industrialisation and other social changes have gradually removed children from working and from seeing adults engaged in work. The result, it is argued, has been to deprive young people of many of the experiences most important to maturation and to learning the full range of skills required for adult life (Coleman, 1972). Experience-based learning about work is viewed as a means of reinstating some of these experiences: of breaking down the barriers that isolate the young from the economic institutions where the main productive activities of society take place, and giving these institutions an explicit role in the education of the young.

The second factor is the revived popularity of a vein of educational philosophy which decries 'inert ideas' and places self-discovery through experience at the heart of the educational process (Whitehead, 1932; Dewey, 1938). Advocates of this point of view argue that the most effective learning is based not on the passive reception of static knowledge but on the dynamic interaction between thought and experience. This has been influentially conceptualised by Lewin (1951) and Kolb (1984) in cyclical form, viewing effective learning as occurring in a four-stage cycle of concrete experience, reflective observation, abstract conceptualisation, and active experimentation (Figure 13.1). 'Action-rich' experiences like experience-based learning about work are seen as making potentially powerful contributions to this cycle, in relation to many aspects of educational curricula.

Extent

The aims of such provision are accordingly not confined to guidance. An analysis of the aims of school-based work-experience schemes, as stated in a variety of

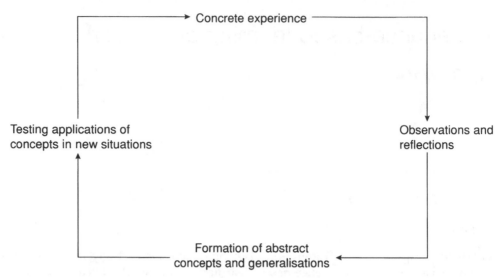

Figure 13.1 The experiential learning cycle

Source: Lewin (1951); subsequently amplified by Kolb (1984).

documents at national, local and school level, identified ten aims and grouped them into five curricular frames, of which careers education is one (Table 13.1). The careers education frame covers three of the aims – 'expansive', 'sampling' and 'anticipatory' – and is also linked to the more controversial 'placing' aim (regarded by some as an abuse of the concept). In practice, careers education seems to be the most common frame for school-based work-experience schemes in Britain. Considerable attention has however been given in recent years to developing the other frames (Miller *et al.*, 1991). It was largely because of this wider curricular base that policy regarding school-based work experience moved from 'work experience for some' to 'work experience for all', reflected most strongly in a 1988 government policy statement that by 1992 all school-leavers should have had two or more weeks' work experience in the course of their compulsory education (Jamieson and Miller, 1991). In the event, a survey in 1992 found that 91 per cent of pupils in their last year of compulsory education were involved in work-experience placements, the average length of placement per pupil being 9–10 days (DfE, 1993).

Work experience is only one form of experience-based learning about work in schools. The growth of the schools–industry movement (Jamieson, 1985) resulted in a massive growth of other forms as well, most notably work simulations (Jamieson *et al.*, 1988) and work shadowing (Watts, 1986). Many of these schemes, too, were not set up as part of careers education programmes. Most however offered potential guidance benefits, particularly when careers education is viewed in a cross-curricular perspective (see Chapters 5 and 12).

In further and higher education, experience-based learning about work has most commonly been found in vocational courses. Some of these are set up on a 'sandwich' basis, with work placements of up to a year being incorporated into the course; others include shorter placements, or other forms of direct experience. Such experiences may be based on a *professional* model, focusing on

Table 13.1 Possible aims of school-based work experience

Curricular frame	Aim	Description
Academic subject(s)	Enhancing	To enable students to deepen their understanding of concepts learned in classroom settings, and to apply skills learned in such settings.
Academic subject(s)	Motivational	To make the school curriculum more meaningful and significant to students, so improving their levels of academic attainment.
Personal and social	Maturational	To facilitate students' personal and social development.
Economic and industrial	Investigative	To enable students to develop their knowledge and understanding of the world of work.
Careers education	Expansive	To broaden the range of occupations students are prepared to consider in terms of their personal career planning.
Careers education	Sampling	To enable students to test their vocational preference before committing themselves to it.
Careers education	Anticipatory	To enable students to experience some of the strains of work so that they will be able to manage the transition to work more comfortably.
Vocational course	Preparatory	To help students to acquire skills and knowledge related to a particular occupational area, which they will be able to apply if they wish to enter employment in that area.
	Placing	To enable students to establish a relationship with a particular employer which may lead to the offer of a full-time job.
	Custodial	To transfer some of the responsibility for particular students for a period.

Source: Adapted from Watts (1991a)

preparation for a predetermined vocational goal, within parameters set by the relevant professional body: these experiences are normally designed to meet requirements for professional practice. Or the experiences may be based on an *academic* model, providing opportunities for exploring the interaction between theory and practice, within parameters set up by the university or college. The notion of using the experiences to explore career areas to which students are not yet committed has traditionally been marginal or absent, largely because the experiences have been mainly concentrated in courses where it is assumed that a prior vocational commitment has been made. Career exploration is barely mentioned, for example, in a review of the literature on experience-based learning within the higher education curriculum (Davies, 1990). In higher education, however, the Enterprise in Higher Education programme has resulted in a considerable growth and diversification of forms of experience-based learning about work, and also in greater attention to its career exploration potential (Watts and Hawthorn, 1992). In further education, too, the growth of more broadly-based forms of vocational preparation has resulted in a strengthening of this facet of such experience.

All of these examples refer to students within educational institutions being given access to experiences of work as part of their preparation for choices and transitions relating to entering (or re-entering) the labour market. Attention to the use of experience-based learning in guidance need not however be confined to such examples. Programmes designed to give adults already in employment an opportunity to experience alternative work settings – secondments, for instance – can have a very similar function. So indeed can forms of experience-based learning about educational opportunities: for example, 'taster' experiences designed to enable adults to consider the possibility of returning to study, or to enable existing students to experience a particular programme of study before committing themselves to it. It is also important to recognise that 'real' experiences – students taking part-time or holiday jobs, for instance – can be powerful forms of career exploration (Varlaam, 1983; Finn, 1984), and that many initial choices – what Super (1957) called 'floundering' or 'trial' behaviour – are exploratory in nature.

Many of the principles discussed in the rest of this chapter can be applied or adapted to these alternative forms of experience-based learning. Nonetheless, for the sake of clarity and coherence, we will continue to confine our main attention to forms of experience-based learning set up within educational institutions through which students are helped to explore the concept and nature of work.

Theoretical basis

The theoretical basis for the use of experience-based learning in guidance programmes can be approached from a number of different starting-points (see Chapter 2). Developmental theories provide general encouragement for interventions designed to facilitate and accelerate career development. Social learning theory (Krumboltz *et al.*, 1976; Mitchell and Krumboltz, 1984) provides more specific support for experience-based learning, because it attends particularly to the importance of the self-views which the individual acquires from learning experiences comprising contact with and cognitive analysis of positively and negatively reinforcing events. Indeed, an attempt by Krumboltz to operationalise his theory took the form of a series of work-simulation kits (Krumboltz and Sheppard, 1969).

Community-interaction theory (Law, 1981) offers an alternative lens for viewing the way in which experience-based learning can contribute to guidance programmes. It emphasises the importance of the plurality of inter-personal transactions experienced by individuals, and the interactions within and between groups of which the individual is a member. It also analyses the way in which individuals and groups exert their influence: through *expectations*, through *feedback*, through *support* (reinforcement and encouragement), through *modelling*, and through transmission of *information*. In this sense, forms of experience-based learning can be seen as a powerful means of extending the network of people and groups to whose varied forms of influence individuals have access. This is particularly true of experiences in the workplace, to which we will turn next. It can also, however, be true of work simulations, which we will examine subsequently – particularly where they involve the participation of 'real workers'.

13.2 EXPERIENCE IN THE WORKPLACE

Methods

Work experience can be defined as describing schemes in which students experience work tasks in work environments, but without taking on the full identity of a worker. This can be contrasted with *work observation*, in which students experience work environments but not work tasks; and with *work simulations*, in which students usually experience work tasks but not work environments (Watts, 1991a). Work simulations will be examined separately in Section 13.3.

Work observation takes two main forms. The first is *work visits*, in which individuals or (often) groups of students are guided around workplaces to watch a range of employee activities and work processes. Such visits have been an accepted educational method in schools in particular for longer than work experience, though lack of adequate structure and planning has sometimes meant that they have fallen into disrepute (Bennett, 1983).

The second form of work observation is *work shadowing*, in which an individual student follows a particular worker for a period of time (usually between two days and a week), observing the various tasks in which he or she engages, and doing so within the context of his or her total role. The late 1980s saw a considerable growth of interest in such programmes, not only in schools (Watts, 1986; 1988) but also in higher education (Jack, 1989). Shadowing may involve students carrying out some tasks for the person they are observing, but this is only a subordinate means to the observational end – i.e. to understanding what it is like to be in his or her shoes. In work experience, the reverse is the case: there may be an element of shadowing – particularly in training the students to carry out the tasks they have been allocated – but this is merely a subordinate means to the task-performance end (Watts, 1986).

Thus not only are work visits and work shadowing different in their nature from work experience: they also focus on different aspects of the workplace. Whereas work experience focuses primarily on work *tasks*, work visits focus primarily on work *processes*, and work shadowing on worker *roles* (Table 13.2). These focuses are not of course mutually exclusive: a student on work experience, for example, is also likely to learn about work processes and worker roles. But because the *primary* focus is different, the nature of what is learned is likely to vary in character.

Even within these categories, the methods can take different forms. Work experience, in particular, can take at least five forms (Watts, 1991a):

1 *Doing an actual job*: being given tasks which are integral to the operations of the organisation, and which another employee would normally have had to carry out if the student were not there.

2 *Providing an 'extra pair of hands'*: this can range from being given 'dogsbody' tasks to being given a series of well-designed tasks drawn from existing jobs.
3 *Helping someone in an actual job*: this incorporates elements of work shadowing and has the merit of ensuring a high level of personal supervision.
4 *Rotating around different departments*: this incorporates elements of work visits and, while it can be fragmented, can give a wider understanding of the organisation as a whole.
5 *Carrying out specifically constructed tasks* (i.e. work-based projects) which, while of possible use to the work organisation, are extraneous to its normal operations.

Table 13.2 Primary focuses of different methods of experience in the workplace

	Work tasks	Work processes	Worker roles	Work environments
Work experience	✓✓	✓	✓	✓
Work visits	✓	✓✓	✓	✓
Work shadowing	✓	✓	✓✓	✓

Source: Watts (1986)

Elements of these five forms may be combined in particular placements, but each involves very different kinds of experience. The ones later in the list tend to leave students in a 'student' role, whereas the earlier ones move them closer to an 'employee' role involving accountability to the employer (rather than the educational institution) for work undertaken. Again, the later ones involve students in a kind of voyeurism in relation to the workplace, whereas the earlier ones offer immersion.

Pros and cons

All these methods have distinctive strengths and weaknesses. The direct experience offered by work experience tends to be stronger than the vicarious experience offered by work shadowing and work visits. On the other hand, the latter offer access to work situations and to occupations which do not lend themselves to work experience: it is possible, for example, to observe highly skilled occupations (e.g. a doctor or senior manager) for which work experience in a direct sense is inconceivable. Work shadowing and work visits tend also to be more economical in terms of time. In addition, they can be used with younger age-groups: work experience is limited by the Education (Work Experience) Act 1973 to students in or beyond the final twelve months of compulsory schooling – i.e. from the age of 15 – whereas work shadowing and work visits are not subject to such restriction.

From a guidance perspective, work shadowing offers particular strengths because of its primary focus on worker roles: in the end, career choices tend to be primarily choices of roles rather than of tasks, processes or environments. Work visits are usually of more limited value for guidance purposes. Work experience can have a powerful impact on career decisions, but poses problems about the extent to which the experience provides an accurate sample of the occupation in question. This is particularly the case because of the limitations imposed on work experience by issues of safety (e.g. in engineering firms), of confidentiality (e.g. in banking), and of skill requirements. The result of the last in particular is that, especially in school-based programmes, occupations may be represented only in terms of their most routine tasks. This can be misleading: one report, for example, expressed concern about a group of students rejecting careers in institutional management because of the repetitive nature of the work of a canteen/kitchen assistant in which they had participated for a week (ICO, 1974). Such limitations are more acute for forms of work experience which move closer to an 'employee' role: they apply less to forms which stay closer to a 'student' role (e.g. work-based projects), though these latter tend to be weak forms of work experience in a strict sense since they have a less strong element of direct experience through task performance.

Selection of placements

In addition to choice of appropriate method, important decisions need to be made within work-experience and work-shadowing schemes about the selection and allocation of placements. Such decisions are not entirely in the hands of the scheme managers: the co-operation of employers is required, and attention is therefore needed to employers' motivations (Watts, 1991b) as well as individuals' guidance needs. Nonetheless, it is important to clarify the principles underlying the choice of employers to be approached and how ensuing placements are to be distributed. Where the placements are set up on an individual basis for guidance purposes, these principles can be negotiated with the individual concerned. Where however the placements are included as part of a curricular programme for a group of students, some prior decisions need to be made, related to the aims of the programme in question.

Many schemes attach importance to students being able to choose their own placements. In some cases, this means choice from within a given pool of placements; in others, it means encouraging students to find their own placements. Such voluntarism can increase the student's motivation for the placement. It also, however, tends to reinforce constraints related to social class, ethnicity, and gender (Miller, 1991a).

In Sweden, very little scope has been provided for freedom of choice by students. All students have been expected to spend six to ten weeks in workplaces between the age of 7 and 16: these include group visits at younger ages, and at least one week's experience at ages 12–16 in each of the three broad sectors of working life (manufacturing, commerce, and social services). The objectives of these latter three placements in particular has been 'to counteract prejudice in vocational decisions'. Accordingly, students are normally expected to accept the places they are allotted, often as a result of a draw (Watts et al., 1989).

The resolution of this issue depends on the nature of the aim that is being pursued (see Table 13.1). If the primary aim is the *sampling* one of enabling students to test their vocational preference before committing themselves to it, then freedom of choice would seem desirable and even essential. If, on the other hand, the aim is the *expansive* one of broadening the range of occupations that students are prepared to consider in terms of their personal career planning, then arguably some constraints on such freedom are needed. Moreover, whereas the sampling aim can be satisfied by one placement, the expansive aim can benefit from multiple placements – as in the Swedish example.

13.3 WORK SIMULATION

Work simulations have tended to be viewed in some circles as acceptable but inferior alternatives to experience in the workplace. This view is misconceived. Certainly work simulations lack the full sensory reality of experiences in the workplace. But they are easier to organise and control, and this may have advantages in constructing learning experiences. As Waddell (1982) claimed: 'simulation is a close representation of reality, but may be superior to reality for teaching/learning purposes' (p. 80).

Simulations are operational models of real systems or processes, which usually simplify and accelerate reality. Work simulations are operating representations of work tasks outside real work situations. In this sense, they combine elements of three more limited concepts:

1 *Case-studies*, presenting situations in order to illustrate particular issues or problems.
2 *Role-plays*, inviting individuals to imagine they are in a particular situation and to act out their imagined behaviour in that situation.
3 *Games*, involving contest (play) among adversaries (players) operating under constraints (rules) for an objective (winning victory or play-off) (Abt, 1968).

Simulations provide more active involvement than case-studies, and more structuring of procedures and relationships than role-plays; they may or may not also involve a game element.

An analysis of work simulations used in schools identified six main types (Jamieson *et al.*, 1988):

1 *'Design and make' simulations*, concerned with design and prototype construction.
2 *Production simulations*, concerned with mass production, typically attempting to mirror assembly lines in manufacturing industry.
3 *Mini-enterprises*, concerned not only with design and production but also with placing these in the context of a total process in which students set up and run their own 'business' for a limited period of time.
4 *Work practice units*, which are designed physically to resemble industrial premises as closely as possible.
5 *Business games*, concerned with decision-making in the running of business enterprises (typically involving students taking the roles of competing teams of managers who have to take decisions about rival products or services operating within the same market).
6 *School work tasks*, where these are viewed as simulating parallel tasks in the outside world, and where the learning potential which ensues from such parallels is harnessed.

As with the different forms of experience in the workplace (Table 13.2), such simulations vary in the relative extent of their focus on work tasks, work

Table 13.3 Primary focuses of different forms of work simulation

	Work tasks	Work processes	Worker roles	Work environments
'Design and make' simulations	✓✓	✓	✓	✓
Production simulations	✓✓	✓✓	✓✓	✓
Mini-enterprises	✓✓	✓✓	✓✓	
Work practice units	✓✓	✓✓	✓	✓✓
Business games	✓✓	✓✓	✓✓	
School work tasks	✓✓	✓	✓	

Source: Jamieson *et al.* (1988)

processes, worker roles and work environments. Work practice units cover all four, and are particularly concerned with simulating work environments. The others usually focus mainly on roles, tasks and processes, with 'design and make' simulations and school work tasks tending to have a particular focus on tasks (Table 13.3).

In terms of worker roles, the range of roles offered to students varies considerably. Business games tend to concentrate on managerial roles; by contrast, production simulations, work practice units and school work tasks tend to be mainly concerned with operator-level worker roles, though they may offer managerial roles as well. 'Design and make' simulations are more concerned with technical roles related to the design process, and some of the other simulations may offer a wider range of technical roles: some production simulations, for example, may offer roles as quality controller, as store/stock controller, as secretary/typist, as accountant, and so on; similarly, business games may offer such roles as marketing/sales manager, personnel manager, production manager, and financial manager/accountant. Mini-enterprises can offer a particularly wide range of roles, since they have to encompass all the functions of a business.

The allocation of such roles raises similar issues to those identified in Section 13.2 in relation to selection of placements. If students allocate the roles themselves, there is a risk of reinforcing gender and other stereotypes. Sensitive teacher allocation of roles, or random role allocation through drawing of lots, can avoid this danger, if the aim is to expand students' views of their capability. At the same time, some simulations – especially those with a number of clearly distinguished but closely interdependent roles – will not operate effectively unless certain key roles are performed competently: this tends to require such roles to be allocated to students with the appropriate skills and motivation; otherwise the other students may become frustrated and the simulation may collapse. Such intrusions of 'reality' tend to constrain the expansive aim.

A distinctive issue for work simulation is the extent to which it simulates accurately the external reality it purports to represent. Simulations in general do not *sample* in a representative way the range and balance of simulations to be found in the working world. Instead, they tend to select examples of reality which lend themselves to the simulation format. Other sampling biases are introduced by the sponsorship source of many simulations (it is noticeable how many business games are based on the oil industry). There are also variations in the *fidelity* of simulations in corresponding directly to the reality they are representing. Some writers argue that such fidelity matters less than the overall felt reality of the simulation itself, but low fidelity can lead to faulty learning. The same is true of the *validity* of the simulation in representing what it purports to represent. The distinction between fidelity and validity is important: some simulations (e.g. STARPOWER) make no pretence at fidelity in terms of content or context, but are still able to encapsulate the essence of key aspects of the world of work in a highly valid way (Jamieson *et al.*, 1988).

Certainly, however, it is easy for students to derive false impressions and false information from work simulations. Mini-enterprises, for example, can give the impression that starting a business is a relatively easy matter. Ways accordingly need to be found of enabling students to test the simulation against the reality it represents. A powerful way of doing this is by involving in the simulation 'real workers' with direct experience of this reality. These may be involved as *consultants*, offering comments and suggestions during the action or after it. Or they may be invited to play *themselves*: in mini-enterprises, for example, students are often expected to present their case for a loan to a bank manager acting *as* a bank manager. Or they may take ordinary *group roles*, as in CRAC Insight courses where young managers take part with the students as ordinary participants (CRAC, 1986). In each of these ways, the 'real workers' are able to help the students to recognise and explore linkages with reality.

13.4 INTEGRATING EXPERIENCE INTO LEARNING

Integration

The nature and the quality of the learning derived from experiences of work are heavily dependent on the ways in which they are integrated into learning programmes. Miller (1991b) suggests a five-stage cycle comprising preparation, briefing, the activity, debriefing, and follow-up.

The *preparation* stage establishes the learning frame for the experience: the 'lens' through which the student is being encouraged to approach it. It also seeks to ensure that students have the knowledge, understanding and skills they require in order to gain access to, cope with, and benefit from, the experience. In the case of the 'expansive' aim, for example, this might include attention to the broad structure of the world of work, and ways of classifying different types of work; in the case of the 'sampling' aim, it might include identifying students' vocational interests and work preferences; in the case of the 'anticipatory' aim, it might include attention to the pressures of work environments and the structure of the working day. Other issues might include stereotyping and discrimination in the workplace. Role-plays can be helpful in preparing students for situations they may confront. In addition, in relation to work experience and work shadowing in particular, the processes students go through in choosing and preparing for their placements can be constructed to offer a 'simulation' of the processes they will subsequently go through in applying for jobs.

The *briefing* stage is concerned with ensuring that students have the operational information they require for the activity. With experiences in workplaces, this includes information on how to get to the workplace, how to dress, to whom to report, and so on; it may also include a pre-placement visit. With work simulations, it includes allocation of roles, and inducting students into their roles.

During the *activity* itself, some support may be provided for recording and reflecting on what is happening. In the case of experiences in workplaces, this may involve maintaining a diary or log or work book; it may also include a teacher visit. In the case of work simulations, it may involve breaks in the action (though these are usually kept to a minimum); more commonly, it comprises systematic observation by nominated observers of the content and/or the process of the simulation, for later analysis at the debriefing stage.

The *debriefing* stage is, in many respects, as crucial to effective learning as the activity itself. It includes two stages of the experiential learning cycle (Figure 13.1): reflective observation and abstract conceptualisation. *Reflection* encourages students to identify what they have experienced, and – where it is conducted in a group setting – to share it with the experiences of other students. This can be followed by an *analysis* sub-stage in which students are encouraged to interpret their experiences in a systematic way, to contrast them with the experiences of other students, and to draw out conclusions which are related to the learning aim(s) of the programme. Debriefing may also include attention to *evaluation*, both of student learning outcomes and of the quality of the activity.

Finally, the *follow-up* stage covers the application of what has been learned from the experience to new areas of learning. It represents the fourth and last stage of the experiential learning cycle: active experimentation.

The framing provided to experiences of work by the learning programme as a whole can shape the learning in very different ways. For example, such experiences can be adaptive in nature, accepting existing opportunity structures, and socialising students into prevailing employer attitudes and values. Or they can provide the basis for critical explorations of labour relations and workplace practices (see Watkins, 1987; Shilling, 1989). Much depends on the nature of the supporting work which is done before and after the experience itself. In this sense, the learning frame set by the teacher can be viewed as an attempt to reassert some element of control over what students learn from the experience. There are, however, constraints on the extent of such control. Part of the power of experience-based learning about work is that the experience is, in the end, owned by the student; moreover, particularly in the case of experiences in the workplace, the experience is largely managed by the employer, not the teacher. The active involvement of students and of employers in determining the nature of experience-based learning about work makes it particularly fertile ground for careers education.

Progression

We have so far viewed the various forms of experience-based learning about work as *alternatives*. There is much merit, however, in seeing them as *complementary* to one another, and in seeking forms of progression which realise the potential synergy when they are combined and sequenced in a coherent way. Such progression can take place *within* particular learning programmes, and also *between* learning programmes (Jamieson *et al.*, 1988; Miller, 1991c).

In terms of progression *within* learning programmes, various combinations can be envisaged. Work simulations can be used as a means of preparation for 'real' work experience: a work practice unit, for example, was viewed by a head teacher as 'a very useful intermediary step between school-based work and work experience' (quoted in Verma, 1985, p. 40). Again, a mini-enterprise project was followed by work shadowing as a way of introducing students to the 'real-life' counterpart of their school-based experience, and this was followed in turn by work experience (Watts, 1986, pp. 35–36). Conversely, experiences of real work environments can be used as part of the preparation for work simulations. Thus in one school, shadowing was used in the build-up to a production simulation, providing an insight into the role of management and unions within a company, so helping students to assume their simulation roles more quickly and effectively (ibid., p. 37). At another school, work visits were used both before and after a simulation: *before* it, in order to orient the students towards the rhythm, pace and atmosphere of a factory; *after* it, to test some of the students' experiences against reality (Smith, 1985).

In terms of progression *between* learning programmes, it is possible to conceive of a series of different experiences of work being built up over, for example, the course of compulsory schooling, which systematically covers a variety of worker roles and work environments. This could include work visits, work shadowing, work experience and work simulations, all mapped against different sectors of the economy (agriculture, manufacturing, services), different types of organisation (public corporation, local-authority department, private limited company, co-operative, etc.), and different levels and types of worker roles. Such multiple experiences, particularly when mapped in this way, would enable students to develop strong and richer constructs (Kelly, 1955) for understanding the world of work. They would also make it possible to attach different primary aims (Table 13.1) to different experiences: it is the over-loading of multiple aims on to single experiences which causes many of the problems in current programmes (Miller *et al.*, 1991).

13.5 CONCLUSION

The distinctive contribution of experience-based learning to guidance programmes is to expand the base of experience on which individuals can draw in making their career decisions. Much guidance provision is engaged in *reflection* on existing experiences: drawing out from such experiences individuals' perceptions of their attributes and their preferences. This is true in particular of careers interviews (Chapter 11) and of recording of achievement and action planning (Chapter 14), but it is also true of many computer-aided guidance systems (Chapter 15) and even of large elements of careers education programmes (Chapter 12). Many individuals, however, are constrained by *experience deficits*. Their awareness both of their capacities and interests, and of the opportunities open to them, is limited by the experiences they have had, which in turn are restricted by their social background. Experience-based learning can reduce such deficits by expanding the range of experience in a planned way.

The power of direct experience is immense. Most forms of information on opportunities are representational in nature – this is true of publications, audio-visual aids and computer-based systems. If they offer experience, it is vicarious in form. Direct experience, however, involves the individual in active interaction with the environment in question: the individual penetrates the sensory complexities of the environment; the environment penetrates the internal psychological processes of the individual. It accordingly provides a potent form of career learning.

REFERENCES

Abt, C. C. (1968) 'Games for Learning', in Boocock, S. S. and Schild, E. O. (eds) *Simulation Games in Learning*, Beverly Hills, CA: Sage.

Bennett, J. (1983) 'Work Visits', in Watts, A. G. (ed.) *Work Experience and Schools*, London: Heinemann.

Careers Research and Advisory Centre (1986) *Inside Insight Courses*, Cambridge: CRAC.

Coleman, J. S. (1972) 'How Do the Young Become Adults?', *Review of Educational Research* 42(4): 431–39.

Davies, L. (1990) *Experience-Based Learning within the Curriculum: a Synthesis Study*, London: Council for National Academic Awards/Association for Sandwich Education and Training.

Department for Education (1993) 'Survey of School Business Links', *Statistical Bulletin*, 10/93, London: DfE.

Dewey, J. (1938) *Experience and Education*, New York: Macmillan.

Finn, D. (1984) 'Leaving School and Growing Up: Work Experience in the Juvenile Labour Market', in Bates, I., Clarke, J., Cohen, P., Finn, D., Moore, R. and Willis, P., *Schooling for the Dole?: the New Vocationalism*, London: Macmillan.

Institute of Careers Officers (1974) *Work Experience in British Secondary Schools*, Stourbridge: ICO.

Jack, A. (1989) *Life at the Top*, London: Industrial Society.

Jamieson, I. (ed.) (1985) *Industry in Education*, Harlow: Longman.

Jamieson, I. and Miller, A. (1991) 'History and Policy Context', in Miller, A., Watts, A. G. and Jamieson, I., *Rethinking Work Experience*, London: Falmer.

Jamieson, I., Miller, A. and Watts, A. G. (1988) *Mirrors of Work*, London: Falmer.

Kelly, G. (1955) *The Psychology of Personal Constructs* (2 vols), New York: Norton.

Kolb, D. A. (1984) *Experiential Learning*, Englewood Cliffs, NJ: Prentice-Hall.

Krumboltz, J. D. and Sheppard, L. D. (1969) 'Vocational Problem-Solving Experiences', in Krumboltz, J. D. and Thoresen, C. E. (eds) *Behavioral Counseling: Cases and Techniques*, New York: Holt, Rinehart and Winston.

Krumboltz, J. D., Mitchell, A. M. and Jones, G. B. (1976) 'A Social Learning Theory of Career Selection', *Counseling Psychologist* 6(1): 71–81.

Law, B. (1981) 'Community Interaction: a "Mid-Range" Focus for Theories of Career Development in Young Adults', *British Journal of Guidance and Counselling* 9(2): 142–58.

Lewin, K. (1951) *Field Theory in Social Sciences*, New York: Harper & Row.

Miller, A. (1991a) 'Matching Students to Placements', in Miller, A., Watts, A. G. and Jamieson, I., *Rethinking Work Experience*, London: Falmer.

Miller, A. (1991b) 'Teaching Strategies', in Miller, A., Watts, A. G. and Jamieson, I., *Rethinking Work Experience*, London: Falmer.

Miller, A. (1991c) 'Progression', in Miller, A., Watts, A. G. and Jamieson, I., *Rethinking Work Experience*, London: Falmer.

Miller, A., Watts, A. G. and Jamieson, I. (1991) *Rethinking Work Experience*, London: Falmer.

Mitchell, L. K. and Krumboltz, J. D. (1984) 'Social Learning Approach to Career Decision Making: Krumboltz's Theory', in Brown, D. and Brooks, L. (eds) *Career Choice and Development*, San Francisco, CA: Jossey-Bass.

Shilling, C. (1989) *Schooling for Work in Capitalist Britain*, London: Falmer.

Smith, K. (1985) 'Alternatives to Work Experience at Hetton School, Sunderland', in Jamieson, I. (ed.) *Industry in Education*, Harlow: Longman.

Super, D. E. (1957) *The Psychology of Careers*, New York: Harper & Row.

Varlaam, C. (1983) 'Making Use of Part-Time Job Experience', in Watts, A. G. (ed.) *Work Experience and Schools*, London: Heinemann.

Verma, G. (1985) 'The Bradford Work Practice Unit', in Jamieson, I. (ed.) *Industry in Education*, Harlow: Longman.

Waddell, G. (1982) 'Simulation: Balancing the Pros and Cons', *Training and Development Journal* 36(1): 80–83.

Watkins, P. (1987) 'Student Participant-Observation in the Contested Workplace: the Policy Dilemmas of In-School Work Experience', *Journal of Education Policy* 2(1): 27–42.

Watts, A. G. (1983) 'Work Experience: Principles and Practice', in Watts, A. G. (ed.) *Work Experience and Schools*, London: Heinemann.

Watts, A. G. (1986) *Work Shadowing*, York: Longman/School Curriculum Development Committee.

Watts, A.G. (1988) *Executive Shadows*, York: Longman/School Curriculum Development Committee.

Watts, A. G. (1991a) 'The Concept of Work Experience', in Miller, A., Watts, A. G. and Jamieson, I., *Rethinking Work Experience*, London: Falmer.

Watts, A. G. (1991b) 'Employers' Perspectives', in Miller, A., Watts, A. G. and Jamieson, I., *Rethinking Work Experience*, London: Falmer.

Watts, A. G. and Hawthorn, R. (1992) *Careers Education and the Curriculum in Higher Education*, NICEC Project Report, Cambridge: Careers Research and Advisory Centre/Hobsons.

Watts, A. G., Jamieson, I. and Miller, A. (1989) 'School-Based Work Experience: Some International Comparisons', *British Journal of Education and Work* 3(1): 33–47.

Whitehead, A. N. (1932) *The Aims of Education*, London: Williams & Norgate.

Chapter 14

Recording achievement and action planning

Bill Law

14.1 INTRODUCTION

For the learner, recording achievement is gathering information about what he or she has done and is doing – a portrayal of a 'self' in 'situations'. It can be entirely one's own perception, but it can usefully involve gathering other points of view. The term 'achievement' implies that the portrayal will be of success – in completing some project, gaining some learning, demonstrating some ability. But most experience is a mixture of 'success' and 'failure'; and not facing up to failure is the most desperate failure of all. The term 'recording experience' is more inclusive in this respect.

Planning can be based upon the record. The learner works through and re-examines the material, comparing one account with another, collating them, and identifying causes and effects: a necessary understanding for anticipating possible selves in possible futures.

Recording and planning are frequently best undertaken with help. In education, such help may come from a teacher or tutor; in guidance, from an adviser or counsellor; in employment, from an appraiser or mentor; in all cases, from a comprehending friend or relative. The whole procedure examines what has happened and is happening in order to anticipate what can happen, what might happen, and what can be made to happen. It can be extended into lifelong use.

The terms 'recording achievement' and 'action planning' had meaning before they became programme titles. The urge to set down a personal record is persistent and pervasive. It stretches from the first painting by *homo sapiens* of a buffalo on a cave wall. It includes Julius Caesar and Samuel Pepys setting down where they came, what they saw and whom they conquered. More significantly, it includes the struggles of all individuals to make some sense of their lives. The vocabulary of recording achievement and planning action has, then, a provenance of some depth and breadth in human experience. It is important that this discourse is not sacrificed to more recent usage. What is fruitful must not be lost to what is momentarily influential.

Programmes for 'recording achievement' and 'action planning' can thus be understood as professional support for what is natural, often informal, and sometimes spontaneous in human experience. The procedures have a particular role as bases for action concerning who is to do what in the working world. Such action is based in part upon understanding the abilities, personality and motivations that a person brings to work. Until recently, these were commonly screened by examination results and resolved by interview, both the applicant and the selector using information to assess the chances of a successful 'match'. This chapter examines more recently developed procedures. It clusters them into four groups:

1 *'Scientific'* methods: such as expert interviews, their supporting psychometric tests, and the resulting reports.
2 *Expanded* methods: looser techniques, capable of use in a wider range of settings, involving 'negotiated statements', 'checklists', 'recording experience' and 'careers portfolios'.
3 *Structured* methods: more specific and focused methods, including 'profiling', 'recording achievement' and 'action planning'.
4 *'Official'* methods: the 'National Record of Achievement' and 'Individual Action Planning'.

All such activities raise complex issues. The chapter identifies eight of these:

1 *Purposes*: Why do we do it? Is it to help selectors to select? Is this reconcilable with helping learners to learn? Are there other purposes?
2 *Effects*: How are these purposes realised? On the basis of information about self? Because we can guess what this means for new and changing situations? Because we are equipping people to know how to do this on a lifelong basis? Are we being realistic about this?
3 *Settings*: Where do we envisage such techniques being used? In private? At school or college? At work? With a careers adviser? On the Internet?
4 *Coverage*: What should records be recording? Is it mainly what people have done and intend to do? Should there be a harder-edged assessment of what they are *able* to do? What about potential? personality? motivations? hopes and fears?
5 *Sources*: Who has a say? The learner, of course! But should a helper also have a say? A teacher? A manager? A relative? A work-experience contact? Any others?
6 *Trustworthiness*: How reliable and valid must the information be? How can we improve the probability that it is 'objective'? Do we need to?
7 *Control*: Who says what goes into the portrayal? Who sees what comes out? Does everybody who sees it see all of it and keep it for ever? Who decides?
8 *Acceptability*: Does it do any good? What good? Is it cost-effective? Is it manageable? Is it understood and accepted by the people who may be expected to work with it?

The issues come into view as we follow each group of procedures through its development. For each group, three stages are described:

1 *Inputs* – the knowledge and experience contributing to the portrayal.
2 *Processes* – how material is exchanged, considered and assembled.
3 *Outcomes* – the emerging portrayal and the uses made of it.

Each group of descriptions is followed by a chart indicating what is happening at each of these stages, for three groups of participants:

1 *Learners* – 'first-person' participants who invest in the procedure and gain personally from it.

2 *Helpers* – 'second-party' participants, who work closely alongside the learners as teachers, tutors, mentors, or advisers.
3 *Others* – 'third-party' participants, such as managers, selectors, or admissions tutors, who take institutional action on the information generated.

We turn first to descriptions of the four clusters of procedures.

14.2 'SCIENTIFIC' METHODS

Early careers work employed matching models, requiring information about people. Much use was made of interviews and psychometric tests, and the reports they generated.

Interview notes

The seven-point plan (Rodger, 1952) was used in both guidance and selection. It invited the helper to attend to the 'physical make-up', 'attainments', 'general intelligence', 'special aptitudes', 'interests', 'disposition' and 'circumstances' of the learner or candidate, and then – using professional skill and judgement – to make observations in each of these categories (see Chapter 11).

Psychometric testing

Since interviewing has not enjoyed a good reputation as a means of gathering such information (Morea, 1972), psychometric tests and other measures have been developed. Such measures can be found for all but one category in the seven-point plan (the exception is 'circumstances'). They have also been developed for 'personality', and – by means of 'projective techniques' – for 'deeper aspects of self' (Kline, 1975).

Most measures are norm-referenced, a person's position in each category being set in a frame-of-reference defined by some known population with which the individual can be compared. The data can be used *nomothetically* – comparing self with an external standard (such as the norm). In competitive situations, this is likely to be at least part of the basis for a report. In guidance situations, it more likely that the data will be used *idiographically*, comparing self-with-self (Fox, 1995).

Most psychometric tests rely on paper-and-pencil or keyboard techniques. This means that we infer that a person is relatively 'numerate' or 'co-operative' from answers to questions, rather than from direct observation of his or her behaviour. This may not be a problem in measures of 'attainment', 'intelligence' and 'aptitudes'. These are, for the most part, challenges to the learner to see whether or not he or she can get the 'right' answers. It is difficult to 'fake good'.

But measures of 'interest' and – perhaps – 'disposition' rely upon disclosure. In a competitive situation, 'faking good' is a possibility. A portrayal derived entirely from disclosure might deceive the unwary helper. More seriously, the process can be *self*-deluding, by – for example – making self-stereotyping responses to inventory items. The computerised equivalent is the 'junk-in-junk-out' syndrome (Law, 1994).

Reports

Processing the information helps: by taking one piece of information with another, a person may find bases for challenging too-easy assumptions. Skilled help can be critical in such a process: noticing and helpfully confronting inconsistencies. Computer systems offer a less developed scepticism.

The report sets down a portrayal of the learner, incorporating a recommendation or suggestion for action. The report might go to the learner, to help the learner decide his or her next action; or it might go to a selector or manager, to assist recruitment or promotion decisions *about* the learner.

Commentary

As Table 14.1 illustrates, all of the elements of what we have come to call 'recording achievement' and 'action planning' are embedded in these long-established procedures. The model represented in the table reflects concerns for the reliability and validity of the portrayal. Part of the rationale is that these techniques protect the individual from the prejudice, poor judgement and even self-interest of teachers, managers, selectors and other gatekeepers. The search is for unbiased data, skilled interpretation and 'neutral' guidance. A specific argument for the *helping* use of the model is that the process can elicit and recognise more possibilities for self-portrayal than *unassisted* disclosure will yield (Fox, 1995).

Table 14.1 Inputs, processes and outcomes of 'scientific' methods

	Input	Process	Outcome
By learner	Introspection and recall	Disclosing	A career decision
By 'helper'	Interviewing and psychometric skills combined with expert knowledge of opportunities	Questioning, attending and clarifying; establishing frames-of-reference; interpreting and matching	Provision of information and advice
By others			A selection decision

14.3 EXPANDED METHODS

There are some doubts about whether 'scientific' methods can adequately portray human subtlety, variety and variability (Morea, 1972). Expanded methods are claimed to be more comprehending in these respects. They include negotiated statements, checklists, discursive writing, graphics and other 'loosened' means of setting down information. All, in different ways, do three things: they move the basis for portrayal closer to the direct observation of behaviour, they extend the range of what might be included, and they develop the processes – in some cases by calling upon curriculum as well as guidance settings.

Negotiated statements

Some argue that tests work better when they are undertaken voluntarily, and interpreted 'in counseling time' (Goldman, 1971). A person can then be active in the process: the input from tests is used in a frame-of-reference influenced by the learner, who can contribute to the interpretation, and set it in context. This is a rationale for the 'negotiated' portrayal of self. It is based on an assumption that an unthreatened learner, engaged in a non-judgemental process, would have no interest in deceiving the helper or deluding his or her self (Rogers, 1965).

A criticism of the seven-point plan (Daws, 1968) was that it was not sufficiently comprehensive in its acknowledgement of the importance of feelings, attitudes and motivations for work. The argument distinguished 'performance' from 'motivation'. *Performance* considerations identify what a person has done, can do and can learn to do. *Motivational* considerations identify what a person wants to do, and the rewards and incentives which attract (or repel) that person. We are speaking here of hopes, fears and the like: portrayals of self which leave out such motivations leave out too much (Law and Ward, 1981).

A feature of all such work is, then, a more active learner, engaged in reflecting upon and shaping the information, in a way which can take account of 'hopes and fears'. It invites the hope that the learner might learn from the *process* as much as from the *content* of portrayal; and that a significant outcome of portraying self is 'learning how to do it' – for example, by learning that self-deception is not going to help.

Checklists and so on

A loosening of approaches to the use of paper-and-pencil (and computer-derived) data invites the development of 'checklists'. Checklists, at their worst, are tick-and-flick exercises for impulsive use. But they also belong to a freer approach to portrayal. The approach includes not only checklists but also graphic portrayal (in maps, charts, time-lines, diagrams and cartoons) together with discursive writing and scattergrams (see also Law, 1993; Law *et al.*, 1995).

These techniques impose minimal technical requirements for validation, norming, administration and interpretation. They are designed exclusively as stimulants to thought and reflection by learners – not with other people. If they yield scores, these scores are used idiographically, not nomothetically.

An early example, developed for use in schools and colleges, invited reflection on 'influences', 'values and needs', 'qualifications', 'mental and physical abilities', and 'personal style' (Law, 1977). It incorporated a workbook, to be held by students, in which a structured portrayal could be made and matched to information about the working world – a prototypical profile (see Section 14.4 below).

A feature of many such methods is that they are designed for group use. Here, introspection and disclosure can be linked to sharing and comparing. Both feedback and modelling are diversified: the former by offering ideas about self from other people's perceptions; the latter by encountering other selves and, therefore, other ways of talking about self. Both offer a wider and more varied social context for learning – in a curriculum. A significant outcome from such work may be learning how to learn about self.

Records of experience

Widespread dissatisfaction has been expressed concerning school reports, which have been seen as unreliable and, by concentrating on 'academic' achievement, too limited in scope (Balogh, 1982; Goacher, 1983; Goacher and Reid, 1983). The argument is that such reports miss too much of importance to the career development of too many children, particularly where achievements cannot be recorded in 'academic' terms.

Stansbury was a pioneer of an alternative way of setting down what can be known about students (see Law, 1984). His methods invited direct observation of participation in a wide range of activities. These activities included curricular, extra-curricular and extra-mural events. The accounts were discursive, unconstrained by ready-made categories, and not subjected to analysis and report. The recorded facts were allowed to speak for themselves. Such untrammelled portrayals were termed 'records of experience'.

The expansion is significant. Instead of relying upon inference drawn from disclosure, test results, introspection, feedback and modelling, this process draws upon directly observed accounts of experience in real tasks and locations. The input is different.

Stansbury has conducted trials to demonstrate the validity of such portrayals for selection purposes (see Law, 1984). It is, however, more likely that such documents are used at the interview rather than the screening stage. There they provide 'something to talk over', increasing comprehension of individuality within the selection process.

Table 14.2 Inputs, processes and outcomes of expanded methods

	Input	Process	Outcome
By learner	Observation and recall of experience, including curriculum experience	Setting down, disclosing, interpreting and negotiating, in both curriculum and guidance settings	A diary. journal or portfolio recording learning; sometimes negotiated with helpers; perhaps with a short-term learning plan, perhaps for partial disclosure; learning how to learn about self
By 'helper'	Design and delivery of learning programme; observation and feedback to learners	Teaching, tutoring, guiding and negotiating	Programme evaluation
By others	Direct observation, feedback and modelling		Selection decision

Careers portfolios

Portfolios are accounts of learning which expand as learning expands, and which are periodically reviewed by the learner – providing springboards for future learning and action (Pike, 1995). They resemble 'scrap-books', 'journals' and 'day-books'. They support a free, words-and-pictures, exploratory and tentative articulation of learning, as and when it occurs. They need all of the checklist and discursive techniques outlined above. They are instruments of disclosure, helping learners to gather, articulate, compare and reflect upon their learning. An important feature is that they are designed for use in both guidance and curriculum settings (Harrison, 1993; Munro and Law, 1994). The techniques are particularly relevant to careers education (see Chapter 12), where they help students – in what is usually non-examined work – to *document* their learning.

The setting of short-term targets is an important feature of portfolios. They invite learners to identify plans that can be implemented and evaluated within a readily foreseeable time-span – a week, a month, not much more.

Careers portfolios are designed wholly for learning, not for selection purposes. Like other 'expanded' procedures, they are concerned more with helping students to learn how to learn about self than with the identification of any absolute and general 'truth' about self. Designs can, however, include help for learners who want to abstract the material into a more public record for use by third parties (Munro and Law, 1994).

'Authoring' software is well suited to portfolio work (Law, 1994). It combines the conventional apparatus of word-processors, databases and spreadsheets with hand-drawn and technology-generated graphics, in both moving and static media. It can integrate all of this into a single, collated, searchable and developing account. There is much potentiality for lifelong portfolio development in the technology of the disc. The Internet will allow the selective release of such information.

Commentary

Expanded methods offer a freedom which learners of all ages need. Much of what people returning to work have to record may be based upon their thoughts, feelings, experiences and achievements in domestic life as much as in formal work-related training. Much of what a person needs to consider in accepting promotion may have more to do with what happens at home than at work. Much of what people learn they learn informally.

The main features are set out in Table 14.2. Among the major preoccupations is the perceived need to do justice to the unique subtlety of human individuality. The distinctive features of this cluster of activities include: an appeal to direct observation of what the learners have done in real situations; the inclusion of 'third parties' not just as selectors but also as helpers – peers, family members and even selectors helping learners more fully to appreciate what their records show; the more active involvement of the learner in the process of interpreting her or his own experience; short-term planning as part of the outcome; and a more exploratory approach, admitting a wider range of feelings and experiences. Significantly, many of these procedures seek to help learners to know how to learn about themselves. Learning the *processes* of portrayal becomes an *outcome* of the procedure.

14.4 STRUCTURED METHODS

The strengthening of pre-vocational education (see Chapters 5–6) has influenced recording and planning procedures. Pre-vocational programmes, and the public funding regimes supporting them, have been accompanied by a movement to more structured records and plans, bringing the terms 'profile', 'record of achievement' and 'action plan' into common use.

Profiles

A series of formats, more structured than records of experience, uses pre-set categories such as 'language', 'use of number', and 'visual understanding and expression'. They also respond to the concerns for wider coverage by acknowledging such attributes as 'leadership' and 'responsiveness'.

A feature of these procedures is that each individual yields a personal 'profile', with distinctive saliences, which might then be offered as a 'match' to work or training and as a way of establishing progress in it (Otter, 1989). The portrayal may be, at the same time, both nomothetic and idiographic: the former because it examines each person's performance on an 'objective' standard ('can he or she do this task, or not?'), the latter because it enables self-with-self comparisons ('she or he demonstrates more of these kinds of abilities than those'). Such designs serve pre-vocational education well. They are articulated to 'skills and competencies' manifest in behaviour. They therefore lend themselves to criterion-referencing (FEU, 1979). Criterion references, often set out as a checklist of 'can do . . .' statements, conjure verifiable images of observable behaviour. A pre-structured 'profile' format can set down what a person 'can do . . .' in each category.

Criterion-referencing is contrasted with grade-referencing, norm-referencing and unstructured or discursive referencing (to say that someone is 5'11" is grade-referenced, that she is above-average in height is norm-referenced, and that she feels that she is too tall is discursive; but to say that she can knock off a policeman's helmet is criterion-referenced). The over-zealous reduction of criterion writing is easy to deride (Education Resources Unit, 1982). Attempts to extend the range of criterion references to unverifiable descriptors are more worrying than risible (for example, 'can understand the moral consequences of actions'!).

Profiling can have a close link to the curriculum. The competency statements incorporated into criteria are reverse representations of curriculum objectives. As such, they can be arranged progressively, beginning with the more basic and moving towards the more demanding. If we are going to assess someone for her ultimate capacity to knock a small helmet off a tall policeman (a demanding criterion), then we should ensure that the curriculum provides her with an opportunity to learn how to do that – beginning, perhaps, with practice in knocking a large helmet off a small policeman. The portrayal and the scheme of work are interwoven.

An arrangement of progressively more demanding criteria in a number of categories yields a grid: a City and Guilds pre-vocational profile is an example (Law, 1984). The complete design combines a number of elements. The procedure is instigated by the learner's diary, into which accounts of experience are entered on a continuing basis. A series of regular review sessions with helpers sifts the material into interim grids, which then become a basis for short-term target-setting – 'such progress having been made, this is the next thing to aim at'. A summative document can be compacted from the interim grids, in nego-tiation with the learner. Such schemes have not, as the Education Resources Unit (1982) suggests, been tried and found wanting; they have been found expensive and not properly tried.

Records of achievement

Pre-vocational education was brought into secondary education largely through the Technical and Vocational Education Initiative (TVEI) (see Chapter 5), the later phases of which required a 'record of achievement' (RoA). Some schools had already responded to concerns regarding the inadequacy of school reports, as expressed by Goacher (1983) and others, by developing 'personal achieve-ment records'. A few early attempts at profiling appeared to assume that students would maintain the record independently: gathering, maintaining and using the portrayal without supporting procedures. However, experiences showed that students required tutoring, which was time-consuming (Broadfoot et al., 1988).

Time is certainly an issue. One strategy is to design systems the outcomes of which can be used concurrently with a variety of audiences: the students, their families, careers officers, and people in selection roles in education, training and employment. This assumes that the same information can be used for a variety of purposes.

Looked at from one point of view, TVEI mandated and claimed credit for procedures which were already well-developed in schools. Looked at from another, TVEI rescued a highly labour-intensive activity that needed significant additional funding. In any event, TVEI's term 'recording achievement' became the standard term for this group of activities.

Action plans

Action plans and the procedures that produce them can be understood as a natural and probably inevitable outworking of any guidance process in which portrayal figures. Indeed, their theoretical and professional roots contain little that has not also been used as part of a general rationale for guidance (Hughes, 1995). Action planning is, then, close in meaning to 'using records in guidance': in this sense, it has always been a feature of guidance. Both guidance in general and action planning in particular assist learning from the portrayal of past action in order to inform future action. Plans are the prospective use of retrospective records (Watts, 1992).

Early approaches to planning work – developed in further education – were known as 'student- (or trainee-) centred reviewing' (Pearce et al., 1981). On joining a learning programme, learners are asked to specify targets, and how they believe the programme can help them; these targets are then periodically reviewed and updated. The range of plans is in principle diverse: they might be for the award of a qualification, better attendance, less aggression with peers, more skill with keyboards, reading *Hamlet* from beginning to end, a developed *curriculum vitae*, or a grasp of rights under benefits legislation. All are plans; all require action; all are career-relevant.

Such target-setting is a teaching-and-learning tool. It entails establishing with a learner what needs to be done, and developing a regime in which teacher and learner each agree to take responsibility for ensuring that the target is reached. Broadfoot *et al.* (1988) report the process as one of ensuring that learners complete certain tasks and achieve certain competencies. The plan can also be *negotiated*, in a more active sense than with recording achievement: on an 'if-you-will-I-will' basis.

There is a bonus. In some cases, attending to what learners say about their experience of learning will change what is provided (Law, 1984). Such 'catalytic' effects of portrayal are brought about in a number of ways, not least through the negotiation that the helper is prepared to enter into with the learner.

Commentary

Features of this and other structured methods for recording and planning are outlined in Table 14.3. The model seeks to reconcile summative, formative and catalytic concerns. The system is therefore busy, producing problems for reducing the range of concerns into a manageable and coherent form. One solution is to try to produce a single document concurrently pursuing a number of purposes. The City and Guilds solution separates formative from summative elements by using a diary and a grid-type profile. But the 'selecting out' process of deciding what is disclosed then becomes a time-demanding process of supportive tutoring or mentoring.

Table 14.3 Inputs, processes and outcomes of structured methods

	Input	Process	Outcome
By learner	Recall and observation	Setting down, interpreting, negotiating; selecting what will be presented	Perhaps a diary or journal; certainly a record of achievement and/or action plan; with new learning, understanding and purpose
By 'helper'	A learning programme and feedback to learner	Tutoring, negotiating, guiding	Programme evaluation; programme change
By others	Feedback to learner		Screening decision; selection decision

Yet the potentiality of such systems is considerable. Systematic recording and target-setting require careful consideration – about the present effects of past causes and the future effects of present causes. This requires thought, not merely awareness; understanding, not merely information; and purpose, not merely preference. This, however, presents a problem: whether in education or employment, 'complicated, expensive and challenging' is not a sure-fire formula for survival.

14.5 'OFFICIAL' METHODS

One of the principal conclusions of an evaluation of recording achievement in schools (Broadfoot *et al.*, 1991) was the need for greater coherence between pre- and post-16 work. The report suggested that coherence might be achieved through the development of a common set of processes and reporting formats, at a national level.

The National Record of Achievement

In 1990, government canvassed a prototype intended to distil the essence of records of achievement into a single meaningful procedure and document. The format, called the 'National Record of Achievement' (NRA), tabulates individual performance in subjects (criterion-referenced), sets out an attendance record (directly observed), and records qualifications and credits (probably norm-referenced). Wider achievements (such as voluntary work, clubs and leisure activities) are represented in more discursive form. There is a summary statement and a personal statement, standing side-by-side. Because the document is intended to begin a record of lifelong learning, there is also an employment history.

It is intended that learners will continuously record and occasionally review the evidence of their achievements. From time to time, with tutorial or mentoring help, they will compact information into the summary record and action plan. The resulting document will, it is expected, recognise achievement (a summative intention), motivate learners (formative), help people in the school, college or place of employment to understand how its provision can be improved (catalytic), and act as a record (again, summative). The claim may be over-ambitious. As we shall see, the reality has proven more complex.

For summative purposes, joint validation schemes have been set up in which Training and Enterprise Councils and universities can co-operate in validating NRA procedures (see e.g. CambsTEC, 1993). But a review (Garforth Associates, 1994) suggested that higher education and employment made little use of the NRA for either recruitment or career-development purposes. A more positive picture emerged in further education and training, where the NRA was more likely to be used as part of the admissions process.

Individual Action Plans

By 1992 the idea of an action plan as part of the NRA was also being canvassed. Action planning is conceived as linking recording achievement to target-setting. It offers, as examples of plans, 'completing a qualification or a course, a particular careers move or other un-certificated achievements'. These are long-term plans, anticipating what is going to happen over months or even a year or more ahead. An objective in the process is to 'determine the learning needs' required to achieve such goals. The aim is to identify and arrange appropriate provision for these needs (NCVQ, 1993). However, the inclusion of an action plan in the NRA is a matter for local discretion.

Table 14.4 Inputs, processes and outcomes of 'official' methods

	Input	*Process*	*Outcome*
By learner	Recall of achievement, examination results and experience of work	Disclosing, selecting	Perhaps an identification of learning needs, leading to a long-term plan, set out with other information in a NRA
By 'helper'	Professional skills	Tutoring, guiding (mainly in guidance settings)	Statistical record
By others			Screening, selection and promotion decisions

The Confederation of British Industry (1993) is more insistent. It advocates a 'careership profile'. The expectation is that this profile, through action planning and recording a broad range of achievement, will develop an account of life-long learning, beginning at age 14. Four general questions are proposed to articulate that procedure: 'where am I now?', 'what do I want to achieve?', 'what will I learn?', and 'how will I get there?'

Meanwhile, arrangements for youth (training) credits have boosted the use of action plans – whether or not they are included in the NRA. The award of youth credits to young people is conditional on completion of an Individual Action Plan, showing how the training is to be used (DfE, 1992). Careers services offer the supporting guidance.

Reports of use (HMI, 1992) suggest that such action planning may frequently not be linked to recording achievement or even to action planning already carried out in schools. Their completion is characterised in some cases as 'abrupt', sometimes in groups of students with little opportunity to relate past experiences to present dilemmas and future needs. The HMI evidence suggests that, because completed action plans are output measures of careers service performance (see Chapter 9), the matter has, in some cases, been bureaucratically treated, for statistical purposes (an administrative chore) rather than as an intrinsically valuable part of guidance.

A survey identifying the visibility and perceived usefulness of action plans reinforces the findings on the NRA. Learners value plans mainly for reflective purposes; for such purposes, the written plan does not need to survive the process. Furthermore, although many colleges, training providers and employers have heard of action plans, significantly fewer actually ask to see them, least of all employers (Weston *et al.*, 1994).

Both NRA and IAPs – whether linked or not – are summative procedures intended to be available to *third* parties, for use in screening and selection. But the very language of individual action *planning* strongly connotes a formative aim, addressed to *first* parties for their own purposes. The CBI's questions require such involvement. A person would need to reflect upon *causes*: asking

'Where did I get the idea of doing this?' and 'What makes me so sure that it is what I want?' That would lead to a consideration of *alternatives*: provoking such questions as 'What makes me think this is the way of getting what I want?' and 'What else is there?' There will be some concern with *effects*: leading to questions such as 'Will it work?', 'Is it the most effective solution?', and 'Suppose it goes wrong, or suppose I change my mind, what then?' Such a line of enquiry raises issues for *dealing with effects*: the questions might be 'Am I ready for this?' and 'What more do I need to be better prepared?' All of this entails thinking about stages: 'How do I get this started?', 'What have I got to do soon?' and 'What can I set aside for now?' And there is always a *social context*: suggesting questions about 'Who else has an interest in what I do?', 'Am I doing right by my parent (or partner, or child) in doing it this way?' and 'Who can help and who might hinder me in this?' The process is personal, layered, and disclosing. It needs more than glib answers, to trite questions, sent to people I may never meet. Setting down information about self in order to compete for a place on a training scheme, or win a youth credit, or to help providers get sustained funding, does not belong to the same discourse.

Commentary

The RoA–IAP procedure is leaner and more focused than what was becoming a sprawling matrix of sometimes contradictory purposes and strategies. Removing the clutter from work that Broadfoot rightly found incoherent has revealed some internal structural tensions. Some of the tensions can be found in Table 14.4.

Coherence has been achieved by articulating portrayal largely to summative purposes. NRA–IAP occupies the same ground as 'scientific' methods. It therefore invites the same concerns for reliability and validity. High standards will be required of a government-mandated system which – because it is part of the selection process – must be seen to be trustworthy. Much of the 'research' into NRA–IAP work fails to mention reliability or validity (see 'Trustworthiness' in Section 14.6 below).

What is missing from the chart is also significant. It is far from clear what relation NRA–IAP work is intended to have in schools and other educational institutions with the curriculum. Other designs are linked to the curriculum, not only because what is learned or needs to be learned appears in the documents, but because the procedures are curriculum procedures. RoA–IAP work can be thought of wholly as guidance provision (DfE/ED, 1994); but should it be?

14.6 ISSUES

Purposes

We return now to the questions raised at the beginning of the chapter. The first of these concerned purposes. We have found three clusters:

1 Records and plans are *formative* in their effects when they offer learners an incentive to learn, feedback on what they have learned, and an opportunity to disclose and reflect upon progress as a basis for setting targets.

2 They have *catalytic* effects when they suggest changes to the programme, because the provider is prepared to negotiate with the learner, because they offer evaluation to the provider concerning what learners actually gain, or because the process of changing the way the programme is assessed will suggest changes to the way it is offered.
3 Their effects are *summative* when they become useful for learners' competitive purposes and selectors' decision-making purposes, so that learners can fairly assess themselves and be fairly assessed by others, supplementing and extending the range of information that traditional assessment covers.

For some time it was assumed that the principal purpose for recording achievement would be summative (cf. Ashforth, 1990; Burgess and Adams, 1985). For reasons set out below, it may prove increasingly difficult to sustain this position.

We have not found a single system that can do everything. We have found systems that have over-ambitiously sought to do so, or have claimed to do so, but have not delivered. The tensions are too great and were clear from the beginning: in the summative procedures, the individual's role is to look good (if necessary by faking), in order to maximise competitive advantage; in formative procedures, the individual's role is to disclose, because disclosure is a requirement for learning. That tension is acknowledged in the distinction between 'private' and 'public' use (Watts, 1995): the former helping individuals to clarify their personal skills and goals; the latter engaging the individual in negotiation with a selector.

Effects

Records and action plans might give effect to a number of purposes:

1 They can portray useful *information* about behaviour and learning in specific contexts, such as on a work task or at the end of a learning experience.
2 They might provide a basis for saying that some of this behaviour and learning is *transferable* to other contexts – such as similar future work tasks or learning experiences.
3 They might even help learners to *learn how to learn* from their experience, so that they can be more open to what their experience teaches them and more used to making decisions based on what they learn.

The simplest is the first of these. A recording and planning procedure can set down what a person has done in known contexts, as a basis for decision-making. There are degrees of specificity: an experience in a known context can be focused more or less sharply on time, task, role and organisation. There are advantages to restricting such portrayal to clear and limited context-located observations: the more focused the observation, the more verifiable the portrayal.

Yet the concept of 'transferable skill' might improve the value of the effect. This concept rests on an assumption that if a person has been observed to do something in one context, there is reason to suppose that she or he might be able to do it – or something like it – in another. The concept is multi-dimensional: the 'transfer' might be to another time, on a different version of the task, in another role, or in another organisation. Transferability relates to other concepts: 'core skills' are generic skills which can be applied in a number of settings; 'portability' is a readiness to carry learned behaviour into new settings. These are attractive ideas. There is the possibility of improved access to opportunity on the basis of existing learning, as well as of a sustained return on what people have already learned.

The concept of learning-to-learn is yet more attractive, for it means that the processes of portrayal can develop useful information about what I have done, and also can help me to continue to reflect upon, learn from and act upon my experience. Such interests are sometimes characterised as the primacy of process over product. There is some reason to suppose that learners of all ages value the process of reflection more highly than the documents which issue from it (Weston *et al.*, 1994); and that some providers share that view (Hughes, 1995). The process–product antithesis is, however, misleading, because a valuing of process and a willingness to continue to do it are themselves products. Among the skills to be learned are those embedded in the processes identified in Tables 14.1–14.4. Learning to become self-propelled in these processes might be among the most significant *outcomes* of portrayal work. Watts (1994) lists such skills; he also suggests that a learner might be developing personal qualities in that process, such as confidence, responsibility and initiative. But if the rhetoric of the careership profile as a basis for lifelong learning is to have any reality, people must not only be *able* to do it, and to have *qualities* that can accommodate it: they must also *want* to do it. This means enjoying it and seeing the value or point of it. The learning-to-learn gains to be made from portrayal must therefore include process skills, qualities *and* motivation.

The second and third sets of effects assume transferability of learning: the second because it assumes that *what is portrayed* is portable; the third because it assumes that *doing reviewing and planning work* is portable. Though laudable, these ideas are problematic: we learn in a context, and transfer means adapting what we have learned for use in another context (Harrison, 1995). Of course, a person can use the same understanding, creativity and commitment in the successive learning of related tasks. But transferability proposes more: that because something has been done earlier, something like it can more readily be done later. The evidence is not overwhelming (Meadows, 1993): people do not readily recognise new contexts for what they can do; and, even if they do so, they do not find it easy to make the adaptations. Indeed, some transfer effects are negative – having done something like this before may actually hinder later adaptation. Transfer, it seems, occurs most readily where the earlier learning is in some depth, and is explicitly related to a range of possible applications. Transferability, then, requires deeply and multiply-encoded learning.

The implications for recording and planning work are twofold: first, that it should be done with support to help an understanding of the underlying principles of its procedures; and second, that it should be done in a variety of settings. In practical terms, this means encoding its processes (possibly) to both 'employment' and 'wider concepts of work', and (probably) to both work and social life. It also means (certainly) that its processes should be engaged in both guidance and curriculum settings. Quick-and-easy procedures in hit-and-run settings will not much serve such effects. Close to the heart of the matter is what we all learn – or think we learn – about ourselves as children. It can take a long time and a lot of help to unravel *that*!

Settings

More than one kind of organisation uses recording and planning techniques. Host organisations include guidance organisations, business organisations, and education and training organisations (NCVQ, 1995).

Guidance organisations have been engaged in recording and planning techniques from their earliest incarnations. Many careers services are now contractual providers of individual action planning (see Chapter 9). Their involvement in expanded techniques, requiring curriculum contact, is likely to be in partnership with schools and colleges.

Business organisations are involved for staff selection and promotion purposes, but also for purposes with an important guidance element – such as appraisal. Smaller organisations and voluntary organisations probably face a more critical cost-benefit calculation. Any organisation offering training and other learning experiences can, in principle, link recording and planning procedures to that 'curriculum'.

Education and training organisations have a curriculum as their primary 'product'. Concepts of lifelong learning can extend such provision, particularly through the use of new information technologies. Most are also providers of guidance, for example through school, college and university careers departments. The most valuable contribution of these procedures to careers work may be to link curriculum and guidance into a coherent provision. Policy-driven statements, unhappily, allocate the procedures entirely to guidance (DfE/ED, 1994). But it has long been understood that good portrayal procedures require curriculum support (Munby, 1989).

The setting within the organisation may, therefore, be important to understanding how well the procedures can become embedded. Examples of how each organisation can link recording and planning work to selection, guidance and curriculum settings are set out in Table 14.5. No portrayal method has yet served equally well in all three settings, any more than they have served all kinds of purposes.

Table 14.5 Uses of recording and planning in different organisations and settings

Settings	Organisation		
	Business	Guidance	Education and training
Selection	Screening applicants	Recommendations to employers	Setting skill targets
Guidance	Career planning	Guidance linked to action planning	Setting learning targets
Curriculum	Changes in training programme	Feedback to providers on value of provision	Portfolio development and curriculum negotiation

Coverage

Purpose and settings raise questions for coverage. To what extent do records and plans cover one or more of four ways of talking about a person: what the person *has done*; what the person *can do*; what the person *is like*; and what the person *wants*.

'*Has done*' statements are 'raw data', free of attempts to assess their value, leaving others to judge what they mean. Such information includes statements of experiences engaged in, examinations passed and courses completed – each transferred uninterpreted from input to output.

'*Can do*' information implies transferability, working from observation in one context to anticipation for another. Easily-scanned 'can do' statements cannot be glibly produced – transferability is not a facile issue. Nonetheless, such statements of potential are of critical importance to planning.

'*Is like*' information speaks more of traits and styles – of disposition – than of abilities. Information about whether a person is usually 'co-operative' or 'sociable' is significant for career-development purposes. Some psychometric tests purport to identify such traits. They may be inferred, with care, from attentive direct observation. This kind of information cannot be fitted to easily scanned formats.

'*Wants*' information is about why a person will approach or avoid different types of work and context. People work for many different reasons. Variations include 'attachment', 'security', 'stimulation' and 'achievement'. Motivation both drives and draws people, and does so both towards and away from particular kinds of work. It is the subject of what may be one of the most commonly asked questions in a selection interview – 'Why do you want this?' Interest inventories skirt its edges, counselling might be trusted enough to explore it; but no selector should assume that she or he will be told the whole truth in answer to this question. Motivation is more a matter for disclosure than for observation. It is what makes autobiography interesting. Plans that ignore it ignore too much.

Sources

The next question is: if this is what we want to know, who or what can tell us? There are two ways of pursuing the question: what sources do we call upon; and in what contexts?

The learner's recollection of events and interpretations of what they mean are *sources*. This is a feature of all methods: making the learner an 'agent' of the record, not merely its 'subject'. Even where examination results and psychometric tests are used, the learner consents in the setting down, interpretation and use of that information. The learner may be the dominant, in some case the sole, contributor. But others are commonly involved: formal helpers (such as careers advisers, teachers, and appraisers); informal helpers (such as lecturers, colleagues, peers, and work-experience contacts); and others (such as family members and friends).

The information collected may derive from different *contexts*. It may record experience in a guidance, selection or curriculum context; in a particular organisation, such as a school or firm; in an outside setting, such as extra-mural work; or in family and leisure life.

Identifying sources for information is a 'sampling' issue. Failure to find evidence is sometimes the result of looking in the wrong place. For example, in the case of a 'returner' with little recent organisation-based experience, experience as a family member or voluntary worker may offer the best available portrayal of significant learning. But the more important issue here may be to ensure that learning is sufficiently sampled to be deeply and multiply 'encoded'. As we have seen, such encoding is a requirement for transferability of learning.

Trustworthiness

Any statement about any person, whether biographical or autobiographical, should be able to meet the challenge 'why do you say that?' The concern is two-fold: for reliability and for validity.

A concern for *reliability* asks: 'Would anybody else, having seen what you've seen, agree that this is what they saw?' Reliability requires that the same data used by other people on another occasion will yield a recognisably similar portrayal. All forms of observation are unreliable to some extent, but some are unacceptably unreliable – they would only be applicable through a once-in-a-while chance.

A concern for *validity* asks: 'Would anybody else, having seen what you've seen, agree that this is what it *means*?' Validity requires that the portrayal is an interpretation, not a misinterpretation of the data, so that the reader can be sure it means what it appears to mean. A common distortion comes from attaching stereotyped or self-stereotyped meanings to evidence. Learners can do that to themselves, as well as having it done to them.

Reliability and validity are most critical where a person who was not been involved in the generation of the information is basing important decisions upon it. A selector needs to be sure that the portrayal is of (say) another person's 'co-operativeness', rather than of (say) his or her own 'gullibility' with a cleverly faking careerist.

Underlying the need for both reliability and validity is the need for *verifiability*. *Evidence* is verifiable if sane and fair people can agree whether or not it is so. A description of observed behaviour ('on this course she has almost always chosen to work with others') is reasonably verifiable – operational, specific, and set in its context. A statement about another person's disposition ('she is generally co-operative') is less so, and is more of an *impression* – less specific and with an interpretive edge. Statements about motivations ('she prefers working with others') are unverifiable because they are about an unobservable state rather than observable behaviour: they are – whether valid or not – *assessments*.

Evidence is verifiable and is of course useful; but it is anecdotal and can be banal. Assessment is interpretive and may be subjective; but if it is trustworthy, it may be insightful and highly pertinent. Learners make all types of statement (see NCVQ, 1995). It is not obvious that any should be excluded. But we do need to be guarded about some of the statements that appear on records and plans.

Such considerations are influenced by the degree of specificity, which may be at three levels:

1 *Task-specific* – e.g. stemming from an observation of a specific task in a particular setting.
2 *Context-specific* – e.g. repeatedly observed in this and similar settings and thought to be applicable in all such settings.

3 *General* – e.g. a personally transferable ability, disposition or motive, observed
   enough times to support the inference to other settings and tasks.

These levels range from requiring simply that observant sources keep their eyes
open and say what they see – no more, no less – to requiring *thought* (comparison and inference) as much as *observation*. Trusting the statement means trusting
the thought.

   Quality is a product of such techniques. A first requirement for the quality of
records and plans is that the statements they contain have acceptable levels of
trustworthiness. Risk can be minimised by helping sources – especially learners
– sensibly to use their 'street-level' versions of such techniques. Then, when
asked 'what makes you say that?', they might know – an important feature of
learning-to-learn.

Control

The interests of different stakeholders – with their different purposes for
portrayal – are often close, but they are not identical. Possible conflicts of interest
raise ethical questions. While purposes identify ends, and procedures are the
means to those ends, we need some ethical means for knowing what social and
moral limits to place on the use of these means.

   Information is power. The ethical questions therefore hinge on matters of
control – specifically, who controls the terms in which information is gathered,
disseminated and used. Total confidentiality would mean not telling anybody,
anything, ever. But all of the procedures set out here involve telling somebody,
something, sometime. It is, then, to the 'who?', 'how much?' and 'when?' that
questions of control relate.

   Few would argue that such control should be exercised by second parties
(such as teachers) or third parties (such as selectors). First-party control means
that it is the learner – perhaps in negotiation with a helper – who will take
account of the fact that, for some purposes, some information can be released
to some people, sometime.

   But the learner must then understand that, once something is placed in any
kind of public record, further control is lost. The learner may not know how
widely it is then circulated, for how long it will remain on the record, what
decisions will be made on the basis of it, how it will be understood, how any
misunderstandings may be corrected, and – perhaps – what false attributions
on the basis of limited evidence can be made (the possibilities for such distortion
are examined in detail in Law, 1984). Assigning ultimate control to the learner
acknowledges absolute confidentiality as a possibility – saying nothing to anyone,
at any time. The evidence cited earlier on the relative invisibility of the NRA
and its associated IAP may be interpreted as suggesting that some learners might
be exercising that caution – by dumping the documents!

   Learner control requires a more sophisticated decision, so that the holder of
the record understands where her or his interests and the interests of second
and third parties coincide, and where they do not; knows how to negotiate an
optimal course between total disclosure and total confidentiality; and is able to
deal with the effects of disclosure. In a society in which the successful presentation of self is a necessary part of negotiation concerning work, such learning
would be a significant outcome of the formative use of such procedures.

These ethical issues have implications for the separation of formative and summative portrayals. The procedures for generating (say) a summative NRA must derive from the procedures for developing (say) a formative portfolio. The root of, and ultimate ethical justification for, portrayal will be in the latter, not the former.

Acceptability

Any procedure is endangered if it is not understood to be worthwhile. Much of the support for the development of records and plans is undertaken by teachers, careers advisers, mentors and the like. They can readily use a *formative* procedure which articulates learning, diagnoses need, sets targets and monitors progress. If it also offers *catalytic* feedback for improvement in the help that is offered, then so much the better. Teachers and others will, of course, do their best to help learners to adopt a good *summative* position for recruitment or promotion; and they will do that for the learner's sake and also because the 'bottom line' of the institution is served. But without some sense of intrinsic value, the activity is a *bureaucratic* chore, to be contained by the minimum expenditure of effort. This chapter has cited evidence acknowledging such a possibility.

Our analysis identifies formative purposes as the core of the procedure, from which all other purposes receive whatever input is reconcilable with that central intention. Figure 14.1 outlines the relationships. It supports the case for a life-long series of procedures, a value of which may well be 'to support individuals between sectors' (Watts, 1995). But it does so by attaching formative and summative purposes to a central formative core.

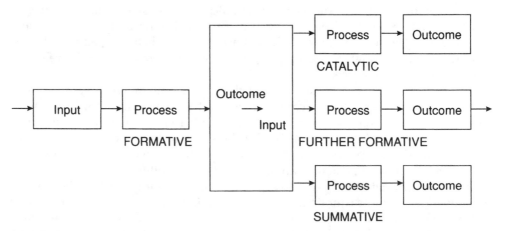

Figure 14.1   Relationships between different aims and processes in recording and planning

Support for such a configuration has been documented in this chapter. In particular:

1 Learner control of action, taken primarily for his or her own 'first-party' purposes, is the only ethically defensible posture that a profession can take on the issues identified here.

2 The lifelong careership profile, whatever it eventually proves to be, is best set in motion in schools, and the most intrinsically valuable purposes for schools are formative.

3 Formative portrayal work can unify the uses in careers work of both curriculum and guidance, as mutually dependent contributions to a careers portfolio.

4 Transferable learning needs to be gathered and processed in a way which deeply and multiply 'encodes' it; this requires sustained formative work.

5 Formative procedures can more readily reach acceptable levels of reliability and validity, since all that is portrayed is generated, checked, adjusted and used by the learner and the immediate contacts he or she chooses to work with.

6 An active careers portfolio is an informed basis for judging what can be released on to more public records, and what must be withheld.

7 Formative procedures can support a more trustworthy summative procedure; indeed, formative procedures can usefully input all subsequent procedures – summative, catalytic, and further formative.

8 The 'shelf-life' of all information expires, and an active formative portfolio can be used to modify and update a summative record.

9 The most significant effect for portrayal is formative – helping learners to learn how to learn.

Within such a framing of purposes, recording and planning can provide a means for reinstating the concept of 'career' in contemporary society. Recording and planning may help people to become learners who can represent themselves and their experience, develop plans on the basis of what they learn, and negotiate with others concerning the new opportunities which implement these plans. Such people are forging for themselves a genuinely developing career – whether conducted in employment or in a wider work scenario. It may be one of the most valuable means we have for enabling people to make continuing sense of increasingly discontinuous experience.

REFERENCES

Ashforth, D. (1990) *Records of Achievement in the Market Place*, Windsor: NFER–Nelson.

Balogh, J. (1982) *Profile Reports for School Leavers*, London: Longman/Schools Council.

Broadfoot, P., Grant, M., James, M., Nuttall, D. and Stierer, B. (1991) *Records of Achievement: Report of the National Evaluation of Extension Work in Pilot Schemes*, London: HMSO.

Broadfoot, P., James, M., McMeeking, S., Nuttall, D. and Stierer, B. (1988) *Records of Achievement: Report of the National Evaluation of Pilot Schemes*, London: HMSO.

Burgess, T. and Adams, E. (1985) *Records of Achievement at 16*, Windsor: NFER–Nelson.

CambsTEC (1993) *National Record of Achievement: Procedures and Guidelines for the Implementation of the Joint Validation Scheme*, Cambridge: CambsTEC.

Confederation of British Industry (1993) *Routes for Success*, London: CBI.

Daws, P. P. (1968) *A Good Start in Life*, Cambridge: Careers Research and Advisory Centre.

Department for Education (1992) *The Implementation of the Pilot Training Credit Scheme in England and Wales: 1990–1992*, London: DfE.

Department for Education/Employment Department (1994) *Better Choices*, London: DfE/ED.

Education Resources Unit (1982) *Assessment in Youth Training: Made-to-Measure?*, Glasgow: Scottish Vocational Preparation Unit.

Fox, G. (1995) 'Psychometrics in Careers Guidance: a Useful Tool or Guidance by Numbers?', *Careers Guidance Today* 3(1): 20–21.

Further Education Unit (1979) *A Basis for Choice*, London: FEU.

Garforth Associates (1994) *The National Record of Achievement: Supporting Life-Long Learning*, Dorchester: Garforth Associates.

Goacher, B. (1983) *Recording Achievement at 16+*, London: Longman/Schools Council.

Goacher, B. and Reid, M. (1983) *School Reports to Parents*, Windsor: NFER–Nelson.

Goldman, L. (1961) *Using Tests in Counseling*, New York: Appleton–Century–Crofts.

Harrison, R. (1993) 'Using Portfolios for Personal and Career Development', in Assiter, A. and Shaw, E. (eds) *Using Records of Achievement in Higher Education*, London: Kogan Page.

Harrison, R. (1995) 'Personal Skills and Transfer: Meanings, Agendas and Possibilities', in Edwards, R., Hanson, A. and Raggett, P. (eds) *Boundaries of Adult Learning*, London: Routledge.

Her Majesty's Inspectorate (1992) *Survey of Guidance 13–19 in Schools and Sixth Form Colleges*, London: Department for Education.

Hughes, J. (1995) 'Where Did the Cycle Begin?: Origins of Action Planning and their Influence on Practice', *British Journal of Guidance and Counselling* 23(3): 347–60.

Kline, P. (1975) *The Psychology of Vocational Guidance*, London: Batsford.

Law, B. (1977) *Decide for Yourself*, Cambridge: Careers Research and Advisory Centre/Hobsons.

Law, B. (1984) *The Uses and Abuses of Profiling*, London: Paul Chapman.

Law, B. (1993) *Teachers' Business: Careers Education and Guidance*, London: Understanding British Industry.

Law, B. (1994) 'On the Importance of Interwagulation!', in *The Future Use of Information Technology in Guidance*, Coventry: National Council for Educational Technology.

Law, B. and Ward, R. (1981) 'Is Career Development Motivated?', in Watts, A. G., Super, D. E. and Kidd, J. M. (eds.) *Career Development in Britain*, Cambridge: Careers Research and Advisory Centre/Hobsons.

Law, B. *et al.* (1995) *Careers Work* (revised edn), Manchester: Open College.

Meadows, S. (1993) *The Child as Thinker*, London: Routledge.

Morea, P. C. (1972) *Guidance, Selection and Training*, London: Routledge & Kegan Paul.

Munby, S. (1989) *Assessing and Reporting Achievement*, Oxford: Blackwell.

Munro, M. and Law, B. (1994) *The Morrisby Careers Education Programme*, Hemel Hempstead: Morrisby Organisation.

National Council for Vocational Qualifications (1993) *Action Planning and the National Record of Achievement: Report on Consultation*, London: NCVQ.

National Council for Vocational Qualifications (1995) *The NRA in Action*, London: NCVQ.

Otter, S. (1989) *Student Potential in Britain*, Leicester: Unit for the Development of Adult and Continuing Education.

Pearce, B., Varney, E., Flegg, D. and Waldman, P. (1981) *Trainee Centred Reviewing (TCR)*, Special Programmes Research and Development Series No. 2, London: Manpower Services Commission.

Pike, S. (1995) 'Supporting Students in Managing their Own Learning 14–19', *British Journal of Curriculum and Assessment* 5(3): 37–42.

Rodger, A. (1952) *The Seven Point Plan*, London: National Institute of Industrial Psychology.

Rogers, C. (1965) *Client Centred Therapy*, New York: Houghton Mifflin.

Watts, A. G. (1992) 'Individual Action Planning: Issues and Strategies', *British Journal of Education and Work* 5(1): 47–63.

Watts, A. G. (1994) 'Developing Individual Action Planning Skills', *British Journal of Education and Work* 7(2): 51–61.

Watts, A. G. (1995) *Helping People to Succeed: the Future of the National Record of Achievement*, CRAC/NICEC Conference Briefing, Cambridge: Careers Research and Advisory Centre.

Weston, P., Tomlins, B., Stoney, S. and Ashby, P. (1994) *An Evaluation of the Use Made of Action Plans*, Sheffield: Employment Department.

Chapter 15

Computers in guidance

A. G. Watts

15.1 INTRODUCTION

Computers offer both a major opportunity and a possible threat to guidance practitioners. The opportunity is that they provide a powerful resource which can potentially improve both the quality of guidance provision and its accessibility to those who need it. The threat is that they may be used to mechanise the human interaction that has been considered central to guidance practice. This is, of course, merely one illustration of a much wider social dilemma. The impact of computer technology on the workplace has caused much of the destabilisation of work structures, from which the increased demand from guidance partly stems (see Chapter 1). It is thus ironic but also appropriate that in seeking to respond to this demand, guidance services should turn to harnessing the very technologies that are its cause. The challenge for such services, as for society as a whole, is to utilise such technologies in ways which supplement and extend human potential rather than acting to restrict or replace it.

The history of computer-aided careers guidance systems can be divided into two periods (Harris-Bowlsbey, 1989). The first period, from 1965 to 1980, might be termed the *demonstration and limited implementation* period. It was characterised by the use of mainframe computers, which made it very expensive for the user to interact directly with the computer. A number of systems based on interactive usage were developed, demonstrating its potential: these notably included, in the UK, the Interactive Careers Guidance System (Butler and Dowsey, 1978; Watts, 1975). But the only systems that proved widely practicable in cost terms were based on batch processing: questionnaires were completed in the guidance location and sent to a computer centre where they were processed; print-outs were then despatched back to the guidance location. The static nature of this process and the delays it involved limited the appeal of such systems.

The second period, starting around 1981, might be termed the *diffusion and extensive implementation* period. The advent of the microcomputer made interactive usage much more economical, and also made it much easier to develop and market limited software packages; its attractions grew as more powerful versions of the personal computer were developed. The result was a huge increase in the number of computer-aided guidance systems. Whereas in 1975/76 there were only seven such systems in the UK (Watts, 1978), by 1990 there were 56 (Offer, 1990). At the same time, the use of these systems developed so that

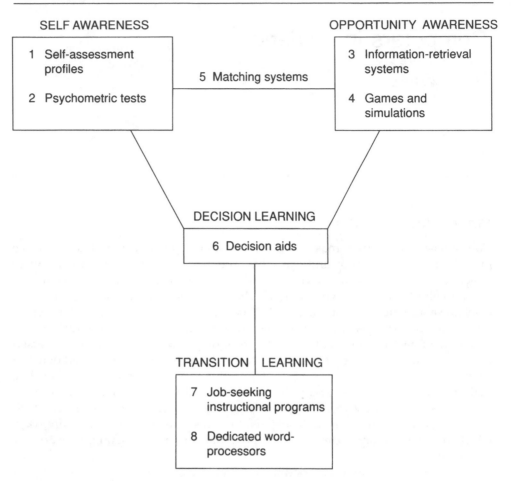

Figure 15.1 Main categories of computer-aided careers guidance systems, mapped on to the DOTS framework

by the late 1980s it was difficult to find a guidance service in any sector which did not make use of one or more such systems.

The rapid growth of interest in the use of computers in guidance has been fuelled not only by the enterprise of some guidance practitioners and commercial software developers, but also by two other factors. One is the interest of policy-makers, who have seen computers as a way of making cost savings or (more plausibly) of increasing the effectiveness of guidance services in a cost-effective way. The other is the recognition that clients – particularly younger ones – who are accustomed to making everyday use of computer technology in other areas of their lives will increasingly expect guidance services to harness such technology, and will regard services which fail to do so as outdated and lacking in credibility.

15.2 THE SYSTEMS

The existing computer systems can be divided into eight categories (adapted from Offer, 1990; 1993). These are mapped in Figure 15.1 on to the DOTS framework (see Chapters 4 and 12). The eight categories are:

1 *Self-assessment profiles*. These are commonly based on an occupational interest questionnaire, and produce a profile in terms of occupational families.
2 *Psychometric tests*. These are mainly on-line adaptations of pencil-and-paper tests, measuring abilities, aptitudes, personality, etc. (see French, 1986).
3 *Information-retrieval systems*. These comprise databases of education and training opportunities, or of occupations, or of employers, with a menu of search factors or key words which enable users to find the data they want. Prominent examples include ECCTIS, MICRODOORS and TAP.
4 *Business games and other work simulations*. These enable users to explore particular occupational areas in an experiential way (cf. Chapter 13). They are only at present available for a very limited number of occupations, and appear if anything to have contracted in usage (Hunt, 1994).
5 *Matching systems*. These match profiles of individuals against profiles of opportunities (usually occupations) and produce lists of the opportunities which match the individual profiles most closely. They have represented the most commonly-used applications of computers in the guidance field. Prominent examples include CASCAID and JIIG-CAL (both of which have now diversified into a range of packages), and (in higher education) GRADSCOPE.
6 *Decision aids*. These are database programs designed to help users to work out their own perceptions of the relative desirability of a small number of options, by defining their own criteria and applying them in a systematic way; they may also relate such desirability to the perceived probability of gaining entry. Early examples included MAUD and SELSTRA (Wooler and Lewis, 1982).
7 *Job-seeking instructional programs*. These teach transition skills related to handling interviews and making job applications.
8 *Dedicated word-processors*. These comprise programs which prompt the user through the process of preparing curricula vitae or completing application forms.

In addition, there are a few *comprehensive learning systems* which cover most of the tasks covered by these eight categories, but do so in an integrated way which enables users to move flexibly between the different tasks. These 'maxi' systems thereby model a career decision-making process through which users can acquire not only information but also skills and concepts which they can apply to present and future career decisions. Such learning potential may be present in the 'mini' systems too, but is greater in these 'maxi' systems. The main UK example is PROSPECT (HE); the main US examples are DISCOVER and SIGI (in addition, the Canadian CHOICES system and the UK CAREER-BUILDER system also include many characteristics of a 'maxi' system, and are perhaps most appropriately regarded as 'midi' systems).

The pros and cons of 'maxi' and 'mini' systems have been a matter of debate (Watts, 1993; Jackson, 1993). In favour of 'maxi' systems, it is argued that the standardisation of concepts and language, and the integrated design, make it possible to move easily between different functions, and to call up information from one part of the system when working in another part; in addition, such systems model directly to the user the potential scope and complexity of the decision-making process and thereby encourage users to address this complexity. In favour of 'mini' systems, it is argued that they encourage diversity and choice: guidance services are able to select the mix of such systems which meets their distinctive needs and preferences. In addition, it is suggested that some degree of coherence and comprehensiveness can be achieved at reduced cost by encouraging the development of 'families' of 'mini' systems, and by the use of software menus to bring together a number of different packages (NCET, 1993).

Certainly the cost of developing and maintaining 'maxi' systems is considerable, and this means that they require a higher level of funding investment than other systems. In addition, because of their greater impact on the guidance process, issues relating to their ownership have more powerful implications (a point to which I will return in Section 15.4). Nonetheless, it is noteworthy that where 'maxi' systems have been developed, they appear to achieve very extensive usage: this is particularly true of the North American 'maxi' systems, which are the clear 'market leaders' in their countries.

An interesting trend with 'maxi' systems in the USA has been their customisation for different sectors. DISCOVER was initially developed for use with high-school students; SIGI for community-college students. Both have now, however, been adapted in a number of different versions, for use with different client-groups in different settings (Harris-Bowlsbey, 1989). These include not only different educational and community settings, but also use by employees in organisations, building on earlier work in developing specific systems for use in such settings (see e.g. Phillips *et al.*, 1981; Minor, 1986). In the UK, the original plans with regard to PROSPECT were to adapt the initial higher education system for use in schools on the one hand and by adults on the other. So far, however, funding for such adaptations has not materialised (Watts, 1993).

The theoretical basis of the different systems (see Chapter 2) varies. Offer (1993), for example, contrasts usage which adopts the static certainties of 'trait-and-factor' matching, in which the computer 'analyses' and 'tells', with usage which views human beings as dynamic entities with the potential to do many different occupations well, depending on what aspect of their 'community of selves' (Mair, 1977) they allow to come to the fore. Again, there is a major contrast between data-less decision-aid systems which work in a phenomenological way with the individual's own constructs, on the assumption that this represents the way in which individuals actually construct their own reality, and data-based systems which seek to describe the self and opportunities 'objectively' in terms of common predetermined constructs derived from traditional social-scientific methods, and to induct users into this way of seeing the world.

More broadly, Law (1994) notes that computers can be used to implement a wide variety of different theoretical approaches. In part, such differences relate to the way in which particular systems are used: the same system can be used for very different purposes, particularly where it is embedded in a wider guidance programme (see Section 15.3 below). In addition, theoretical assumptions are built into the design of the systems themselves. One of the merits of the application of computers to guidance is that it requires a systematic approach to guidance design, and means that basic theoretical decisions have to be addressed more explicitly and more rigorously than is the case with other guidance interventions. These include decisions relating to the overall aim of guidance, and the model of career decision-making which is being used. They also include more detailed matters: within matching systems, for example, decisions need to be made on the domains that are to be covered, the hierarchy and sequence to be established between them, the dimensions to be covered within these domains, the relative emphasis to be placed on psychometric test ratings and on client self-ratings, and the decision rules to be used in determining which opportunities meet clients' characteristics and preferences (Katz and Shatkin, 1983; see also Sampson, 1994b).

In many respects, computer-aided guidance systems simulate a guidance interview. In principle, the computer can deliver any predesigned interview sequence that the system developer wishes to construct. But whereas counsellors within an interview situation can respond flexibly and intuitively to any given situation, with computer systems any such flexibility has to be consciously built into the system itself, on principles which are potentially transparent and open to inspection. The power of the 'Barnum' effect – whereby individuals accept positive feedback, assuming that it is based on a valid assessment procedure (Crowley, 1992) – makes it important that such transparency is insisted upon, and that not only the reliability and validity of any computer-generated data but also the underlying assumptions and principles incorporated in the system are made explicit. This is accentuated by the fact that computer systems reach many more people than any single counsellor can do, and so are capable of more widespread help or harm (Katz, 1993). In the privacy of the individual interview, basic theoretical issues can be blurred or ducked; with computer systems, they have to be confronted, and the outcomes of the confrontation should be made public.

15.3 INTEGRATING COMPUTER SYSTEMS INTO GUIDANCE PROGRAMMES

Possible roles of the computer

There are three ways in which the relationship of computer systems to guidance programmes can be conceived: as a tool, supplementing the various other tools used in such programmes; as an alternative, replacing other elements of the programme; or as an agent of change, altering the design of the programme in a fundamental way (Watts, 1986).

As a *tool*, computer systems are viewed as one among a range of resources which can be used in the guidance programme. They take their place alongside other media including printed resources and audio-visual resources. If regarded solely in these terms, however, there is a danger that they may not be used very extensively, and may indeed be left in corners within information rooms where they slowly gather dust. This danger is exacerbated by the fact that they may not be as susceptible to quick and casual scanning as are print materials.

As an *alternative*, computer systems may be viewed as a means of replacing, for example, the counselling interview. This view underlies the interest of some policy-makers, noted in Section 15.1, in using computers as a means of achieving cost savings. Certainly there are some aspects of a counselling interview – repetitive information-giving, for example – which a computer can arguably cover with greater efficiency and reliability than a counsellor can. But whether the computer can adequately deal with the complexities of career decision-making, and in particular its affective as well as cognitive complexities, is an issue to which we shall return shortly.

As an *agent of change*, computer systems are viewed as a means of providing an opportunity to review the basic design of the guidance programme as a whole. As Walz (1984) notes, 'the very discussion necessary for the appropriate use of computers can sharpen the programmatic emphasis to a degree that strengthens the entire guidance program' (p. 135). In principle, the relationship between the technical development of computer systems and the organisational development of guidance programmes should be viewed as an interactive process of 'joint optimisation' (Trist, 1981), in which technical possibilities are regularly reviewed in the light of organisational needs, and organisational structures are regularly reviewed in the light of technical developments (Ballantine and Watts, 1989).

In general, 'mini' systems which model only a limited part of the guidance process are likely to be regarded as additional 'tools', whereas 'maxi' systems which model most of the process are more likely to be regarded as an alternative or as an agent of change. If they are viewed as an agent of change, and if their potential in this respect is to be maximised, careful attention needs to be given to the way in which the system is introduced and to managing the change process. Guidance practitioners need from the outset to be fully involved in decisions relating to the system, to be given opportunities to familiarise themselves with it, and also to review their present services in the light of it. Sampson (1994b) suggests an implementation model divided into seven phases: programme evaluation; software selection; software integration; staff training; trial use; operation; and evaluation. Each phase should include attention to the principle of 'joint optimisation' between the computer system and the guidance programme as a whole.

The choice between the three conceptions of the role of the computer outlined above depends to a significant degree on the view that is taken of the potential strengths of the computer, and of its limits. It is to this that I now turn.

Strengths and limits of the computer

The strengths of the computer in relation to guidance usage are considerable. It can *store* immense quantities of data, and *update* these data quickly and easily. It can *retrieve* information speedily and accurately. It can *converse* with users, helping them to clarify their needs. It can *collate* a wide range of such needs, and, where necessary, *compute* permutations between them. It can *search, assemble* and *edit* the data which meets these needs.

At the same time, the computer can only work with the information it is given. Hofstadter (1979) stated that 'computers by their very nature are the most inflexible, desireless, rule-following of beasts' (p. 26). The flexibility of computers has grown significantly since then, but the basic force of Hofstadter's statement remains valid. Computers reduce knowledge, wisdom, common-sense and experience to data. They manipulate such data according to strict logic, and subordinate this logic to the set purposes for which they are programmed.

These are important limitations in relation to career decision-making. Such decisions have an important cognitive component, but they are also bound up very closely with people's feelings about themselves, their sense of their identity, and their dreams and aspirations. The essential rationale for counselling in relation to these decisions is that the individual can best be helped by working with another human being who provides a reflection of their humanity and has the skills to enable them to confront their own distinctive identity. This is why the counselling interview (see Chapter 11) has often been seen as the core of the guidance programme. An American study revealed that even where computer-based systems were perceived by clients as comparable to counsellors in providing expert information, they were not seen as comparable in 'attractiveness' (including positive regard for the client) or 'trustworthiness' (recognition that they were working for the client's benefit) (Sampson et al., 1992).

On the other hand, interviews with skilled counsellors are an expensive and scarce resource. Moreover, *some* aspects of the guidance process can be carried out very effectively in other ways: hence the interest in, for example, careers education in the curriculum (Chapter 12) and experience-based learning about work (Chapter 13). The computer provides a further powerful resource. In addition, the relationship with the counsellor is more than a reflection process: it is, to some extent, a power-based relationship. Some users of computer-aided systems have reported that such systems do not 'put them down' as some careers advisers do (e.g. Watts, 1975, p. 21): the users feel in control of the process, in a way they do not in the counselling interview. Also, computer systems do not discriminate between particular users: in that sense, they are more impartial and objective than counsellors may be.

In general, however, it seems that the more affective and deeply personal aspects of career decision-making cannot be adequately addressed by the computer. Katz and Shatkin (1983) indeed condemn systems which repeatedly address clients by name and appear to personalise each message ('Hello, John, glad to see you'): 'a machine pretending to be a person seems no more tolerable than a person pretending to be a machine' (p. 24). In the end, the best applications of artificial intelligence are only able to *mimic* the empathy, warmth and genuineness which research has consistently shown to be crucial to effective counselling (e.g. Truax and Carkhuff, 1967).

In view of this, it seems likely that in principle a combination of the computer and direct interaction with a counsellor will be more effective than either on its own. There is indeed some research evidence to support this (e.g. Marin and Splete, 1991). This means that both counsellor and computer can be used to play to their distinctive strengths. Sampson and Pyle (1983) characterised these in the following terms:

> Aspects of the helping process that are repetitive, as in information dissemination, or that follow a uniform sequence of steps, as in decision making instruction or administration of assessment instruments, are more effectively handled by the computer. Aspects of the helping process that involve exploring the nature of client concerns, facilitating an understanding of the factors involved, and identifying and following up on various action-oriented strategies are more effectively handled by a counselor.
>
> (Sampson and Pyle, 1983, p. 284)

It is, however, evident that individual responses to the computer vary considerably. Some are so averse to it, and feel so dehumanised by it, that they become 'computerphobic' (Jay, 1981; Meier, 1985). There is also evidence, for example, that individuals with relatively stable goals and a relatively strong sense of independence are more satisfied with computer-aided guidance systems and benefit more from them than do individuals with less stable goals and less sense of independence (Kivlighan *et al.*, 1994).

This suggests that there are two alternative ways of viewing the use of the computer in relation to other guidance interventions. One is that there are some *kinds of users* who are happier using the computer than other sources of help. The other is that there are some *forms of help* which the computer is better able to provide. The stance taken on these issues is likely to influence the way in which the computer system is integrated into guidance programmes.

Integrating computer systems into guidance programmes

There are broadly four models of integration of computer systems into guidance programmes:

1 The *stand-alone* model, in which the computer system is used in isolation from other guidance interventions.
2 The *supported* model, in which the user is seen – usually for a brief period – immediately before and/or after using the system.
3 The *incorporated* model, in which the computer system is used within another guidance intervention.
4 The *progressive* model, in which the use of the computer system is preceded and/or followed by other guidance interventions in a developmental sequence.

Within careers education programmes, the 'incorporated' model would seem of particular value, making it possible to address, within the group context, the essentially individual nature of career decision-making. The JIIG-CAL system, for example, has been widely used on a batch-processing basis within a structured programme of classroom sessions (Closs, 1986). It is also now increasingly possible for banks of machines on a network within the classroom to allow individuals to work interactively through a programme singly or in pairs, and then to share their experiences on a group basis. The peer-counselling opportunities offered by paired usage seem to offer particularly rich possibilities (Watts and Ball, 1990), which can be effectively harnessed within a group context.

Use of computer systems can also be 'incorporated' within interviews, enabling counsellor and client to work with the computer system together. Such 'shoulder to shoulder' rather than 'eyeball to eyeball' interviewing[1] can ease the relationship between client and counsellor, symbolising physically their collaborative interaction with the information embodied in the computer system. In the early days of using computers in guidance, some systems were indeed devised to be

1 I am indebted to Marcus Offer for this image, which is adapted from C. S. Lewis's characterisations of eros ('face to face, absorbed in each other') and friendship ('side by side, absorbed in some common interest') (Lewis, 1960, p. 73).

dependent on the counsellor: 'interpretation' by the counsellor was required, for example, to make print-outs intelligible to the user (Watts, 1978). But using a computer system within the interview may mean that, far from reducing the counsellor time required by the client, the system increases it. In addition, it is clear that some users prefer to use such systems on their own.

On the other hand, there are ethical issues relating to using computer systems on a totally 'stand-alone' basis. As Sampson (1987) argues:

> Computers cannot notice when someone is sad or scared, or when a non-verbal behavior is completely incongruent with what is being said. If we let people have access to computers without access to counselors, this over-cognitive emphasis may not only restrict but also dehumanize the counseling process.
>
> (Sampson, 1987, p. 24)

The ethical standards produced by the American Association for Counseling and Development (1988) accordingly state that:

> When computer applications are used as a component of counseling services, the member must ensure that (a) the client is intellectually, emotionally, and physically capable of using the computer application; (b) the computer application is appropriate for the needs of the client; (c) the client understands the purpose and operation of the computer application; and (d) a follow-up of client use of a computer application is provided to both correct possible problems (misconceptions or inappropriate use) and assess subsequent needs.
>
> (AACD, 1988, p. 5)

This is a demanding and, arguably, over-protective standard. It would seem to require at least 'supported' usage on a mandatory rather than optional basis. Some may indeed go further and seek a 'progressive' framework in which sequences of computer usage and direct counsellor interventions (on an individual or group basis) are interspersed. Harris-Bowlsbey (1987) and Sampson *et al.* (1989), for example, have developed cyclical models in which a series of direct interventions alternate with computer usage. Where the direct interventions are on a group basis, the costs may be acceptable. Where they comprise individual interviews, however, such models are again very demanding of resources. In practice, therefore, many services may restrict themselves to 'supported' usage and indeed make such support available on a more flexible basis. If, for example, a computer system is in use within an information room, a counsellor or information officer can be available for short interventions if the user requests or seems to require it.

It is worth noting that the AACD guidelines do not wholly rule out 'stand-alone' usage, but insist that systems used in this way should be designed from the outset to function in a stand-alone manner, and should include within the computer program 'a description of the conditions under which self-help computer applications might not be appropriate, and a description of when and how counseling services might be beneficial' (AACD, 1988, p. 5). This is important, because it enables computer systems to be based outside guidance services. There have, for example, been some interesting experiments in placing such systems in libraries (e.g. Johnson, 1991; Watts *et al.*, 1991). It has also been suggested that the PROSPECT system, for instance, might be networked throughout a university campus, including teaching departments and halls of residence (Watts, 1993). Indeed, some limited systems have been designed for use in the home, particularly in the case of the Minitel structure in France (Aubret and Guichard, 1989).

This kind of 'stand-alone' usage seems likely to increase greatly the extent to which such systems are used, because it takes them to where potential users habitually are. Moreover, if the systems include strong references to the availability of guidance services, they could provide a valuable marketing device for such services. Some services, however, fear that the systems will satisfy people's perceived needs and so *deter* them from taking advantage of the additional provision the services have to offer. They are also anxious that users may be more likely to misuse the computer system or misinterpret the information they receive from it. Certainly there is some evidence that 'outreach' usage results in a substantial increase in *quantity* of usage, but makes it more difficult to encourage *quality* of usage (Watts *et al.*, 1991). Attempts to restrict such 'outreach' usage are, though, open to attack as representing a form of restrictive practice seeking to protect the services' own vested interests. This raises the wider issue of the 'ownership' of such systems, to which I will return in Section 15.4.

Implications for the role of the counsellor

The impact of computer systems on guidance delivery could take two different forms. It could result in growing *convergence* between such systems and other guidance interventions, with the characteristics of the computer – its relentless logic and cognitive emphasis, for example – gradually influencing the nature of the other interventions. Or it could result in growing *divergence*, with the assumptions and purposes underlying the other interventions being seen as complementing those of the computer.

This reflects a more general human dilemma in response to the computer. Turkle (1984) argues that computers present human beings with a side of their own nature:

> Because they stand on the line between mind and not-mind, between life and not-life, computers excite reflection about the nature of mind and the nature of life. They provoke us to think about who we are. They challenge our ideas about what it is to be human, to think and feel. They present us with more than a challenge. They present us with an affront, because they hold up a new mirror in which mind is reflected as machine.
>
> (Turkle, 1984, p. 320)

The effect of this mirror-image could be to constrain or to liberate. People may increasingly conform to the image, so giving way to 'the imperialism of instrumental reason' (Weizenbaum, 1976). Or they may be released by it to develop and value the other parts of their nature: their emotions, their capacity to relate to one another, their moral sense.

In relation to guidance, the computer has considerable implications for the role of guidance practitioners. Traditionally their professional credibility has often lain largely in the repositories of career information to which they are perceived to have access, and in the methods they use for assessing individuals' suitability for particular options. Both of these roles are to some extent being 'taken over', or at least made more 'transparent', by the computer.

Instead, there would seem henceforth to be two major roles for the guidance practitioner (Watts, 1986). The first is as a *counsellor* in the strict sense of the word: helping students to express and explore their feelings and concerns, to reflect on the information they have collected, and to work on the emotional difficulties which many people experience in making career decisions – difficulties which often cannot be resolved by simply providing further information. Paradoxically, while challenging the central role of the interview within the guidance pro-gramme, as the main delivery vehicle for information and assessment, the com-puter could also strengthen the position of counselling within the interview.

The second emerging role is as a *manager of guidance resources*. Such resources will include computer systems, alongside individual counselling, group activi-ties, experience-based learning programmes, and the like. The critical skill of the guidance practitioner in this respect will be to manage these diverse resources in ways which enable individuals to find the means through which their personal needs can best be met.

These two roles should enable guidance practitioners to base their work on higher-order skills than in the past. They also challenge such practitioners to demonstrate that their distinctively human skills can deliver higher-quality services than computers alone can do. The computer can at least deliver assured and consistent standards. It is by no means self-evident that counsellors currently demonstrate, for example, consistently high levels of empathy, warmth and genuineness. The advent of the computer should provide them with the oppor-tunity, and the incentive, to do so.

15.4 CONCLUSION

The possible applications of computer-aided guidance systems have certainly not been exhausted. Advances in technology are offering many new possibili-ties. Developments such as the advent of CD-ROM have greatly expanded the data-storage capacity of such systems and the speed at which they can access data, so increasing their potential scale and power. In addition, the use of coloured graphics, 'windows' and the like have considerably improved the attrac-tiveness and flexibility of displays. At the same time, the emergence of interactive video, multi-media and hypermedia are now enabling still photographs, video sequences and sound to be added to text and graphics. Sampson (1994a) notes that 'while interactive video technology is not currently a common resource used in CACG [computer-aided career guidance] systems, the significant reductions in hardware costs that are expected over the next few years should make this technology a more common component of future CACG systems' (p. 93). The Internet, too, is offering new opportunities for making careers information more readily accessible than ever before.

In the longer run, it is likely that computers will offer as yet unforeseen oppor-tunities for developing new forms of help in career decision-making. 'Virtual reality', for example, will offer new ways of developing computer-generated simulations of the physical world as well as any imaginary world, with rich opportunities for extending access to experience (Heim, 1993): this may mean that career exploration will increasingly be conducted through such experience rather than through the representational forms of words and visual images (cf. Chapter 13). To date, computer-aided guidance systems have largely used computers to do more effectively what is already being done in other ways. Technological advances, along with more creative approaches to computer usage, are likely to reveal new possibilities, and indeed may challenge some of the statements about the limitations of computers that have been made earlier in this chapter.

These developments and possibilities accentuate the importance of questions about the 'ownership' of such systems. With the current systems, it seems that 'mini' systems can be left largely to the market, though quality standards are needed to ensure that the interests of the user are protected. In the case of 'maxi' systems, however, the level of financial investment required is much greater, and their power and comprehensiveness mean that they have much wider implications for the organisation and structure of the guidance programmes in which they are located; this is likely to become even more the case as the potency of such systems grows. This suggests that there is an important development role for government (as the main funder of guidance services), and also – as noted earlier – for guidance professionals (as the providers of such services). In relation to the latter, the growing literature on socio-technical approaches to integrating technology into organisations attaches considerable significance to the active involvement of users in the design as well as the implementation of technological systems (Walton, 1989). The role of government in the funding of PROSPECT (HE), and the role of the Association of Graduate Careers Advisory Services and the Central Services Unit (see Chapter 7) in managing its development, provide a possible model, as well as a rich case-study of the political and economic difficulties that can arise (Watts, 1993).

These difficulties include the tensions between professional ownership and individual access, to which we have already alluded in Section 15.3. Professional ownership can be viewed as protecting the interests of the clients or the interests of the guidance providers themselves. Computers sharpen this issue. They have the potential for moving guidance away from professional control. 'Expert systems' can simulate the role of the counsellor and make it available to all. If there is sufficient demand for such systems, a market may emerge in which existing guidance professional structures are by-passed. The challenge for guidance professionals is to demonstrate that the effective integration of computer systems in wider guidance programmes significantly improves the *quality* of the help delivered to clients, but at the same time to avoid being open to attack for attempting to restrict the potential of the computer for extending *access* to such help. In the long run, any such attempts are almost certainly doomed to failure.

Computers have considerable potential both for increasing the quantity and quality of data to which individuals have access and also for supporting the individual's ownership of his or her career development. A critical task for the future will be to reconcile these two roles. This can be illustrated in two respects. First, reference was made earlier to the distinction between systems which work with 'objective' constructs and those which work with the individual's own subjective constructs. Effective thesauri are now needed which will enable individuals working with their own constructs to 'call up' data related to these constructs. Second, alongside the attention to developing 'maxi' systems to take full advantage of the power of the computer, attention is also needed to using authoring software to enable individuals to build up their own customised records of their own career development, including their records of achievement and action plans (Chapter 14) and other data they want to retain for their own purposes, downloading material from other systems where they want to do so. This may presage the transition to a third age in the history of computer-aided guidance systems presented in Section 15.1: a period in which the locus of control in the usage of such systems – which in the first period belongs to the system, and in the second to the interactive interface between system and individual – passes to a much more significant extent to the individual.

REFERENCES

American Association for Counseling and Development (1988) 'Ethical Standards (3rd Revision, AACD Governing Council, March 1988)', *Journal of Counseling and Development* 67: 4–8.

Aubret, J. and Guichard, J. (1989) 'Minitel and Careers Guidance', in Watts, A. G. (ed.) *Computers in Careers Guidance*, Cambridge: Careers Research and Advisory Centre/ Hobsons.

Ballantine, M. and Watts, A. G. (1989) 'Computers and Careers Guidance Services: Integrating the Technology into the Organisation', in Watts, A. G. (ed.) *Computers in Careers Guidance*, Cambridge: Careers Research and Advisory Centre/Hobsons.

Butler, A. M. and Dowsey, M. W. (1978) 'Using a Computer with a Careers Education Model of Guidance: the Interactive Careers Guidance System', *Journal of Occupational Psychology* 51(1): 57–68.

Closs, S. J. (1986) 'Current and Future Developments of the JIIG–CAL System', *British Journal of Guidance and Counselling* 14(1): 53–65.

Crowley, T. (1992) 'Computer-Aided Careers Guidance: an Investigation Involving an Artificial System', *British Journal of Guidance and Counselling* 20(3): 344–51.

French, C. C. (1986) 'Microcomputers and Psychometric Assessment', *British Journal of Guidance and Counselling* 14(1): 33–45.

Harris-Bowlsbey, J. A. (1987) 'The Counselor and the Computer as Service Providers', *Career Planning and Adult Development Journal* 3(2): 43–48.

Harris-Bowlsbey, J. A. (1989) 'Computer-Based Careers Guidance Systems: their Past, Present and a Possible Future', in Watts, A. G. (ed.) *Computers in Careers Guidance*, Cambridge: Careers Research and Advisory Centre/Hobsons.

Heim, M. (1993) *The Metaphysics of Virtual Reality*, Oxford: Oxford University Press.

Hofstadter, D. (1979) *Gödel, Escher, Bach: an Eternal Golden Braid*, Hassocks: Harvester Press.

Hunt, M. R. (1994) 'The Present and Future Use of Information Technology to Support Guidance', in *The Future Use of Information Technology in Guidance*, Coventry: National Council for Educational Technology.

Jackson, C. (1993) 'The Case for Diversity in Computer-Aided Careers Guidance Systems: a Response to Watts', *British Journal of Guidance and Counselling* 21(2): 189–95.

Jay, T. B. (1981) 'Computerphobia: What To Do About It', *Educational Technology* 21(1): 47–48.

Johnson, C. S. (ed.) (1991) 'Adult Career Development: Alternative Delivery Systems', *Journal of Career Development* 18(1): 3–87.

Katz, M. R. (1993) *Computer-Assisted Career Decision Making: the Guide in the Machine*, Hillsdale, NJ: Erlbaum.

Katz, M. R. and Shatkin, L. (1983) 'Characteristics of Computer-Assisted Guidance', *Counseling Psychologist* 11(4): 15–31.

Kivlighan, D. M., Johnston, J. A., Hogan, R. S. and Mauer, E. (1994) 'Who Benefits from Computerised Career Counseling?', *Journal of Counseling and Development* 72(3): 289–92.

Law, B. (1994) 'On the Importance of Interwagulation!', in *The Future Use of Information*

Technology in Guidance, Coventry: National Council for Educational Technology.

Lewis, C. S. (1960) *The Four Loves*, London: Geoffrey Bles.

Mair, J. M. M. (1977) 'The Community of Selves', in Bannister, D. (ed.) *New Perspectives in Personal Construct Theory*, New York: Academic Press.

Marin, P. A. and Splete, H. (1991) 'A Comparison of the Effect of Two Computer-Based Counseling Interventions on the Career Decidedness of Adults', *Career Development Quarterly* 39(4): 360–71.

Meier, S. T. (1985) 'Computer Aversion', *Computers in Human Behavior* 1(2): 171–79.

Minor, F. J. (1986) 'Computer Applications in Career Development Planning', in Hall, D.T. (ed.) *Career Development in Organizations*, San Francisco, CA: Jossey-Bass.

National Council for Educational Technology (1993) *Using Software Menus in Careers Education and Guidance*, Coventry: NCET.

Offer, M. (ed.) (1990) *Careers Software Review*, Coventry: National Council for Educational Technology.

Offer M. (1993) 'Developments in the Field of Vocational Guidance Software from Cambridge to Nuremburg 1989–1992', in *New Tendencies, Challenges and Technologies in Transnational Careers Guidance*, Report of the Third European Conference on Computers in Careers Guidance, Nürnberg: Bundesanstalt für Arbeit.

Phillips, S. D., Cairo, P. C. and Myers, R. A. (1981) 'Computer-Based Career Planning for Adults', *British Journal of Guidance and Counselling* 9(1): 100–07.

Sampson, J. P. (1987) 'Computer Use or Abuse: Ethics in the Use of Computers', in Walz, G. R. and Bleuer, J. C. (eds) *The Growth Edge: Creative Use of Computers for Facilitating Learning and Enhancing Personal Development*, Ann Arbor, MI: ERIC Counseling and Personnel Services Clearinghouse.

Sampson, J. P. (1994a) 'Factors Influencing the Effective Use of Computer-Aided Career Guidance: the North American Experience', *British Journal of Guidance and Counselling* 22(1): 91–106.

Sampson, J. P. (1994b) *Effective Computer-Assisted Career Guidance: Occasional Paper Number 2*, Tallahassee, FL: Center for the Study of Technology in Counseling and Career Development, Florida State University (mimeo).

Sampson, J. P. and Pyle, K. R. (1983) 'Ethical Issues Involved with the Use of Computer-Assisted Counseling, Testing, and Guidance Systems', *Personnel and Guidance Journal* 61(5): 283–87.

Sampson, J. P., Peterson, G. W. and Reardon, R. C. (1989) 'Counselor Intervention Strategies for Computer-Assisted Career Guidance: an Information-Processing Approach', *Journal of Career Development* 16(2): 139–54.

Sampson, J. P., Peterson, G. W., Reardon, R. C., Lenz, J. G., Shahnasarian, M. and Ryan-Jones, R. E. (1992) 'The Social Influence of Two Computer-Assisted Career Guidance Systems: DISCOVER and SIGI', *Career Development Quarterly* 41: 75–83.

Trist, E. (1981) *The Evolution of Socio-Technical Systems*, Toronto: Ontario Quality of Working Life Centre, Ontario Ministry of Labour.

Truax, C. B. and Carkhuff, R. R. (1967) *Toward Effective Counseling and Psychotherapy*, Chicago: Aldine.

Turkle, S. (1984) *The Second Self: Computers and the Human Spirit*, London: Granada.

Walton, R. E. (1989) *Up and Running: Integrating Information Technology and the Organization*, Boston, MA: Harvard Business School Press.

Walz, G. (1984) 'Role of the Counselor with Computers', *Journal of Counseling and Development* 63(3): 135–38.

Watts, A. G. (1975) *The IBM/Cheshire Interactive Careers Guidance System: an Independent Review*, IBM Scientific Centre Report UKSC-0072, Peterlee, Co. Durham: IBM.

Watts, A. G. (1978) 'Using Computers in Careers Guidance in Schools', *Journal of Occupational Psychology* 51(1): 29–40.

Watts, A. G. (1986) 'The Role of the Computer in Careers Guidance', *International Journal for the Advancement of Counselling* 9(2): 145–58.

Watts, A. G. (1993) 'The Politics and Economics of Computer-Aided Careers Guidance Systems', *British Journal of Guidance and Counselling* 21(2): 175–88.

Watts, A. G. and Ball, D. (1990) *Towards a PROSPECT (16–19) System?: a Trial of PROSPECT (HE) in Two Colleges*, Cambridge: National Institute for Careers Education and Counselling.

Watts, A. G., Kidd, J. M. and Knasel, E. (1991) 'PROSPECT (HE): an Evaluation of User Responses', *British Journal of Guidance and Counselling* 19(1): 66–80.

Weizenbaum, J. (1976) *Computer Power and Human Reason: from Judgment to Calculation*, San Francisco, CA: Freeman.

Wooler, S. and Lewis, B. (1982) 'Computer-Assisted Counselling: a New Approach', *British Journal of Guidance and Counselling* 10(2): 125–35.

Part IV

Development

This part of the book addresses processes designed to support the development of guidance practice.

Chapter 16 examines staff development. It identifies ten main forms which staff development takes, ranging from long courses to consultancy and mentoring. It explores the *outcomes* sought, including preparation for tasks, for roles, and for developing understanding, as well as accreditation. It discusses the *inputs* that need to be invested, including physical, ideational and human resources. Finally, it looks at the *processes* of staff development, including the different learning styles involved. It is noted that any staff development, to be effective, will need to be accompanied by programme development and organisation development.

This latter is discussed in Chapter 17, which focuses on developing careers programmes in organisations. It is argued that the nature of such programmes will be strongly influenced by whether they are seen as primary, ancillary, additional or marginal activities, and by whether they are formal, semi-formal or informal. It discusses factors that influence the success of programme ideas within organisations. It also examines key considerations for effective programme management. It notes the importance of taking account of the interests of stakeholders. In addition, it emphasises the significance of communication channels within the organisation, and of access to decision-making.

Chapter 18 explores the role of evaluation. It examines different conceptions of this role, relating in part to the extent to which evaluation is viewed as a 'scientific' process, and in part to the varying interests of different stakeholders in the evaluation process. It looks in detail at different methodological approaches to process and outcome evaluation respectively, and at some of the problems they have to confront. It explores the relationship between evaluation and quality assurance. Finally, it examines the role of evaluation by guidance practitioners themselves, and ways in which they might be supported by the more formal work of external evaluators.

Chapter 16

Staff development

Bill Law

16.1 INTRODUCTION

Staff development is intended to change behaviour, so that people can do something different, or differently. A common form of staff development is training, wherein individuals are sent on a course in order to gain new learning, which they will then implement in their work. This chapter will demonstrate that this is not the only way of helping them; that courses are not the only form in which that help may be offered; that careers staff are not the only people who need to be helped; and that changed behaviour is not the only significant outcome of such help.

The chapter will refer mainly to staff development for guidance work in educational settings. Most of the concepts and issues presented were developed in relation to careers work in schools (Chapter 5), but can be readily extended to further and higher education (Chapters 6–7). Many can also be extrapolated to careers guidance within work organisations (Chapter 8) and to 'external' guidance agencies including the Careers Service (Chapters 9–10).

The role of staff development in the field of careers education and guidance is, however, complicated by the diversity of roles and of professional structures within the field (Hawthorn and Butcher, 1992). For many guidance workers, guidance is a secondary adjunct to their primary professional role – as a teacher, for example (Watts, 1992). Within schools, all teachers are required to have a substantial initial training; this is not yet the case in further and higher education. Subsequent staff development in guidance may therefore be building on an existing professional teaching base, or it may not. For some careers workers, on the other hand, guidance itself is their primary professional role: this is true of careers officers in the Careers Service, for instance, and of careers advisers in higher education. Again, though, the training structure varies: the former are required to have a professional qualification in careers guidance before being permitted to practise; the latter are not.

The structures of staff development are accordingly very diverse. The experience might be on a long course requiring up to a year of full-time study. Some have the option of a distance- or open-learning programme. However, most of these participants will also participate in shorter programmes, for as a little as a day at a time, in pursuit of specific pieces of learning. They might, on occasion, do this in their own organisation or in a partner's so that team members can work together on their contributions to shared work. Despite this complexity, there are – as we shall see – some unifying features in staff development for

Table 16.1   Staff-development provision as a system

Input	*Process*	*Outcome*
What material resources? location, equipment, material	*By what activities?* workshops, lectures, others	*For what tasks?* in guidance, curriculum, management
What ideas? from theory, practice, policy, social change	*On what aspect of change?* programme, organisation, people	*In what roles?* practitioners, managers, partners
What human resources? tutors, mentors, others		*With what gains?* understanding, skill, accreditation

careers work: all draw upon common theoretical disciplines, employ parallel delivery strategies and skills, and are driven by similar ideologies.

In this chapter, we will first look in more detail at the different forms of provision. Each provision can be viewed as a system (Table 16.1). The rest of the chapter will then examine each of the elements within this system, looking first at the outcomes sought, next at the resources required, and finally at the activities which use the resources to achieve the outcomes.

16.2 FORMS OF PROVISION

Staff-development provision can be divided into ten main forms: long courses; research-based provision; short courses and conferences; modularised events; support-network activities; consultancy and mentoring; materials-based provision; experience-based provision; organisation-based events; and integrative events. Much provision incorporates elements of two or more of these forms.

Long courses

Long courses are located in institutions of higher education. For careers officers they are one-year full-time or equivalent part-time postgraduate-level courses leading to a diploma (Hawthorn and Butcher, 1992). There are also long courses for other careers workers, including careers teachers, educational guidance workers, and careers advisers in higher education: these are usually on a part-time basis or on an 'open learning' basis incorporating substantial materials-based provision (see below). All offer general coverage for the field of work they address, whether careers guidance, careers education or educational guidance. All tend to have more substantial theoretical components than other forms of provision (Hughes, 1977; Kidd *et al.*, 1994). The full-time version of such courses has been characterised as an 'immersion' experience (Law, 1977). Part-time versions are usually on an in-service basis, with similar coverage to the full-time courses, but allowing continued contact with guidance practice in the workplace.

Research-based provision

The location of courses in higher education permits the expansion of activity in host departments to include research activity. In many cases the work is undertaken by alumni of the long courses, although other suitably qualified careers officers, teachers and others may carry out research too. Other higher education departments also support research by guidance workers. Action research, undertaken in careers-work locations, is – as we shall see – an important variant of this activity.

Short courses and conferences

Short courses for careers workers may be fairly general in their awareness-raising coverage of a theme or issue, or more tightly focused on a specific practical strategy or skill. Some interleave visiting lecturers with variants of the 'discussion group'. Others set up more task-oriented group work, perhaps practising a skill or developing a strategy. Where the intention is awareness-raising rather than skill development, they are more likely to be called conferences than courses; conferences may be cross-sectoral, bringing different careers-work roles together.

Modularised events

Modularised events are almost always focused on a specific task or role, and addressed substantially to practical skills. They are modularised in the sense that a person can undertake a series of selected but related events on a 'bespoke' basis. Other forms of provision listed here – for example, short courses and conferences, support-network activity and organisation-based events – sometimes 'buy in' modularised elements.

Support-network activities

In networks, participants share information, contacts and insight on an inter-organisational basis. In some cases, directories of who-can-provide-what are developed. The idea of forming a network of organisations to support and share resources, including staff-development resources, has been strongly developed by adult guidance agencies (Hawthorn and Wood, 1988). Professional associations commonly build such network activities into the services they offer to their members.

Consultancy and mentoring

Consultancy and mentoring bring an expert helper into contact with guidance workers in their workplace. The relationship may be focused on roles or on specific tasks. In schools, advisory teachers based in careers-service or LEA teams provide consultancy services of both kinds. Mentoring is commonly an important element of open-learning professional qualifications (Graham, 1994; Jones, 1995).

Materials-based provision

Re-usable task-oriented 'handouts' are a common feature of staff-development events. Such material has been developed into more extensive study guides and interactive distance- and open-learning packs which can be purchased as free-standing bases for staff development (Law *et al.*, 1995). 'Open learning' implies that participants engage in the use of the material in their own time, in their own location, and on whatever tasks are locally identified as appropriate.

Experience-based learning

Experience-based learning uses 'real' tasks, situations and encounters as learning resources. Its staff-development use includes placing participants in new work locations where they can discover and develop new approaches to their own work. This may include placements in industry and commerce.

Organisation-based events

The argument for organisation-based training is that the knowledge, skills, commitments and ethics of a profession are best learned where they are used (Hargreaves, 1994). In careers work they are set up by the organisation for its own staff. The simplest and perhaps most common example is the staff conference. More elaborate versions for careers work in schools have included 'consultations' (Law and Watts, 1977) developed as an action-research method, using the event as a laboratory. Organisation-based events may also involve partners from other agencies and the wider community. At their most pervasive, organisation-based events lead to the development not only of new skills, but also of new programme activities and new organisational arrangements to support them (see Section 16.5).

Integrative events

Other forms of provision, too, can incorporate features designed to link staff development to programme and organisation development. Resources can be provided for training groups to become planning groups (Hawthorn and Wood, 1988), aimed directly at producing changes in guidance programmes and the organisational arrangements which support them. The CRAC 'Learning for a Changing World' programme, for example, included various features of this kind (Andrews *et al.*, 1995, pp. 9–10).

16.3 OUTCOMES

Outcomes will be examined as preparation for tasks, for roles, and for developing understanding. Finally in this section, accreditation as an outcome will be considered.

Table 16.2   Tasks of careers workers

Tasks	Skills
1 *Taking a general view*	Appreciate the range of possible careers education and guidance practice Understand careers-related social and community change Keep up-to-date on developments in careers-related policy Understand careers education and guidance needs and readiness in the organisation Understand the career-development needs and readiness of learners Understand careers education and guidance theory
2 *Providing (in print etc.) careers information*	Provide a resource or learning centre Make and use local information resources Enable learners to access and use information Use computers in this area of the work
3 *Offering guidance to learners*	Use individual guidance skills Provide support for learners in planning and implementing a course of action Structure learning opportunities for individuals Provide a structured counselling setting Negotiate with learners Help learners to review achievement Enable placements Follow up learners
4 *Working with information about learners*	Use standardised assessments, such as test results and computer printouts Enable recording achievement and its use by learners Enable individual action planning by learners
5 *Working with small groups*	Set up and conduct group work
6 *Providing a programme of careers education*	Develop careers education programmes Prepare materials for careers education Teach careers education Make the programme participative Make the programme experiential Negotiate the careers education curriculum
7 *Developing inter-departmental action*	Manage and co-ordinate a programme Nurture links with colleagues Form active working partnerships across departmental boundaries Negotiate specific inter-departmental actions Inform, support and train non-specialist colleagues
8 *Developing informal work*	Enable informal careers-related activities
9 *Working with other providers of help*	Support informal guidance sources Liaise with other providers Liaise with learners' families Liaise with employers Establish community-based learning resources Involve community contacts as partners in programme development Operate referral procedures
10 *Evaluating provision*	Monitor practice Evaluate practice Assess own contribution

Table 16.2   continued

Tasks	Skills
11 *Managing and co-ordinating provision*	Manage the whole careers programme Contribute to the organisation's careers education and guidance policy Build teams Establish new targets Establish support systems Inform and influence institutional management

For what tasks?

Outcomes can be stated in terms of the tasks that careers workers undertake. Table 16.2 draws upon a number of analyses of careers education and guidance in such terms (Law *et al.*, 1991; Hawthorn and Butcher, 1992; Advice, Guidance, Counselling and Psychotherapy Lead Body, 1995; Humberside Careers and Guidance Services, 1995; Law *et al.*, 1995; Andrews *et al.*, 1995). Each task implies one or more skills to which the staff-development programme might be directed. An analysis of tasks provides a functional list of possible outcomes for staff development.

The role of the Advice, Guidance, Counselling and Psychotherapy Lead Body, with its government mandate for a National Vocational Qualification-type assessment, seems likely to prove influential in this respect. Its analysis, however, may have a significance beyond assessment. If there is any tendency at all to 'teach to the assessment', then such analyses will influence the way in which the field itself is defined and can develop. It is important, therefore, to note three significant features of the Lead Body's work. First, its contributions to the analysis in Table 16.2 inevitably fall in the *guidance* rather than the *education* areas. Any comprehensive list of careers-work abilities must, however, acknowledge the distinctive character and mutual dependence of *both* ranges of activity (see Chapter 12). Second, like other NVQ-type analyses, the Lead Body defines competence in terms of operational *behaviours* rather than abilities to manage and apply underpinning *understanding*. Third, again like other NVQ-type analyses, it portrays tasks in *reductive* terms, attending to modular parts more than their interrelationships in the molar whole. As we shall see in later sections of this chapter, these features of NVQ-type assessment need not, however, present insuperable problems to vigilant staff-development providers.

The analysis in Table 16.2 identifies tasks that any careers worker might need to undertake at some time, though in different balances and to different degrees. Some of this diversity reflects between-sector variations in practice, particularly between primarily guidance- and primarily curriculum-based delivery. There are also variations within sectors. Some schemes allow for core-and-option activity, on the assumption that not everybody in an organisation needs to be able to do everything. Again, some schemes are constructed on the principle of 'finding-the-best-next-thing-to-do' (e.g. Law *et al.*, 1995), on the assumption that different organisations will be ready for different developments at different stages. Generic, everybody-learns-everything approaches may be appropriate for initial training.

All other provision needs to take account of the fact that different people are doing different things, in different organisations, at different stages of development.

In what roles?

Identifying outcomes in role-related terms has the advantage of setting delivery in the context of a position in an organisation. As the task list in Table 16.2 acknowledges, careers work is a networking activity, drawing upon a wide variety of resources – formal and informal, specialist and non-specialist – within the organisation and in the wider community. The organisation's management is a significant part of such a network. The guidance service's referral system depends on the links offered by the network, as do business organisations' links with education, and education's use of adults-other-than-teachers. Such links often offer leading-edge development possibilities for careers work. Staff development, particularly where it is organisation-based, needs to involve as much of this network as possible wherever it can.

Different roles in the network have different needs. Some require an opportunity properly to appreciate careers work. Some need to understand it in greater depth. Some need to learn how to do it. A plan for a staff-development programme needs simultaneously to pursue outcomes related to both tasks and roles. Useful planning devices may be based on matrices indicating who (in what *role*?) needs to learn about what (on what *task*?) (Law *et al.*, 1995).

The gains: a place for theory?

Task-related outcomes are 'doing' – rather than 'knowing' or 'understanding' – gains. They do not necessarily imply that knowledge and understanding are rejected; they do, however, imply that, at best, knowledge and understanding are means to operational ends. Theory may, then, be a useful *input* to such a programme, but mere understanding of theory is not the sought *outcome*.

Theory is, though, recognised as an important element of staff development for careers work (Andrews *et al.*, 1995; Kidd *et al.*, 1994). Elliott (1993) identifies three perspectives for analysing the role of theory in this context.

First, what we have called task-related outcomes accord well with what Elliott calls a *production–consumption* perspective, pursuing quantifiable, and therefore behavioural, outcomes. Discrete practical skills and competencies define what people will learn. Elliott argues that this perspective fits well to the concept of a market for training, where purchasers specify needs and locate appropriate providers. More broadly, it fits well to a culture requiring ready identification of clear value-for-money effects.

Second, role-related outcomes offer some parallels with what Elliott calls the *hermeneutic* perspective. This calls for specific action based upon a 'situational understanding' of where the work is to be done. Learning is from reflective experience or action research. The situation is assumed to be complex and subtle, and the response must therefore be local and specific. This perspective is more interested in understanding the specific situation than in the identification of universal or objective 'truths'. One does not understand in order to act; one acts in order to understand – in 'a kind of practical science'. This perspective does not promulgate reductive, easy-to-market ideas.

Third, Elliott also suggests a *rationalist* perspective, rooted in general theoretical principles, independent of everyday manifestations and, it is hoped, free from situational bias. An autonomous professional is thus able to approach her or his work with a learned basis for applying and adapting these principles to any setting. This perspective tends, therefore, to minimise the importance of organisation-based learning. Elliott suggests that the movement of the centre of gravity for teacher education, away from higher education and into school-based work, is a symptom of disenchantment with the rationalist perspective. This movement is visible in other areas.

Research indicates that the use of theory in careers education and guidance has as much a hermeneutic as a rationalist resonance. Such theory can hardly be promoted as objective and universal 'truth': it must be presented as a conversation between complementary perspectives (see Chapters 2 and 3). In indicating the difficulties careers officers have in relating theory to practice, Kidd *et al.* (1994) report its use as a means of making *retrospective* sense of experience in their working roles, employing different theoretical formulations with different clients. In similar vein, Watson (1994) observes that careers officers come to the complexity of theory most effectively with the benefit of experience. She concludes that they might best be helped to reintegrate theory with their work if there were in-service opportunities for them to re-examine theoretical issues in the light of their experience and in the context of their practice.

In reviewing or planning the place of theory in staff development, it is possible to expect one or more of the following gains:

1 It helps practitioners rationally to understand causes and effects, and therefore to assess the probable consequences of their own and other people's actions.
2 In a field riven with a multiplicity of policy initiatives, it can suggest whether these suggested means are likely to realise the favoured ends.
3 Where staff development is fragmented by modular provision and careers work itself is fragmented by separate funding regimes, it can provide more general frameworks for attaching the fragments to a coherent whole. The whole is more than the sum of the parts.
4 By identifying coherence, it can help to identify what is missing from any current or proposed careers provision. In a changing world it can, similarly, suggest new actions for untried circumstances.
5 It develops a range of understandings useful for framing reflection on differential experience.

In these ways, theory represents a challenge to vendors of snake oil and purveyors of, often recycled, nostrums. It also serves as an important anti-reductive influence. Theory is, however, an input, not an outcome. Few of the above objectives are achieved simply by preparing people to write an examination script or dissertation. Nonetheless, the interdependence of 'intellectual skills, attitudes and manual skills' is increasingly urged upon training regimes, along with the concomitant need to design assessment procedures which adequately acknowledge the interrelated nature of these gains (Gonczi, 1994).

The gains: a place for accreditation?

As already noted, the importance of accreditation varies between different sectors. In some – notably the Careers Service – practice is not permitted without accreditation. The long courses and their equivalents lead to a postgraduate diploma-level award. Similar awards at different levels have been developed for practitioners in other sectors (Hawthorn and Butcher, 1992; Ford and Graham, 1994). There are also opportunities to pursue a programme leading to the award of a higher degree by undertaking original research, including action research.

In addition, serial participation in modular or open-learning programmes can lead to certificate and diploma awards (Ford and Graham, 1994). These have frequently been established within credit accumulation and transfer schemes. Such arrangements favour not only serial programmes but also the accreditation of prior learning.

Even in relation to roles for which accreditation is not essential, it is increasingly regarded as desirable (Andrews *et al.*, 1995). Moreover, there is growing pressure to develop more flexible forms of accreditation which enable enhanced competence, based on practice as well as formal learning, to be recognised and valued. In addition to traditional means of assessment – such as essays and dissertations, which provide evidence of theoretical understanding – careers practice also requires supervised practical experience that provides a basis for assessing delivery skills. Integration between the theory and practice is gained from an account of the practitioner's professional reflections. Further integration is possible where the resulting account is linked to a role, in a workplace, taking account of prior experience, and indicating further action to be taken (Wyatt, 1993; Jones, 1995). Such an activity has many of the features of what Elliott calls hermeneutic action research.

The format is, increasingly, not a research 'report' but an evidence portfolio. Portfolios are collections of annotated and referenced working materials (including reports, schemes-of-work and audio- or video-recordings) which participants assemble from their work. Task-related statements of competence provide verifiable criteria for the assessment of the material. There may be an additional requirement that each piece of material attests to theoretical understanding as well as competence (Jones, 1995; MacDonald, 1995; Kent Careers and Guidance, 1995).

Such accreditation arrangements provide a more user-controlled procedure. It is, of course, important that this does not compromise professional and intellectual standards. But, that being so, there is no reason why such arrangements could not be used in any programme – including part-time long courses interleaved with professional practice.

16.4 INVESTMENT

The outcomes of staff development are the task- and role-related skills and understanding that people gain, and the accreditation they acquire to acknowledge these gains. We now turn to the *input* for staff development: the resources that need to be invested in order to achieve the gains. These include *physical*, *ideational* and *human* resources.

Physical and ideational resources

Access to, and the appropriate use of, physical resources is, of course, important. The value of information technology to staff development deserves particular attention. Its use in the transmission of ideas and information, in networking contacts, in creating virtual realities, in responding interactively with users, and in assembling, collating and presenting new learning, is at the leading edge of staff-development technology (cf. DfE/DTI/ED, 1995). In these and in other ways, it is important not to disregard the significance of material resources. But well-equipped training suites are mere glitz without ideas for their use.

At the input stage, the pursuit of ideas is for an understanding of what participants should do, answering the question, 'What makes us think that this is such a good idea?' Two further questions present themselves: 'What ideas?' and 'Generated by whom?'

Ideas informing staff development

The roots of what careers workers do lie in an understanding of what their clients need to do. This is often expressed in terms of the thoughts, feelings and actions people engage in when accomplishing their own decisions and transitions. More specifically, it is an experience of seeking a stake in their communities, in establishing their attachment to their society, and in discovering and re-discovering motivation for career-related action. More generally, such understanding takes account of the shape of the labour economy, with its changing levels and patterns of recruitment, and its organisation and re-organisation of workplaces. More deeply, this includes an understanding of the impact of changed work – on both personal and community experience. More broadly, it links all of these events to multinational trading, the regulation and deregulation of work, changing patterns of unifying and fragmenting the workforce, and their concomitants for social cohesion. All can be analysed in terms of what is cyclical and what is structural. All can be extrapolated to future scenarios, and emergent concepts of work which will support them. Staff development must be invested with an understanding of how careers work can usefully help learners to deal with these layered and dynamic realities.

The generation of ideas

Theory is important for such purposes, and draws upon a wide range of disciplines (see especially Chapters 2 and 3; also Arthur et al., 1989). But a position once mainly occupied by theory is now increasingly also inhabited by policy interests (see Chapter 21). Careers work is about 'who does what' in the working world, and therefore influences national economic interests. Furthermore, because 'what people do' is a major means by which people achieve their stake in society and their interest in maintaining its stability, careers work is also a contributor to the social fabric. Policy cannot afford to ignore either matter. Of course, theory and policy are both capable of partiality with regard to how they order priorities for careers work. Their supporting ideologies and constituencies require no less of them (cf. Chapter 19).

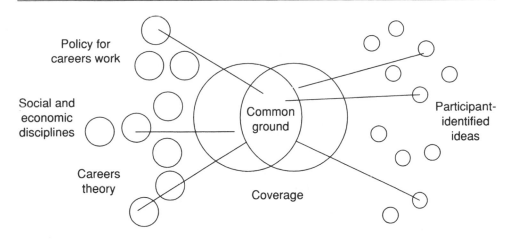

Figure 16.1   The search for common ground in staff development

Theory and policy may offer complementary or competing rationales for staff development. They have, however, a commonality: they both represent a 'top-down' and deductive process, working from general principles and offering the 'expert' considerable influence on attentive participants.

But practitioners also influence staff development. Practitioners are theorists and policy-makers, at least in the sense that they too need to make some usable sense of experience and to order priorities concerning what should be done. What Elliott (1993) calls a production–consumption orientation to staff development is responsive to the practitioner concerns of participants. In contrast with theoretical and policy influences, participants are more likely to move inductively, from widely scattered fragments of information. Such 'bottom-up' processes are most readily engaged by staff-development action which can be undertaken close to the point of delivery: organisation-based events, consultancy, networks and integrative events.

Formal providers of staff development are, then, not the only source of ideas. Experience has long suggested that teachers significantly influence each other (Hargreaves, 1972); furthermore, peer relationships in staff development have long been known to be important sources of satisfaction and usefulness (Law, 1977). There is much legitimate authority to be reconciled here: of experts on theory and policy, and of participants who speak with manifest authority on their own experience. The task is represented in Figure 16.1, reconciling (on the left) provider-led with (on the right) user-led ideas. A review or plan for any staff-development programme needs to attend to the terms in which such common ground is found.

Human resources

The forms of staff development are diverse, and the people who provide it have evolved a correspondingly diverse range of methods. Figure 16.2 identifies a sample of such methods, suggesting where examples might stand on two dimensions relating to the sources of influence. Towards the left, matters are

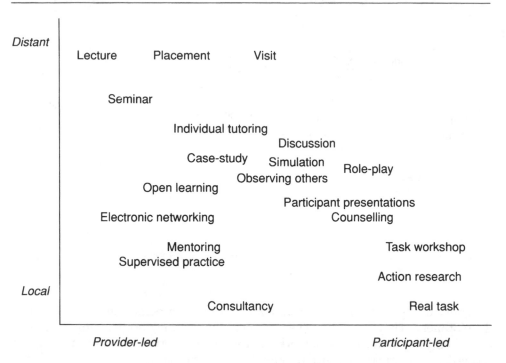

Figure 16.2 Methods of staff development

much in the hands of the provider – the lecturer, tutor, consultant or mentor. Towards the right, matters are more in the hands of the participants – whether careers advisers, teachers or their managers. Towards the top, the focus is general, concerned with what is transferable between settings, and – perhaps – theory-, policy- or ideology-led. Towards the bottom, the focus is on local concerns: what is happening in a specific organisation at a specific time.

The reality is, of course, more variable than the figure suggests. Lectures lend themselves to the delivery of provider-influenced material which is thought to be generally applicable. But not all lectures can be located in this way. A lecture certainly presents *expertise*. But its influence is modified by the extent to which participant expectations and reactions are *consulted*. Furthermore, different lecturers infuse their presentation to different degrees with a *personal* presence. They are prepared to different extents to *negotiate* form and content in response to participant reactions. Some presenters are attended to because of the perceived importance of their *position* – if not wise, then merely influential. Different lecturers manage all these matters in different ways, and thoughtful and sceptical audiences are able to modify their effects. Any of these five ways of managing influence (each examined in more detail in Chapter 17) can suggest other places for 'lecture' on the figure (although there are limits: lecturing cannot do everything!). All of the other methods have similarly diverse possibilities.

Figure 16.2 is a model, not a description. It analyses *influence* in a staff-development system, offering a way of locating methods used in a particular programme, and a stimulus for wondering whether the balance is right. Influence in systems is brought into focus by MacDonald and Walker (1976), who develop Havelock's (1971) explanation of managing change. They identify three broadly distinguishable approaches to bringing about change: research, development and diffusion; social interaction; and problem-solving. Each requires different mixes of the staff-development methods set out in the table.

In *research, development and diffusion*, the 'sender' has the idea for change. That idea has been developed independently of the 'receiver', who is viewed as being relatively passive and powerless. The approach therefore relies on 'expert' influence. It is assumed that the idea will be appropriate to a wide range of settings, irrespective of receiver reactions. The approach has some resonance with Elliott's (1993) rationalist perspective. However, not all disseminated ideas are rational, researched or particularly expert. The centre of gravity in the concept is the notion of a general idea *thought* to be worth disseminating, on a 'top-down' basis.

In *social interaction*, the sender identifies a need and, on this basis, puts forward a message for change. The receiver's response then determines what further messages are sent. Successful change therefore depends upon effective channels of communication, principally those which depend upon personal contact. Social interaction is also a top-down model: at its narrowest, no more than dissemination with a winning smile and careful tongue! A broader-based variation is that the sender will have a repertoire of off-the-shelf 'solutions', from which something can be selected and negotiated to fit specific conditions. This dissemination is, therefore, adaptive, with some resonance with what Elliott calls a production–consumption perspective. MacDonald and Walker highlight three aspects of its effectiveness: the presentation of a personal self with which the audience can identify; a careful negotiation of the content of communication; and the ability personally to demonstrate or model any proposed change.

In *problem-solving*, the receiver initiates the process by identifying a concern or need for change. The sender works with the receiver to identify what is needed and how it can be achieved. The sender is characterised as a 'change agent', engaged in co-operation with the receiver. The receiver is therefore the sender's client, and in control of the outcomes of the process. This insistence upon referring action to the specifics of the work situation offers considerable resonance with Elliott's hermeneutic perspective.

The variations, within as well as between these models, strongly suggest that they are multidimensional. Figure 16.2 offers two of the dimensions, referring to the extent of provider control and of local reference. A strong combination of provider control and general applicability are features of 'top-down' influence on behalf of ready-made solutions. A strong combination of user control and local applicability are features of 'bottom-up' influence on behalf of bespoke solutions. A line combining these non-orthogonal effects runs from top-left to bottom-right in Figure 16.2.

Staff development cannot be wholly undertaken at either extreme. In particular, the centre is where common ground – between the 'general and disseminable' and the 'specific and local' – will be found. Here providers and participants work most closely together, each on the basis of their own authority. Table 16.3 assembles the elements into three broadly distinguishable but interdependent approaches.

Table 16.3 Three approaches to staff development

	Top-down	Common ground	Bottom-up
Provider role	Policy or theory expert	Consultant	Process-expert
User role	Receiver	Negotiator	Protagonist
Modal form of provision	Short course, long course	Module, network, materials-based	Consultancy, experience-based, organisation-based
Examples of method	Lecture, seminar	Workshop, discussion	Action research
Closest perspective (Elliott)	Rationalist	Consumer–producer	Hermeneutic
Closest approach (MacDonald and Walker)	Research, development and diffusion	Social interaction	Problem-solving

The authority of participants in a staff-development event is an essential feature of such an event. They know what formal providers cannot know. The emergence of forms of staff development in which participant input is strong (the final two columns in Table 16.3) acknowledges this mutual dependence of provider and participant. But no review or plan for staff development can for long afford to ignore any of the columns in the analysis.

16.5 PROCESSES

If input is the investment in staff development, and outcome is the gain, then process is the activity which translates the investment into the gain. A conventional view of this throughput is that somebody first identifies what the training needs of the worker are and buys a place on an appropriate course; that the worker attends the course and engages in activities which can develop those understandings and skills; and that the worker returns better able to deal with his or her work. The reality is more complex. This section examines the variety of activities which translate resources into gains. It does so by considering staff-development activities and the aspects of change these activities address.

What staff-development activities?

The core activity is 'learning'. A number of complex learning scenarios have been developed. They variously invite providers to attend to learning in terms of its 'concrete experience' and 'abstract conceptualisation', as well as in terms of 'active experimentation' and 'reflective observation' (Kolb, 1984). Scenarios visualise a single learner as, by turns, 'active', 'reflective', 'theoretical' and 'pragmatic' (Honey and Mumford, 1986). In these cases, learning is envisaged in part as *cyclical* – where learners are thought of as moving through recurring kinds of learning experience. But in part they are *differential* – thinking of different people as moving through the cycle in different orders. Learning may also be conceived wholly as *sequential* – where learning progress moves from 'basic' beginnings to more 'advanced' continuations, and so on. An example of such a progressive sequence is set out in Chapter 3 as 'sensing', 'sifting', 'focusing' and 'understanding'. There is much complexity here: notions along the lines 'tell-'em-and-then-they'll-know' find little support.

A strongly differential analysis has been developed as a design specification for an open-learning pack for careers work (Law *et al.*, 1995). It suggests that learners can be broadly analysed in four groups.

First, some people may want to *look at the possibilities* for the work, in concrete, pragmatic and operational terms. Their intention is to identify appropriate models for their work. Such participants will value staff development for its ability to deliver information about what can be done to provide practical activities they can try out, and to develop specific skills in the identified tasks. The approach is circumspect in the sense that they are seeking to be convinced before action is undertaken.

Second, some will want to appreciate work tasks, seeking affective, open-ended and empathetic opportunities to *sense the experience* of the work. They will be ready to become personally involved in their work and in staff-development activities that help them with it. They may be ready to do so in some depth and with some appreciation of both its rewards and its strains. Such participants value the opportunity to reflect upon the values and meanings of their work, to explore different points of view concerning it, and to develop insights into the consequences of involvement for the people engaged in it – both themselves and other people. The approach is immediate rather than circumspect, the participant being ready to get involved in something in order to appreciate its depth and breadth.

Third, some will want to *consider the ideas* embedded in the work, in informed, reasoned and generalisable terms. Such participants seek an understanding of careers education and guidance by means of which they can assemble its elements into coherent frames-of-thought. They will value evidence for the causes and effects of action, concepts for organising the evidence into theory, and an opportunity to develop an understanding of what makes action transferable from one setting to another. They might be interested in theory and policy as bases for action; but, as we have hinted, not all theory and policy can expect to satisfy the most thoughtful and sceptical in this group. Such thinking is circumspect, needing to be convinced.

Finally, some participants will learn best from an opportunity to *act on a strategy*, organising themselves, and perhaps others, around action in a workplace. They may welcome help with developing team roles. They seek help in dealing with a defined situation and its specific problems. This is not circumspect but immediate – learning by doing.

Some of these activities favour concreteness in learning, some abstraction. Some are immediate and involving, some require a more circumspect approach

Table 16.4   Four learning styles

	Concrete	Abstract
Immediate	Act on a strategy	Sense the experience
Circumspect	Look at the possibilities	Consider the ideas

to learning. These features of the different learning styles are suggested as two dimensions in Table 16.4.

Any staff-development programme might be planned or reviewed for its ability to accommodate these differences. It is important to do so, in two respects. First, careers work has enough breadth and depth that different aspects of the work need to be learned in different ways. A learning scenario built on the analysis will provide for the use of different learning styles in different parts of the programme.

Second – the point strongly identified in the analysis – different people learn in different ways. Accordingly, different people need different learning scenarios, moving through each activity in different sequences. Information technology now permits participants to do this. There are also implications for team building in organisation-based work: an understanding of such differences helps to identify who might best do what in shared activities.

Any form of staff development, including both long and short courses, can be designed to accommodate such styles. If the aim is for the participants to change their behaviour, the arguments for what have been called 'immediate' styles are based on a suggestion that changed behaviour is, hermeneutically, a cause as well as an effect of learning – 'You won't really know it until you've done it' (Fullan, 1991; see also Chapter 17).

What aspects of change?

Such thinking moves us forward to a consideration of aspects of change. Change can be brought about in a number of scenarios: they include an opportunity to listen and talk about new actions, a role-play or simulation, an off-site experience, a virtual-reality representation, and an actual implementation *in situ*. What will actually be changed will vary according to how staff development engages in these different 'theatres'.

Plainly, learning in the place where the work is to be done can be linked to the specific organisational and programme arrangements in that place. Furthermore, changed behaviour depends upon changes in the institution. If, when they return from 'training', or as a result of it, participants find changed arrangements supporting new actions, then training is more likely to be effective. The institution is both a recipient of changed behaviour and a contributor to changed behaviour. Strong forms of learning need to be supported by changed institutional structures.

Where institutional change is an *intended* effect of the programme, we are speaking of more than staff development. Organisation-based work provides a rationale not only for learning-by-doing, but also for action research, with its intention to change role and task behaviour and in addition to change institutional structures. Thus attending to the importance of learning in a specific setting becomes progressively more important as each of the following assumptions is made:

1 That staff development is intended strongly to change behaviour.
2 That what is learned for one setting may not be possible in another.
3 That behaviour is modified by the situation in which it is delivered.
4 That where behaviour is changed, this has consequences for change in the institution where the work is done.

5 That other people – partners in the organisation and its community – may also need to change their behaviour.
6 That some behaviour cannot change unless the situation is also changed.
7 That agendas for change are best addressed concurrently to the institution as well as to the individual behaviour of the careers worker.

A review or plan for staff-development programmes can ask how far the programme attends to each of these considerations. Even where participants are sent on a long course, a different impact will be made where management takes account of the need to re-accommodate them. Not to do so can lead to what has been called 're-entry' effects (Law, 1979) and can lose part of the programme's value-for-money.

What sorts of changes are entailed here? A threefold analysis of development identifies the options:

1 *Staff development* helps people to do different work or do their work differently, by helping them to improve their commitment, understanding and skills. This can be done by sending people on a course but, as we have seen, it can also be done in other ways.
2 *Programme development* (Chapters 11–15) creates or adapts guidance procedures or schemes-of-work which will accommodate the new approaches to work that staff development suggests. This might include identifying new objectives, developing or adapting materials which support them, and supporting the new activities with appropriate evaluation and appraisal.
3 *Organisation development* (Chapter 17) re-examines institutional policy and priorities for its fit with the new activities, if necessary re-defining roles and providing additional time, organisational links and money to support them. In so doing, the organisation sponsors a culture which will help rather than hinder the new activities.

Any effective staff development will require – to a greater or lesser extent – some adjustment in programme and organisation. In this way, its effects are re-attached to the institution. Emerging eagerly from staff development is frustrating and damaging where people find that their programme will not accommodate the learning, or that they are simply not in a position in their organisation to implement it. It is an open question whether change is best brought about by concentrating first on behaviour, on programme, or on organisation development. The need for changes in the programme and organisation may be required before anything else much can be changed. Nothing happens in a vacuum. The environment, as much as the staff involved, stores and releases much of the energy for change. The dynamic interdependence of aspects of change is suggested in Figure 16.3. Change in any part of the circle can be supported by, and might require, change elsewhere.

Some forms of staff-development provision can more readily be brought close to the organisation and programme where the work is done. This applies, for example, to consultancy, organisation-based work and open learning; by contrast, short and long courses are relatively more distant. Forms of provision which can be used at close quarters can take more account of, and more directly influence, programme and organisation development. Figure 16.4 represents these relationships.

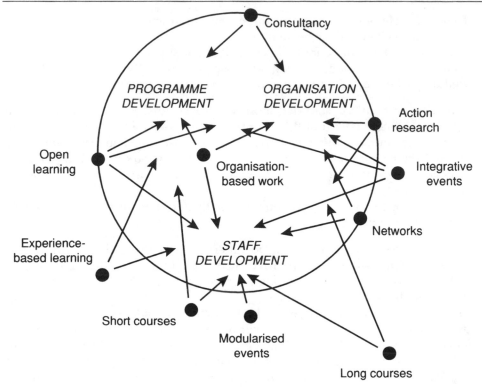

Figure 16.3 An interdependent model of change

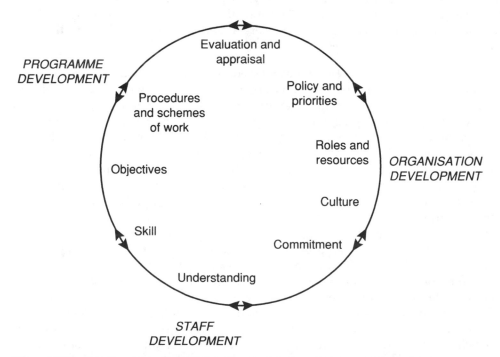

Figure 16.4 Relationships of staff development to programme and organisation development

16.6 CONCLUSION

This chapter has argued that 'training' is not the only way of helping careers workers to change their behaviour; that courses are not the only form in which that help may be offered; that careers staff (diverse though they are) are not the only people who need to be helped; and that changed behaviour is not the only significant outcome of that help.

The conclusions emerge from an input–process–outcome analysis of the elements. The model suggests causes and effects, proposing that change in one element will lead to changes elsewhere. It provides a frame for analysing the respective contributions of initial and in-service work, of long- and short-course provision in part-time and full-time forms, and of other forms of provision, in any sector. This structure for planning and reviewing staff development can be undertaken by participants, evaluating their own experience of staff development, or by providers, thinking about their provision.

REFERENCES

Advice, Guidance, Counselling and Psychotherapy Lead Body (1995) *First Release of Standards*, London: AGCPLB.

Andrews, D., Barnes, A. and Law, B. (1995) *Staff Development for Careers Work*, NICEC Project Report, Cambridge: Careers Research and Advisory Centre.

Arthur, M. B., Hall, D. T. and Lawrence, B. S. (eds) (1989) *Handbook of Career Theory*, Cambridge: Cambridge University Press.

Department for Education/Department for Trade and Industry/Employment Department (1995) *Getting Involved in Careers Work* (interactive video), London: DfE/DTI/ED.

Elliott, J. (1993) 'Three Perspectives on Coherence and Continuity in Teacher Education', in Elliott, J. (ed.) *Reconstructing Teacher Education*, London: Falmer.

Ford, C. and Graham, B. (1994) 'The New Qualification in Careers Guidance in Higher Education: a Collaborative Partnership', *British Journal of Guidance and Counselling* 22(1): 127–41.

Fullan, M. (1991) *The New Meaning of Educational Change*, London: Cassell.

Gonczi, A. (1994) 'Competency Based Assessment in the Professions in Australia', *Assessment in Education* 1(1): 27–44.

Graham, B. (1994) 'Mentoring and Professional Development in Careers Services in Higher Education', *British Journal of Guidance and Counselling* 22(2): 261–71.

Hargreaves, D. (1972) *Interpersonal Relations and Education*, London: Routledge & Kegan Paul.

Hargreaves, D. (1994) *The Mosaic of Learning: Schools and Teachers for the Next Century*, London: Demos.

Havelock, R. G. (1971) *Planning for Innovation through the Dissemination and Utilisation of Knowledge*, Ann Arbor, MI: Center for the Research and Utilisation of Knowledge.

Hawthorn, R. and Butcher, V. (1992) *Guidance Workers in the UK: their Work and Training*, NICEC Project Report, Cambridge: Careers Research and Advisory Centre.

Hawthorn, R. and Wood, R. (1988) *Training Issues in Educational Guidance for Adults*, Leicester: Unit for the Development of Adult Continuing Education.

Honey, P. and Mumford, A. (1986) *The Manual of Learning Styles*, Maidenhead: Ardingley House.

Hughes, P. (1977) 'Changing Perspectives in Full-Time Training', *The Counsellor* 2(2): 4–7.

Humberside Careers and Guidance Services (1995) *Competence in Careers Education and Guidance*, Hull: HC&GS.

Jones, M. (1995) 'Training for Careers Work in Birmingham Schools', *NICEC Careers Education and Guidance Bulletin* 44: 24–27.

Kent Careers and Guidance (1995) *Supporting Careers Work*, Maidstone: KC&G.

Kidd, J., Killeen, J., Jarvis, J. and Offer, M. (1994) 'Is Guidance an Applied Science?: the Role of Theory in the Careers Guidance Interview', *British Journal of Guidance and Counselling* 22(3): 385–403.

Kolb, D. A. (1984) *Experiential Learning*, Englewood Cliffs, NJ: Prentice-Hall.

Law, B. (1977) 'What Do Teachers Learn from In-Service Guidance Training?', *The Counsellor* 2(2): 8–31.

Law, B. (1979) 'The Contexts of System Orientation in Secondary-School Counselling', *British Journal of Guidance and Counselling* 7(2): 199–211.

Law, B. and Watts, A. G. (1977) *Schools, Careers and Community*, London: Church Information Office.

Law, B. Andrews, D. and Barnes, A. (1995) *Making Careers Work*, NICEC Users' Guide, Cambridge: Careers Research and Advisory Centre.

Law, B., Sims, N. and Watkins, C. (1991) 'Competent in Guidance: Says Who?', *NICEC Careers Education and Guidance Bulletin* 38: 16–22.

Law, B. *et al.* (1995) *Careers Work* (revised edn), Manchester: Open College.

MacDonald, B. and Walker, R. (1976) *Changing the Curriculum*, London: Open Books.

MacDonald, J. (1995) 'Developing a Portfolio for an Advanced Diploma in Careers Education and Guidance', *NICEC Careers Education and Guidance Bulletin* 44: 29–33.

Watson, C. (1994) 'Improving the Quality of Careers Guidance: Towards an Understanding of the Development of Personal Models', *British Journal of Guidance and Counselling* 22(3): 357–72.

Watts, A. G. (1992) *Occupational Profiles of Vocational Counsellors*, Berlin: CEDEFOP.

Wyatt, J. (1993) 'Portfolio Development in InSET: Using Open-Learning Materials with Careers Teachers', *NICEC Careers Education and Guidance Bulletin* 41: 19–22.

Chapter 17

Developing careers programmes in organisations

Bill Law

17.1 INTRODUCTION

Careers education and guidance occurs in organisations. It can be found, for example, in schools, colleges, business corporations and specialist guidance agencies (see Chapters 5–10). This chapter is about what sorts of careers education and guidance development can be undertaken in what kinds of organisation. It includes a method for identifying how the impact and survival of careers programmes in an organisation can be optimised.

Organisations have cultures. The culture influences what is acceptable and how it can be implemented. Very different careers programmes might be expected in 'Comanche' from those in 'Pueblo' organisational cultures (Musgrove and Taylor, 1969). A Comanche culture expects people to be courageous, individualistic, enterprising, and full of dash, initiative and achievement. Careers programmes can be driven and shaped by such values. A Pueblo culture, by contrast, encourages co-operation, favours group work, values creativity, and places the common good above individual reputation. Such a culture is likely to support careers programmes with very different emphases.

Organisational cultures can be changed, but they cannot safely be ignored. Different development strategies would, for example, be needed for each of the four cultures usefully developed from Harrison (1972) by Handy (1976; 1984). A 'power' or 'club' culture is dominated by a central group, acceptance by whom is the key to influence, unfettered by rules and procedures, where responses can be quickly adapted to meet new challenges, until the next challenge comes along. A 'role' culture is more orderly, maintaining rules and procedures which give each member a clear idea of what she or he is supposed to do, but which may be slow to change, and where any change might then become a matter of routine. A 'task' culture focuses on finding solutions, so that people who can help will be 'networked' into the problem-solving group, making the organisation adaptable but harder to map on a day-to-day basis. A 'person' culture is rare: said to be prepared to risk support for individual vision and aspiration. Each person works in networks of his or her formation or choice. Such a culture is, therefore, difficult to manage, and offers management roles less-than-fully-professional status.

Of course, twofold and fourfold analyses of culture are too simple. The elements of culture are multifarious. They include variations on how *priorities* are set, on how *roles* are assigned and achieved, on what kinds of *influence* are exerted and respected, on how *communication* of information and expectations is undertaken, on what internal and external *links* are thought to be worthwhile, on what *barriers* are thought to be necessary, on what *authority* decision-making is founded and carried through, and on how *conflict* is resolved. This is the very stuff of organisations: it can frustrate people who try to change them.

All cultures change. Developing a careers programme will shape and hasten certain kinds of change in the organisation. But the programme also needs to be shaped to optimise its chances of survival and effectiveness in that particular organisation. This chapter addresses both of these tasks. It begins by suggesting how the careers programme in the organisation can usefully be mapped. It then approaches programme and organisation development as a sequence of 'nested' approaches, beginning with the most specific and easiest to change, and ending with the most general and most difficult to change.

17.2 MAPPING ORGANISATIONS AND LOCATING CAREERS PROGRAMMES

Organisations are not homogeneous. All organisations have a range of products – goods and services for which different roles and structures are evolved. Furthermore, different people attach different importance to different components within that range. Thus all organisations evolve both a culture and a number of sub-cultures.

There is potential for change both in the variability of the product range and in the dynamics of the culture and sub-cultures. Taking account of this internal variability may be significant for developing careers programmes.

Primary production and other activities

A product range includes the goods and services produced for customers and for the organisation's own staff. There can be disagreement about what is primary. A primary product of a careers service is guidance; but a majority of its members may also be interested in supporting schools in curriculum development, which they see as an essential back-up to a good guidance service. In a fast-food franchise, the primary product might be thought to be 'burgers'; however, others might consider job enrichment as important, partly because it maintains the quality of the product, but partly because people should be treated like people. An educational organisation might be said to exist to maintain the integrity of the knowledge, concepts and skills of its disciplines, and to impart them to its students; some, however, might strenuously argue that ensuring that students can recognise the relevance of their education to their lives not only helps academic achievement, but is intrinsically valuable.

The position of careers programmes in an organisation can be mapped in terms of four types of activity or product:

1 *Careers guidance* is a primary activity for few organisations. Many organisations, however, offer guidance as an ancillary or additional activity.
2 *Careers education* is a primary activity of no organisation. It may, however, be easier to attach to organisations which have other learning programmes.
3 *Social-fabric support* covers a wide range of activities, in some of which almost all organisations engage. They are often ancillary activities which support the functionality of the work and maintain the habitability of its environment.

Some are undertaken because they are held to be intrinsically worthwhile. On either count, relatively modest examples include the provision of crèche facilities; ambitious examples include the implementation of an environment-friendly policy. For some organisations – such as welfare services, citizens' advice bureaux and pressure groups – social-fabric support is a primary activity.

4 *Other goods and services* are what most organisations have as their primary products. These may include selling insurance – or careers guidance; maintaining cars – or academic integrity; and making television programmes – to transmit to television sets manufactured by yet other organisations. Producing financial margins – for technological investment or for dividends – may also be seen as the primary product of some organisations.

Different organisations will thus attach different levels of importance to these different activities, according to whether they are regarded as:

1 A *primary* activity: the essential reason for the organisation's existence.
2 An *ancillary* activity: useful, perhaps necessary, for the support of the primary activity.
3 An *additional* activity: though not necessary, a valuable enrichment of the organisation.
4 A *marginal* activity: of little value to the primary activity, and with little perceived intrinsic value.

In a few organisations, careers education and guidance is a primary activity. But in most organisations, it occupies a different position: the challenge is to keep it out of the 'marginal' category.

Degrees of formality

Careers education and guidance in organisations where it is not a primary product appears at first to be part of a sub-culture, embodying values, procedures and skills not yet known or understood in the mainstream. Emerging cultures often emerge informally. Informal action is what people do not so much because it is part of their job description, but because it seems useful or valuable. What Handy (1976) calls 'person' cultures will readily accommodate such activity; but, as already pointed out, such cultures are rare. Permitting useful informal development is one of the means by which any organisation, with any culture, innovates.

Careers education and guidance is not a stranger to informality. Indeed, it can be understood historically as an activity which, as society has become more diversified and complex, has moved from informal to formal provision (see Chapter 20). Much influential careers help is still provided in peer relationships and families. Middle-range settings, between formality and informality, include voluntary organisations, 'job clubs', trade-union branches, staff associations, and ethnic and other cultural affiliations.

Organisations can host both formal and informal careers activities. An example of less formal activity is where an aspect of guidance is loosely attached to an existing role: for instance, where it is loosely expected that line managers or form tutors will take an interest in the career development of their charges. Some such activity may be 'extra-curricular' or 'satellite' activity, for example in an out-of-hours information or counselling service provided by enthusiasts. 'Extra-mural' activities often develop at first informally, for example in the provision of a pilot outreach programme, or where teachers set up contacts in the community for students whose work experience has proven a disappointment. The organisation is not strongly mandating any of these activities: they may indeed be seen as discretionary rather than required; they may not appear in the organisation's reports or brochures; they may not have resources formally assigned to them. Some of them will nonetheless be important leading-edge developments in any organisation's programme.

The relationship between formality and informality is a layered and subtle continuum. Three broad levels can be distinguished:

1 Highly *informal* careers education and guidance, like that undertaken in family and peer groups, is undertaken within organisations on the basis of trusted encounters between people whose roles may not require it, and in which both the providers and the beneficiaries are participating voluntarily.
2 *Semi-formal* careers education and guidance is based on the assumption that people will take it on voluntarily. The instigators are probably enthusiasts, but as the organisation begins to recognise the value of the activity, it may become loosely expected even of people who are less enthusiastic and do not see it as a part of their role. It is not, however, strongly mandated and may not be properly resourced by the organisation.
3 Fully *formal* careers programmes assign roles and resources to designated people, who may well have applied for the work because they are both committed and skilled, and see themselves as specialists, if not necessarily full-time.

The evolution of careers programmes can often be traced through stages based on these levels (see e.g. Chapter 5). What cannot be launched as a formal mainstream programme might at first be set up on the basis of less formal commitments from some part of the sub-culture of the organisation. The semi-formal stage is critical. Some people will welcome and respond to such a challenge; others will dismiss it. Their response will, over time, influence whether evolution proceeds to the formal stage.

Locating careers programmes in organisations

Figure 17.1 relates the four levels of activity to the three levels of formality noted above, and locates the four types of activity or product within the resulting two-dimensional space. Example (a) is a commercial business: most such organisations would have strong entries for primary products and social-fabric support; some would have no entries at all for careers education and guidance. Different commercial businesses would thus have different configurations, but would be likely to be more like each other than like the careers service, school and voluntary agency 'mapped' in (b), (c) and (d) respectively.

Specific organisations would usefully be able to enter specific programme titles on to such a chart (e.g. a line-manager mentoring programme, a pre-retirement course, a learning resources centre, succession planning appraisals, a personal and social education programme, a service-level agreement, consultancy to schools). Different members of the organisation might locate these programmes in different positions. A useful development event would be to explore these differences on the basis of a shared chart with movable plaques for each programme element.

Where careers education and guidance appears as a primary or ancillary activity, roles are likely to be mandated and resourced from senior levels, people doing the work are likely to be specialist and trained in the field, and other members of the organisation are likely to know about the work and to see it as a valued part of the organisation's culture. It will appear in the top-left of the charts in Figure 17.1. There are dangers here: of complacency, bureaucratisation and compliance with the merely routine. There may still be renewal work to be done. But where careers education and guidance does not appear at all, or is elsewhere in the chart, more radical work may be required, to move the activity leftward and upward.

The remainder of this chapter will examine how this work might be accomplished. It proposes four sets of tasks:

1 Coming up with a good *programme idea*. This includes identifying actions which simultaneously pursue worthwhile careers education and guidance objectives and can be understood to be effective and valuable within the organisation. It may relate to only one development; but it requires intensive short-term attention while the action is being developed into a sustainable form.
2 Carrying out effective *programme management*. This includes ensuring that the idea is integrated with the whole programme. Once an idea for action is in train, something must be done to optimise its impact and chances of survival. This means exercising influence which is skilfully measured, paced and communicated. It needs at least one careers programme manager or co-ordinator, and some breadth of attention in the organisation.
3 Attending to *programme stakeholders*. This includes ensuring that people who potentially can help (and be helped by) the programme are able to do so, willing to do so, and have a role or are in a position which permits them to do so. It may not be something that can be accomplished in the short term, but it is valuable to aim for medium-term effects. The remit is wider, longer-term and more demanding. It probably requires some management 'clout' and not a little 'wisdom'.
4 Working with the *organisation's structure*. This means ensuring that the big organisational decisions which influence the programme are properly informed and comprehending of its value. It includes helping people to make necessary links, across departmental and organisational boundaries. This is a broad remit requiring a long-term strategy. It is difficult to achieve wholly from a specialist careers education and guidance position, even as programme manager; senior management will need to know and support what is happening.

This analysis can be used as a basis for examining a specific situation. Any development work will encounter both helping and hindering elements for each of these tasks.

(a) A commercial business

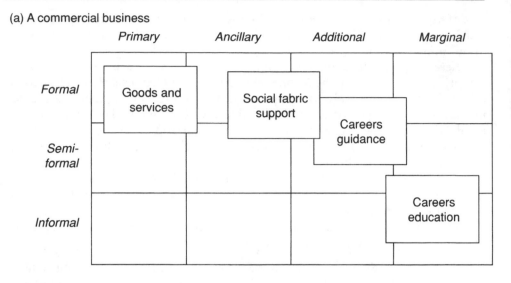

(b) A careers service

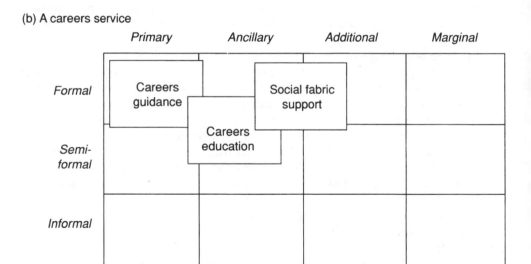

Figure 17.1 The place of careers programmes within four organisations

17.3 WORKING ON THE PROGRAMME IDEA

The programme idea describes what people are going to do different or differently. This might be an idea for guidance (see Chapter 11), for the curriculum (Chapter 12) or for an associated activity (Chapters 13–15). Few ideas remain unchanged after the first 'eureka' experience: this is followed by a development process. It has been argued that the period between inception and delivery is not sufficiently attended to by innovators, on the assumption that once an idea is launched, people can be left to get on with it (Fullan, 1985). But there is much to be done to adjust any programme once it is in train. Separation of planning

(c) A school

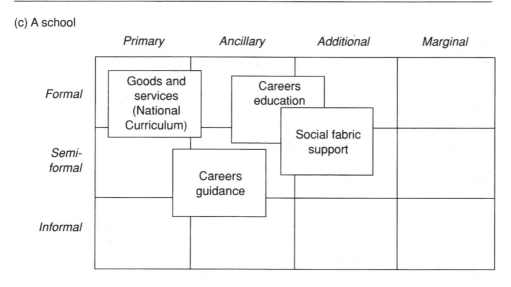

(d) A voluntary agency

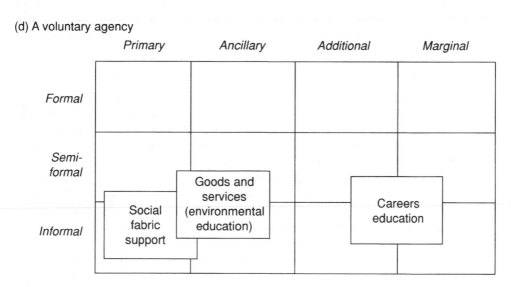

Figure 17.1   (continued)

and practice is argued to be a cause of failure in much innovation, success depending upon the support of what will prove defensible in a particular organisation (Fullan and Hargreaves, 1992).

Three variations on this issue are suggested here. First, will anyone gain anything worthwhile from the idea – will it *work*? Second, can people see their own concerns dealt with in it – does it make *common ground*? Third, how *clearly* is it put forward – will everybody know what is being talked about?

Knowing whether it will work

Knowing whether it will work means knowing whether beneficiaries will gain from it. The search is for *practical* programme ideas.

There is no shortage of suggestions for careers education and guidance actions. Policy-makers advocate actions which they can defend with their constituents; publishers advertise materials they want to sell; experts stake their reputations. The only case that matters here is one that cogently links affordable causes to probable gains. To appeal to such arguments is to support practice with theory. Not to do so may posture as practicality, but it is – in reality – irresponsibility.

Theory is a contributor to such thought (see Chapters 2–3), as is formative evaluation (see Chapter 18). Both can be home-grown. Locally-generated understanding may be as valuable as more distant and more prestigious voices (see Chapter 16). It is in the nature of careers education and guidance that providers learn about the organisation's impact on its people's lives. Co-ordinating this information is an important part of any careers programme manager's work.

Careers education and guidance has few sure-fire solutions that are bound to work in all circumstances. But no idea for action deserves to be taken seriously unless it can be shown that, right here, it is likely to have a useful impact.

Finding common ground

Though necessary, such argument is unlikely to prove sufficient. Other concerns will make an idea-for-action, however cogent, unwelcome. It may be opposed, not because it will not work, but because it *might*! Desirability, not effectiveness, is now the issue – for the people who can influence the action, or be influenced by it. The question is, 'Can they see any value in it?'

This is a serious consideration. Anything that is not wanted can be thwarted by sceptical and resourceful people at ground level; if not thwarted, hijacked to some other purpose; if not hijacked, cosmeticised to the appearance of compliance. Such scepticism and resourcefulness deserve to be better used.

It is commonly argued that successful innovation must be based on an appreciation of such ground-level thought. Innovators should restrict themselves to placing knowledge, material and consultancy at the disposal of a 'bottom-up' process. Despite the yearnings of the naive for recommendations for 'good practice', no idea-for-action is infinitely transferable to all settings. The significant variables for their viability are too subtle, too complex – and too many! The implication is that proposals should be understood in their own terms by the people who are to implement them. Solutions should be 'relevant to the members of the target user group and bring major benefits to them . . . a matter of both reassuring practitioners and yet not buttressing previous practice' (MacDonald and Walker, 1976; see also Chapter 16).

There is a dilemma here. To respond only to ground-level concerns would be to collude with the 'not-invented-here' syndrome, which arbitrarily rejects everything but home-grown solutions to narrowly-defined problems. Moreover, some problems do not require, and cannot afford, a 'bottom-up' but inefficient reinvention of the wheel. Reassuring practitioners cannot just mean re-using self-enclosed assumptions about what is valuable. The converse of 'bottom-up' is 'top-down'. Some top-down innovation is successful. Sometimes other people's solutions *are* useful (Fullan, 1985). Publishing careers materials and strategies depends absolutely upon the validity of that assumption.

The resolution of the dilemma is what takes the time. Its resolution may be wholly rejection, but it is rarely wholly adoption: it is usually adaptation, informed by local knowledge. An innovator needs to understand when to assert and when to defer, a point to which we will return. The unifying concept here is 'finding common ground' (Law, 1986): looking for overlap between what people can identify as worthwhile and what is being proposed by others. Adaptation increases this area of overlap. The requirement is that people recognise and acknowledge their own concerns. The strategy is to develop ideas which, although they may be challenging and novel, can also be seen as solutions.

PROGRAMME IDEA	Its clarity	Understanding is . . . VAGUE ├─┼─┼─┤ EXPLICIT
	Its common ground	Overlap with concerns is . . . LOW ├─┼─┼─┤ HIGH
	Its likely impact	That the idea actually works is . . . ASSUMED ├─┼─┼─┤ DEMONSTRATED

Figure 17.2   A framework for examining the viability of a programme idea

Making it clear

In implementing change, what people most need is repeatedly found to be the opportunity to make the innovation explicit to themselves and to work on it in their own situation (Fullan and Pomfret, 1977). A framework for examining the viability of a programme idea is set out in Figure 17.2. The implication here is that putting forward a vague idea, about action which is of no particular concern to anybody, and for which no case has been made concerning its likely effectiveness, is not likely to be effective.

17.4 MANAGING THE PROGRAMME

Management roles are deeply entangled in questions of influence, authority, communication, priorities and conflict. Managers are said 'to make strategic choices regarding the speed of the effort, the amount of preplanning, the involvement of others, the relative emphasis they will give to different approaches there may be to change' (Kotter and Schlesinger, 1979, p. 100); possible strategies include:

1 *Education–communication*, which persuades people.
2 *Participation–involvement*, which increases commitment.
3 *Facilitation–support*, which deals with adjustment problems.
4 *Negotiation–agreement*, which offers compensation for the cost of change.
5 *Manipulation–co-option*, which selectively uses information and consciously structures events.
6 *Explicit–implicit coercion*, which requires compliance.

Managers are said to have preferred styles (Ball, 1990):

1 *Interpersonal* styles, relying on face-to-face contacts.
2 *Managerial* styles, using the bureaucratic machinery.
3 *Political–adversarial* styles, relishing conflict, acknowledging ideology, celebrating challenge.
4 *Political–authoritarian* styles, stifling argument in favour of dictate, so that opposition is avoided, disabled or ignored, and 'Mach' (-iavellian) scores are high.

Not all of these options are open to careers education and guidance managers. Fewer still will help to improve the position of a marginal programme currently relying on informal goodwill.

Middle management has distinctive contributions to make, including establishing high expectations, reviewing the programme, pacing development, maintaining an open climate, and acknowledging problems. An effective middle manager is said to be a good team leader, able to support and inspire, an enabler, a person open to and prepared for change, a successful deployer of resources, a cultivator of good atmosphere, and ambitious for his or her own people (Earley and Fletcher-Campbell, 1989).

Three key considerations for effective programme management are embedded in these characterisations. They are the management of:

1 *Authority* – where considerations of 'wisdom', 'clout' and 'personality' come into play.
2 *Finesse* – knowing when boldly to 'push' against resistance, and when cautiously to 'duck'.
3 *Communication* – knowing what to bring to the attention of whom.

Finding bases for authority

The minimum qualification for leadership is having one follower. A manager needs other people to have a reason for paying attention to what she or he says and does. Contemporary analyses of such power or influence have come to us from Weber (1922), through Etzioni (1961), to Handy (1976). The main elements have been analysed for programme management in careers education and guidance, as follows (Law, 1995):

1 *Positional* influence derives from a senior role, which people accept should – in some sense or other – be 'obeyed'.
2 *Exchange* influence negotiates with people on an 'if you will I will' basis, offering rewards or help as a basis for co-operation.

3 *Personal* influence attracts support on the basis of liking or respect for the person who proposes the idea.
4 *Consultative* influence understands and reflects upon people's concerns by shaping proposals for action to respond to them.
5 *Expert* influence knows and understands what is entailed in careers education and guidance and can develop a rational case for change.

This is a continuum. At one end, positional power and resource power bring about change by means of leverage in the system – colloquially known as 'clout'. At the other end, expert and consultative influence bring about change by knowing what is going on, and knowing what to do about it – in a word, 'wisdom'. No manager can inexhaustibly draw on all parts of the range. Some specialise in clout rather than wisdom. Fortunately, for the lowly careers programme manager, wisdom can be successfully exercised without much clout. Some of the management strategies, styles and preferences cited above rely on such wisdom, which understands the organisation, its people, their needs and concerns, and how careers education and guidance can be a solution to some of these problems. This might not move the careers programme from bottom-right to top-left (in Figure 17.1) at a stroke, but it can often break inertia.

There are two dimensions, not one, in the analysis. Some authority can be exercised at a distance: wisdom and clout can be displayed without actually meeting anybody. In Figure 17.3, these are at the extremes. The middle part of the continuum, however, usually requires personal contact.

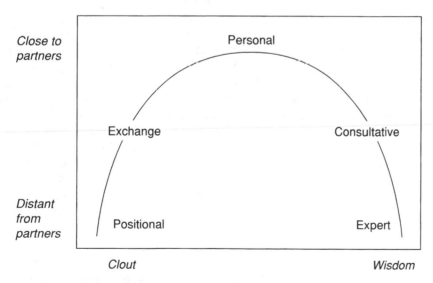

Figure 17.3 Authority relations

Much useful change is negotiated here, between people who find it easy to talk to each other, can understand each other, trust each other, and can recognise meaning in 'presence' as well as in 'words'. The implication of the analysis is that a not-very-powerful programme manager can set things moving with some combination of wisdom and personality – by consulting, understanding and 'finding a friend'.

Using finesse

All programmes engender both support and resistance. Resistance has been said to stem from parochial self-interest, a misunderstanding of what is being proposed, a lack of trust in the idea or in the person proposing it, a different assessment of the need for change, or a low personal tolerance for change (Kotter and Schlesinger, 1979). Resistance to overload, fear of the unknown, anxiety about the untried, doubt about the value of the work, and resentment of threatened autonomy, may also feature (Fullan, 1991). Much of this has to do with *doubt* about the validity of the proposal and *fear* of its consequences. Resistance is a natural and useful response to doubt and fear. People may be obstructing a proposal which *should* be obstructed. No manager should ignore such reactions. The manager might be wrong.

We are speaking here of authority relations, requiring 'finesse'. Finesse knows when, and when not, to propose, to argue and to require action. Not doing these things offers other people room to work out their own positions and reactions. The problem is that this may or may not be useful. Management 'finesse' is, then, not the avoidance of conflict: it is knowing when to take it on and when to wait (Law, 1986).

Some situations require bold action, in a short time, with rigorous standards and controls, cajoling reluctant people. Other situations can be managed more cautiously, with people ready, who have self-selected themselves, drawing on available energy, in what will seem a natural and easy development, perhaps pursued on no more than a pilot basis. Finesse takes measured action on this continuum.

Any part of it can be effective. In careers education and guidance as much as in any programme, people must be free to develop their own approach. Yet on occasions such workers are found to value '"harder", "more searching", "deeper", "more critical" comments – with "a bit more bite"!' (Elliott *et al.*, 1981). People reporting their attempts to help such workers refer to the dilemma between 'the passive reaction' and 'being a more interventionist chaser' (Davies, 1981).

There may be habitual preferences here. Different guidance workers have, themselves, been found to be spread out on this factor. At one end, they are interventionists: active in exchanges, seeking decisive results through access to administrative machinery, using control of information, accepting risk of conflict, pursuing behaviour modification. At the other, they are prepared to wait, will maintain silence rather than risk conflict, avoid the use of administrative machinery, and look for long-term personal growth in others rather than short-term behavioural change (Law, 1979).

But neither habitual boldness nor habitual caution will serve. Finesse needs access to both ends of the spectrum. To be too bold might be to expose the unready to too much change too soon, risking backlash, and – most seriously – denying the legitimate authority of others. There is a particular risk in the ill-considered pursuit of 'quick-fix faddism' (Fullan and Hargreaves, 1992). Early caution can lay the foundations for later boldness. But to be too cautious may be to postpone too much, and to miss opportunities. A particular risk is waiting too long for what the organisation needs now (Burgoyne, 1988).

Figure 17.4 suggests a way of mapping an approach to a specific change in a careers programme. A skilful manager might be able to move anywhere in the chart. But a specific action in a particular organisation will require one of these styles more than the others. The analysis also draws upon Handy's (1976) characterisation of organisational cultures. Whatever action is taken might gather support from the culture. But it might also establish the beginning of a new sub-culture.

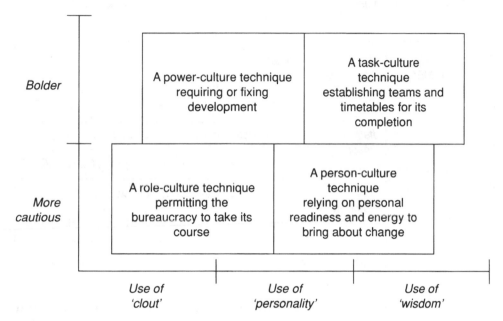

Figure 17.4   Approaches to managing change

Communication

All authority and intervention ultimately depend upon communication. This is an organisational as well as an interpersonal process. Programme managers need to know what to say, and what not to say, to whom. Change is said to be success-fully brought about, not by saying everything to everybody, but by altering the content of communication so that it contains what specific people need to hear. The communicators are not inconsistent: they are just careful about what they say to whom (MacDonald and Walker, 1976).

Certainly, programme managers engage in more than one kind of communi-cation. The variety of messages has been characterised as (Law, 1995):

1 *Informing* on the 'what?', 'where?', 'how?', 'when?', 'who?' and 'why?' of the action.
2 *Canvassing* how the proposed action is being received – listening as well as talking.
3 *Enquiring* about the current situation – a common hazard for innovation in complex organisations is that the change will interfere with what is already happening.
4 *Inviting action* by new people – asking or directing people to do something different or differently.

5 *Reflecting* people's disclosure of their experience of the action – a *post hoc* form of canvassing.
6 *Helping* with personal and material resources – for example, materials training and acknowledgement.

This suggests a difficulty for managers who rigidly stick to one approach. Figure 17.5 frames the choices.

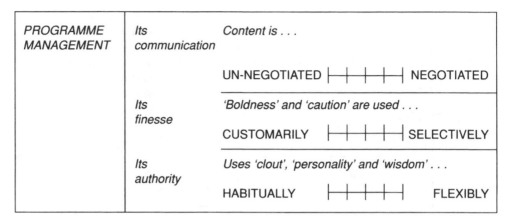

Figure 17.5 A framework for examining approaches to programme management

Knowing what to communicate to whom, on the basis of what authority, and with what finesse, is a matter of management skill. It is at least as important to middle managers as to senior managers; more critical to people managing marginal programmes than to those in primary production; and therefore, often, more necessary to careers education and guidance than to much other work.

17.5 WORKING WITH STAKEHOLDERS

Setting the programme in an organisation means taking account of other people's interests. There are three broadly distinguishable groups:

1 *Providers*: people who are expected to do the careers work. These may be 'staff', such as line managers in a business organisation. But they may be more distant partners, such as work-experience contacts in a school careers programme.
2 *Beneficiaries*: people who are expected to gain from the work. These are the students, customers or workers for whose direct benefit the provision is made. There are also more distant beneficiaries, such as direct beneficiaries' family and future employers.
3 *Audiences*: people who have an interest but are not directly involved in the action. These include colleagues and people not yet involved in the work; they also include senior management. More distantly, they include members of society-at-large and their representatives – for example, in the media and among policy-makers. In outreach work, this group includes people who are not members or clients of any formal work-related organisation, and whose needs for careers help may be more pressing than anyone else's.

Table 17.1   Stakeholders in careers programmes

	More proximate	More distant
Beneficiaries	Students, workers, customers	Family members, line managers, future employers
Providers	Advisers, mentors, teachers	Providers in other organisations, work-experience contacts
Audiences	Potential 'in-house' providers and beneficiaries, senior management	Other colleagues, external policy-makers, regulators and funders, potential 'outreach' providers and beneficiaries

All have a stake in the programme. A programme manager can identify the stakeholders along the lines suggested in Table 17.1.

There is a welter of concerns here. But the interests of some audiences are often overlooked. The views of potential providers and beneficiaries may be critical to programme development. The needs of potential outreach beneficiaries, often attended to by careers services, could be included in the programmes of other organisations.

Three issues for working with stakeholders can be posed. What do they need to be *able* to do? Do they *want* to do it? And are they in a *position* to do it?

Who can do what?

Both providers and beneficiaries need to know what they are being asked to do (Ruddock, 1991). They need the *capacity* to do something about it and to be able to *understand* the programme.

Attempted improvement fails, it is reported, because providers can make neither head nor tail of it, so that they do not know what they are supposed to do, or – significantly – why they are supposed to do it. They are unable to speak of the essential principles of an innovation, and they therefore try to implement new actions on the basis of habitual thinking. 'The most fundamental breakthrough occurs when people can cognitively understand the underlying conceptions and rationale with respect to "why this new way works better"' (Fullan, 1985, p. 396).

Beneficiaries who are helped to understand what they are going to do, and why, are then pursuing foreseeable gains, rather than merely engaging in something to be got-done-and-out-of-the-way. The programme's impact will be strengthened. Where they cannot see the point, their reaction can put the programme's survival at risk.

Providers who first become involved may have the required abilities. But as the work evolves, the ability of new 'recruits' becomes critical (Roberts and Law, 1985). Training and other forms of staff development have been found to be most effective where theory, operations, practice, feedback and coaching all contribute to a programmed series of events, over a period of time (Fullan and Pomfret, 1977; see also Chapter 16). A practical use of stakeholder analysis is to list the people significantly involved in a programme in order to review who needs to be able to understand what, and do what, and to receive what help.

Wanting to help

'Wanting' is a feeling. Plainly it is better to work with the people who 'feel good' about the proposal than to waste time banging one's head against unyielding doors, and – as a result – becoming a plaintive nuisance. Finding the people who can appreciate the value of the programme, and starting with them – perhaps at first informally – is characterised as 'following the energy' (Law, 1995).

But as the programme moves from informal commitment to formal assignment, change in people's attitudes may be sought. Providers sometimes change their attitudes in training; but that change does not invariably survive re-entry into the dominant culture of the surrounding organisation (Law, 1979). Hands-on involvement has been observed to calm fears and anxieties, so that positive attitudes can develop. A conclusion from the observation reverses what might have been expected: 'Changes in attitudes, beliefs and understandings tend to *follow* rather than *precede* changes in behaviour' (Fullan, 1985, p. 393).

Involvement not only in delivery but also in initiating, adapting, planning and operationalising a programme are commonly reported as significant for generating a positive attitude. It is a matter of 'ownership': not wanting to carry what is perceived as 'other people's baggage'. If providers, beneficiaries and other audiences feel no sympathy with a programme, which is perceived as being 'rammed down people's throats', then negative attitudes can turn to outright hostility. Not to take account of this is not only bad professional method: it is also bad organisational politics.

In a position to help

Capacity-to-help refers to understanding and skills. Wanting-to-help refers to attitudes and motivation. Being-in-a-position-to-help refers to a role in the organisation.

As Handy (1976) points out, some organisations are assembled bureaucratically around role. But all organisations identify roles, making explicit what is thought appropriate, setting relationships with other roles, providing resources, and by all these means giving a sense of what people feel in a position to do. A person who is to be involved in a careers programme will need to have some such sense. At a formal level it represents something that can be mentioned in a report or in a professional curriculum vitae. Resistance to involvement is not uncommonly based on a variation of 'I am simply not in a position to do this!' In a role culture, this can be decisively restrictive.

Acceptance of involvement is more likely where (1) the new behaviour is *expected* of a person's role, or (2) the role makes it *possible* for her or him to do it. But other people's expectations are not the only basis for this sense. There are also role *conceptions* – ideas which people develop for themselves about what they should do. Roles are therefore not just assigned by the organisation: they are achieved by role occupants. Guidance workers who are role achievers are found to have low 'system orientation' – a disposition not to assume that the current organisational system must be legitimated in every respect. The disposition correlates with inner-directedness as a person; with tolerance of internal conflict between elements in one's own role; and with preparedness to risk conflict with colleagues (Law, 1977; 1978a; 1978b; 1979). In a person culture, such role achievement is pervasive; in any organisation, it is an innovative, if informal, force.

Providers in particular need a sense of mandate, time, resources and position for the work. But not only they do so: beneficiaries can psychologically withdraw without that sense (Fullan, 1991); so can more distant stakeholders, who have no sense of attachment to the organisation (Law, 1986). The elements entailed in working with stakeholders are set out in Figure 17.6. The emphasis will work best where it is applied separately to each sub-group.

STAKEHOLDER INTERESTS	Their role	Stakeholder positions are . . . INAPPROPRIATE ├─┼─┼─┼─┤ APPROPRIATE
	Their willingness	Motivation and ownership is . . . FEEL BAD ├─┼─┼─┼─┤ FEEL GOOD
	Their ability	Ability to help is . . . UNDEVELOPED ├─┼─┼─┼─┤ DEVELOPED

Figure 17.6   A framework for examining approaches to working with stakeholders

Ability and motivation are personal characteristics. They are, in principle, transportable with the person to other work settings. Role is, however, a feature of an organisation. A person's leverage on the situation changes when he or she leaves or joins the organisation, or when a role is redefined. The implication of this is that developing understanding, skills and attitudes can be frustrating where a stakeholder is left in no position to do anything about it (see Chapter 16).

17.6 WORKING ON THE ORGANISATION

Working with the organisation is the broadest, most pervasive task in which the management of careers programmes is engaged. A good programme idea is 'nuclear', its management is 'atomic', dealing with stakeholders is 'molecular', but working with the organisation is 'molar'.

Yet achieving change is as responsive to the organisation as to any of the factors we have yet considered. In particular, change is more likely to occur in an open organisation which exchanges communication and influence with its environment, with other organisations, and – not least – within itself. The circulation of ideas and information catalyses change. As people understand what is happening 'out there' or 'over there' – economically, socially, politically or technologically – they will better understand the need for change (Hartley, 1995).

This section identifies two features of organisation important to developing careers work: whether communication and influence is open or contained; and in particular, whether there is access to decision-making.

Opening doors

There are good reasons for assuming that any organisation managed in an 'open' way will favour the development of careers education and guidance. Of its nature, careers education and guidance is a linking activity – joining learning to its use, education to training, training to work, individual to opportunity, past to present, and present to future. These are all inter-departmental and inter-organisational matters. Understanding that, and building programmes to support it, almost always requires new links to be made within and between organisations.

It has long been understood that an organisation which is responsive to external events will be innovative (Burns and Stalker, 1966). Following Durkheim (1972 edn), such analyses contrast 'organic' and 'mechanistic' systems. Organic systems are willing to respond to changing environmental conditions, to acknowledge the new and unforeseen, to use networks rather than hierarchy as structures for control, to use the interaction of people in redefining roles, and to consider other-than-contractual (i.e. informal) commitments as bases for action. A similarly derived analysis has been developed specifically for schools (Bernstein, 1971; 1973; see Chapter 5).

But openness can also be destabilising, evoking doubts and fears concerning change, and permitting the entry and cross-flow of what might prove arbitrary and transient influences. Some degree of closure does, and must, become embedded in any organisation.

Organisations are increasingly opened to external accountability, exposing providers to scrutiny and pressure (Nixon, 1992). The apparatus of accountability includes externally-generated quality standards, 'kitemarks', statements of entitlement, performance indicators, evaluation criteria, and attainment targets. It is mediated through appraisal procedures and policy guidelines. It is sanctioned by regulatory offices, contingent funding, and statutory instruments (Law, 1995). Much of this represents reform rather than innovation (Ruddock, 1991). It is a political reaction to what is perceived to be failed professionally-led provision – 'producer capture'.

However, innovation is qualitatively different from reform. Reform draws on the pessimistic assumptions about motives for work which are part of McGregor's (1960) 'theory X'. Such pessimism is not entirely ill-founded: people do resist the spotlight of unwanted scrutiny (Evans and Law, 1984). But innovation is part of the more optimistic 'theory Y'. In it, people may be disposed to acknowledge the importance of contact with a wider community (Fullan and Hargreaves, 1992).

Links and boundaries of organisations can be usefully mapped for management purposes. Figure 17.7 suggests, in simplified form, how this can be done, indicating with boundaries the organisations and departments, with connecting lines the links made for the purposes of careers programmes, and with circles the position of the decision-makers who shape and support the action. All organisations (e.g. 'A', 'B' and 'C') have all three features, but they are differently configured in each.

The most specialised careers education and guidance organisations – careers services – have always been relatively open organisations, their flat hierarchies and extensive networks well adapted to deal with the need to maintain links. They most resemble 'A' in the diagram. Schools are more bureaucratic, boundary

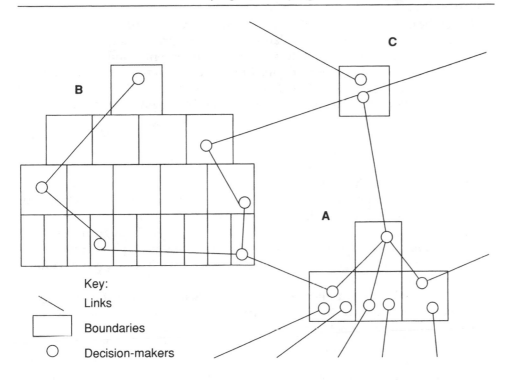

Figure 17.7 Mapping links and boundaries for organisations

railings and timetables symbolising closure, setting clear limits on what people are supposed to do. Organisations in education and business can be like this, most resembling 'B' in the diagram. Education-based partnerships, themselves relatively frail structures, must somehow negotiate with all of these elements of organisation (Law, 1986; King *et al.*, 1991). They resemble 'C' in the diagram. Such mapping can be elaborated: with enough detail, the map becomes a model, a way of understanding why certain things do and do not happen in a specific careers programme.

The future of careers education and guidance may depend, in considerable measure, upon what we do about accommodating it in organisational terms. The open organisation of careers services has been finely tuned to meet the needs of careers education and guidance delivery. That has been so because its product line has been focused, its institutional management and programme management have been highly symbiotic, and non-competitive organisations have been able to operate with relatively open climates. Other organisations – schools, colleges and corporations – have not usually been structured in this way; and their pursuit of careers education and guidance has required organisational adjustment. This chapter's assumptions – in this as in other respects – predict that such adjustments will continue. Whether such conditions can long survive in the newly privatised careers services, committed to the commercial pursuit of a diversified product line (see Chapters 9 and 21), remains to be seen.

The implications here are vast. They include the proposition that in order to develop careers education and guidance in a bureaucratic organisation, it may be necessary first to help people to see across departmental and organisational boundaries, because that is where much of the understanding of the need for careers-related change will be found. This is, of course, a tall order for a lowly manager in a multinational corporation. It is not easy, either, for a classroom teacher in a medium-sized school.

Accessing decision-making

Institutional decision-making is made distant by bureaucracy and proximate by networking. Bureaucracy closes around a small number of high-level decision-makers, whom others cannot influence or even know about. That is safe, but slow: characterised by Handy (1976) as a 'role' culture. Through networking, decision-making is opened to a perpetual state of review in all parts of the organisation. That is fast, but precarious: Handy characterises it as a 'person' culture. Most organisations combine elements of both.

It is commonly argued that senior decision-making support would guarantee the development of the careers programme. It certainly would do so in a 'power' culture; it probably would do so in a bureaucracy, such as a 'role' culture; it might do so where the bureaucracy is modified by networking into a 'task' culture; but it may have no effect whatever in a 'person' culture, which offers minimum bureaucratic control to almost entirely networked procedures.

Table 17.2 Possible contrasts between institutional and programme management

	Institutional management	Programme management
Framing image, policy and philosophy	Canvassing ideas and setting the frame	Influencing policy and maintaining the programme's relationship with it
External and internal communication	Promoting the organisation for survival, expansion, and impact	Offering services, canvassing resources, consulting reactions
Allocating human resources	Establishing a 'hiring-and-firing' policy	Setting expectations, co-ordinating roles
Staff development	Mandating a framework and allocating budgets	Identifying needs, providing and co-ordinating support
Allocating physical resources	Winning investment and allocating budgets	Seeking allocations, deciding on spending
Programme development and delivery	Monitoring	Designing, developing, pacing, co-ordinating, communicating
Evaluation	General measurement – largely for summative purposes	Specific enquiry – in part for formative purpose

Furthermore, decision-making at different levels in any organisation is focused in different ways. Table 17.2 suggests contrasts between institutional and programme-management decision-making in relation to careers education and guidance. Plainly, active support on the left of the table will help. But even here, senior management is vulnerable and overloaded (Fullan, 1991). Indeed, inept senior managers can actually hinder change (Nicholls, 1985). Overloaded senior managers with organisation-wide responsibilities are net consumers, rather than producers, of programme solutions. Neither pressure from, nor pressure on, senior managers guarantees anything – at best, they make things more probable.

We need a more subtle formulation. Symbiosis is achieved where the senior manager needs meetings with the programme manager because the programme manager is offering solutions. This is not pressure: it is access. In Figure 17.7 it would involve more circles close to programme delivery, connected to circles at institutional-management level.

Programme management's interest in climate is threefold:

1 To assess the level of appreciation of the need to do this work.
2 To locate departments within the organisation that are sufficiently open to offer needed support and co-operation.
3 To use the careers programme as part of the organisation's movement from closure to openness.

The key concept for openness in organisations is access. In Figure 17.8, it is found on the right. Analyses based on this figure can usefully be made on a department-by-department basis.

ORGANISA-TIONAL CLIMATE	Its decision-making	Decision-making is . . . INACCESSIBLE ├─┼─┼─┤ ACCESSIBLE
	Its internal boundaries	Inter-departmental exchange is . . . RARE ├─┼─┼─┤ COMMON
	Its external boundary	Understanding of and exchange with environment is . . . UNUSUAL ├─┼─┼─┤ FREQUENT

Figure 17.8 A framework for examining organisational climates

All organisations have some features of both network and bureaucracy. All need both. A healthy organisation needs to be able both to stand and to move. Increasing pressure for full-scale change increases the temperature but, as so many of the accountability measures outlined earlier have already done, may also erode the voluntary spirit upon which sustainable leading-edge developments often depend.

PROGRAMME IDEA	Its clarity	Understanding is . . . VAGUE ├──┼──┼──┤ EXPLICIT
	Its common ground	Overlap with concerns is . . . LOW ├──┼──┼──┤ HIGH
	Its likely impact	That the idea actually works is . . . ASSUMED ├──┼──┼──┤ DEMONSTRATED
PROGRAMME MANAGEMENT	Its communication	Content is . . . UN-NEGOTIATED ├──┼──┼──┤ NEGOTIATED
	Its finesse	'Boldness' and 'caution' are used . . . CUSTOMARILY ├──┼──┼──┤ SELECTIVELY
	Its authority	Uses 'clout', 'personality' and 'wisdom' . . . HABITUALLY ├──┼──┼──┤ FLEXIBLY
STAKEHOLDER INTERESTS	Their role	Stakeholder positions are . . . INAPPROPRIATE ├──┼──┼──┤ APPROPRIATE
	Their willingness	Motivation and ownership is . . . FEEL BAD ├──┼──┼──┤ FEEL GOOD
	Their ability	Ability to help is . . . UNDEVELOPED ├──┼──┼──┤ DEVELOPED
ORGANISA-TIONAL CLIMATE	Its decision-making	Decision-making is . . . INACCESSIBLE ├──┼──┼──┤ ACCESSIBLE
	Its internal boundaries	Inter-departmental exchange is . . . RARE ├──┼──┼──┤ COMMON
	Its external boundary	Understanding of and exchange with environment is . . . UNUSUAL ├──┼──┼──┤ FREQUENT

Figure 17.9 Four tasks for working with the organisation

17.7 CONCLUSION

There is a better way. It relies upon addressing four sets of tasks – but not all at once! The tasks range in scope from the 'nuclear' to the 'molar'. Work on any task will eventually depend on the others. But there is no particular place to start.

The conditions identified by the four sets of diagnoses presented earlier (repeated in Figure 17.9) will rarely be perfect – with high levels of readiness plotted to the right of each scale. Development must usually be accomplished in 'less than perfect' conditions. But to try to push a bold development against a 'mass of unreadiness' – all plotting to the left – will be hard, probably fruitless, and possibly counterproductive.

More carefully targeted finesse might achieve more. This chapter argues that there is never only one thing that can be done to improve the chances of success – but that there is usually one thing that can be done now! Programme management is characterised here in terms of its 'feel for the process'. The model supports flexible, adaptive action willing to slow down as well as speed up; to try again but in another way; and, in all of this, understanding why the shortest distance between two points is not necessarily a straight line.

All of the elements in the models used here can help or hinder the impact of the programme, and its chances of survival. Without survival, development is transient; without impact, it is futile.

REFERENCES

Ball, S. J. (1990) *The Micropolitics of the School: Towards a Theory of School Organisation*, London: Routledge.

Bernstein, B. B. (1971) 'Open Schools, Open Society', in Cosin, B. R., Dale, I. R., Esland, G. M. and Swift, D. F. (eds) *Schools and Society*, London: Open University/Routledge & Kegan Paul.

Bernstein, B. B. (1973) 'On the Classification and Framing of Educational Knowledge', in Brown, K. (ed.) *Knowledge, Education and Cultural Change*, London: Tavistock.

Burgoyne, J. (1988) 'Management Development for the Individual and the Organisation', *Personnel Management*, June, 40–43.

Burns, T. and Stalker, G. H. (1966) *The Management of Innovation*, London: Tavistock.

Davies, J. P. (1981) *The SITE Project in Northampton 1978–80*, Northampton: Nene College.

Durkheim, E. (1972 edn) *Selected Writings* (ed. Anthony Giddens), Cambridge: Cambridge University Press.

Earley, P. and Fletcher-Campbell, F. (1989) *The Time to Manage*, London: NFER–Nelson.

Elliott, J. *et al.* (1981) *Cambridge Accountability Project: a Summary Report*, London: Social Science Research Council.

Evans, K. and Law, B. (1984) *Careers Guidance Integration Project: Final Report*, Hertford: National Institute for Careers Education and Counselling (mimeo).

Etzioni, A. (1961) *A Comparative Analysis of Complex Organisations*, London: Macmillan.

Fullan, M. (1985) 'Change Processes and Strategies at the Local Level', *Elementary School Journal* 85(3): 391–421.

Fullan, M. (1991) *The New Meaning of Educational Change*, London: Cassell.

Fullan, M. and Hargreaves, A. (1992) *What's Worth Fighting for in Your School?: Working for Improvement*, Milton Keynes: Open University Press.

Fullan, M. and Pomfret, A. (1977) 'Research on Curriculum Instruction Implementation', *Review of Educational Research* 47(1): 335–97.

Handy, C. (1976) *Understanding Organisations*, Harmondsworth: Penguin.

Handy, C. (1984) *Taken for Granted?: Understanding Schools as Organisations*, London: Longman/Schools Council.

Harrison, R. (1972) 'Understanding Your Organization's Character', *Harvard Business Review* 50(3): 119–28.

Hartley, J. (1995) 'Organisational Change', in Warr, P. (ed.) *Psychology at Work*, Harmondsworth: Penguin.

King, B., Lea, C. and Moroney, G. (1991) *The Partnership Handbook*, Sheffield: Department of Employment.

Kotter, J. and Schlesinger, L. A. (1979) 'Choosing Strategies for Change', *Harvard Business Review* 57: 100–12.

Law, B. (1977) 'System Orientation: a Dilemma for the Role Conceptualisation of "Counsellors" in Schools', *British Journal of Guidance and Counselling* 5(2): 129–48.

Law, B. (1978a) 'Counselling and Teaching Identification', *British Journal of Guidance and Counselling* 6(1): 59–74.

Law, B. (1978b) 'The Concomitants of System Orientation in Secondary School Counsellors', *British Journal of Guidance and Counselling* 6(2): 161–74.

Law, B. (1979) 'The Contexts of System Orientation in Secondary-School Counselling', *British Journal of Guidance and Counselling* 7(2): 199–211.

Law, B. (1986) *The Pre-Vocational Franchise*, London: Paul Chapman.

Law, B. (1995) *Key Concepts for Careers Work*, Manchester: Open College.

MacDonald, B. and Walker, R. (1976) *Changing the Curriculum*, London: Open Books.

McGregor, D. (1960) *The Human Side of the Enterprise*, New York: McGraw-Hill.

Musgrove, F. and Taylor, P. H. (1969) *Society and the Teacher's Role*, London: Routledge & Kegan Paul.

Nicholls, A. (1985) *Managing Educational Innovations*, London: Allen & Unwin.

Nixon, J. (1992) *Evaluating the Whole Curriculum*, Milton Keynes: Open University Press.

Roberts, C. and Law, B. (1985) *No Certain Place to Go*, Hertford: National Institute for Careers Education and Counselling (mimeo).

Ruddock, J. (1991) *Innovation and Change*, Milton Keynes: Open University Press.

Weber, M. (1922) 'Three Types of Legitimate Rule', *Preussische Jahrbuecher*, 187; reprinted in Etzioni, A. (ed.) (1970) *A Sociological Reader on Complex Organisations* (2nd edn), London: Holt, Rinehart & Winston.

Chapter 18

Evaluation

John Killeen

18.1 INTRODUCTION

Evaluation is often thought to be the process by which we form judgements about the value of things like guidance. Considered in this way, it is easy enough to identify examples of 'pseudo-evaluation' (Suchman, 1972): the 'eyewash' of favourable but superficial description, and the 'whitewash' which obscures faults; the empty ritual, means of postponing decisions, or way of justifying decisions that have already been taken. Evaluation is tangled up in the macro-politics of national resource allocation and the micro-politics of organisational preferment. For this reason it may be done in outright bad faith, although the reality may more often be that the evaluator is led to bias the outcome without being fully conscious of what is happening. Here, we are concerned with the attempt to do it in good faith and the techniques we can use to minimise the possibility of self-deceit. We shall first consider the scope of evaluation, before looking at the way in which process and outcome evaluation respectively are done and the methodological difficulties they encounter. We shall then go on briefly to consider the connection of evaluation to the task of quality assurance in guidance, and conclude by considering the ways in which practitioners can use it.

18.2 THE SCOPE OF EVALUATION

Controversy

Evaluation is controversial in its purpose, the power relationships it manifests, and the manner in which it should be conducted. Two contrasting views of evaluation illustrate the way in which opinions can become polarised. Cook *et al.* (1977) assume that the purpose of evaluation is either to 'provide a program director ... with ways to improve a program or its management' (p. 104), in which case the accent may be upon speed rather than scientific propriety; or to assess the impact of a programme on behalf of those who are paying for it, in which case external researchers, with a greater concern for scientific validity, are likely to collect data 'within a planned experimental framework' in order to determine whether it serves the purpose for which it was instituted. The first element of Cook *et al.*'s description refers to a 'managerialist' variant of what is often called *formative* evaluation; the second part of what is called *summative* evaluation. As part of this general overview, we can also identify *evaluability assessment* (Wholey, 1977), which is intended to show that a programme is functioning, that it is not so puny as to make it incredible that it should have a worthwhile impact, and that we can clearly define its objectives and other possible effects, to the point at which they can be 'operationalised' (observed and measured) for the purpose of summative evaluation. From this perspective, the aims of formative evaluation can come to include helping those responsible for a programme to develop it in a way which ensures a positive evaluability assessment, and to identify the range of effects which it would be sensible to consider at the summative stage (Rutman, 1977).

This conception approximates to what Guba and Lincoln (1989) call 'third-generation' evaluation: a 'top-down', judgemental approach, with a strong emphasis on techniques for making valid judgements. Evaluation is often an exercise of power: the same power that can cancel a project, send in inspectors, close a school, tell guidance practitioners or teachers how they should do their jobs, and punish them when they do not do as they are told. It dramatises the limits both of professional discretion and of job security. When this is so, an obvious strategy is that of 'low-trust' evaluation: the external expert and the minutely detailed scepticism of the experimental method.

Compare the passionate defence of the University of East Anglia style of educational evaluation made by a leading member of that school (Elliot, 1990). It should 'realise educational values', with the purpose of fostering worthwhile educational change. As these attempts are always dependent for their success on sensitivity to context, it should be grounded in the qualitative study of particular cases. Educational values are contested, and researchers should guard against biases and interpretations which arise from the unconscious imposition of their own values. Teachers and students are participants in, not merely subjects of, research; in consequence, even if change is led by policy-makers, evaluation – to be successful – should be democratic. This is a radical variant of the sort of thinking Guba and Lincoln (1989) associate with 'fourth-generation' evaluation, in which the concerns of all 'stakeholders' serve as the basis for determining what information is needed, and evaluation is regarded as a form of negotiation between stakeholders, rather than a 'top-down' judgemental process. But even those instinctively drawn to the latter can find something in such an approach, because low-trust evaluation tends also to be high-threat evaluation. If those under evaluation are to give their detailed knowledge of working realities, their invention and their enthusiasm to improving practice, and hence to the evaluation process, surely they must act out of something more than fear?

The dispute over 'science'

Those with a science orientation are likely to conduct evaluation in a way which is as transparent and replicable as possible. They aim to squeeze out subjective interpretation, and to conduct their studies in such a way that anyone trained in the techniques they have employed would, they believe, obtain the same results.

Others view the 'scientific' approach as ponderously slow, as too wedded to what can be quantified, and as producing results which lack generalisability, even when this is their only ostensible virtue. Some take this view because they see evaluation primarily as formative or developmental, and as a collaborative venture. Kemmis (1983) characterises 'action research' in much the same terms as Elliot's (1990) description of educational evaluation: as 'emancipatory' and involving a 'spiral of self-reflection'. Others, however, reach the same conclusions through a more pragmatic route, believing that the only satisfactory way in which to come to conclusions is to take a more open approach: often one that rests upon the acuteness of observation and the gifts of interpretation of particular individuals, and in which transparency and replicability take a back-seat.

Diversity of stakeholders and purposes

Another way of putting this is to say that evaluation is extraordinarily diverse, and that this diversity is to some extent, but not inevitably, associated with the diversity of interests of the stakeholders. Even if we consider evaluation as *making judgements* (Cook *et al.*, 1977), we quickly find that these are not inevitably 'top-down'. When we make judgements of 'worth' or 'value', we may indeed be trying to determine whether the activity under evaluation is worth doing, and this may boil down to asking if or how much it fulfils the objectives for which it has been instituted, in order to decide whether it should be continued. But more generally, we measure, or attach a value to, guidance in terms of the criteria we adopt for the decisions we make about it. These are the things we take into account when we decide to offer, or not to offer, guidance, and to spend more or less money on it; but they are also the things we use to decide to use it or not to use it, to do it this way or that way, to say that it is or is not of acceptable quality, to say that it has or has not improved, and so on. In this sense, almost everyone involved in the guidance process may be said to 'evaluate' it.

When we characterise the stakeholders who may wish to make judgements, the reasons they typically have for making these judgements, and thus the purposes they might impose upon evaluation, we commonly distinguish:

1 *Sponsors*, who require guidance evaluation to be conducted, either by specialist evaluators or by guidance agencies themselves, for the purpose of accountability, sometimes in the (rather optimistic) belief that 'cost-benefit' calculations can be performed, but often more simply to ensure that implementation is occurring satisfactorily.
2 *Guidance managers and agencies* (including schools etc.), which conduct evaluation in order to monitor implementation of existing activities, or improve the effectiveness with which they operate.
3 *Practitioners*, who perform evaluation in order to improve their own competence, assess new techniques, or simply monitor their own activities.

Conventionally, we have paid little attention to:

4 *Clients or consumers*, whose judgements are often sought and collated in the process of evaluation, but who are less often regarded as people who might require evaluation to be conducted in order to inform their own decisions about it.

If we add the latter, we can say, despite the unfortunate associations of the term, that evaluation can play a role in *marketing* guidance.

It is also important to note that a large number of studies are conducted, mostly in the United States, and mostly by counselling psychologists, which consider guidance outcomes at least as much in a spirit of scholarly enquiry as from any of the perspectives outlined above. Thus, for example, the robust evidence we currently have of the learning outcomes of guidance (see Chapter 4) arises almost exclusively from such scholarly activity. When studies of this kind are conducted, the questions posed are, in descending order of frequency: first, does a newly-developed intervention have at least some effects consistent with its objectives? Second, how do competing techniques compare, in relation to outcomes which appear to be a 'fair test' of their relative effectiveness? And third, does a particular intervention produce different effects, or different scales of effect, among clients of differing types? (For reviews, see Myers, 1971; Oliver and Spokane, 1988; Killeen and Kidd, 1991). These studies tend to be superior, in a technical sense, to studies carried out by, for example, policy-directed programme evaluators, where little more than lip-service is sometimes paid to the methodological concerns which *should*, but repeatedly *do not*, govern the way in which programme evaluation is conducted. It is to consideration of these concerns that we turn in the next three sections. We will adopt a distinction between process and outcome evaluation, recognising as we do so that real projects usually include at least a little of both.

18.3 PROCESS EVALUATION

Most evaluation reports contain some sort of description of the processes under evaluation. But quite often, evaluation is confined to consideration of these processes. From the standpoint of 'evaluability assessment', the purpose is, as already indicated, to answer the question: 'Is it worth attempting summative evaluation?' But as should already be clear, the scope of process evaluation is much wider than this. We can distinguish seven forms.

The first is *quantitative process description*, in which one asks 'how much?' or 'how often?' For example, King (1981) used the survey method to chart rising careers education provision in a sample of schools, and Ballantine and Strebler (1989) to examine the extent of implementation of information technology in the Careers Service.

The second is *qualitative process description*. This is better adapted to considering emerging systems, relationships and forms of organisation. Samples are usually small (indeed, there may be only one system or organisation in view) and are intensively studied. The method asks 'What is happening?' and is often a necessary precursor to quantitative approaches. Comparison frequently plays a role. Knasel *et al.* (1982) used comparison to identify variations in organisation, working relationships, the roles of different guidance providers, and the perceived role of guidance, in provision for young people on government training programmes. Fleming and Lavercombe (1982) used a semi-structured interview method to examine practitioners' differing perceptions of their roles in relation to unemployed young people. Detailed analysis of tape-recorded guidance interviews has been used to describe variations in guidance style (Hughes and May, 1985). From a critical perspective, qualitative methods have been used to identify the ways in which teachers use guidance to align young people's perceptions of options with their own perceptions of young people's abilities, or to meet option recruitment targets (Woods, 1979; Shilling, 1986).

The third is *provider quality-of-process perceptions*. Often, participants are regarded as having privileged insight into the quality of processes, and into the factors which contribute to or undermine it. Ballantine and Strebler (1989) gathered this sort of data, reporting the view of principal careers officers that lack of training and technical support was hindering the successful implementation of information technology. Innes (1985) reported a study in which teachers in a single school reflected upon some of the weaknesses of the organisation and provision of guidance and the reasons they perceived for these weaknesses.

The fourth is *client reaction to process*. The supposition is that, under many circumstances, the 'quality' of a process depends as much upon how it is perceived and interpreted by clients, as upon what practitioners do. Client reactions to process were included, for example, in an evaluation of the use of repertory-grid techniques in guidance (Edmonds, 1979). They have also been included in studies of the expectations young people have or their perceptions of, and their feelings during, guidance. Early studies of this sort claimed that young people expected to be given information about specific job opportunities, rather than the guidance they actually received (Jahoda and Chalmers, 1963; Carter, 1966). The fifth is *process assessment based on mastery*. This includes the conventional methods of inspection adopted for schools and the Careers Service, but it is often also included in evaluation projects. Published examples include the assessment of the technical qualities and user interfaces of competing computer-aided guidance systems made by NCET (1988).

The sixth is *process assessment based on analysis*. The dividing line between this and other forms of assessment is easier to draw in principle than in practice. The essential point is that either criteria are predefined in a way that makes them 'inexpertly' observable, or they are developed in the course of process evaluation on the basis of both internal and ancillary evidence. This is evident in the study by Knasel *et al.* (1982), and also in a study by Kushner and Logan (1985) which argued that imbalances of power, conflicting priorities and dissent observable in the relationships between schools and careers services made it unlikely that the latter would achieve the more central role in schools that was implied by programmes for closer integration.

The seventh is *dynamic process involvement*. This equates to some interpretations of the term 'formative evaluation', in which evaluation plays a role in forming or shaping the processes to which it is applied, and in which the relationship between the evaluator and those responsible for these processes is likely to be an intimate and 'facilitative' one. It is based at least as much on the traditions of organisational development, as on expertise in guidance or in evaluation *per se* (Kemmis, 1983; Stronach, 1986).

When new ventures are undertaken, these are the first, and may for some time be the only, forms of evaluation. When we are confident about effectiveness, they may be thought the only forms of evaluation that need to be performed.

18.4 OUTCOME EVALUATION

Since, however, guidance is an instrumental activity, this implies that we can only know its worth through its effects. It is 'as good as its effects'. This seems to favour the process of summative judgement described by Cook *et al.* (1977) (see Section 18.2 above). But a distinction has so often been drawn between the lack of scientific or experimental propriety commonly employed in formative evaluation, and the rigour with which effects should be demonstrated in summative evaluation, that an entirely false conception has arisen that non-experimental evaluation cannot play a role in the latter. This seems, in turn, to preclude practitioner evaluation for the purpose of demonstrating effectiveness, since experimentation as commonly understood is likely to conflict with or hinder them in their primary purpose. Yet most evaluation with a 'summative' purpose is *not* experimental in character. Six forms of outcome evaluation can be identified.

The first is *outcome identification*. A distinction can be made between the *manifest* effects of guidance (the effects it is expected to have and which generally correspond to its objectives), and its *latent* effects (the unanticipated and unintended effects it has, both positive and negative). A programme may achieve its stated objectives, but defeat those of another policy, or have unanticipated 'side-effects' which seriously undermine its value. Equally, a programme which fails to achieve its stated objectives may inadvertently confer benefits which justify its continuation. For example, in the 1980s it came to be recognised that employment and training measures for young people had beneficial effects upon their psychological health or 'well-being' (e.g. Stafford, 1982; Banks and Jackson, 1982). One of the ways in which providers seek their own survival is by persuading their sponsors to allow 'goal substitution', and the discovery of latent benefits is one means to this end: the unintended outcome becomes the intended one (although at national level, the Treasury tends to resist attempts by one ministry [e.g. employment] to justify its programmes according to the responsibilities of another [e.g. health]). Thus an important part of the task of evaluating guidance may be to identify its effects. Experimentation is not suitable for this purpose: *exploratory* methods of research, often relying on the perceptions of those involved, are required.

The second is *opinion surveys*. In their simplest form, opinion surveys ask people merely to rate the 'usefulness' of guidance, or their 'satisfaction' with it, on the assumption that if the results are positive, it must have had beneficial effects. This is so often done that one may assert with some confidence that there is scarcely a form of guidance practice, a service or an initiative for which at least some data of this sort are not available (e.g. Pollock and Nicholson, 1981; Varlaam, 1984; Curragh and McGleenon, 1980; Gray, 1980; McCartney and Whyte, 1984; MORI, 1980; Closs *et al.*, 1985; NFER, 1987). The problem with general ratings of this type is that they do not tell us *what* guidance has accomplished. Also, satisfaction with outcomes may be conflated with satisfaction with processes. Again, the same guidance may be seen as more or less useful, or to have had a greater or larger effect, dependent upon *when* people are questioned. Helpfulness and satisfaction ratings tend to decline with the passage of time (e.g. West and Newton, 1983). As opinion surveys are often retrospective, and retrospective to differing degrees, this makes data difficult to interpret and compare. A related difficulty in making comparisons between, for example, the ratings given to formal careers education and guidance activities, and other sources of help such as family and friends (e.g. Gray, 1980; Cherry and Gear, 1987; Kirton, 1976), is that the latter forms of help are not merely more intensive but also more extensive through time. Studies which look at the relationship between stage of vocational development, what each source is used for, and utility ratings, ameliorate some of these problems (Kidd, 1984; Arnold *et al.*, 1988).

The third is *attributed-effect studies*. It is often not practicable to devise objective tests, or to define a small number of objective variables, which correspond to the criteria of judgement we wish to adopt. It is one thing to *name* an objective – for example, that students or clients should become more aware of the world of work – but quite another to *measure*, or obtain *demonstrations* of, increased awareness, particularly with the degree of sensitivity which is required. Not unnaturally, therefore, evaluators repeatedly rely upon the perceptions of those involved. For example, studies of enterprise education (Harris, 1989; Williamson, 1989) have been conducted in this way to show that teachers rated it a useful teaching tool and valuable teaching method, and that students believed they had become more aware of the world of work and had gained teamwork, interpersonal, and specific business skills. But are we really *aware* of the effects guidance has upon us?

The fourth is *process-outcome observation*. When people are exposed to guidance, certain obvious changes may result. They may, for example, come into possession of information that they have lacked, or they may demonstrate a change of mood – notably, increased optimism. Guidance practitioners repeatedly see these sorts of things happening, and the simplest kinds of evaluation merely formalise such observations so that they are freed from the accusation of over-optimistic or biased reporting. In schools and colleges, an obvious and potentially routine course of action is to 'evaluate' by monitoring and recording learning, or rather the knowledge and competencies thought to arise from learning (e.g. Careers Service Quality Assurance and Development Unit, 1995), but there are degrees to which the 'connection' between process and outcome is genuinely observed. Bedford (1982) devised an objective (behaviourally-anchored) method for an observer to record learning as it happened in the course of vocational guidance interviews, which disclosed gains in awareness, planning, focus, and realism. By working with behavioural data in 'real time', the intimacy of connection between process and outcome was maintained within a single observational field. Often, however, this essential condition cannot be met. The difficulties here are threefold: first, that the process, particularly in the case of careers education, may not occur 'in isolation' and over a short timescale; second, that the intended outcome may be more generalised than can be observed in this way; and third, that retention or persistence may be part of our conception of the intended outcome. This means that there is often a problem of validly recording or measuring processes and outcomes, and of establishing their connection to one another.

But there is a further difficulty, even if we can 'see' guidance 'working'. Intended changes *may* happen in some other way, if guidance is not available. Moreover, the things we can 'see' are only a sub-set of the objectives associated with guidance (see Chapter 4). In both respects, we find ourselves forced to consider the less obvious or less palpable effects of guidance. In the first, we need to consider not merely the changes made by guidance, but its 'additionality' – its capacity to make changes which would not have occurred in some other way, or to make them happen more rapidly than would otherwise have been the case. For example, after ten sessions of careers education, sixth-formers in four schools increased by 19 per cent their commitment to a preferred occupation and were able to identify a wider range of their own work values (Curragh and McGleenon, 1980): would they have done so in any event, over this length of time, at this stage in their lives? In the second, we need to consider 'additionality' against much more remote criteria (see Chapter 4) – often ones which are not likely to be observed by guidance practitioners unless they deliberately set out to observe them.

There are many 'threats' to conclusions about 'additionality'. One group of threats is to the internal validity of such conclusions: in other words, the contention that it was specifically *this* careers education and guidance which had *this* effect on *these* people in *this* time-period and in *this* place. People develop and change whether we will it or not *(maturation)*. Similarly, it may have been something else in the environment which brought the effect about *(history)*. Moreover, if we assume well-founded baseline data which tell us that, on average, young people in the cohort from which a careers education class was drawn did not make as much progress as those exposed to it, there remains the possibility that the careers education class group was made up of young people who would, in any event, show the most improvement *(sample selection)*.

We can simplify the problem of sample selection through two opposing general hypotheses: (1) that those people who suffer relative deficits pass through guidance; and (2) that people who are 'well-placed' or wise option-seekers and decision-makers use guidance. In the first case, positive outcomes (or gains) to guidance may be compatible with apparent losses, in comparison to individuals not exposed to guidance: this is because guidance may remedy *part* of the deficit, leaving its clients better off, but not as well-off as people who did not suffer the deficit to begin with. In the second case, guidance may benefit, in any comparison, from the superior *general* performance of those who use it.

The strategy used to minimise these and some other threats is the fifth form of outcome evaluation: the *random-assignment-controlled trial*. Here an experimental group given the 'treatment' is compared to a control group which is not. As random samples tend to be representative of the populations from which they are drawn, two random samples drawn from the same population tend to be similar, both as to their starting characteristics and as to their likely future maturation and history, at the moment they are drawn. Thus differences evolving thereafter can be attributed to the 'treatment'. But even this method is not free from threats. Most obviously, since the two samples only tend towards similarity, there is always a chance that they will differ significantly in some respect material to the outcome. Moreover, an unconsidered component of the 'total treatment difference in experience' between the samples, such as the personal qualities of the guidance practitioner, might be responsible for the effect we attribute to careers education and guidance. Similarly, the result might be produced by the experiment itself, perhaps by enhancing motivation. The longer the timescale between treatment and outcome (e.g. income effects), and the more widespread the availability of alternative treatments, the more likely it is that the control will break down, in the sense that control subjects will seek alternatives, thus deflating additionality estimates. And so the list of threats may be continued. Once identified, each of these threats gives rise to further strategies for the reduction of doubt, and hence for raising confidence in the internal validity of the conclusion.

Alongside the threats to internal validity noted above are threats to external validity. These are encountered when we try to generalise the results of such a trial. Doubt reduction here involves both setting limits on generalisation and using samples consistent with the degree of generalisation we intend. Most obviously, one might seek representative samples both of careers education and guidance and of the relevant group of individuals, and ways of measuring outcomes that are consistent with the generalisation. However, while the conclusion drawn may hold in the aggregate, this does not mean it is true under all circumstances. So one may also compare specific sub-samples or different kinds of sample across different studies, in order to determine the scope of generalisation in more detail.

Resistance to the principle of random assignment to 'no-treatment control groups' can sometimes lead to compromises which preserve randomisation, such as 'alternative treatment trials' and 'waiting-list trials' which do not deny help, or do not deny it permanently. These designs involve restrictions which can sometimes be tolerated. For example, some of the earliest UK attempts to evaluate psychometrically-based 'scientific guidance' were in fact alternative treatment trials, as the control samples continued to be given the conventional forms of help available from schools and the (then) Juvenile Employment Service (Earle, 1931; Allen and Smith, 1932; Hunt and Smith, 1944). This was acceptable because it was the 'additionality' of the new methods relative to the old which was in question, not their additionality to 'no guidance'.

It is often the case, however, that randomised trials are not possible or practicable. When this is so, the sixth form of outcome evaluation – *quasi-experiments* – may be conducted. The simplest form of quasi-experiment considers a single unit, be it a person or a 'pilot' area or organisation, which is monitored over a period long enough to establish the 'stability' or otherwise of the outcome variable before guidance occurs (pre-test). The guidance intervention is then made, or the guidance programme instituted, and the outcome variable is monitored for a further, preferably lengthy period (post-test). If a change follows directly after the guidance which is of a magnitude greater than previous or later fluctuations, or if the trajectory of change is decisively altered just once, directly after guidance, this is taken as evidence of a linkage. A search for 'counterfactual evidence', or evidence of other possible causes which might 'explain away' any apparent change attributable to guidance (maturation, history), can then be used to build confidence, but is of course limited to specific competing explanations. If the quasi-experiment is repeated on more than one occasion, and if the same pattern is found, confidence is further raised.

A possible additional step is to introduce *comparison*. Pilot areas in which guidance provision has been introduced may be compared with those in which it has not. In like fashion, samples of people exposed to guidance may be compared to those who have not, as in the more tightly specified conditions of controlled trials. Providing that pre- to post-test changes are compared, these designs may diminish one or more of the threats posed by maturation and history. For example, comparing a careers education class group to the rest of the school cohort from which it was drawn, or to a comparison sample also drawn from that cohort, reduces such threats. The care with which comparison samples are matched is of some importance (see Section 18.5). Often inadequate attention is paid to such matching. Thus Pearson (1988) compared the employment durations of unemployed professionals who had attended a 'bridging course' inclusive of guidance, to those of the general unemployed population at the time. Even more dubiously, West and Newton (1983) followed up school-leavers who had experienced contrasting forms of careers education – 'traditional' and 'developmental' – finding differences not merely in attitudes to careers education, but in decision-making, work adjustment, and reactions to transition. The study involved two schools: an ex-secondary modern lacking a sixth form, in which the 'developmental' careers curriculum was used; and an ex-grammar school located in a different sort of community. The problem should be obvious. The technique used here did not cope with the threats of sample selection, or with its interaction with maturation and history. Many ingenious devices can be used to diminish these sorts of threat, but none is conclusive, and quasi-experiments are generally regarded as the poor relations to random-assignment controlled trials.

18.5 PROBLEMS OF EXPERIMENTAL AND ASSOCIATED TECHNIQUES

In addition to the quite routine problem that random assignment is difficult to achieve, leading to the adoption of weaker methods, there are a number of additional difficulties to be considered.

One is the problem of *multiple goals*. Guidance has a range of goals. In the extreme case, the evaluator may assess outcomes which do not coincide with the goals actually pursued by practitioners. This has led (e.g. Oliver, 1979) to the advocacy of multiple outcome measurement. This is rational, but it does mean that for any particular outcome, effects become a little more difficult to demonstrate, as sample sizes must be raised to cope with variability of goals across treatments. It also raises the spectre of false positives, because as the number of outcomes tested increases, so does the probability that at least one of them will be 'significantly' related to guidance by chance.

A second is the problem of *'unique' clients*. It is an article of faith for most guidance practitioners that each client is a unique individual whose situation, starting-point and needs must be understood in order for guidance objectives to be negotiated and agreed. For some practitioners, this means that objectives set externally (e.g. by government) are not relevant. But from a technical point of view, it potentially amplifies the problem of multiple goals. Goals may become so numerous and idiosyncratic that either the precondition of clearly defined, measurable outcomes breaks down, or a very partial set of often inappropriate outcome indicators is applied. Results will be attenuated and effectiveness underestimated. It has accordingly been suggested that evaluation should be based upon clients' estimates of the degree to which aims negotiated at the outset of guidance are reached. In addition, of course, the types and situations of clients vary across guidance agencies in ways largely beyond the agencies' control. The danger is, therefore, that agencies or techniques may be judged against the nature of their clients, rather than against what they themselves do.

A third problem is *multiple methodologies*. Guidance techniques and their intensity vary. This is in part because there are legitimate differences about the way in which guidance should be done (see e.g. Chapter 11). There is always a consequent danger that guidance will be treated as a 'black box', and individuals simply classified as either exposed or not exposed to it. In strict experimental settings, everything possible is done to standardise treatments, or to vary them in a highly controlled and fully recorded way. This is less easy in the natural settings with which evaluation must deal, where it may be difficult to record the guidance to which individuals have been exposed. This is likely to attenuate results. If the question is simply 'Does guidance as it *now is* "work"?', then this does not matter. But if the question is 'Can guidance of a specified *quality* "work"?', then the problem is more acute.

A fourth problem is *client autonomy*. When we say that the outcomes of guidance are its 'effects', we do not mean that these are mechanically produced. Far from it: guidance 'works' only so far as it influences, and is used by, its clients, and incorporated in some way in what they do.

A fifth problem is *external determination of outcomes*. Many of the objectives of guidance, such as improved employment chances, are largely determined by factors outside its control, such as local economic conditions. Guidance is often a very modest contribution, when set against the other factors internal and external to the individual that are likely to be the main determinants of remote outcomes. This raises the spectre of false negatives. For example, guidance provision for adults has sometimes been introduced on a pilot area basis and assessed accordingly (e.g. Coopers & Lybrand, 1994). As such interventions are 'puny' relative to the other factors determining local employment, training and allied patterns, one would not expect their effects to be demonstrable with any degree of confidence. Thus evaluation of these sorts of effects at a pilot area level is not attempted, and studies of effects on individuals are substituted – though even at this level, the problem persists.

This gives rise to two further means of exerting control, which can be used in both experimental and non-experimental evaluation. The first is control by *selection*, either by 'matching pairs' prior to random assignment, or by other 'case control' procedures in which non-random comparison samples are designed which are explicitly similar to those who receive guidance. For example, Kent (1984) compared the effect of integrated and special-school education on the occupational decision-making of ESN children: pairs were matched on age, sex, IQ, parental occupational prestige and location of home. The second is control by *calculation*, when measured differences material to the outcome are 'allowed for' in an adjustment of the crude differences of outcome in those exposed and not exposed to guidance. This can be used in general population surveys in which data on exposure to guidance are gathered, but it can also be used to supplement explicit matching in comparison sample designs.

Each of these methods is as good as our existing knowledge of the alternative or competing causes of outcomes, since matching on irrelevant factors, or 'allowing for' irrelevant factors, does not change the result. Even when factors are relevant, they are usually an incomplete set, and may be measured with some degree of error. Thus when applied in quasi-experiments, surveys, and so on, these methods do not reveal the 'true' magnitude of the effects of guidance: they simply improve on the estimate which would be obtained in their absence, by providing a partial control for selection and its interactions with maturation and history.

A second group of problems, which apply even more widely, are those of quantification, which is inherent to the attempt to produce a 'final summing-up' of the value of guidance by the methods we have considered. Some important examples are:

1 The objective may be stated in terms which do not correspond to anything we can 'measure', in the sense in which the term 'measurement' is popularly understood. This can be because outcomes are too vaguely defined, or too subjective, or too 'qualitative', or are 'public goods' which are not exchanged on the market and therefore do not have a 'market price'. We may therefore be forced to use indicators which imperfectly relate to our objectives.

2 Outcomes may not be quantifiable on a common scale. Evaluators with a psychological background react to this problem by 'standardisation' (z-scoring), so that the average gain in a sample on each outcome can be expressed in terms of its deviation away from the preceding or control sample average, in units which describe the amount of variability, or deviation from the mean, that already existed. This makes it possible to 'count' in similar units. For example, Oliver and Spokane (1988) showed that over a large sample of studies, the mean 'effect size' of careers education and guidance interventions on career-related knowledge was 0.88 when calculated in this way, but on appropriateness or realism of choice it was 0.51. This is, however, only a solution to some of the technical problems of statistical analysis, and no sane psychologist would go on to claim that this created a common scale of *value*. Economists, on the other hand, go to extraordinary (and to their critics, dubious) lengths to assign monetary values to all outcomes (these imputed values are called 'shadow prices'). If everything is measured monetarily, it is by definition measured on a common scale of value. Economists then compare benefits expressed in this way to the *cost* of guidance, so that a monetary cost-benefit may be calculated (to the best of my knowledge, this has not been attempted for guidance).

3 We may be able to measure only 'fractionally' – i.e. we may be able only to measure part of the objective, and be left asking nervous questions about the relationship between what we have measured and what we are really trying to evaluate.

4 We may attempt to evaluate a variety of objectives, but be unable (if we refuse to impute money values) to combine them into a summary measure of value, because we do not know which relative weights to apply to each of them.

This returns us to one of the disputes noted in Section 18.2. Problems of this kind tend to be treated in two ways. Those with BA degrees conclude that the quantitative approach to evaluation is irredeemably flawed, and that priority should be given to the style of informed, judicious, and essentially qualitative review of the evidence for which their education has prepared them. Those with BSc degrees attempt to counter an ever-widening range of threats to validity, and to solve the measurement problems confronting them, and in doing so create methodologies which only they can understand. It is no longer fashionable to refer to the 'two cultures' of arts and science, but evaluation, particularly of things associated with education, does seem to be a pretty good example of what C. P. Snow (1959) had in mind.

18.6 EVALUATION AND QUALITY ASSURANCE

It is sometimes assumed that evaluation and quality assurance are similar or indeed the same thing. This is unhelpful, because it prevents us from thinking about their proper relationship. Historically, in the United Kingdom, quality assurance was largely a matter of inspection by external expert observers. This was the form favoured by government, which inspected the fire brigade, police, social services departments, and careers education and guidance (notably the Careers Service), in much the same way. There is now, however, a growing insistence that quality assurance should be formally incorporated into the normal activities of guidance agencies. Indeed, the very use of the term 'quality assurance' (QA), imported from industry and commerce, has been associated with this development (for a review, see Hawthorn, 1995).

An important example is the guidelines to TECs for the quality assurance of their suppliers (and hence of guidance suppliers) which propose that objective standards should be applied to inputs, delivery processes, and outputs (ED, 1993). There has been some resultant confusion between industrial terminology, in which 'processes' produce guidance, which is the 'output' – so that another term (e.g. 'outcomes') must be applied to the effects of guidance (e.g. AGCAS, 1991) – and the use of the term 'outputs' to describe effects, or immediate effects, with 'outcomes' referring to the more remote effects of guidance. But terminology aside, it is evident that some statements of quality standards include reference to the effects of guidance: for example, the FEU (1994) quality standards for adult guidance include the development and use of decision-making skills by users, and propose measurement of evidence of such skills, subsequent entry into learning programmes, and other personal outcomes.

Plainly, any conception of quality which is detached from the idea of effectiveness is hollow. The task of quality assurance should be to ensure that the conditions are reproduced under which guidance is known to be effective. If quality assurance is to reach its full potential in the United Kingdom, it should be developed in parallel with, and in close connection to, all kinds of outcome research, whether intended as 'evaluation' or not.

We can thus conceive one of the main tasks of outcome research as providing secure assumptions upon which quality assurance can be based. These assumptions minimally concern the relationships between: (1) the conditions under which guidance occurs; (2) the clients to whom it is offered; (3) guidance processes; (4) immediate (often, learning) outcomes; and (5) the 'economic' outcomes which guidance is intended to produce (see Chapter 4). Providing that it is able to refer to an adequate body of condition–client–process–outcome evidence, quality assurance can confidently attend both to process issues and to non-experimental indicators of performance which can be efficiently assessed during or immediately after guidance.

18.7 EVALUATION BY PRACTITIONERS

We do not know how much formal evaluation is undertaken by guidance practitioners in the United Kingdom. A recent Canadian study disclosed that, in that country, 40 per cent of practitioners never did any sort of evaluation, and about 40 per cent did it only in a very informal way, perhaps by asking their clients how helpful they thought their guidance sessions had been. Less than a quarter ever did any sort of formal evaluation. In consequence, there was a fair degree of uncertainty amongst practitioners as to whether the expectations of their sponsors were being met (Conger et al., 1993). It is unlikely that things are significantly better than this in the United Kingdom, and they may be a good deal worse.

Formal evaluation consumes resources which might otherwise go to service delivery, and practitioners may in any event lack the encouragement or discretion to institute it. Hiebert (1994) believes that the process orientation communicated to practitioners in their training may be contributory: that is, the tendency to conceptualise guidance in terms such as 'helping relationship', 'facilitation' and 'empowering', rather than in outcome-oriented language. This is likely to direct practitioners' attention to issues of 'process quality', almost irrespective of the outcomes of that process.

Guidance practitioners are also unlikely to be trained in methods of outcome evaluation, but may know enough about the difficulties involved to believe that the pretence to evaluation by the outcomes central to policy is futile. They may know, for example, that each year the agency in which they are employed dutifully follows up its clients, and reports the numbers entering work or education, presenting this to sponsors either (sensibly) as information about what happened or (suspectly) as something which the agency has *done*. Who is better placed than a guidance practitioner to know that this year the agency 'did well' because there was an upturn in the local economy, or in the graduate labour market, or in the provision of training for unemployed people, whereas last year the agency 'did badly' because unemployment rates were rising faster? Practitioners may think such reporting no more than pseudo-evaluation, in which they are being judged against criteria over which they have negligible control.

This puts guidance into a dangerously paradoxical position: an apparent refusal to be judged against the objects for which it is instituted, on the grounds that it does not exert much influence upon them. However, the paradox is not a real one (see Chapter 4). When set in its proper perspective (for example, in comparison with the national education budget), guidance is a very small investment, intended to exert a small but worthwhile effect upon the 'economic outcomes' in question. The problem with client follow-up data is that they do not measure this small effect: they measure global outcomes which are determined in the main, and which vary in the main, in response to causes other than guidance. How, then, should guidance practitioners address the task of evaluation by outcomes? There are at least two important avenues for exploration, both of which will depend upon an accumulation of good-quality research evidence: opinions and attributed effects; and learning outcomes.

Opinions and attributed effects

Elsewhere I and colleagues have been critical of excessive reliance upon client satisfaction as a criterion of evaluation (Killeen and Kidd, 1991), and sceptical about the interpretation of subjective self-report learning outcome scales which have not yet been validated against more objective measures (Killeen et al., 1994). This is not because client opinion, or subjective measures in general, are necessarily without value, but because we do not yet know what their value is.

But as we have seen, the practical reality is that evaluators of all kinds, including practitioner-evaluators, often have to rely upon the opinions of participants. Opinion data take a variety of forms, including satisfaction or utility ratings, beliefs about current state (e.g. of career decidedness), and specific attributions of effects to guidance. It may be gathered in a variety of ways, and with greater or lesser attention to its validity. Commonly, those who use large-sample survey methods pay no attention at all to this issue. Those who devise evaluation strategies for schools, where the outcome may itself be a matter for identification, sometimes urge verification by, for example, the 'triangulation' of multiple sources and forms of evidence (Law, 1994). Standardised outcome self-report scales, such as the Measure of Guidance Impact (NFER, 1993), or similar US scales such as the Career Decision Scale (Osipow, 1987) (for a review, see Killeen *et al.*, 1994), have the advantage over *ad hoc* questioning methods that greater attention has been paid to measurement properties. Their corresponding disadvantage is their rigidity.

We can, in principle, use self-report and opinion data to cover a wide range of outcomes. One problem is, of course, that we may be more deceived about ourselves than we know. For example, many unemployed adults experience a change of mood during guidance. They become more hopeful, happier and, perhaps as a result of this, say that they are 'satisfied' with their guidance and that it has been 'helpful'. If they find work soon after guidance, they may – perhaps falsely – connect the two events: believing that one led to the other, regardless of whether it did or not.

A vitally important task for practitioner-evaluators is, therefore, to establish at a general level the *meaning* of opinion data. What is the relationship between satisfaction and outcomes rather than processes? What is the relationship between *beliefs* about outcomes, and outcomes themselves? If we discover how much reliance can be placed on such data, the basis will exist for important developments in practitioner evaluation. But there is a second problem, as we know. People do not know what their experience and behaviour would have been, if they had *not* been exposed to the guidance in question. This is the problem of 'additionality'.

Learning outcomes

Guidance practitioners cannot routinely assess economic effects. So should they abandon all hope of outcome evaluation? There is a middle path: one increasingly taken in the United Kingdom in recent years, although far from new in principle. 'Learning outcomes' are more directly sensitive to and rapidly influenced by guidance than are 'economic' ones. They tend to correspond to the sorts of changes practitioners hope to produce in their clients in the short run, and which practitioners view as being more under their control than longer-run economic effects. When adopted as criteria, measures of these outcomes make the controlled trial a viable practitioner-evaluation strategy; when standardised, these measures can be inspected for pre-/post-test stability in control samples and, if stable, used in pre-/post-test only (uncontrolled quasi-experimental) studies of effectiveness. They are *legitimate*, precisely because they correspond to things guidance practitioners say they try to achieve. They make methodologically adequate outcome evaluation a real possibility for practitioners, who no longer need feel restricted only to 'quality of process' questions.

As noted in Chapter 4, however, there is a general question which needs to be answered: do learning gains predict economic ones? There is *some* evidence that they may (Killeen *et al.*, 1992), but this is far from adequate. If the eventual answer (or set of answers) is positive, then learning outcomes will to some extent be able to substitute (or act as proxies for) economic ones. There needs to be, therefore, both a division of labour and an interchange between summative economic evaluators and practitioner-evaluators. The latter should insist that the former provide the data upon which the connection of learning outcome gains to the 'economic' effects demanded by policy can be established. This will make it possible to assess the viability of the assertion that evaluation by learning outcomes simultaneously fulfils an educational and practice-related end, and provides 'proxies' for the economic assessment which a summative programme-evaluator might essay.

REFERENCES

Allen, E. P. and Smith, P. (1932) *The Value of Vocational Tests as Aids to Choice of Employment: Report of Research*, Birmingham: City of Birmingham Education Committee.

Arnold, J., Budd, R. J. and Miller, K. (1988) 'Young People's Perceptions of the Uses and Usefulness of Different Sources of Careers Help', *British Journal of Guidance and Counselling* 16(1): 83–90.

Association of Graduate Careers Advisory Services (1991) *Performance Management and Measures*, Edinburgh: AGCAS.

Ballantine, M. and Strebler, M. (1989) *The Use of Information Technology in the Careers Service*, London: Birkbeck College, University of London (mimeo).

Banks, M. H. and Jackson, P. R. (1982) 'Unemployment and Risk of Minor Psychiatric Disorder in Young People: Cross-Sectional and Longitudinal Evidence', *Psychological Medicine* 12: 789–98.

Bedford, T. (1982) *Vocational Guidance Interviews: a Survey by the Careers Service Inspectorate*, London: Department of Employment.

Careers Service Quality Assurance and Development Unit (1995) *Careers Education and Guidance: an Evaluative Framework*, London: Employment Department.

Carter, M. C. (1966) *Into Work*, Harmondsworth: Penguin.

Cherry, N. and Gear, R. (1987) 'Young People's Perceptions of their Vocational Guidance Needs: II. Influences and Interventions', *British Journal of Guidance and Counselling* 15(2): 169–81.

Closs, S. J., Maclean, P. R. and Walker, M. V. (1985) *An Evaluation of the JIIG–CAL System*, Sevenoaks: Hodder & Stoughton (mimeo).

Conger, D. S., Hiebert, B. and Hong-Farrell, E. (1993) *Career and Employment Counselling in Canada*, Ottawa, Ont.: Canadian Labour Force Development Board.

Cook, T. D., Cook, F. L. and Mark, M. M. (1977) 'Randomised and Quasi-Experimental Designs in Evaluation Research', in Rutman, L. (ed.) *Evaluation Research Methods: a Basic Guide*, London: Sage.

Coopers & Lybrand (1994) *Gateways to Learning: Summary of Findings from First Round Pilots*, London: Coopers & Lybrand.

Curragh, E. F. and McGleenon, C. F. (1980) 'Towards the Development and Conceptualisation of Vocational Values in a Careers Education Programme: a Curricular Approach', *Durham and Newcastle Research Review* 9(44): 67–73.

Earle, F. M. (1931) *Methods of Choosing a Career*, London: Harrap.

Edmonds, T. (1979) 'Applying Personal Construct Theory in Occupational Guidance', *British Journal of Guidance and Counselling* 7(2): 225–33.

Elliot, J. (1990) 'Educational Research in Crisis', *British Educational Research Journal* 16(1): 3–18.

Employment Department (1993) *TEC Quality Assurance: Supplier Management*, Sheffield: ED.

Fleming, D. and Lavercombe, S. (1982) 'Talking about Unemployment with School-Leavers', *British Journal of Guidance and Counselling* 10(1): 22–33.

Further Education Unit (1994) *Quality in Guidance for Adults*, London: FEU.

Gray, J. (1980) 'Guidance in Scottish Secondary Schools: a Client Evaluation', *British Journal of Guidance and Counselling* 8(2): 129–45.

Guba, E. G. and Lincoln, Y. S. (1989) *Fourth Generation Evaluation*, London: Sage.

Harris, A. (1989) 'Teachers' Evaluation of Enterprise Education in the Secondary School', *British Journal of Education and Work* 3(1): 83–97.

Hawthorn, R. (1995) *First Steps: a Quality Standards Framework for Guidance Across All Sectors*, London: Royal Society of Arts/National Advisory Council for Careers and Educational Guidance.

Hiebert, B. (1994) 'A Framework for Quality Control, Accountability, and Evaluation: Being Clear about the Legitimate Outcomes of Career Counselling', paper presented to the Symposium on Issues and Solutions for Evaluating Career Development, Halifax, Nova Scotia.

Hughes, D. and May, D. (1985) 'Some Limitations of the Interview Form in Careers Counselling for the Mildly Mentally Handicapped', *British Journal of Guidance and Counselling* 13(2): 178–90.

Hunt, E. P. and Smith, P. (1944) *Scientific Vocational Guidance and its Value to the Choice of Employment Work of a Local Education Authority*, Birmingham: City of Birmingham Education Committee.

Innes, D. R. (1985) *The Perception of Pupils and Staff of the Provision of Guidance and Counselling in a Scottish Secondary Comprehensive School*, Edinburgh: University of Edinburgh.

Jahoda, G. and Chalmers, A. D. (1963) 'The Youth Employment Service: a Consumer Perspective', *Occupational Psychology* 37(1): 165–74.

Kemmis, S. (1983) 'Action Research', in Anderson, D. S. and Blakers, C. (eds) *Youth, Transition and Social Research*, Canberra: Australian National University Press.

Kent, A. J. (1984) 'Occupational Choice and Occupational Success in Slow-Learning School Leavers', *British Journal of Guidance and Counselling* 12(2): 175–85.

Kidd, J. M. (1984) 'Young People's Perceptions of their Occupational Decision-Making', *British Journal of Guidance and Counselling* 12(1): 25–38.

Killeen, J. and Kidd, J. M. (1991) *Learning Outcomes of Guidance: a Review of Research*, Research Paper No. 85, Sheffield: Employment Department.

Killeen, J., White, M. and Watts, A. G. (1992) *The Economic Value of Careers Guidance*, London: Policy Studies Institute.

Killeen, J., Kidd, J. M., Hawthorn, R., Sampson, J. and White, M. (1994) *A Review of Measures of the Learning Outcomes of Guidance*, Cambridge: National Institute for Careers Education and Counselling.

King, R. A. (1981) 'Secondary Schools: Some Changes of a Decade', *Educational Research* 23(3): 173–76.

Kirton, M. (1976) *Career Knowledge of Sixth Form Boys*, London: Careers and Occupational Information Centre.

Knasel, E. G., Watts, A. G. and Kidd, J. M. (1982) *The Benefit of Experience*, Special Programmes Research and Development Series No. 5, London: Manpower Services Commission.

Kushner, S. and Logan, T. (1985) 'The Careers Service and the Curriculum: Trapped in the Corridor', *Cambridge Journal of Education* 15(1): 22–31.

Law, B. (1994) *Evaluating Your Learning Outcomes Project*, Maidstone: Kent County Council (mimeo).

McCartney, J. R. and Whyte, J. (1984) *Opportunity and Choice, Part One: 15 Year Olds in Schools and Further Education Colleges*, Belfast: Northern Ireland Council for Educational Research.

Market & Opinion Research International (1980) 'Career Attitudes of Final Year Undergraduates', *Employment Gazette* 88(1): 13–15, 22.

Myers, R. A. (1971) 'Research on Educational and Vocational Counseling', in Bergin, A. E. and Garfield, S. L. (eds) *Handbook of Psychotherapy and Behavior Change: an Empirical*

Analysis, New York: Wiley.

National Council for Educational Technology (1988) *Computer Aided Guidance Evaluation: an Evaluation of the Place of Computer Aided Guidance in the TAP Context and Evaluation of Specific Packages Trialled,* London: NCET (mimeo).

National Foundation for Educational Research (1987) *Job Ideas and Information Generator: Computer Assisted Learning (JIIG–CAL): Evaluation Report,* Slough: NFER (mimeo).

National Foundation for Educational Research (1993) *Measure of Guidance Impact: Manual,* Slough: NFER.

Oliver, L. W. (1979) 'Outcome Measurement in Career Counseling Research', *Journal of Counseling Psychology* 26(3): 217–26.

Oliver, L. W. and Spokane, A. R. (1988) 'Career Intervention Outcome: What Contributes to Client Gain?', *Journal of Counseling Psychology* 35: 447–62.

Osipow, S. H. (1987) *Career Decision Scale Manual,* Odessa, FL: Psychological Assessment Resources.

Pearson, R. W. (1988) 'Creating Flexible Careers: Some Observations on a "Bridge" Programme for Unemployed Professionals, *British Journal of Guidance and Counselling* 16(3): 250–67.

Pollock, G. J. and Nicholson, V. M. (1981) *Just the Job: a Study of the Employment and Training of Young School Leavers,* London: Hodder & Stoughton.

Rutman, L. (1977) 'Formative Research and Program Evaluability', in Rutman, L. (ed.) *Evaluation Research Methods: a Basic Guide,* London: Sage.

Shilling, C. (1986) 'Implementing the Contract: the Technical and Vocational Education Initiative', *British Journal of Sociology of Education* 7(4): 397–414.

Snow, C. P. (1959) *The Two Cultures and the Scientific Revolution,* Cambridge: Cambridge University Press.

Stafford, E. M. (1982) 'The Impact of the Youth Opportunities Programme on Young People's Employment Prospects and Psychological Well-Being', *British Journal of Guidance and Counselling* 10(1): 12–21.

Stronach, I. (1986) 'Practical Evaluation', in Hopkins, D. (ed.) *Evaluating TVEI: Some Methodological Issues,* Cambridge: Cambridge Institute of Education.

Suchman, E. (1972) 'Action for What?: a Critique of Evaluative Research', in Weiss, C. H. (ed.) *Evaluating Action Programs,* Boston: Allyn & Bacon.

Varlaam, C. (1984) 'Provision for CSE Failures', in Varlaam, C. (ed.): *Rethinking Transition: Educational Innovation and the Transition to Adult Life,* Lewes: Falmer.

West, M. and Newton, P. (1983) *The Transition from School to Work,* Beckenham: Croom Helm.

Wholey, J. S. (1977) 'Evaluability Assessment', in Rutman, L. (ed.) *Evaluation Research Methods: a Basic Guide,* London: Sage.

Williamson, H. (1989) 'Mini-Enterprises in Schools: the Pupils' Experience', *British Journal of Education and Work* 3(1): 71–82.

Woods, P. (1979) 'How Teachers Decide Pupils' Subject Choices', in Eggleston, J. (ed.) *Teacher Decision-Making in the Classroom,* London: Routledge & Kegan Paul.

Part V

Policy

The final part of the book deals with policy-related issues.

Chapter 19 examines socio-political ideologies in guidance. It distinguishes four such ideologies: liberal (non-directive), conservative (social control), progressive (individual change) and radical (social change). It then explores these in relation to the issues of unemployment, of gender and of ethnicity. It notes that all four ideological positions are vulnerable to attack, and that most guidance interventions are likely to contain some mix of the approaches.

Chapter 20 presents a framework for looking at guidance systems in an international perspective. It examines in particular the extent to which differences between guidance systems relate to five factors: the state of economic development, the political system, social and cultural factors, education and training systems, and professional and organisational structures. It notes that the development of formal guidance services is linked to industrialisation, to democratisation, to social mobility, and to cultural individualism. It discusses whether such forces are likely to lead to greater convergence between guidance systems in the future.

Chapter 21 explores the role of public policy in relation to guidance provision. It identifies three functions of policy – funding, influence, and regulation – and notes that the balance between these functions varies between different sectors. It distinguishes three policy models: a social-welfare model, a market model, and a quasi-market model. It then analyses the application of these models to guidance practice in the UK, and in particular the application of quasi-market mechanisms in the form of contracts and vouchers. It contends that, even within a market framework, the notion of a 'market (or quasi-market) in guidance' is only defensible if it delivers the public interest in guidance as a 'market-maker' (i.e. a means of making the labour market, and education and training market, work more effectively). It concludes that while market principles may have a role to play in public policy on guidance provision, they are too narrow to encompass the social functions of such provision.

Chapter 19

Socio-political ideologies in guidance

A. G. Watts

19.1 INTRODUCTION

Careers education and guidance is a profoundly political process. It operates at the interface between the individual and society, between self and opportunity, between aspiration and realism. It facilitates the allocation of life chances. Within a society in which such life chances are unequally distributed, it faces the issue of whether it serves to reinforce such inequalities or to reduce them.

In principle, the more choice individuals have, the more scope there is for guidance. This is illustrated in Figure 19.1, which outlines a spectrum of gradually increasing scope for choice and exercise of self-determination (within competitive constraints). Madsen (1986) suggests that the model can be applied *historically*, demonstrating the shift from pre-industrial societies with a social order based largely on ascription to industrial societies with a social order based more extensively on achievement. This helps to explain why formal guidance services have tended to emerge as a product of industrialisation (see Chapter 20). Within societies based on achievement rather than ascription, with increasingly complex and volatile occupational structures, the family's capacity to communicate

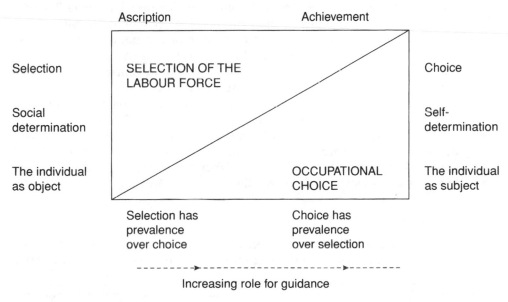

Figure 19.1 Selection and choice
Source: Adapted from Madsen (1986)

information on opportunities becomes inadequate. Individuals are likely to need guidance from more formal sources in order to make effective use of their increased freedom to choose; conversely, the social structure is more likely to require arrangements which support the free choice of the individual but relate it to social needs.

Madsen also suggests that within industrial societies the model can be applied in *social–structural* terms, indicating the greater choice available for the middle class than for the working class, to whites than to blacks, to males than to females. This implies that guidance is more relevant to the first group in each of these pairs than to the second. On the other hand, part of the concern of guidance services has often been to maximise the capacity for choice for groups with constrained opportunities.

Indeed, the origins of the vocational guidance movement in the USA were as a process of gradualist social reform, seeking to improve the work conditions of the lower classes (Brewer, 1942). Such reform was designed to restructure society so that 'the human potentialities of all members may be more fully utilised in the interest of each and in the interest of all' (Williamson, 1965, p. 43). It was set within a democratic ideal which respected the rights of individuals to make free choices about their own lives, sanctioning 'neither the exploitation of the individual by society, nor the disregard of the interests of society by the individual' (quoted in Stephens, 1970, p. 112).

Despite these origins, and the complex issues they raise, the socio-political nature of guidance has tended to be given limited attention in the professional literature or in the professional training of guidance counsellors. In part this can be attributed to the way in which guidance services have become institutionalised within schools or other organisations, or within government bureaucracies. In part, too, it can be attributed to the way in which the theoretical basis of professional guidance practice has been dominated by psychologists. Particularly in the USA, but in most other countries as well, the dominant guidance theories – and the theories of career development on which they have been based – have been psychological rather than sociological or economic in nature (see Chapter 2). This is perhaps understandable, since at the point of intervention the focus of attention is the individual. But it means that the social context of the intervention, and the socio-political nature of the intervention itself, tend to be neglected and implicitly regarded as unproblematic.

In reality, the socio-political nature of guidance is highly problematic. Guidance can be a form of social reform; it can also be a form of social control. There are important choices to be made. To clarify the nature of these choices, the present chapter will offer four alternative approaches to guidance from a socio-political perspective. These approaches will then be elaborated in relation to the challenge posed by unemployment, and also in relation to the issues of gender and ethnicity.

19.2 FOUR APPROACHES

Most writers on guidance have tended to view it in *liberal*[1] terms as a *non-directive* process concerned with helping individuals to choose the opportunities

---

1 The use of the term 'liberal' here - as with the subsequent use of the terms 'conservative', 'progressive' and 'radical' - is specific to guidance ideologies and does not imply any necessary association with political Liberalism.

appropriate not only to their abilities and skills but also to their interests and values. This approach has been strongly influenced by the models of non-directive counselling developed by Carl Rogers (1961): while it recognises the desirability of a wider range of interventions, it holds to the ideal of respecting and valuing the right of individuals to make decisions concerning their own lives. Guidance is seen as *facilitating* this process, not influencing it in a particular direction (Daws, 1967). Careers education, for example, is viewed as an appropriate complement to counselling, helping individuals to develop the skills, knowledge and understanding they need in order to make their own informed decisions (Watts, 1973).

Such views tend to be criticised by sociologists, who commonly view guidance as an essentially *conservative* force, operating as an agent of *social control*. Its main function is seen as adapting individuals to the opportunities appropriate for them (Roberts, 1977). According to this view, its primary concern is to meet the needs of the labour market: Brown (1985), for example, writing from a neo-Marxist perspective, sees the Careers Service as part of a state apparatus designed to habituate entrants to the workforce to the requirements of capital.

Other writers use less ideological language to make much the same kind of point. They emphasise that counsellors act as 'gatekeepers' to opportunities (Erickson, 1975; Wrench, 1991). They also note that one of the main functions of guidance is to discourage students from seeking opportunities regarded as 'unrealistic' and to lower their expectations. Guidance is seen as an effective if insidious means of 'cooling out' excessive aspirations (Clark, 1960). It masks inequalities in society by making them seem matters of individual choice, thereby reconciling people to their roles. In doing so, it propagates myths, such as the 'dignity of work' and the concept of 'choice' itself. Thus to suggest to young people 'that there is satisfaction and dignity in that which is their probable economic destiny is not making it possible for them to have "freedom to choose" – it is rather telling them that they should be satisfied with their lot in life' (Sessions, 1975, pp. 315–16; also Grubb and Lazerson, 1975).

Such comments, it should be noted, refer to the *functions* of guidance rather than to *conscious intentionality*. The comments tend to be made by brief visitors to the field, who are concerned with pointing out the gulf between its liberal rhetoric and what they see as being its conservative reality. At the same time, the reality they describe does have some direct congruence with policy-makers who view guidance as being concerned primarily with serving the needs of the labour market, and with guidance writers and practitioners who emphasise ' realism'.

To counter the sociological critique of the liberal position, some guidance writers have adopted a more *progressive* stance, viewing guidance as a means of *individual change*. The emphasis shifts to a proactive approach, seeking in particular to raise the aspirations of individuals from deprived backgrounds. This incorporates attention to using active role models so as to increase expectations, to adopting forms of coaching and assertiveness training so as to improve self-confidence, and to engaging in forms of advocacy designed to remove obstacles to the individual's progress. The assumption tends to be that the individual's interests are best met by seeking to achieve the highest level that is possible within the status hierarchy of the opportunity structure. The conflict of identity and loyalty that, for example, young people from working-class backgrounds may experience in moving into middle-class roles (Jackson and Marsden, 1962) are regarded as difficulties to be overcome rather than as legitimate objections to seeking advancement.

The progressive approach is open to the criticism that encouraging some degree of movement of individuals within the status hierarchy merely reinforces the hierarchy itself, with no benefits for those who remain at the lower levels within it. Some have accordingly argued that guidance should seek to adopt a more *radical* stance, concerned with promoting *social change*. The basic assumption here is that it is not possible to advance the interests of certain groups of individuals without some change in social structures. This might materialise in guidance practice as a more generalised advocacy role on behalf of groups of individuals (Ranson and Ribbins, 1988), or as a feedback role which seeks to change the opportunity structure in the interests of such groups (Oakeshott, 1990).

More radically still, it might involve seeking to help such individuals to view their situation in group rather than individual terms: enabling them to understand, for example, the unequal and exploitative nature of the employment system. Such an approach has drawn sustenance from the work of Willis (1977) with working-class boys, showing how personal choices are bounded by norms and perceptions linked to shared identity: this has been interpreted by some as implying the need for interventions to engage with the group culture and develop its socio-political consciousness. Thus some careers teachers in London schools were reported as indicating that they were not disposed to co-operate with any 'tinkering' efforts to improve individual prospects but that their concern was rather to 'conscientise' young people (*New Society*, 14 May 1981).

A broadly similar position was elaborated within the Schools Council Careers Education and Guidance Project:

> Society and the range of job and other opportunities were regarded as more incompatible than compatible with the goal of encouraging the development and expression of human potential. This led to an emphasis on stimulating pupils to assess critically society and the occupational roles available and to act as an influence for social change, particularly in the world of work.
>
> (Bates, 1990, p. 71)

Bates analyses the political conflicts which surrounded the Schools Council project, and particularly the tensions between the radical and liberal positions. She also describes how teachers tended to ignore the different political nuances evident in the project publications and to regard them in a pragmatic and politically uncritical way as a source of lesson materials which could lift careers education out of its job-information rut. She further notes how even this was modified by pressure from pupils to revert to the traditional job-information approach. This provides a valuable reminder of how even sharply defined ideological stances can become modified by the practical constraints of the context in which they are implemented and by the negotiation with clients which effective guidance arguably requires.

The four approaches we have identified can be arranged on two dimensions, according to whether their core focus is on society or on the individual, and according to whether their concern in each case is with accepting the status quo or changing it in prescribed directions. This is illustrated in Table 19.1, with the former dimension represented vertically and the latter one horizontally.

Table 19.1   Four socio-political approaches to careers education and guidance

	Core focus on society	Core focus on individual
Change	Radical (social change)	Progressive (individual change)
Status quo	Conservative (social control)	Liberal (non-directive)

Source: Adapted from Watts and Herr (1976)

It is worth noting that there is also some lateral correspondence within the table. Thus both the conservative and progressive models tend to assume what Katz (1993) terms a 'single optimisation model' for meeting both societal and individual interests: the notion that opportunities are arranged in a single hierarchy, and that the issue is who 'wins' or 'loses' particular places within this hierarchy. The liberal and radical approaches, by contrast, question in different forms the dominance of the hierarchy: the liberal approach by arguing that differences in values mean that individuals can 'win' in different ways; the radical approach by questioning the 'game' itself. The extent to which it is feasible and/or legitimate for guidance to adopt a *fully-fledged* social-change approach is open to question. Certainly it is likely to attract political opposition, as when a Minister of State for Employment accused careers officers of being 'social engineers . . . incapable or unwilling to help employers by encouraging young people to take up opportunities on offer' (Morrison, 1983). More fundamentally, Halmos (1974) argued that there is an intrinsic incompatibility between the personalist orientation of counselling (in its various forms) and political activism. He contended that any attempt at 'hybridisation' of the roles was a serious mistake. Halmos further argued that the radical critique of counselling was misconceived: 'no social system, least of all the favoured utopias, can come about and subsist without a generously staffed personal service to individuals' (p. 147).

This leaves open, however, the issue of whether some *elements* of the social-change approach might be necessary to achieve the personal emancipation valued by the liberal approach. We will explore this issue further in the sections that follow.

19.3 THE CHALLENGE OF UNEMPLOYMENT

Of the four approaches outlined in the previous section, the liberal and progressive approaches tend to be dominant in most careers education and guidance practice at the level of conscious intentionality. This is mainly because they focus on the individual, which – as noted earlier – is the natural focus of attention at the point of guidance intervention. When opportunities are relatively plentiful and/or expanding, this dominance is more likely to be uncontested. When, however, opportunities contract, it tends to come under growing pressure. This is particularly the case when levels of unemployment rise. Unemployment calls into question the concepts of 'opportunities' and 'choice' on which the liberal and progressive approaches are essentially based. Responses to unemployment thus provide a particularly fruitful area in which to explore the impact of different socio-political ideologies on educational provision in general and on guidance practice in particular (Watts, 1978, 1983; Fleming and Lavercombe, 1982; Watts and Knasel, 1985).

The most common immediate response of guidance services to rising unemployment is to pay more attention to active ways of helping their clients to secure the opportunities that remain available. In particular, there tends to be increased focus on *employability*. This includes job-search skills, and skills of self-presentation on paper and in selection interviews. It also includes exploration of possibilities for education and training which may increase employability. Eventually, however, guidance services have to confront the fact that while guidance along these lines may be helpful and effective for some of the individuals concerned, it does little or nothing to increase the number of jobs, and that many clients may remain unemployed. In such cases, guidance programmes limited to employability may only increase the stress and sense of inadequacy that stem from repeated failure, making it seem that this failure is due to personal inadequacy.

Attention may accordingly extend to focus on *coping*. This may include helping people to claim the benefits to which they are entitled, and to survive on a limited budget. It may also include helping them to explore opportunities for making good use of their increased 'leisure' time – hobbies, voluntary work, skill exchanges, and non-vocational educational opportunities – and helping them to cope in mental-health terms. Excessive focus on coping is, however, open to attack on the grounds that it is encouraging people to tolerate the intolerable, particularly in a society in which employment remains the chief source of status, of social identity, and of income.

A further extension therefore focuses on *opportunity creation*. This involves helping people to explore possibilities for becoming self-employed or setting up a small business or co-operative. The rise of unemployment in the early 1980s indeed saw a huge growth of attention to such possibilities, linked to the 'education for enterprise' movement (Watts and Moran, 1984). Again, however, too much focus on encouraging people to be 'enterprising' in this sense could imply that this represents a societal solution to unemployment, and that people who do not take up this option are feckless: this could be aligned to political arguments for reducing or withdrawing their benefits, so again becoming a classic case of 'blaming the victim'.

In each of these cases, therefore, options which appear liberal–progressive in nature are open to attack on the grounds that they are hidden forms of social control. This is reflected clearly in the attitude taken to hidden-economy activity. For many unemployed people, activities within the hidden economy are important forms both of coping and of opportunity creation. Because, however, they are officially proscribed, they tend to be ignored in guidance programmes (Watts, 1981).

Some careers teachers, careers officers and other guidance workers find it acutely uncomfortable to accept the social-control nature of their work. They are aware that their efforts to help people with their individual problems fail to address the social context from which these problems largely stem. Moreover, they may begin to feel that they are helping to reinforce the social context by shifting attention away from it: by suggesting that what is needed is not socio-political reform but ways of making good the inadequacies of individuals.

In response to this, they may seek to focus also on the *context* itself. This may involve helping people to understand the extent to which responsibility for unemployment lies at a societal rather than individual level, and to explore possible forms of social, political and community action in response to it. This may be justified in liberal–progressive terms: if unemployed people understand that unemployment is not due to personal inadequacy, this may make it easier to avoid the destructive effect which unemployment may have on their confidence and self-respect. But it may also be justified in more radical terms, as raising people's consciousness of the social causes of unemployment and helping them to work collectively for social change. This too, however, is open to objections: increased awareness of the size and complexity of the forces that cause unemployment could lead unemployed people to feel a sense of impotence in the face of these forces; this in turn could lead to a fatalism which not only reduces their personal chances of finding a job but also produces a more general sense of alienation and disenchantment; it is likely to attract opposition from the public authorities on whose support most guidance provision depends; and it places the unemployed in the forefront of political pressures for change, which may expose them to risk and may mean that excessive expectations are raised for a group whose power is relatively limited.

In the end, resolving these dilemmas is a question of finding the optimal balance between the different options that is appropriate to the particular guidance context in question. To focus exclusively on any one option poses considerable ethical and professional difficulties. But an appropriate balance between them may make it possible to avoid or at least minimise such difficulties. In this sense, the difficulties tend to be more acute in careers education programmes than in, for example, the counselling interview, where the balance between the various options can be more flexibly negotiated with the individual client. On the other hand, socio-political context issues tend to be difficult to address in one-to-one counselling sessions and may be easier to tackle in group situations. For our present purposes, however, the various guidance options available in response to the challenge of unemployment illustrate very clearly the socio-political dilemmas that lie beneath all guidance provision.

19.4 GENDER ISSUES

Issues of socio-political ideology also arise in relation to gender. Here they assume a particularly acute form because of the fixed nature of gender allocation: whereas people can move between social classes, they cannot do so (*pace* transsexualism) between genders. Since gender segregation in the labour market is still strong, with many women confined to relatively low-paid and low-status jobs (Martin and Roberts, 1984; Rees, 1992; see Chapter 1), guidance is faced with the question of whether it serves to reinforce or challenge such segregation.

Traditionally, guidance clearly tended to reinforce the segregation. Prout (1983) argues that until the mid-1970s guidance not only reflected gender-stereotyped assumptions about male and female roles in society, but overtly encouraged them. The Youth Employment Service (now the Careers Service) had separate sections for boys and girls, with distinct staff, records and job-vacancy lists. Careers literature referred to 'girls' jobs' and 'boys' jobs'. Pictures in such literature tended to show men at work doing positive and demanding tasks, whereas women were shown in supportive roles as secretaries, in caring roles as nurses, or in decorative roles as florists and hairdressers. Child-rearing and home-making were assumed to play central roles in women's careers but not in men's.

These practices and assumptions have been strongly challenged by the feminist movement and changes in social mores. The more overtly segregated practices were abandoned, and explicit stereotyping is now scrutinised much more critically. Nonetheless, there is some evidence that in practice guidance services still tend to perform a conservative, social-control function in relation to gender issues. Several studies have shown, for example, that careers officers and teachers have been perceived as offering little help, and often positive discouragement, to girls who want to choose gender-atypical occupations (Benett and Carter, 1982; Breakwell and Weinberger, 1987; Cockburn, 1987; Devine, 1993).

The stance of careers advisers themselves is often liberal in nature. Most of them claim to be following equal-opportunities policies, at least in a passive sense. But their adherence to a non-directive approach means that they are inclined to take their clients' interests and preferences at face value. They are concerned about whether it is ethically legitimate for them to seek 'to reshape youngsters' aspirations and views of themselves' (Gottfredson, 1981, p. 577). They are also anxious to avoid rejection or ridicule from their clients (Cockburn, 1987). They accordingly may be reluctant to present gender-atypical options to those who do not volunteer an interest in such options. On the other hand, they may feel that with those who do indicate an interest in gender-atypical options, they should ensure that the individuals concerned are aware of the difficulties involved (Breakwell and Weinberger, 1987). This is easily perceived by such individuals as discouragement. In such ways, the liberal stance of careers advisers can serve conservative ends.

There has accordingly been pressure to adopt a more progressive approach, based on more active equal-opportunities policies (Watts and Kant, 1986). This includes active ways of increasing awareness of gender-atypical options. A particularly common approach is the use of positive role models, through talks, group discussions or work-shadowing schemes. Attention may also be given to providing support to those who want to pursue gender-atypical options, helping them to confront discrimination. Sometimes such programmes include work in single-sex groups, where issues specific to the gender in question can be addressed more directly. This runs the risk of reintroducing segregation and reinforcing gender stereotypes.

There is some evidence that progressive programmes of these kinds have only limited success in terms of direct impact on immediate choices (Brooks et al., 1985; HMI, 1982; Sultana, 1990). This demonstrates the strength and persistence of gender stereotypes. Gottfredson's (1981) theory of career development (see Chapter 2) emphasises that gender-role conceptions are fundamental to people's sense of personal identity and that this produces strong resistance to relinquishing gender-type perceptions in choosing an occupation. It seems likely that such resistance will be particularly strong during adolescence, when young people are still developing their sexual identity and beginning their sexual careers. Such concerns seem to pose even greater problems for boys than for girls in choosing gender-atypical options for their occupational careers: such choices are viewed as irrational in selecting lower-status and lower-paid 'feminine' occupations, and tend therefore to be regarded as casting doubts on the individual's sexual identity (Hayes, 1986). Yet, arguably, the movement of males into 'feminine' occupations is critical if females are to be able to move more easily into 'masculine' occupations.

A common progressive response to these difficulties in relation to careers education programmes in schools is to seek to start them much earlier, before gender stereotypes are rigidly formed. Indeed, this forms one of the chief arguments for beginning careers education programmes in primary schools, in advance of puberty. A second response is to argue that such programmes need to be broader in approach, incorporating attention to domestic and child-rearing roles as well as occupational roles (Van Dyke, 1981). This enables the interaction between such roles to be addressed, and the gender distribution of work in the home as well as in employment to be brought into question.

Such responses can be incorporated within a liberal–progressive approach, but some writers have suggested that a more radical stance needs to be taken. It is argued that the concept of equal opportunities is not adequate as a framework for countering gender discrimination and women's disadvantage: that instead an anti-sexist approach is required based on challenging patriarchal power bases (Weiner, 1985). Attempts have been made to develop curriculum units based on anti-sexist principles designed to influence occupational choice by developing a broader critical consciousness of gender divisions and stereotyping (Chisholm and Holland, 1986; Blackman, 1987). Griffin (1985), by contrast, attached importance to such critical consciousness as an end in its own right. She argued that careers advisers and teachers should not try to force young women into non-traditional jobs where they will be detached from the support of other women: instead they should develop the students' understanding of *why* their choices are so limited.

Beneath these different approaches, two key issues can be identified. The first is whether it is the responsibility of guidance to represent the world of work as it is, or as it might be. The conservative and liberal approaches tend to be concerned with presenting the world as it is, with its existing inequalities and discrimination. Thus the fact that certain occupations are gender-segregated is regarded as valid occupational information. The progressive approach, on the other hand, tends to place more emphasis on the world as it might be from the individual's perspective, attaching particular importance to positive images and role models. Thus significance is attached to representing occupations non-stereotypically or even counter-stereotypically, so that a male-dominated occupation is represented visually by equal numbers of men and women. This makes it easier for girls to see the occupation as accessible to them, even though it misrepresents the current reality (Birk et al., 1979) and pays no attention to the structural changes required to achieve change. The radical approach, by contrast, sees it as important to address the current reality but to expose its structural foundations to radical critique.

The second issue is the balance between the approaches which is most likely to encourage individual autonomy. Such autonomy requires individuals to be able to envisage a range of possible selves in possible futures and to transcend the prescriptions of their situation and their socialised self (Law, 1981). It is important to recognise that the test of such autonomy must include the possibility of choosing conventional as well as non-conventional options, but choosing them as an act of informed volition rather than as a result of conditioning. The danger with the progressive and radical approaches is that they tend implicitly to devalue traditionally feminine occupations, and the traditionally feminine roles of home-making and child-rearing, and to impose on women a male definition of career achievement (Hashizume and Crozier, 1994). On the other hand, it is arguable that the critical understanding of traditionally feminine roles developed by such approaches, and the awareness of alternatives, are essential if these roles are to be assumed as a matter of genuine choice. In other words, some elements of the progressive and radical approaches are necessary to detach liberal approaches from their conservative tendencies, but in the end the progressive and radical approaches have to be reconciled with the liberal one if individual autonomy is to be affirmed. It may be that the recognition of this point explains why a survey of teacher attitudes found stronger support for the statement 'It is important that careers education should encourage people to look critically at sex roles in society', which is concerned with awareness-raising at the exploration stage, than for the statement 'A careers teacher should make positive efforts to encourage pupils to consider taking up subjects or careers that are not normally done by their sex', which suggests directive intervention closer to the point of decision-making (Pratt, et al., 1984, pp. 185–86).

19.5 ETHNICITY ISSUES

Ethnicity is a particularly socio-political issue for the 'visible ethnic minorities', i.e. people 'likely to be discriminated against on the basis of colour' (Forbes and Mead, 1992, p. 1). By 1989 such people constituted about 4.7 per cent of the total population of Britain. Most are systematically disadvantaged in the labour market, although the nature and degree of such disadvantage varies according to the country of origin (ibid.). As with gender, ethnic identity is in principle immutable; but in contrast to gender disadvantage, ethnic disadvantage applies to whole families and communities. This, along with the fact that some ethnic groups arrived in Britain only relatively recently, means that they may have only limited quantities of relevant 'cultural capital' (Bourdieu and Passeron, 1977) on which to draw. Accordingly, they may need more active support in order to secure access to opportunities.

One of the results is that black youngsters of Afro-Caribbean or Asian descent tend to be much more dependent on formal guidance services than do white youngsters. They are less likely to be able to obtain from their family or friends the informed help they need in order to gain access to opportunities. They are accordingly more likely to have recourse to careers officers or teachers (Brooks and Singh, 1978: Lee and Wrench, 1983; Sillitoe and Meltzer, 1985; Verma and Darby, 1987).

In response to such demands, some careers officers and teachers adopt the liberal 'colour-blind' stance that 'we treat them all the same'. Such a stance tends to deny the existence of systematic discrimination against ethnic minorities within the labour market, and to attribute any lack of success on the part of these minorities to their cultural attributes (Cross et al., 1990). There appears to be little if any evidence of overt ethnic discrimination on the part of guidance services (Roberts et al., 1981). Nonetheless, there is evidence that careers advisers tend to assess the occupational aspirations of ethnic-minority young people less favourably than those of white young people with similar qualifications, and to be more likely to regard such aspirations as unrealistic. Moreover, they are inclined to engage in 'protective channelling', directing ethnic-minority young people away from opportunities where they suspect these youngsters will be rejected (Cross *et al.*, 1990). This means that discrimination on the part of employers is not even tested, let alone challenged. In such ways, careers advisers operating within a liberal framework which rejects racism nonetheless can help to produce racist outcomes. Concepts such as 'realism' act to conceal the underlying racism. Indeed, Brown (1985) argues that such 'racist non-racism' is able to hold the racist model together precisely because it represents itself as an individualistic, meritocratic and informal set of practices based on common sense.

In response to such critiques, one or more of three rather different positions seem to be adopted. The first is a reformed liberal approach based on pluralistic *multicultural* principles. This seeks to pay more attention to understanding and accepting the cultural background of ethnic-minority groups. It may include acceptance of cultural factors that constrain the range of opportuni-ties. It might also, however, include training for careers advisers in avoiding cultural stereotypes, and strategies for recruiting careers advisers from ethnic-minority groups.

The second is a progressive approach based on active *assimilation*. This may include providing compensatory teaching for ethnic-minority groups in employability skills and/or knowledge of the labour market. It may also include providing access to positive role models, and extending the range of informal networks to which ethnic-minority individuals have access (Watts and Law, 1985).

The third is a more radical approach based on *anti-racist* principles. This seeks to develop a stronger critical understanding of the power relations underlying racism. It might include 'racism awareness training' for careers advisers, seeking to help them to confront their own latent racism, though this has sometimes alienated careers staff and been counter-productive in its effects. 'Anti-racist training', aimed more at organisational strategies for combating racism, has been suggested as being more fruitful in practical terms. This might include strategies for combating racist recruitment practices on the part of employers (Cross *et al.*, 1990). At the level of guidance interventions, strategies might include examining within careers education programmes socio-political issues related to the opportunities open to ethnic minorities, and preparing ethnic-minority individuals to confront discrimination and racism (Watts and Law, 1985).

As in the case of gender, the choice of strategies in relation to ethnicity has to wrestle with complex issues related to identity as well as social context. This is particularly the case when there are tensions between attitudes and behaviours valued within the ethnic-minority subculture, and attitudes and behaviours required to achieve success within the white-dominated labour market. Liberal approaches tend to attach more importance to the former, and progressive approaches to the latter; attempts may be made to reconcile these by seeking to help ethnic-minority groups to become effectively bicultural. Radical approaches, by contrast, seek to address the tensions themselves within a broader critical analysis.

19.6 CONCLUSION

During most of this chapter, the four different approaches to careers education and guidance have been presented as alternatives. In these terms, each is vulnerable to attack.

The *conservative* approach, focused on social control, accepts and seeks to reinforce the social status quo. It thereby conserves existing inequalities which constrain opportunities for many individuals.

The *liberal* approach is in practice closely aligned with the conservative one. It tends to regret any inequalities, but its non-directive character means that it avoids confronting them.

The *progressive* approach, focused on individual change, seeks to alter the distribution of opportunities but not the opportunity structure itself. It therefore accepts the social status quo in a more direct way than the liberal approach does. On the other hand, it in some respects places more pressure on the opportunity structure by raising expectations which this structure may be unable to meet. This is a familiar feature of the 'diploma disease' (Dore, 1976): expectations of vocational advancement lead more individuals to apply for higher levels of education; this leads to an expansion of educational opportunities at a rate which exceeds the pace of change in the skill-mix of the economy; the result is frustration of the very vocational aspirations which have set the process in motion. This is likely to increase individual discontent: the *objective* degree of social inequality needs to be distinguished from the *felt* inequality, which is experienced only in relation to the reference groups with which those at the lower levels of the hierarchy compare themselves; the effect of raising aspirations is to extend these reference groups, thus increasing the sense of relative deprivation (Runciman, 1966). Moreover, because the progressive approach focuses on the individual without questioning the social context, the individual is left carrying the full weight of the deprivation.

The *radical* approach addresses the social causes of inequality and seeks to remedy them through social change. In its more extreme forms, it is prepared to increase individuals' sense of relative deprivation and alienation, on the grounds that this is necessary in order to achieve the level of social consciousness which will stimulate change. In this sense, it may be prepared to sacrifice immediate individual satisfaction in the interests of possible future social reform. This can be aligned to a dogmatism which views alternative viewpoints as 'false consciousness'. It also tends to be utopian in nature: if such utopias turn out to be chimerical, the individual sacrifice it has demanded will be in vain.

Such arguments are, however, based on narrow extrapolation to *reductio ad absurdum* extremes. In reality, no guidance intervention is likely to be sufficiently powerful to achieve the effects envisaged here. Moreover, most guidance interventions are likely to contain some mix of the approaches, particularly if they are to involve some negotiation with clients. Indeed, the argument developed in relation to gender at the end of Section 19.4 can be applied more broadly: elements of the progressive and radical approaches can help to rescue liberal approaches from their conservative inclinations, particularly for individuals and groups whose immediate access to genuine choices is limited; but in the end they need to be reconciled with the liberal approach if the autonomy of the individual is to be respected and supported. The appropriate mix is likely, however, to vary in different situations and with different clients. The professional task of the guidance practitioner is to identify what is morally and pragmatically appropriate in particular contexts. The discussion in this chapter may be helpful in thinking through the options and the issues involved.

REFERENCES

Bates, I. (1990) 'The Politics of Careers Education and Guidance: a Case for Scrutiny', *British Journal of Guidance and Counselling* 18(1): 66–83.

Benett, Y. and Carter, D. (1982) *Sidetracked?: a Look at the Careers Advice Given to Fifth Form Girls*, Manchester: Equal Opportunities Commission.

Birk, J. M., Tanney, M. F. and Cooper, J. F. (1979) 'A Case of Blurred Vision: Stereotyping in Career Information Illustrations', *Journal of Vocational Behavior* 15(2): 247–57.

Blackman, S. J. (1987) 'The Labour Market in School: New Vocationalism and Issues of Socially Ascribed Discrimination', in Brown, P. and Ashton, D. M. (eds) *Education, Unemployment and Labour Markets*, Lewes: Falmer.

Bourdieu, P. and Passeron, J. C. (1977) *Reproduction in Education, Society and Culture*, London: Sage.

Breakwell, G. M. and Weinberger, B. (1987) *Young Women in 'Gender-Atypical' Jobs: the Case of Trainee Technicians in the Engineering Industry*, Research Paper No. 49, London: Department of Employment.

Brewer, J. M. (1942) *History of Vocational Guidance*, New York: Harper.

Brooks, D. and Singh, K. (1978) *Aspirations versus Opportunities: Asian and White School Leavers in the Midlands*, London: Commission for Racial Equality.

Brooks, L., Holahan, W. and Galligan, M. (1985) 'The Effects of a Nontraditional Role-Modeling Intervention on Sex Typing of Occupational Preferences and Career Salience in Adolescent Females', *Journal of Vocational Behavior* 26: 264–76.

Brown, K. M. (1985) 'Turning a Blind Eye: Racial Oppression and the Unintended Consequences of White "Non-Racism"', *Sociological Review* 33(4): 670–90.

Chisholm, L. A. and Holland, J. (1986) 'Girls and Occupational Choice: Anti-Sexism in Action in a Curriculum Development Project', *British Journal of Sociology of Education* 7(4): 353–65.

Clark, B. (1960) *The Open Door College*, New York: McGraw-Hill.

Cockburn, C. (1987) *Two-Track Training: Sex Inequalities and the Youth Training Scheme*, Basingstoke: Macmillan.

Cross, M., Wrench, J. and Barnett, S. (1990) *Ethnic Minorities and the Careers Service: an Investigation into Processes of Assessment and Placement*, Research Paper No. 73, Sheffield: Department of Employment.

Daws, P. P. (1967) *A Good Start in Life*, Cambridge: Careers Research and Advisory Centre.

Devine, F. (1993) 'Gender Segregation and Labour Supply: On "Choosing" Gender-Atypical Jobs', *British Journal of Education and Work* 6(3): 61–74.

Dore, R. (1976) *The Diploma Disease*, London: Allen & Unwin.

Erickson, F. (1975) 'Gatekeeping and the Melting Pot: Interactions in Counseling Encounters', *Harvard Educational Review* 45(1): 44–70.

Fleming, D. and Lavercombe, S. (1982) 'Talking about Unemployment with School-Leavers', *British Journal of Guidance and Counselling* 10(1): 22–33.

Forbes, I. and Mead, G. (1992) *Measure for Measure: a Comparative Analysis of Measures to Combat Racial Discrimination in the Member Countries of the European Community*, Sheffield: Employment Department.

Gottfredson, L. S. (1981) 'Circumscription and Compromise: a Developmental Theory of Occupational Aspirations', *Journal of Counseling Psychology* 28(6): 545–79.

Griffin, C. (1985) *Typical Girls?: Young Women from School to the Job Market*, London: Routledge & Kegan Paul.

Grubb, W. N. and Lazerson, M. (1975) 'Rally Round the Workplace: Continuities and Fallacies in Career Education', *Harvard Educational Review* 45(4): 451–74.

Halmos, P. (1974) 'The Personal and the Political', *British Journal of Guidance and Counselling* 2(2): 130–48.

Hashizume, L. and Crozier, S. (1994) 'A Feminine Definition of Career Achievement', in Crozier, S., Gallivan, J. and Lalande, V. (eds) *Women, Girls and Achievement*, North York, Ont: Captus Press.

Hayes, R. (1986) 'Men's Decisions to Enter or Avoid Nontraditional Occupations', *Career Development Quarterly* 35(2): 89–101.

Her Majesty's Inspectorate (1992) *The Preparation of Girls for Adult and Working Life*, London: Department for Education.

Jackson, B. and Marsden, D. (1962) *Education and the Working Class*, London: Routledge & Kegan Paul.

Katz, M. (1993) *Computer-Assisted Career Decision Making: the Guide in the Machine*, Hillsdale, NJ: Erlbaum.

Law, B. (1981) 'Careers Theory: a Third Dimension?', in Watts, A. G., Super, D. E. and Kidd, J. M. (eds) *Career Development in Britain*, Cambridge: Careers Research and Advisory Centre/Hobsons.

Lee, G. and Wrench, J. (1983) *Skill Seekers: Black Youth, Apprenticeships and Disadvantage*, Leicester: National Youth Bureau.

Madsen, B. (1986) 'Occupational Guidance and Social Change', *International Journal for the Advancement of Counselling* 9(1): 97–112.

Martin, J. and Roberts, C. (1984) *Women and Employment: a Lifetime Perspective*, London: HMSO.

Morrison, P. (1983) 'Parting Clouds: or All Our Futures?', *Careers Journal* 4(2): 6–11.

Oakeshott, M. (1990) *Educational Guidance and Curriculum Change*, London: Further Education Unit/Unit for the Development of Adult Continuing Education.

Pratt, J., Broomfield, J. and Seale, C. (1984) *Option Choice: a Question of Equal Opportunity*, Windsor: NFER–Nelson.

Prout, G. (1983) 'Careers', in Whyld, J. (ed.) *Sexism in the Secondary Curriculum*, London: Harper & Row.

Ranson, S. and Ribbins, P. (1988) *Servicing Careers in the Post-Employment Society*, Lewes: Falmer.

Rees, T. (1992) *Women and the Labour Market*, London: Routledge.

Roberts, K. (1977) 'The Social Conditions, Consequences and Limitations of Careers Guidance', *British Journal of Guidance and Counselling* 5(1): 1–9.

Roberts, K., Duggan, J. and Noble, M. (1981) *Unregistered Youth Unemployment and Outreach Careers Work*, Research Paper No. 31, London: Department of Employment.

Rogers, C. (1961) *On Becoming a Person*, London: Constable.

Runciman, W. G. (1966) *Relative Deprivation and Social Justice*, London: Routledge & Kegan Paul.

Sessions, J. A. (1975) 'Misdirecting Career Education: a Union View', *Vocational Guidance Quarterly* 23(4): 311–16.

Sillitoe, K. and Meltzer, H. (1985) *The West Indian School Leaver, vol. 1: Starting Work*, London: HMSO.

Stephens, W. R. (1970) *Social Reform and the Origins of Vocational Guidance*, Washington, DC: National Vocational Guidance Association.

Sultana, R. (1990) 'Gender, Schooling and Transformation: Evaluating Liberal Feminist Action in Education', *New Zealand Journal of Educational Studies* 25(1): 5–25.

Van Dyke, R. (1981) 'Patriarchy and Careers Education', *Schooling and Culture* 10: 16–24.

Verma, G. K. and Darby, D. S. (1987) *Race, Training and Employment*, Lewes: Falmer.

Watts, A. G. (1973) 'A Structure for Careers Education', in Jackson, R. (ed.) *Careers Guidance: Practice and Problems*, London: Arnold.

Watts, A. G. (1978) 'The Implications of School-Leaver Unemployment for Careers Education in Schools', *Journal of Curriculum Studies* 10(3): 233–50.

Watts, A. G. (1981) 'Careers Education and the Informal Economies', *British Journal of Guidance and Counselling* 9(1): 24–35.

Watts, A. G. (1983) *Education, Unemployment and the Future of Work*, Milton Keynes: Open University Press.

Watts, A. G. and Herr, E. L. (1976) 'Career(s) Education in Britain and the USA: Contrasts and Common Problems', *British Journal of Guidance and Counselling* 4(2): 129–42.

Watts, A. G. and Kant, L. (1986) *A Working Start: Guidance Strategies for Girls and Young Women*, York: Longman/School Curriculum Development Committee.

Watts, A. G. and Knasel, E. G. (1985) *Adult Unemployment and the Curriculum*, London: Further Education Unit.

Watts, A. G. and Law, B. (1985) 'Issues for Careers Education in the Multi-Ethnic Classroom', *Pastoral Care in Education* 3(2): 119–27.

Watts, A. G. and Moran, P. (eds) (1984) *Education for Enterprise*, Cambridge: Careers Research and Advisory Centre/Hobsons.

Weiner, G. (ed.) (1985) *Just a Bunch of Girls: Feminist Approaches to Schooling*, Buckingham: Open University Press.

Williamson, E. G. (1965) *Vocational Counseling: Some Historical, Philosophical, and Theoretical Perspectives*, New York: McGraw-Hill.

Willis, P. (1977) *Learning to Labour: How Working Class Kids Get Working Class Jobs*, Farnborough: Saxon House.

Wrench, J. (1991) 'Gatekeepers in the Urban Labour Market: Constraining or Constrained?', in Cross, M. and Payne, G. (eds) *Work and the Enterprise Culture*, London: Falmer.

Chapter 20

International perspectives

A. G. Watts

20.1 INTRODUCTION

There are at least three reasons for studying guidance systems in other countries than one's own. The first is that it demonstrates the *cultural relativity* of one's own practices. By showing that things are done differently elsewhere, it causes one to question practices which otherwise tend to be taken for granted. The second is that it permits *policy borrowing*. While direct transplanting of practice from one country to another is problematic, new possibilities can be indicated which can be adapted to one's own situation. The third is that it facilitates *international co-operation*. Within an increasingly global economy, the growing mobility of students, trainees and workers between countries means that guidance services need to work more closely together: understanding the similarities and differences between guidance systems can help to facilitate such co-operation and make it more effective.

Studying guidance systems can be a revealing lens through which to seek to understand another country. It brings into focus the education and training system and the economic system, and the relationship between the two. It also illuminates the social and political structure, and cultural factors concerning the relationship between the individual, the family, and the wider society.

Despite all this, the comparative literature on guidance systems is remarkably limited. There are a number of 'travel reports', based on studies conducted by brief visitors. Because these tend to be limited to single countries, however, they usually lack a strong comparative framework. The same is true of collections of country-studies such as Drapela (1979). Some studies have attempted to develop a comparative framework from separate country-studies provided by other authors (e.g. Watts and Ferreira-Marques, 1979; Plant, 1990; Watts, 1992). In other cases, the methodology has included first-hand visits by the main author(s), so strengthening the comparative frame (e.g. Keller and Viteles, 1937; Reubens, 1977; Watts *et al.*, 1988; 1994). Further reports and commentaries have drawn more impressionistically from conferences, visits made over a period of time, and the like (e.g. Reuchlin, 1964; Super, 1974).

The paucity of comparative guidance studies contrasts with the now very extensive and theoretically sophisticated literature on comparative education (for a useful overview, see Halls, 1990). Comparative guidance studies can draw on this literature, of course, but they need a broader frame of reference.

The present chapter attempts to develop a framework for looking at guidance systems in an international perspective. It draws from the existing studies, and particularly from various studies in which I have been personally involved over the last twenty-five years. It pays particular attention to the key differences between guidance systems in different countries, and the reasons for these differences. It looks in turn at the extent to which such differences relate to stage of economic development, to the political system, to social and cultural factors, to the education and training system, and to professional and organisational structures. Finally, it explores the pressures towards convergence and divergence between guidance systems. Many of the points made in the chapter are effectively hypotheses based on selective illustrative evidence rather than conclusions based on exhaustive enquiry. It is hoped, however, that they will encourage more rigorous comparative studies in the future.

20.2 IMPACT OF STAGE OF ECONOMIC DEVELOPMENT

Formal guidance services are, in part at least, a product of economic development. In relatively primitive societies, based on a subsistence economy, there is little division of labour. As agrarian-based societies become more wealthy and sophisticated, with more trade, there is a greater diversity of roles, but allocation of such roles is determined largely by the family, caste or class into which one is born. It is with the growth of industrialisation that the division of labour eventually extends to a point where such traditional mechanisms of role allocation start to break down, and formal guidance services may be developed to supplement them.

It was accordingly at the end of the nineteenth century and in the early years of the twentieth century that the first vocational guidance services began to appear both in the USA and in Europe (Brewer, 1942; Keller and Viteles, 1937; Heginbotham, 1951). In Third World countries, formal guidance services are a much more recent development, and are still very limited in nature (Drapela, 1979).

Stage of economic development can influence not only the extent of guidance services but also their orientation. For countries still in the early stages of economic development, guidance services tend to be dominated by labour-utilisation considerations, channelling individuals into fields of education, training and work that are deemed necessary for the national economy. A common policy role for formal guidance in developing countries, for example, is to encourage young people to move into technical and vocational education rather than aspiring to higher education (Watts and Ferreira Marques, 1979; UNESCO, 1980). It is only in conditions of relative affluence that greater attention may begin to be given to individual human development (Super, 1954; 1985).

More speculatively, it seems possible that as societies move into a post-industrial stage, with more emphasis on knowledge occupations (Drucker, 1969) and more flexible educational and occupational structures (Handy, 1989), the role of guidance may become more salient and more pervasive than it has been in the past. In industrial societies, labour has tended to be concentrated in large organisations, individuals have tended to stay in such organisations for long periods of time, and any career progression they may have experienced has tended to be managed by the organisation; much the same has been true of the system of education, which has preceded employment rather than being interwoven with it; guidance has tended to be concentrated at the interface between the two systems, supporting individuals in their passage between them. In post-industrial societies, all these generalisations are likely to be less valid. The case for lifelong access to guidance in support of continuous career development, in mediating the 'psychological contract' between individuals and organisations (Argyris, 1960; Herriot, 1992) on an iterative basis, and in supporting the construction of self as a 'reflexive project' (Giddens, 1991), accordingly becomes stronger and more pressing (Watts, 1994, 1996; Collin and Watts, 1996).

20.3 IMPACT OF POLITICAL SYSTEMS

If the development of formal guidance services is linked to industrialisation, it also seems to be linked to democratisation. Unless there is some degree of free choice for citizens, guidance services have no role to play. In Maoist China at the time of the Cultural Revolution, for example, all guidance services were disbanded (Weiyuan, 1994). All school-leavers were sent to the countryside, without any choice, to spend a period working in agriculture. Those who went to university were assigned to courses with no consideration for what they were interested in – 'that would be individualism, a capitalist vice' (Chang, 1993 edn, p. 605). Neighbourhood councils decided what training and occupations a member of the community should embark upon. To quit one's job was to incur severe social disapproval (Brammer, 1985). Individuals, in short, had little or no say in the direction of their working lives.

This is an extreme example, but countries with planned economies and totalitarian political systems, whether right-wing or left-wing, tend to have no space for guidance or to view it as a conservative, social-control process, using directive methods to meet labour-utilisation needs. In the USSR under Communist rule, for instance, there was an obligation on all citizens to work, and on the authorities to find work for them. Jobs were commonly assigned by placement commissions. Advancement was dependent significantly on membership of the Communist Party, and 'careerism' in terms of personal quest for career success was disparaged (Skorikov and Vondracek, 1993). The concept of vocational guidance was blurred with vocational selection (Nowikowa, 1991; Zajda, 1979); the task of vocational guidance was to adjust the individual's subjective view of reality to make it consistent with the objective needs of society (Machula, 1989). Teachers in schools were made responsible for vocational guidance, but their programmes tended to be no more than general orientation on current manpower needs along with appeals to fill the labour quotas (Drapela, 1979).

In Germany in the 1930s, the guidance system was strongly influenced by the overtly racist (and ultimately genocidal) policy of the National Socialist regime. The concern was not just for *social* but for *biological* selection. Even before the concentration camps, Jews and other non-Aryans were forced into the least desirable jobs. Keller and Viteles (1937) reported – in terms that in retrospect seem chillingly portentous – that in testing programmes, great stress was laid upon heredity: 'Entire family trees are reconstructed. The characteristics of all the relatives are given, and on the basis of the general pattern the boy is advised as to the kind of work in which he is mostly likely to succeed' (p. 135). They also recorded that counsellors were selected with great care and 'must have the quality of leadership, as expressed in the tenets of the National Socialist Party' (p. 137).

In South Africa under apartheid, a sophisticated guidance system for the white community – strongly influenced by Christian Nationalist ideology – co-existed with a limited or non-existent service for the black community. Severe restrictions were placed on the choice of work for blacks within the white areas – which was where most employment opportunities were located. Migrant workers were classified by labour bureau officers into particular categories of employment, in which they were likely to have to stay for the rest of their working lives. In 1975 there were 30 trained counsellors to provide all psychological services for nearly 3.75 million black school children. Much of their time was spent administering tests, the results of which were used largely for statistical and research rather than guidance purposes. A section on 'vocational guidance' was included in the social studies curriculum: it included a heavy emphasis on 'cultivating realistic attitudes, ideals and expectations' and on 'the importance of manual labour' (Watts, 1980; Dovey, 1980; Dovey and Mason, 1984). The emphasis was thus on bringing students to accept politically-constructed reality: any attempt to encourage a critical approach to this reality was taboo (much the same has been true of counselling in Arab schools in Israel – see Mar'i, 1982).

All of these are clear examples of the constraints placed on guidance services by totalitarian regimes. South Africa under apartheid was, however, different from the earlier examples because it aspired to liberal–democratic principles even though it confined the application of these principles to the white community. This led it to permit the establishment of a small number of community agencies, funded mainly by overseas governments and foundations and by large international companies, which developed careers guidance services for black people. These were part of a wide range of non-governmental organisations in a variety of fields, which played an important role both in developing services and in contesting apartheid (Harding, 1994). The careers centres were concerned to make information on opportunities and on the obstacles to opportunities available, partly to help black people to make career decisions but partly also to encourage them to agitate for political change (Walters, 1989). In the terms outlined in Chapter 19, therefore, they provided an example of community-based guidance agencies pursuing a radical social-change agenda in reaction to an official guidance system operating a conservative social-control strategy. With the end of apartheid and the advent of a new black-dominated government in South Africa, the experience of the community-based careers centres may be crucial in developing an official guidance system capable of addressing the needs of the black communities. The South African case thus provides an example both of contrasting socio-political models within the same country, and of how such models become recontoured when the political system changes.

In general, countries with market economies and democratic political regimes are inclined to attach more importance to guidance. They are also more likely to view it in liberal–progressive terms, seeing it as an non-directive process or as a process designed to maximise individual achievement (see Chapter 19). In these terms, guidance can be seen both as a way of making the labour market work more effectively and as a means of affirming the value attached in democratic societies to the rights of individuals to make free choices about their own lives.

In practice, tensions between societal needs and individual needs mean that even within liberal–democratic societies, guidance sometimes comes under pressure to revert to a conservative social-control model (see Chapter 19). Some countries, however, may attain a sufficient level of democratic sophistication to view these tensions in a different way, and to recognise the validity of guidance as a more radical process of ongoing social change. The most notable case is Sweden, where an official policy statement on guidance issued in 1971 (quoted in Watts, 1981a) included radical as well as liberal–progressive aims. It suggested, for example, that guidance should develop a critical awareness of sources of information and influences on choice:

> Among other things, a critical attitude implies the querying by pupils of the facts selected in the information they are given and the theoretical foundations of that information. For instance, it is important for them to be made aware of the unreliability of forecasts and tests and critical of categorical statements concerning labour market developments.

It placed individual decision-making within a pluralistic social context in which issues of conflict and inequality were not to be avoided:

> Pupils should ask questions and obtain facts concerning social relations and work-places, the values of different groups, problems such as the goal of activities, pay differentials, occupational status, relations between superiors and subordinates, sex roles, etc., and then discuss these matters and relate them to their own problems of vocational decision.

It did not regard obstacles to freedom of choice as given, but instead specifically charged the counsellors to work against them wherever possible:

> SYO [educational and vocational guidance] should counteract restrictions of vocational choice due, e.g., to social background, sex, lack of motivation for the analysis of one's own situation etc., even if this involves questioning decisions taken by the pupil and even if, by increasing the number of alternatives apparent to the pupil, it has the effect of making it more difficult for him [sic] to choose.

It recognised that individual choices could themselves act as agents of change in society, and positively supported such effects:

> One of the tasks of SYO is to supply the individual with true and detailed information, and this may also result conceivably in an increased labour shortage in certain sectors coupled with a labour surplus in others, e.g., due to greater light being shed on the differences between different occupations in terms of remuneration and prospects of job satisfaction. This in turn may lead to long-term changes in the labour market.

Finally, it recognised that some of the social changes necessary to meet the career interests of individuals could not be achieved through individuals working alone, and asserted the links between guidance and the development of political consciousness:

> SYO should among other things be related to instruction and debate concerning trade union and political organisations, and the ability of the individual to influence developments.

In all of these respects, it recognised officially the positive role that guidance could play in promoting constructive social change on a continuous basis. The reality of guidance practice, however, tended to be more prosaic and limited than these radical aims would suggest (Watts, 1981a).

A further recent example of the impact of political systems is the attempt in some countries influenced by the 'New Right' to explore the application of market principles to the organisation of guidance delivery. This has included encouraging the growth of guidance services within the private sector, and moving public guidance services into quasi-market situations where they have been exposed to the forces of competition. Such developments have been particularly evident in the United Kingdom (see Chapter 21), but they have also been visible in Australia (Pryor, 1991), in New Zealand (Hesketh and Kennedy, 1991) and to a lesser extent in some other European countries, notably the Netherlands (Watts et al., 1994).

20.4 IMPACT OF SOCIAL AND CULTURAL FACTORS

In addition to economic and political factors, the significance attached to guidance and its nature are also strongly influenced by social and cultural factors. In social–structural terms, for example, countries with strong social stratification are likely to have relatively limited needs for formal guidance services: individuals tend to make choices within socially circumscribed limits, and are able to get much of the help they need from their family and from informal networks. In societies with relatively high levels of social mobility, on the other hand, formal guidance assumes greater importance: individuals have a wider field of choice available to them, and their family and informal networks are less likely to provide informed help in relation to the full range of opportunities; accordingly, there is likely to be more recourse to formal guidance services to provide the help that is required.

In countries with traditionally strong class systems, the contestation of such systems seems to lead to more attention being paid to sociological dimensions in guidance (see Chapter 19). This is certainly the case in Britain and Scandinavia, where sociologists have made influential contributions to the theoretical guidance literature (see Chapter 2). In the USA, on the other hand, the guidance field has been almost entirely dominated by psychologists. This seems linked to cultural and historical factors. Even though social mobility rates in the USA are not substantially different from those recorded in other economically advanced societies (Blau and Duncan, 1967), the USA has from the beginning of its independent existence been committed to the proposition that 'all men [sic] are created equal' and that any American, however humble his or her origin, can become President. Moreover, the existence of a frontier moving gradually westwards long sustained the possibility of escaping economic and social oppression and becoming wealthy and self-respecting through effort and native wit alone (Turner, 1921). The psychological dominance of guidance thus seems closely linked to the individualism on which American culture is based (Watts, 1981b). Counsellors in the USA appear to have more difficulty than those in Britain in recognising the relevance of socio-political issues to their work.

Individualism is not, however, confined to the USA. In most western industrialised countries, it is an important element of national culture (Hofstede, 1984). In many eastern and Third World cultures, on the other hand, the role of the individual is subordinated to the collectivity, whether to the nuclear family, the extended family, or the tribe. This is linked to Tönnies' (1957 edn) classic distinction between *Gemeinschaft* (a community based on strong common ties in which the individual is not sharply differentiated) and *Gesellschaft* (a society based on individuals forming associations for different purposes). Where *Gemeinschaft* survives, guidance in its individualist form is unlikely to find a place. Esen (1972), for example, pointed out that in Nigeria the central concept of guidance – that of the self-determining individual – was inappropriate, since individual identity was considered subordinate to group – and especially tribal – identity:

> Since the group embodies reality and is the framework within which the people can hope for a degree of self-actualization that would be difficult to attain otherwise, the views of the group's accredited spokesmen tend to become the conscience of the people. Authority, rather than reason or free choice, becomes the guiding principle of the individual's life.
>
> (Esen, 1972, p. 795)

Again, Moracco (1979) noted that in Arab families, individuals were subordinated to the group and in decision-making were influenced strongly by the values and needs of the family. If these conflicted with their own, individuals were expected to conform to family values, expressed in most cases by the father. Similar points have been made in relation to Latin America (Espin, 1979) and to Chinese communities (Scaff and Ting, 1972; Saner-Yui and Saner-Yui, 1985).

In some cases, the concept of individual choice may be further limited by religious fatalism. Amongst the Yoruba in Nigeria, for example, it is believed that all individuals have a predestined occupation as part of their *ori* – a detailed 'blueprint' of the life they will lead and the role they will play within the tribe. To discover this blueprint, it is necessary at each decision point to consult the *batalawo*, an Ifa priest (Ipaye, 1989).

All of these traditions can influence what happens when, as part of the process of industrialisation, formal guidance services grow up in eastern or Third World countries. Thus in countries with a strong emphasis on respect for authority, such guidance is likely to be directive in nature. In Latin America, for instance, students tend to expect the counsellors to tell them exactly what to do, and may judge the counsellor to be incompetent if this does *not* happen. Extensive emphasis on psychometric testing fits well into this tradition (Espin, 1979). The extent to which guidance services are inevitably in conflict with traditional structures, or could and should seek to accommodate themselves to such structures, is an important issue to which we shall return in Section 20.7.

20.5 IMPACT OF EDUCATION, TRAINING AND EMPLOYMENT SYSTEMS

Within these broad economic, political and social structures, and cultural mores, the organisational structure of education, training and employment systems also have an impact on careers guidance provision. Turner (1960) distinguished between educational systems based on 'contest mobility', with weak and late tracking, and those based on 'sponsored mobility', with strong and early tracking.

The former are likely to attach much more importance to guidance than the latter. Thus schools in America, Turner's exemplar of a contest-mobility model, historically developed much more sophisticated guidance and counselling systems than did schools in England, his exemplar of a sponsored-mobility model. It was the introduction of comprehensive schools in Britain, with their greater flexibility and less rigid tracking, which gave rise to a significant increase in the importance of guidance systems (Daws, 1968).

The curriculum theory adopted by a particular educational system is also likely to influence the place of formal guidance within it. Nicholas (1983) distinguished three models: European classicism, in which objective knowledge is pursued for its own sake, and the search for wisdom, truth and beauty is regarded as the highest form of human activity, which should not be sullied or tainted by the practical world; Marxist–Leninism, in which the political purpose of schooling is to act as an agent in the production of the new Communist society, inculcating the skills, knowledge, attitudes and behaviour which will be needed; and liberal–pragmatism, in which schools are seen as servicing the needs of the individual, in his or her pursuit of freedom and social mobility. Formal guidance would seem likely to have very little place in relation to European classicism, a limited and highly directive place in relation to the Marxist–Leninist model (as already noted in Section 20.3), and a much more central, though less directive, role in relation to liberal–pragmatism. This helps to explain why careers education has been able to establish a place within the curriculum more readily in some countries (e.g. the USA, Denmark, Netherlands, and *Realschulen* in Germany) than in others (e.g. France, and *Gymnasien* in Germany).

The nature of the vocational education and training system is relevant too. Systems which are largely based on apprenticeship within the workplace are likely to locate their main guidance services within labour-market institutions, whereas those which are largely education-based tend to locate them within education. Thus in Germany, with its strong apprenticeship system, vocational guidance is a formal monopoly of the Bundesanstalt für Arbeit, a labour-market organisation. In France, with its structure of vocational education, on the other hand, the main guidance services are part of the education system (Watts *et al.*, 1994).

The issue of whether formal guidance services are located in educational or labour-market institutions is important, because it tends to influence their orientation. Services based within education tend to focus on educational-choice processes, to be somewhat detached from the world of work, and to emphasise personal-development aspects of guidance. Services based within labour-market institutions, by contrast, tend to focus on occupational choice and job placement, and to emphasise labour-market realities. The choice of location may not only influence such considerations but also be influenced by them: countries with strong labour-utilisation rather than individual-development concerns (see Section 20.2) are more likely to base guidance services within employment services and other labour-market institutions rather than within education. Many countries, of course, have guidance services in both sectors, and/or in 'agency' structures located between them.

The nature of the employment system also has an effect on the structure and nature of guidance services. In Japan, for example, the 'lifetime employment system' means that men in particular tend to make their primary commitment to an organisation rather than to an occupation, and to stay in the same organisation throughout their career (Watts, 1985). Indeed, their corporate membership tends to occupy a major part of their self-identity (Ishiyama and Kitayama, 1994). The result is that guidance and placement services for facilitating movement *between* organisations are not well developed, whereas there has been a growth of services designed to facilitate career development *within* organisations. In addition, in guidance services for young people there is a much heavier emphasis than in most other countries on choice of organisation. Much of the careers information made available in guidance services for young people entering the labour market is accordingly classified by organisation rather than by occupation (Watts, 1985).

20.6 IMPACT OF PROFESSIONAL AND ORGANISATIONAL STRUCTURES

A final set of international differences in guidance provision is related to the professional and organisational structures within which guidance is located. The professional identity and training of those occupying formal guidance roles varies considerably. In many cases their primary professional identity is as psychologists, as teachers, or as labour-market administrators. In such cases, their guidance training is regarded as being incorporated into, or supplementary to, the training for their primary professional role. This explains why their guidance training is sometimes limited in scale and even optional in nature. It is only in a residual number of cases that the primary professional identity of guidance professionals is as counsellors or guidance workers, with their own specialist training (Watts *et al.*, 1988; Watts, 1992).

To some extent, of course, professional identity is linked to sectoral location: services based in educational institutions will tend to be staffed by teachers; services in labour-market organisations by labour-market administrators; services in separate agencies by psychologists or specialist counsellors. This is not, however, invariably the case. In Sweden, for example, the SYO counsellors are based in schools but are not trained as teachers (Watts, 1981a). Again, psychologists are to be found in schools and in labour-market organisations as well as in separate agencies. Reuchlin (1964) points out that the delivery of services by psychologists tends to be related to an emphasis on psychometric testing.

The definition of the focus of the counsellor's role also varies between countries. A common conceptual distinction is between *educational* guidance (e.g. on educational options, or on learning problems), *vocational* guidance (e.g. on choice of occupations and work roles), and *personal* and *social* guidance (e.g. on behaviour problems, or emotional issues). In some cases – Germany, for example – there is clear-cut distinction between these forms of guidance, which are allocated to wholly separate agencies. In other cases, all three forms of guidance are brought together: in Belgium, through different roles based in one agency (the Psycho-Medico-Social Centre); in schools in such countries as Ireland, through a single role (the school counsellor or guidance counsellor) (Watts *et al.*, 1994).

The combined effect of professional identity, sectoral location and role focus leads to very varied models of provision across countries in relation to schools in particular. Broadly, there are three main ways in which careers guidance provision is organised within schools (Watts, 1988a).

First, it can be based on specialists outside the school. These specialists may be based in education authorities (e.g. France) or in labour-market authorities (e.g. Germany). They may cover all three forms of guidance (e.g. Belgium) or they may focus mainly on educational or vocational guidance (e.g. France and Germany respectively). They commonly go into schools to offer interviews, give talks, and so on, but they do so from an external base.

Second, careers guidance can be provided by specialists inside the school. In some cases these are non-teachers (e.g. Sweden). In others, they are initially trained as teachers but have had substantial in-service training in counselling and now spend most of their time on guidance and counselling activities: in effect, their guidance role has taken on the attributes of a sub-profession within the teaching profession. In such cases, their roles usually cover educational and personal/social as well as vocational guidance: this is true of school counsellors in such countries as Canada, Ireland, the Philippines and the USA. Where the role is confined to educational and vocational guidance, the level of specialist training in guidance and of time allocated to guidance roles tends to be much more limited: this is the case, for example, with careers teachers in Greece and the Netherlands.

Third, careers guidance can be more fully integrated into the school, by encouraging most or all teachers to be involved in it. This may be attempted by seeking to integrate it into academic-subject teaching, which has been tried in such countries as Germany (Busshoff, quoted in Watts and Ferreira-Marques, 1979) and the USA (Watts and Herr, 1976), though it has proved difficult to implement successfully. Alternatively, careers guidance can be integrated into the 'pastoral' structure of the school: this is the case, for instance, in Japan, where it is regarded as part of the responsibility of the 'home-room' teacher (Watts, 1985); in Venezuela, where all teachers are expected to take on the role of guidance counsellor in addition to that of specialist teacher of a specific subject (Kim, 1987); and in Singapore, where careers education is delivered through a curriculum in pastoral care implemented by form tutors (Watts, 1988b).

These organisational models are not mutually exclusive, and many countries have elements of more than one model. In England and Wales, for example, there are elements of all three: careers education and guidance is offered by careers officers based outside the school, by careers teachers based inside the school, and by tutors who form the basis of the school's pastoral-care structure.

The same kinds of distinctions can be drawn in relation to guidance services available to young people and adults after leaving school. These services are in many countries less well-developed than services for young people in schools. But a study of guidance systems within the European Community found significant between-country differences in guidance services in tertiary education, in guidance services for young people based outside full-time education (in apprenticeship structures, in transition programmes, and in youth and community services), and in guidance services for adults (within public employment services, in adult education, in the voluntary and private sectors, and in the workplace) (Watts et al., 1994).

20.7 CONVERGENCE OR DIVERGENCE?

Much of this chapter has focused on variations between formal guidance systems in different countries. Some of these variations have been essentially organisational in nature; others have been more conceptual and ideological. They have been linked to economic, political, socio-cultural, educational and professional factors. Across societies, these factors are interwoven in complex ways: the implications of these textures needs more detailed exploration than has been possible here.

The focus on variations requires, however, to be balanced by a recognition that there are some tendencies to professional convergence which may transcend such differences. Thus a four-stage model of the development of conceptions of careers guidance in schools (from a focus on information, through a focus on interviewing and then the addition of careers education to the curriculum, to the integration of careers education across the curriculum) which was originally developed in relation to the UK (Law and Watts, 1977), appears to have a wider validity as a way of explaining such development in other countries too (Watts, 1988a).

Again, it seems that across the guidance systems within the European Community, three common trends can be identified. The first is towards guidance as a continuous process, which should start in schools and be accessible throughout adult and working life. The second is towards a more open professional model, in which the concept of an expert guidance specialist working with individual clients in a psychological vacuum is replaced or supplemented by a more diffuse approach in which a more varied range of interventions is used and more attention is given to working with and through networks of other individuals and agencies. The third is a greater emphasis on the individual as an active agent, rather than a passive recipient, within the guidance process (Watts *et al.*, 1994). These trends are evident in advanced industrialised countries in other parts of the world too.

Such convergence is supported by international links as mediated through such organisations as the International Association for Educational and Vocational Guidance (IAEVG) and the International Round Table for the Advancement of Counselling (IRTAC). It is also fostered by aid programmes and international use of consultants. Many countries with less developed guidance systems have looked to countries with more developed systems for models and support. International borrowing of this kind can lead to difficulties. In countries such as Ghana and Malaysia, for example, individualistic client-centred models of guidance were imported from the USA and Britain which seemed inappropriate to the culture and meant that insufficient attention was paid to basic priorities such as the provision of occupational information (Bolger, 1978; Watts, 1978; see also Kim, 1987).

Underlying the issue of convergence or divergence is the extent to which guidance is a technique or a philosophy. Morris (1955) suggests 'that guidance is purely a technique, that it is only a means, and that the ends which it serves will be determined both by the cultural tradition within which it operates and by the detailed way in which it interprets that tradition in its modes of operation' (p. 124). Patterson (1978), on the other hand, takes the view that counselling 'is neither time-bound nor culture-bound; it transcends time and culture, since it is based upon the universal unity of human nature' (p. 231). According to Patterson, counselling is concerned essentially with self-actualisation, which 'is an ultimate, universal value, not one that is man-made or culture-bound'. He is careful to note that self-actualisation is not necessarily identified with western culture and with its 'extreme individualism, selfish aggrandizement, and competitive dog-eat-dog ethics, with the devil taking the hindmost'. But he argues that the values and forms of every culture 'must be judged or evaluated in terms of their contribution to the self-actualization of the individual' (pp. 237–38). In this sense, the goals of counselling are universal, not culture-specific. These arguments are developed in relation to counselling in general, but could equally be applied to careers education and guidance in particular.

The arguments and evidence we have presented in this chapter offer some support for both these views. Guidance is able to take many different forms. Certainly its organisational features vary considerably, as do its techniques and approaches. But at the heart of the concept of guidance is a set of values which call into question whether guidance services in, for example, Nazi Germany represented guidance in a 'true' or 'complete' sense.

Formal guidance services, as we have seen, are linked to industrialisation, to democratisation, to social mobility, and to cultural individualism. In societies where these processes are less evident, the values which are central to guidance philosophy – of respect for the individual, and of concern for individual growth and development – may still be present, if within a very different cultural context. As the pace of change encourages the growth of guidance services in such countries, it is important that such services respect and work with elements of the culture which are congruent with their own.

REFERENCES

Argyris, C. (1960) *Understanding Organizational Behavior*, Homewood, IL: Dorsey.
Blau, P. M. and Duncan, O. D. (1967) *The American Occupational Structure*, New York: Wiley.
Bolger, A. W. (1978) 'Guidance and Counseling in a Developing Country', *International Journal for the Advancement of Counselling* 1(3): 225–29.
Brammer, L. M. (1985) 'Counselling Services in the People's Republic of China', *International Journal for the Advancement of Counselling* 8(2): 125–36.
Brewer, J. M. (1942) *History of Vocational Guidance*, New York: Harper.
Chang, J. (1993 edn) *Wild Swans* (first pub. 1991), London: Flamingo.
Collin, A. and Watts, A. G. (1996) 'The Death and Transfiguration of Career – and of Career Guidance?', *British Journal of Guidance and Counselling* (in press).
Daws, P. P. (1968) *A Good Start in Life*, Cambridge: Careers Research and Advisory Centre.
Dovey, K. A. (1980) 'Politics and Guidance: an Overview of the South African School Guidance Service', *British Journal of Guidance and Counselling* 8(1): 1–10.
Dovey, K. and Mason, M. (1984) 'Guidance for Submission: Social Control and Guidance in Schools for Black Pupils in South Africa', *British Journal of Guidance and Counselling* 12(1): 15–24.
Drapela, V. (ed.) (1979) *Guidance and Counseling around the World*, Washington, DC: University Press of America.
Drucker, P. (1969) *The Age of Discontinuity*, London: Heinemann.
Esen, A. (1972) 'A View of Guidance from Africa', *Personnel and Guidance Journal* 50(10): 792–98.
Espin, O. M. (1979) 'A Changing Continent', in Drapela, V. (ed.) *Guidance and Counseling Around the World*, Washington, DC: University Press of America.
Giddens, A. (1991) *Modernity and Self-Identity*, Cambridge: Polity Press.
Halls, W. D. (ed.) (1990) *Comparative Education: Contemporary Issues and Trends*, London: Jessica Kingsley/UNESCO.
Handy, C. (1989) *The Age of Unreason*, London: Business Books.

Harding, D. (1994) *From Global to Local: Issues and Challenges Facing NGOs*, Durban: Olive.
Heginbotham, H. (1951) *The Youth Employment Service*, London: Methuen.
Herriot, P. (1992) *The Career Management Challenge*, London: Sage.
Hesketh, B. and Kennedy, L. (1991) 'Changes and Responsibilities: Policy Challenges Confronting Careers Guidance in New Zealand', *British Journal of Guidance and Counselling* 19(3): 246–57.
Hofstede, G. (1984) *Culture's Consequences*, Beverly Hills, CA: Sage.
Ipaye, B. (1989) 'Vocational Guidance in Nigeria', *Prospects* 69: 65–73.
Ishiyama, F. I. and Kitayama, A. (1994) 'Overwork and Career-Centered Self-Validation among the Japanese: Psychosocial Issues and Counselling Implications', *International Journal for the Advancement of Counselling* 17(3): 167–82.
Keller, F. J. and Viteles, M. S. (1937) *Vocational Guidance throughout the World*, London: Cape.
Kim, Y. M. (1987) 'Student Guidance in Secondary Education in Latin America', *Prospects* 17(1): 107–14.
Law, B. and Watts, A. G. (1977) *Schools, Careers and Community*, London: Church Information Office.
Machula, C. S. (1989) 'The Soviet School Reforms of 1984: Making Career Development a Matter of State Control', *Career Development Quarterly* 38(1): 39–56.
Mar'i, S. K. (1982) 'Cultural and Socio-Political Influences on Counseling and Career Guidance: the Case of Arabs in the Jewish State', *International Journal for the Advancement of Counselling* 5(4): 247–63.
Moracco, J. (1979) 'Arab Countries', in Drapela, V. (ed.) *Guidance and Counseling Around the World*, Washington, DC: University Press of America.
Morris, B. (1955) 'Guidance as a Concept in Educational Philosophy', in *The Year Book of Education 1955*, London: Evans.
Nicholas, E. J. (1983) *Issues in Education: a Comparative Analysis*, London: Harper & Row.
Nowikowa, T. (1991) 'Problems of Vocational Orientation in the USSR', *Educational and Vocational Guidance* 52: 8–15.
Patterson, C. H. (1978) 'Cross-Cultural or Intercultural Counseling or Psychotherapy', *International Journal for the Advancement of Counselling* 1(3): 231–47.
Plant, P. (1990) *Transnational Vocational Guidance and Training for Young People and Adults*, Berlin: CEDEFOP.
Pryor, R. G. L. (1991) 'When the Luck Runs Out: Policy Challenges Confronting Careers Guidance in Australia', *British Journal of Guidance and Counselling* 19(3): 283–97.
Reubens, B. (1977) *Bridges to Work: International Comparisons of Transition Services*, Montclair, NJ: Allanheld, Osmun.
Reuchlin, M. (1964) *Pupil Guidance: Facts and Problems*, Strasbourg: Council for Cultural Co-operation of the Council of Europe.
Saner-Yui, R. and Saner-Yui, L. (1985) 'Value Dimensions in American Counseling Theory: a Taiwanese–American Comparison', *International Journal for the Advancement of Counselling* 8(2): 137–46.
Scaff, M. K. and Ting, M. G. (1972) 'Fu Tao: Guidance in Taiwan Seeks a Value Orientation', *Personnel and Guidance Journal* 50(8): 645–53.
Skorikov, V. and Vondracek, F. W. (1993) 'Career Development in the Commonwealth of Independent States', *Career Development Quarterly* 41(4): 314–29.
Super, D. E. (1954) 'Guidance: Manpower Utilization or Human Development?', *Personnel and Guidance Journal* 33: 8–14.
Super, D. E. (1974) 'The Broader Context of Career Development and Vocational Guidance: American Trends in World Perspective', in Herr, E. L. (ed.) *Vocational Guidance and Human Development*, Boston, MA: Houghton Mifflin.
Super, D. E. (1985) 'Guidance and Mobility in the Educational Systems of Developing and Developed Countries', *Educational and Vocational Bulletin* 44: 24–28.
Tönnies, F. (1957 edn) *Community and Society* (trans. C. P. Loomis) (first pub. 1887), New York: Harper & Row.
Turner, F. J. (1921) *The Frontier in American History*, New York: Holt.
Turner, R. H. (1960) 'Modes of Social Ascent through Education: Sponsored and Contest Mobility and the School System', *American Sociological Review* 25(5): 855–67.

UNESCO (1980) *Sub-Regional Seminar on the Promotion of Educational and Vocational Guidance in the Arab States: Final Report*, Beirut: UNESCO (mimeo).

Walters, S. (1989) *Education for Democratic Participation*, Cape Town: Centre for Adult and Continuing Education, University of the Western Cape.

Watts, A. G. (1978) 'Careers Guidance in a Developing Country: Malaysia', *International Journal for the Advancement of Counselling* 1(2): 97–105.

Watts, A. G. (1980) 'Careers Guidance under Apartheid', *International Journal for the Advancement of Counselling* 3(1): 3–27.

Watts, A. G. (1981a) 'Careers Guidance in Sweden: a British Perspective', *International Journal for the Advancement of Counselling* 4(3): 187–207.

Watts, A. G. (1981b) 'Introduction', in Watts, A. G., Super, D. E. and Kidd, J. M. (eds) *Career Development in Britain*, Cambridge: Careers Research and Advisory Centre/Hobsons.

Watts, A. G. (1985) 'The Japanese "Lifetime Employment System" and its Implications for Careers Guidance', *International Journal for the Advancement of Counselling* 8(2): 91–114.

Watts, A. G. (1988a) 'The Changing Place of Careers Guidance in Schools', *Prospects* 18(4): 473–82.

Watts, A. G. (1988b) 'Changing Conceptions of Careers Guidance and a Proposed Model for Singapore Schools', *Singapore Journal of Education* 9(1): 28–36.

Watts, A. G. (1992) *Occupational Profiles of Vocational Counsellors in the European Community*, Berlin: CEDEFOP.

Watts, A. G. (1994) *Lifelong Career Development: Towards a National Strategy for Careers Education and Guidance*, CRAC Occasional Paper, Cambridge: Careers Research and Advisory Centre/Hobsons.

Watts, A. G. (1996) 'Towards a Policy for Lifelong Career Development: a Trans-Atlantic Perspective', *Career Development Quarterly* (in press).

Watts, A. G. and Ferreira-Marques, J. H. (1979) *Guidance and the School Curriculum*, Paris: UNESCO (mimeo).

Watts, A. G. and Herr, E. L. (1976) 'Career(s) Education in Britain and the USA: Contrasts and Common Problems', *British Journal of Guidance and Counselling* 4(2): 129–42.

Watts, A. G., Dartois, C. and Plant, P. (1988) *Educational and Vocational Guidance Services for the 14–25 Age Group in the European Community*, Maastricht: Presses Interuniversitaires Européennes.

Watts, A. G., Guichard, J., Plant, P. and Rodriguez, M. L. (1994) *Educational and Vocational Guidance in the European Community*, Luxembourg: Office for Official Publications of the European Communities.

Weiyuan, Z. (1994) 'The History and Current State of Careers Guidance in China', *Educational and Vocational Guidance Bulletin* 55: 1–7.

Zajda, J. (1979) 'Education for Labour in the USSR', *Comparative Education* 15(3): 287–99.

Chapter 21

Careers guidance and public policy

A. G. Watts

21.1 INTRODUCTION

At the point of delivery, careers education and guidance is addressed to the welfare of individuals. Most guidance services, however, are funded by government, whether directly or indirectly. They are accordingly the *object* of public policy. Moreover, in presenting the case for such funding, it is commonly argued that guidance is a public as well as a private good, in economic and/or social terms. In this sense, guidance services are also potentially an *instrument* of public policy.

The beneficiaries of guidance are, in principle, multiple. The *immediate* beneficiary is the individual, in making and implementing decisions which maximise their potential and accord as closely as possible with their personal interests and values. There are also *intermediate* beneficiaries. These include education and training providers: guidance can increase the effectiveness of such provision by linking learners to programmes which meet their needs and inspire their motivations, so improving learning performance. They further include employers: guidance can filter employees whose talents and motivations are suited to the employer's requirements. The *ultimate* beneficiary – from a policy perspective – is the society as a whole, in ensuring that optimum use is made of its human resources, reconciled with its social values. In democratic polities, governments are the custodians of this wider societal interest.

The main broad aims which governments tend to seek through guidance provision are twofold. The first is *economic efficiency* in the allocation and use of human resources. It is argued, for example, that guidance can support the individual decisions through which the labour market operates, can reduce some of its market failures, and can support reforms designed to improve its normal functioning (Killeen *et al.*, 1992) (see Chapter 3); it is also argued that guidance is an important mechanism for linking the educational system to the labour market, so optimising the economic yield from the state's investment in education. The second aim is *social equity* in access to educational and vocational opportunities. Guidance can perform a valuable role in raising the aspirations of individuals from disadvantaged backgrounds, making them aware of opportunities, and supporting them in securing entry to such opportunities (see Chapter 19).

The balance between these two aims tends to vary between different guidance services, and under different political regimes. Left-wing governments tend to attach more weight to social equity, whereas right-wing governments tend to focus more strongly on economic efficiency. In either case, however, it is possible to seek to implement such aims through structural solutions (tax systems and the like). It is only when faith in such structural solutions breaks down, and/or when it is believed that these aims are best pursued through free but informed individual choices, that 'softer' and more process-focused interventions such as guidance are given prominence.

In this sense, guidance can be viewed in a policy perspective as a kind of *brokerage* between individual needs and societal needs. It addresses both individual rights and individual responsibilities within a societal context. It is a means of encouraging individuals to participate in determining their role within, and their contribution to, the society of which they are part. This emphasis on the 'active individual' provides a third and more distinctive rationale for policy interest in guidance, which helps to explain why countries with market economies and liberal–democratic regimes have tended to pay more attention to this field than countries with planned economies and totalitarian political systems (see Chapter 20).

An important issue for policy is the extent to which it seeks to emphasise public interests which go beyond, and may at times be at variance with, the direct interests of the individuals who are the direct recipients of the guidance service. In relation to the Careers Service, for example, Chapter 9 shows that the roots of the service – and a recurrent theme through its history – have been a concern to convince more young people to take a longer-term view of their future and to invest more strongly in education and training, rather than taking immediate jobs on offer. This can be represented as being in the individual's long-term interests as well as meeting societal needs for upgrading of skills. At other times, however, the government has emphasised the need for the service to meet the immediate demands of the labour market, encouraging young people to take up whatever opportunities are available. This tension was particularly acute during the 1980s when the performance of the service was significantly measured in terms of placement into government training schemes, many of which were widely regarded as low-skill and dead-end in nature. The result was that the service was viewed by some young people as a coercive functionary of youth training, resulting in hostility and suspicion towards it (Mizen, 1995).

It is for these kinds of reasons that guidance professionals have tended consistently to argue that their *primary* client must be the individual, rather than employers or indeed government. There are practical as well as ethical reasons for this, not the least of which is that guidance services can only serve the interests of their secondary clients (the intermediate and ultimate beneficiaries noted earlier) if they retain the confidence and trust of the individuals with whom they are working (the direct beneficiaries) – whose interests must accordingly be given primacy.

This requires a self-denying ordinance on the part of government. It may justify public support for guidance services on the grounds that they serve public purposes, but it has to abnegate these purposes as the operating principles on which the practice of the services should be based. This means that careers guidance needs to be viewed not as a direct *instrument* of public policy, but more as a *lubricant* of such policies and of the operations of the labour market (Watts, 1980). Under this view, guidance services have a responsibility to ensure that individual choices are well-informed in terms of the opportunity structure, but they have

no responsibility for directing or encouraging individuals to meet the requirements of educational institutions or employers, or the behest of government. In
other words, the main concern of guidance is seen as being to enable individuals
to take responsibility for their choices in terms of what is in their own best interests. The assumption is that this will ultimately serve the public interest too. It is,
in principle, a classic case of Adam Smith's (1776) famous dictum that individuals encouraged to pursue their own interests are led by an 'invisible hand' to promote an end which is no part of their intention – the public interest – and to do
so more effectually than when they intend to promote it.

The remainder of this chapter will explore some applications of public policy
in relation to careers guidance. First, it will examine the *functions* of policy in this
area, including their relevance to different sectors of guidance provision. Next, it
will identify a number of different *models* of public policy in relation to guidance.
Finally, in the light of this analysis, it will review the major policy *applications*
which have influenced guidance developments in the UK, with particular emphasis on the policy changes which took place in the late 1980s and early 1990s.

21.2 POLICY FUNCTIONS

There are three possible functions of policy in relation to guidance provision.
The first is funding. The second is influence. The third is regulation.

As already noted, most guidance services are *funded* by government. This
funding may be provided *directly* from central or local government, whether to
fulfil statutory provision (as in the case of the Careers Service) or on a shorter-
term programme basis. Or it may be provided *indirectly* – as, for example, where
educational institutions are funded by government and choose to devote some
of this funding to the provision of guidance services.

Whether or not its funding is direct or indirect, the government may seek to *influence* the nature of guidance provision. Such influence can be exerted in a variety of
ways, ranging from exhortation in ministers' speeches to formal policy guidelines.

In some cases, government may seek to intervene more strongly through *regulation*. This is particularly likely where it is directly responsible for funding and
can exert financial sanctions for non-compliance. It may also, however, seek to
regulate services funded indirectly – through inspection procedures, for instance.
It could also in principle seek to regulate services provided on a market basis,
by requiring licences to offer such services.

The balance between these functions varies in relation to the three main sectors
of guidance provision identified in Part II of this book. *Employer-based guidance*
(Chapter 8) is still fairly embryonic, and since it has been provided on a voluntary basis by employers who consider it relevant to their organisational aims,
the role of government has been limited to influence, mainly in the form of
exhortation and kite-marking (notably the Investors in People programme) plus
some limited pump-priming funding (notably the Skill Choice programme).

Education-based guidance (Chapters 5–7) is normally included in the general
funding of educational institutions. Accordingly, decisions on the extent of
investment in guidance services, and the form which these services should take,
are made independently by each institution. The role of government is again
usually confined to influence, through publication of policy guidelines and the
like, sometimes supported by inspection procedures which provide some degree

of regulation (see Hawthorn, 1995). In the case of further education, guidance has been tied more closely into the funding mechanism, as a means of making the institutional culture more learner-centred: this means a stronger regulatory role (see Chapter 6).

It is, however, the area of 'external' or *free-standing guidance* (Chapters 9–10) that is the main focus for government policy in terms of funding and regulation. Since such guidance is not provided by intermediary organisations, government has to take direct decisions regarding the extent to which it wishes to fund guidance services or to leave them to the free play of the market. Where it decides to provide funding, its direct responsibility for such funding means that it is likely to impose a relatively strong degree of regulation.

Since 'free-standing' guidance is, paradoxically, the sector in which the role of public policy tends to be most direct, this will provide the main focus for our examination of recent policy developments in the remainder of this chapter. This examination will draw heavily from earlier analyses (Watts, 1991; 1995), but with some extension and updating.

21.3 POLICY MODELS

Within the 'free-standing' guidance sector, government can in principle adopt one of three models. The first is a *social-welfare* model, in which guidance is fully funded and controlled by government as part of the welfare state. The second is a *market* model, in which guidance is paid for by its direct beneficiaries – individuals – or perhaps in some cases by employers (as part of redundancy counselling packages, for example). The third is a *quasi-market* model, in which there may be varied sources of funding, with a greater degree of autonomy for services than in the social-welfare model, and more room for a non-profit ethos than in the market model.

In the UK, as in most other countries, careers guidance services have traditionally been conceived as part of public-sector social-welfare provision. The main services have accordingly been funded by government, whether central or local, and have been free to the individual at the point of delivery.

The rationale for including guidance as part of social-welfare provision is in principle twofold. The first is that guidance is a 'worthy good' (Savas, 1987) which is so intrinsically desirable that individuals have a right to have access to it regardless of the resources at their disposal. The second is the one already discussed earlier in this chapter: that guidance offers public as well as private benefits. In either case, as with other parts of the welfare state, the taxation system is used to ensure that some elements of private income are 'devoted to purposes of common advantage' (Tawney, 1964 edn, p. 124). These purposes include 'the desire for a more socially just, more materially equal, more truly democratic society' (Thane, 1982, p. 253).

In the late 1970s and early 1980s, a strong critique of the welfare state in general was launched by the New Right in the UK and a number of other countries. The bureaucratic structures of the welfare state were alleged to reduce freedom in six respects: by infringing the freedom of taxpayers to dispose of their property as they pleased; by limiting the range of services; by paternalistically directing citizens towards defined choices; by imposing bureaucratic and/or legal restrictions on individuals; by producing dependency among welfare recipients; and by creating its own supporting interest groups among bureaucrats and beneficiaries, who then opposed alternative social and political arrangements (Goodin, 1982). The last point was developed by public choice theorists (e.g. Niskanen, 1971), who argued that the welfare state induced its bureaucrats to be self-interested budget maximisers, and that this – allied to the absence of profit criteria, and pressures on politicians to promise goods and services to voters in order to secure election – encouraged the public sector to expand in a reckless manner. While this 'backlash against professional society' (Perkin, 1989) emanated largely from the New Right, it also reflected critiques from anarcho-Left writers such as Illich (1973; 1977).

The result of this critique was a political move to restore market principles to social and economic activities wherever it was possible to do so. The assumption was that the market-based production of goods and services ensured greater responsiveness to consumer choice and greater efficiency because of the profit incentive (see King, 1987). For writers such as Hayek (1944), individualism was allied with market relations because the latter maximised liberty as voluntary choice and reduced coercion to a minimum. In particular, it was argued that the market, by encouraging plurality of provision, enabled consumers to exert pressure on providers through 'exit' (i.e. going elsewhere) as well as through 'voice' (i.e. consumer feedback) (Hirschmann, 1970).

These arguments, applied to guidance provision, lead to the notion that independent guidance is best assured where the service is paid for directly by the user rather than indirectly by the taxpayer. This suggests in turn that existing public-sector guidance services should be privatised, and a *market in guidance* be encouraged to develop. There has long been a limited sector of private fee-charging careers guidance services (see Chapter 10): this, it is contended, should now be encouraged to grow.

This leaves open, however, the question of the public interest in guidance as a public good. In market language, guidance can be viewed in these terms as a *market-maker*: a means of making other markets – notably the labour market, and the education and training market – work more effectively by ensuring that the supply-side actors within these markets have access to market information and are able to read market signals. The issue then is whether a market in guidance is likely to deliver the public interest in guidance as a market-maker. If it does not do so, public intervention needs to be maintained.

Some advocates of market principles accept this argument, but contend that such interventions need to take a different form. They accept the state's role in *paying* for these and other services through the taxation system, but argue that it should apply market principles wherever possible to the administrative mechanisms through which the goods are *delivered* to their customers (Osborne and Gaebler, 1992; Savas, 1987). The result of this line of thought is the concept of 'quasi-markets' (Le Grand, 1991) or 'social markets' (Davies, 1992). These can take a variety of forms. One is *contracts*, where the services are contracted out to external agencies, which may be commercial or non-profit in nature. Another is *vouchers*, where the public funding is channelled not to the provider but to the user, who is then able to take it to whichever service he or she chooses. The assumption is that the competitive mechanism implicit in such arrangements drives up quality. In the case of vouchers, it is further assumed that channelling funding through individuals empowers them in their relationships with guidance agencies and so makes it more likely that the guidance provided is designed to meet their interests.

Quasi-markets, it should be noted, can have attractions to the political Left as well as to the Right. Le Grand and Estrin (1989), for example, promote the concept of market socialism, in which market means are applied to socialist ends – preventing exploitation of the weak by the powerful, securing greater equality of income, wealth, status and power, and assuring the satisfaction of basic needs. They point out that vouchers can be used for redistributive purposes, and that the fact that the idea of vouchers has in recent years been colonised almost exclusively by the New Right does not mean that there is anything inherently right-wing in what is perhaps their principal potential merit – empowering the welfare client.

These arguments have obvious potential applicability to guidance services. Indeed, as we shall see in Section 21.4, there have been experiments in applying both contracts and vouchers to such services. An important issue, however, is the extent to which the application of market or even quasi-market arguments engages with the essence of their professional nature. Gorz (1989) argues that the rationality of 'cost and return' which comprises 'economic reason' has over time been expanding its territorial domain, yet is 'unaware of how narrow its proper limits are' (p. 2). The important question is to determine 'which activities can be subordinated to economic rationality without losing their meaning and for which activities economic rationalisation would be a perversion or a negation of the meaning inherent in them' (pp. 132–33). In Gorz's view, the infiltration of economic reason is particularly inappropriate with regard to the 'caring professions', which include education and health (and, we might add, guidance). For these types of profession, Gorz argues, efficiency is impossible to quantify: indeed, it is 'possible for the efficiency of "carers" to be in inverse proportion to their visible quantifiable output'. This is because the service 'depends on a person-by-person relationship, not on the execution of predetermined, quantifiable output' (p. 143). Such jobs 'are only done well when they are performed out of a "sense of vocation", that is, an *unconditional* desire to help other people' (p. 144). Accordingly, they need to be uncoupled from a direct and narrowly-defined cash nexus.

Such arguments can be framed in quasi-religious terms. Economic reason is viewed as a 'secular' or 'profane' attempt to infiltrate, colonise or control the 'sacred' essence of certain professional activities. This 'secularisation process' must be resisted to prevent the 'sacred' being compromised (Broadbent et al., 1993; cf. Eliade, 1959). Such notions are clearly open to abuse, providing a mystical cover for professional self-interest. But there is an essential truth at their heart: that economic gain is not the only source of personal motivation, and in relation to some professional activities – including, arguably, guidance – may be less appropriate, and less effective, than other motivations. Public policy needs to keep this possibility in its sight.

21.4 POLICY APPLICATIONS

In the light of the models we have outlined, what have been the main applications of policy to careers guidance, particularly 'free-standing' guidance? We will analyse in turn the evolution of the social-welfare model, the development of market and quasi-market concepts, and the application of market principles in practice.

The social-welfare model

The notion of a statutory careers guidance service for young people is long-established. As outlined in Chapter 9, the two key watersheds were the Employment and Training Acts of 1948 and 1973 (see also Bradley, 1990). The 1948 Act reformed the previous Juvenile Employment Service into the Youth Employment Service, extended its legal coverage to embrace young people up to age 18, and sought to make it a comprehensive service, with the Ministry of Labour providing it if Local Education Authorities did not choose to do so. The 1973 Act further transformed the service into the Careers Service, and made it mandatory for Local Education Authorities to provide it, under the guidance and inspection of the Department of Employment. It also removed the upper age limit of 18 and made it possible for the new service to operate a guidance and placement function for any client-group, regardless of age – though the statutory requirement remained confined to individuals engaged in full-time education (other than higher education) plus young people under 21 who had left education up to two years previously.

The key policy questions in the period following the 1973 Act were whether the Careers Service should continue to be administered by Local Education Authorities, and whether the statutory client-group should be extended to make it an all-age service. Periodic reviews were undertaken, without producing any basic change in the structure. A number of careers services developed a limited service for non-statutory adults, but without any direct funding support from central government. An all-age Occupational Guidance Service, which had been set up on a limited basis in 1966, remained a separate service within the Department of Employment and was dismantled in 1980/81 as a casualty of public-expenditure cuts. The general pressures on public expenditure made a significant extension of the Careers Service's statutory client-group less and less likely, particularly as careers guidance remained low on the public-policy agenda. In short, careers guidance was firmly established as part of social-welfare provision for young people, but within these terms was at risk of gradual erosion as a result of general political and economic pressures on the welfare state, and certainly seemed unlikely to attract the significant increased resources needed to extend the statutory entitlement to wider client-groups.

The development of market and quasi-market concepts

Towards the end of the 1980s, however, market concepts began to be applied more directly to careers guidance provision, in ways which opened up new policy options. The starting-point was the Confederation of British Industry's seminal report *Towards a Skills Revolution* (CBI, 1989). The CBI argued that if Britain is to compete effectively in world markets, a quantum leap will be required in the nation's education and training performance. It suggested that the way to achieve this was to 'put individuals first': to motivate and empower individuals to improve their skills throughout their working lives. Among the measures it proposed to promote this concept of 'careership' was a system of credits which would give all post-16 young people a publicly-funded right to education and training, and control over the form it should take. The CBI viewed effective careers guidance as the essential means of ensuring that such individuals' decisions were well-informed, and proposed that careers guidance required 'a new rationale, reinvigoration and extra investment' (p. 23).

The CBI's arguments moved guidance significantly up the public-policy agenda. Instead of being viewed as a rather marginal area of social-welfare provision, it became transformed into what in New Right terms could be viewed as 'that most politically acceptable of professions: the market-makers' (McNair, 1990). The CBI's 'skills revolution' analysis had a significant influence on government policy, and resulted in due course in the establishment of a programme of training credits for young people, and a set of National Targets for Education and Training. These and parallel developments brought enhanced attention to the policy significance of careers guidance. Because the CBI's 'careership' proposals became associated with training or learning credits for young people, the force of their influence was mainly to advance the case for improved provision for the traditional statutory client-group. Potentially, however, their emphasis on the importance of lifelong skill development provided a rationale for re-examining the extension of statutory provision.

Alongside the 'guidance as market-maker' argument, though, a case began to be mounted for developing a market in guidance itself. This view was developed in a series of seminars organised by Full Employment UK (1991a; 1991b). It was argued that those interested in developing guidance services for adults should move away from the notion that guidance was a free service. Instead, services should be fee-charging: in some cases (for example, the unemployed) the fees would be paid by government, in some cases by the employer, and in some cases by individuals themselves. Considerable interest was expressed in the notion of guidance credits to target the government expenditure: for some groups, these credits might cover the full costs of the guidance offered; for other groups, they might provide a subsidy. One of the expressed advantages of such an approach was that it 'would encourage a healthy degree of competition between different counselling providers for the custom of counselling credit-holders' (Full Employment UK, 1991a, p. 29).

The CBI was attracted by these arguments, and in a later report not only adopted them but extended them to cover young people as well as adults. It suggested that 'creating an effective and informed market in careers guidance provision is the best way to guarantee that the range of individuals' needs can be satisfied, that individual choices are maximised and that customers remain the focus' (CBI, 1993, p. 22). It argued that guidance vouchers should be issued to all young people aged 16–19, as well as to specific older groups. Indeed, it subsequently suggested that guidance vouchers should also be issued to all students in higher education, to enable them to use services outside their own institution (CBI, 1994). However, it accepted that guidance vouchers for the pre-16 age-group were inappropriate. Instead it suggested that a competitive tendering process should be adopted under which accredited providers within local guidance markets would be invited to bid for contracts for delivery of guidance services in schools. Alternatively, it proposed that funds might be allocated directly to schools so that they would have autonomy in the choice of guidance provider, again possibly through a competitive tendering process (CBI, 1993).

The view eventually adopted by the CBI, therefore, appeared to be that the role of guidance as market-maker could be best performed by stimulating a market in guidance. This model included some real-market components, in the sense that some users were expected to pay full costs. It also, however, included significant quasi-market components, in the sense that the costs of guidance for significant groups were paid for by the state, but administered through quasi-market mechanisms. The favoured mechanism was guidance vouchers. The residual mechanism, for young people up to 16, was competitive tendering for contracts.

The application of market principles

The Government was strongly influenced by these ideas, but chose to apply them more tentatively, and with a different balance between the competing quasi-market mechanisms of contracts and vouchers. Education-based guidance has not been 'marketised' at all: it remains, effectively, part of social-welfare provision. The Careers Service, on the other hand, was removed by the Trade Union Reform and Employment Rights Act 1993 from the mandatory control of Local Education Authorities, with the Secretary of State for Employment being given powers to determine what form arrangements for its operation should take. In England and Wales, the model adopted was competitive tendering to provide careers services in local areas; in Scotland, joint tenders were invited in the first instance from partnerships between education authorities and Local Enterprise Companies, with competitive tendering reserved as a fallback option. The contracts covered services for the existing statutory client-group (see Chapter 9).

In relation to individuals outside this client-group, the Government launched experiments in guidance vouchers. It did so particularly within two development programmes: Gateways to Learning, aimed mainly at the unemployed; and Skill Choice, aimed more strongly at individuals in employment. Specified groups of individuals were given access to guidance vouchers which they could take to a range of guidance providers accredited by the local Training and Enterprise Council. The vouchers provided a significant contribution towards the cost of guidance but, particularly in the case of Skill Choice, individuals and/or their employers were expected to meet part of the costs of the services used.

The experiment in guidance vouchers can be seen in two ways: as a new form of social-welfare provision which could be more truly user-centred than the old, or as a half-way house to a real market in guidance. To explore the latter possibility, a research project was commissioned by the Government from PA Cambridge Economic Consultants (1993). The report concluded that there would be difficulties in moving quickly towards a self-sustaining guidance market. It noted that many people were unclear about the nature of guidance and its benefits, and tended to associate it with the role of the Employment Service in relation to the unemployed (which was placement- rather than guidance-oriented and included strong elements of official surveillance regarding rights to benefit). It found that most would not expect to be charged for any guidance services they might use, and that only a minority could conceive of any circumstances in which they would consider paying. Moreover, the perceived need for guidance tended to be strongest among unemployed people and younger individuals, whereas willingness to pay tended to be strongest among those with higher-level academic qualifications and those with higher incomes. Circumstances in which employers would consider paying for their employees to receive guidance tended to be limited to specific situations, notably redundancy and training/skills enhancement. Some of these obstacles could be regarded as transitional, but others seemed likely to be enduring in nature.

In the light of this study and other similar findings, the notion that the public interest in guidance as a market-maker could be adequately delivered by a market in guidance began to look seriously flawed. Moreover, the evaluations of the experiments in guidance vouchers within the Gateways to Learning and Skill Choice programmes provided little evidence of their claimed benefits (Coopers & Lybrand, 1994; 1995). There was, for example, little sign that clients felt empowered by their use of guidance vouchers. It was also not evident that individuals were currently capable of, or particularly interested in becoming capable of, making informed choices between competing *guidance* providers: what they wanted was assurance of high-quality guidance to help them in making informed choices between competing *opportunity* providers.

At the same time, it was clear that there was little possibility, in the light of continued public-expenditure constraints, of extending statutory free access to a full guidance service. Accordingly, a possible compromise model was developed (TEC National Council, 1994; Watts, 1994). This suggested that limited *foundation* guidance provision, including open-access information centres and brief diagnostic guidance designed in particular to identify further guidance needs, should be made available on a universal, free basis. This should be complemented by *customised* guidance provision (e.g. counselling interviews, group sessions, psychometric testing) which should be provided on a charged basis to those able to pay, and on a free basis to those not able to do so. In other words, the proposal sought to assure the general availability of core elements of guidance as a public good, but also saw this as providing a base on which extended provision could be marketed to those able to pay for it, thus stimulating a market in guidance where this was feasible. At the time of writing (early 1996), it was unclear whether the Government would accept this model or not.

The position in early 1996, then, was that there were two distinct strands of government policy towards 'free-standing' guidance provision. In relation to young people, the notion of a statutory free entitlement remained unchallenged, but some quasi-market elements had been introduced to the concept of competitive tendering for what were in effect monopoly contracts to deliver the service in specified local areas. In most cases, this had resulted in the service being run by the existing services under new more independent structures involving various forms of partnership between Local Education Authorities and Training and Enterprise Councils. In a few cases, however, it had involved contracts being offered to private-sector or voluntary-sector organisations, or to services from other areas, thus providing some experiments in 'market entry' and 'expansionism' respectively.

In relation to adults, experiments in an alternative quasi-market notion, that of vouchers, had proved largely unsuccessful. Policy nonetheless continued to be based on encouraging competition at the level of the user between multiple providers, with a limited government role. The nature of this role, however, remained unresolved. It was unclear, for example, what level of funding government would seek to provide for adult guidance. It was also unclear whether government would seek to regulate the market element directly, or would encourage a body such as the new National Advisory Council for Careers and Educational Guidance (founded in 1994 by the key interest groups in the field, with government departments as observers) to do so (cf. Hawthorn, 1995). It was also unclear what the relationship was between adult guidance policy and youth guidance policy: whether, for instance, the careers services holding the monopoly contracts for youth guidance had a *primus inter pares* role in relation to adult guidance strategies, or were to be kept at arm's length to prevent exploitation of their market advantage.

21.5 CONCLUSION

This analysis of the application of policy to 'free-standing' guidance illustrates many of the points made earlier in the chapter about the role of public policy in relation to guidance provision. The adoption of market and quasi-market concepts has challenged, sometimes constructively but sometimes destructively, the professional ethos which characterised the social-welfare model. At the same time, however, it has given guidance a higher policy profile than ever before. Moreover, it has on the whole demonstrated a high degree of respect for the 'self-denying ordinance' regarding the imposition of public interests on individual choices, outlined in Section 21.1. A key issue for the future is whether the virtuous aspects of the professional ethos within the social-welfare model of guidance can be reasserted, detached from excessive bureaucracy, and reconciled with the reinvigoration of the policy debate introduced by the application of the market and quasi-market models.

In the end, market principles may have a role to play in public policy on guidance provision, but are too narrow to encompass the social functions of such provision. This is true not only of the concept of a market in guidance, but also of that of guidance as a market-maker. Guidance does not only make markets work: it also makes the wider structure of society work, by linking individual needs to societal needs on a voluntaristic basis. Public policy relating to guidance needs to question the recent hegemony of market concepts, and to address this broader social purpose.

REFERENCES

Bradley, S. (1990) 'The Careers Service: Past, Present and Future', *British Journal of Guidance and Counselling* 18(2): 137–55.

Broadbent, J., Dietrich, M. and Laughlin, R. (1993) *The Development of Principal–Agent, Contracting and Accountability Relationships in the Public Sector: Conceptual and Cultural Problems*, Discussion Paper No. 93.34, Sheffield: Sheffield University Management School (mimeo).

Confederation of British Industry (1989) *Towards a Skills Revolution*, London: CBI.

Confederation of British Industry (1993) *A Credit to Your Career*, London: CBI.

Confederation of British Industry (1994) *Thinking Ahead: Ensuring the Expansion of Higher Education into the 21st Century*, London: CBI.

Coopers & Lybrand (1994) *Gateways to Learning National Evaluation: Final Report*, London: Coopers & Lybrand (mimeo).

Coopers & Lybrand (1995) *National Evaluation of Skill Choice: Final Report*, London: Coopers & Lybrand (mimeo).

Davies, H. (1992) *Fighting Leviathan: Building Social Markets that Work*, London: Social Market Foundation.

Eliade, M. (1959) *The Sacred and the Profane: the Nature of Religion*, New York: Harcourt, Brace & World.

Full Employment UK (1991a) *Investing in Skills, Part Four*, London: Full Employment UK (mimeo).

Full Employment UK (1991b) *Investing in Skills, Part Seven: Developing Fee-Charging Adult Guidance Services*, London: Full Employment UK (mimeo).

Goodin, R. E. (1982) 'Freedom and the Welfare State: Theoretical Foundations', *Journal of Social Policy* 11: 149–76.

Gorz, A. (1989) *Critique of Economic Reason* (trans. G. Handyside and C. Turner), London: Verso.

Hawthorn, R. (1995) *First Steps: a Quality Standards Framework for Guidance Across All Sectors*, London: Royal Society of Arts/National Advisory Council for Careers and Educational Guidance.

Hayek, F. A. (1944) *The Road to Serfdom*, London: Routledge.

Hirschmann, A. O. (1970) *Exit, Voice and Loyalty*, Cambridge, MA: Harvard University Press.

Illich, I. (1973) *Deschooling Society*, Harmondsworth: Penguin.

Illich, I. (1977) *Disabling Professions*, London: Boyars.

Killeen, J., White, M. and Watts, A. G. (1992) *The Economic Value of Careers Guidance*, London: Policy Studies Institute.

King, D. S. (1987) *The New Right: Politics, Markets and Citizenship*, London: Macmillan.

Le Grand, J. (1991) 'Quasi-Markets and Social Policy', *Economic Journal* 101(408): 1256–67.

Le Grand, J. and Estrin, S. (1989) *Market Socialism*, Oxford: Clarendon Press.

McNair, S. (1990) 'Guidance and the Education and Training Market', in Watts, A. G. (ed.) *Guidance and Educational Change*, Cambridge: Careers Research and Advisory Centre/Hobsons.

Mizen, P. (1995) *The State, Young People and Youth Training: In and Against the Training State*, London: Mansell.

Niskanen, W. A. (1971) *Bureaucracy and Representative Government*, Chicago, IL: Aldine-Atherton.

Osborne, D. and Gaebler, T. (1992) *Reinventing Government*, Reading, MA: Addison-Wesley.

PA Cambridge Economic Consultants (1993) *Research on the Labour Market Need for Advice and Guidance Services: Final Report*, Cambridge: PACEC (mimeo).

Perkin, H. (1989) *The Rise of Professional Society: England Since 1880*, London: Routledge.

Savas, E. S. (1987) *Privatisation: the Key to Better Government*, Chatham, NJ: Chatham House.

Smith, A. (1776) *An Enquiry into the Nature and Causes of the Wealth of Nations*, Edinburgh: Black.

Tawney, R. H. (1964 edn) *Equality* (first pub. 1931), London: Allen & Unwin.

TEC National Council (1994) *Individual Commitment to Lifetime Learning*, London: TEC National Council.

Thane, P. (1982) *Foundations of the Welfare State*, London: Longman.

Watts, A. G. (1980) 'Careers Guidance and Public Policy', *Careers Journal* 1(2): 14–18.

Watts, A. G. (1991) 'The Impact of the "New Right": Policy Challenges Confronting Careers Guidance in England and Wales', *British Journal of Guidance and Counselling* 19(3): 230–45.

Watts, A. G. (1994) *A Strategy for Developing Careers Guidance Services for Adults*, CRAC Occasional Paper, Cambridge: Careers Research and Advisory Centre.

Watts, A. G. (1995) 'Applying Market Principles to the Delivery of Careers Guidance Services: a Critical Review', *British Journal of Guidance and Counselling* 23(1): 69–81.

Author index

Subject index